Criminal Law in Singapore and Malaysia

Text and materials

Criminal Law in Singapore and Malaysia

Text and materials

KL Koh, LL B (Hons) (Malaya), LL M, Ph D (Sing),
Dipl de Hautes Etudes Internationales (Gev)
Advocate and Solicitor, Supreme Court of Singapore
Professor, Faculty of Law
National University of Singapore

CMV Clarkson, BA, LL B (Cape T), LL M (Lond)
Lecturer in Law, University of Bristol
Former Visiting Senior Fellow, Faculty of Law
National University of Singapore

NA Morgan, BA(Oxon)(Sheffield) MA
Lecturer in Law, University of Western Australia
Former Lecturer, Faculty of Law
National University of Singapore

Malayan Law Journal Pte Ltd
Malayan Law Journal Sdn Bhd
Singapore • Kuala Lumpur
1989

THE BUTTERWORTH GROUP OF COMPANIES

SINGAPORE	BUTTERWORTH & CO (ASIA) PTE LTD
	MALAYAN LAW JOURNAL PTE LTD
	30-Robinson Road #12-01 Tuan Sing Towers
	Singapore 0104
MALAYSIA	MALAYAN LAW JOURNAL SDN BHD
	10th Floor Wisma Hamzah Kwong Hing
	No 1 Leboh Ampang
	50100 Kuala Lumpur
AUSTRALIA	BUTTERWORTHS PTY LTD
	Sydney, Melbourne, Brisbane, Adelaide, Perth,
	Canberra and Hobart
CANADA	BUTTERWORTHS CANADA LTD
	Toronto and Vancouver
IRELAND	BUTTERWORTH (IRELAND) LTD
	Dublin
NEW ZEALAND	BUTTERWORTHS OF NEW ZEALAND LTD
	Wellington and Auckland
UK	BUTTERWORTH & CO (PUBLISHERS) LTD
	London, Edinburgh
UNITED STATES	BUTTERWORTH LEGAL PUBLISHERS
OF AMERICA	St Paul, Minnesota
	Seattle, Washington
	Boston, Massachusetts
	Austin, Texas
	D & S Publishers Company
	Clearwater, Florida

©

Malayan Journal Law Pte Ltd
1989

ISBN 9971-70-069-7
ISBN 9971-70-071-9 (pb)

Typeset in Singapore by Superskill Graphics Pte Ltd and printed in Singapore by General Printing Services Pte Ltd.

Preface

This book is aimed primarily at students studying criminal law in Singapore and Malaysia. It is nevertheless hoped that practitioners will find it of assistance and that it will be useful for students and practitioners in all those jurisdictions with criminal law *in pari materia* with Singapore's and Malaysia's – in particular India, Pakistan, Sri Lanka, Nigeria, Sudan and Kenya.

There are several distinctive features about this book. First, it is a book on the criminal law; it is not simply a commentary on the Penal Code. While the Penal Code is obviously the most important source of criminal law, it is not a complete source. Accordingly, other important offences, including some contained in separate road traffic statutes, and strict liability offences, are considered.

Further, because it is not a commentary on the Penal Code, the authors have been highly selective in the topics covered and no attempt has been made to cover all offences, even within the Penal Code. However, the offences dealt with do broadly cover the territory of the criminal law. They include most offences of significance.

The approach adopted throughout has been in line with this non-commentary format. Effort has been made to try and expose the rationale and objectives of the law. To facilitate this, a whole chapter has been included on punishment. This is based on the premise that the substantive rules of criminal law and punishment are two sides of the same coin. Without a clear understanding of the objectives of the criminal justice system it is hard to understand the structure and definition of particular offences.

A second distinctive feature of this book is its format. It is neither a textbook, nor a "cases and materials" book; but, hopefully, it combines the best features of each, providing "two books in one". This is an ideal format for students, but it is hoped that practitioners will also benefit from a book which combines a substantial text with access to the primary materials.

The final distinctive feature is that this is not a book by three co-authors each jointly responsible for the whole. While a basic format and common style have been adopted, it must be emphasized that each author is fully and solely responsible only for those chapters written by that author. No author assumes responsibility for the chapters of a co-author. This book should perhaps be viewed as a collection of essays, each by its own author – but cumulatively covering the main areas of the criminal law.

The authors would like to thank Ms Carol Wee of the National University of Singapore Law Library for her kind assistance.

of Singapore Law Library for her kind assistance.

KL Koh dedicates her portion of this book to law students at the Faculty of Law, National University of Singapore.

Chris Clarkson dedicates his share of this book to his friends at Kingston Polytechnic and at the National University of Singapore.

Neil Morgan dedicates his share of this book to Irene, Isabelle and Liana.

This book is written with reference to the law as at 14 June 1988. All references to the "Penal Code" should be understood as references to the Penal Codes of both Singapore and Malaysia, unless otherwise stated.

KL Koh
CMV Clarkson
NA Morgan
Singapore
April 1989

Acknowledgments

Grateful acknowledgment is given to the following authors and publishers for permission to reproduce extracts from their works:

Brabyn, JM
Brown, BJ
Canagarayar, JK
Clarkson, CMV
Douglas, Gillian
English, Peter
Keating, HM
Koh, KL
Koh, TTB
Mckillop, BA
Sornarajah, M
The Attorney-General, Singapore
Wright, Shelley
Yeo Meng Heong, Stanley

All India Reporter Ltd, Nagpur, India
Allahabad Weekly Reporter, India
Asia Publishing House, Bombay, India
Butterworths, Singapore
Controller of Publication, High Court of Delhi, India
Department of Government Printing, Sri Lanka
Eastern Book Co, Lucknow, India
Indian Law Reports, High Court of Calcutta, India
Indian Law Reports, Bombay, Government Printing & Stationery,
    India
Jaisingh & Mehta Publishers Private Ltd
Trustees of Indiana University, Bloomington, USA
Law Book Co, Allahabad, India
Law Publishers, Allahabad, India
Law Times Press, Orissa, India
Malaya Law Review, Singapore
Malayan Law Journal (Pte) Ltd, Singapore
Ministry of the Environment, Ontario, Canada
National University of Singapore, Singapore
Oxford University Press, Oxford, UK
Printing & Stationery, Uttar Pradesh, India
Quin Pte Ltd, Singapore
Scottish Academic Press Limited, Edinburgh, Scotland
Sweet & Maxwell Limited, London, UK
The All Pakistan Legal Decisions, Lahore, Pakistan
The Bombay Law Reporter Pte Ltd, India

vii

The Incorporated Council of Law Reporting for England and
    Wales, London, UK
The Indian Law Institute, New Delhi, India

    We would also like to thank the following publishers in accordance with the
format requested by them:

Bottoms, AE, "An Introduction to the 'Coming Crises'" in Bottoms, AE & Preston,
    RH *The Coming Penal Crises* (1980). Reprinted with permission of Scottish
    Academic Press Ltd.

Fletcher, George, P, *Rethinking Criminal Law* (1978).
    Reprinted with permission of Little, Brown and Company.

Hart, HLA, and Honore, AM, *Causation in the Law* (2nd edn, 1985)
    Reprinted with permission of Oxford University Press.

Kadish, SH, "Excusing Crime" (1987) 75 Cal LR 257
    Copyright © 1987 by the California Law Review Inc. Reprinted with per-
    mission of California Law Review Inc.

Malaysian Current Law Journal Sdn Bhd, *Leong Siong Sun and Anor* v *PP* [1985]
    2 MCLJ 250.
    Reprinted with permission of MCLJ.

Mulia SN, and Gupta, CL (eds), *Nelson's The Indian Penal Code* (7th edn, 1985).
    Reprinted with permission of The Law Book Company (P) Ltd.

Robinson, PH, *Criminal Law Defenses* (1984). Copyright ©
    Reprinted with permission of West Publishing Co.

Williams, Glanville, *Textbook on Criminal Law* (1978 and 1983).
    Reprinted with permission of Sweet & Maxwell Ltd.

Contents

PART II   GENERAL EXCEPTIONS

Chapter 4   Introduction   **103**
by NA Morgan

Table of cases

Table of statutes

Others

Ceylon (Sri Lanka)

Hong Kong

India

England

Bibliography

Books

Archbold, *Criminal Pleading, Evidence and Practice* (36th edn, 1966) Sweet & Maxwell.

Ashworth, Andrew, *Sentencing and Penal Policy* (1983) Weidenfeld and Nicolson.

Atchuthen Pillai, PS, *Criminal Law* (6th edn, 1983) Tripathi Pte Ltd.

Balasubrahmanyam, V, "Group Liability" in *Essays on the Penal Code* (1962) Indian Law Institute.

Balasubrahmanyam, V, "The Guilty Mind" in *Essays on the Indian Penal Code* (1962) Indian Law Institute.

Clarkson, CMV, *Understanding Criminal Law* (1987) Fontana Press.

Clarkson, CMV and Keating, HM, *Criminal Law: Text and Materials* (1984) Sweet & Maxwell.

Clive, John, *John Macaulay: The Shaping of the Historian* (1973) Vintage Books.

Criminal Law Revision Committee, *Report on Offences Against the Person* (1980) HMSO.

Criminal Law Revision Committee, *Working Paper on Sexual Offences* (1980) HMSO.

Criminal Law Revision Committee, *Working Paper on Offences Against the Person* (1976) HMSO.

Dickinson, J, *Administrative Justice and the Supremacy of the Law in the United States* (1927) Cambridge Harvard University Press.

Devlin, Lord, *The Enforcement of Morals* (1965) Oxford University Press.

Fitzgerald, PJ, (ed) *Salmond on Jurisprudence* (12th edn, 1985) Sweet & Maxwell.

Fletcher, George P, *Rethinking Criminal Law* (1978) Little, Brown and Co.

Foster, M, Sir, *Crown Law* (3rd edn).

Gaur, KD, *Criminal Law: Cases and Materials* (2nd edn, 1985) NM Tripathi.

Gour, HS, *Penal Law of British India* (1st edn, 1909).

Gour, HS, *Penal Law of British India* (2nd edn, 1917).

Gour, HS, *Penal Law of British India* (3rd edn, 1925).

Gour, HS, *Penal Law of British India* (5th edn, 1936).

Gour, HS, *Penal Law of India* (6th edn, 1955) Law Book Co.

Gour, HS, *Penal Law of India* (10th edn, Vol 1, 1982; Vol II, 1983; Vol III, 1983; Vol IV, 1984) Law Publishers.

Hale, Sir Matthew *Pleas of the Crown* (1736).

Halsbury's *Laws of England* (3rd edn, 1951-1954) vol 10, Butterworths.

Hanbury and Maudsley, *Modern Equity* (12th edn, 1985) Stevens & Sons.

Hart, HLA, *Law Liberty and Morality* (1963) Oxford University Press.

Hart, HLA, *Punishment and Responsibility: Essays in the Philosophy of Law* (1968) Clarendon Press.

Hart, HLA and Honore, T, *Causation in the Law* (2nd edn, 1985) Clarendon Press.

Howard, Colin, *Criminal Law* (3rd edn, 1977) Law Book Co.

India (Republic) Law Commission, *42nd Report* 1971, Minister of Law and Justice.

The Law Commission of India (42nd Report, Indian Penal Code) 1971.

Kadish, SH and Paulson, MG, *Criminal Law and its Processes* (1969) Little, Brown & Co.

Keeton, GW and Sheridan, LA, *The Law of Trusts* (10th edn, 1974) Professional Books Ltd.

Kenny, *Outlines of Criminal Law* (18th edn, 1962) Cambridge University Press.

Koh, KL, *Criminal Law* (1977) Singapore Law Series, Malaya Law Review.

Koh, KL and Molly Cheang, *The Penal Codes of Singapore and Malaysia, Vol II* (1976) Quins Ltd.

Koh, KL and Myint Soe, *The Penal Codes of Singapore & States of Malaya: Cases, Materials and Comments, Vol I* (1976) Law Book Co.

Law Commission (1973), Law Commission Working Paper No 50, *Inchoate Offences: Conspiracy, Attempt and Incitement* (1973) HMSO.

Law Commission (1978), Law Commission Working Paper No 89, *Report on the Mental Element in Crime* (1978) HMSO.

Law Commission (1980), Law Commission Working Paper No 102, *Attempt and Impossibility in Relation to Attempt, Conspiracy and Incitement* (1980) HMSO.

Law Commission (1985), Law Commission Working Paper No 143, *Codification of the Criminal Law. A Report to the Law Commission* (1985) HMSO.

Law Commission Working Paper No 55, *Defences of General Application* (1974) HMSO.

Leigh, LH, *Strict and Vicarious Liability* (1982) Sweet & Maxwell.

Macaulay, Lord, *The Works of Lord Macaulay* (1898) Vol II.

Macaulay, Lord, "Introductory Report upon the Indian Penal Code" in *The Works of Lord Macaulay, Speeches, Poems and Miscellaneous*, Vol II (Albany edn) (1837).

Macaulay, TB and other Indian Law Commissioners, *A Penal Code Prepared by the Indian Law Commissioners* (1937) Longmans.

Mayne, JD, *Criminal Law* (2nd edn, 1901) Higginbothams Ltd.

Mayne's Criminal Law of India. Swaminadhan S (ed) (4th edn, 1914) Higginbothams Ltd.

Mehrotra, KC, *Culpable Homicide and Legal Defences* (1967) Eastern Book.

Mill, JS, *On Liberty* 1859.

Myint Soe, *General Principles of Singapore Law* (1978) Institute of Banking and Finance.

Nelson's The Indian Penal Code (7th edn, 1985), revised by Suresh Narain Mulla and Chheda Lal Gupta, Law Book Co.

Ratanlal, R and Dhirajlal, KT, *The Indian Penal Code* (Vol I, 26th edn, 1987; Vol II, 1988) Bombay Law Reporter.

Ratanlal, R and Dhirajlal, KT, *The Law of Crimes* (21st edn, 1966) The Bombay Law Reporter (Pte) Ltd.

Ratanlal, R and Dhirajlal, KT, *Law of Crimes* (23rd edn, 1987) Wadwhu and Co Pte Ltd Law Publishers.

Ricquier, WJM and Yeo, S, *Breaches of Trust in Singapore and Malaysia* (1984) Butterworths.

Robinson, PH, *Criminal Law Defences* (1984) West Publishing Co (Criminal Practice Series).

Smith and Hogan, *Criminal Law* (2nd edn, 1969) Butterworths.

Stephen, Sir J, *History of the Criminal Law of England* Vols II and III (1883) Macmillan.

Stephen, Sir J, *Digest of Criminal Law* (3rd edn, 1883) Macmillan.

Taylor, Alfred Swaine, *Principles and Practice of Medical Jurisprudence* (11th edn, 1956), Vol 1, J & A Churchill, 1956-57.

Trivedi, HDD, *Indian Penal Code, 1860 (Act No 45 of* 1860) (2nd edn, 1981) Eastern Book Co.

West, DJ, *Murder Followed by Suicide* (1965) Heinemann.

Wily, HJ and Stallworthy, KR, *Mental Abnormality and the Law* (1962) Peryer Ltd.

Williams, Glanville, *Textbook of Criminal Law* (1978) Stevens & Sons.

Williams, Glanville, *Textbook of Criminal Law* (2nd edn, 1983) Stevens & Sons.

Woon, Walter, "Stare Decisis and Judicial Precedent in Singapore" in AJ Harding (ed) *The Common Law in Singapore and Malaysia* (1985) Butterworths.

Wootton, B, *Crime and the Criminal Law: Reflections of a Magistrate and Social Scientist* (2nd edn, 1981) Stevens & Sons.

Yeo, Stanley, "The Application of Common Law Defences to the Penal Code in Singapore and Malaysia" in AJ Harding (ed) *The Common Law in Singapore and Malaysia* (1985) Malaya Law Review and Butterworths.

Articles

Brabyn, JM, "Intoxication in Singapore: An Alternative to Majewski" (1986) Lawasia 60.

Brett, Peter, "Mistake of Law as a Criminal Defence" (1966) 5 Melbourne ULR 197.

Brown, BJ, "'Chance Medley' and the Malayan Penal Codes" (1961) 3 Mal LR 73.

Brown, BJ, "Diminished Responsibility" (1961) Mal LR 331.

Canagarayar, JK, "Breach of Trust by Partners" (1986) 28 Mal LR 214.

Canagarayar, JK, "Dishonored Cheques and the Offence of Cheating – A Singapore Perspective" (1987) 29 Mal LR 41.

Canagarayar, JK, "Recent Developments in the Law Relating to Criminal Negligence in Singapore and Malaysia" [1981] 2 MLJ clxii. (See also amendment to the article in [1982] 1 MLJ lxxii.)

Canagarayar, JK, "The Plea of Insanity: Some Observations on the Application of the 'Wrong or Contrary to Law' Test in Singapore, Malaysia and India" [1985] 2 MLJ iii.

Cheang, Molly, "The Intoxicated Offender under Singapore Law" (1986) 35 ICLQ 106.

Cheang, Molly, "The Insanity Defence in Singapore" (1986) Anglo-American Law Review 245.

Davies, WED, "The Defences of Insanity and Intoxication in Malayan Criminal Law" (1958) MLJ lxxvi.

Douglas, Gillian, "Joint Liability in the Penal Code" (1983) Mal LR 259.

Edwards, J LL J, "Constructive Murder in Canadian and English Law" (1959) Mal LR 17.

Edwards, Susan SM, "Pre-Menstrual Tension" (1982) 146 JPN 476.

English, Peter, "The Defence of Duress under the Penal Code" (1983) 25 Mal LR 404.

Friedman, M, "Unscrambling the Judicial Egg: Some Observations on Stare Decisis in Singapore and Malaysia" (1980) 22 Mal LR 227.

Harbarjan Singh, "Stare Decisis in Singapore and Malaysia – a Review" [1971] 1 MLJ xvi.

Hart, HLA, "Immorality and Treason" 62 Listener 163 (30 July 1959).

Hatchard, "The Law Concerning Intoxication in Zambia" [1983] 12 Anglo-Am L Rev 41.

Hughes, Graham, "Criminal Omissions" (1958) 67 Yale LJ 590.

Kadish, Sanford H, "Excusing Crime" (1987) 75 Calif LR 257.

Koh, KL, "Doctrine of Consent in Criminal Law" (1967) 9 Mal LR 188.

Koh, KL, "Consent and Responsibility in Sexual Offences" (in 2 parts) [1968] Crim LR 81, 150.

Koh, KL, "Joint Liability and Section 397 of the Penal Code of Malaya" 19 Mal LR 383.

Koh, TTB, "The Misuse of Drugs Act, 1973" [1973] 1 MLJ xlviiili.

McKillop, Bron, "Insanity under the Penal Code" (1966) 7 Me Judice 65, 71.

McKillop, Bron, "Strict Liability Offences in Singapore & Malaysia" (1967) 9 Mal LR 118.

Mooney, Peter, "Intoxication as a Defence under the Penal Code" (1961) 27 MLJ xxxvi.

Myint Soe, "Some Aspects of Common Intention in the Penal Code of Singapore and West Malaysia" (1972) 14 Mal LR 163.

Orchard, "Agreement in Criminal Conspiracy" [1974] Crim LR 297.

Sayre, FB, "Public Welfare Offences" (1933) 33 Col LR 55.

Schulhofer, SJ, "Harm and Punishment: A Critique of Emphasis on Results of Conduct in the Criminal Law" (1974) 122 Univ of Pennsylvania Law Review 1497.

Sornarajah, M, "Defences to Strict Liability Offences in Singapore and Malaysia" (1985) 27 Mal LR 1.

Sornarajah, M, "Towards a Liberal View of Provocation" [1985] 2 MLJ cxliv.

Stuart, Donald, "Mens Rea, Negligence and Attempts" [1968] Crim LR 647.

Turner, JW Cecil, "Attempts to Commit Crimes" (1934) 5 Cambridge LJ 230.

Wasik, M, "Partial Excuses in the Criminal Law" (1982) 45 MLR 516.

Williams, Glanville, "Recklessness Redefined" [1981] CLJ 252.

Williams, Glanville, "The Theory of Excuses" [1982] Crim LR 732.

Woon, Walter, "Precedents that Bind – a Gordian Knot: Stare Decisis in the Federal Court" (1982) 24 Mal LR 1.

Wright, Shelley, "Attempt and Abandonment where there are Several Participants in the Commission of a Crime" (unpublished).

Yeo, S, "Homicide in Singapore" (1985) 27 Mal LR 113.

Yeo, S, "The Provoked 'Reasonable' Singapore/Malaysian: An Update" [1987] 2 MLJ cclxxxv.

Part I

General background and principles

Chapter 1

Introduction

By KL Koh

> ... there is no department of law which so early attracted the attention of philosophers or which still excites so general an interest among reflecting and reading men....

> Lord Macaulay, on devising a new Penal Code for India, in Minute of 4 June 1835 to the Indian Council.

This book deals with the main offences and defences under both the Penal Codes of Singapore and of Malaysia, in addition to some non-Penal Code offences.

A. Historical sketch of Singapore and Malaysia

A historical sketch of the two countries is necessary in order to understand the history of the two Penal Codes, viz the Penal Code of Singapore (Cap 224) and the FMS Penal Code (FMS, Cap 45).

Singapore and Malaysia are not only geographical neighbours (at least the "States of Malaya" and Singapore are), but have had a shared political history. Penang and Malacca, which are now part of Malaysia, were at one time part of the "Straits Settlements" together with Singapore and a few other territories (see below, p 4). On 16 September 1963 Singapore merged with the then Federation of Malaya, the Borneo States (now Sabah and Sarawak) to form the Federation of Malaysia. However, on 9 August 1965 it separated from Malaysia and became an independent Republic.

At this juncture, we may trace the history of Singapore from the time of its founding by Sir Stamford Raffles of the British East India Company in 1819. Sir Stamford Raffles entered into a treaty of friendship and alliance with Johore to establish a trading post in Singapore. In 1824, Singapore was ceded to the British Crown, and so was Malacca under the Anglo-Dutch Treaty in 1824. Penang had been ceded to the British by the King of Kedah in 1791.

In 1824 the Straits Settlements comprising Singapore, Penang (then known as Prince of Wales' Island), Province Wellesley and Malacca came into existence, and were governed by the East India Company. In

3

1826 the administration of the Straits Settlements came under the government of Bengal in India. There was dissatisfaction over the Bengal administration and finally, in 1867, the Straits Settlements were transferred from Bengal to the direct control of the Colonial Office in London (see the Straits Settlements Act 1866) and remained such until the Japanese occupation during World War II. After the Japanese occupation in 1945, the Straits Settlements were under the British Military Administration until their disbandment in 1946 by the Straits Settlements (Repeal) Act 1946. Singapore, together with a few other territories, became the Colony of Singapore; Malacca and Penang became the "Settlements" of the Malayan Union which was formed in 1946. In 1959 Singapore became a self-governing state and on 16 September 1963 it became part of Malaysia. In 1965 Singapore separated from Malaysia and became an independent, sovereign republic.

Malaysia now comprises 13 states: the "States of Malaya" in the Malay Peninsula, viz Johore, Kedah, Kelantan, Malacca, Negri Sembilan, Pahang, Penang, Perak, Perlis, Selangor, Trengganu; and the "Borneo States" comprising Sabah and Sarawak.

British influence in the "States of Malaya" was in the form of protection or advice.

In 1895 Perak, Selangor, Pahang and Negri Sembilan formed the Federated Malay States (FMS). The other Malay States, viz Johore, Kedah, Perlis and Kelantan, were known as the unfederated Malay States.

After the Japanese occupation in World War II a British Military Administration was set up until 1946 when the Malayan Union was formed. The Union comprised the Federated Malay States and the unfederated Malay States together with Penang and Malacca. In 1948 the independent Federation of Malaya came into existence.

Sabah was a Crown Colony from 1946 until it joined Malaysia in 1963. Sarawak was ceded to Sir James Brooke in 1841. In 1946 sovereignity was transferred to the British Crown who retained it until 1963.

On 16 September 1963 the then Federation of Malaya joined with Singapore, Sabah (formerly North Borneo) and Sarawak to form the Federation of Malaysia. Singapore, as noted earlier, separated from Malaysia in 1965.

B. History of the Penal Codes of Singapore and Malaysia

The precursor of the Penal Codes of Singapore and of Malaysia is the Penal Code of the Straits Settlements (SS Penal Code) which was passed by the Legislative Council of the Straits Settlements in 1871 and came into force on 16 September 1872.

The SS Penal Code (SS, Cap 20) applied to the Settlements of

Singapore, Penang, Malacca and Labuan. When Singapore became a Crown Colony in 1946 the Penal Code became the Penal Code of Singapore but the SS Penal Code continued to apply to Penang and Malacca until 1948.

The SS Penal Code was adopted by most of the Federated and unfederated Malay States in separate enactments.

In 1935 the FMS Penal Code (FMS Cap 45) came into existence and applied to the Federated Malay States, and the individual Penal Code enactment of each of these states was repealed. In 1948 when the Federation of Malaya was formed, the FMS Penal Code was extended throughout the Federation of Malaya and the individual enactments of the then unfederated Malay States and also the SS Penal Code were repealed. Subsequently, the FMS Penal Code was extended throughout Malaysia by the Penal Code (Amendment and Extension) Act 1976 (Act A327). As the FMS Penal Code was already applicable to the "States of Malaya" the Act was effectively extended to Sabah and Sarawak only, and therefore repealed the Penal Codes of these two states.

The Singapore Penal Code and the FMS Penal Code have been amended from time to time but still retain their main original provisions.

C. Criminal jurisprudence in the making

Being codes, it would seem obvious that they are intended to deal exhaustively with all the offences and the defences contained in them. The long title of the Penal Codes of Singapore and of Malaysia each states that it is "[a]n Act to consolidate the law relating to criminal offences", and s 2 of both the Penal Codes provides that "every person shall be liable to punishment under this Code and not otherwise ...." One interpretation of this section is that it repeals all former laws for the punishment of offences now punishable by the Penal Code. This means, for example, that it would exclude the application in Singapore of any English criminal law that was applicable by virtue of the Second Charter of Justice dated 27 November 1826, which deals with the reception of the English common law. This interpretation is supported by cases. In *Lee Siong Kiat* (1935) Terrell J said: "In criminal matters the law in the colony [ie the Straits Settlements] is provided by the Penal Code to the exclusion of the English law or English Statute Law." This does not of course mean that the whole of the criminal law in Singapore and Malaysia is contained in the Penal Codes of the respective countries for there are many other non-Penal Code statutes in these two countries. The Penal Codes of these two countries, however, are the most comprehensive criminal law statutes, each statute comprising 511 sections.

Thus, for example, both the Penal Codes deal with the following matters, unless otherwise indicated:

Chapter I (ss 1-5):	Preliminary
Chapter II (ss 6-52):	General explanations
Chapter III (ss 53-75):	Punishments
Chapter IV (ss 76-106):	General exceptions
Chapter V (ss 107-120):	Abetment
Chapter VA (ss 120A-120B):	Criminal conspiracy
Chapter VI (ss 121-130A):	Offences against the state
Chapter VII (ss 131-140B):	Offences relating to the armed forces
Chapter VIII (ss 141-160):	Offences against the public tranquillity
Chapter IX (ss 161-171):	Offences by or relating to public servants
Chapter X (ss 172-190):	Contempts of the lawful authority of public servants
Chapter XI (ss 191-229):	False evidence and offences against public justice
Chapter XII (ss 230-263):	Offences relating to coin and investment stamps
Chapter XIII (ss 264-267):	Offences relating to weights and measures
Chapter XIV (ss 268-294):	Offences affecting the public health, safety, convenience, decency and morals
Chapter XV (ss 295-298):	Offences relating to religion
Chapter XVI (ss 299-377A):	Offences affecting the human body
Chapter XVII (ss 378-462):	Offences against property
Chapter XVIII (Singapore: ss 463-489E; Malaysia: ss 463-489D):	Offences relating to documents and to currency notes and bank notes
Chapter XIX (Malaysia: ss 490-492; Singapore– there is no Chapter XIX)	Criminal breach of contracts of service
Chapter XX (ss 493-498):	Offences relating to marriage
Chapter XXI (ss 499-502):	Defamation
Chapter XXII (ss 503-510):	Criminal intimidation, insult and annoyance
Chapter XXIII (s 511):	Attempts to commit offences

The Penal Codes are based on the Indian Penal Code (1860) which was first drafted by the Indian Law Commission of which Lord Macaulay was President. Macaulay was a famous historian, essayist, politician, poet and, not least, a lawyer. Clive (1973), writing on Lord Macaulay's work on the Indian Penal Code said:

> The idea of drawing up a complete criminal code for India was Macaulay's. The Charter Act of 1833 had conceived of the inquiries undertaken by the law commissioners as preliminary to whatever alternatives of the law might be judged necessary....
>
> Reform of the English criminal law had indeed engaged the attention of leading statesmen–Mackintosh, Romilly, Peel and Brougham among others....

English criminal law was still in a state of chaos, with serious reforms just being put in train. And it was no doubt because it was still both "undefined" and "loose" that Macaulay suggested to the Council that its instruction to the law commissioners should emphasize that the Indian code was to cover all contingencies. "Not only ought everything in the code to be law; but nothing that is not in the code ought to be law." The code was to be more than a mere digest of existing usages and regulations, and this comprise all the reforms that the Law Commission might think desirable....

The terminology to be employed in the proposed code was to be clear and unequivocal, the language concise and perspicuous. The Council [ie Governor-General of India in Council] was to warn the commissioners against using vague terms such as "treason" or "manslaughter", taken from English law–"words which include a great variety of offences widely differing from each other...."

Despite a cutting of the English umbilical cord in many areas of criminal law dealt with in the Indian Penal Code it had somehow got connected in its interpretation in India as well as in those jurisdictions which derive their Penal Codes from the Indian subcontinent. Again, despite the avoidance of the use of words such as "manslaughter", it had somehow crept into its interpretation (see the Singapore case of *Francis* (1960)).

In drafting the Indian Penal Code, some inspiration was drawn from the English criminal law, the Penal Code of France and Livingston's Code for Louisiana. Although the criminal laws of France and Louisiana have hardly, if ever, been resorted to in the interpretation of the local or Indian Penal Codes, English criminal law has been relied upon not only in the interpretation of the Penal Codes but also in the face of express provisions. Balasubrahmanyam (1962, p 56) speaking on the Indian Penal Code bemoans that "it is a tragedy that sometimes the Indian Penal Code is called to bear the oppressive weight of English case law." Courts in Singapore and Malaysia have also at times unjustifiably looked to English case law either in the interpretation of their Penal Codes or in utter disregard of express provisions contained in them or in other criminal law statutes. For example, in the interpretation of s 300 Exception 1 of the FMS Penal Code (defence of provocation) the former Court of Appeal in Malaya in *Mat Sawi b Bahodin* (1958) cited with approval a passage from the English case of *Holmes* (1946), in which the test of provocation under English law was measured by the reasonable man. This is in face of the absence of the mention of reasonable man in the section. Even if the concept of a reasonable man were introduced into the section, who is a reasonable man in the Malayan context in *Mat Sawi b Bahodin* (1958)? Should the court impose the concept of the English reasonable man on to the Malaysian and Singapore societies which are not homogeneous but consist of different races, viz Chinese, Malays and Indians, with each race having its own different culture?

Still on s 300 Exception 1, this time the Court of Criminal Appeal of Singapore in *Vijajan* (1975, p 10) said: "Exception 1 of section 300 is quite obviously based on the common law of England" and "it is desirable to examine English cases which define provocation." Choor

Singh J, delivering the judgment of the court, then reviewed the following English cases: *Mancini* (1942); *Holmes* (1946) on the concept of the English reasonable man.

While there may be some aspects of provocation in the two Penal Codes which may be the same as those in the English law on provocation s 300 Exception 1 is certainly not entirely based on the English law.

There are clear instances where courts have ignored entirely the provisions of the Penal Codes and proceeded to decide a case simply by applying English criminal law. Thus in *Kee Ah Bah* (1979) where the question at issue was attempt, s 511 of the FMS Penal Code was not even mentioned; the High Court in Johore, Malaya, proceeded to examine the following English authorities on attempt: *Haughton* v *Smith* (1973); *Hope* v *Brown* (1954) and *Eagleton* (1855).

In the recent case of *Zainal Abidin b Ismail* (1987), the High Court of Brunei ignored the provisions of ss 79 and 375 of the Penal Code of Brunei on the issue of consent in rape. (The Penal Code of Brunei is *in pari materia* with the Penal Codes of Singapore and Malaysia.) After making reference to these two sections Dato Sir Denys Roberts applied the English case of *Morgan* (1976). A few months later when a similar issue was raised in the Singapore case of *Teo Eng Chan* (1988), P Coomaraswamy J rightly rejected the approach in *Zainal* (1987) and decided the case according to the law on mistake under s 79 of the Penal Code of Singapore.

There are other courts which have been acutely aware of the differences that exist between the Penal Code and other criminal statutes on the one hand and English criminal law on the other. In the Singapore case of *Woo Sing and Sim Ah Kow* (1954), Murray-Aynsley CJ, in deciding a case under s 304A of the Penal Code which deals with criminal negligence, said:

> The Penal Code is not a codification of English law. In numerous respects its provisions resemble the corresponding English law. In others, particularly as regards homicide, its provisions differ very greatly and deliberately so. In my opinion it is always dangerous to introduce English cases into the consideration of the Penal Code. The English law as to homicide remains unwritten and is still in a confused state.... But there still remain, in theory at least, constructive murder and constructive manslaughter. The Penal Code deliberately excluded the constructive offences and in sections 299–300 required certain specific intentions. In England involuntary manslaughter has always been very much tied up with the notion of constructive offences, in early times entirely so. It was the doing of an unlawful act, not the doing of a negligent act, that rendered a person guilty of manslaughter. In these circumstances the English law of manslaughter has no relevance in the interpretation of section 304A. In England negligence in any ordinary sense of the word is not the criterion of manslaughter. In *Bateman*'s case (1925), Lord Hewart CJ said: "It is most desirable that in trials for manslaughter by negligence it should be impressed on the jury that the issue is not negligence or no negligence, but felony or no felony." I do not think that once this source of confusion is removed Courts need have any difficulty in the application of this section to particular cases. Different degrees of gravity can be treated by a suitable variation in the penalty, bearing in mind that

s 304A involves offences of much less gravity than such as would come within the scope of manslaughter in England.

It is significant that the above passage occupied the greater part of the judgment in *Woo Sing and Sim Ah Kow* (1954), where his Lordship was at pains to point out the position under English law in order to compare it with that under the Penal Code. This underlines how demanding the administration of criminal law could be in Singapore and also in Malaysia as it requires one to understand fully both the English criminal law as well as the Penal Code in order to determine what English criminal law principles are or are not relevant in the interpretation of the Penal Code. The vast majority of judges presiding over the courts in Singapore and in Malaysia have had their legal education in England and are more familiar with the English criminal law rather than the criminal law in Singapore or Malaysia. The Law Faculty in the National University of Singapore produced its first batch of graduates in 1961 and the University of Malaya, in 1976. There have been three other law schools set up in Malaysia since. No doubt, with more lawyers being locally qualified there should be more awareness of the need to appreciate the similarities and differences in the criminal law of Singapore and Malaysia on the one hand and England on the other. The problem is not altogether solved with the local training of lawyers. The absence of local textbooks on criminal law has also been a culprit. Without a textbook, English textbooks and those from other common law jurisdictions are relied on rather indiscriminately and it is not easy to find out exactly what English cases or those from other jurisdictions are relevant in the interpretation of the Penal Codes. Although there are many books on the Indian Penal Code, notably Gour, *Penal Code of India* (1982–84, 4 vols), and Ratanlal and Dhirajlal, *Law of Crimes* (1987–88, 2 vols), all of which cite numerous English cases, there is no attempt to analyse systematically their relevance or otherwise to the Penal Code. Indeed, sometimes English cases are cited as being analogous to the Penal Code and this could be misleading, as noted by Murray-Aynsley CJ in the Singapore case of *Vincent Lee* (1949) where his Lordship, pointing out that extortion under the Penal Code of Singapore is different from that under English law, said:

> It is to be regretted that the use of the word "extortion" in this connection, which is very different from the technical use in English law ... had led to confusion. It will be seen that the authorities cited in the commentary both in Gour and Ratanlal are mostly English cases and they are examples of offences very different from that defined in the section.

Although the Penal Code is not a codification of English criminal law this does not mean that the principles and concepts of English criminal law are never relevant. They are relevant and of persuasive authority in the construction of the Penal Code and other criminal law statutes, provided that they are not inconsistent. There are, for example, a number of concepts in the Penal Code that are not defined or are defined inadequately and resort may be had to those concepts as they have developed in England or in other jurisdictions. Examples are "cause", "act" and "intention" to mention a few. What is more important in the construction of the Penal Code are cases on the Indian Penal Code and other Penal Codes which are derived from the Indian Penal Code, such as the Penal Code of Sri Lanka, and those of some African countries. The cases from these jurisdictions are of highly persuasive authority. There are, however, conflicting decisions, particularly those under the Indian Penal Code and it is difficult sometimes to determine what exactly the law is. If appeals have gone to the Privy Council they would be binding on Singapore and Malaysian courts if the law is *in pari materia* (see *Khalid Panjang (No 2)*, 1962; *Wo Yok Ling*, 1979).

There is, then, a dire need for a local textbook on criminal law. It must be a textbook with a difference in that it should involve, in certain areas, a comparative study of English law in order to determine the relevance or otherwise of English law. Also, a selection has to be made from a welter of decisions, at times conflicting, from other jurisdictions with similar Penal Codes.

The aim of this book is to present an explanatory text along with the materials produced. In view of what has been said above, some of the conclusions reached may be only tentative and the reader is encouraged to pursue his own conclusions. In the preparation of this book the writers have become acutely aware of the wealth of moot points and the different constructions that can be given to the Penal Code and other non-Penal Code offences. The vitality of statute law cannot be overlooked. A code ought not to be construed so narrowly that the law might be fossilized. There should be some flexibility within the bounds of statutory construction.

The foregoing excursus into the way courts have interpreted the Penal Codes and the possible reasons for the problems encountered is necessary as the approach taken in this book is influenced by what courts have done or not done. Of necessity, therefore, our analysis of a given aspect may be more detailed than that found in traditional textbooks, which attempt simply to state the law. Criminal jurisprudence in Singapore and in Malaysia is still in the making, and we hope this book will provide some contribution.

D.   Doctrine of stare decisis in criminal cases in Singapore and Malaysia

A word on the doctrine of *stare decisis*, ie binding precedent, as it applies in criminal cases in Singapore and Malaysia is necessary. (See Harbajan Singh, 1971; Koh, 1977; Friedman, 1980; Woon, 1982 and 1985.)

The English doctrine of *stare decisis* generally forms part of the judicial systems in Singapore and in Malaysia. According to the doctrine, decisions of the highest court in a judicial system binds all courts in the lower hierarchy. Appellate courts bind themselves (subject to exceptions) and lower courts. High courts do not bind themselves but they bind lower courts. Lower courts do not bind themselves.

In *Mah Kah Yew* (1971) the High Court in Singapore approved the doctrine of *stare decisis* in criminal cases as it applies to the Court of Criminal Appeal in England. Regarding the practice in England, the court noted that the general rule is that the Court of Criminal Appeal in England would follow a decision of its own unless the exception in *Taylor* (1950) applied (compare Woon, 1982). There, Lord Goddard stated:

> ... questions involving the liberty of the subject, and if... in the opinion of a full court... the law has been either misapplied or misunderstood in a decision which it has previously given, and that, on the strength of that decision, an accused person has been sentenced and imprisioned it is the bounden duty of the court to reconsider the earlier decision with a view to seeing whether that person had been properly convicted. The exceptions which apply in civil cases ought not to be the only ones applied in such a case ....

In a somewhat earlier case of *Gideon Nkambule* (1950), the Privy Council stated that it would not follow an earlier decision of its own, if it were satisfied that all relevant considerations and historical circumstances were not before it. This is a wider exception than that in *Taylor* (1950). *Gideon Nkambule* (1950) was noted by the Federal Court of Malaysia in *Ooi Hee Koi* (1966). In departing from its previous decision in *Lee Hoo Boon* (1966), decided only a few days before, the Federal Court said that it would follow the same principle as applied in *Gideon Nkambule* (1950) (see Woon, 1982).

The doctrine is dependent on a system of courts. The predecessor courts, particularly those of the Court of Criminal Appeal of Singapore and of the Supreme Court of Malaysia brought about by constitutional changes, have complicated the application of the doctrine.

A summary of the judicial systems and the doctrine of *stare decisis* as it applies in Singapore and in Malaysia is given below.

Judicial system in Singapore

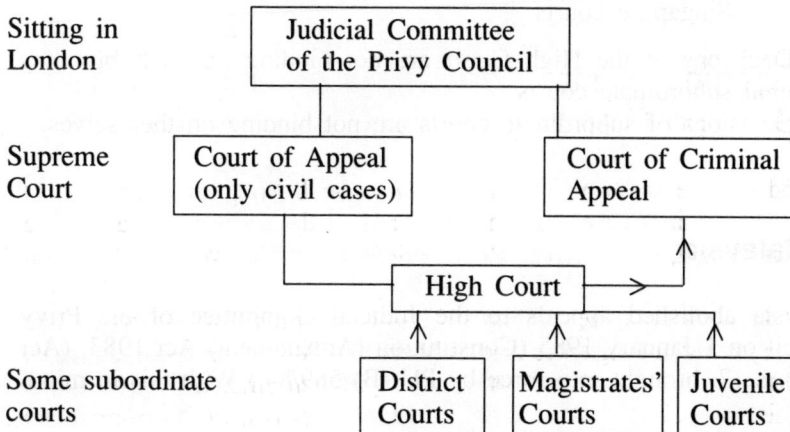

1. Singapore

(1) Decisions of the Privy Council on appeal from Singapore are binding on all Singapore courts. The Privy Council, being an advisory body, in not bound by its past decisions.

(2) "Applicable" decisions (ie where the law is *in pari materia*) of the Privy Council in appeals from other jurisdictions are binding on all Singapore courts (see *Khalid Panjang* (1964) and s 13, Republic of Singapore Independence Act (Act 9 of 1965) (1985 Rev Ed)).

(3) Decisions of the Court of Criminal Appeal are binding on itself, the High Court and subordinate courts, unless the *Taylor* and *Gideon Nkambule* exceptions apply.

(4) Decisions of the following predecessor courts in respect of criminal matters are binding on the Court of Criminal Appeal (subject to the exceptions above), the High Court and subordinate courts:

    (a) Supreme Court of the Straits Settlements.

    (b) Court of Criminal Appeal of the Straits Settlements.

    (c) Court of Appeal of the Straits Settlements.

    (d) Court of Appeal of the Federation of Malaya.

    (e) Court of Appeal of Sarawak, North Borneo and Brunei before Malaysia Day, ie 16 September 1963.

    (f) Court of Criminal Appeal of Singapore before Malaysia Day.

    (g) Federal Court of Malaysia between Malaysia Day and 9 August 1965. *Quaere* are decisions of the Federal Court of Malaysia between 9 August 1965 and the date of coming into force of the Supreme Court of Judicature Act of Singapore (see now Cap 322), ie 9 January 1970, binding? See Harbajan Singh (1971), compare Koh (1977) and Woon (1985).

    (h) Decisions of the former FMS Court of Appeal are not binding as the court was not expressly stated in s 88(3) of the Malaysia Act (Act 26 of 1963). However, they are of persuasive authority. It has not been decided judicially whether decisions of the Court of Appeal of the Malayan Union are binding on Singapore courts.

(5) Decisions of the High Court are not binding on itself but they bind subordinate courts.

(6) Decisions of subordinate courts are not binding on themselves.

2. Malaysia

Malaysia abolished appeals to the Judicial Committee of the Privy Council on 1 January 1985 (Constitution (Amendment) Act 1983, (Act A566), s 17, brought into force by PU (B) 589/84.) With this in mind,

Judicial system in Malaysia

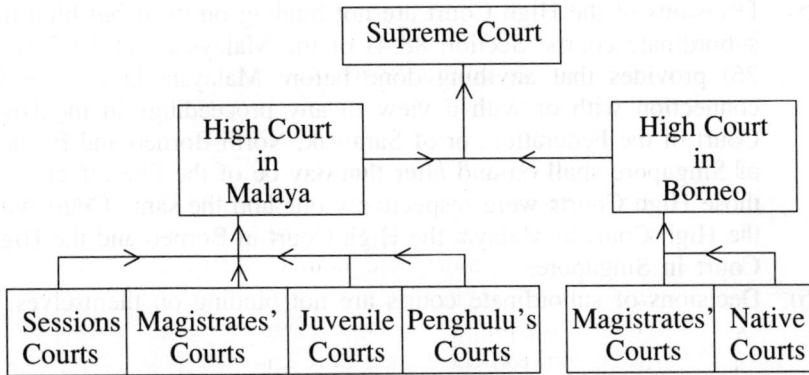

```
                        ┌─────────────────┐
                        │  Supreme Court  │
                        └─────────────────┘
                                 ↑
       ┌──────────────┐          │          ┌──────────────┐
       │  High Court  │    ───→ ─┴─ ←───     │  High Court  │
       │     in       │                      │     in       │
       │   Malaya     │                      │   Borneo     │
       └──────────────┘                      └──────────────┘
              ↑                                     ↑
    ┌────→ ─┴─ ←──── ←───┐              ┌────→ ─┴─ ←───┐
```

Sessions Courts	Magistrates' Courts	Juvenile Courts	Penghulu's Courts	Magistrates' Courts	Native Courts

the following is a summary of the doctrine of *stare decisis* as it applies in criminal cases in Malaysia:

(1)   Decisions of the Privy Council on appeal from Malaysia before 1 January 1985 are binding on all Malaysian courts (but see *Viro*, 1978).

(2)   "Applicable" decisions (ie where the law is *in pari materia*) of the Privy Council in appeals from other jurisdictions before 1 January 1985 are binding on all Malaysian courts (see *Khalid Panjang* (1964)).

(3)   Decisions of the Supreme Court in criminal matters are binding on itself, the High Court of Malaya and the High Court of Borneo and all subordinate courts in Malaysia, subject to certain exceptions.

(4)   Decisions of the following main predecessor courts in respect of criminal matters are binding on the Supreme Court, the High Court in Malaya, the High Court in Borneo and subordinate courts:

   (a)   Supreme Court of the Straits Settlements.
   (b)   Court of Appeal of Johore.
   (c)   Court of Appeal of Kedah.
   (d)   Court of Appeal of Trengganu.
   (e)   Sultan's Court of Kelantan (when it acts as an appellate court).
   (f)   Court of Raja in Council of Perlis (when it acts as an appellate court).
   (g)   Court of Appeal of the Malayan Union.
   (h)   Court of Appeal of the Federated Malay States.
   (i)   Court of Appeal of the Federation of Malaya.
   (j)   Court of Appeal of Sarawak, North Borneo and Brunei.
   (k)   Court of Criminal Appeal of Singapore (before Malaysia Day, ie 16 September 1963).
   (l)   Federal Court in appeals from Singapore, ie 16 September 1963, when Singapore was part of Malaysia until the Supreme Court of Judicature Act of Singapore, ie 9 January 1970.

(m) Federal Court of Malaysia (Courts of Judicature (Amendment) (No 2) (Act 1984 (Act A606)).

(5) Decisions of the High Court are not binding on itself but bind the subordinate courts. Section 88(4) of the Malaysia Act 1963 (Act 26) provides that anything done before Malaysia Day in or in connection with or with a view to any proceedings in the High Court of the Federation, or of Sarawak, North Borneo and Brunei, of Singapore shall on and after that day be of the like effect as if those High Courts were respectively one and the same Court with the High Court in Malaya, the High Court in Borneo and the High Court in Singapore.

(6) Decisions of subordinate courts are not binding on themselves.

Chapter 2

Crime and punishment

By CMV Clarkson

A. Introduction

The criminal law could be loosely defined as a body of rules prohibiting certain conduct on pain of punishment. The essence of the criminal law is that when it is alleged that someone has committed the prohibited act it must be established, using rules of criminal procedure designed to ensure fairness to the accused, that he did commit the alleged act or cause the forbidden harm and had no legally recognized excuse or justification for what he did. Once liability is established the accused becomes liable to punishment by the state, the type and level of such punishment varying with the seriousness of the crime committed.

Some local statutes are often thought by lay observers to relate to the criminal law–largely because they involve the physical detention of persons which appears to resemble the punishment of imprisonment. Thus in Singapore the Internal Security Act (Cap 143), s 8 permits the detention without trial for up to two years of any person "with a view to preventing that person from acting in any manner prejudicial to the security of Singapore ... or to the maintenance of public order or essential services therein ...". (See also the Criminal Law (Temporary Provisions) Act (Singapore) (Cap 67) and the preventive detention laws in ss 149 and 150 of the Malaysian Constitution both of which statutes permit detention without trial in specified circumstances.) None of these provisions deals with the criminal law as they are not concerned with the establishment in a court of law that the accused committed an offence for which he can be punished. They do of course raise fundamental issues relating to the rule of law and whether it can ever be permissible to detain an innocent man (all persons are necessarily innocent in the eyes of the law until found guilty of an offence by a court of competent jurisdiction) in the interests of "security", etc; these issues, however, belong more appropriately in a constitutional law book.

This book is primarily devoted to an examination of the substantive rules of the criminal law. However, any examination that limited itself to such substantive law without attempting to expose the rationale and purpose of the law and without examining the structure and relationship of the various rules to each other would be sterile. Accordingly, efforts have been made at various stages in this book to explain these rules in the context of the purposes of the criminal law. This involves addressing the following questions: how should a crime be defined and what level of punishment should it carry? ie who may be punished and how much punishment and of what type can be imposed? What is the purpose of such punishment? How should the level of seriousness of an offence (say, whether the crime is murder or culpable homicide), with concomitant levels of punishment, be measured? Is it by the harm caused (for instance, whether someone has been killed or seriously injured) or by the blameworthiness of the accused (for instance, whether he meant to cause the harm or was negligent)?

As the above list of questions reveals, the rules of the criminal law and the punishment of offenders for violating such rules are "two sides of the same coin". For this central theme of the book to be clear, it is accordingly necessary that this chapter be devoted to a few introductory words about the concept and purpose of punishment.

B. Function of punishment

What is important to an understanding of the substantive criminal law is not the procedural details concerning each type of punishment but, rather, the philosophical rationalization of the institution of punishment and of each individual punishment. Nevertheless, it is useful to list the different types of punishment available in Singapore and Malaysia:

(1) death penalty;
(2) caning;
(3) imprisonment;
(4) probation;
(5) fine;
(6) compensation order to victim;
(7) binding over;
(8) absolute and conditional discharge.

Two points will be made in relation to this list. First, the range of available dispositions, compared to many other countries, is rather narrow. For example, neither Singapore nor Malaysia has the suspended sentence or the community service order (see Morgan, 1987). Second, it must be observed that while criticism of the death penalty and caning is muted in Singapore and Malaysia, such sentences are extremely controversial–both as to their morality and their efficacy as a deterrent, quite apart from any controversy as to their constitutionality (Pannick, 1982). The present writer has expressed his views on these matters elsewhere and will not repeat them here (see Clarkson, 1987).

What, however, is the purpose of the whole institution of punishment and what factors will determine which particular sentence (and the level thereof) is appropriate? The traditional view is that there are four "theories" of punishment:

1. Retribution

TTB Koh, "The Sentencing Policy and Practice of the Singapore Courts" (1965) 7 Mal LR 291, 294

The courts seldom articulate what they regard as their objectives in imposing a sentence. My impression is that the dominant penal philosophy of our judiciary is a retributionist one and when they say that a punishment is excessive, they generally mean that it exceeds some unpublished tariff which they follow.

Some 16 years later, English (1981) concluded that this was still the dominant philosophy underlying sentencing in Singapore.

"Retribution" is a loose word. It is still often used in its older sense as indicating vengeance, the idea being that it is right to hate criminals and to strike back at them on an "eye for an eye and a tooth for a tooth" basis. A manifestation of this philosophy can be seen in the role of caning which is extensively used in Singapore, mainly in response to crimes of violence. It is a form of "striking back in kind".

Apologists for this rationale tend to assert that the desire for vengeance is strongly felt at two levels. First, there is the victim or his relatives and friends in the case of death. The state by acting on their behalf relieves their need for vengeance and protects them from having to resort to private retaliation. Second, the public itself has a need for vengeance. Punishment by the state is a socially acceptable outlet for aggressions that would otherwise become repressed and perhaps break out in an unacceptable manner.

A more acceptable (philosophically) variant of the retributive theory is that an offender *deserves* punishment. Under a general theory of political obligation all persons owe duties to others not to infringe their rights. Justice and fairness insist that all persons must bear the sacrifice of obeying the law equally. By committing a crime the offender has gained an unfair advantage over all the others who have "toed the line" and restrained themselves from committing crime. Social equilibrium in society must be restored. The offender deserves and must receive punishment in order to destroy his unfair advantage.

John Finnis, "The Restoration of Retribution" (1971) *Analysis*, 32.4, 131

Jeffrie G Murphy (1971) argues that the retributivist claim that crime deserves punishment may be taken, not as the assertion of an intuited, primitive and unanalysed proposition, but as one particular application of, or theorem within, a general theory of political obligation. Thus, if political obligation is based on the justice of reciprocity or fair play in the sharing of the burdens and benefits of social life, then crime may be analysed as gaining (or putting oneself in a position to gain: Murphy is not specific about this) an unfair advantage over those who, even when they do not desire to do so, voluntarily obey the law; and punishment can be analysed as the attempt "to maintain the proper balance between benefit and obedience by insuring that there is no profit in criminal wrongdoing"; and the general principle of fairness between citizens then justifies punishment for crime....

These obscurities about the nature and occasion of the criminal's profiting can be cleared up if we go further than Murphy, and say that

(1) what the criminal gains in the act of committing crime (whatever the size and nature of the loot, if any, and indeed quite apart from the success or failure of his overall purpose) is the advantage of indulging a (wrongful) self-preference, of permitting himself an excessive freedom in choosing–this advantage (of exercising a wider freedom and of acting according to one's tastes ...) being something that his law-abiding fellow citizens have denied themselves insofar as they have chosen to conform their will (habits and choices) to the law even when they would "prefer" not to;

(2) this advantage is gained at the time of the crime, because and insofar as the crime is ... a free and "responsible" exercise of self-will; the wrongfulness of gaining this advantage is the specifically relevant moral turpitude adverted to in the retributivist's talk of criminal "guilt"; and the advantage is one that cannot be lost, unless and until ...

(3) the criminal has the disadvantage of having his wayward will restricted in its freedom by being subjected to the representative "will of society" (the "will" which he disregarded in disregarding the law) through the process of punishment; a punishment is thus to be defined not, formally speaking, in terms of the infliction of pain (nor as incarceration), but rather in terms of the subjection of will (normally, but not necessarily, effected through the denial of benefits and advantages of social living: compulsory employment on some useful work which the criminal would not of himself have chosen to do would satisfy the definition)....

It is not just the victim and the wrongdoer who should be put back on a footing of equality: the "satisfaction" which the wrongdoer gains is an advantage not only as against the victim but also as against all those who might have been wrongdoers but restrained themselves ....

Aquinas ... [said,] "anyone who has indulged his will more than he ought [*plus voluntati suae indulsit quam debuit*], by transgressing the law, should either of his own accord or without his consent undergo something opposed to what he wills–so that the equality of justice may thus be restored [*reintegretur*]."

On this view ... we can say ... that the restoration of a fair distribution of advantages and disadvantages as between citizens is *an aim* of punishment....

At the end of a period one should be able to look back over the *whole* period and say that, because of the adjustments that were made in response to criminal disruption of that order, no one has (overall and taking the period as a whole) been disadvantaged unfairly by attempting to live in strict accordance with that basic order of fairness....

In the classical and more standard view, represented by Aquinas for example, while it is clear that crime should ordinarily be punished, the questions of time, place, circumstance and degree are a matter of pure positive law, and cannot be determined by abstract moral reasoning. (See eg *Summa Theologiae*, 1a 2ae, q95, a2.) And this position seems more reasonable than Kant's. For although fairness is a component of the overall social good, it is only a component, and it would be silly to sacrifice important social goods simply to secure a scrupulously restored order of fairness. Indeed, if it is unfair to law-abiding citizens not to punish criminals, it is more unfair to them to punish criminals when it is clear that the punishment will lead to more crime, more unfairness by criminals and more danger and disadvantage to law-abiding citizens.

In short, ... where Kant is keen to insist that it is *wrong not to punish the guilty*, we should say that it is more reasonable morally (and more representative of Western commonsense) to argue that it is *unfair not to aim at punishing the guilty*.

The critical point about this just deserts philosophy is that it necessitates a continual measuring of the punishment against the crime committed. The punishment must be proportionate to the crime for the simple reason that if the purpose of punishment is to destroy the unfair advantage of the offender, he should only be punished to that extent necessary to destroy such advantage. Excessive punishment would be undeserved and unfair and tip the social equilibrium against the offender. Insufficient punishment would not completely destroy the offender's advantage. In short, a strictly interpreted just deserts philosophy would lead to relatively fixed and inflexible sentences–a development which has occurred in the USA. Indeed, advocates of fixed and mandatory minimum sentences in Singapore and Malaysia have resorted to such ideas in support of their claims (see below, pp 20–22; 24–25; 34).

However, it should be stressed that the concept of just deserts does *not* mean that everyone who commits a particular offence, say, robbery, deserves an identical sentence. Individual characteristics of the offender could be critical in determining how much punishment is deserved. An offender with 20 previous convictions might *deserve* more punishment than a first-time offender who commits an identical crime. It need not be a question of his dangerousness justifying extra punishment (see below, pp 24–27), but rather, because of his failure to learn lessons from previous convictions and punishment, he deserves more punishment. Such a person has persisted in criminal behaviour after being specifically warned and already punished. Perhaps such repeated defiance of the law could even be viewed as an additional harm. Alternatively, viewed negatively, a first offender deserves *less* punishment because of the following reason:

> We wish to condemn the person for his act but accord him some respect for
> the fact that his inhibitions against wrongdoing have functioned on previous
> occasions, and show some sympathy for the all-too-human frailty that can
> lead someone to such a lapse. This we do by showing a reduced disapproval
> of him for his first misdeed (Von Hirsch, 1985).

Further, it is a manifest absurdity to suggest that, apart from the above considerations relating to previous convictions, all persons committing the same offence deserve the same punishment. Suppose two offenders are convicted of a crime falling under the same offence definition, say, robbery. One offender who could be impoverished, and needing food for his child, threatens to punch a passer-by if he does not give him $10. The other offender, armed with a machine-gun, could be executing a sophisticated plan for robbing a security van of $10m. In short, most offences are so broadly framed and cover so wide a variety of human wrongdoing that it would be naive to assert that there was a deserved punishment for any particular crime. At the same time, however, it would be foolish to assert that there can be no criteria to structure the sentencing judge's discretion. Simply leaving the sentencing decision to the judge on the basis that because of his "expertise" he "knows best" is opening the door to sentencing disparity. Respect for the criminal law is not enhanced when two offenders with substantially similar backgrounds committing similar crimes in similar circumstances receive hugely different sentences. In the last decade this has been the major issue in criminal justice both in the USA and in England: how can one ensure that there is justice, ie equality of treatment for all offenders in the sense that like cases are treated alike and unlike cases treated differently–and how and on what basis can one measure "likeness"? Implicit in this whole debate has been acceptance to a certain extent of the just deserts philosophy.

2.   Deterrence

The aim of deterrence is that the threat of punishment will deter people from committing crime. *Individual deterrence* is where the individual offender is discouraged from committing a further crime as a result of his unpleasant punishment. In the case of *general deterrence* the punishment of an offender serves as an example and a threat to others of what will happen to them if they commit crimes. General deterrence operates in two ways. First, regular and normal levels of punishment keep the constant threat of punishment alive. Second, courts will occasionally pass "exemplary sentences". These are disproportionately severe penalties usually imposed when a particular type of activity is perceived to be on the increase.

There can be no doubt that general deterrence is regarded as one of the central aims of the institution of punishment in Singapore and Malaysia.

Peter English, "Sentencing in Singapore" (1981) 22 Mal LR 1, 24

Singapore's courts are not unique in placing faith in the value of deterrent sentences but if it be thought that they sometimes place too much faith in that direction it must be said that the Legislature in Singapore has adopted a similar attitude. The extent of mandatory punishments for certain crimes is explicable on the basis that the legislators believe in the efficacy of deterrent sentences. It amounts in effect to an assertion that the public interest requires such measures. Courts, it has been said, "may not perhaps have to wholly reflect public opinion but they certainly must not be indifferent or disregard it". Nor are courts likely to be indifferent to or disregard clear indications of the views of the elected representatives in the Legislature. It is not surprising therefore that deterrence continues to be an important element in sentencing practice in Singapore.

Shelly Wright, "The New Mandatory Minimum Penalties in Singapore: A Comment" (1985) Lawasia 131

The Penal Code (Amendment) Act 1984 and the Arms Offences (Amendment) Act 1984 both seek to provide more deterrent penalties for certain offences, in the case of the Arms Offences (Amendment) Act, by providing mandatory minimum penalties (prison sentences and caning) for the unlawful possession and use of arms and ammunition, and, in the case of the Penal Code (Amendment) Act, mandatory minimum penalties (again both prison sentences and, in most instances, caning) for aggravated rape and outraging modesty, robbery, snatch theft, extortion and housebreaking. In addition the amendment to the Penal Code creates a new offence of theft of a motor vehicle or any component part of a motor vehicle with a mandatory minimum prison sentence of one year, a fine and driving licence disqualification....

The result of imposing mandatory minimum penalties may very well be "too many hard cases, too many injustices to be swallowed, and therefore too much evasion and twisting of the law by all concerned". Offenders may be more likely to plead not guilty and demand trial, leading to a further clogging of an already over-burdened court system. On the other hand, plea bargaining may become more widespread, thus evading the mandatory minima altogether. Offenders who would previously have received discharges or probation may spend extended periods of time in prison, which may lead to an increase in prison population and consequent undesirable results such as over-crowding, young or first-time offenders being "criminalized" and greater stress and un-happiness for the offenders and their families than can be justified. It is pos-sible, of course, that the deterrent and potential rehabilitative effects of manda-tory minimum prison terms and corporal punishment will have the desired result of lowering the number of persons going through the criminal justice system....

It is too soon yet to know whether any of these more practical problems have developed, but there would seem to be a need for careful monitoring and reappraisal at some future date.

Some difficulties in relation to offenders who are not appropriate candidates for minimum prison sentences may be dealt with by the exercise of the Attor-ney General's discretion. This exercise of discretion has always allowed the prosecuting authorities the necessary margin in which to deal with individual cases. However, the decision of the Attorney General as to how and whom he wishes to charge is not subject to any appeal whereas sentences imposed by the judiciary are. In other words, the discretion in relation to sentence moves from the open courtroom which is under the supervision of the higher courts to the closed doors of the Attorney General's Chambers from which no review or appeal is possible....

Is there any evidence that increased penalties have in the past led to drops in the recorded crime rate in Singapore...?

It is impossible to tell from these figures whether the "success" of Sin-gapore's drug campaign has to do with the increased penalties, massive police action to curtail drug activities, other factors or a combination of factors. Even more interestingly, there is no indication from the figures that the drug cam-paign has in fact been successful....

The figures which have been examined seem to demonstrate that more severe penalties may result in a temporary drop in the amount of recorded crime, but that they do not in and of themselves greatly affect the rate of recorded crime over the long term.

Stanley Yeo Meng Heong, "Mandatory Minimum Sentences: A Tying of Judicial Hands" [1985] 2 MLJ clxxxvi

The main justification for mandatory minimum sentences is to deter persons from committing those offences which attract such sentences. In respect of the offender who is apprehended and convicted, sterner punishment in the form of a minimum sentence is claimed to be likely to deter him from reverting to crime. However, the real value of such a sentence concerns general deterrence. Certain incarceration for a specified period of time is assumed to have a definite deterrent effect, not so much on the affected offenders, as on all who might be tempted to violate the law. Our parliamentary debates on the various bills introducing mandatory minimum sentences are replete with statements to this effect. For example, in the parliamentary debates preceding the implementation of the Misuse of Drugs Act, it was said of drug traffickers that "[t]hey and their trade must be stopped. To do this effectively, heavy penalties have to be provided for trafficking .... We have therefore expressly provided minimum penalties and the rotan for trafficking."

Beginning with the assumption that the certain nature of such sentences deters, it is not at all clear that this has been proven....

With regard to drug trafficking ... the available criminal statistics reveal that there was a sudden increase of thirty-eight reported cases in 1976 (despite the raising of minimum sentences and the introduction of the death penalty in late 1975) and the number has generally been above thirty cases per year since then. It could, of course, be argued that the number of trafficking cases would have been much higher had minimum sentences not been prescribed, but until further evidence is tendered in support of this claim, it remains unproven.

Minimum prison sentences were also introduced by the Penal Code (Amendment) Act 1984 to deter persons from committing housebreaking for the purpose of theft. Yet, recent statistics indicate that these sentences have had no immediate impact on the rising rate of housebreaking....

It is therefore submitted that mandatory minimum sentences have failed to display any concrete deterrent effect on the crimes sought to be eradicated. Arguably, it is the efficiency of police detection, ensuring that offenders are apprehended and convicted, which has a far greater impact. In other words, the certainty of punishment, not the severity, is the deterrent to crime.

Despite this local faith in deterrence, there has been growing scepticism in other countries of the value of punishment as a general deterrent. The whole theory of deterrence presupposes that criminals act rationally in the sense that they "weigh the odds" before committing an offence. However, crimes of violence in particular are often committed by persons in highly charged emotional states. Further, deterrence can only operate on a person's conscious mind if he thinks there is a realistic chance that he will be apprehended. Because of the large number of crimes never reported to the police it is impossible to estimate exact chances of apprehension or criminal's estimates thereof but it seems clear that many criminals over-estimate their chances of avoiding detection and to that extent are not amenable to the deterrent threat of punishment.

Internationally, there is now a broad consensus on the limited effectiveness of punishment as a deterrent: nothing has been or can be proved—but *perhaps* the threat of punishment can deter *some* people *sometimes* from committing *some* crimes (Beyleveld, 1980; Walker, 1985). In view of the inconclusive nature of the evidence, it would seem naive to place over-reliance on the value of punishment as a general deterrent.

There is a third species of deterrence–*An educative-deterrence*. While individual and general deterrence hope to operate at a conscious level inducing people to refrain from committing crimes, educative deterrence operates on the subconscious; it seeks to educate people into the habit of not committing crimes; it is a mechanism whereby social values or morality are underwritten. General deterrence aims at frightening people into not committing crime. Educative deterrence tries to mould people's moral values so that they do not want to commit crime.

CMV Clarkson, *Understanding Criminal Law* (1987), 177–179

All laws have a symbolic or expressive function....

Simply declaring an activity to be criminal can, in itself, have a symbolic effect in influencing attitudes and moral beliefs. This point is illustrated by the research of Kaufmann (1970) who asked a group of subjects to evaluate the morality of certain behaviour (failing to rescue a drowning man). Some subjects were told that this behaviour was criminal; others were told that there was no legal duty to rescue. The former group judged the inaction more harshly than the latter group. Breaking the law was in itself viewed as immoral. Similarly, Walker and Marsh (1984) discovered that subjects stated that their disapproval of not wearing a seat-belt would increase when this became an offence.

While the mere existence of criminal laws has important expressive consequences, it is enforcement of that law and the punishment of offenders that gives the criminal law its real "sting". Through punishment society is emphatically condemning and thereby disavowing the offender's acts. Failure to punish, on the other hand, amounts to an endorsement or approval of such actions. Feinberg (1965) uses a telling example: suppose an aeroplane from nation A shoots down an aeroplane from nation B over international waters. If nation A were to punish its pilot this would amount to a disavowal of the pilot's action: the actions would simply be those of a deranged pilot. But a failure to punish the pilot would amount to an endorsement of his actions. Nation A would effectively be admitting that it was responsible for the act and approved of it.

Such disavowals of criminal acts have an important socializing effect in reinforcing attitudes and social values. They are part of the conditioning process that creates conscious and unconscious inhibitions against committing crime. In this way the criminal law can have the effect of strengthening the public's moral code. Every time a person is punished for, say, theft, our underlying conviction that theft is wrong is reinforced. The aim of punishing drunken drivers is not simply to deter other would-be drunken drivers but to try and induce a social climate in which it is regarded as morally unacceptable to drive after drinking too much alcohol....

A lesser, but related, claim is that even if criminal law and punishment does not actually mould morality, it nevertheless induces an automatic, habitual response of obeying the law. A soldier in the army might not believe in the justice or morality of every order he receives, but he has been indoctrinated into a knee-jerk habit of obeying all orders. The criminal law and punishment can induce such law-abiding conduct "purely as a matter of habit, with fear, respect for authority or social imitation as connecting links" (Andenaes, 1952).

Punishment for the purpose of inducing the habit of conformity to the law might be necessary for other psychological reasons. Durkheim (1964) has argued that those who obey the law need support. At a subconscious level there might be a temptation to commit crime. By abstaining therefrom, the conformist has been able to maintain internal control. To sustain this balance within the personality and ensure the dominance of internal control, the conformist needs to be able to identify with the police and the courts; the offender must be made unattractice as a role model. The inhibition of deviant impulses must be made to seem worthwhile. The punishment of offenders reassures the conformist that it was worth obeying the law. His morale and habit of not breaking the law are maintained.

3. Incapacitation

The central idea here is that society needs protection from "dangerous criminals", ie those criminals likely to reoffend. Accordingly, society is justified in taking whatever steps are necessary to protect itself from the danger. This might involve as minor a penalty as disqualifying a dangerous driver from driving again (Malaysian Road Traffic Ordinance 1958 (Ord 49 of 1958), s 30; Singapore, Road Traffic Act (Cap 276), s 42). More typically, however, giving "dangerous offender" its more commonly accepted meaning, long terms of imprisonment are used to keep such persons out of society. (Capital punishment can be viewed as a species of incapacitative sentence. However, arguments in favour of judicial homicide have their roots mainly in the soil of retributive and deterrent philosophies.)

There are three ways, all employed in Singapore and Malaysia, that imprisonment can be employed as an incapacitative sentence.

First, there is life imprisonment where even though "life" does not mean actual life (compare Criminal Justice Ordinance 1953 (Malaysia) (Ord 14 of 1953)) whereby a sentence of imprisonment for life shall be deemed for all purposes to be a sentence of imprisonment for 20 years), it nevertheless involves the incapacitation of the offender for a substantial period of time.

Second, the new mandatory minimum sentences discussed above, can be viewed not only as deterrent sentences but as efforts to incapacitate certain types of dangerous offender.

Stanley Yeo Meng Heong, "Mandatory Minimum Sentences: A Tying of Judicial Hands" [1985] 2 MLJ clxxxvi

Another justification lies in community protection. A minimum sentence guarantees that offenders convicted of certain crimes will be removed from society for at least a specified duration. During this period, the community will be protected from further depredations by these offenders. At this juncture, one might ask why the legislature should intervene when it is within the powers of the courts to impose sentences which deter as well as protect the community against certain types of offences. The answer is that the legislature has found the sentencing practice of the courts to be too lenient for its liking....

Turning now to the rationale that mandatory minima provide for community protection, public clamour for such protection and the political capitalization on it which feeds its growth ignores the fact that it is at most only some offenders from whom the public needs this protection and that the legislature is not in a position to identify the precise individuals who pose the feared risk. The offender who robs to feed his starving family does not pose the same danger to the community as the one who robs as a convenient way of making a living. The effect of mandatory minimum prison sentences is to incarcerate offenders who pose no threat to the community in order to incapacitate the smaller percentage of offenders who are community threats. This is not only a costly waste of human resources but is intrinsically immoral.

The final way in which imprisonment can be used as an incapacitative sentence is by enabling courts to sentence dangerous offenders to longer periods of imprisonment than justified for the crime. In other words, the dangerous offender is sentenced not just for the crime he has committed but also for his dangerousness. There are several devices, particularly in Singapore, enabling the courts to achieve this objective.

(a) Singapore

(i) Corrective training

Section 12(1) of the Criminal Procedure Code (Singapore) (Cap 68) authorizes a court to sentence persons with specified previous convictions (at least two), (or specified multiple offenders with a previous conviction) to a sentence of corrective training (five to fourteen years) if "satisfied that it is expedient with a view to his reformation and the prevention of crime that he should receive training of a corrective character for a substantial period of time, followed by a period of supervision".

(ii) Preventive detention

Section 12(2) of the Singapore Criminal Procedure Code authorizes a court to sentence older persons (ie at least 30 years old) with previous convictions (at least three) (or multiple offenders with a previous conviction) to a sentence of preventive detention (seven to twenty years) if "satisfied that it is expedient for the protection of the public that he should be detained in custody for a substantial period of time, followed by a period of supervision".

(iii) Consecutive sentencing

A further mechanism for incapacitating the dangerous for as long as possible is to be found in the new Singapore amendment (1984) to the Criminal Procedure Code, s 18, which provides that where a person is convicted at the same trial of at least three distinct offences and sentenced to imprisonment for each, it is *mandatory* for the court to order that at least two of those sentences shall run consecutively.

(iv) Enhanced sentencing

Under s 75 of the Penal Code, where the accused has a previous conviction for an offence under Chapter XII or Chapter XVII of the Penal Code punishable with imprisonment of three years' imprisonment or more (viz offences relating to coins and government stamps and offences relating to property respectively) then if he is convicted of another offence punishable with at least three years' imprisonment under either of those chapters, he becomes subject to double the amount of punishment he would otherwise have received. (This is subject to a maximum of ten years imprisonment but, strangely, life imprisonment is an alternative.)

It is difficult to see why this is limited to coin and property offences. Presumably it was felt that the potential penalties for the various offences of personal violence are set sufficiently high that previous convictions can simply be taken into account by the sentencing judge in exercising his sentencing discretion.

(v) Police supervision

Section 11 (2),(4) and (6) of the Singapore Criminal Procedure Code provides that a person convicted of an offence punishable with two or more years imprisonment who has previously already been convicted of such an offence may be subjected to police supervision for up to three years *after* the expiration of the sentence passed on him.

(b) Malaysia

In Malaysia there is no provision for corrective training or preventive detention, or for mandatory consecutive sentences. ("Preventive detention" does exist but involves detention without trial: see above, p 15.) The only special provisions allowing the courts to deal with an offender differently (as opposed to previous convictions simply being an aggravating factor) because of his dangerousness (judged by previous convictions) are as follows:

(i) FMS Penal Code

FMS Penal Code, s 75 (enhanced sentences) is the same as its Singapore equivalent but without the ten-year maximum (or the life imprisonment alternative).

(ii) FMS Criminal Procedure Code

FMS Criminal Procedure Code (Cap 6), s 295 provides for police supervision in similar circumstances to those set out in s 11 of the Singapore Criminal Procedure Code.

FMS Criminal Procedure Code, s 294 provides that offenders may be bound-over, ie "released on his entering into a bond with or without sureties" if it appears "expedient that the offender be released on probation of good conduct". The marginal note to s 294 reads "first offenders". While this does not of course provide any heavier punishment for offenders with previous convictions that nevertheless is its effect, albeit viewed negatively. The offender with previous convictions is not eligible for immediate release into the community. (It should be noted that s 294 itself makes no actual reference to first offenders. Compare FMS Criminal Procedure Code, s 2 "The marginal notes of this Code shall not affect the construction thereof".)

It was suggested above (p 19) that it is possible to assert that those with previous convictions *deserve* greater punishment than first-time offenders. However, the main rationale for all the above extended sentences is that persons with previous convictions are thought to be more likely to reoffend and therefore need restraining. It also appears clear that Singapore is more committed than Malaysia to the notion that it is justifiable to restrain "dangerous" offenders for long periods.

There are, however, several problems associated with this approach. Dangerousness is defined locally in terms of number of convictions. Such definition raises two issues. In trying to predict dangerousness it is clear that a wider range of factors such as unemployment and drug or alcohol use should be investigated (Greenwood, 1982). Second, it appears that all such efforts at prediction are little more than "guesses in the dark" which run the risk of yielding too many "false positives", ie persons locked up for longer than they deserve because it is wrongly predicted they will reoffend (Von Hirsch, 1985).

However, none of these addresses the central issue. Assuming that one were able to predict accurately who was dangerous, and what constituted dangerousness (eg would repeated stealing of a neighbour's flowers from his garden qualify?), one would still be left with the question whether it was justifiable to punish a person for what he might do in the future as opposed to what he had done in the past.

4. Rehabilitation

The purpose of rehabilitative sentencing is to try and reform the offender so that, being rehabilitated, he can resume a normal and useful role in society. Under this philosophy it is necessary that the sentencer find the appropriate sentence that will reform the particular offender. It does not matter what sentence other offenders receive. The punishment must fit the offender, not necessarily the crime. This is known as *individualized sentencing*.

Teo Siew Peng v PP [1985] 2 MLJ 125 (HC, Kuching, Malaysia)

The five appellants were young first offenders. They pleaded guilty to the offence of gang robbery punishable under s 395 of the Penal Code.

After calling for probation reports four of the appellants were sentenced to one year's imprisonment and two to three strokes of the rotan. The fifth appellant, being a youthful offender was sentenced to one year's detention in the Sarawak Boys' Home and two strokes of the rotan. The appellants appealed against sentence.

Tan Chiaw Thong J: Now, it is clear that the objects of sentence are three-fold, namely, in order to prevent any recurrence of an offence the offender must be dealt with by taking from him the power of offending, ie incapacitation; secondly, by taking away the desire of offending (reformation); and thirdly, by making him afraid of offending (intimidation)....

The lower court, apart from mentioning that careful consideration had been given to the probation reports, came to the conclusion that a custodial sentence was the only proper one in the particular circumstances in respect of each of the appellants. As earlier stated, although on the one hand it is right and correct that the deterrent factor must be taken into account, on the other hand, in respect of each individual offender, particularly in the case of young offenders, the reformative factor should also be adequately considered. In this respect, I do not consider that the lower court, having regard to the record of proceedings, had adequately considered the reformative factor involved in sentencing.

Now, in respect of each of the appellants here, there is a favourable probation report. The Probation Service is ready to undertake their supervision if the appellants are placed on probation. The matter for consideration is whether, in order to give the best chance of realizing the object of turning the appellants into good citizens, they should be sent to prison or given another chance to turn over a new leaf, behave themselves and keep out of trouble having regard, as earlier observed, to the fact that all of them were young offenders at the time of the commission of the offence. The *Smith* case (1964) laid emphasis that the public have no greater interest than that young offenders should become good citizens. Having regard to the circumstances of the offence, the character and antecedents of each of the appellants and the probation reports, I am of the opinion that the object of turning the appellants into good citizens could be better achieved by not sending them to prison and imposing whipping at the same time. It is noted that each of them had been in custody for over 80 days. This no doubt, having regard to the evidence before this court, would have had a salutary effect on each of the appellants....

I have come to the conclusion, for the reasons given, and bearing in mind that an appellate court does not alter the sentence of a lower court unless it had erred in principle or that the sentence is manifestly excessive, that in the particular circumstances, for the reasons that the reformative factor involved in sentencing and the probation reports and character and antecedents of the appellants do not appear to have been adequately considered, the lower court had erred in principle and therefore this court should interfere in the sentences.

Sentences reduced to probation

Raja Izzuddin Shah v PP [1979] 1 MLJ 270 (HC, Ipoh, Malaysia)

The appellant pleaded guilty to the offence of assaulting a public servant and was sentenced to three months' imprisonment. He appealed against the sentence.

Hashim Yeop A Sani J: Considering all the facts before the court I have come to the conclusion that the public interest is in no way better served by committing the appellant to prison. The primary purpose of punishment is reformatory and it is clear in this case that the appellant has realized the fact that notwithstanding his status he is not above the law. He has also clearly stated that he has repented and would not make the same mistake again. Under the circumstances it is my opinion that the public interest is best served by setting aside the sentence of imprisonment and substituting therefor an order under section 294(i) of the Criminal Procedure Code that the appellant enter into a bond with one surety in the sum of one thousand dollars for a period of two years and in the meantime to keep the peace and be of good behaviour.

Order accordingly

In Western Europe and the USA rehabilitation has been regarded as an important goal over the last few decades and, realizing the futility of attempting rehabilitation within the confines of a prison, several new types of sentence involving treatment of the offender within the community have been introduced. Probation and community service orders are the most notable among such sentences.

In Singapore there are a few sentences that pay lip-service to the rehabilitative ideal. The Probation of Offenders Act (Cap 252) does permit an offender to remain in the community subject to some supervision which can in theory assist in the rehabilitative process. However, it appears that such sentences are used primarily in relation to youthful offenders.

Section 13(1) of the Criminal Procedure Code permits persons between the ages of 16 and 21 to be sentenced to "undergo a period of training in a reformative training centre" (for a period between 18 months and three years). Finally, it should be noted that s 12(1) dealing with corrective training provides that in addition to the prevention of crime, one of the criteria for the imposition of such a sentence is that "it is expedient with a view to his reformation" that he "should receive training of a corrective character". It nevertheless seems clear, given the limited nature of these provisions and their usage, that the central thinking in Singapore is that while juveniles and young persons may be amenable to rehabilitation, such efforts in relation to adults are either ineffective or inappropriate. It is interesting that while there are even fewer provisions on the statute book aimed at rehabilitation in Malaysia, nevertheless the courts there in making use of probation orders and in exercising their discretion in sentencing do appear to pay more attention to rehabilitation as a possible goal of punishment.

While rehabilitation has long been regarded as important in the shaping of sentencing policy in Western Europe and North America, there has, however, been mounting scepticism over the last two decades as to whether punishment can ever be justified on such a basis.

AE Bottoms, "An Introduction to 'The Coming Crisis'" in AE Bottoms and RH Preston, *The Coming Penal Crisis* (1980), 1–3

First, and the dominant factor in much current penal consideration, comes *the collapse of the rehabilitative ideal....* A succession of negative research reports has–with a few exceptions which do not seriously disturb the conclusion–

suggested that different types of treatment make little or no difference to the subsequent reconviction rates of offenders.... As the Serota Report (ACPS 1977) succinctly put it:

> "A steadily accumulating volume of research has shown that, if reconviction rates are used to measure the success or failure of sentencing policy, there is virtually nothing to choose between different lengths of custodial sentence, different types of institutional regime, and even between custodial and non-custodial treatment; (para 8)."

Very recently, the Home Office's *Review* has endorsed this view....

But the objections to the treatment (or rehabilitation) ethic have not been solely based on empirical demonstrations of lack of efficacy. Strong theoretical objections have also been raised, perhaps most influentially in the American Friends Service Committee's (1971) *Struggle for Justice*, which argued that there was:

> "compelling evidence that the individualized-treatment model, the ideal towards which reformers have been urging us for at least a century, is theoretically faulty, systematically discriminatory in application, and inconsistent with some of our most basic concepts of justice (p 12)."

What lies behind these claims?

(i) *'Theoretically faulty'*–because, it can be claimed, the treatment model implies that criminal behaviour has its roots in the deficiencies of the individual and his upbringing, and that if these are remedied, the crime rate will be cut; but this medical analogy is inappropriate, and crime is far more a result of the overall organization of society than of the deficiencies of the individual.

(ii) *'Systematically discriminatory'*–because the treatment model typically takes more severe coercive action in cases of "unsatisfactory" home circumstances or "dubious" moral background; but these judgments are made by middle-class workers who unwittingly but systematically discriminate against the poor and the disadvantaged, and in favour of the "good" homes of the privileged.

(iii) *'Inconsistent with justice'*–because judgments involving the liberty of the individual are made (in the name of "casework" or whatever) on the basis of extremely impressionistic evidence which is usually not revealed to the offender, and which he cannot therefore challenge; and the result may be, for example, that some will serve long sentences for trivial crimes because their "attitudes have not improved", while others convicted of serious crime but who have allegedly "responded" are let out.

Underneath criticisms like these, it will be noted, lies a fundamental conviction by the critics as to the essentially *coercive* nature of the rehabilitative ideal .... Many adherents of the ideal blinded themselves as to this coerciveness, in the false belief that benevolent intentions preclude a coercive result....

For all these reasons it seems unlikely that the importance of rehabilitation as the underlying rationale of punishment will increase in Singapore and Malaysia. However, it can only be hoped that the jettisoning of such ideals will not be accompanied by an increase in over-retributive, in the sense of vindictive, attitudes towards punishment and the implementation thereof:

> A civilized and humane society cannot afford to ignore the importance of rehabilitating offenders. What this means is that while one might be punishing for other reasons such as deterrence or incapacitation, rehabilitation must

remain a desirable *collateral objective*. When espoused as a *purpose* of punishment, rehabilitation becomes vulnerable and in danger of being jettisoned if found to be ineffective. But if clearly understood as a desirable by-product or collateral purpose, the rehabilitative ideal becomes immune from attack on grounds of inefficacy (Clarkson, 1987).

C. Aim v justification

A troubling issue in relation to the above "theories" is that of the punishment of the innocent. The argument runs as follows. If one subscribed to, say, general deterrence, as the goal of punishment, then one might be justified in punishing an innocent person to deter others. Similarly, if one's goal were incapacitation, one might be justified in punishing an innocent person on the basis of a prediction that he was dangerous and about to commit a crime.

The committed utilitarian does have a response to this. Particularly with regard to the punishment of the innocent to achieve deterrent objectives, an obvious retort is that this could not be an effective deterrent as punishment would become a lottery; there would be no disincentive to would-be offenders because one would be just as likely to be picked up and punished as an innocent as if one had committed a crime. And as Cross and Ashworth (1981) have stated:

> [T]he object of state punishment is to reduce crime by means which will command the respect of most citizens. Most citizens would not respect the reduction of crime by means of the punishment of those known to be innocent. If it be said that most citizens would not know that an innocent man was being punished, the correct retort is "truth will out and confidence in the legal system as a whole would be undermined." (p 123)

However, what if it were possible to hoodwink the general public in believing that it was the guilty who were being punished? It would still not be justifiable to punish the innocent for the simple reason that such punishment would be totally *undeserved* and therefore *unjust*.

And what of those adjudged dangerous? Assertions that this could be justified on the basis of being "non-punitive detention" have been rightly dismissed by Walker (1970) as "double think". A person who has not committed any crime will hardly accept his detention with equanimity because he is reassured that it is not "punishment", but rather "non-punitive detention"! Again, the short point about such punishment is that a person who has as yet committed no crime does not *deserve* any punishment; it would be *unjust*.

Following such reasoning there has been increasing acceptance, especially since the writings of Hart (1968) and Ross (1975), of the view that the above "theories" are in reality addressing two separate questions. The *justifying aim* of punishment (ie the purpose of the whole institution of punishment) is utilitarian (incapacitation, deterrence, etc) but any individual punishment can only be justified on the basis of retribution. This means that whatever the general goals of state punishment are, they must be limited by *retribution in distribution*. No matter how effective a punishment might be as a deterrent, one is only justified in punishing a person who deserves it and only justified in punishing *to the extent* that it is deserved. Punishment beyond what is deserved is tantamount to punishment of innocence.

Such a philosophy is hard to reconcile with extended sentences for dangerous criminals or exemplary sentences: with both of these one is punishing the individual beyond what is deserved. However, the examination of the substantive criminal law in this book does tend to reveal an implicit acceptance of this basic philosophy. In the main, offences are defined (eg as requiring a blame) and structured (eg voluntarily causing grievous hurt (s 322) as contrasted with voluntarily causing hurt (s 321) with concomitant levels of punishment) in a manner that reflects retributive thinking. The greater the harm or blameworthiness of the accused, the greater the punishment. Offences with levels of punishment are not defined and structured so as to reflect a utilitarian philosophy. Thus, for instance, the definition and relationship between the above two offences, ss 321 and 322, is *not* based upon any utilitarian assessment that defining voluntarily causing grievous hurt in that manner and punishing it with a maximum of seven years imprisonment (as opposed to the one-year maximum available for voluntarily causing hurt) would provide any extra deterrent effect or additional protection for the public. The rationale is simple. The offender who causes a much more serious harm (grievous hurt) and who possessed that high degree of blameworthiness (ie intended to cause or knew himself likely to cause *grievous* hurt) *deserves* more punishment than he who causes a lesser harm (hurt) and/or acts with a less blameworthy state of mind (ie only intends or knows himself likely to cause hurt *simpliciter*). Such *distribution* in punishment is inherently retributive in nature.

D. Sentencing disparity

Zulkifli b Puasa v PP [1985] 1 MLJ 461 (HC, Brunei)

Sir Alan Huggins JA: It is, of course desirable that there should be a measure of consistency in the sentences passed upon different defendants for comparable offences and this court will not hesitate to interfere where that is necessary to maintain consistency.

Sentencing disparity occurs when two persons committing similar crimes receive very different sentences.

TTB Koh, "The Sentencing Policy and Practice of the Singapore Courts" (1965) 7 Mal LR 291, 291–292

Let me bring to light a remarkable inconsistency in the results of two similar cases. They both concern offences committed during the disturbances in Singapore last year. In the first case, *Anwar* (1965) the accused, Anwar, was found to be in possession of an offensive weapon, a knuckle duster, in the vicinity of Alexandra Road–an offence under s 25(1) of the Public Order (Preservation) Ordinance 1958. Anwar's submission that he was carrying the knuckle duster for the purpose of defending himself was rejected. The Magistrate convicted Anwar and sentenced him to one year's imprisonment and six strokes of the cane. On appeal to the High Court, the Chief Justice of Singapore, altered the sentence of imprisonment to one of three months and affirmed the sentence of caning.

In another case, Criminal Appeal No 178 of 1964, the accused person, Seah Ah Poh, was also charged with having contravened s 25(1) of the Public Order (Preservation) Ordinance 1958. Seah was found one night in the same month of September along a back-lane off Prince Philip Avenue, a proclaimed security area, with a motor-cycle chain equipped with a handle. Seah was convicted by a District Judge who imposed a sentence of one year's imprisonment and six strokes of the cane. On appeal to the High Court, the Judge hearing the appeal, not the Chief Justice, affirmed the conviction but altered the sentences to one day's imprisonment. The one day's imprisonment was deemed to have been served by the presence of Seah in court during the day. The result was that Seah walked out of court at the end of the day, a free man, whereas Anwar would have to suffer three months' imprisonment and four strokes of the cane.

Can these different sentences be explained by reference to some principle or criterion? The second judge did not attempt to do so and, in my view, they are not reconciliable. The argument in favour of the individualization of punishment does not appear to have been relevant. The Chief Justice did not decide on the sentences of three months' imprisonment and four strokes of the cane for Anwar on the ground that they were designed to rehabilitate him. Neither did the second judge choose the sentence of one day's imprisonment for that reason. Neither judge appears to have considered the social background of the offenders and what the best treatment was for each of them.

PP v Loo Choon Fatt [1976] 2 MLJ 256 (HC, Ipoh, Malaysia)

Hashim Yeop A Sani J: In respect of sentencing there can be only general guidelines. No two cases can have exactly the same facts to the minutest detail. Facts do differ from case to case and ultimately each case has to be decided on its own merits. In practice sentences do differ not only from case to case but also from court to court. All things being equal these variations are inevitable if only because of the human element involved. But of course, there must be limits to permissible variations.

As long as the rehabilitative model of sentencing was given prominence there could be little criticism of sentencing disparity. Sentences needed to be individualized. The punishment had to fit the offender and not the crime.

However, over the past two decades deep cynicism has set in, particularly in the USA. Research into sentencing and the psychology of sentencing revealed that widespread sentencing disparity existed and that it was mostly *not* attributable to "individualized sentencing", but rather to different judges having very different notions as to what the purposes of punishment were and what sentence could best achieve that objective. In tandem with this realization came the demise of the rehabilitative model of sentencing and the revival of the just deserts concept. Offenders should be punished according to what they deserve which means, *broadly speaking* (see above, p 19), that all offenders committing the same crime should receive the same punishment. Justice insists on equality of treatment. Sentencing disparity is unjust.

The response in the USA has been dramatic with a majority of states introducing "guideline models of sentencing" which drastically limit the sentencing judge's discretionary powers. In the UK the same debate has been waged, albeit with less intensity, and in order to counteract sentencing disparity, the Court of Appeal (Criminal Division) has started issuing "guideline judgments" in which sentencing guidelines are laid down for particular offences. These and other cases can now be cited as precedents (which would be patent nonsense if one were still adhering to individualized sentencing) and the hope is that consistency will be achieved by the emergence of a "common law of sentencing". Following judicial guidelines as opposed to the statutory guidelines in the USA gives the sentencing judge some flexibility to take account of the multitude of factors that distinguish cases, but nevertheless greatly limits the opportunity for capricious sentences with resultant injustice.

The debate on sentencing disparity has not commenced in Singapore and Malaysia other than that the reduction of disparity has been cited as one of the justifications for the introduction of mandatory minimum sentences (Yeo, 1985). Perhaps the debate will never start. The physical size and population of the two countries (particularly Singapore) and the small number of sentencing judges ensures that there can never be the degree of disparity that was found to exist in the USA. Further, both prosecution and defence can appeal against sentence locally which is a guarantee that gross disparity can be eliminated in individual cases. Another factor is that while the true causes of sentencing disparity are to be found mainly in the different perspectives and attitudes of the sentencing judges, such disparity is encouraged and becomes entrenched under a system committed to individualized sentencing. While lip-service is occasionally paid to this and the goal of rehabilitation in Malaysia and Singapore, it nevertheless seems clear that it is retribution and deterrence that is paramount in the minds of most sentencers here when exercising their sentencing discretion, and thus the seeds of the sentencing revolution will not easily be planted nor will they flourish here. The introduction of the mandatory minimum sentences and the fixed death penalty for certain drug offences underlines this philosophy under which the room for disparity is reduced. And finally, the attack on sentencing discretion in the West must be understood as being part of a wider attack on broad discretionary powers exercised by officials, judicial and otherwise. Such an attack has not occurred in either Malaysia or Singapore where broad discretionary powers are regarded as integral to the administration of justice.

Chapter 3

Basic elements of criminal liability

By CMV Clarkson

A. Introduction

Every crime has its own definition. For instance, the definition of murder in s 300 is, naturally, quite different from that of rape in s 375. Nevertheless, most crimes do possess broadly similar characteristics–or are subject to common exceptions–which can loosely be described as the basic elements or general principles of criminal liability.

Generally speaking, most legal systems adopt the position that criminal liability is only justifiable if a person commits a prohibited act or causes a forbidden harm and his actions are accompanied by a blameworthy state of mind. This is often stated in the form of a Latin maxim *actus non facit reum nisi mens sit rea* (an act does not make a person legally guilty unless his mind is legally blameworthy). From this it can be deduced that as a general rule criminal liability is only imposed if there is a coincidence of the following two ingredients:

(1) *actus reus:* the conduct or action of the accused which produces or constitutes the forbidden harm, for instance, firing the gun and killing the victim; and
(2) *mens rea:* a blameworthy state of mind, for instance, intending to kill when firing the gun.

It must be emphasized that this is no more than a general working proposition. The terms *actus reus* and *mens rea* are useful shorthand to convey fundamental themes. They must *not*, however, be taken literally. Their precise meanings and role in the criminal law of Singapore and Malaysia are the subject matter of most of this chapter. Further, as will be seen at the end of this chapter, there are clear and established exceptions to the so-called rule, namely, cases where no or only a minimal mental element is required. However, as the terminology of *actus reus* and *mens rea* is so well established in criminal jurisprudence, it will be employed in this book to introduce the fundamental principles of Singapore and Malaysian criminal law.

B. Actus reus

Before imposing criminal liability there must be conduct. The accused must have done something. The criminal law does not engage in punishing thought-crime. No matter how wicked one's intentions, the law insists upon a physical manifestation of those evil intentions before it will intervene. The Penal Code, however, does contain one dramatic exception to this rule.

Penal Code, s 121A

Whoever compasses, imagines, invents, devises, or intends the death of or hurt to or imprisonment or restraint of the President, shall be punished with death, and shall also be liable to fine.

How could simply imagining the death of the President ever be proved? Is such imagination, without more, sufficiently dangerous or alarming to justify the imposition of criminal liability? Consider the *actus reus* requirement of the crimes of attempt and conspiracy (see below, p 264 et seq); these are both crimes where, as in s 121A, the ultimate harm need not occur. Is there any material distinction between those crimes and s 121A with respect to the requirement that criminal liability ought only to be imposed where there has been some *conduct*?

As has already been seen, the *actus reus* of every crime is different, making a definition of an "*actus reus*" impossible. However, the nature of an *actus reus* can be exposed by exploring those elements common to most crimes.

Broadly, there are two types of crime:

(1) *Conduct crimes*:   this is where criminal liability is imposed simply because the accused has done something that is prohibited by law. These actions need have no result. For example, under s 6(a) of the Misuse of Drugs 1973 (Singapore) (now Cap 185) it is an offence to possess a controlled drug. This possession need not lead to any directly harmful result such as sale or consumption of the controlled drug. The essence of the crime lies in the conduct of possessing the controlled drug. Similarly, under s 64 of the Road Traffic Act (Singapore) (now Cap 276) it is an offence to drive a motor vehicle on a road in a reckless or dangerous manner. Again, such driving need have no result; the offence is a conduct crime.

(2) *Result crimes*:   here the definition of the crime requires the conduct of the accused to cause a prohibited result. For instance, for culpable homicide, as defined in s 299 of the Penal Code, the act of the accused must cause death. Similarly, under s 66 of the Road Traffic Act (Singapore) it is an offence for a person to drive a motor vehicle on a road in a reckless or dangerous manner if he thereby causes the death of a person. The causing of the prohibited result is the critical element in the offence.

The main distinction between conduct crimes and result crimes is that with the latter it must be established that the conduct of the accused caused a particular, prohibited result. This issue of causation gives rise to complex problems, discussion of which is reserved until later (see below, ch 18).

Apart from this distinction relating to causation, the common element in the definition of crimes is that there be some act or conduct on the part of the accused. However what is meant by an "act" or "conduct"?

No comprehensive definition is provided in the Penal Code. The only sections of any relevance here are s 32 (discussed below, p 44) and s 33. This latter section states that "The word 'act' denotes as well a series of acts as a single act...".

Gour, *Penal Law of India* (10th edn, 1982) Vol 1, 262

The word "act" ... must be construed in the light of commonsense .... "Act" is nowhere defined. It must necessarily be something short of a transaction which is composed of a series of acts, but cannot, in the ordinary language be restricted to every separate willed movement of a human being; for when courts speak of an act of shooting or stabbing, it means the action taken as a whole and not the numerous movements involved. Where an accused has done more than one act closely following upon, and intimately connected with, each other, they are not to be separated and assigned the one to one intention and the other or others to another intention.

In considering the meaning of an "act" or "conduct" it is, however, necessary to consider two important issues, namely, the requirement that the conduct of the accused be voluntary and, second, the fact that an "act" may be broadly interpreted to include certain omissions to act.

1. Conduct must be voluntary

The Penal Code does contain a definition of "voluntarily" in s 39. This, however, refers to *mens rea* and is of no assistance here (see below, p 59). Accordingly, it is necessary to turn to established common law principles.

(a) The common law approach

The very notion of an "act" or "conduct" connotes *voluntary* action or conduct. Holmes (1881) defined an "act" as a "willed muscular contraction". The mind is in control of bodily movements; it sends instructions to the muscles; an "act" is thus a physical movement resulting from an operation of the will. If one has been pushed and is falling uncontrollably down a flight of stairs, it is a negation of common sense to assert that one is *acting*; one's physical movements are not the result of an exercise of the will. It follows that criminal liability would be most inappropriate in such cases. Where physical movements were involuntary but caused a harm, punishment would be undeserved and could serve no useful utilitarian purpose: involuntary conduct clearly cannot be deterred and such an "actor" is in no need of incapacitation or rehabilitation. Accordingly, most legal systems have exempted such persons from criminal liability. They have not "acted"; there is no *actus reus*. The common law has developed a shorthand term for such cases: they are afforded the defence of *automatism*.

The real problem has been to define the concept of "voluntariness". The example of someone being pushed down the stairs is an "easy" one. There is no control at any level of will over physical movements. However, what of someone in a state of somnambulism? In the Australian case of *Cogdon* (1951) Mrs Cogdon, in a somnambulistic state, dreaming that her daughter was being attacked by ghosts, spiders and North Korean soldiers, axed her daughter to death. Is this involuntary "conduct"? The physical movements of a sleepwalker are controlled by some form of mental power, albeit subconscious. They are not the same as those of someone falling uncontrollably down a flight of stairs.

The common law has not attempted to face these complex problems and has instead simply used the requirement of voluntariness as a mechanism to exclude certain cases from its ambit. It has, in effect, "defined" voluntariness by example. Certain human conduct is simply perceived as too abnormal to be brought within the ambit of the criminal law. Punishment in such cases is so pointless that the "conduct" can safely be regarded as "involuntary" and the accused afforded a defence of automatism. It is widely accepted that the following categories of involuntary conduct will give rise to a defence of automatism in English law:

(1)   physical compulsion: for example, being pushed down a flight of stairs;
(2)   reflex movements of an external origin: for example, reflexive movements while being attacked by a swarm of bees (*Hill* v *Baxter*, 1958);
(3)   concussion;
(4)   unconsciousness: for example, movements while under the effect of a general anaesthetic;
(5)   hypnosis;
(6)   somnambulism (*Cogdon*, 1951);
(7)   hypoglycaemia: where a diabetic with a blood-sugar deficiency acts in an uncoordinated manner (*Quick*, 1973).

However, common law courts have exercised extreme caution in this regard. An accused found to be acting in a state of automatism is entitled to a complete acquittal. Accordingly, in drawing up the category of persons entitled to such a defence the courts have been careful only to include those who are safe to release in that they are unlikely to repeat their automatic behaviour. This means that two categories of involuntary conduct have *not* been included on such list:

(i)   Involuntary conduct caused by disease of mind

In the English House of Lords decision of *Sullivan* (1983) it was held that if the involuntary movements had an internal cause resulting in a mental impairment the accused should not be acquitted on grounds of automatism but should instead receive the special insanity verdict (see below, ch 12) which would result in indefinite detention "at Her Majesty's pleasure". In this way control can be maintained over persons thought dangerous. If they are suffering from a disease of the mind there is always the risk that they may repeat their anti-social behaviour. Indefinite detention until they are "cured" is perceived as the best method of protecting society.

(ii) Involuntary conduct caused by accused's own fault

If an accused does something, such as take drugs, or if he fails to do something, such as when a diabetic fails to eat after taking insulin, and he knows or ought to know that there is a risk of resultant involuntary conduct, the law will not allow him to hide behind the protective umbrella of the defence of automatism (*Quick*, 1973; *Bailey*, 1983). He is to blame for bringing about the involuntary conduct; the criminal law is concerned with the punishment of the blameworthy who causes harm.

(b) The Penal Code

As has already been seen, the Penal Code provides no comprehensive definition of an "act" nor is any defence of automatism expressly provided. What then is the local position?

In the only local case to date it was assumed that if an accused acted in an involuntary manner during an epileptic fit the only possible defence available to him would be that of insanity under s 84 of the Penal Code (see ch 12.)

Sinnasamy v PP (1956) 22 MLJ 36 (CA, Malaya)

Good J: This is an appeal against the conviction of the appellant for the murder of his daughter aged 21 months ....

There is no discoverable motive for the killing of the child. The appellant, though he remembered in considerable detail the events and circumstances immediately preceding and immediately following the act, maintained that he had no recollection of the act itself or why he did it.

There is a medical history ... that the appellant is an epileptic.

The defence was that the appellant did the act when in a state of automatism, which is a temporary loss of consciousness associated with some types of epilepsy. The onus was on the appellant to set up this defence, and the question is, whether he has succeeded in bringing himself within the exceptions set out in section 84 of the Penal Code....

Argument (was based) on two main grounds:

> "That the appellant, if he did the act may have done it in a state of automatism, which would bring him within section 84 of the Penal Code; and that the prosecution failed to prove the necessary intention or knowledge to support a conviction for murder"....

In the course of his argument he criticized the judgment of the learned trial judge in two respects:

"Where in disagreeing with the assessors, he says that their answers to the questions put to them were completely contrary to the medical evidence; and where he refers to the learned Deputy Public Prosecutor's suggestion that the appellant killed his child on an irresistible impulse possibly caused by the children annoying him for a moment."

As regards the first main ground of appeal, and the objection to the passage in the judgment which is connected with it, we are of the opinion that the learned trial judge was right in his conclusion. The doctor, while accepting that the appellant was an epileptic and that automatism is associated with some cases of epilepsy, stated unequivocally that a person acting under a state of automatism will not be conscious at the time. Turning to the appellant's own evidence, we find that he had the clearest recollection, going into considerable detail, of the events surrounding the act of killing: he remembered leaving his place of work to go to his quarters to get a drink, meeting his youngest child on the way and taking her with him, unlocking the door and entering the house where he noticed that the two elder children had followed him letting go the youngest child and snatching up the knife, holding her behind him with one hand while he held the knife in the other, hearing the eldest child ask "what is the matter" and replying to her "wait", seeing the blood in the kitchen in front of the back door, feeling concerned at having left his work before the proper time, and locking up the house again and returning to his work. The doctor was not, perhaps, questioned in as much detail as might have been desirable on the form of unconsciousness associated with automatism, but it is difficult to see how, in face of the appellant's own evidence, the assessors could reasonably have found that the appellant was in a state of unconsciousness when he did the act, and in our view, the learned trial judge, in his summing up, was right in rejecting the defence of automatism in favour of the theory that the appellant acted on an irresistible impulse.

Once the defence of automatism failed, there were only two alternatives left: that the appellant killed his child on an irresistible impulse or that he killed her for an undisclosed reason; the second alternative is, on the evidence of the appellant's temperament and his relations in general with his children so remote that the only reasonable conclusion is that he acted on irresistible impulse. It was, perhaps, unnecessary for the learned Deputy Public Prosecutor to speculate as to the cause of the irresistible impulse, but we see nothing objectionable in his having suggested one. We would add that irresistible impulse *per se* is no defence, and can only be a defence when it is proved to have been the result of insanity in law. The onus of proving this lay on the appellant and, in our view, he did not succeed in discharging it....

For the reasons which we have given the appeal is dismissed.

Appeal dismissed

Indian cases are to the same effect. If an accused commits a harm during an epileptic fit, the insanity defence is the only one available to him (*Nga Ant Bwe*, 1936; *Ahmadulla*, 1961). This is consistent with the prevailing English approach. In *Sullivan* (1983) the accused was suffering from an epileptic fit when he attacked a friend. The House of Lords held that during an epileptic fit the sufferer was insane, it being irrelevant that the mental impairment was only temporary. It was indicated by the House of Lords that an acquittal on grounds of automatism should be reserved for those cases where the involuntary conduct was caused by "some external factor such as a blow on the head causing concussion or the administration of an anaesthetic for therapeutic purposes".

Authority of the consequences of other forms of involuntary conduct is sparse, the only other case being the following Indian decision where the consequences of a killing during a state of somnambulism were dealt with *obiter*.

Re Pappathi Ammal (1959) Cri LJ 724 (Madras HC, India)

The accused, who had recently given birth to a child, jumped into a well with the child at night. An alarm was raised and the accused rescued, but the child drowned. The accused was charged with murder and attempted suicide. In her defence she pleaded that she was a sleepwalker and that during such sleepwalking she must have walked into the well with her child. It was ruled that such an allegation of somnambulism had not been substantiated. Nevertheless, the following observations were made.

Ramaswami J: Somnambulism is the unconscious state known as sleepwalking and its characteristics are thus set out ....

MA Kamath's Medical Jurisprudence (5th edn) at p 375:

> "Somnambulism ... is an abnormal condition allied to epilepsy and the artificially induced state of mesmerism or hypnotism. In this condition the higher or intellectual nerve centres appear to be in a state of partial activity only; or, as in the higher form of somnambulism, in a state of full activity to one particular train of impressions, but inactive as regards others ...."

Bearing these medical observations in mind, though there is no decided case law on the subject, somnambulism if proved will constitute that unsoundness of mind, attracting the application of s 84, IPC.

From these cases it would seem that the defence of automatism does not exist under the Penal Code, the insanity provision of s 84 being the only relevant one and applying to all cases of involuntary conduct.

However, there is a strong opposing argument.

Stanley Yeo Meng Heong, "The Application of Common Law Defences to the Penal Code in Singapore and Malaysia" in AJ Harding (ed), *The Common Law in Singapore and Malaysia* (1985), 149–152

One might venture to suggest that non-insane automatism may be pleaded in the form of the rarely used defence of accident under s 80 of the Code.

The word "accident" in this provision does not mean a mere chance but rather an unintentional or unexpected act. In order for this defence to succeed, it must be shown that the act was an accident or misfortune, and was not accompanied by any criminal intention, but that, on the other hand, it was the outcome of a lawful act which was done in a lawful manner, by lawful means and with proper care and caution.

The case of a licensed driver who suffers a concussion as a result of which he loses control of his vehicle and kills a pedestrian may illustrate how non-insane automatism could fall within this defence provision. The act of colliding with the pedestrian was an accident in that it was both unintentional and unexpected on the part of the driver. It was, furthermore, the result of a lawful act, namely, driving, which was done in a lawful manner by lawful means. The driver should then be allowed to plead the defence of accident if he shows that he had exercised proper care and caution while driving. If, however, his concussion was the result of a blow on the head by goods left unsecured in the back seat of his vehicle, his defence would fail for want of care and caution on his part. It may well be that s 80 was only meant to cover cases where the accident sprang from a conscious act such as the use of a hatchet, the head of which flies off and kills a bystander. However, it is submitted that the wording of the section is sufficiently wide to cover cases involving unconscious acts brought about by non-insane automatism.

Another way in which non-insane automatism may be introduced locally is to consider it as a defence relating to the *actus reus* of an offence rather than as part of the *mens rea*. Under this view, the voluntariness of the accused's conduct should be regarded as an essential constituent of the act, which is part of the *actus reus*. This being the case, once an accused suggests that he may have acted automatically, the prosecution is left to discharge the ultimate burden. When non-insane automatism is treated in this manner, it raises the contention that the prosecution has not proved its case; it is therefore not a defence which the accused himself has to prove, such as those defences prescribed in the Code. It may then be argued that the Code was meant to be exhaustive only in respect of defences which negate the *mens rea* of an offence. Accordingly, submissions that the prosecution has not proved the *actus reus* of an offence (such as when automatism is pleaded) have not been ruled out by the Code.

As a final comment, it is noted that the defence of automatism is a recent one which was never in the contemplation of the 19th Century jurists concerned with criminal law. Had the defence then been present under English law, it is probable that Macaulay and the other Indian Commissioners would have expressly included it in the Penal Code. It is however never too late for the legislature to do so.

It is submitted that one of these arguments by Stanley Yeo (1985) must be accepted (see also, Ratanlal and Dhirajlal, 1987, Vol 1). However, which one? If automatism is introduced into the law under the broad umbrella of the defence of accident in s 80, the onus will be on the accused to establish his defence on a balance of probabilities. Under the alternative argument in the above extract, however, the onus will remain on the prosecution to establish beyond reasonable doubt that the accused "acted" and that there was therefore an *actus reus*. In many ways this latter view is the more attractive. The wording of s 80 seems inapt to cover all cases of automatism. Take, for instance, the case of *Cogdon* (1951, above, p 38). It is surely inappropriate to assert that Mrs Cogdon killed her daughter by "accident" or "misfortune" and odd to allege that this occurred "in the doing of a lawful act in a lawful manner, by lawful means". On the other hand, the alternative argument that there is no *actus reus* in such cases is clear and well established at common law. In most cases one will be interpreting an undefined word in the Penal Code such as "an act" in s 299. In such cases it is permissible to receive established English common law provided such reception is not incompatible with the structure of the Penal Code. No such incompatibility exists. On the contrary, the English common law approach makes sense. It is nonsense to describe unconscious movements as "acts" and simply inconceivable that anyone who caused a harm while in a state of unconsciousness (say, concussion after a car accident) could either be convicted or detained as insane after an appropriate finding under s 84.

Accepting this view that the "defence" of automatism is available in Singapore and Malaysia, the precise parameters of the defence still need to be established. It would seem clear that certain categories of involuntary conduct will give rise to the full "defence" of automatism:

(1) physical compulsion;
(2) reflex actions of external origin;
(3) concussion;
(4) unconsciousness having external origin.

On the other hand, where the involuntary conduct is caused by "unsoundness of mind" only s 84 may be used. Those causing a harm while in the throes of an epileptic fit will fall within this category. This will inevitably have the consequence of forcing such persons to plead guilty to the offence charged. In *Sullivan* (1983, above, p 40) the accused changed his plea to one of guilty as soon as it was ruled that he was suffering from a disease of the mind. He was sentenced to three years' probation–and of course avoided indefinite detention in a secure mental institution!

More controversial are the three remaining categories:

(1) hypnosis;
(2) somnambulism;
(3) hypoglycaemia.

At present each of these gives rise to a defence of automatism under English law, while there are dicta in the Indian case of *Re Pappathi Ammal* (1959) that the first two categories (and therefore one would have thought the third as well) can only give rise to a defence of insanity under s 84. Bearing in mind the respective consequences of automatism and insanity, there must be a strong case for classifying these three species of involuntary conduct as non-insane automatism.

Finally, again assuming that the "defence" of automatism is available at least in relation to certain of the above categories of involuntary conduct, is it subject to the common law restriction that it will be negated by preceding fault?

It is submitted for the following reasons that the defence of automatism will not be available if it was the accused's own fault that he got himself into the state of automatism. First, if using Stanley Yeo's (1985) argument that the "defence" of automatism may be imported into the Penal Code under s 80, it must be established that the accused when he caused the harm was acting with "proper care and caution". An accused who negligently allows himself to get into a state wherein he commits involuntary actions can hardly be said to be acting with "proper care and caution". Second, if using Stanley Yeo's (1985) argument that involuntariness leads to a negation of the *actus reus*, then as this is an argument based on the reception of the English common law in interpreting a word such as "act" in the Penal Code, it ought to be the whole of that English common law which is received, ie including the limitation on the "defence" in cases where it was the accused's own fault that the involuntary conduct occurred. Further, there are strong policy arguments to support such a view. It is the business of the criminal law to punish the blameworthy who cause harm. Where a person has in a blameworthy manner allowed himself to get into a state of automatism and then causes a harm it would be highly unrealistic to expect any court to accede to the technical argument that as the movements were involuntary, the accused must be acquitted. This was why the English courts in *Quick* (1973) and *Bailey* (1983) rejected such arguments. The courts in Singapore and Malaysia can confidently be expected to follow the same direction.

2. Omissions

Penal Code, ss 32 and 43

    32. In every part of this Code, except where a contrary intention appears from the context, words which refer to acts done extend also to illegal omissions.
    43. The word "illegal" is applicable to every thing which is an offence, or which is prohibited by law, or which furnishes ground for a civil action: and a person is said to be "legally bound to do" whatever it is illegal in him to omit.

The Penal Code thus makes it plain that while criminal liability always flows from positive acts of commission (provided causation and *mens rea* are established), there is no liability for omissions to act unless the omission can be said to be "illegal" as defined by s 43. This means that a stranger can with impunity watch a small child drown in a shallow pool even though he could have saved the child's life with a minimum of effort and with no risk to himself. His omission is not "illegal" within s 43 and thus there is no *actus reus* of any offence.

    The crucial matter thus becomes one of determining the precise circumstances in which an omission is "illegal'. Section 43 deals with three situations:

(a) Failure to act which is "an offence"

This must refer to omissions that are independently made criminal offences by the Penal Code or other statutes. For example, s 289 of the Penal Code provides:

    Whoever knowingly or negligently omits to take such order with any animal in his possession as is sufficient to guard against any probable danger to human life ... shall be punished....

Thus if an accused failed to exercise the requisite control over such an animal in his possession with the result that it killed a person, the accused's failure to act would be an "illegal omission" which could constitute the requisite *actus reus* of the offence of culpable homicide.

Lee Sai Yan v PP (Unreported. Magistrate's Appeal No 90 of 1980 Subordinate Courts, Singapore)

The accused, a site engineer on a building worksite, did nothing to prevent the deceased entering a bored hole which needed cleaning. The deceased, wearing no breathing apparatus, was lowered into the deep hole in a bucket where he died from asphyxia due to insufficient oxygen. The accused was charged under s 81(12) of the Factories Act 1973 with the offence of facilitating a crime under s 34(8) of the Factories Act 1973. Section 34(8) provides that "No person ... shall require, permit or direct any other person to enter or remain in, any confined space in which the preparation of oxygen in the air is liable to have been substantially reduced unless either–(a) he is wearing a suitable breathing apparatus...". The Company, Penta Ocean, for whom the accused worked had already been convicted of this offence. The question arose as to whether the accused had "facilitated" this offence.

Alfonso Ang, Magistrate: For the charge to succeed, the accused must have facilitated the offence of Penta Ocean. The prosecution's case was that by making no attempt to stop the deceased from going down when he was not wearing breathing apparatus, the accused was said to have facilitated. To facilitate, the accused contended, required active participation....

The statutory duty imposed upon the accused was in s 34(8) Factories Act. His neglect was that he omitted to perform the duty imposed by law, ie permitting the deceased to enter the bored hole when he was not wearing a breathing apparatus and when no tests were conducted....

The absence of breathing apparatus on the site is immaterial. The law imposes an absolute obligation–either to conduct tests to ensure adequate supply of oxygen ... or a suitable breathing apparatus is worn. Any person who contravenes these obligations is said to have breached the Act....

A fine of $1,000 was thus imposed on the accused.

Order accordingly

The accused's omission to act in this case was thus held to be an offence. Accordingly, under s 43 it was an "illegal" omission. It follows that if the prosecution had wished to charge the accused with a more serious homicide offence under s 299 or s 304A there would have been no problem in establishing the requisite *actus reus* of these offences (subject to causation being established). Both require the accused to have committed an "act". Under s 32 this illegal omission would have constituted such an "act".

(b)   Failure to act which is "prohibited by law"

Many failures to act which are "prohibited by law" are offences and will thus fall under the category already discussed. However, the two terms are not synonomous. Certain failures to act could be "prohibited by law", yet not be offences. For instance, s 115 of the Women's Charter (Singapore) (Cap 353) in Singapore provides that "it shall be the duty of a parent to maintain or contribute to the maintenance of his or her children... either by providing them with such accommodation, clothing, food and education as may be reasonable ...". While such a failure to act is prohibited by law, it is not in itself an offence. However, being "prohibited by law" it will constitute an illegal omission capable of forming the *actus reus* of a criminal offence. (Note, such a failure would probably furnish grounds for a civil action and thus come within the third category as well. Note, also, that wilful neglect of a child is a separate offence under s 4(1) of the Children and Young Persons Act (Cap 38).)

De'Souza v Pashupati Nath Sarkar (1968) Cri LJ 405 (Calcutta HC, India)

The defendant was captain of a ship which arrived at Sandhead 110 miles off the port of Calcutta and had to wait there for pilotage. While there the deceased, a junior engineer on the ship, fell ill. When his condition deteriorated, several requests were made of the captain to remove the sick man to Calcutta. For five days, from the first requests for removal, nothing was done. During this period at least five ships, including some belonging to the same company as the accused's ship, left Sandhead daily for Calcutta. No request was made for any medical help from any of these ships. On the fifth day the ship was piloted into Calcutta Port and the accused radioed for the deceased to be removed to hospital. The following day the deceased died of infective hepatitis with hepatic coma with hepato revel failure. The accused was charged, inter alia, with an offence contrary to s 304A Indian Penal Code but petitioned the High Court to have the proceedings against him quashed.

TP Mukherji J: [T]he petitioner contends that the process so far as it related to an offence under s 304A, IPC is wholly misconceived in as much as the passivity of his client in the matter of the treatment of the sick engineer can by no stretch of imagination be held to be the efficient and proximate cause of the latter's death. He conceded that an illegal omission may constitute an "act" in law, but when no legal duty is cast in the matter, failure to perform that duty is not illegal. As the petitioner in the case ... had no legal obligation to provide for the treatment of the sick person over and above the facility available in his ship, his failure to remove the ailing engineer to Calcutta for better treatment cannot be construed as an illegal omission in that regard. If the omission to act was not illegal that omission would not constitute an "act" and however negligent the petitioner might have been in the matter of that omission it would not be a negligent act as contemplated in s 304A, IPC....

Section 304A, IPC provides for punishment of the offence of causing death by a rash or negligent act. Under s 32, IPC an illegal omission would constitute an "act" in law and under s 43 of the Code the word "illegal" is applicable to everything which is an offence and which is prohibited by law or which furnishes ground for a civil action. An illegal omission thus is an "act" under s 304A, IPC and may constitute an offence if it is negligent.

Mr Choudhury appearing for the opposite party referred to s 190 of the Merchant Shipping Act which according to him casts a duty on the master of a ship to do any lawful act proper and requisite to be done by him for preserving any person belonging to or on board the ship from danger to life. He contended that this section imposes on the master of a vessel the duty of taking proper and requisite action for preserving any person on board the ship from danger to life and in that regard, in the background of the facts of this case, it was the duty of the petitioner as the master of the ship to take all possible steps, care and precaution in the matter of the treatment of the ailing engineer and to try to arrange for his removal to Calcutta for better treatment when such arrangement could easily have been made by him.

The relevant provision of s 190 of the Merchant Shipping Act, runs as follows:

"No Master, Seaman, or Apprentice belonging to an Indian Ship wherever it may be or to any other ship while in India shall knowingly....

(b) refuse or omit to do any lawful Act, proper and requisite to be done by him for preserving the ship from immediate loss, destruction or serious damage, or for preserving any person belonging to or on board the ship from danger to life or from injury."...

When, therefore, s 190 of the Act imposes on the master of a ship the duty of doing all lawful acts proper and requisite to be done for preserving persons belonging to or on board the ship from danger to life, it demands of him to take every possible legal step....

In my view s 190 (b) embodies a statutory obligation of the Master of a vessel to take all possible steps when a person on board the ship becomes sick, to arrange for his best available treatment for the purpose of preserving his life. Whether all possible steps in that regard were taken in this case or not is a question of fact which has to be determined by the Magistrate, if and when the case comes to trial....

[The process issued against the accused under s 304A was nevertheless quashed on grounds of lack of causation.]

Order accordingly

(c) Failure to act "which furnishes ground for a civil action"

To discover whether an omission to act furnishes "ground for a civil action" necessitates reference to the civil law of Singapore and Malaysia –primarily the law of tort. Such law is for present purposes virtually identical to English law. This, however, by no means solves the problem for two reasons. First, the English civil law on this topic is far from clear. Second, the extent to which it is permissible to rely on English *criminal* cases on this matter is controversial. These English cases initially based themselves on the English civil law, thus inducing all the Indian commentators to assume that reference to them is permissible. However, there has been a growing awareness in the UK that great caution needs to be exercised before indulging in any cross-referencing between criminal law and civil law as the objects of these two branches of the law are so diverse. The result has been that English criminal cases have developed independently of civil cases. The Penal Code, however, (wisely or not) specifically links criminal liability for omissions to civil liability. It thus follows that before any English case can be used in Singapore or Malaysia care must be taken to ensure that it reflects the civil law as well as the criminal law.

Bearing this important caveat in mind, it would appear that the law is as follows: an omission only furnishes ground for civil action and thus criminal liability if the accused is under a *duty to act*. Such a duty to act arises in the following circumstances:

(i) Special relationship

Om Prakash v State of Punjab AIR (1961) SC 1782 (SC, India)

The accused starved his wife by omitting to feed her and denying her permission to leave the house.

Raghubar Dayal J: [C]ounsel for the appellant ... concedes that it is only when a person is helpless and is unable to look after himself that the person having control over him is legally bound to look after his requirements and to see that he is adequately fed. Such persons, according to him, are infants, old people and lunatics. He contends that it is no part of a husband's duty to spoon feed his wife, his duty being simply to provide funds and food. In view of the finding of the court below about (the victim wife) being confined and being deprived of regular food in pursuance of a scheme of regularly starving her in order to accelerate her end, the responsibility of the appellant for the condition to which she was brought ... is clear. The findings really go against any suggestion that the appellant had actually provided food and funds for his wife ....

What is the basis of the duty in such cases? Is it that the blood and marriage relationship is so strong that it generates a duty to act? This cannot be the case because no duty would be owed to one's separated spouse or one's emancipated child (*Shepherd*, 1862). Presumably, the better rationale is that one owes a duty to those who are dependent on and reasonably expect assistance from one. To this extent it could thus be argued that this whole category can be subsumed within the following broader one.

(ii) Duty voluntarily assumed

Even though there may be no special relationship between the parties, if one person voluntarily assumes a responsibility towards another, a legal duty to act will have been created. As seen above, the real basis of the duty in such cases is the dependence and reasonable expectation of assistance springing from such a gratuitous assumption of responsibility.

R v Instan [1893] 1 QB 450 (Court for Crown Cases Reserved, England)

The accused lived with her 73 year old aunt. The aunt who had been healthy until shortly before her death developed gangrene in her leg. During the last twelve days of her life she could not fend for herself, move about or summon help. Only the accused knew of her state and gave her aunt no food and did not seek medical assistance. The accused was charged with manslaughter and convicted.

Lord Coleridge CJ: We are all of the opinion that this conviction must be affirmed. It would not be correct to say that every moral obligation involves a legal duty; but every legal duty is founded on a moral obligation. A legal common law duty is nothing else than the enforcing by law of that which is a moral obligation without legal enforcement. There can be no question in this case that it was the clear duty of the prisoner to impart to the deceased so much as was necessary to sustain life of the food which she from time to time took in, and which was paid for by the deceased's own money for the purpose of the maintenance of herself and the prisoner; it was only through the instrumentality of the prisoner that the deceased could get the food. There was, therefore, a common law duty imposed upon the prisoner which she did not discharge.

Nor can there by any question that the failure of the prisoner to discharge her legal duty at least accelerated the death of the deceased, if it did not actually cause it. There is no case directly in point; but it would be a slur upon and a discredit to the administration of justice in this country if there were any doubt as to the legal principle, or as to the present case being within it. The prisoner was under a moral obligation to the deceased from which arose a legal duty towards her; that legal duty the prisoner has wilfully and deliberately left unperformed, with the consequence that there has been an acceleration of the death of the deceased owing to the non-performance of that legal duty. It is unnecessary to say more than that upon the evidence this conviction was most properly arrived at.

If two people go jungle trekking together, can it be said that they have assumed a responsibility towards each other that, in the event of any emergency, each will act to rescue the other? Certainly, there would be a reasonable expectation of assistance in such cases. By the same token, if one goes shopping in Orchard Road with a business colleague, one will certainly expect assistance from him should an accident befall one, but how does the act of simply going shopping with another generate a duty to act? It is unlikely, however, that these intractible problems will ever trouble the courts as a criminal prosecution is only likely to be brought in clear cases such as *Instan* (1893) where a helpless person has been taken into the home of the accused and being thus isolated from the rest of the world is *totally* dependent on the accused.

(iii) Duty assumed by contract

R v Pittwood (1902) 19 TLR 37 (Taunton Assizes, England)

The accused was a railway gatekeeper who was employed to keep the gate shut whenever a train was passing during the period 7 am to pm.

Not many trains used to pass during this day period. One day he left the gate open with the result that a train hit a hay cart crossing the line killing one man and injuring another seriously. The accused was charged with manslaughter.

Mr Simon, on behalf of the prisoner, submitted that it was necessary that the duty to take care should be towards the person who complained; and that, in the present case, the prisoner only contracted with his employers–the railway company ....

Mr Justice Wright, ... said he was clearly of opinion that in this case there was gross and criminal negligence, as the man was paid to keep the gate shut and protect the public ....

A man might incur criminal liability from a duty arising out of contract .... (*Instan*, 1893) clearly governed the present charge ....

[The accused was found guilty and sentenced to three weeks' imprisonment.]

(iv) Creating dangerous situation

R v Miller [1983] 2 AC 161 (HL, England)

One night while squatting in someone else's house, the appellant lit a cigarette and then lay down on a mattress in one of the rooms. He fell asleep before he had finished smoking the cigarette and it dropped onto the mattress. Later he woke up and saw that the mattress was smouldering. He did nothing about it; he merely moved to another room and went to sleep again. The house caught fire. The appellant was rescued and subsequently charged with arson, contrary to s 1(1) and (3) of the Criminal Damage Act 1971. At his trial he submitted that there was no case to go to the jury because his omission to put out the fire, which he had started accidentally, could not in the circumstances amount to a sufficient *actus reus*. The judge ruled that once he had discovered the mattress was smouldering the appellant had been under a duty to act. The appellant was convicted. The Court of Appeal upheld his conviction on the ground that his whole course of conduct constituted a continuous *actus reus*. The case went on appeal to the House of Lords.

Lord Diplock: The first question is a pure question of causation ... If ... the question ....

"Did a physical act of the accused start the fire which spread and damaged property belonging to another?" is answered "Yes," as it was by the jury in the instant case, then for the purpose of the further questions the answers to which are determinative of his guilt of the offence of arson, the conduct of the accused, throughout the period from immediately before the moment of ignition to the completion of the damage to the property by the fire, is relevant; so is his state of mind throughout that period.

Since arson is a result-crime the period may be considerable, and during it the conduct of the accused that is causative of the result may consist not only of his doing physical acts which cause the fire to start or spread but also of his failing to take measures that lie within his power to counteract the danger that he has himself created. And if his conduct, active or passive, varies in the course of the period, so may his state of mind at the time of each piece of conduct. If, at the time of any particular piece of conduct by the accused that is causative of the result, the state of mind that actuates his conduct falls within the description of one or other of the states of mind that are made a necessary ingredient of the offence of arson by s 1(1) of the Criminal Damage Act 1971 (ie intending to damage property belonging to another or being reckless whether such property would be damaged), I know of no principle of English criminal law that would prevent his being guilty of the offence created by that subsection. Likewise I see no rational ground for excluding from conduct capable of giving rise to criminal liability conduct which consists of failing to take measures that lie within one's power to counteract a danger that one has oneself created, if at the time of such conduct one's state of mind is such as constitutes a necessary ingredient of the offence....

I cannot see any good reason why, so far as liability under criminal law is concerned, it should matter at what point of time before the resultant damage is complete a person becomes aware that he has done a physical act which, whether or not he appreciated that it would at the time when he did it, does in fact create a risk that property of another will be damaged, provided that, at the moment of awareness, it lies within his power to take steps, either himself or by calling for the assistance of the fire brigade if this be necessary, to prevent or minimize the damage to the property at risk.

Let me take first the case of the person who has thrown away a lighted cigarette expecting it to go out harmlessly, but later becomes aware that, although he did not intend it to do so, it has, in the event, caused some inflammable material to smoulder and that unless the smouldering is extinguished promptly, an act that the person who dropped the cigarette could perform without danger to himself or difficulty, the inflammable material will be likely to burst into flames and damage some other person's property. The person who dropped the cigarette deliberately refrains from doing anything to extinguish the smouldering. His reason for so refraining is that he intends that the risk which his own act had originally created, though it was only subsequently that he became aware of this, should fructify in actual damage to that other person's property; and what he so intends in fact occurs. There can be no sensible reason why he should not be guilty of arson. If he would be guilty of arson, having appreciated the risk of damage at the very moment of dropping the lighted cigarette, it would be quite irrational that he should not be guilty if he first appreciated the risk at some later point in time but when it was still possible for him to take steps to prevent or minimize the damage....

The recorder, in his lucid summing up to the jury ... told them that the accused, having by his own act started a fire in the mattress which, when he became aware of its existence, presented an obvious risk of damaging the house, became under a duty to take some action to put it out. The Court of Appeal upheld the conviction, but its ratio decidendi appears to be somewhat different from that of the recorder. As I understand the judgment, in effect it treats the whole course of conduct of the accused, from the moment at which he fell asleep and dropped the cigarette onto the mattress until the time the damage to the house by fire was complete, as a continuous act of the accused, and holds that it is sufficient to constitute the statutory offence of arson if at any stage in that course of conduct the state of mind of the accused, when he fails to try to prevent or minimize the damage which will result from his initial act, although it lies within his power to do so, is that of being reckless whether property belonging to another would be damaged.

My Lords, these alternative ways of analysing the legal theory that justifies [the] decision ... provoked academic controversy. Each theory has distinguished support. Professor JC Smith (1982, p 528) espouses the "duty theory"; Professor Glanville Williams (1982) ... now prefers that of the continuous act. When applied to cases where a person has unknowingly done an act which sets in train events that, when he becomes aware of them present an obvious risk that property belonging to another will be damaged, both theories lead to an identical result; and, since what your Lordships are concerned with is to give guidance to trial judges in their task of summing up to juries. I would for this purpose adopt the duty theory as being the easier to explain to a jury; though I would commend the use of the word "responsibility", rather that "duty" which is more appropriate to civil than to criminal law since it suggests an obligation owed to another person, ie the person to whom the endangered property belongs, whereas a criminal statute defines combinations of conduct and state of mind which render a person liable to punishment by the state itself....

[A] suitable direction to the jury would be that the accused is guilty of the offence under s 1(1) of the 1971 Act if, when he does become aware that the events in question have happened as a result of his own act, he does not try to prevent or reduce the risk of damage by his own efforts or if necessary by sending for help from the fire brigade and the reason why he does not is either because he has not given any thought to the possibility of there being any such risk or because having recognized that there was some risk involved he has decided not to try to prevent or reduce it.

Appeal dismissed

This is an English criminal case basing the accused's liability (or, at least, the *actus reus* element thereof) on his *omission* to act. How would a civil court handle the facts of *Miller* (1983)–bearing in mind the necessity for the failure to act to furnish "ground for a civil action" under s 43? It is clear that there would be liability in such a case at civil law–but the civil courts would approach the problem in a different manner focusing on the defendant's negligent *positive act* of going to sleep with a lit cigarette. He owed a duty of care to anyone who might be injured by such positive actions. However the result is achieved, the end-product is the same: there are grounds for civil action in the circumstances, rendering the omission "illegal" for purposes of s 43. Indeed, there is no reason why the criminal courts could not also base liability upon such positive acts of commission (especially if the only *mens rea* that need be established were negligence). Miller's positive act would be going to sleep with a lit cigarette. Of course, he might have had no subjective *mens rea* at that stage, but it would clearly be a negligent course of action (and, arguably, since the House of Lords decision of *Caldwell*, 1982, such negligence could be the equivalent of the recklessness required under the Criminal Damage Act 1971– see below, p 61).

Benoy Chandra Dey v State of Calcutta (1984) Cri LJ 1038 (Calcutta HC, India)

The accused (petitioner) applied for revision of the judgment dismissing his appeal and confirming his conviction under s 304A Indian Penal Code. A naked, live galvanized electric wire had been connected from the house of one Gopal to that of the petitioner. A 13-year-old boy while passing in front of the petitioner's house touched the wire and died instantly from electric shock.

J N Chaudhuri J: [T]he petitioner has submitted that there is no evidence to show that either the petitioner was personally responsible for taking the electric connection from Gopal's house or that he knew that such a connection was there.

It is not necessary on a charge under s 304A IPC, as in the present case, that the petitioner must have personally got the electric connection from Gopal's house. Allowing the AC connection to remain in this bare, uninsulated danger-ous situation, is sufficient negligence on his part to bring him within the ambit of the section, even if he was not personally responsible for procuring the electric connection in question. Under s 32 IPC acts include illegal omissions. In the case of *SN Hussain* v *Andhra Pradesh* (1972) ... the Supreme Court has laid down that "Culpable negligence lies in the failure to exercise reasonable and proper care and the extent of its reasonableness will always depend upon the circumstances of each case."

The fact that an electric bulb was burning in the petitioner's room at the time of the incident and that the connection had been taken 2/3 days before, leaves little room for doubt as to the knowledge of the petitioner about the electric connection .... We are satisfied of the petitioner's criminal negligence within the meaning of s 304A IPC in this case....

[Sentence: six months plus fine.]

Order accordingly

The principle established in such cases is potentially extremely broad. Many of the classic tort examples, such as building a swimming pool without erecting a fence around it with the result that a small child falls in and drowns, could give rise to criminal liability. The failure to erect a protective fence would furnish "ground for a civil action" rendering such failure to act an "illegal omission". However, in most such cases the requisite degree of *criminal* negligence would not be established and even if there were a chance that it could be, it is unlikely that a criminal prosecution would be brought.

Two final, and more general questions, present themselves. First, ought the level of punishment to be less when criminal liability is based on omissions than when based on positive acts of commission? Do you find convincing the argument that it is worse to "kill" than to "let die"? (Fletcher, 1978).

Second, bearing in mind the need for some correlation between law and morality, do you find it acceptable that a person can sit and watch a baby drown in two feet of water when with a minimum of effort and inconvenience he could have saved the child's life? To put it another way, should there be a general duty to act? If there were such a general duty would there be any particular problems, say, in relation to causa-tion or *mens rea*? (See Hughes, 1958; Clarkson and Keating, 1984.)

Macaulay and other Indian Law Commissioners, A Penal Code Prepared by the Indian Law Commissioners, Note M 53–56 (1837)

On the other hand, it will hardly be maintained that a man should be punished as a murderer because he omitted to relieve a beggar, even though there might be the clearest proof that the death of the beggar was the effect of this omis-sion, and that the man who omitted to give the alms knew that the death of the beggar was likely to be the effect of the omission.... It is difficult to say whether a Penal Code which should put no omissions on the same footing with acts would produce consequences more absurd and revolting.... It is plain, therefore, that a middle course must be taken.... What we propose is this, that where acts are made punishable on the ground that they have caused, or have been intended to cause, or have been known to be likely to cause a certain evil effect, omissions which have caused, which have been intended to cause, or which have been known to be likely to cause the same effect shall be punishable in the same manner; provided that such omissions were, on other grounds, illegal. An omission is illegal ... if it be an offence, if it be a breach of some direction of law, or if it be such a wrong as would be a good ground for a civil action....

We are sensible that in some of the cases which we have put our rule may appear too lenient. But we do not think that it can be made more severe, without disturbing the whole order of society. It is true that the man who, having abundance of wealth, suffers a fellow creature to die of hunger at his feet, is a bad man,–a worse man, probably, than many of those for whom we have provided very severe punishment. But we are unable to see where, if we make such a man legally punishable, we can draw the line. If the rich man who refuses to save a beggar's life at the cost of a little copper is a murderer, is the poor man just one degree above beggary also to be a murderer if he omits to invite the beggar to partake his hard earned rice? Again: if the rich man is a murderer for refusing to save the beggar's life at the cost of a little copper, is he also to be murderer if he refuses to save the beggar's life at the cost of a thousand rupees? ....

It is, indeed, most highly desirable that men should not merely abstain from doing harm to their neighbours, but should render active services to their neighbours. In general however the penal law must content itself with keeping men from doing positive harm and must leave to public opinion, and to the teachers of morality and religion, the office of furnishing men with motives for doing positive good. It is evident that to attempt to punish men by law for not rendering to others all the service which it is their duty to render to others would be preposterous. We must grant impunity to the vast majority of those omissions which a benevolent morality would pronounce reprehensible, and must content ourselves with punishing such omissions only when they are distinguished from the rest by some circumstance which marks them out as peculiarly fit objects of penal legislation.

C. Mens rea

1. Introduction

CMV Clarkson, *Understanding Criminal Law* (1987), 56–58

Generally criminal liability is only imposed upon a *blameworthy* actor whose conduct has caused a forbidden harm. It is not enough that a defendant has simply done the forbidden act or caused the prohibited harm. He must have done so in circumstances in which he can properly be blamed for his conduct. Without such blame or fault he is regarded as "innocent"–and a civilized society is offended at the notion of punishing the innocent. Further, punishment of the blameless would probably be an ineffective deterrent: the law cannot hope to deter innocent actions, and those who are blameless are in no need of help or rehabilitation; and their very "innocence" indicates that they present no threat to others and thus society has no need to protect itself from such persons. In short, not only would it be unjust, but also there would be little purpose served in punishing the blameless....

[M]an is viewed today as a moral agent and not simply as an instrument of causing harm. He is regarded as *responsible* for his actions. Being a responsible agent means that man is capable of reason; he is capable of understanding the social and legal norms to which he is subject; he possesses free will. He can thus control his actions and can choose whether to comply with the law or not....

It follows that because man is this responsible agent exercising control and choice over his actions, we are able to judge those actions. We can evaluate and discriminate between different actions and attribute praise or blame to the actor–in a manner that would be quite inappropriate if dealing with a non-responsible agent. In an artificial sense one might praise or blame a baby for being good or not, or praise or blame a dog for being quiet or not–but we do not hold the baby or the dog *responsible* for their actions in any meaningful way because their actions are not the product of reason, control and choice. We can judge the *result* (and disapprove of the noise made by the baby or the dog), but not the *agent* because of its non-responsibility.

This notion of responsibility and view of man as a moral agent led to wide acceptance of the view that blame and punishment were only justified if a person had *chosen* to commit a crime. If I deliberately throw my glass on the floor breaking it, you can blame me for my actions because you can disapprove of my choice to act in that way. But if I, acting in a normal, careful manner were to slip on a loose carpet and drop my glass and break it, blame would be inappropriate; I was not in complete control of my actions and did not choose to break the glass.

This process of choosing to break the law is, of course, a mental process. Such persons are said to have a morally blameworthy *state of mind*–or, in legal shorthand, *mens rea*. Where a person acts with *mens rea* he is a responsible agent who has chosen to break the rules; he is thus blameworthy and deserves punishment. Or to put it another way: the presence of *mens rea* indicates that the defendant is blameworthy. There are other indicators of blame but before exploring them we should examine this main indicator of blame, *mens rea*, in more detail.

Mens rea is the mental element required by the definition of a particular crime. As seen in the preceding section, it clearly embraces those who have made a decision and chosen to break the law. However, *mens rea* is not limited to such states of mind. It also covers those who act realizing there is a chance (perhaps only a small chance) of their conduct causing the prohibited result. And in some cases it could even extend to persons who do not anticipate causing any harm, but who really ought to have realized the risks involved in their actions. In short, *mens rea* does not refer to any single state of mind. There are degrees of *mens rea*....

2. The law

Many modern criminal codes contain general clauses stating that in the absence of an express provision to the contrary, *mens rea* is to be implied as an element of every offence. For example, s 2.02 of the Model Penal

Code in the USA provides (subject to an exception that need not detain us here) that "a person is not guilty of an offence unless he acted purposely, knowingly, recklessly or negligently, as the law may require, with respect to each material element of the offence".

There is no such general provision in the Penal Codes of Singapore, Malaysia or India or in any other legislative provision in those jurisdictions. Under the Penal Code and other local legislation a specific form of *mens rea* is sometimes required for an offence and this is stated. At other times a statutory provision may be silent as to whether any *mens rea* is required–and if so, what species of *mens rea* is required. In this section the meaning of these various specific *mens rea* terms will be explored and then attention will be directed to the problem of an offence being silent as to whether *mens rea* is necessary.

(a) Specific mens rea terms

(i) Introduction

Many sections of the Penal Code (and of other statutes creating criminal liability) specifically spell out the need for *mens rea* and indicate exactly which species of *mens rea* must be proved. For instance, s 142 of the Penal Code makes it an offence if a person "*intentionally* joins" an unlawful assembly. Section 275 makes it an offence if a person "*knowing* any drug or medicinal preparation to have been adulterated ...*" sells, etc such drug. Section 304A makes it an offence if a person "causes the death of any person by doing any *rash or negligent* act ...". Section 378 defines theft as "*intending to take dishonestly* any movable property ...".

Numerous other *mens rea* terms are to be found in the Penal Code and in other statutes creating criminal liability, eg *recklessness* (s 64, Road Traffic Act (Singapore) (Cap 276); *voluntarily* (Penal Code, s 377); *fraudulently* (s 415); *wantonly* (s 153); *malignantly* (s 270); *corruptly* (s 220); *maliciously* (s 219); *dangerously* (s 64, Road Traffic Act (Singapore).

The meaning of the more important of these *mens rea* terms such as intention, knowledge and dishonesty will be dealt with fully in relation to those statutory provisions to which they have most application. At this stage, however, it is necessary to provide at least a working definition of some of the main terms found in the criminal statutes of Singapore and Malaysia.

(ii) Intention

The concept "intention" is nowhere defined in the Penal Code. The following case is the culmination of a long line of controversial English decisions attempting to define "intention".

R v Nedrick [1986] 3 All ER 1 (CA, Criminal Division, England)

The accused, after threatening to burn out a woman against whom he bore a grudge, poured paraffin through the letter box of her house and set it alight. The woman's child was killed in the resulting fire and the accused was charged with murder. He claimed that he merely wanted to frighten the woman and did not want anyone to die. The question arose as to whether knowledge as to the consequences of his actions was the equivalent of an intention to cause those consequences.

Lord Lane CJ: We have endeavoured to crystallize the effect of their Lordships' speeches in *Moloney* (1985) and *Hancock* (1986) in a way which we hope may be helpful to judges who have to handle this type of case.

It may be advisable first of all to explain to the jury that a man may intend to achieve a certain result whilst at the same time not desiring it to come about. In *Moloney* (1985) Lord Bridge gave an illustration of the distinction:

"A man who, at London Airport, boards a plane which he knows to be bound for Manchester, clearly intends to travel to Manchester, even though Manchester is the last place he wants to be and his motive for boarding the plane is simply to escape pursuit."

The man who knowingly boards the Manchester aircraft wants to go there in the sense that boarding it is a voluntary act. His desire to leave London predominates over his desire not to go to Manchester. When he decides to board the aircraft, if not before, he forms the intention to travel to Manchester.

In *Hancock* the House decided that the *Moloney* guidelines require a reference to probability. Lord Scarman said:

"They also require an explanation that the greater the probability of a consequence the more likely it is that the consequence was foreseen and that if that consequence was foreseen the greater the probability is that that consequence was also intended."

When determining whether the defendant had the necessary intent, it may therefore be helpful for a jury to ask themselves two questions. (1) How probable was the consequence which resulted from the defendant's voluntary act? (2) Did he foresee that consequence?

If he did not appreciate that death or serious harm was likely to result from his act, he cannot have intended to bring it about. If he did, but thought that the risk to which he was exposing the person killed was only slight, then it may be easy for the jury to conclude that he did not intend to bring about that result. On the other hand, if the jury are satisfied that at the material time the defendant recognized that death or serious harm would be virtually certain (barring some unforeseen intervention) to result from his voluntary act, then that is a fact from which they may find it easy to infer that he intended to kill or do serious bodily harm, even though he may not have had any desire to achieve that result.

As Lord Bridge said in *Moloney* (1985):

"... the probability of the consequence taken to have been foreseen must be little short of overwhelming before it will suffice to establish the necessary intent."

Later he uses the expression "moral certainty" and says, "will lead to a certain consequence unless something unexpected supervenes to prevent it."

Where the charge is murder and in the rare cases where the simple direction is not enough, the jury should be directed that they are not entitled to infer the necessary intention unless they feel sure that death or serious bodily harm was a virtual certainty (barring some unforeseen intervention) as a result of the defendant's actions and that the defendant appreciated that such was the case.

Where a man realizes that it is for all practical purposes inevitable that his actions will result in death or serious harm, the inference may be irresistible that he intended that result, however little he may have desired or wished it to happen. The decision is one for the jury to be reached on a consideration of all the evidence.

Appeal allowed

Under the Penal Code it is clear that foreseeing or knowing a consequence to be *likely* or *probable* is *not* the equivalent of intending that result. Section 39 draws a sharp distinction between the two states of mind in defining "voluntarily" as encompassing *either* an intention to cause a result *or* knowledge that it is likely to be caused.

In *Nedrick* (1986) it was decided that foreseeing a consequence as a *"virtual certainty"* *was* the equivalent of intending that consequence. It is an open question whether such a conclusion is supportable under the Penal Code. Section 300, in defining murder, draws a distinction between intending death (s 300(a)) and knowing that one's acts are *so imminently dangerous* that they *must in all probability* cause death (s 300(d)). This latter state of mind does not amount to intention: if it did, s 300(d) would be unnecessary. The line between "knowing that one's actions must in all probability" cause a result (s 300(d)) and knowing that one's actions are "virtually certain" to cause a result (*Nedrick*, 1986) is, at best, an exceedingly thin one. If it is felt to be too thin a line to draw then there seems little alternative but to limit the concept of "intention" to those cases where the defendant *meant* to cause the result–where it was his *aim* or *purpose* in acting. Anything less such as foreseeing a consequence as even "virtually certain" would then not amount to intention, but only to knowledge or recklessness.

Such an approach would have the advantage of certainty and simplicity but such a definition of intention would be so narrow as to be open to the serious criticism that there can be little, if any, moral distinction between a man who wants to achieve a result and one who foresees that result as virtually certain.

(iii) Knowledge

No definition of the term "knowledge" is provided in the Penal Code.

RC Nigam, *Law of Crimes in India* (1965) Vol I, 77

To know a thing means to have a mental cognition of it. To believe a thing is to assent to a proposition or affirmation or to accept a fact as real or certain without immediate personal knowledge. Thus knowledge and "reason to believe" are to be clearly distinguished. For example, a man you know to be poor brings to you for sale a valuable gold ornament and offers it to you for one-tenth of the real price. He comes to you at night under suspicious circumstances. Here you may not know that the article is stolen, but you have reason to believe that it is stolen. Thus belief is somewhat weaker than knowledge but a well-grounded belief that certain consequences will follow a certain act is ordinarily as good as knowledge.

Section 26 of the Indian Penal Code states that "a person is said to have reason to believe a thing if he has sufficient cause to believe that thing, but not otherwise." Thus, for example, A sets fire during the night to an inhabited house in a large town for the purpose of facilitating robbery and thus causes the death of a person. Here in this case, the person had not the knowledge that the house was inhabited, but he had reason to believe that it was inhabited. Belief is somewhat weaker than knowledge. "Knowledge," says Locke, "is the highest degree of the speculative faculties and consists in the perception of the truth of the affirmative or negative propositions."

Knowledge and reasonable grounds of belief in most cases supply the place of intention. Intention is purely an operation of the mind and is often difficult to prove. Therefore, it is inferred from the surrounding circumstances and the acts of the person. Every man is supposed to intend the natural consequences of his act. Such inferences are sometimes based on certainty, sometimes on different degrees of probability. Where an inference is more or less certain, we say it is based on knowledge; where it is only probable, it is based on belief. In many cases, however, a reasonable ground of belief for all practical purposes is as good as knowledge.

As the above extract indicates, strictly speaking, one cannot know something unless that something is in fact so. One cannot know that goods are stolen unless they are stolen. This is an extremely strict test which would mean that no knowledge could be imputed to a handler of stolen goods even if he were 100% certain that the goods were stolen–unless it could be affirmatively established that the goods were indeed stolen. The Penal Code avoids this problem in relation to stolen goods by s 411 adopting the broader *mens rea* test that that the accused will be liable if he knows or has *reason to believe* the goods are stolen.

The test is also difficult to apply to many sections of the Penal Code where the requisite knowledge must relate to the consequences of the accused's actions. For instance, how can one *know* (as strictly defined above) that one's actions are "so imminently dangerous that" they "must in all probability cause death" contrary to s 300(d)? One can suspect, think or believe that they will be so dangerous, but one simply cannot *know* anything speculative.

Accordingly, it is submitted that a more flexible interpretation of "knowledge" and its grammatical variants needs to be adopted–perhaps along the lines of the proposal put forward in cl 22(a) of the English Draft Criminal Code Bill (1985):

a person acts in respect of an element of an offence–"knowingly" when he is aware that it exists or is almost certain that it exists or will exist or occur.

(iv) Voluntarily

Penal Code, s 39

A person is said to cause an effect "voluntarily" when he causes it by means whereby he intended to cause it, or by means which, at the time of employing those means, he knew or had reason to believe to be likely to cause it.

Illustration

A sets fire, by night, to an inhabited house in a large town, for the purpose of facilitating a robbery, and thus causes the death of a person. Here A may not have intended to cause death, and may even be sorry that death has been caused by this act; yet, if he knew that he was likely to cause death, he has caused death voluntarily.

The term "voluntarily" is given an artificial meaning for the purposes of the Penal Code, a meaning that approximates to the English *mens rea* term, "wilfully". It covers *mens rea* in its widest sense in that a person can be said to act "voluntarily" in any of the following situations:

(1)   when he intends to cause a result;
(2)   when he knows he is likely to cause a result;
(3)   when he has reason to believe he is likely to cause a result.

In traditional common law these three "states of mind" ((1) to (3) above) correspond to intention, recklessness and negligence respectively. When the only *mens rea* required for an offence is that the accused acted "voluntarily" (eg s 339 Penal Code) it is unnecessary to draw sharp distinctions between these different degrees of *mens rea*. However, many offences in the Penal Code restrict the wide scope of s 39. For instance, for the offence of voluntarily causing hurt contrary to s 321 of the Penal Code the requirement of "voluntariness" is qualified in that the accused must intend to cause hurt or know that he is likely to cause hurt. Without such subjective *mens rea* there can be no liability; the mere fact that he has reason to believe he is likely to cause hurt is not sufficient *mens rea*.

(v)   Recklessness

This concept is unknown to the Penal Code but has been introduced into other local legislation, such as the Road Traffic Act (Singapore), as a direct borrowing from English law.

In English law "recklessness" used to bear a subjective meaning in the sense that the accused had himself to realize that there was a chance of the harmful consequence occurring and the taking of the risk must have been unjustifiable in the circumstances (*Cunningham*, 1957). The House of Lords has now, however, reversed this and given a new meaning to the concept, "recklessness".

R v Lawrence [1982] AC 510 (HL, England)

Lord Diplock: In my view, an appropriate instruction ... on what is meant by driving recklessly would ... (involve) two things:

First, that the defendant was in fact driving the vehicle in such a manner as to create an obvious and serious risk of causing physical injury to some other person who might happen to be using the road or of doing substantial damage to property; and

Second, that in driving in that manner the defendant did so without having given any thought to the possibility of there being any such risk or, having recognized that there was some risk involved, had nonetheless gone on to take it....

[W]hether the risk created by the manner in which the vehicle was being driven was both obvious and serious ... (depends on) the standard of the ordinary prudent motorist....

A similiar test (but without the qualification that the risk be "serious") was laid down by the House of Lords in *Caldwell* (1982). Further, in *Seymour* (1983) the House of Lords ruled that this test applies to all crimes in English law that can be committed recklessly.

This new test is a radical departure from the old subjective test of recklessness. It is no longer necessary that the accused himself should have foreseen the possibility of the risk occurring. As long as the risk was "obvious" to the reasonable man the accused has acted recklessly. In *Elliott* v *C (A Minor)* (1983) a 14-year-old girl who was in a remedial class at school and had not slept an entire night was held to be reckless when she poured white spirit on the floor of a garden shed and threw lighted matches on the spirit. This was so despite the fact that the judges hearing the case at first instance had concluded that because of her age, understanding, lack of experience and exhaustion, she *was not capable* of appreciating the risks attached to her actions. This, however, was irrelevant: the risk would have been obvious to the reasonably prudent man and that was all that was involved in the *Caldwell/Lawrence* (1982) test of recklessness. Similarly, in *Bell* (1984) an accused was adjudged to be reckless because he had failed to give thought to the obvious consequences of his actions. The fact that he was in the throes of a schizophrenic attack and thought he was being driven on by God was dismissed as irrelevant under the objective *Caldwell/Lawrence* (1982) test.

Although some theoretical distinctions remain (Glanville Williams, 1981), the practical effect of these developments is that the test of recklessness is virtually synonymous with that of negligence–or, at the very least, with that of gross negligence.

(vi) Rashly and negligently

While each of these terms has a separate meaning the Penal Code generally uses them jointly as in "causing death by a rash or negligent act" contrary to s 304A.

Full discussion of these terms, their relationship to other *mens rea* concepts, and whether negligence is a justifiable ground for the imposition of criminal liability, is reserved until later (see below, ch 21), the classic definition here sufficing:

Re Nidamarti Nagabhushanam (1872) 7 Mad HCR 119 (Holloway and Kindersley JJ)

Judgment of court: Culpable rashness is acting with the consciousness that mischievous and illegal consequences may follow, but with the hope that they will not and often with the belief that the actor has taken sufficient precautions to prevent their happening. The imputability arises from acting despite the consciousness *luxuria*. Culpable negligence is acting without the consciousness that the illegal and mischievous effects will follow, but in circumstances which show that the actor has not exercised the caution incumbent on him, and that, if he had, he would have had the consciousness. The imputability arises from the neglect of the civic duty of circumspection....

Rashness is thus advertence to the possibility of the consequence occurring. Negligence is inadvertence to such a possibility.

It should be noted that the above definition of negligence requires that if the accused had stopped to think about the consequences of his actions "he would have had the consciousness". Applying this to the facts of *Elliot* v *C (A Minor)* (1983), if the girl had stopped to consider the consequences of her actions she would still not, because of her retardation, have had the necessary "consciousness". She would thus not be negligent under this test. This serves to emphasize yet again how strict the new test of recklessness under *Caldwell/Lawrence* (1982) has become.

(vii)　Malignantly

RC Nigam, *Law of Crimes in India* (1965) Vol I, 107

This term ... means "maliciously".... A thing is done "maliciously", if it is done wickedly or in a depraved or perverse or malignant spirit, regardless of social duty and deliberately bent on mischief.

The term "maliciously" itself appears in ss 219 and 220 of the Penal Code. Being undefined, it is permissible to look at English law where one discovers that the term bears a meaning significantly different from that attributed to it by Nigam in the above passage.

R v Cunningham [1957] 2 All ER 412 (CCA, England)

Byrne J: We have considered ... the following principle which was propounded by the late Professor CS Kenny ....:

> "... in any statutory definition of a crime 'malice' must be taken not in the old vague sense of 'wickedness' in general, but as requiring either (i) an actual intention to do the particular *kind* of harm that in fact was done, or (ii) recklessness as to whether such harm should occur or not (ie the accused has foreseen that the particular kind of harm might be done, and yet has gone on to take the risk of it). It is neither limited to, nor does it indeed require, any ill-will towards the person injured." ...

We think that this is an accurate statement of the law.... In our opinion, the word "maliciously" in a statutory crime postulates foresight of consequences....

It should be noted that references to "recklessness" in the above passage were of course references to the old subjective test of recklessness adopted by English law before *Caldwell/Lawrence* (1982), under which it was necessary that the accused himself foresee the possibility of the consequence occurring.

(viii) Wantonly

Kari v State (1952) Cri LJ 449 (Patna HC, India)

Imam J: The expression "wanton" ... means recklessly, thoughtlessly without regard for right or consequence. Today, I think it must be recognized that to kill or to sacrifice a cow in the open exposed to the view of the public would cause needless offence .... A person who so kills or sacrifices a cow obviously does so recklessly, thoughtlessly and without regard for the sentiment of those who do not approve of such an act.

Gour, *Penal Law of India* (10th edn, 1983) Vol II, 1363

The expression "wanton" ... implies a disposition not evil, but reckless or mischievous. A man may do a thing wantonly when he has no reason to do it, but he does it because he takes pleasure in doing though he knows that its consequences to others may be serious.

Is there any difference between "wantonly" and "recklessly" (in either its subjective or objective formulation)?

The remaining specific *mens rea* terms, such as dishonesty and fraudulently have technical meanings best understood when dealing with the offences to which they apply. Accordingly, discussion of these terms is postponed until then. (See below, pp 530–531; 592–594; 604–607.)

The above analysis of these statutory *mens rea* provisions clearly reveals that the law in Singapore and Malaysia has committed itself to the ideas articulated in the introduction to this section: criminal liability ought to be based upon a premise of blame and this is best evidenced by a finding of one of the above mental elements.

(b) Applicability of general doctrine of mens rea

Numerous statutory provisions do not expressly contain any specific provision for *mens rea*. Nowhere in the Penal Code or elsewhere is there any general provision endorsing the concept of *mens rea*. Does this mean that liability in all such cases must be "strict" in the sense that no mental element or other criterion of blameworthiness need be established?

Penal Code, s 375

A man is said to commit "rape" who, except in the case hereinafter excepted, has sexual intercourse with a woman under circumstances falling under any of the five following descriptions:
(a) against her will;
(b) without her consent;
(c) with her consent, when her consent has been obtained by putting her in fear of death or hurt;
(d) with her consent, when the man knows that he is not her husband, and her consent is given because she believes that he is another man to whom she

is or believes herself to be lawfully married or to whom she would consent;

(e) with or without her consent, when she is under fourteen years of age.

This offence of rape (carrying a maximum penalty of life imprisonment under s 376) makes no reference to any mental element. What is the position of an accused who honestly believes that the woman is consenting to intercourse when in fact she is not? And what of the accused who honestly thinks the girl is over 14 years of age when in fact she is not? Must such an accused person be convicted on the basis that the doctrine of *mens rea* is inapplicable under the Penal Code? This indeed was (and is) the view of many commentators.

Ratanlal and Dhirajlal, *Law of Crimes* (23rd edn, 1987) Vol 1, 216

The maxim *actus non facit reum, nisi mens sit rea* has, however no application to the offences under the Code; because the definitions of various offences contain expressly a proposition as to the state of mind of the accused. The definitions state whether the act must have been done "voluntarily", "knowingly", "dishonestly", or "fraudulently" or the like. Every ingredient of the offence is stated in the definitions. So *mens rea* will mean one thing or another according to the particular offence.... If, in any case, the Indian legislature has omitted to prescribe a particular mental condition, the presumption is that the omission is intentional. In such a case the doctrine of *mens rea* is not applicable.

This approach used to be widely endorsed (see Balasubrahmanyam, 1962), but has been firmly rejected in Singapore and Malaysia. Local courts have committed themselves to a "general doctrine" of "*mens rea*". Unfortunately, however, there has been no consistency in their approach to *how* a *mens rea* requirement should be incorporated. Further, it has been made plain that this is no more than a "general" doctrine: in some cases it does not apply and strict liability without any degree of fault can be imposed.

Essentially two quite different approaches have been applied: the "Chapter IV approach" (which very much confines itself to the Penal Code) and the "presumption of *mens rea* approach" (which goes beyond the Penal Code and draws on established common law principles).

(i) Chapter IV, Penal Code involves mens rea:

The central argument here is that while the Penal Code does not contain a neat, single section incorporating a general doctrine of *mens rea* as, for instance, in the Model Penal Code (see above, p 56), nevertheless its chapter of general exceptions (Chapter IV) achieves much the same effect.

V Balasubrahmanyam, "Guilty Mind" in *Essays on the Indian Penal Code* (1962), 61

While the specific *mens rea* found in the definitions of particular offences gives effect to the doctrine in a positive way the general exceptions in Ch IV like mistake, accident, etc emphasize–in a negative way–the same doctrine, ie that where there is no *mens rea* there can be no criminal liability. The general exceptions (based upon absence of *mens rea*) are but the enunciation of the doctrine of *mens rea* in a statutory form....

The two most important sections introducting *mens rea* "via the back door" in Chapter IV are ss 79 and 80.

Penal Code, ss 79 and 80

79.   Nothing is an offence which is done by any person who is justified by law, or who by reason of a mistake of fact and not by reason of a mistake of law in good faith believes himself to be justified by law in doing it.

80.   Nothing is an offence which is done by accident or misfortune, and without any criminal intention or knowledge, in the doing of a lawful act in a lawful manner, by lawful means, and with proper care and caution.

Illustration

A is at work with a hatchet; the head flies off and kills a man who is standing by. Here, if there was no want of proper caution on the part of A, his act is excusable and not an offence.

Provisions such as these apply to every offence in the Penal Code or in any other statute irrespective of whether any *mens rea* term has been used in the definition of the statutory offence.

Penal Code, s 6

Throughout this Code every definition of an offence, every penal provision, and every illustration of every such definition or penal provision, shall be understood subject to the exceptions contained in the Chapter entitled "General Exceptions", though those exceptions are not repeated in such definition, penal provision or illustration.

Penal Code, s 40(2)

In Chapters IV ...., the word "offence" denotes a thing punishable under this Code or under any other law for the time being in force.

It thus appears clear that the general exceptions, including ss 79 and 80, are applicable to every offence in Singapore and Malaysia whether it be a Penal Code offence or not. The effect of applying these general exceptions to offences such as rape is to introduce a *mens rea* require-ment via the back door in that an accused who lacked the necessary *mens rea* could avail himself of such exceptions and thereby escape liability.

Abdullah v R (1954) 20 MLJ 195 (CCA, Singapore)

Murray-Aynsley CJ (with whom Whitton J agreed): This case turns on the construction of s 79 of the Penal Code. The appellant was charged with rape. It was clear at the trial that the offence, if committed, was only within the scope of s 376 by reason of the fact that the complainant was under 14 years of age. There was no doubt that appellant had carnal knowledge of the complainant and that her age was under 14. The appellant contended that he thought she was over 16. At the trial the learned Judge ruled that this belief, if it existed, was immaterial and refused to leave the matter to the consideration of the jury. He was convicted and now appeals on this point of law.

There is no equivalent to s 79 in English law. This section applies to all offences whether under the Penal Code or otherwise (s 40 PC). It is clear that if the appellant believed "in good faith" that the complainant was over 16 it would be a case of mistake of fact. In this case what he did would not be an offence had the facts been as he supposed them to be; would he be "justified by law"? If on this supposition he would have committed some other offence, eg, if he had thought the girl to be over 14 but under 16, he would clearly not have been justified by law. I think that if the act would have been a tort though not an offence, he would not have been "justified by law". On the other hand, in the present case, if his belief had been correct he would have committed neither a crime nor a tort. Is such an act always "justifiable by law"? In my opinion this is so. According to modern ideas, as embodied in the Penal Code, an act only acquires its criminal character by being forbidden by law. What the law does not forbid it allows, and what a law allows is I think justified by law. I do not think that it is possible to have an intermediate area that is not forbidden but not justifiable. I think that the question should have been left to the jury and I should order a new trial.

MV Sankaran, "*Mens Rea* in Rape: An Analysis of Reg v Morgan and ss 375 and 79 of the Indian Penal Code" (1978) 20 JILI 438, 457–458

Not only have the framers of the code incorporated into the definition of each crime the *mens rea* required for it, but they have given further effect to the doctrine of *mens rea* by providing in chapter IV of the code for general exemption from liability in certain circumstances which are inconsistent with the existence of a guilty mind.

Therefore, even though, say, the second clause of s 375 is silent with respect to the *mens rea* requisite for the offence, where a man had sexual intercourse with a woman under the belief that she was consenting to the act while in fact she was not, he can set up the defence of mistake of fact within the ambit of s 79 of the Indian Penal Code. A mistake of fact is a form of absence of *mens rea* and so excusable. The onus of proving the mistake as under s 79 is, however, on the accused.

PP v Teo Eng Chan [1988] 1 MLJ 156 (HC, Singapore)

The four accused drove a girl in a lorry to a deserted quarry and there each had sexual intercourse with her. The accused persons were charged with rape punishable under s 376(2) of the Penal Code. Their defence was that the girl had consented, or if she had not, that they believed she had consented.

Coomaraswamy J: In my view, the law on consent and mistake of fact are contained in the Penal Code itself ....

The next question for me to consider is whether there was a mistake of fact in the minds of the accused persons when they presumed that she consented. The law on this is contained in s 79 of the Penal Code which provides that "nothing is an offence which is done by any person ... who by reason of a mistake of fact ... in good faith believes himself to be justified by law, in doing it."

The implications of this approach are extremely far-reaching and if consistently applied would mean that *mens rea* (admittedly introduced in this negative fashion) was a necessary ingredient of *every* crime in Singapore and Malaysia–unless the legislature expressly stated otherwise. This conclusion has been endorsed by the Supreme Court of Ceylon.

Perera v Munaweera (1955) 56 NLR 433 (SC, Ceylon) (Gratiaen J, Swan J, de Silva J, Sansoni J and Fernando J)

The facts appear from the judgment of the court. Note that s 72 of the Ceylon Penal Code is identical to s 79 of the Penal Code of Singapore and Malaysia.

Judgment of court: The appellant was charged with having sold a loaf of bread purporting to weigh 16 ounces, but in fact weighing only 15 1/4 ounces, at a price which was 1 7/32 cents in excess of the maximum control price fixed under a Food Price Order in force at the time; this sale, it was alleged, constituted a contravention of s 8(1) of the Control of Prices Act, No 29 of 1950 and was punishable under s 8(6) of the Act.

The appellant gave evidence, however, to the effect that, as a responsible person employed by a reputable bakery, he had taken all reasonable precautions to avoid selling bread at prices beyond the controlled price; that he honestly believed that the weight of the offending loaf was in fact 16 ounces, and that, in demanding and receiving 26 cents for its sale, he acted in good faith and intended to charge only what was in truth the controlled price fixed for a 16 ounce loaf. In other words, he set up a defence under s 72 of the Penal Code the relevant provisions of which are as follows:

"72. Nothing is an offence which is done by any person who ... by reason of a mistake of fact and not by reason of a mistake of law in good faith believes himself to be justified by law in doing it".

The learned Magistrate did not reject the appellant's version of the circumstances relating to the sale. He took the view, however, that the Food Price Order in question contained words of absolute and unqualified prohibition, and that in regard to such offences, as in England, the defence of "*bona fide* mistake of fact" was not available to an accused person against whom the commission of the *actus reus* had been established. In reaching this conclusion, the learned Magistrate adopted the *ratio decidendi* of Soertsz J's judgment in *Perumal* v *Arumugam* (1939). In that case a person charged under s 28 of the Poisons, Opium, and Dangerous Drugs Ordinance (Cap 172) explained by way of defence that his possession of an article containing ganja was due to a *bona fide* mistake of fact. Soertsz J decided that s 72 of the Penal Code was not applicable to offences punishable under s 28 of the Ordinance because:

"As regards Common law offences, which so far as we are concerned have been made statutory to the extent that they have been codified in our Penal Code, *mens rea* is necessary as s 72 of the Penal Code indicates. Section 38 makes s 72 applicable to offences punishable under "any law other than this Code" as well, but in my opinion, this does not mean that it necessarily applies to all offences outside the Penal Code. It is not an inflexible rule. Whether it applies or not must as I have pointed out on the authority of the cases I have referred to depend on the particular Legislative Enactment. If I may repeat myself and use the words of de Sampayo J 'there are many branches of social and municipal legislation in which an act is made criminal without any *mens rea*. The Poisons, Opium, and Dangerous Drugs Ordinance is such an Ordinance."

It was argued before us that this decision was wrong, and that it is in conflict with the earlier judgment of the same distinguished Judge in *Letchman* v *Murugappa Chettiar* (1936). In that case the accused was charged with plying an omnibus along a route not approved by the licensing authority. His defence was he honestly believed that he had a valid licence authorizing him to proceed along the particular route. Soertsz J, in quashing the conviction, said:

"The accused has given evidence and his defence is that he had not been informed, and he was not aware, that the licensing authority had withdrawn his approval of a section of the route. There is no reason whatever for rejecting the accused's evidence on this point. The only question is whether his defence is good in law. I am of opinion it is. In *Weerakoon* v *Ranhamy* (1921), a Bench of four Judges considered the question of *mens rea* in relation to our law. They held that s 72 ... applies to all enactments alike, including those enactments which impose absolute obligations. The English Law drew a distinction and made the plea of absence of *mens rea* inoperative in the case of charges framed under 'certain exceptional enactments containing prohibitions which are interpreted as unqualified'. Our law knows no such distinction."

In our opinion this passage correctly sets out the general principle as to the applicability of s 72 of the Penal Code not only to offences punishable under the Penal Code but also to offences punishable under all other criminal statutes enacted in Ceylon. Section 38(2) of the Code unambiguously declares that the word "offence" in Chapter 4 of the Code (dealing with "General Exceptions") includes "a thing punishable in Ceylon under any law other than this Code". Accordingly, s 72 equally applies to every statutory offence even if its definition does not contain a particular state of mind or knowledge as one of its elements. (*Weerakoon* v *Ranhamy*, 1921). It is therefore wrong to say that the rule laid down in s 38 of the Code in its present form is "not inflexible". Where the definition of an offence contains words of absolute and unqualified prohibition, the prosecution need only establish beyond reasonable doubt the commission of the prohibited act, and it is not required in addition to establish that the accused acted with any specific intention or knowledge. But this does not mean that in such a case the accused is to be denied the right to plead any of the general exceptions set out in Chapter 4 of the Code. The accused would therefore be entitled to an acquittal if he proved on a balance of probability that by reason of a mistake of fact, and not by reason of a mistake of law, he had in good faith believed himself to be doing something which was not prohibited by law. The accused must, of course, prove affirmatively the existence of each of these circumstances, and he will not be entitled to the benefit of s 72 if he fails to do so, or merely leaves that issue in doubt. *Chandrasekera* (1942) ....

We were invited to consider the undesirability of s 38 of the Penal Code making s 72 inflexibly applicable to offences to which, under modern conditions, Parliament may, in the interests of justice, consider the defence of *bona fide* mistake to be inappropriate. This argument does not impress us. In such a contingency, it is always open to Parliament to enact that, in regard to any particular criminal statute, Chapter 4 of the Penal Code or any part of it shall not apply: s 38(2) would then stand repealed or amended to that extent. No such repeal or amendment having been enacted in the case of offences punishable under the Control of Prices Act, No 29 of 1950, it was not open to the learned Magistrate to convict the appellant without rejecting the appellant's evidence that he believed in good faith, and by reason of a mistake of fact, that he was justified in law in charging 26 cents for a loaf of bread which he honestly but erroneously believed to be 16 ounces in weight. We allow the appeal and quash the conviction.

Appeal allowed

This approach would mean that there could be no strict liability offences in Singapore or Malaysia. The general defences could be pleaded in relation to *every* offence whether the offence be one under the Penal Code (s 6) or under any other law (s 40(2)). However, as will be seen (see below, p 84), it is clear that strict liability offences *do* exist both in Singapore and Malaysia and are backed by such strong precedents that it is really "too late" (Sornarajah, 1985) to argue they have no place in local law.

(ii) Presumption of mens rea

Totally misunderstanding the scheme and structure of the Penal Code with regard to the mental element, courts both in India and in Singapore and Malaysia have largely ignored the Penal Code in these matters and have instead turned to English Law and applied the now well-established principle that in the absence of any express statutory provision there is a clear presumption that *mens rea* is implied. In certain circumstances this presumption may be rebutted with the result that liability is strict (see below, p 76 et seq). However, in all other cases the general rule is that *mens rea* is required.

Lim Chin Aik v The Queen [1963] AC 160 (PC, appeal from HC, Singapore)

The facts and fuller extracts from the judgment in this case are set out below, pp 93–94.

The Privy Council was concerned to construe s 6 of the Singapore Immigration Ordinance 1952 which contained no specific reference to any *mens rea* requirement.

Lord Evershed: [I]t is with the question whether a guilty mind is a necessary requisite for the establishment of an offence under the relevant section that their Lordships are alone concerned ....

That proof of the existence of a guilty intent is an essential ingredient of a crime at common law is not at all in doubt. The problem is of the extent to which the same rule is applicable in the case of offences created and defined by statute or statutory instrument ....

Mr Gratiaen founded his argument upon the formulation of the problem contained in the judgment of Wright J in *Sherras*'s case (1895). The language of that learned and experienced judge was as follows:

"There is a presumption that *mens rea*, or evil intention, or knowledge of the wrongfulness of the act, is an essential ingredient in every offence; but that presumption is liable to be displaced either by the words of the statute creating the offence or by the subject matter with which it deals, and both must be considered."...

Their Lordships accept as correct the formulation cited from the judgment of Wright J. They are fortified in that view by the fact that such formulation was expressly accepted by Lord du Parcq in delivering the judgment of the Board in the case in 1947 of *Srinivas Mall Bairoliya* (1947)–a case which unfortunately has not found its way into the Law Reports. That was a case in which one of the appellants had been charged with an offence under the rules made by virtue of the Defence of India Act 1939, consisting of the sale of salt at prices exceeding those prescribed under the rules, the sales having in fact been made without that appellant's knowledge by one of his servants. The Indian High Court had held the appellant to be nonetheless liable upon the terms of the rules; but the Board rejected the view of the High Court. Lord du Parcq, after citing with approval the judgment already quoted of Wright J, also adopted the language of Lord Goddard CJ in the case of *Brend* v *Wood* (1946):

"It is in my opinion of the utmost importance for the protection of the liberty of the subject that a court should always bear in mind that unless a statute either clearly or by necessary implication rules out *mens rea* as a constituent part of a crime a defendant should not be found guilty of an offence against the criminal law unless he has got a guilty mind."

Numerous cases have followed this approach: *Mohamed Ibrahim* (1963, Malaysia); *Kochu Muhammad Kunju Ismail* v *Mohammed Kadja Umma* (1959, India); *CT Prim* (1961, India); *Sim Poh Ho* (1966, Borneo); *Phua Keng Tong* (1986, Singapore).

PP v Zainal Abidin b Ismail [1987] 2 MLJ 741 (HC, Brunei)

The four accused took a girl to the beach and there had sexual intercourse with her. They were charged with rape contrary to s 375 of the Penal Code but claimed that she was consenting or that they believed she was consenting.

Roberts CJ: In relation to ... (the accused) I have to consider only whether the prosecution has satisfied me, so that I am sure, that these acts of intercourse took place in such circumstances as to constitute rape under s 376 of the Penal Code–ie did Miss X consent to what was done to her?

It is, I think, appropriate at this point that I should refer to *Morgan* (1976) which sets out the principles which have to be applied by a judge when deciding the issue of consent on a charge of rape. The majority view of the House of Lords, which was subsequently overruled by the Sexual Offences Act 1967 [sic: Sexual Offences Act 1976], which does not apply in Brunei, was that the crime of rape consisted in having sexual intercourse with a woman, with intent to do so, without her consent or with indifference to whether or not she consented. The offence could not be committed if that essential intention was absent. Accordingly, if an accused in fact believed that the woman had consented, whether or not that belief was based on reasonable grounds, he could not be found guilty of rape.

It should be noted that there is no reference to the fact that s 376 specifies no *mens rea* terms; there is no reference to the fact that the accused persons were in fact claiming to have made a mistake and therefore Chapter IV of the Penal Code should have been applicable. The court simply turns to the English common law and applies it directly.

This approach has become so widespread that in India Gour, who wrote: "But no question of *mens rea* arises where the legislature has omitted to prescribe a particular mental condition as an ingredient of an offence because the presumption is that the omission is intentional" (Gour, 1955), has recanted in his latest edition.

HS Gour, *Penal law of India* (10th edn, 1982) Vol 1, 111–112:

Mens rea is an essential ingredient of a criminal offence. Doubtless a statute may exclude the element of *mens rea*, but it is a sound rule of construction adopted in England and also accepted in India to construe a statutory provision creating an offence in conformity with the common law rather than against it unless the statute expressly or by necessary implication excluded *mens rea* ....

A statutory crime may or may not contain an express definition of the necessary state of mind .... [I]t may be silent as to any requirement of *mens rea*, and in such a case in order to determine whether or not *mens rea* is an essential element of the offence, it is necessary to look at the objects and terms of the statute. In some cases, the Courts have concluded that despite the absence of express language the intention of the Legislature was that *mens rea* was a necessary ingredient of the offence ....

It is possible to defend the importation of such common law principles.

Stanley Yeo Meng Heong, "The Application of Common Law Defences to the Penal Code in Singapore and Malaysia" in AJ Harding (ed), *The Common Law in Singapore and Malaysia* (1985), 145–146

It should be noted that these *dicta* merely state that English common law offences or defences cannot be invoked when there are express provisions covering the matter. However, this does not mean that *principles* derived from the common law cannot be considered for the purposes of construction. The courts would also have been prevented from such reliance on the common law had Macaulay, the principal draftsman among the Indian Commissioners who drafted the Indian Penal Code, had his way. Macaulay proposed that whenever an appellate court reversed a lower court on a point of law not previously determined or whenever two judges of a higher court disagreed on the interpretation of a provision of the Code, the matter should be referred to Parliament, which should decide on the point and, if necessary, amend the Code. This proposal was not adopted in India, nor in Singapore or Malaysia, so that the courts of these jurisdictions have been given the task of determining the meaning to be given to an ambiguous provision. In such cases, the common law has occasionally been resorted to partly because the Indian Commissioners had themselves drawn some of their inspiration from English law and also because many of the judges and legal practitioners, at least prior to the independence of these nations from British rule, were most familiar with the criminal law of England.

It is submitted that such reliance on common law principles is quite acceptable and reference may be made to s 5 of the Criminal Procedure Code as indicative of when these principles might be applied by local courts. This section provides for the English law relating to criminal procedure to be applied when there does not exist any special provision on the matter either in the Code or in any other existing local law. No such provision exists in the Penal Code. What is important to note, however, is the proviso to this section which states that English law is applicable insofar as it "does not conflict or is not inconsistent with [the] Code and can be made auxiliary thereto". Similarly, in respect of the Penal Code, it is arguable that English law may be referred to for guidance in the construction of a particular section provided that the law is not inconsistent with the wording of the section and the spirit of the subject matter involved.

This suggestion of how aspects of the common law might be considered under the Code accords with general principles of statutory interpretation. The basic rule is that the essence of a code is to be exhaustive on the matters in respect of which it declares the law and the courts cannot disregard or go outside the letter of the enactment according to its true construction. Hence the courts are to examine the words in the first instance, and where the words are plain, they are to decide the case accordingly. There is a secondary rule of statutory interpretation which governs instances when the words of a provision allow for two constructions. In such cases the courts should not adopt a construction which would lead to an absurdity, but should adopt that construction which appears to be most in accord with reason and convenience, having regard to the subject matter in question. Common law principles may assist in the application of this rule of interpretation, provided always that those principles are generally consistent with the statutory provisions concerned.

On the other hand, many commentators have roundly condemned this whole approach. For instance, Balasubrahmanyam (1962) states:

> Applying the common law doctrine of *mens rea*, as an interpretive principle while dealing with offences under the Penal Code, and relying on English authorities for that purpose, really means that the scheme of the Code in regard to the mental element in criminal responsibility is not properly appreciated .... The general exceptions (based upon absence of *mens rea*) are but the enunciation of the doctrine of *mens rea* in a statutory form and there can be no justification for deriving inspiration from English law .... It is a tragedy that some times the Indian Penal Code is called upon to bear the oppressive weight of English case law.

These views were accepted and there was an emphatic rejection of this whole "presumption of *mens rea*" approach in the most recent Singapore decision on the subject.

PP v Teo Eng Chan [1988] 1 MLJ 156 (HC, Singapore)

(The facts are set out above, p 66.)

Coomaraswamy J: [T]he defence of each accused ... was that ... each had reason to believe that she consented (to intercourse). For this, reliance was placed on the English case of *Morgan* (1976) where the House of Lords, by a majority of three to two, held that if an accused in fact believed that the woman had consented, he could not be found guilty of rape, whether or not that belief was based on reasonable gounds. Counsel placed heavy reliance on the decision of the learned Chief Justice, Dato Sir Denys Roberts, sitting as a trial judge in Brunei Darussalam in the case of *Zainal Abidin b Ismail* (1987). The

Chief Justice applied the *Morgan* principle in this case of rape against the accused. Counsel before me relied upon the case of *Zainal Abidin* (1987) because the Penal Code of Brunei is, with differences immaterial for present purposes, similar to ours. Section 375 is identical in the two Penal Codes. They therefore argued that I should follow the decision in *Zainal Abidin* (1987).

In my view, the law on consent and mistake of fact are contained in the Penal Code itself under Chapter IV dealing with exceptions, ...

In view of these specific provisions in our law, the majority decision of the House of Lords in *Morgan* (1976) does not, in my humble view, have any application in Singapore. There is also nothing in the transcript of Dato Sir Denys Roberts' decision in *Zainal Abidin*'s case (1987) that he was referred to the provisions of the Penal Code to which I have just referred and will here-after refer.

This is an important decision and one that spells the death-knoll for the "presumption of *mens rea*" approach. It is confidently predicted that this Chapter IV approach is the one that will be used in Singapore and Malaysia in the future. However, this approach leaves open a major question. Coomaraswamy J completely overlooked the leading Privy Council decision, *Lim Chin Aik* (1963), which was binding on him. This problem and that of the implications of this decision for crimes of strict liability will be dealt with shortly.

(iii) Meaning of "mens rea"

One final problem remains for consideration. Bearing in mind that there are many different types or degrees of *mens rea*, which of these vari-ous forms is to be adopted when a statutory provision does not specify any particular species of *mens rea*? For example, s 375 of the Penal Code is silent as to the *mens rea* requirement for rape. What *mens rea* is required for this offence?

The meaning to be attributed to the concept *mens rea* depends en-tirely on which of the above two methods has been used to incorporate the concept into the offence.

First, if one adopts the view that Chapter IV of the Penal Code involves *mens rea*, it becomes clear that the meaning of *mens rea* must be found in Chapter IV itself.

MV Sankaran, "Mens Rea in Rape: An Analysis of Reg v Morgan and ss 375 and 79 of the Indian Penal Code" (1978) 20 JILI 438, 458–461

Under s 79 of the Indian Penal Code, a mistake made by the accused would be a good defence if:

(i)   the accused's mistake was "a mistake of fact and not a mistake of law";

(ii) the accused made the mistake in "good faith" (as defined under section 52 of the code); and

(iii) the accused had under the mistake of fact in good faith "believed himself to be justified by law in acting as he did".

Taking into consideration the first ingredient of s 79 insofar as it pertains to our inquiry, that is, in a case of rape as under the second clause of s 375, any question whether the woman consented to the intercourse or not would be a question of fact. Therefore, any mistaken belief on the part of the accused as to the consent of the woman would be a mistake of fact and not a mistake of law.

Taking into consideration the second ingredient of s 79, the term "good faith" is defined under s 52 of the code as follows: "Nothing is said to be done or believed in 'good faith' which is done or believed without due care and attention."

The Law Commissioners who drafted the Indian Penal Code state:

> "To satisfy the court of his good faith a person must show at least that he acted advisedly and that he had reasonable ground *prima facie* for believing that he ought to do what he did."

According to *Webster's Third New International Dictionary*, "due care" means: "The care that an ordinarily reasonable and prudent person exercises under all circumstances for his own protection."

The same dictionary explains "attention" to mean, "the application of the mind to any object of sense or thought" or simply, "observant care" ....

Taking into consideration the third ingredient under s 79, we find that the accused's act must be justifiable in law under the state of things as supposed by him. The question then arises: "What is justified by law?" The code does not define this term. The Law Commissioners who drafted the Indian Penal Code state:

> "Under both (ss 76 and 79) there must be a *bona fide* intention to advance the Law, manifested by the circumstances attending the act which is the subject of the charge; and the party accused cannot allege generally that he had a good motive, but must allege specifically that he believed in good faith that he was bound by law (s 76) to do as he did, or that being *empowered by law* (s 79) to act in the matter, he had acted to the best of his judgment exerted in good faith."

The Law Commissioners thus equate the expression, "justified by law" with that which is "empowered by law". This does not seem clear enough as again the question may be raised: "What is empowered by law?" It seems safer to say that an act which is not "illegal" within the meaning of s 43 of the code would be an act "justified by law"....

To conclude, in the *Morgan* case (1976), the House of Lords has held, yielding to sound logic and the weight of academic opinion, that an honest but mistaken belief entertained by the accused that the woman was consenting to sexual intercourse, would preclude the *mens rea* required in rape and hence negative the charge of rape itself.... [T]he court held that reasonableness of the mistaken belief is irrelevant except as a matter of evidence to show that the accused genuinely held that belief. The court also held that recklessness as to the woman's consent would form part of the *mens rea* in rape. The decision is obviously sound because if *mens rea* is a subjective element according to modern notions, then the absence of *mens rea* should equally be subjective.

However, the *Morgan* case (1976) cannot be followed by our courts, until a statutory change is made in this regard. Section 375 of the Indian Penal Code dealing with rape on the whole leaves the *mens rea* to be presumed from the circumstances described therein. The defence of mistake of fact as under s 79 of the code is circumscribed by the term, "good faith", which is not equivalent to an "honest belief" as under the General Clauses Act 1897, whether negligent or not. However "honestly" a mistaken belief is held by the accused, if it fails the test of "due care and caution" as under s 52 of the code, the defence of mistake would fail. This requirement of due diligence does bring in an objective element into the plea of the "absence of *mens rea*" based on mistake of fact.

PP v Teo Eng Chan [1988] 1 MLJ 156 (HC, Singapore)

(The facts are set out above, p 67.)

Coomaraswamy J: (Section 79 requiring "good faith" is applicable) .... "Good faith" is further defined by s 52 of the Penal Code which reads: "Nothing is said to be done or believed in good faith which is done or believed without due care and attention." ...

Section 79 of the Penal Code appears in Chapter IV of the Code. This chapter deals with "General Exceptions". Section 107 of the Evidence Act provides that the burden of proving the existence of circumstances bringing a case within the general exceptions in the Penal Code is upon the accused person and the court shall presume the absence of such circumstances.

In the light of the provisions to which I have referred, the burden of proof under s 79 is upon the accused. Acknowledgedly, the quantum of proof with which this burden is to be discharged is on a balance of probabilities and not beyond a reasonable doubt.

My finding is that even on this lesser burden, not one of the accused has rebutted the presumption of the absence of circumstances enabling him to bring himself within the exception under 's 79. The respective evidence of each was carefully considered by me. So was the respective evidence against each, one separate from the other.

Even without resort to the presumption in s 107 of the Evidence Act, there was ample evidence for me to hold as a fact that not one of the accused in his respective claimed belief that Kay consented, in good faith believed that she consented to his having sexual intercourse with her. If any of them held that belief, my finding is that he did so without due care and attention.

The meaning of *mens rea* becomes quite different if one adopts the second solution discussed above, namely, the "presumption of *mens rea* approach". Under this approach one is not introducing *mens rea* "via the back door" by using s 79 and therefore there is no limitation that the accused have acted "in good faith" as defined by s 52. *Mens rea* is being implied positively in accordance with the English common law and accordingly must bear such meaning as would be ascribed by the common law. Continuing with the rape example of s 375, this would mean that the *mens rea* of rape is that as defined by the leading English decision, *Morgan* (1976). According to this the accused must know that the woman was not consenting or must at least have realized that there was a chance that she was not consenting (subjective recklessness under English law). If he honestly thought that she was consenting then he lacks the *mens rea* necessary for rape. Under *Morgan* (1976) the *reasonableness or otherwise of the belief is irrelevant* (other than in evidential terms).

Further, because *mens rea* is being positively implied, the burden of proving such *mens rea* is on the prosecution throughout. This of course is a burden that has to be discharged beyond all reasonable doubt.

This was the approach adopted in *Zainal Abidin b Ismail* (1987, above, p 70). The common law meaning of *mens rea* for the crime of rape was simply transposed upon s 375 of the Penal Code. Had the court confined its analysis within the four corners of the Penal Code it would have reached the different result that the accused's belief would have to have been "in good faith".

However, it now seems more likely that courts will follow *Teo Eng Chan* (1988) and insist on the Chapter IV approach. Under this approach it will be far easier to secure convictions for two reasons. First, only a lesser degree of blameworthiness need be established, namely, that the accused acted without "due care and attention" and second, the prosecution has no evidential burden to discharge here, the burden being on the accused to establish on a balance of probabilities that he was acting with the requisite "due care and attention".

D. Strict liability

1. Meaning of strict liability

(a) Introduction

An offence of strict liability is one where an element of *mens rea* is dispensed with. Such crimes represent an exception to the general rule discussed in the preceding section whereby proof of blame is normally a prerequisite to the imposition of criminal liability. With crimes of strict liability an accused can be convicted even though he had no *mens rea* and was not blameworthy in any other way.

PP v Osman b Apo Hamid [1978] 2 MLJ 38 (HC, Kuala Trengganu, Malaysia)

The respondents were found carrying bags of rice in excess of that allowed by the permits which they produced. They were detained and subsequently charged. Both respondents admitted knowledge of the fact that they carried 130 bags of rice but they denied knowledge of the number allowed in the permits, that is, 80 bags only.

The prosecution appealed against the decision of the lower court acquitting the accused.

Abdul Razak J: It was submitted by the defence that the defendants had no knowledge that they were allowed to carry 80 bags only and should not be convicted. I do not think I can agree with that contention. In my view the offence is one of strict liability in which the mental element is negatived by the legislature. I have no doubt that the legislature intended that the category of physical acts of this nature must itself constitute an offence if only because the alternative would mean that the apprehension of offences of this nature would be well nigh difficult if not impossible. The creation of absolute offences is not new. Indeed *Sweet* v *Parsley* (1970) which I shall refer to takes cognizance of this fact. Lord Reid says:

"Our first duty is to consider the words of the Act: if they show a clear intention to create an absolute offence that is an end of the matter." ...

And Lord Morris at page 152 in the same vein had this to say on the requirement of *mens rea*:

"But as Parliament is supreme it is open to Parliament to legislate in such a way that an offence may be created of which someone may be found guilty though *mens rea* is lacking. There may be cases in which as Channell J said in *Pearks, Gunston & Tee Ltd* v *Ward* (1902):

'... the Legislature has thought it so important to prevent the particular act from being committed that it absolutely forbids it to be done; and if it is done the offender is liable to a penalty whether he had any *mens rea* or not, and whether or not he intended to commit a breach of the law. Thus in diverse situations and circumstances and for any one of a variety of reasons Parliament may see fit to create offences and make people responsible before criminal courts although there is an absence of *mens rea*.'

Lord Pearce has given us some of the requisites to look for in offences of strict liability. He said:

"But the nature of the crime, the punishment, the absence of social obloquy, the particular mischief and the field of activity in which it occurs, and the wording of the particular section and its context, may show that Parliament intended that the act should be prevented by punishment regardless of intent or knowledge."

I have been asked to say that by the decision of *Sweet* v *Parsley* (1970) the rationale that mental element of *mens rea* can be excluded by statute has seen its last days and that that case has finally laid down the rule which now is settled law that a presumption of *mens rea* must always be implied even in cases where the legislature merely makes the commission of the prohibited act an offence. But this apparently does not seem to be true even after the case. In the case of *Alphacell Ltd* v *Woodward*, (1972) the courts seem to have quite firmly and categorically viewed *Sweet* v *Parsley* (1970) as merely laying a general proposition of law and that courts are still free to determine whether a given statute is intended to oust the requirement of *mens rea* or not. In that case the statute provides that:

"a person commits an offence (under the Rivers Pollution Act 1951) if (a) he causes or knowingly permits to enter a stream any poisonous, noxious or polluting matter ...".

The defendants owned a factory which operated to discharge industrial effluents which they made to flow and collect in a tank by the side of the river. The apparatus was worked in such a manner that the water was returned to the factory to be circuitously reused and its capacity in the tank maintained at a level as not to overflow into the river. At some stage or another the tank overflowed and the effluent was discharged into the stream although precaution was earlier taken and examination made by the defendants' employees to see that the water level in the tank remained the same. The defendants were, nevertheless, held liable for polluting the stream by their discharge....

In other words, Widgery LJ, was saying that short of any third-party intervention once it is established that the defendant has caused the pollution he is liable regardless of whether he had knowledge of the defect or whether he had been negligent or not. He was clearly stating in terms that the mental element or *mens rea* has no relevance or consequence in such type of offence where the legislature expressly provides that the offence is committed by the commission of the physical act. Considering the scope and extent to which the court nevertheless was prepared in that case to consider a statute as excluding *mens rea*, especially bearing in mind that the word "cause" therein was inextricably linked with the word "knowingly" connoting thereby the requirement of *mens rea*, how could it ever be said that in our case which is not even remotely near those words and phrases it was not intended to exclude the mental element of *mens rea*. Bearing in mind also that the act contemplated is the act of the defendant or the doer himself and not unlike *Sweet* v *Parsley* (1970) or that in *Alphacell Ltd* v *Woodward* (1972) the act or omission of the defendant's servant or agent.

One has to study the purport of the LPN Act 1971 under which PU(A) 320/71 was promulgated and I think it is obvious that looking at the statute and the regulations under which it was made, it must have been intended that the latter be of strict liability if only because in the context in which the Government deems it necessary in order to maintain a stable and proper price for padi and rice for the consumer and the padi planter by having their prices fixed at different levels at different States, that the movement of rice and padi in the States and particularly that from the border State of Thailand should not be allowed unrestricted as to offset the balance of distribution of that commodity in the country as a whole and therefore to upset its expected price levels in the various States. There is always a temptation in a situation like this to circumvent the regulation by unauthorized smuggling and therefore it is of the utmost importance that the regulation should be as strict as possible as to offer the minimum opportunity for evasion and deception.

The learned judge then went on to hold that in any event the respondents probably did have the requisite knowledge or at least were grossly negligent.

Appeal allowed

A striking recent example of strict liability can be seen in the English House of Lords decision of *Pharmaceutical Society of Great Britain* v *Storkwain Ltd* (1986). The appellants, retail chemists, supplied prescription-only drugs in accordance with a forged prescription. They were convicted of an offence contrary to s 58(2) of the Medicines Act 1968 which provides that "(a) no person shall sell by retail ... a medicinal product (defined) ... except in accordance with a prescription given by an appropriate practitioner ...". It was accepted that the appellants were in no way to blame. However, the offence was construed to be one of strict liability and criminal liability accordingly ensued despite a complete absence of *mens rea*.

(b) Strict liability v absolute liability

An offence of absolute liability would be one where no mental or fault element *at all* was required, and one to which there could be no defence. All that would be necessary to establish would be the *actus reus* of the offence. On the other hand, an offence of strict liability is one that simply dispenses with the mental or fault element in relation to one aspect of the *actus reus* (admittedly, usually the crucial element); further, it is possible that certain defences may be raised to strict liability offences (see below, p 94).

The case of *Mohamed Ibrahim* (1963, see below, p 85) illustrates this well. The accused was charged with possession for purposes of sale of an allegedly obscene book contrary to s 292(a) of the Penal Code. The accused's defence that he had no knowledge of the book's obscenity was rejected as s 292(a) was construed to be an offence of strict liability. However, close analysis of s 292(a) reveals three separate elements to the *actus reus* of the crime:

(1)   for purposes of sale
(2)   has in his possession
(3)   any obscene book.

Section 292(a) was held to create an offence of strict liability because it was unnecessary to prove knowledge of obscenity. However, a mental element would still be necessary in relation to the first two *actus reus* elements: the accused would not be liable if the purpose in possessing the obscene books was his own private gratification. Similarly, it would be necessary to establish "possession". If the book had been slippped into his shop without his knowledge, he would not be in possession of the book and accordingly would not be liable.

Of course, many words necessarily involve proof of some mental element. Take, for instance, s 18(1)(g) of the Environmental Public Health Act 1987 (Singapore) (Act 14 of 1987) which makes it an offence to "spit or expel mucous from the nose upon or onto any street or public place". This would clearly be an offence of strict liability in that it would be unnecessary to establish knowledge that it was a street or public place that was being spat upon. So one would be liable even if one thought one was spitting in one's own garden if that spit landed upon any public place. However, one could not "spit" or "expel" mucous without intending to (or at least being negligent thereto). Thus if a sneeze resulted in the expulsion of mucous from the nose onto the street, one would not be liable because there would be no mental element in relation to the expulsion (or, perhaps, because the defence of automatism was available).

In *Gammon Ltd* (1984) builders were charged with an offence of diverging or deviating in a material way from any work shown in a plan approved by the building authority. When the building was constructed part of the lateral support system, required by the plans, was removed. The Privy Council ruled that the offence did involve an element of *mens rea*, namely, there had to be knowledge of the approved plan and of the fact of deviation–but the offence could be regarded as one of strict liability because no knowledge of the *materiality* of the deviation was necessary. Again, dispensing with *mens rea* in relation to one element of the *actus reus* (the materiality of the deviation) rendered the offence one of strict liability. Had it been an offence of absolute liability, no *mens rea* in relation to *any* of the *actus reus* elements would have been necessary.

(c) Strict liability v ignorance of the law

The doctrine of strict liability must be carefully distinguished from the well-known maxim "ignorance of the law is no excuse" (see below, pp 177–178) as in many cases it might not be obvious whether an accused's lack of knowledge is in respect of an *actus reus* element or in respect of the existence of a law.

In *Koo Cheh Yew* (1980) the accused was charged with being concerned with the importation into Malaysia of pianos from South Africa contrary to s 135(1)(a) of the Customs Act 1967 (Rev 1980, Act 235 of 1967). He denied all knowledge of the prohibition. It was held that it was necessary to distinguish between:

(1)   knowledge of the existence of the law prohibiting the importation of pianos into Malaysia; and
(2)   knowledge of the existence of the *actus reus* elements of the offence, namely, "being concerned in importing ... any prohibited goods ...".

With regard to (1), ignorance of the existence of a law is no excuse and an accused cannot escape liability on such a ground (see, however, p 178 below for an exception to this rule). With regard to (2) it becomes necessary to determine whether the offence is one of strict liability. If it is, then lack of knowledge here is similarly no defence. If, however, some degree of *mens rea* is required, then the requisite knowledge must be proved. This would mean proof that the accused knew he was (1) concerned in; (2) importing; (3) prohibited goods. With regard to "prohibited" goods the accused must know those facts that make the goods prohibited (in this case that the pianos were from South Africa, as opposed to, say, New Zealand), rather than being aware of the existence of a law making South African goods prohibited.

As this analysis demonstrates where the offence is one of strict liability it will generally not matter whether the accused's lack of knowledge relates to the law or to the facts. However, if the offence requires any degree of *mens rea*, as was the case in *Koo Cheh Yew* (1980), it becomes crucial to distinguish the two.

The same issue was at stake in the leading Privy Council appeal from Singapore, *Lim Chin Aik* (1963, see below, p 93). The accused had entered Singapore lawfully. After his entry the Minister of Labour and Welfare made an order prohibiting him from entering or remaining in Singapore. The accused had no knowledge of this order; no effort was made to bring it to his attention. He was charged with contravening s 6(2) of the Immigration Ordinance in that he remained in Singapore when he had been "prohibited". The Privy Council held that this was an offence requiring *mens rea* which meant the accused had to have *mens rea* in relation to all the *actus reus* elements, namely:

(1)   remaining in Singapore;
(2)   being prohibited.

The problem here was that knowing one was prohibited would surely amount to knowing the law–which under the general maxim is irrelevant. The Privy Council extricated itself from this thorny dilemma by holding, inter alia, that a prohibition order from the Minister was not "law". The doctrine "ignorance of the law is no excuse" is confined to *legislative* commands and does not extend to executive or administrative commands such as those of the Minister. *Mens rea* in relation to being prohibited meant knowing the *fact* that he was a prohibited person. He lacked such knowledge. His conviction was accordingly quashed.

2. Rationale and development of strict liability

CMV Clarkson, *Understanding Criminal Law* **(1987) 93–94**

The development of most strict liability offences dates from the nineteenth century. In the aftermath of the industrial revolution a great deal of regulatory legislation was enacted dealing with the new areas of public health, safety and welfare. The trend increased in the twentieth century as an increasingly complex society demanded social regulation. Legislation dealing with traffic regulation, consumer protection, control of impure food and drugs, protection of the environment and so on was steadily passed.

Much of this developing regulation could have been placed under administrative control without involving the criminal law. For instance, local authorities could have been given powers to close down or in some other way to restrict the operations of companies causing polluted matter to enter rivers. But instead of adopting such an approach, it was felt that the criminal law would be the most effective instrument for enforcing such regulations. Invocation of the criminal sanction would best stimulate the required diligence and cause persons engaged in such activities to police their enterprises to ensure compliance with the law. Also, of course, many of these activities do cause real and serious harms: causing polluted matter to enter rivers clearly harms the environment. The criminal law has always been one of the traditional mechanisms of social control and prevention of harms.

But, accepting such a view for the moment, why were the traditional principles of the criminal law not incorporated into such regulatory offences? Why was the requirement of blame or fault dispensed with? The true reason relates to problems of law enforcement. Proof of blame could have undermined the efficacy of the law. Take, for instance, offences relating to the sale of impure or adulterated food or drugs. Advances in chemical analysis meant that adulteration became easier to detect but the huge increase in the standard of products, and the increased complexity of their component ingredients made it extremely difficult to prove that a manufacturer or merchant knew that the goods did not conform to standards (Leigh, 1982). If *mens rea* needed to be proved, the law would become a dead letter.

While these practical considerations of enforcement were the real reason for the proliferation of strict liability offences, other justifications were soon added. Strict liability would promote increased care and efficiency. Knowledge of strict liability is a cost to be weighed when setting up a trade or business. It will encourage enterprises to appoint experts, say chemists or bacteriologists, to ensure that their products are safe. It is preferable to place the burden on such enterprises who are in a position to prevent the harm than on the innocent public.

Another line of justification is that no injustice is caused as strict liability offences are not "real crimes". They are only quasi-criminal offences, "regulatory violations". Conviction does not entail the same stigma as for real crimes. The penalties are usually slight. Prosecutorial discretion usually insists upon prosecution only of those who are in some way to blame. In other cases, should the truly blameless be prosecuted and convicted, a minimal sentence such as an absolute discharge would be appropriate.

And, finally, it is argued that the sheer volume of regulatory offences necessitates dispensing with *mens rea* or other indicators of blameworthiness. It would simply be too time-consuming if blameworthiness had to be proved in every case of, say, parking on a double-yellow line.

M Sornarajah, "Defences to Strict Liability Offences in Singapore and Malaysia" (1985) 27 Mal LR 1, 2

The creation of strict liability offences confers a "Robin Hood" image on the state in that the state appears to assume a paternalistic role and protects the weak against the strong and for that reason alone will prove to be popular and lasting despite criticism. That image will come to be accentuated particularly in new areas such as economic crimes and environmental protection. The presentation of statutory offences as proceeding from a paternalistic concern of the state to protect the weak from the strong will give it enough political strength to withstand the liberal criticism that the aim of such social protection is achieved at the cost of convicting the innocent: Strict liability offences protect the consumer from the manufacturer and the large chain stores, the young from international drug syndicates, society from conglomerate corporations which create environmental hazards, the small investor from the predators in the stock markets and the innocent passer-by from hazards created by careless contractors at building sites. The popular appeal of strict liability ensures the continued life of the policies on which it is based.

CMV Clarkson, *Understanding Criminal Law* (1987), 96–98

The case against strict liability is a strong one. It is unjust and morally indefensible to punish the blameless. A person who does not know he is doing wrong and who has taken all reasonable precautions to avoid harm (ie was not negligent) does not deserve criminal conviction and punishment. Describing such offences as "quasi-criminal" or "violations" is no more than a semantic evasion which "seems rather like saying that it is all right to be unjust so long as you are not too unjust" (Brett, 1963). No matter how trivial, a strict liability offence is still a crime which can result in prosecution and conviction in the criminal courts. Such moral condemnation is unjustifiable in the absence of blame.

Further, it is simply not true to assert that all offences of strict liability are minor offences carrying lesser penalties....

Turning to the utilitarian arguments, there appears to be little evidence that the imposition of strict liability makes people more careful. Some persons involved in the sorts of activities generally regulated by strict liability offences will simply regard any fines incurred (the typical penalty) as a licence fee for operating as they do. Others, if they are to retain their competitiveness in the market, will generally only be able to afford to take such precautions *as are reasonable*. In other words, the imposition of strict liability achieves nothing in deterrent terms that could not be achieved by making all such crimes ones of negligence. Further, a blameless operator does not need rehabilitation or incapacitation (the other two established objectives of the criminal sanction)–or if he did, this could be better achieved by administrative control and sanction.

What, finally, of the arguments of expediency–that it would be too difficult and time-consuming to have to prove *mens rea* or other blame in each case? Clearly, administrative convenience cannot be allowed to dictate the contours of the criminal law: no one would suggest making theft an offence of strict liability simply because of the vast number of prosecutions that are regularly brought and the difficulty of establishing *mens rea*. Also, it it doubtful whether the existence of strict liability saves that much time and money in many cases as *after conviction* there needs to be some enquiry (albeit not subject to the same burden of proof) as to blameworthiness in order to fix the appropriate sentence.

M Sornarajah, "Defences to Strict Liability Offences in Singapore and Malaysia" (1985) 27 Mal LR 1, 1–2

An old justification for the creation of statutory offences without reference to the mental element involved in the offence is that these offences are really not criminal in nature, that they deal with minor infractions in the area of traffic, sale of food and the like, that no moral stigma are attached, and that they usually involve fines of small amounts. That justification, which has been advanced in recent decisions, does not hold good as far as many statutory offences in Singapore and Malaysia are concerned. Severe penalties may flow from the violation of acts prohibited by statutes. A new phenomenon in Singapore is the imposition of mandatory minimum sentences for strict liability offences. The Arms Offences Act 1984 imposes a mandatory minimum sentence of five years for unlawful possession of firearms. In Malaysia, a discretion exists in the prosecutor to treat the same offence as an offence which falls under the Internal Security Act. The penalty for such an offence may be death. It is unrealistic to confine strict liability offences to a dark corner of the criminal law by referring to them as a species of "administrative offences" which "are not criminal in any real sense" when the penalties involved for these violations are so severe.... An illustration is provided by the recent Singapore legislation, Water Pollution Control and Drainage (Amendment) Act 1983 which provides for a penalty of $10,000 or a penalty of six months imprisonment or both for the first offence and a minimum of one month imprisonment and a fine of a minimum of $20,000 for each subsequent offence.

3.   Strict liability and the Penal Code

We saw earlier (see above, pp 66–69) that the general exceptions under the Penal Code, particularly ss 79 and 80, apply to every offence in Singapore and Malaysia thereby ensuring that some form of blame, albeit only negligence, should be required for every offence. Acceptance of such a view would mean that there could be no strict liability offences in Singapore or Malaysia. However, as we again saw, local courts led by the Privy Council decision of *Lim Chin Aik* (1963) have not adopted such an approach and, ignoring the structure of the Penal Code, have followed English law and held that in certain circumstances strict liability offences can and do exist.

M Sornarajah, "Defences to Strict Liability Offences in Singapore and Malaysia" (1985) 27 Mal LR 1, 1, 3–6

The proliferation of statutory crimes is inevitable in Singapore and Malaysia given the bustling economic and industrial activity that goes on within these states and the many social problems that arise from rapid economic development within their communities....

Theoretically, the Penal Codes of Singapore and Malaysia contain exhaustive statements of the criminal law of these states....

[There follows an explanation of how Chapter IV of the Penal Code ought to preclude strict liability.]

But the opportunity for adopting such a solution in Singapore and Malaysia has passed. The course of development of case law in these two states has been such that it is now too late to argue that the cases accepting strict liability were wrongly decided. The situation, perhaps, calls for the application of the maxim, *communis error ius facit*. Hence, it is best to proceed with the acceptance of strict liability in the law of this region as a *fait accompli* and look to the avenues of redressing any injustice that may accrue from the imposition of strict responsibility.

Judges in Singapore and Malaysia have relied exclusively on English authority in construing certain statutes as creating strict liability. They have effectively removed strict liability offences from the control of the principles of the Penal Codes and created an autonomous category of offences. In the formulation of future law, it is imperative that this silent evolution be acknowledged. There are several reasons for accepting this view. Firstly, the Penal Code itself was drafted at a time when the law did not recognize the notion of strict liability offences. The Code was designed prior to the advent of the modern welfare state which in the playing of a more paternalistic role has assumed many regulatory functions. Secondly, even within the common law, strict liability offences are recognized as constituting an autonomous category. The removal of strict liability offences from the control of the Penal Code can be justified on the ground that its objectives are different in that it is based entirely on a utilitarian philosophy which may condone the punishment of even the innocent in the hope of securing the goal of social protection from certain harmful activities.

Once it is recognized that there is a two-track system of criminal law in Singapore and Malaysia—one tract consisting of the Penal Code and other statutory offences subject to it and the second track consisting of statutory offences regarded by the courts as involving strict liability—then courts will be free to develop the second track of the criminal law untrammelled by any technicalities in the Codes. The Codes were designed at a time when social pressures did not make the imposition of strict liability necessary. They should not stand in the way of developing a modern principle in a relevant and just manner.

It has been suggested that only offences outside the Penal Code can be construed as strict liability offences (McKillop, 1967). Such a view is, however, difficult to support. While s 6 mandates the application of the general exceptions to Penal Code offences, s 40(2) also mandates their application to all other offences. Further, in the following case, one of the leading local decisions on strict liability, the offence in question fell under the Penal Code but s 79 was ignored. Further, it would make little sense to argue that an offence, say adulteration of drugs contrary to s 274 of the Penal Code, must require *mens rea* simply because it is a Penal Code offence–whereas if an identical crime had been created in other legislation it might be acceptable to impose strict liability.

Mohamed Ibrahim v PP (1963) 29 MLJ 289 (HC, KL, Malaysia)

The appellant was convicted of an offence contrary to s 292(a) of the Penal Code of having in his possession for purposes of sale 65 copies of a book entitled "Tropic of Cancer", which was found to be an obscene book. He appealed against his conviction on the ground that he could not read nor write English and thus did not know, nor have any reason to know, that the book was obscene.

Thomson CJ: The appellant said, and this has not been contradicted and there is no reason why it should not be accepted, that he is ignorant of the English language and that therefore he was ignorant of the contents of the book. There is here, of course, a fallacy in reasoning. There is implied that reading is the only means by which one can acquire knowledge of the content of a printed article. That is not true. Knowledge can come to the mind through the ear as well as through the eye. The appellant had the benefit of the assistance of an English-speaking lawyer's clerk in ordering books and there is no reason why he should not have had the assistance of the same person in ascertaining their contents. And in any event it would be more than passing strange that he should for any length of time have kept his employment as manager of a bookshop without any knowledge of the nature of the wares he was selling.

Nevertheless, the argument is there, and it has to be considered. It is that *mens rea* and intention are of the essence of the offence charged as of any offence, that it was for the prosecution to prove the existence of these ingredients and that having regard to the fact that the appellant did not speak English they had failed to do so....

The relevant portion of section 292 of the Penal Code is as follows:

"Whoever–(a) ... for purposes of sale ... has in his possession any obscene book ... shall be punished with imprisonment ... for a term which may extend to three months, or with fine, or with both."

and that provision is subject to the exception, which has no application in the present case, that it does not extend to any book kept or used *bona fide* for religious purposes.

Little assistance is to be derived from construing the words of the section itself although it is to be noted that it does not include the word "knowingly" (see *Frailey* v *Charlton* (1920), *Sherras* v *De Rutzen* (1895) and it does contain an exception to its own generality (see *Brooks* v *Mason* (1902). Both these are criteria which have been held to be of assistance in such cases.

More assistance, however, is to be had from a consideration of the line of cases where it has been held that the public interest demands a construction of considerable strictness.

In the case of *Woodrow* (1846), a dealer in tobacco was convicted for having in his possession adulterated tobacco although he had purchased it as genuine and had no knowledge, or cause to suspect, that it was not so. The Court of Exchequer was of the opinion that the conviction was correct. Pollock CB said in the course of discussion (at p 42):

> "There can be no doubt that every stringent law, which is made for the purpose of working some great public good, will be attended with frequent cases of hardship, and sometimes with cases of apparently great injustice. That, however, is a matter for the consideration, either of those who make the laws, or of those who call for the execution of them. Suppose it a case, not of protecting the revenue, but of protecting the public health, as where the Beer Act forbids persons to have certain things in their possession at all. So, you are not allowed to have Bank paper in your possession: it is so dangerous that any person should be allowed to have it, that it is absolutely prohibited."

Later he said (at p 415):

> "If this were the case of provisions, or of any matter that affected the public health, it would not be at all unreasonable to require persons dealing in them to be aware of their character and quality and to be responsible for their goodness, whether they know it or not; they are bound to take care."

Then in the case of *Bishop* (1879), the defendant was convicted of receiving two or more lunatics into her house which was not licensed for that purpose, but it was specially found by the jury that although the persons so received were lunatics the defendant honestly and on reasonable grounds believed that they were not lunatics. It was held by the Court of Crown Cases Reserved that the conviction was right. Lord Coleridge said (261):

> "I think the conviction was right. If the knowledge of the parties so receiving lunatics is the only question, it is quite plain."

Then Denman J said:

> "The question reserved was whether the fact that the defendant thought the person not lunatic was a defence. If we were to so hold, the object of the statute might be frustrated."

In the case of *Baker* v *Tillstone* (1894), the defendant was convicted for having in his possession for sale meat which was unsound and unfit for the food of man. There was no evidence that he had seen the meat or knew of his own knowledge what its condition was although he might have known if he had exercised reasonable care. The conviction was upheld. Lord Coleridge CJ distinguished the case from previous "broad-arrow" cases which were decided under a statute having a different object, namely the protection of the Queen's Stores. With regard to the case before him he said:

> "The question for us is whether the magistrate is bound to insist on direct proof of knowledge on the part of the seller of the bad condition of the stuff sold. Perhaps it might be an answer to this contention to say that the Act of Parliament would be nugatory if such proof were insisted on, for it would then always be open to the defendant to say that he was not aware of the condition of the article sold, and that it was not his duty under the statute to make any inquiries on the point, with the obvious result that a man might in practice go on selling meat which was positively injurious without the possibility of getting a conviction against him."

In the case of *Hobbs* v *Winchester Corp* (1910), a butcher had been acquitted for selling for human consumption meat condemned as unsound apparently on the ground that he was unaware of the fact and could not have discovered it by any examination which he could reasonably have been expected to make. In the circumstances he claimed for compensation against the local authority in respect of the condemnation of the meat. The Court of Appeal after considering a number of previous cases including *Baker* v *Tillstone* (1894) came to the conclusion that an offence had been committed, Farwell LJ said (at p 481):

> "The knowledge or possible means of knowledge of the butcher is not a matter which affects the public; it is the unsound meat which poisons them; and I think that the Legislature intended that butcher should sell unsound meat at his peril."

It is clearly one object of section 292 of the Penal Code to protect those members of the public, particularly the younger members of the public who may be tempted to buy and so expose themselves to the corrupting influence of obscene books. To adopt the language of Lord Coleridge in *Baker* v *Tillstone* (1894), it is clear that any enactment forbidding possession for sale of obscene books would be nugatory if in every case it was open for the person in possession to say that he did not know the contents of the books he was selling and if it were for the prosecution to negative that assertion. In every case it would be open to any person wishing to sell such books to employ as his vendor persons ignorant of the English language who would be immune from punishment. I can see no reason for differentiating between the person who sells books and the person who sells beer or beef or tobacco. It is his business to ensure that his merchandise is such that the public who buy from him do not suffer and the most the prosecution can be expected to prove is not knowledge but the existence of means of acquiring knowledge.

Such a case can be clearly distinguished from the recent Singapore case of *Lim Chin Aik* (1963), where the appellant could not have had knowledge that he was committing an offence.

To adopt the language of Farwell LJ in the case of *Hobbs* v *Winchester Corp* (1910), *supra*, the knowledge of the bookseller is not a matter which affects the public. It is the obscene books which he sells which poison their minds.

The appeal is dismissed.

Appeal dismissed

When faced with a statutory provision which is silent as to *mens rea*, the first task of the court is to ascertain whether the offence is one of strict liability or not. If the offence is construed as one of strict liability that is the end of the matter. Any objection that this is not giving effect to the structure of the Penal Code must be countered with the retort that the Penal Code was not drafted with the needs of a modern industrialized society with its concomitant hazards in mind. For policy reasons some offences of strict liability are inevitable. (If, on the other hand, the offence is *not* construed as being one of strict liability, then some degree of blame must be required–and it is at this stage that the question arises whether to apply the "presumption of *mens rea*" or the "Chapter IV approach".)

4. Principles of interpretation

How does one determine whether a particular offence is one of strict liability or one requiring *mens rea*? In *Lim Chin Aik* (1963) the accused was charged with an offence contrary to s 6(2) of the Immigration Ordinance 1952 under which the following is prohibited:

> for any person other than a citizen of Singapore to enter Singapore from the Federation or having entered Singapore from the Federation to remain in Singapore if–
> (b) such person has been prohibited by order ....

The issue before the Privy Council was whether this was an offence of strict liability. Was it an offence simply "to remain" in Singapore even in ignorance of the prohibition order–or was it necessary to establish that the accused deliberately remained after knowing that he was a prohibited person?

This is ultimately a problem of statutory interpretation. The question is one of ascertaining the legislature's intention. Was the crime meant to be one requiring some degree of *mens rea* or did parliament intend to create an offence of strict liability? Of course, where a *mens rea* word, such as intention or knowledge, is used there is generally little problem. However, if the offence, as in *Lim Chin Aik* (1963), is silent on the point it does *not* necessarily follow that the offence is one of strict liability. Even though a *mens rea* word were omitted it might not be clear that parliament did indeed intend the offence to be one of strict liability.

As with all statutory interpretation the wording of the provision and its statutory context can be critical.

Pharmaceutical Society of Great Britain v Storkwain Ltd (1986) 83 Cr App R 359 (HL, England)

The appellants, retail chemists, supplied a prescription-only drug in accordance with a forged prescription. They were charged with an offence contrary to s 58(2)(a) of the Medicines Act 1968 which provides that "no person shall sell by retail, or supply in circumstances corresponding to retail sale, a medicinal product of a description, or falling within a class, specified in an order under this section except in accordance with a prescription given by an appropriate practitioner ...". As the appellants were blameless, it was necessary to establish whether s 58(2)(a) was an offence of strict liability.

Lord Goff of Chieveley: It is, in my opinion, clear from the Act of 1968 that Parliament must have intended that the presumption of *mens rea* should be inapplicable to s 58(2)(a). First of all, it appears from the Act of 1968 that, where Parliament wished to recognize that *mens rea* should be an ingredient of an offence created by the Act, it has expressly so provided. Thus, taking first of all offences created under provisions of Part II of the Act of 1968, express requirements of *mens rea* are to be found both in s 45(2) and in s 46(1)(2) and (3) of the Act. More particularly, in relation to offences created by Part III and Parts V and VI of the Act of 1968, section 121 makes detailed provision for a requirement of *mens rea* in respect of certain specified sections of the Act, including ss 63 to 65 (which are contained in Part III), but significantly not s 58, nor indeed ss 52 and 53.... It is very difficult to avoid the conclusion that, by omitting s 58 from those sections to which s 121 is expressly made applicable, Parliament intended that there should be no implication of a requirement of *mens rea* in s 58(2)(a).

In addition to the normal principles of statutory interpretation, in construing offences to ascertain whether strict liability is to be imposed, certain particular and now fairly well-established principles of interpretation have been developed. It should be noted in this regard that local cases here have relied entirely on English decisions. Such a practice in relation to this particular issue is unobjectionable as, for once, one is stepping outside the Penal Code and is applying common law principles of interpretation. Given the continuing reception of English law into Singapore and Malaysia, such principles must necessarily be found in the English law.

(a) Presumption of mens rea

It is a fundamental rule of statutory interpretation that penal statutes should be narrowly construed in favour of the accused. Thus if there is any doubt, a penal statute should be interpreted so as to require *mens rea*. This has led to the courts holding that there is a presumption of *mens rea*. It is presumed that parliament did not intend to punish the blameless. This presumption was strongly reaffirmed by the House of Lords in the leading decision of *Sweet* v *Parsley* (1970) with Lord Reid holding:

> There has for centuries been a presumption that Parliament did not intend to make criminals of persons who were in no way blameworthy in what they did. That means that whenever a section is silent as to *mens rea* there is a presumption that, in order to give effect to the will of Parliament, we must read in words appropriate to require *mens rea*.

This presumption of *mens rea* has been widely supported and affirmed by both Singapore and Malaysian cases. (See *Lim Chin Aik*, 1963; *Osman b Apo Hamid*, 1978; *Koo Cheh Yew*, 1980. See further McKillop, 1967; Sornarajah, 1985.)

PP v Phua Keng Tong [1986] 2 MLJ 279 (HC, Singapore)

The first accused, Tan, was director of Protocol at the Ministry of Foreign Affairs. He and the second accused, Phua, were friends and became involved in speculating in foreign currencies. In order to assist in such speculations Tan sent certain confidential documents to Phua. He was charged with communicating confidential documents contrary to s 5(1) of the Official Secrets Act. Section 5(1) makes no reference to *mens rea* but simply makes it an offence if such a person "communicates ... any such information".

Thean J: The issue of *mens rea* really turns on the true construction of s 5(1) of the Act, and the rule of construction is that where a statutory provision creates an offence there is a presumption that *mens rea* is a constituent of such an offence unless it is displaced expressly or by necessary implication by the language of the statute or by the subject matter with which the statute deals. In *Sherras* v *De Rutzen* (1895) Wright J said:

> "There is a presumption that *mens rea*, an evil intention, or a knowledge of the wrongfulness of the act, is an essential ingredient in every offence; but that presumption is liable to be displaced either by the words of the statute creating the offence or by the subject matter with which it deals, and both must be considered."

This pronouncement was approved and adopted by the Privy Council in *Lim Chin Aik* (1963).... The same view was expressed by the House of Lords in *Sweet* v *Parsley* (1970). There the accused who was a tenant of a farmhouse let out several rooms to various tenants. She was charged and convicted with being concerned in the management of the house used for the purpose of smoking cannabis resin contrary to s 5 of the Dangerous Drug Act 1965. It was conceded that she did not know that the house was so used. The House of Lords held that s 5 did not create an absolute offence and *mens rea* was an essential ingredient of the offence; the conviction was accordingly quashed. Lord Morris of Borth-y-Gest expressed a very emphatic view on the point right at the commencement of his speech at p 152, where he said:

> "My Lords, it has frequently been affirmed and should unhesitatingly be recognized that it is a cardinal principle of our law that *mens rea*, an evil intention or a knowledge of the wrongfulness of the act, is in all ordinary cases an essential ingredient of guilt of a criminal offence. It follows from this that there will not be guilt of an offence created by statute unless there is *mens rea* or unless Parliament has by the statute enacted that guilt may be established in cases where there is no *mens rea*."

More recently the same point came up for consideration before the Privy Council in the case of *Gammon Ltd* (1984) and there it was held that *mens rea* was to a certain extent not an essential ingredient of the offences under s 40(2A) and (2B) of the Building Ordinance of Hong Kong. In delivering the judgement of the Board, Lord Scarman stated the law in the following propositions:

> "(1) there is a presumption of law that *mens rea* is required before a person can be held guilty of a criminal offence; (2) the presumption is particularly strong where the offence is "truly criminal" in character; (3) the presumption applies to statutory offences, and can be displaced only if this is clearly or by necessary implication the effect of the statute; (4) the only situation in which the presumption can be displaced is where the statute is concerned with an issue of social concern, and public safety is such an issue; (5) even where a statute is concerned with such an issue, the presumption of *mens rea* stands unless it can also be shown that the creation of strict liability will be effective to promote the objects of the statute by encouraging greater vigilance to prevent the commission of the prohibited act."

I now turn to consider the Act and in particular s 5(1) thereof. The subject matter of the Act is the prevention or prohibition of disclosure of official documents and information; it is not one dealing with an issue of social concern, such as public safety or public welfare, and there does not appear any indication that the presumption of *mens rea* should be displaced. Looking at the section itself, the language is silent as to the requirement of *mens rea*. There is, therefore, nothing either in the subject matter or the language of the Act which necessarily displaces the presumption that *mens rea* is a necessary ingredient of an offence under s 5(1). In my judgment, on the basis of the principles laid down in those cases, *mens rea* is a necessary ingredient of the offence which the prosecution must prove.

(b) Rebutting the presumption

As indicated by the above case the presumption of *mens rea* can be rebutted. In deciding whether or not the presumption should be rebutted the courts have developed the following two guiding criteria:

(i) Public welfare offences

If the offence is a "public welfare offence" there will be a greater readiness on the part of the courts to allow the presumption of *mens rea* to be rebutted and strict liability to be imposed. An archetypal "public welfare offence" is one that:

(1) relates to matters of social regulation such as public health, safety and welfare, traffic regulation, etc;
(2) is broadly regarded as only "quasi-criminal", ie carries no stigma; and
(3) carries a relatively light punishment, typically a fine.

Sweet v Parsley [1970] AC 132 (HL, England)

Lord Pearce: Since the Industrial Revolution the increasing complexity of life called into being new duties and crimes which took no account of intent. Those who undertake various industrial and other activities, especially where these affect the life and health of the citizen, may find themselves liable to statutory punishment regardless of knowledge or intent, both in respect of their own acts or neglect and those of their servants. But one must remember that normally *mens rea* is still an ingredient of any offence. Before the court will dispense with the necessity for *mens rea* it has to be satisfied that Parliament so intended. The mere absence of the word "knowingly" is not enough. But the nature of the crime, the punishment, the absence of social obloquy, the particular mischief and the field of activity in which it occurs, and the wording of the particular section and its context, may show that Parliament intended that the act should be prevented by punishment regardless of intent or knowledge.

Lim Chin Aik v R (1963) 29 MLJ 50 (PC, appeal from Singapore)

Lord Evershed: Where the subject matter of the statute is the regulation for the public welfare of a particular activity–statutes regulating the sale of food and drink are to be found among the earliest examples–it can be and frequently has been inferred that the legislature intended that such activities should be carried out under conditions of strict liability. The presumption is that the statute or statutory instrument can be effectively enforced only if those in charge of the relevant activities are made responsible for seeing that they are complied with. When such a presumption is to be inferred, it displaces the ordinary presumption of *mens rea*. Thus sellers of meat may be made responsible for seeing that the meat is fit for human consumption and it is no answer for them to say that they were not aware that it was polluted. If that were a satisfactory answer, then ... the distribution of bad meat (and its far-reaching consequences) would not be effectively prevented. So a publican may be made responsible for observing the condition of his customers, *Cundy* v *Le Cocq* (1883-84).

M Sornarajah, "Defences to Strict Liability Offences in Singapore and Malaysia" (1985) 27 Mal LR 1, 8–9

A more methodical categorization was made on the basis of American case law by Sayre in 1933. It is useful to set out Sayre's categories and point out that they are supported by case law in the Commonwealth. Sayre's categories ... were: (1) illegal sales of intoxicating liquor, (2) sales of impure or adulterated food or drugs, (3) sales of misbranded articles, (4) violation of narcotic acts, (5) criminal nuisances, (6) violation of traffic regulations, (7) violation of motor vehicle laws, (8) violation of general police regulations, passed for safety, health or well-being of the community. Legislation under these categories exists in Singapore and Malaysia and the chances are that offences created by such legislation will be construed as creating strict liability offences.

The categories mentioned by Sayre do not constitute a closed list. The growing importance of the subject of strict liability is evidenced by the fact that almost as many categories could be added on the basis of case law in the fifty years since Sayre wrote. There is authority for criminal legislation falling under the following categories being regarded as creating offences of strict liability: (1) environmental pollution: this has been an area of intense activity in most Western States but in Singapore, concern with litter and waste disposal will lead to the creation of an increasing number of offences: (2) company and securities legislation: in Singapore, where statutory offences have been seen as a means of ensuring the protection of Singapore's image as an international investment centre, recent amendments to the Companies Act may be seen as initiating a trend towards strict liability in this area, (3) safety at building and industrial sites: again, intense building activity in Singapore, as in Hong Kong, may give rise to more regulatory offences related to safety standards at construction sites, (4) controlling inflation, (5) customs regulations, (6) fisheries regulations, particularly in Malaysia, (7) immigration control, (8) possession of firearms.

The operation of this guiding criterion of rebuttal can be seen clearly by contrasting the two following recent cases:

In *Pharmaceutical Society of Great Britain* v *Storkwain Ltd* (1986, see above, p 88) the House of Lords in holding s 58(2) of the Medicines Act 1968 (supplying certain medicines without proper prescriptions) to be an offence of strict liability was clearly influenced by the fact that this was a "public welfare offence" in the sense that pharmacists were in a position to put illicit drugs on the market; the public have no means of protecting themselves; strict liability was necessary to make pharmacists extra careful.

On the other hand, in *Phua Keng Tong* (1986, see above, p 89) the court was ready to uphold the presumption of *mens rea* because the offence in question (disclosing official documents and information) was "not one dealing with an issue of social concern, such as public safety or public welfare".

It must, however, be stressed that these are no more than "guiding criteria". In particular, offences of strict liability can be created which are stigmatic and which do carry severe penalties (see Arms Offences Act (Singapore) (Cap 14)). In *Gammon Ltd* (1984) it was argued that because the offence (deviating in a material way from approved plans contrary to s 40(2A)(b) of the HK Building Ordinance) carried a heavy penalty (a fine of $250,000 and imprisonment for three years) it was unlikely that the legislature intended the offence to be one of strict liability. Responding to this, Lord Scarman stated:

> The severity of the maximum penalties is a more formidable point. But it has to be considered in the light of the ordinance read as a whole. For reasons which their Lordships have already developed, there is nothing inconsistent with the purpose of the ordinance in imposing severe penalties for offences of strict liability. The legislature could reasonably have intended severity to be a significant deterrent, bearing in mind the risks to public safety arising from some contraventions of the ordinance. Their Lordships agree with the view on this point of the Court of Appeal. It must be crucially important that those who participate in or bear responsibility for the carrying out of works in a manner which complies with the requirements of the ordinance should know that severe penalties await them in the event of any contravention or non-compliance with the ordinance by themselves or by anyone over whom they are required to exercise supervision or control.

(ii) Effectiveness in promoting statutory objectives

Lim Chin Aik v R (1963) 29 MLJ 50 (PC, appeal from Singapore)

The accused was convicted at his trial of contravening s 6(2) of the Immigration Ordinance 1952 by remaining in Singapore after he had been declared a prohibited immigrant. There was no evidence that the prohibition order had ever been brought to his attention or that any effort so to do had ever been made.

Lord Evershed: But it is not enough in their Lordships' opinion merely to label the statute as one dealing with a grave social evil and from that to infer that strict liability was intended. It is pertinent also to inquire whether putting the defendant under strict liability will assist in the enforcement of the regulations. That means that there must be something he can do, directly or indirectly, by supervision or inspection, by improvement of his business methods or by exhorting those whom he may be expected to influence or control, which will promote the observance of the regulations. Unless this is so, there is no reason in penalizing him, and it cannot be inferred that the legislature imposed strict liability merely in order to find a luckless victim.... Their Lordships prefer ... (this) to the alternative view that strict liability follows simply from the nature of the subject matter and that persons whose conduct is beyond any sort of criticism can be dealt with by the imposition of a nominal penalty ....

Where it can be shown that the imposition or strict liability would result in the prosecution and conviction of a class of persons whose conduct could not in any way affect the observance of the law, Their Lordships consider that, even where the statute is dealing with a grave social evil, strict liability is not likely to be intended.

Their Lordships apply these general observations to the Ordinance in the present case. The subject matter, the control of immigration, is not one in which the presumption of strict liability has generally been made. Nevertheless, if the Courts of Singapore were of the view that unrestricted immigration is a social evil which it is the object of the Ordinance to control most vigorously, their Lordships would hesitate to disagree. That is a matter peculiarly within the cognizance of the local Courts. But Mr Le Quesne was unable to point to anything that the appellant could possibly have done so as to ensure that he complied with the regulations. It was not, for example, suggested that it would be practicable for him to make continuous inquiry to see whether an order had been made against him. Clearly one of the objects of the Ordinance is the expulsion of prohibited persons from Singapore, but there is nothing that a man can do about it if, before the commission of the offence, there is no practical or sensible way in which he can ascertain whether he is a prohibited person or not....

Their Lordships have accordingly reached the clear conclusion, with all respect to the view taken in the courts below, that the application of the rule that *mens rea* is an essential ingredient in every offence has not in the present case been ousted by the terms or subject matter of the Ordinance and that the appellant's conviction and sentence cannot stand.

5.   Defences to strict liability offences

The effect of holding an offence to be one of strict liability is that generally the defences of mistake and accident do not apply. Thus as we have seen the general exceptions based on ss 76, 79 and 80 have no application here. But what of the other general exceptions? Could one plead necessity, duress, superior orders, infancy, insanity, automatism, intoxication or private defence if charged with an offence of strict liability?

M Sornarajah, "Defences to Strict Liability Offences in Singapore and Malaysia" (1985) 27 Mal LR 1, 11, 12–14, 18–19

If the aim of strict liability is the deterrence of socially harmful behaviour, this aim cannot be furthered by the punishment of the obviously innocent. In fact, the punishment of the innocent could attract public opprobrium to the law....

The recognition of defences to strict liability is a way of avoiding this....

(1) *Necessity*
The theory of defences to crime proceeds on the basis that if circumstances which negative either the *actus reus* or the *mens rea* of the crime had existed at the time of the crime, the accused should be acquitted. Statutory offences of strict liability exclude the need for proof of *mens rea* and, *a fortiori*, exclude the defences based on *actus reus*. Alternatively, using the analysis made by Fletcher of defences to criminal liability, a distinction could be made between justification and excuse. Excuses are those defences which are based on the law's compassion towards offenders who had committed the offence under overwhelming pressures and offenders who suffer from some disability like insanity or intoxication. Justificatory defences, like self-defence and necessity are based on the existence of a right in the offender. The accused who acts in self-defence or in circumstances of necessity is excused because he exercises a right. Necessity in effect is the wider defence, for self-defence is an aspect of

necessity. Statutes creating strict liability exclude excusing conditions but should not be read as excluding the justificatory defences. The latter defences, being dependent on rights, should not be regarded as displaced unless there is a clear indication in the statute that they do not apply....

It is necessary to find authority for the view that necessity is a defence to strict liability. Authority is meagre and is confined to dicta in cases. The most cogent argument is in the logical absurdity involved in not recognizing the defence. Take for example, the prohibition order involved in *Seah Eng Joo* (1961). The statute made it an offence of strict liability for a person subject to the prohibition order to leave his home during the hours specified in the order. Had a fire broken out at the offender's house, it would be highly illogical to argue that the offender should have continued to remain in the burning house than violate the prohibition order. Necessity must provide a defence in such circumstances....

(3) *Involuntariness*
It is generally accepted that criminal liability can only be based on a conscious and voluntary act. An involuntary commission of a prohibited act cannot be the basis of liability even for strict liability offences. This has been recognized in a series of English decisions. An opportunity for formulating a similar doctrine for strict liability offences was missed in *Ayavoo* (1966). In that case, the accused had been subjected to an order under the Prevention of Crime Ordinance to remain indoors after dusk. Cycling home after a dinner so that he could get back to his home before the hour specified in the order, the accused fell over a bridge and became unconscious. He recovered consciousness only after being taken to hospital. He was charged with having breached the prohibition order. The case should have been disposed of on the simple ground that the prohibition order could not have been breached by a person in a state of unconsciousness. Instead, knowing that a conviction on such facts was not morally acceptable, the judge adopted a rather convoluted reasoning. He held that the statute did not create strict liability. Hence, since *mens rea* was relevant, the judge held that the accused could not have entertained the relevant *mens rea* as he was unconscious. He acquitted the accused on this basis. The result was sound, but the reasoning was faulty.

In Singapore, the corresponding legislation, a provision in the Criminal Law (Temporary Provisions) Ordinance 1951, was held to create a strict liability offence in *Seah Eng Joo* (1961). This was correct for the purpose of the legislation was the prevention of crime by confining certain types of persons to their homes. The reasoning adopted in *Ayavoo* (1966) was perhaps influenced by the misapprehension that once an offence is characterized as a strict liability offence, no defences are possible. That, as has been demonstrated, is not so.

An actual instance where a defence akin to involuntariness was attempted was in *Wong Swee Chin* (1981) where the accused was charged under the Internal Security Act of Malaysia with the possession of firearms. There had been a gun battle between a gang and the police in the course of which the police had used tear gas. The case for the accused was that when he was found by the police he was unconscious as a result of having sustained seven gun shot wounds and having inhaled the tear gas. He argued that he was not in "conscious possession or control" of the weapons and ammunition found on him. The court, however, found as a matter of evidence that the accused was in fact conscious. The need, which the appellate court felt, to examine the evidence at the trial may be taken as an indication that the argument was taken

seriously and that had the accused really been unconscious the decision may
have been different. But this is unlikely. On such facts, the inference can be
drawn that the accused had the arms in his possession prior to losing consciousness and such an inference is sufficient to result in conviction unless, of
course, the accused is able to show that the firearms were planted on him after
he had lost consciousness. *Wong Swee Chin* (1981) can be interpreted as providing for this possible defence.

In the above extract, Sornarajah (1985), drawing on Fletcher (1978),
argues that justificatory defences should be available to crimes of strict
liability–but that excusatory defences should not be so available. There
is much to be said for such a view. The effect of an excusatory defence
is that it destroys *blame*; the whole point of strict liability is that it is
not concerned with blame. It would therefore be contradictory to allow
excusatory defences to strict liability offences.

Following this analysis, it would appear that the following should be
defences to strict liability offences because they are justificatory in
nature: private defence; necessity; superior orders; public authority (ss
76–78) and consent. On the other hand, the following excusatory defences would not be defences to strict liability offences: infancy; insanity; and intoxication.

This approach does not, however, solve all problems. For instance,
there is controversy as to whether duress gives rise to a defence which
is justificatory or excusatory in nature. In the USA duress is generally
treated as an excuse. This would mean that a driver who exceeded the
speed limit because someone was pointing a loaded gun at his head and
insisting he drive faster would have no defence to a charge under
s 63(4) of the Road Traffic Act (Singapore) (Cap 276) (exceeding permitted speed limit)–presumably a strict liability offence. Such a result
would be little short of asinine.

Similar problems arise with automatism and other forms of involuntary conduct. In the above extract Sornarajah (1985) argues that involuntariness ought to be a defence to strict liability offences. However,
involuntariness is usually regarded as an *excuse*–and thus would be no
defence to a strict liability offence.

Sanford H Kadish, "Excusing Crime" (1987) 75 Cal LR 257, 259

If involuntariness is the touchstone of excuse, then literal involuntariness, of
course, represents the paradigm case. But such extreme instances of involuntariness may also be viewed as raising a bar to liability more fundamental even
than excuse–namely, that there is no *action* at all, only bodily movement, so
that there is nothing to excuse. Under this view, which represents the conventional characterization of the involuntary act defense, the defense comes to an
"I-didn't-do-it" defense, a failure of the prima facie case.

Thus, there are two ways to classify cases of physical compulsion or involuntariness. On the one hand, these cases can be interpreted as exculpatory
because there was no *actus reus*, and hence no crime to excuse. This interpretation rests on the distinction between genuine human actions, which are susceptible of praise and blame, and mere events brought about by physical causes

which happen to involve a human body. Such events can be harmful or harmless, but they are not human actions and therefore are not subject to moral judgment. On the other hand, there is bodily movement in these cases, and it may have done harm. To that extent the involuntary-act exculpation is not identical with the failure of the prima facie case. When a person denies doing the act the usual expectation is that if he didn't do it, someone else must have. When a person claims the involuntary-act defense he is conceding that his own body made the motion but denies responsibility for it. Therefore, however we characterize the involuntary-act exculpation, whether as a failure of the prima facie case or as a defense, the reason it exculpates belongs to the rationale of excuse: the defendant had no choice in the matter.

The problem with this whole approach is that it forces one to accept the notorious English decisions of *Larsonneur* (1933) and *Winzar* v *Chief Constable of Kent* (1983) as "right"–a somewhat unpalatable conclusion.

In *Larsonneur* (1933) the accused was convicted of being a prohibited alien who was "found in the United Kingdom". She had been deported from the Irish Free State and physically brought to England in police custody. Her presence in England was thus completely involuntary. Nevertheless she was convicted, the circumstances of her being brought to England being described as "perfectly immaterial".

In *Winzar* v *Chief Constable of Kent* (1983) the accused was brought into a hospital on a stretcher. When the doctor discovered that Winzar was merely drunk he ordered him to leave. When he failed to go, the police were summoned. They removed him to the roadway, "formed the opinion he was drunk", and he was arrested and subsequently convicted of the offence of being found drunk on the highway. Again, the fact that his presence on the highway was involuntary was dismissed as immaterial.

A final possibility which will be only briefly mentioned is that there is no such clear-cut solution to the present problem. The only way to determine what defences are available to strict liability offences is to examine each defence in turn and explore its rationale. This would then need to be contrasted with the rationale of strict liability and a decision made on a defence by defence basis as to whether each was available to offences of strict liability.

One example will illustrate how this approach would operate. The defence of infancy (for children aged between 7 and 12) under s 83 of the Penal Code is a classic *excuse*. Such children, who do not understand the nature and consequences of their actions, are blameless and are to be excused from punishment. However, the essence of strict liability is that it is prepared to permit the punishment of the blameless–hence the view that infancy as an excuse ought to be no defence to a strict liability offence. However, if one looks at the rationale of strict liability and asks whether that rationale is satisfied by the punishment of such children, one perhaps reaches a different conclusion. Strict liability is primarily concerned with the promotion of greater care. Can this greater standard of care be achieved by the punishment of a child who does not understand the nature and consequences of his actions? The whole point about strict liability is that one punishes the sane adult even though he had no *mens rea* because he is to be encouraged to be more careful–and being a sane adult he is amenable to such encouragement. Viewed in this manner the punishment of a child coming within s 83 seems pointless as well as unjust. Accordingly infancy under s 83 should be a defence to all strict liability offences.

6. The future for strict liability

CMV Clarkson, *Understanding Criminal Law* (1987), 98–99

It would be naive to contemplate the decriminalization of all offences of strict liability or their wholesale conversion into offences involving fault. Some minor regulatory crimes, such as parking offences, that are widely perceived as not being "truly criminal" and that carry a minimal penalty must clearly remain as offences of strict liability. But for the remainder, there are two possible courses of action.

The first alternative is to decriminalize the conduct as such and make it subject to administrative regulation by administrative processes. Such procedures are already extensively used. Factory inspectors, health and safety officers and other such persons regularly inspect premises and often seek improvement by cooperation and persuasion. Other administrative remedies are at their disposal. planning permissions can be revoked or modified, enforcement and stop notices issued and so on. Leigh (1982), for example, cites the enforcement scheme created by the Health and Safety at Work Act 1974 which in 1977 resulted in 6233 improvement notices and 2666 prohibition notices being issued, compared with only 1600 prosecutions being commenced. Such non-criminal alternatives could be far more effective than prosecutions. Faced with the threat of closure of their premises, for example, a business will quickly effect the necessary improvements–and far sooner than if they merely had to pay a fine as the cost of their infraction.

The other alternative is to convert existing offences of strict liability into ones requiring some degree of blame–most probably, negligence. Such an approach has already been adopted in relation to many former strict liability offences by the introduction of "due diligence" defences. The crime remains prima facie one of strict liability, thus not increasing the prosecutor's burden–but if the defendant can show that he was not negligent, he will escape liability. Thus the crime effectively becomes one of negligence–except in relation to the burden of proof. Canadian and Australian law have developed general due diligence defences applicable to all crimes of strict liability. English law, on the other hand, has preferred a more selective use of such defences with notable examples to be found in such important legislation as the Trade Descriptions Act 1968 and the Misuse of Drugs Act 1971.

Clearly there is room for further expansion along such lines. What is needed is a conscious reappraisal of all strict liability offences with a view to determining which can be decriminalized and made subject to administrative regulation, which need to remain as criminal offences but with due diligence defences added, and, finally, which *minor* offences can remain as pure strict liability offences.

A good local example of a "due diligence defence" in operation is to be found in the following Malaysian case.

Melan b Abdullah v PP [1971] 2 MLJ 280 (HC, KL, Malaysia)

The accused was editor-in-chief of a group of newspapers in one of which was published an article relating to the abolition of Tamil and Chinese medium schools. He was convicted of the offence of publishing a seditious publication contrary to s 4(1)(c) of the Sedition Act and appealed against his conviction.

Ong CJ: Section 4(1)(c) read by itself, would appear to create an offence of absolute liability. This was the submission made by the prosecution. The first appellant, in answer thereto, relied on the provisions of s 6(2) which reads:

> "No person shall be convicted of any offence referred to in s 4(1)(c) or (d) if the person proves that the publication in respect of which he is charged was printed, published, sold, offered for sale, distributed, reproduced or imported (as the case may be) without his authority, consent and knowledge and without any want of due care or caution on his part, or that he did not know and had no reason to believe that the publication had a seditious tendency."

The prosecution conceded that this appellant had no prior knowledge of the publication of the offending subheading, but submitted that, although he had delegated his authority to the subeditors under him, he was still responsible as he had the power of veto and in the circumstances he had failed to exercise due care and caution: he could not therefore be held exonerated by the provisions of s 6(2).

The first appellant gave evidence of the responsibilities of his office, as editor-in-chief, over as many as ten publications of the *Utusan Melayu* Group, employing a staff of over 140 persons. He had perforce to delegate authority to trusted subordinates. On the Sedition Act he had organized seminars and discussions, relating in particular to the "sensitive issues" and had instructed his staff on the relevant law as he understood it. He had sponsored a talk to journalists given on this subject in February 1971 by the Attorney General as well as the Solicitor General–although he was himself unable to attend by reason of illness. Although responsible for all *Utusan* publications it was impossible for him to read all of them every day....

I have no hesitation in holding that the first appellant ought not to have been convicted. The submission unfortunately made by the prosecution, that s 4(1)(c) creates an offence of absolute liability, might have caused some obfuscation of the real issue at the trial. An offence of strict or absolute liability is one where proof of the *actus reus* alone suffices for a conviction, however morally free from blame the defendant may be. Section 6(2), however, refers specifically to s 4(1)(c) and exculpates any person who succeeds in proving that the act constituting the offence was committed, not only without his knowledge, but also without any negligence on his part. This, in my view, is a striking instance of the type of cases where, as Dr Glanville Williams put it:

> "There is a half-way house between *mens rea* and strict responsibility which has not yet been properly utilized, and that is responsibility for negligence."

For this view Lord Pearce gave the stamp of his approval when he said in *Sweet* v *Parsley* (1970):

"If it were possible in some so-called absolute offences to take this sensible half-way house, I think that the courts should do so."

That case unfortunately was not brought to the attention of the special president. At page 163, the judgment of Lord Diplock contains a passage which I think is particularly applicable as follows:

"Where penal provisions are of general application to the conduct of ordinary citizens in the course of their every day life the presumption is that the standard of care required of them in informing themselves of facts which would make their conduct unlawful, is that of the familiar common law duty of care. But where the subject matter of a statute is the regulation of a particular activity involving potential danger to public health, safety or morals in which citizens have a choice as to whether they participate or not, the court may feel driven to infer an intention of Parliament to impose by penal sanctions *a higher duty of care* on those who choose to participate and to place upon them *an obligation to take whatever measures may be necessary to prevent the prohibited acts*, without regard to those considerations of cost or business practicability which play a part in the determination of what would be required of them in order to fulfil the ordinary common law duty of care. But such an inference is not lightly to be drawn, nor is there any room for it *unless there is something that the person on whom the obligation is imposed can do directly or indirectly, by supervision or inspection, by improvement of his business methods or by exhorting those whom he may be expected to influence or control*, which will promote the observance of the obligation (see *Lim Chin Aik*, 1963"....)

Carrying on with the quotation from *Lim Chin Aik* (1963), Lord Evershed in that case went on to say:

"... Unless this is so, there is no reason in penalizing him, and it cannot be inferred that the legislature imposed strict liability merely in order to find a luckless victim. This principle has been expressed and applied in *Reynolds* v *GH Austin & Sons Ltd* (1951) and *James & Son Ltd* v *Smee* (1954). Their Lordships prefer it to the alternative view that strict liability follows simply from the nature of the subject matter and that persons whose conduct is beyond any sort of criticism can be dealt with by the imposition of a nominal penalty."

In the instant case I cannot think of any further precautionary measures, over and above what the first appellant had done, which he ought to have taken to ensure that his publications would not infringe against the Sedition Act. The learned special president, however, appeared to have thought that the principle *respondeat superior* was sufficient. Applying the principles in negligence to this appellant's conduct, I do not think he had failed in the higher standard of care and caution required of him. His conviction and sentence must, therefore, be set aside....

Part II

General exceptions

Chapter 4

Introduction

By NA Morgan

A. Conceptual background

Chapter IV of the Penal Code provides for several "general exceptions" to criminal liability which provide a complete defence to a criminal charge. In addition, s 300 provides various "special exceptions" or "partial defences" to charges of murder (five in Malaysia, seven in Singapore), which formally reduce an offence of murder to culpable homicide not amounting to murder, with a consequent reduction in punishment. The burden of proof in establishing both the general and special exceptions lies on the accused who must establish the defence on the balance of probabilities (Evidence Act (Singapore) (Cap 97), ss 107 and 3(3); Evidence Act 1950 (Malaysia) (Reprinted 1983, Act 56) ss 105 and 3; *Jayasena*, 1970; *Govindasamy*, 1976).

These complete and partial defences provide interesting and often controversial examples of the criminal law delineating cases where the accused is to be "exculpated" in whole or in part by virtue of the circumstances in which he acted, the reasons for his acting in such a manner, or factors suggesting that he was not fully responsible for his behaviour. Robinson (1984, ch 2) points out that such defences are to be distinguished from, inter alia, defences based on factors such as diplomatic immunity, double jeopardy or illegally obtained evidence; in such cases, the issue is not one of exculpation–indeed, the harm caused by the accused and his culpability may both be admitted. It is, rather, that some important public policy consideration is furthered by not convicting. Non-exculpatory defences of this sort obviously raise fundamental issues of public policy, evidence, procedure and international law, but they fall outside the scope of this book. Our focus is on the exculpatory defences contained in the Penal Code. The detailed provisions relating to these exceptions are considered below; the purpose of this section is to provide the conceptual background to these defences and to raise issues of general importance. The "special exceptions" are also considered separately in ch 20.

In recent years, particularly following the pioneering work of Fletcher (1978), there has been much debate on how different defences are characterized. What is their conceptual basis? Are they rather random concessions to accused persons which happen to share a few common features, or are they systematic applications of fundamental general

103

principles? In searching for a systematic conceptual analysis, the key distinction, already noted in the context of defences to strict liability, is between justifications and excuses. Fletcher (1978) drew attention to the concepts of "*wrongdoing*" and "*attribution*" which, in his view, had not been properly distinguished, at least in common law jurisdictions. Broadly speaking, a judgment of "wrongdoing" is an assessment that the *type of conduct* in question is to be judged "wrong". By contrast, questions of "attribution" concern the culpability or blameworthiness of the *particular offender*; they are questions of the individual actor's "*moral accountability*". Although other writers do not generally adopt the language of wrongdoing and attribution, this distinction is analytically helpful and lies at the root of the conceptual difference between justifications and excuses; justifications involve judgments of wrongdoing, excuses concern attribution.

George P Fletcher, *Rethinking Criminal Law* (1978), 459 and 576–577

A justification negates the wrongfulness of the act and denies the element of wrongdoing. An excuse negates the actor's accountability for the act. The implication of either a justification or an excuse is that the actor is not culpable, but the reasons are different. In the case of a justification, there is no wrongful act to render the actor culpable. In the case of an excuse, the act is wrongful, but the absence of personal accountability negates the actor's culpability....

The violation of the prohibitory norm does not entail liability unless it is wrongful. In the typical case, the violation of the definition is wrongful. Yet in extraordinary cases, the conduct might be justified by appeal to a conflicting norm permitting the violation. The paradigmatic instances of justification are lesser evils, self-defence and acting in the name of the law to effect an arrest or prevent an escape from custody. Claims of justification always require a union of objective elements and a subjective intent. The nature of a justification is that the actor has good and sufficient reasons for violating the norm constituting the definition. Justified conduct in violation of the definition is not wrongful, but neither is it perfectly legal, as is conduct that falls outside the scope of the definition. This type of harmful conduct might, for example, support tort liability for the harm done....

Claims of justification negate the dimension of wrongdoing; claims of excuse negate the element of attribution or culpability. The underlying theory of excusability is that it is unfair to hold the particular suspect accountable for his wrongful act. The diverse grounds of excuse ... include insanity, duress and various forms of mistake.... A claim of justification is a privileged violation of the prohibitory norm. The functional impact of a justification is to modify the norm by carving out a limited field where the conduct is not wrongful. Valid claims of excuse do not modify the prohibited norm. Excused conduct is still wrongful: the norm against the conduct remains in tact. To recognize an excuse is to judge that the particular suspect cannot be fairly held liable for the violation.

P Robinson, *Criminal Law Defences* (1984), 83, 86–8, 91–3

(a) *A system of justifications*

[J]ustification defences do not define the harm sought to be prevented or punished by an offence. The harm caused by the justified behavior remains a legally recognized harm that is to be avoided wherever possible. Under the special justifying circumstances, however, that harm is outweighed by the need to avoid an even greater harm or to further a greater societal interest.

A forest fire rages towards a town of 10,000 unsuspecting inhabitants. The actor burns a field of corn located between the fire and the town; the burned field then serves as a firebreak, saving 10,000 lives. By setting fire to the field with the purpose of destroying it, the actor satisfies all the elements of the offence of arson. The immediate harm he has caused–the destruction of the field–is precisely the harm that the statute serves to prevent and punish. Yet the actor is likely to have a complete defence because his conduct and its harmful consequences are justified. The conduct in this instance is tolerated, even encouraged, by society.

The forest fire case provides an example of the "lesser evils" or "choice of evils" justification (also called "necessity" when the threat of greater harm stems from natural forces)....

(b)   *Internal structure of justifications*
All justification defences have the same internal structure:

triggering conditions permit a necessary and proportional response

Triggering conditions are the circumstances that must exist before an actor will be eligible to act under a justification. For example, in defensive force justifications the justification is triggered if an aggressor presents a threat of unjustified harm to a protected interest, as by attempting to burn the defendant's chicken coop. Similarly, public authority justifications are triggered when circumstances arise that evoke the use of the actor's delegated authority. A train conductor is given a general authority to maintain order and safety on a train. Thus, a situation of potential disruption triggers the conductor's justification to use force to prevent the disturbance....

The triggering conditions of a justification defence do not give an actor the privilege to act without restriction. To be justified, the responsive conduct must satisfy two requirements:

(1)   it must be *necessary* to protect or further the interest at stake, and
(2)   it must cause only a harm that is *proportional* or reasonable in relation to the harm threatened or the interest to be furthered.

The *necessity requirement* demands that the defendant act only when and to the extent necessary to protect or further the interest at stake....

The *proportionality requirement* places a limit on the maximum harm that may be used in protection or furtherance of an interest. It bars justification when the harm caused by the actor may be necessary to protect or further the interest at stake, but is too severe in relation to the value of the interest.

(a)   *Excuses–generally*
Excuses, like justifications, are usually general defences applicable to all offences. They exculpate even though the elements of the offence are satisfied. Excuses admit that the deed may be wrong, but excuse the actor because conditions suggest that he is not responsible for his deed....

(b)   *Internal structure of excuses*
Each of the excuse defences has the following internal structure:

a disability causing an excusing condition

(1)   *Disability.*   The *disability* is the abnormal condition of the actor at the time of the offense. It frequently gives the excuse its name. We say, for

example, that an actor is suffering from insanity, intoxication, subnormality, or immaturity. The disability is a real condition with a variety of observable manifestations apart from the conduct constituting the offense. It may be a long-term or even permanent condition, such as subnormality, or it may be a temporary state like intoxication, somnambulism, automatism, or hypnotism. Its cause may be internal, as in insanity, or external, as in duress.

(2)   *Excusing condition.* Having a recognized disability at the time of the offense will not alone qualify an actor for an excuse, for it is not his disability that is central to the reason for exculpating him. An actor is not excused because he is intoxicated, but because the *effect* of the intoxication is to create a condition that renders him blameless for his conduct constituting the offense. An *excusing condition*, then, does not require an element independent of the actor's disability, but rather requires that the actor's disability cause a particular result; his particular exculpating mental state must relate directly to the conduct constituting the offense.

Society is generally willing to excuse an actor under four types of such excusing conditions:

(1)   when the conduct constituting the offense is simply not the product of the actor's voluntary effort or determination (eg the actor is having a seizure);

(2)   when the conduct is the product of the actor's voluntary effort or determination, but he does not accurately perceive the physical nature or consequences of the conduct (eg the actor thinks his gun is a paint brush, or accurately sees the physical characteristics of the gun but does not know that the gun shoots bullets that injure people);

(3)   when the actor accurately perceives and understands the physical nature of the conduct, its physical results, and physical surroundings, but does not know that the conduct or its results are wrong or criminal (eg the actor thinks God has ordered him to sacrifice a neighbour for the good of mankind, or believes, because of paranoid delusions, that the man waiting for a bus is about to assault him); or

(4)   when the actor perceives the conduct accurately and fully, understands its physical consequences, and knows its wrongfulness or criminality, but lacks the ability to control his conduct (eg because of an insane compulsion or duress) to such an extent that it is not proper to hold him accountable for it.

B. Defences in Singapore and Malaysia

1. Justifications

The accused is clearly justified (as opposed to excused) where he is bound or justified by law (ss 76 and 79) or where he is acting judicially (s 77) or in pursuance of a court order (s 78). These are all circumstances in which the conduct in question is considered socially desirable and a greater societal interest is furthered by allowing the defence. Private defence of person and property (ss 96–106) is also justificatory.

Although the law generally forbids the causing of harm, the conduct of a person who acts in private defence is not adjudged wrong; indeed, to adopt the words of Glanville Williams (1982), reasonable action in self-defence is "socially approved". The detailed provisions relating to private defence also provide the clearest illustration in the Penal Code of Robinson's comments on the "internal structure" of justifications; the defence is "triggered" by a "reasonable apprehension of danger" to person or property (ss 102 and 105(1)). It is limited, however, by specified limits on the extent to which the aggressor may be pursued, eg the right "in no case extends to the inflicting of more harm than it is necessary to inflict for the purpose of defence" (s 99(4)).

Necessity (s 81) is generally regarded as a justification. In cases such as Robinson's example of the forest fire, where the accused has clearly prevented a greater evil than he has caused, the defence appears obviously justificatory. However, if the two evils were more evenly balanced, such a defence (if allowed–see ch 7) would appear excusatory; in such cases, the conduct is not justified by reference to some greater societal good, but the accused may be less blameworthy because of the circumstances in which he acted.

Defences based on consent and benefit to the "victim" (ss 87–92) are also justificatory. Society approves and values my acting in good faith for the benefit of a third party, either where that person consents or in certain situations where consent cannot be obtained. Where the question is not one of benefit but simply of consent, the actor's conduct may be justified because society, even if it does not approve the conduct, may at least tolerate it. Such ambivalence may stop short of certain types of consensual act (eg mercy killings), at which point the full defence will cease to apply. Clarkson and Keating (1984, p 320) also point out that recognition of consent as a justification demonstrates society's recognition of the high value placed on human autonomy and freedom of choice.

2. Excuses

Automatism, if it is available as a defence in Malaysia and Singapore (see ch 12), is clearly an excuse. The accused's disability (eg somnambulism) renders him blameless. The defence of accident (s 80) is also an excuse; we do not attribute blame to those who accidentally cause harm. Although s 80 does not appear broad enough to embrace automatism, it is in certain respects similar; in both defences, to adopt Robinson's words (1984, above): "the conduct ... is simply not the product of the actor's voluntary effort or determination." Those who, at the time of the offence, lacked sufficient age or understanding (ss 82–83), or were of unsound mind or intoxicated (ss 84–86) are also excused; we do not attribute blame to such persons–or in some circumstances may blame them less–even though we do not approve of their conduct.

The provisions relating to the mistake of fact defence are contained in the same sections (76 and 79) as defences where the accused was bound or justified by law. This is unfortunate because these defences are conceptually different. Where the accused was bound or justified, his conduct is not adjudged wrong. If he acts under a mistake of fact, we are excusing the individual actor, not justifying his conduct.

Duress (s 94) is generally recognized by academic writers as an excuse: suppose A commits robbery because another person is threatening him with instant death. If he is afforded a defence of duress, it is not because his behaviour is justified by reference to some societal good, but because, in Kadish's words (1987), "some disability in ... [his] freedom to choose the right [thing] makes it inappropriate to punish ... [him]."

C. Importance of distinguishing excuses and justifications

The distinction between justifications and excuses is of more than theoretical interest. A clear recognition of the conceptual difference can significantly affect the scope afforded to a particular defence. Since excuses involve a concession to the individual on the facts of the case, rather than a mark of approval of such conduct generally and for the future, they may be more widely favoured by legislators and judges than justifications. Thus, Clarkson and Keating (1984, pp 318–325) argue that a wider scope may be afforded to defences of duress and necessity if they are conceptualized as excuses rather than justifications; the accused is either blameless or at least less blameworthy, because of his plight at the time of the offence. As will become clear in the chapter on the special exceptions, excuses are also perhaps more flexible than justifications in that judgments of blameworthiness need not be absolute. Obviously the different *mens rea* terms, the key indicators of blame, indicate degrees of culpability; since excuses concern attribution, it is perfectly tenable to hold in certain circumstances that although the accused is not blameless, he is less culpable. By contrast, in the case of justifications, it is harder to develop degrees of "right and wrong".

It must also be emphasized that justifications, as indicated in the previous paragraph and the earlier extracts, effectively modify the substantive law, setting precedents for accused persons acting in similar circumstances in the future. By contrast, the availability of an excuse depends on the accused proving his disability on the facts of the particular case. As Fletcher (1978, above, p 104) puts it: "The functional impact of a justification is to modify the norm by carving out a limited field where the conduct is not wrongful. Valid claims of excuse do not modify the prohibited norm."

Another area of significance concerns strict liability offences (see ch 3) but the basic point bears repeating. Conceptually, it is much easier to apply justificatory defences to offences of strict liability because they "modify the prohibited norm" in the type of situation in which the conduct occurred. It requires greater dexterity to use excuses because the essence of truly strict liability offences is that they impose liability irrespective of blame. Nevertheless, when the purposes of strict liability are considered, there will be situations, such as automatism and infancy, where it would be manifestly absurd and unjust to impose liability even though the defence is an excuse.

The distinction is also important in cases where the accused A is charged with an offence against a person X who was acting under an exculpatory defence. A is only likely to succeed in his defence where X's defence is one of excuse rather than justification. This is recognized in part by the Penal Code; s 98 provides that A will have the right of private defence against X where X's excuse is lack of age/understanding, unsound mind, intoxication or mistake of fact. While the Penal Code makes no express provision for such cases, it is submitted that the same principle should apply to other excuses (duress, accident or automatism). Suppose X, acting under duress, attempts to injure A. Although X may have an excuse on the facts of the case, A should also have the right to defend himself. By contrast, if X's defence is justificatory, A is unlikely to have a defence. Suppose, now, that X was bound by law to act in a certain manner or was exercising his own right of private defence against A's initial aggression. Since X's conduct is *justified*, he has committed no wrong; it is therefore difficult to maintain that A can have the right of private defence. However, A would have the right if X had exceeded his right of private defence so that his conduct had gone beyond what was justified (*Abdul Manap*, 1956).

Similar problems arise with regard to participation and abetment. If one party has an excuse (eg insanity) he alone should derive its benefit; the focus is on his personal blameworthiness. In line with this, s 108, particularly in the illustrations to Explanation 3, recognizes that an abettor may be liable even where a defence of lack of age/understanding, unsoundness of mind or mistake exculpates the perpetrator. Other excusing defences should be dealt with in the same way. By contrast, if the defence is justificatory, it is very likely that the abettor will derive its benefit; if no wrong has been committed, it is hard to see how one can abet a non-existent crime. Thus, if A acts for V's benefit and/or with his consent, in circumstances which give A a defence, the benefit of that defence should also extend to his abettor B. A's defence has nothing to do with disabilities which are personal to him but concerns the judgment that his conduct is right in the circumstances.

A final point to which Clarkson and Keating (1984, p 324) draw attention is that if an actor is excused from criminal liability, society may nevertheless wish in some cases to take preventive action against him. The classic example is unsoundness of mind where the accused will be committed to a mental institution. Similarly, it is not inconceivable for a scheme whereby an offender who suffers from a serious drug dependency may be required to attend a "detoxification centre" even though he was acquitted on grounds of intoxication. By contrast, where the conduct in question is justified–approved or accepted by society– this should not happen.

Justifications

Chapter 5

Private defence

By KL Koh

A. Introduction

Penal Code, ss 96–106

96. Nothing is an offence which is done in the exercise of the right of private defence.

97. Every person has a right, subject to the restrictions contained in section 99, to defend–
(a) his own body, and the body of any other person, against any offence affecting the human body;
(b) the property, whether movable or immovable, of himself or of any other person, against any act which is an offence falling under the definition of theft, robbery, mischief or criminal trespass, or which is an attempt to commit theft, robbery, mischief or criminal trespass.

98. When an act, which would otherwise be a certain offence, is not that offence, by reason of the youth, the want of maturity of understanding, the unsoundness of mind, or the intoxication of the person doing that act, or by reason of any misconception on the part of that person, every person has the same right of private defence against that act which he would have if the act were that offence.

Illustrations
(a) Z, under the influence of madness, attempts to kill A. Z is guilty of no offence. But A has the same right of private defence which he would have if Z were sane.
(b) A enters, by night, a house which he is legally entitled to enter. Z, in good faith, taking A for a housebreaker, attacks A. Here Z, by attacking A under this misconception, commits no offence. But A has the same right of private defence against Z, which he would have if Z were not acting under that misconception.

99.–(1) There is no right of private defence against an act which does not reasonably cause the apprehension of death or of grievous hurt, if done, or attempted to be done, by a public servant acting in good faith under colour of his office, though that act may not be strictly justifiable by law.

(2) There is no right of private defence against an act which does not reasonably cause the apprehension of death or of grievous hurt, if done, or attempted to be done, by the direction of a public servant acting in good faith under colour of his office, though that direction may not be strictly justifiable by law.

(3) There is no right of private defence in cases in which there is time to have recourse to the protection of the public authorities.

113

(4)   The right of private defence in no case extends to the inflicting of more harm than it is necessary to inflict for the purpose of defence.

Explanation 1–A person is not deprived of the right of private defence against an act done, or attempted to be done, by a public servant, as such, unless he knows, or has reason to believe, that the person doing the act is such public servant.

Explanation 2–A person is not deprived of the right of private defence against an act done, or attempted to be done, by the direction of a public servant, unless he knows, or has reason to believe, that the person doing the act is acting by such direction; or unless such person states the authority under which he acts, or, if he has authority in writing, unless he produces such authority, if demanded.

100.   The right of private defence of the body extends, under the restrictions mentioned in section 99, to the voluntary causing of death or of any other harm to the assailant, if the offence which occasions the exercise of the right is of any of the following descriptions:
(a)   such an assault as may reasonably cause the apprehension that death will otherwise be the consequence of such assault;
(b)   such an assault as may reasonably cause the apprehension that grievous hurt will otherwise be the consequence of such assault;
(c)   an assault with the intention of committing rape;
(d)   an assault with the intention of gratifying unnatural lust;
(e)   an assault with the intention of kidnapping or abducting;
(f)   an assault with the intention of wrongfully confining a person, under circumstances which may reasonably cause him to apprehend that he will be unable to have recourse to the public authorities for his release.

101.   If the offence is not of any of the descriptions enumerated in section 100, the right of private defence of the body does not extend to the voluntary causing of death to the assailant, but does extend, under the restrictions mentioned in section 99, to the voluntary causing to the assailant of any harm other than death.

102.   The right of private defence of the body commences as soon as a reasonable apprehension of danger to the body arises from an attempt or threat to commit the offence, though the offence may not have been committed; and it continues as long as such apprehension of danger to the body continues.

103.   The right of private defence of property extends, under the restrictions mentioned in section 99, to the voluntary causing of death or of any other harm to the wrongdoer, if the offence, the committing of which, or the attempting to committ which, occasions the exercise of the right, is an offence of any of the following descriptions:
(a)   robbery;
(b)   house-breaking by night;
(c)   mischief by fire committed on any building, tent or vessel, which building, tent or vessel is used as a human dwelling, or as a place for the custody of property;
(d)   theft, mischief or house-trespass, under such circumstances as may reasonably cause apprehension that death or grievous hurt will be the consequence, if such right of private defence is not exercised.

104. If the offence, the committing of which, or the attempting to commit which, occasions the exercise of the right of private defence, is theft, mischief, or criminal trespass, not of any of the descriptions enumerated in section 103, that right does not extend to the voluntary causing of death, but does extend, subject to the restrictions mentioned in section 99, to the voluntary causing to the wrongdoer of any harm other than death.

105.–(1) The right of private defence of property commences when a reasonable apprehension of danger to the property commences.

(2) The right of private defence of property against theft continues till the offender has effected his retreat with the property, or till the assistance of the public authorities is obtained, or till the property has been recovered.

(3) The right of private defence of property against robbery continues as long as the offender causes or attempts to cause to any person death or hurt or wrongful restraint, or as long as the fear of instant death or of instant hurt or of instant personal restraint continues.

(4) The right of private defence of property against criminal trespass or mischief, continues as long as the offender continues in the commission of criminal trespass or mischief.

(5) The right of private defence of property against house-breaking by night continues as long as house-trespass which has been begun by such house-breaking continues.

106. If, in the exercise of the right of private defence against an assault which reasonably causes the apprehension of death, the defender is so situated that he cannot effectually exercise that right without risk of harm to an innocent person, his right of private defence extends to the running of that risk.

Illustration

A is attacked by a mob who attempt to murder him. He cannot effectually exercise his right of private defence without firing on the mob, and he cannot fire without risk of harming young children who are mingled with the mob. A commits no offence if by so firing he harms any of the children.

It is not possible for any society to come to the aid of its citizens in every conceivable situation. Where the law is unable to help, self-help, based on the instinct of self-preservation, is recognized within circumscribed limits by the right of private defence.

JD Mayne, *The Criminal Law of India* (1901), 437

The whole law of self-defence rests on these propositions: (1) that society undertakes, and, in the great majority of cases, is able to protect private persons against unlawful attacks upon their person or property; (2) that, where its aid can be obtained it must be resorted to; (3) that, where its aid cannot be obtained the individual may do everything that is necessary to protect himself; but (4) that the violence used must be in proportion to the injury of vindicative or malicious feeling. It is evident that proposition (1) is the basis of the entire law. No one would dream of applying the refinements of the Indian Penal Code to an unsettled country where everyone carries his life in his hand; and proposition (2), rests upon and assumes proposition (1).

B. The law

The law of private defence contained in ss 96–106 of the Penal Code extends both to persons and property whether of one's own or of another within defined limits. The sections cover matters such as when the right commences (ss 102 and 105); when it extends to causing death (ss 100 and 103); when it extends to causing harm other than death (ss 101 and 104); and its limits (s 99).

In a case of murder, even though the accused may have exceeded the right of private defence he may rely on s 300 Exception 2 of the Penal Code to reduce the charge to culpable homicide not amounting to murder (see ch 20).

1.   Private defence of person

Section 97 of the Penal Code provides that a right of private defence arises either in defending one's own body, or the body of any other person, against any offence affecting the human body. The right commences as soon as a reasonable apprehension of danger to the body arises from an attempt to commit the offence and continues as long as such apprehension of danger to the body continues (s 102). In certain circumstances under s 100 such right can extend to the causing of death; otherwise the right of private defence extends only to the causing of harm other than death (s 101).

(a)   Reasonable apprehension of danger and mistake

English law has steered away from the objective standard of reasonableness (see *Williams (Gladstone)*, 1984; *Beckford*, 1987); so that if the accused genuinely believes he is defending himself he must be judged according to his honest but mistaken belief. However, under s 100 of the Penal Code, reasonable apprehension of danger is to be viewed objectively, and so is a mistaken belief that caused the apprehension of danger. Commenting on an identical provision in the Penal Code of Nigeria, Brown CJ stated in *Josiah Onyeamaizu* (1958):

> It is to be observed that the defence of self-defence is only available if there is *reasonable* apprehension of death or grievous harm and if the person who claims to have exercised that right had *reasonable grounds for* believing that the only way to protect himself from death or grievous harm was to kill his assailant. It is not open to an abnormally nervous or excitable person who, on being assailed by a comparatively minor assault or an assault of any nature which falls short of that which is described in the section, *unreasonably* believes that he is in danger of death or grievous harm .... The legal right to kill in self-defence cannot be made to depend upon the temperament, nervous or courageous, robust or weak, phlegmatic or excitable, of the individual killer. For those who claim to have exercised this legal right to kill, the law insists upon one standard: it is the standard of the reasonable man.

R v Cumming (1891) SLR [NS] 41 (Assizes, Singapore)

HWH Cumming was charged under s 304 with the culpable homicide not amounting to murder, of Gee Ah Tong.

The prisoner and Dr Middleton lived together, and two "boys" slept below on the ground floor. Early on 1 October, before day light, Dr Middleton heard shouting below: he went to call the prisoner who armed himself with a revolver and a hunting crop, and followed Dr Middleton downstairs: the prisoner on reaching a turn in the stairs, saw Dr Middleton nearly at the bottom, and beyond him two Chinese, the nearer one within 7 feet of Dr Middleton reaching down a spear from the wall: the prisoner, who did not speak much Malay, shouted in English "What are you doing there"? but receiving no answer, he fired and hit the Chinese who was then holding the spear which was pointed towards Dr Middleton. The man was fatally wounded, and proved to be the *tukan ayer*, or water carrier of the house. It was evident that the prisoner had made a mistake, thinking that the man was taking down the spear to plunge it into Dr Middleton.

O'Malley CJ: Here the case for the defence seemed to be that by reason either of the act or the threatened act, or the attempted act of the man who was shot, Dr Middleton was, in the eyes of a reasonable man, in the prisoner's position, in peril of his life or of grievous hurt. A great deal had been said about a "mistake". If a man made a mistake as to fact: if, for instance, the prisoner in the case was really under the impression that these men were burglars: and the jury thought that he had taken reasonable and proper precautions to ascertain whether they were burglars, they might consider the case as regards just as if the men really had been burglars. A man who acted in good faith under a misapprehension of facts was not responsible any more than he would be if the facts were as he believed them to be.

A man was justified in defending the life of his friend, or in defending his friend from grievous injury if that friend was actually attacked or if there was from the acts that had been done, or were being done, reasonable grounds to believe that that friend's life was in danger, and he has no other means of averting it. Did the prisoner see the deceased threaten or attempt to kill or grievously hurt Dr Middleton at the time he fired that shot? Did he see him threaten or attempt to commit a murderous or seriously dangerous assault such as to cause reasonable apprehension of death or grievous hurt? Was there such an act or such an attempt of threat as would give cause to apprehend death or serious hurt to Dr Middleton? If there was, the prisoner was justified, if he could do nothing else to avert the danger. The fact that he believed him to be a burglar was material. As had been pointed out a burglar was presumably a dangerous man and the consideration was one which a reasonable man would carry in his mind. Was there any reasonable possibility of defending Dr Middleton other than by shooting the deceased? It was for the jury to say,—(1) Was there at the time the prisoner fired the shot such a threat or attempt to commit such an assault as would cause reasonable apprehension of death or grievous hurt? (2) Was there any possibility of defending Dr Middleton, and of averting death or grievous hurt short of shooting?

The jury, returned a general verdict of *Not guilty*.

[See s 98 of the Penal Code.]

GFL Ewin v PP (1949) 15 MLJ 279 (CA, Malaya)

The appellant was a police sergeant in an area near Ipoh which was known for terrorist activity. He went, along with others, to a mine to search for terrorists. He entered a hut into which he believed, according to his evidence, that six "bad men" had just gone. In his own words: "I entered the hut with my sten-gun at the ready fully expecting to see six armed men. It was dark inside the hut. The bed seemed to take up most of the room. I saw something move on the bed and fired ...." He shot dead a five-year-old boy.

Willan CJ: In this Court the main ground of appeal was that the learned trial judge had not directed the assessors that the appellant, in acting as he did under the circumstances as he, in good faith, believed them to be, might have been exercising the right of private defence....

The provisions of the law relating to the right of private defence are contained in section 96 *et sequitur* of the Penal Code. Section 96 reads:

"Nothing is an offence which is done in the exercise of the right of private defence."

The first paragraph of s 100 reads:

"The right of private defence of the body extends, under the restrictions mentioned in the last preceding section, to the voluntary causing of death or of any other harm to the assailant if the offence which occasions the exercise of the right be of any of the descriptions hereinafter enumerated–
     First–such an assault as may reasonably cause the apprehension that death will otherwise be the consequence of such assault."

Assault is defined in s 351 as follows:

"Whoever makes any gesture or any preparation, intending or knowing it to be likely that such gesture or preparation will cause any person to apprehend that he who makes that gesture or preparation is about to use criminal force to that person, is said to commit an assault."

That definition is relevant because the appellant at his trial said there was a movement by the figure on the bed.

In our view, on the evidence given in this case, the assessors should have been directed to consider whether or not the appellant was exercising the right of private defence. In fairness to the learned trial Judge it should be stated that Counsel for the appellant at the trial made no reference to any of the sections of the Penal Code relating to that right.

Had the assessors been directed that, if, in the circumstances, they were of opinion that the mistake of fact under which the appellant acted (assuming that they accepted the evidence of such mistake) was such as to make it appear to him in good faith to be necessary to shoot in self-defence, they could find him not guilty. It is impossible for us to say whether or not they would have reached the conclusion which they did....

Re-trial ordered

(b) Right of private defence of aggressor

The right of private defence is based on a defensive right of self-help in certain circumscribed limits. Section 97 provides that such a right arises against acts which are offences. Is it available to an accused who strikes the first blow?

PP v Abdul Manap (1956) 22 MLJ 214 (HC, KL, Malaya)

The accused was charged with voluntarily causing grievous hurt by stabbing the complainant in the course of a dispute about some rent payable by the complainant for a padi field. Both parties had lost their tempers. The accused, being incensed by something which the complainant had said, struck him with his fist. On being struck the complainant, a "tall, young and strong man" hit the accused a number of times and was about to throttle him, when the accused took a dagger and stabbed the complainant once in the chest.

Briggs J: Now, on these facts I am of opinion, first, that although the accused struck the first blow and therefore the complainant was himself entitled to exercise the right of private defence, the retaliation which the complainant in fact made for that single blow was on a much larger scale and much more serious that would possibly be justified in the circumstances. It is true that in law the complainant was entitled to use enough force to prevent any repetition of the blow by the accused; but in fact, having regard to the disparity of physique, any question of really defending himself did not seriously arise, and I am convinced that his real frame of mind was that, the accused having had the nerve to strike him, he would teach the accused a real lesson. That is not private defence. It is true that one does not "weigh in golden scales" the quantum of force which is or is not permitted, but the frame of mind in which the force is applied is of importance. I am entitled to infer what that frame of mind was from the evidence, and I do not consider that the complainant was acting properly within the limits of private defence. This, of course, is fundamental, for if he was acting properly within those limits he was not committing any offence against the accused, and therefore no right of private defence in the accused would ever arise. I believe, however, that he did commit an offence against the accused and that the right of private defence did arise in the accused.

Accused acquitted and discharged

The complainant committed an *offence* against the accused who struck him first because he (the complainant) had exceeded his right of private defence and wanted to teach the accused a "real lesson".

The accused had a knife with him. The court held that "there is no reason whatever to suppose that the accused was carrying the weapon with a view to this particular encounter. It is common knowledge that many people do carry such weapons...". If there was evidence that the accused had carried a weapon for the purpose of confronting the complainant, it might have been different. It might then show a vindictive or retributive purpose and the right of private defence would not have been available. In *Munney Khan* (1971), Dua J said:

> The right of private defence is essentially a defensive right circumscribed by statute, available only when the circumstances clearly justify it. It should not be allowed to be pleaded or availed of as a pretext for a vindictive, aggressive or retributive purpose. This right is available against an offence

and, therefore, where an act is done in exercise of the right of private defence such act cannot give rise to any right of private defence in favour of the aggressor in return. This would be so even if the person exercising the right of private defence has the better of his aggressor provided he does not exceed his right, because the moment he exceeds it, he commits an offence.

Thus, where an act which is done in the exercise òf the right of private defence is not an offence it does not give rise to any right of private defence in return (see also, *Gorie Sanker* v *Sheikh Sultan* (1917)).

What is the position in a free fight? In a free fight, it may be diffi-cult to determine who is an aggressor. In *Munney Khan* (1971), Dua J stated:

> In the case when two parties are having a free fight without disclosing as to who is the initial aggressor it may be dangerous as a general rule to clothe either of them or his sympathizer with a right of private defence. If, however, one of them is shown to be committing an offence affecting human body then that would of course seem to give rise to such right.

(c) Restrictions on right of private defence

The restrictions on the right of private defence are laid down in s 99. Where the limits are exceeded in cases of murder, any unpremeditated excess is protected under s 300 Exception 2. This section is a necessary corollary of s 99 which states that the right of private defence in no case extends to the inflicting of more harm than is necessary for the purpose of defence.

The factors which courts have taken into consideration in determin-ing whether a right of private defence arises under s 100 or 99, eg questions as to whether the person exercising the right has reasonable cause of apprehension of death or of grievous hurt or whether the person exercising the right is inflicting more harm than is necessary are: the relative physique of the parties; the frame of mind and conduct of the parties, the nature of the wound inflicted; whether there was any other way of averting danger.

Macaulay, *The Works of Lord Macaulay* (1898) Vol II, 55–56

We propose (clauses 74 to 84 [ss 96–106 IPC]) to except from the operation of the penal clauses of the code large classes of acts done in good faith for the purpose of repelling unlawful aggressions. In this part of the chapter we have attempted to define, with as much exactness as the subject appears to us to admit, the limits of the right of private defence. It may be thought that we have allowed too great a latitude to the exercise of this right; and we are ourselves of opinion that if we had been framing laws for a bold and high-spirited people, accustomed to take the law into their own hands, and to go beyond the line of moderation in repelling injury, it would have been fit to provide additional restrictions. In this country the danger is on the other side; the people are too little disposed to help themselves; the patience with which they submit to the cruel depredations of gang-robbers and to trespass and mischief committed in the most outrageous manner by bands of ruffians, is one of the most remarkable, and at the same time one of the most discouraging symptoms which the state of society of India presents to us. Under these circumstances we are desirous rather to rouse and encourage a manly spirit among the people than to multiply restrictions on the exercise of the right of self-defence. We are of opinion that all the evil which is likely to arise from the abuse of that right is far less serious than the evil which would arise from the execution of one person for overstepping what might appear to the Courts to be the exact line of moderation in resisting a body of dacoits.

We think it right, however, to say that there is no part of the code with which we feel less satisfied than this. We cannot accuse ourselves of any want of diligence or care. No portion of our work has cost us more anxious thought or has been more frequently re-written. Yet we are compelled to own that we leave it still in a very imperfect state; and though we do not doubt that it may be far better executed than it has been by us, we are inclined to think that it must always be one of the least exact parts of every system of criminal law.

PP v Yeo Kim Bok [1971] 1 MLJ 204 (HC, Muar, Malaysia)

The accused was charged with culpable homicide not amounting to murder. The deceased, a man of better built and strength than the accused, had lent some money to the accused and had demanded its payment. He did so in a very aggressive manner, and on seeing the accused remaining calm and passive went to pick up a knife and rushed towards the accused, who had no way to escape. Finding himself in that desperate situation the accused picked up a wooden ladle and hit the knife which the deceased was carrying. The knife dropped; both the accused and the deceased started to grapple with each other and fell down rolling on the ground endeavouring to pick it up. Although there was some conflict in the evidence as to whether the accused had managed to retrieve the knife, this made no difference.

Sharma J: I have no doubt that there was a reasonable apprehension of danger to the life of the accused when the deceased rushed at him with the knife in his hand and at that stage he had the right of private defence which extended even to the killing of the deceased by the accused. The difficult question, however, is whether that right continued to exist at the time he dealt with the fatal blow to the deceased. I think I can do no better than quote a few passages from "Culpable Homicide and Legal Defence" by *KC Mehrotra*:

> "Section 100 does not lay down grievous hurt must be actually caused by the assailant before the right of private defence is available to the accused. All that the section requires is that the person claiming the right of private defence be under a *bona fide* apprehension of fear that death or grievous hurt would otherwise be the consequence of the assault on him if he does not defend himself.
>
> What constitutes a reasonable apprehension of death or grievous bodily injury is always a question of fact to be decided upon the peculiar facts and circumstances of each case. The source of apprehension can be the weapon, the manner of its use, the mental and the physical attitude of the person uttering the threat, his capacity to execute the threat and so on and so forth. The relative strength of the combatants is sometimes material....
>
> It is for the court to decide if the violence threatened was under the circumstances sufficient to have caused in the mind of the accused a reasonable apprehension of grievous injury...."

To begin with the person exercising the right of private defence must consider whether the threat to his person is real and immediate. If he reaches the conclusion reasonably that the threat is real and immediate, he is entitled to exercise the right. One of the requisites of section 100 is that a person must feel a reasonable apprehension of death or grievous hurt as a result of the assault contemplated on him. As soon as he is faced with an assault which causes a reasonable apprehension of death or grievous hurt, allowance has necessarily to be made for his feelings at the relevant time and it would be inappropriate to adopt tests of detached objectivity which would be so natural in a court room."

The author goes on to give some tests to serve as guidelines to determine whether a person has or has not exceeded his right of private defence or has inflicted more harm than was necessary in the exercise of his right of private defence and again I quote from the same work:

"(1) A defender need not wait till he is actually attacked.
(2) He is not obliged to run away, the law does not require a citizen to behave like a coward.
(3) A defender may pursue the aggressor. A defender is not only not obliged to retreat but he may even pursue his enemy till he finds himself out of danger.
(4) If the defender is unable to escape, he may turn round and attack.
(5) A defender need not coolly reflect on his right or measure his blows. The law does not require that the accused should have exercised a calm and cool judgment and that he should weigh his acts in golden scales.
(6) A defender can make sure that his defence is effective.
(7) A defender may inflict injuries on his aggressor for the purpose of defence as well as for preventing further aggression. It is not only the injuries already inflicted but the injuries the attacker might inflict if the defender does not exercise his right of self-defence that must be taken into consideration. Even if the aggressor is disarmed, if there is a possibility of his wrestling the weapon from the defender, the latter has a right to use violence, but of course not to cause his death. But he can even cause death if one of the two aggressors is still armed. It would be circumscribing the right of private defence of the body with meticulous and unjustifiable restrictions if it were to be held that, when the person attacked had managed to obtain the weapon from the grasp of the attacker, he was not to be allowed to use that weapon in his defence in order to prevent the attacker from regaining possession of it."
(The underlining is mine.)

In the light of the evidence produced by the prosecution in this case I think there was a reasonable possibility, nay probability, that if the deceased had himself managed to get hold of the knife, he would have struck some blows with the knife on the accused. In the circumstances and in the situation in which the accused found himself there was bound to be in his mind a reasonable apprehension of death or grievous hurt being caused to him by the deceased unless he got out of the reach of the deceased. It is not a case where there was an exchange of abuse between the borrower and the lender when the latter went to the house of the borrower in order to collect the debt and the borrower without any more picked up a knife and stabbed the lender with it. That certainly will be a case of exceeding the right of private defence. *Mehrotra* in his book already cited by me continues to say:

"Where a right of private defence is pleaded the essence of the case should be to ascertain who was the aggressor and whether the accused party acted in the exercise of his right of private defence or otherwise. But he who is assaulted is not bound to modulate the defence step by step according to the attack before there is reason to believe that the attack is over. He is entitled to secure his victory as long as the contest lasts. He is not obliged to retreat, but may pursue his adversary till he finds himself out of danger, and if in any conflict between them, he happens to kill, such killing is justifiable. And, of course, when the assault assumed a dangerous form every allowance should be made for one who with the instinct of self-preservation strong upon him, pursues his defence a little further than to a perfectly cool bystander would seem absolutely necessary. The question in such cases will not be whether there was an actually continuing danger, but whether there was a reasonable apprehension of such danger.... Under certain circumstances exaggeration of the danger that the accused was facing will not be unreasonable and the law will always make just allowance for the sentiment of the person placed in situation of peril, who has no time to think. His blood then is hot and his sole object is to strike a decisive blow so as to ward off the danger. But courts should not at the same time forget that the right of private defence is a very limited right. It cannot be converted into a right of reprisal."

It is for the party setting up the right of self defence to prove either by independent evidence or from the prosecution evidence or the surrounding circumstances that what he did was in the exercise of his right of self defence. In this case the defence has through the prosecution witnesses proved that the accused was acting in his right of private defence. It is reasonable to suppose that the accused thought in the critical situation in which he was that the deceased might wrest the knife from his hand and use it against him. The reasonable apprehension of death at the hands of the deceased cannot thus be said to have left the mind of the accused. In the circumstances I hold that there is no case to meet. The accused is discharged.

Accused discharged

(i) Some basic assumptions

Jai Dev and Hari Singh v State of Punjab AIR (1963) SC 612 (SC, India)

Gajendragadkar J: (13) There can be no doubt that in judging the conduct of a person who proves that he had a right of private defence, allowance has necessarily to be made for his feelings at the relevant time. He is faced with an assault which causes a reasonable apprehension of death or grievous hurt and that inevitably creates in his mind some excitement and confusion. At such a moment, the uppermost feeling in his mind would be to ward off the danger and to save himself or his property, and so, he would naturally be anxious to strike a decisive blow in exercise of his right. It is no doubt true that in striking a decisive blow, he must not use more force than appears to be reasonably necessary. But in dealing with the question as to whether more force is used than is necessary or than was justified by the prevailing circumstances, it would be inappropriate to adopt tests of detached objectivity which would be so natural in a Court room, for instance, long after the incident has taken place. That is why in some judicial decisions it has been observed that the means which a threatened person adopts or the force which he uses should not be weighed in golden scales. To begin with, the person exercising a right of private defence must consider whether the threat to his person or his property is real and immediate. If he reaches the conclusion reasonably that the threat is immediate and real, he is entitled to exercise his right. In the exercise of his right, he must use force necessary for the purpose and he must stop using the force as soon as the threat has disappeared. So long as the threat lasts and the right of private defence can be legitimately exercised, it would not be fair to require, as Mayne has observed, that "he should modulate his defence step by step, according to the attack, before there is reason to believe the attack is over". [Mayne, 1914] The law of private defence does not require that the person assaulted or facing an apprehension of an assault must run away for safety. It entitles him to defend himself and law gives him the right to secure his victory over his assailant by using the necessary force. This necessarily postulates that as soon as the cause for the reasonable apprehension has disappeared and the threat has either been destroyed or has been put to rout, there can be no occasion to exercise the right of private defence. If the danger is continuing, the right is there; if the danger or the apprehension about it has ceased to exist, there is no longer the right of private defence, (Vide ss 102 and 105 of the Indian Penal Code).

(ii) Physique of parties

PP v Abdul Manap (1956) 22 MLJ 214 (HC, KL, Malaya)

(For facts of case, see above, p 119.)

Briggs J: At this stage it is necessary to consider the respective physiques of the parties. The complainant, in his evidence, describes it quite clearly in this way: that the accused is a very small man, elderly and of poor physique, while he, the complainant, is tall, young and normally strong. He agreed that he could kill the accused with his hands alone if he wanted. The complainant had no weapon, but the accused had, either on his person or in immediate reach, a small dagger. On being struck by the accused, the complainant seized him with one hand by his baju below the collar and hit him with his fist three times. That was his first account of it, but he also said "I do not remember how often I punched him", so it may well have been much more. The question how his grip on the accused's clothes affected the accused is best understood by the evidence of the acccused's son, Isahak, who though only nine was intelligent and in my opinion was a witness of truth. He said that the complainant had caught the accused by the neck and was throttling him. Later, in answer to me, he said "When I saw the complainant throttling my father, I was frightened. I did not know what would happen." I then asked. "If your father had not stabbed him what do you think would have happened?" and he replied "My father would die; I mean the complainant would have killed him." It is not necessary to suppose that his assumption was correct in fact; but that he could, as I am sure he did, make that assumption, shows that the situation was at any rate substantially serious for the accused. At that stage, the accused took the dagger and stabbed the complainant once in the chest.

Now, if this is so, what degree of force was necessary to be used and has the accused exceeded it? The accused was being throttled. He was held by a much larger and more powerful assailant, and there is no reason to suppose that he had any way of getting away or escaping; meanwhile he was being subjected to blows of the fist, and there seems every reason to suppose that the assault on him would have continued, perhaps with increasing gravity, unless he took immediate action. Again having regard to the disparity of the physique, I cannot conceive that any action other than that which he took would have been effective to enable him to escape from the predicament from which he found himself.

As the complainant did not die no other considerations than this arise on the question of quantum of force used. Where there is no death the only issue is: Was more force used than necessary?–and I am clearly of opinion that it was not. The fact that he almost killed the complainant or might have killed the complainant is really beside the point. If you stab a man at all you expect to do him serious damage, but serious damage was the only way by which the attack of the complainant could be stopped. There is no reason whatever to suppose that the accused was carrying the weapon with a view to this particular encounter. It is common knowledge that many people do carry such weapons, although it may be a very undesirable practice....

I am, however, after considerable thought, of opinion that the evidence given for the prosecution makes it appear to me much more probable than not that the accused did act in private defence and did not do so excessively. The accused is accordingly acquitted and discharged.

Accused acquitted and discharged

[See also *Ngoi Ming Sean*, 1982 and *Lee Thian Beng*, 1972, below.]

(iii) Conduct of deceased and type of weapon used

PP v Ngoi Ming Sean [1982] 1 MLJ 24 (HC, Seremban, Malaysia)

The accused, a police detective, was charged with culpable homicide not amounting to murder. He had gone to a bar where words were exchanged with the deceased. An argument then broke out in the toilet when the deceased claimed he was unable to urinate while the accused was standing there. The accused showed his police authority card but the deceased continued to be aggressive. The accused retreated to the bar but was pursued by the deceased, whereupon he shot the deceased in the course of a struggle when "cornered" by him.

Ajaib Singh J: The defence case is that the accused did no more than exercise his right of private defence. In his evidence on oath the accused said that when the deceased tried to snatch his revolver he became frightened and thought that if the deceased got hold of the revolver he would kill him. The accused said that at that stage he genuinely feared for his life at the hands of the deceased because of the threats and aggression with which the deceased had confronted him from the time that he had entered the bar. He had no intention of killing the deceased but had fired the shot in self-defence.

The Penal Code provides that nothing is an offence which is done in the exercise of the right of private defence of a person's body. But there is no such right where the person has time to seek the protection of the public authorities. Nor will this right of private defence extend to the inflicting of more harm than is necessary for the purpose of defence. Subject to these limitations the right of private defence of the body extends even to the voluntary causing of death or any other harm to the assailant if the person who exercises his right of private defence is under a reasonable apprehension that death or grievous hurt would be caused to him by the assailant. The right of private defence commences as soon as there is reasonable apprehension of danger to the body and this right continues so long as such apprehension of danger continues. (See ss 96 to 102 of the Penal Code). And it goes without saying that the right of private defence ceases and is not available when there is no more apprehension of danger to the body....

[His Lordship referred to *Musa b Yusof* (1953) and Mayne, 1914, and continued:]

The accused is of slight build and his superior officer has said that he is a very passive man who would not involve himself in any trouble. The deceased who was a bigger and stronger person than the accused was the aggressor throughout this unhappy episode. The accused was at the receiving end and at one stage when they were on the opposite sides of the counter the accused even apologized to the deceased in order to avoid trouble. But the deceased would not be pacified. According to the evidence of his own friend Loi Ngok Wan the deceased was quarrelling and shouting almost non-stop. And the fact that the accused was armed with a revolver while the deceased was unarmed cannot affect the right of private defence which was available to the accused. The question which the court has to decide is whether in all the circumstances of this case the accused had a reasonable apprehension that the deceased would cause his death or inflict grievous hurt to his body. The law on this point was stated in the case of *Survade* v *State of Gujarat* (1972) as follows:

> "There is nothing in the law of private defence to suggest that the right of private defence of body cannot be claimed against an assailant who is not armed with some sort of weapon. Looking to the plain language of s 100 of the Indian Penal Code it appears that, the question whether a person has a right of private defence in a given case depends on the manner in and the ferocity with which he is attacked and the apprehension in his mind resulting from such an attack and not on the question whether, he was armed or otherwise. If in view of the attack he has a genuine apprehension that the person assaulting him would either cause his death or grievous hurt to him he would be justified in causing the death of his assailant in exercise of the right of private defence irrespective of the fact whether the assailant was armed or not."

On the evidence as a whole I find that at the stage when the accused and the deceased were struggling for the revolver the accused had a reasonable apprehension of death or grievous hurt at the hands of the deceased. There was no way out for the accused as he was cornered in the small space near the toilet. The assault by the deceased had indeed assumed a dangerous form and the accused was placed in a situation of such great peril that he had no time to think or do anything else but to fire the shot from his revolver. His act which caused the death of the deceased was done in the exercise of his right of private defence and was not in excess of that right. The accused is accordingly entitled to an acquittal and I hereby order that he be acquitted and discharged.

Accused acquitted and discharged

Lee Thian Beng v PP [1972] 1 MLJ 248 (FC, KL, Malaysia)

The appellant was charged with culpable homicide not amounting to murder arising out of an incident in a bar. He was a chief inspector of police but was off duty and out of uniform at the time of the offence. The deceased was sitting at a nearby table. Some glasses were thrown and the deceased complained to the appellant. The appellant made no attempt to identify himself.

Ong Hock Sim FJ: The prosecution had therefore established beyond any shadow of doubt that the appellant used a weapon capable of penetrating to a depth of 3 cm aimed at the face of the deceased and that it was the injury so caused which resulted in death....

In this appeal reliance was placed on the right of private defence.... In this connection the appellant's own evidence is most important. He justified his action solely on this ground:

"I rushed forward to grab the gun. I did this because I considered it my duty as a police officer to disarm him for the safety of his life as well as for the safety of the lives of the people in the bar. At that time I also thought of self-defending myself (sic)."...

Turning to the plea of private defence, s 99 of the Penal Code provides that the right of private defence in no case extends to the infliction of more harm than is necessary to inflict for the purpose of defence.

Subject thereto, s 100 provides that the right of private defence extends to the voluntary causing of death or of any other harm to the assailant if the offence which occasions the exercise of the right be such an assault as may reasonably cause the apprehension that death will otherwise be the consequence of such assault. Section 102 provides that the right of private defence of the body commences as soon as a reasonable apprehension of danger to the body arises from an attempt or threat to commit the offence; and it continues as long as such apprehension of danger to the body continues....

We have, on the whole of the evidence, come to the conclusion that the right of private defence cannot avail the appellant. In the first place, any use of force was absolutely unnecessary at any time–even if it was a fact as alleged by the appellant and inspector Kwok Kit Leng (which we disbelieve) that the deceased did point his gun at the appellant. Had the appellant announced that he was a police inspector when the deceased came over to his table to complain, the argument or altercation would in all probability have been nipped in the bud. According to both Teoh Kim Seng and Teo Ching Siong (supported by the bar-girl on this point) it was the threatening attitude of the appellant and his friends which frightened the deceased and made him get up and retreat two steps before he fired a shot into the air, after which he was floored the next moment by the blow which killed him. Where, then, was the occasion or opportunity for the deceased to aim his gun in a threatening gesture?

Even when threatened the deceased fired, not at or towards his advancing foes, but up in the air. After this shot, would not peace have been restored, had the appellant or his brother officer called out that they were police officers? Announcing their identity is the very first lesson imparted to a police constable. It is, therefore, wholly inconceivable that both officers, each with nearly 20 years of experience, could have failed to do so, from force of habit, unless the appellant deliberately refrained because he wanted to teach the deceased a lesson and give him a thrashing. As he had testified he considered it his duty as a police officer to disarm the deceased. Before taking any forcible action should he not have identified himself first? In the case of inspector Kwok, it was plain that he deliberately set out to help his friend. Unaware of the true identity of the advancing foe, who might have been thugs, was the deceased not acting reasonably when, fearing for his own safety, he fired only into the air? The plain and easy way out of the dangerous situation was for the appellant simply to disclose his identity....

In the instant case the use of force was manifestly unnecessary. The appellant had only to say he was a police officer to nip even the verbal argument in the bud. In the use of force, the appellant would have a decided advantage over the deceased. As he admitted "I am much bigger in size than him". He naturally denied using any weapon because he must have realized that its use was excessive and cruel. In our view the appellant had made a dastardly attack on a man physically very much his inferior, using a vicious weapon when no resort to force was necessary. The deceased after remonstrating to the appellant over the throwing of glasses had apologized and returned to his own table. There the matter should have ended but for the appellant's own conduct in going over to the deceased's table and there creating occasion for the infliction of the fatal injury. The plea of private defence therefore fails and the appeal must be dismissed. With regard to sentence, in the light of the observations we have just made, we do not consider the term of three years in any way excessive and we accordingly affirm it.

Appeal dismissed

[See also *Abdul Manap* (1956, above, p 119.)]

In *Ngoi Ming Sean* (1982), one of the factors which the court took into consideration in determining whether or not the right of private defence was available to the accused was the aggressive and threatening manner of the deceased and also the fact that he had tried to snatch the revolver from the accused. Private defence was successfully pleaded by the accused. In *Lee Thian Beng* (1972) the court held that the right of private defence did not avail the appellant: he had frightened the deceased by his threatening manner. The deceased retreated and fired two shots, not at the appellant but up in the air as a warning not to get near him. The appellant, however, floored and killed the deceased. Also, the deceased was a man much smaller in built than the appellant. The court also took into consideration the vicious weapon used by the appellant.

(iv) Attacker disarmed and weapon passed to the attacked

One is not deprived of one's right of private defence the moment the attack ceases as when the weapon used by the attacker changes hands.

Musa b Yusof v PP (1953) 19 MLJ 70 (CA, KL, Malaya)

The appellant was convicted of culpable homicide not amounting to murder. He pleaded private defence.

Mathew CJ: ... It was most important, bearing in mind that the appellant's defence was a plea of private defence, that the law on the question of private defence should be fully explained to the assessors, in particular the law regarding this right when the attacker had been disarmed and the weapon had passed from the attacker to the attacked....

The law which is applicable in this country is fully set out in *Alingan Kunhinayan & Anor*, (1905). The learned Sessions Judge in that case made the following observations:

"It is urged on behalf of the first accused that he was justified in the exercise of his right of private defence of his person in stabbing deceased when he attacked him with a knife. First accused had undoubtedly a right to defend himself but I think it is clear that he exceeded the right of private defence which he possessed. First accused was certainly not justified in wresting the knife from deceased and inflicting a dangerous wound in the chest. There is no reason, I think, to suppose that first accused could not have escaped further injury by resorting to less violence or by running away. It was not necessary for first accused's own preservation that he should have inflicted such grievous bodily harm."

The Court of Appeal commented on this passage as follows:

"On the facts of the case we cannot agree with the view of the law taken by the learned judge. We do not think it can be said that the first accused exceeded the right of private defence. The learned judge suggests that the first accused could have escaped further injury by resorting to less violence or running away. But, this is placing a greater restriction on the right of private defence of the body than the law requires."...

The principle applicable to a case like this is that laid down by Mayne (1914):

"But a man who is assaulted is not bound to modulate his defence step by step, according to the attack, before there is reason to believe the attack is over. He is entitled to secure his victory, as long as the contest is continued. He is not obliged to retreat, but may pursue his adversary till he finds himself out of danger; and if, in a conflict between them, he happens to kill, such killing is justifiable. And, of course, when the assault has once assumed a dangerous form every allowance should be made for one, who, with the instinct of self-preservation strong upon him, pursues his defence a little further than to a perfectly cool by-stander would seem absolutely necessary. The question in such cases will be, not whether there was an actually continuing danger, but whether there was a reasonable apprehension of such danger."...

The all important facts in connection with the question whether the first accused exceeded the rights of private defence of his body when he gave the stab with his knife which proved fatal to the deceased, are that the deceased was the first to use the knife and had inflicted a wound on the first accused which might well have proved fatal.

On the facts we are of opinion that the first accused did not exceed the right of private defence and that his conviction under ss 304 and 326 of the Indian Penal Code cannot be upheld.

Accepting, as the assessors must have done, that it was the deceased who first attacked the appellant, we cannot but feel that, had the assessors been directed that if they believed that the one blow which the appellant gave to the deceased with the trident was for the purpose of preventing a renewed attack upon him, he was entitled to acquittal, the assessors might well have come to a different conclusion.

We consider that this appeal should be allowed. The conviction is accordingly quashed, the sentence set aside, and the appellant ordered to be released.

Appeal allowed

(v) Nature of wound inflicted

Wong Lai Fatt v PP [1973] 2 MLJ 31 (FC, KL, Malaysia)

The appellant stabbed to death a man who had attempted to rape his wife. He pleaded guilty to a charge of murder and was sentenced to 4 years' imprisonment. The evidence was that he had acted in exercise of his right of private defence. Unfortunately, this was not referred to by his counsel.

On appeal against the legality of the sentence.

Ong CJ: The more serious omission, however, was failure by defence counsel to refer to and lay stress on the provisions of s 100 of the Penal Code which *inter alia* provides that, in the case of an assault with the intention of committing rape, the right of private defence extends, if necessary, to the voluntary causing of death or any other harm to the wrong-doer. With all respect to counsel, the plea in mitigation was nothing if not feeble. Here was a man defending his bride of 4 months who was forcibly being raped. There was only one fatal wound, the others being superficial–which went to prove that no more force was intended than necessary to defend the wife from further attack. Pulling off the deceased, without actually disabling him, would have had dangerous consequences, for the deceased had two able-bodied companions in attendance who could have beaten the appellant and his wife to a pulp. Above all, the extreme provocation offered–in such contemptuous fashion as the deceased did by attempting rape on a wife as if the presence of her husband counted for nothing–was so outrageous that the degree of force used in defence of the women ought not to be measured in delicate scales to be judged as excessive....

In the instant case, where the prosecution case itself clearly raised the right of private defence, which justified infliction of the fatal injury in defence of the appellant's own wife–and it was never suggested that any more force was used than was necessary to prevent the rape from being carried out.

Appeal allowed

In *Wong Lai Fatt* (1973) there was only one fatal wound, the others being superficial; this shows that no more force was intended than necessary to defend the wife from further attack. Pulling off the deceased, without disabling him could have had dangerous consequences, for the deceased had two able-bodied companions in attendance who could have beaten the appellant and his wife to a "pulp".

A simple injury received by an accused does not cause the apprehension of death or grievous hurt under s 100 (a) or (b), and hence does not extend to causing the death of the assailant. It is also important to consider the interval of time between the attack by the assailant and the act of the accused as it would determine whether the act of the accused is one of reprisal. If it is, no right of private defence exists and by parity of reasoning the accused cannot plead the right of private defence under s 300 Exception 2 of the Penal Code.

In *Hazara Singh* (1981), the deceased had attended a public meeting in connection with elections to the Legislative Assembly of the State of Janimu and Kashmir. A quarrel started between two rival groups and Piyara Singh snatched a gun from Hazara Singh and shot Harbans Singh, the deceased. The High Court of Janimu held that the shooting of the deceased, who at the relevant time was not carrying any arms, not even a stone, was a retaliatory action. The court said:

> It is trite law that the right of private defence is a defensive right. It is neither a right of aggression, nor of reprisal. The gunshot fired by Hazara Singh, therefore, could not be said to be an act done in the exercise of his right of private defence.

2.   Private defence of property

The right of private defence of property under s 105 commences when a reasonable apprehension of danger to the property commences. The wording is similar to that in s 102 in respect of the right of private defence to the body. However, the circumstances under which there can be said to be a reasonable apprehension differ. A mere threat is sufficient in the case of an attack on the person, whereas in the case of an attack on property there must be something more than a mere threat–it must be a threat so imminent as to amount to an attempt to commit an offence. (See comparison of ss 100 and 103, below.)

Mohd Rafi v Emperor AIR (1947) Lah 375 (HC, Lahore, India)

A party of persons including the deceased armed with deadly weapons were advancing towards the accused's house in a threatening manner. At the same time they were shouting out threats of setting fire to the house. But they had neither torches nor inflammable materials nor was any attempt of any kind to set fire made. The accused who was standing in front of his house shot and fatally wounded the deceased at a distance of about 11 to 14 feet while he was advancing towards him.

Falshaw J: The question which then arises is whether the accused has in shooting Ibrahim exceeded any right which he may have enjoyed under ss 100 and 103, Penal Code which lay down the circumstances in which death may be voluntarily caused in the exercise of the right of defence of the body and of property respectively....

Similarly there is a difference in the wording of ss 100 and 103. The relevant portion of s 100 reads: "If the offence which occasions the exercise of the right be of any of the description hereinafter enumerated" while the relevant portion of s 103 reads: "If the offence, the committing of which, or the attempting to commit which, occasions the exercise of the right." From this it would appear that although in both cases the right commences when there is a reasonable apprehension of harm, the circumstances under which there can be said to be a reasonable apprehension differ, a mere threat being sufficient in the case of an attack on the person, whereas in the case of an attack on property there must be something more than a mere threat and it must be a threat which is so imminent as to amount to an attempt to commit the offence. In the circumstances of the present case, it would seem that even if the allegation of the accused and his witnesses that Ibrahim and his party were uttering threats of setting fire to his house is true, there is no evidence that any members of the party had made preparations to carry out this threat in the form of carrying torches or inflammable material, or that any attempt of any kind was made, and therefore the threat had not become so imminent that the accused was entitled to shoot in order to repel it.

The question which remains is whether there was a reasonable apprehension that he or any of the persons in the house might suffer grievous hurt at the hands of Ibrahim and his companions....

In the circumstances whether the party of Ibrahim numbered five, as the prosecution witnesses allege, or seven, as the defence alleges, it is almost certain that some of them at any rate were armed with deadly weapons and their advance in a threatening manner must undoubtedly be held to have given rise in the mind of the accused to a reasonable apprehension that he was about to sustain grievous injury at their hands, and it must accordingly be held that in firing his gun so as to cause fatal injuries to Ibrahim he did not exceed the right of defence of the body which he enjoyed according to law and I would accordingly accept the appeal and acquit him.

Appeal allowed

(a) Restrictions on right of private defence

Section 105(2) provides that the right of private defence of property against theft continues till the offender has effected his retreat with the property, or till the assistance of the public authorities is obtained, or till the property has been recovered.

(i) "Till assistance of public authorities is obtained"

Punjabrao v King-Emperor (1945) ILR (Nagpur Series) 881 (HC, Nagpur, India)

A dispute arose between the accused, Punjabrao and Jankibai, and the victim over some property. The victim and her friends had cut crops in two of the disputed fields. When he heard this, the accused gathered some friends. Armed with lathis, they went to the market where they attacked the victim's party.

Pollock J: Under s 105, Indian Penal Code the right of private defence of property against theft continues till the offender has effected his retreat with the property or either the assistance of the public authorities is obtained or the property is recovered. In *Jarha Chamar* v *Surit Ram* (1907) Stanyon AJC held that the right continues after the offender has effected his retreat with the property until the property has been recovered. As I have said in a previous case, that view, with great respect, appears to be open to the criticism passed on it in *Mir Dad* (1925). The meaning of the section is not altogether clear, but in my opinion it should be interpreted as meaning that the right of private defence of property against theft comes to an end if the offender has effected his retreat with the property or the assistance of the public authorities has been obtained or the property has been recovered. Otherwise it seems meaningless to say that the right of private defence continues till the offender has effected his retreat with property if in fact it always continues till the property has been recovered. It is also not altogether clear what is meant by the expression "the offender has effected his retreat with the property". In the first Report on the Penal Code, quoted in Ratanlal's *Law of Crimes*, on pages 232 and 233 of the 15th edition, it was suggested that the offender can probably be said to have effected his retreat when he has once got clear off, having escaped immediate pursuit or pursuit not having been made. In that view it could be said that Jankibai's party had effected their retreat with the property.

I will, however, assume that Jankibai's party had not effected their retreat and that the crops were stolen property, though this is open to doubt. Section 105, Indian Penal Code deals with the commencement and continuance of the right of private defence of property, but section 99, Indian Penal Code, which is the more general section, lays down that there is no right of private defence at all when there is time to have recourse to the protection of the public authorities. The burden of proof is on the accused. They themselves have not stated that they acted in exercise of their right of private defence but left it to be gathered from the evidence in the case. It would also be for them to prove that there was no time to have recourse to the protection of the public authorities. The fight took place at about 2 pm or perhaps a little earlier at the orange market, which is 3 to 4 furlongs or about 10 minutes' walk from the police station-house. The learned Magistrate of the appellate Court was entirely right, in my opinion, in his view that if Punjabrao had had time to collect his followers and go to the orange market to waylay Jankibai's party he could also have had time to go to the station-house and ask for police assistance. I therefore agree that there was no right of private defence in this case....

Application dismissed

(ii) "Till offender has effected his retreat with the property"

The wording under the second limb of s 105 of the Indian Penal Code is slightly different. It reads:

> The right of private defence of property against theft continues till the offender has effected his retreat with the property or *either* the assistance of the public authorities is obtained, or the property has been recovered.

Under the Indian Penal Code there appears to be two instances where the right ceases, viz:

(1) when the offender has effected his retreat with the property or
(2) either
    (a) the assistance of the public authorities is obtained, or
    (b) the property is recovered (ie "or" is read disjunctively).

In contrast, there appear to be three instances under the Penal Code in Singapore and the FMS Penal Code where the right ceases, viz:

(1) when the offender has effected his retreat with the property, or
(2) till the assistance of the public authorities is obtained, or
(3) till the property has been recovered.

Despite the apparent difference, there may be little or no significance in practice. Depending on the circumstances, the person exercising the right of private defence has an option whether to resort to the assistance of the public authorities or to recover the property on his own. He cannot after having resorted to public authorities continue to exercise the right of private defence by proceeding to recover the property. Of course, when he exercises the right and recovers property from the offender the right ceases as the object of the right is to enable recovery of the property. If after recovering the property he attacks the offender in revenge the right does not exist to protect him.

The more problematic question is in regard to an apparent conflict between the first limb, "till the offender has effected his retreat" and the phrase "the property has been recovered". Where the property is recovered during the course of retreat, no problem arises. However, at what stage can the offender be said to have retreated? If he has escaped hot pursuit or if pursuit is not made, can the person whose property has been taken subsequently exercise the right of private defence in recovering the property? Is the right of recovery independent of the first condition? (See *Amar Singh*, 1968, below p 134.)

(iii) "Till property has been recovered"

Amar Singh v State of Rajasthan (1968) Crim LJ 79(HC, Rajasthan, India)

A she-camel belonging to the complainant was taken to the jungle for grazing but was apparently stolen. The footprints were traced to the accused's house. The complainant tried to catch hold of his she-camel, which was being ridden by the accused. The accused opened fire and also used a sword to effect his escape.

VP Tyagi J: The only contention raised by learned counsel is that the complainant has no right to forcibly take away the she-camel from the possession of the accused appellants as the thieves had effected their retreat with the she-camel after the theft was committed by them and the stolen property was brought to their own home in village Satara. In these circumstances, it is urged that even if it is held that the accused persons forcibly took away the she-camel by not permitting the search party and the complainant to snatch it away from their possession, it cannot be said that they did commit any offence.

On the contrary, according to learned counsel, the force used by the accused persons was in the right of their private defence in protecting the property over which they had a complete domain and it could not be taken away from their possession by any other means except by taking recourse to the assistance of the public authorities. In this connection, my attention has been drawn to the provisions of s 105 of the Indian Penal Code....

From the perusal of s 105 Indian Penal Code it is clear that the duration of the right of private defence of property against theft continues (1) till the offender has effected his retreat with property, or (2) the assistance of the public authorities is obtained, or (3) the property has been recovered. The primary object of this provision of the law appears to be that the owner of the stolen property may not be deprived of it when the same may be recovered by the owner by using force against the thief but this right of using force is subject to the aforementioned three conditions.

Learned Deputy Government Advocate urged that even if the offender has effected his retreat with the property the owner has a right to recover it by using force as the third condition permits the continuance of this right till the stolen property is recovered, and it is in support of this proposition that he has relied on *Jarha*'s case (1907).

In *Jarha*'s case (1907) it has been held that if A runs away with B's watch, B may chase him until he effects his retreat, but the right of self-defence does not end with his escape. If B sees A the next day, the next month or the next year, wearing the stolen watch, B may forthwith seize A and recover his watch, using for the purpose as much force as the case allows, and if a policeman be found at hand, B's proper course would be to hand over A to him and let him recover his watch. But B is not bound to put off the capture of A until he can find assistance of the public authorities.

Again, suppose on a day after the theft B sees his watch lying on a table in a house or a garden, and if he can get the assistance of the police, without losing sight of it, no doubt he would be bound to do so, but he would be under no legal obligation to risk a further loss or removal of the stolen property for the purpose of having recourse to the public authorities, and if the circumstances are such that immediate seizure seems to offer the only reasonable prospect of recovery, B is entitled to enter the house or garden and recover the watch.

(11) The proposition laid down in *Jarha*'s case (1907) has not been followed in later cases. In *Mir Dada*'s case (1926), two learned Judges in their separate judgments expressed the view that the right of private defence of property subsists as long as the offender has not effected his retreat with the property, and as soon as the offender has completed his retreat the right ceases....

This view has been followed again by the Lahore High Court in *Rakhia* (1934) wherein it has been observed that if the thief runs away after leaving the property, the right of private defence comes to an end and the owner would not be justified in pursuing him and assaulting him. Allahabad High Court has also adopted the same view in AIR 1959 All 233.

(12) It is contended by learned counsel for the State that s 105 Indian Penal Code also envisages that the right continues till the property is recovered from the possession of the thief and his further contention is that the primary object of giving this right of private defence to the property is that the stolen property must be recovered from the illegal possession of the thief and, therefore, even if the thief has reached his home with the property and if the chasing party or the owner in the hot pursuit finds the thief with the stolen property even in his house he has a right to snatch the property from the possession of the thief by using necessary violence even if he had taken shelter in his own home because his home should not be treated as a citadel for him.

This argument of learned counsel brings me to the real meaning of the phraseology used by the Legislature in s 105 "till the offender has effected his retreat with the property". "Will it mean the disappearance of the thief after an unsuccessful pursuit by the owner of the property? In my opinion, the plain meaning of the words used by the Legislature is that the right of defending the property would come to an end when the offender has finally succeeded in finding an escape from the hot chasers. It will depend on the circumstances of each case as to when the offender can be said to have finally escaped from the hot chase of the searching party. In some cases it is possible that the offender may be chased up to his own house, but it is very doubtful if the pursuers in that event shall have a right of forcible entry in the offender's house. In such a case it shall, in my opinion, be taken that the offender has successfully effected his retreat and the rights of private defence came to an end.

(13) Another question yet remains to be answered and it is as to how the third portion of the clause "that the right continues till the property is recovered" shall be interpreted. In my opinion, the third condition that "the right continues till the property is recovered from the offender" is not independent of the first condition, namely, "till the offender has effected his retreat with the property". In *Jarha*'s case (1907), Justice Bossignol's observations referred to above were based on the apprehension that if such a liberty is given to the owner so as to use violence even after the offender has successfully effected his retreat for recovering the stolen property then serious disorders are likely to arise and therefore the law-makers have put a restraint on this private defence to recover the stolen property from the offender till one of the conditions as mentioned above is completed.

There is no doubt that this view which has been consistently taken by the Courts is likely to benefit the offenders in certain circumstances, but this consideration cannot guide the Courts to interpret the statute differently from what it obviously means. I am, therefore, inclined to agree with the view taken by the Lahore, Nagpur and Allahabad Courts while interpreting the clause "till the offender has effected his retreat with the property" and hold that the complainant in the instant case had no right to forcibly take possession of the she-camel from the accused party after the accused had reached his home with the stolen property and if the accused party by using force succeed in finding an escape with she-camel from their bara they cannot be said to have committed any offence in the eye of law. In this view of the matter, the conviction of the appellants cannot be sustained.

Appeal allowed

Chapter 6

Consent

By KL Koh

A. Introduction

The question of the freedom of the individual to consent to physical harm caused and the interest of the criminal law to protect the individual against violations of his body require a fine balance between two competing interests–individual freedom and the social utility of an activity. Under the Penal Code, suicide itself is not a crime (though attempt and abetment of suicide are punishable under ss 306 and 309 respectively). Why should consent not be a complete defence to murder under s 300 but only a mitigating circumstance (s 300 Exception 5)? Why is it that a person cannot enjoy having an injury inflicted on himself to the point of causing grievous hurt (s 87)?

Libertarians like Mill (1859) would argue that when a bodily harm is consented to by a victim, the criminal law ought not to intervene even on a paternalistic ground. According to Mill, the ground for intervention is "harm to others". However, Devlin's (1965) attitude to the criminal law's response to the victim's consent is simply that it is the law's function to enforce a moral principle and nothing else–the moral principle being the upholding of the sanctity of life and the physical integrity of the person. Hart (1959, 1963) disagrees with Devlin and states that we must ask whether a practice which offends moral feelings is harmful, independently of its repercussion on the general moral code. Also, whether it is really true that failure to translate this item of general morality in criminal law would jeopardize the whole fabric of morality and so of society. While Hart recognizes that Mill's criterion of "harm to others" is an important factor in the law's intervention, he points out that it is not a single criterion. Kadish and Paulson (1969) pose the following questions: To what extent can the distinctions which courts have made as to when to recognize consent as a defence ... be explained on the ground of paternalism rather than legal moralism? Is it physical injury to persons, even those consenting, that the courts are protecting against, or physical harm in the course of immoral behaviour? These questions may also be asked in regard to the defence of consent and its limits in the Penal Code.

B. The law

It is to be noted that in some crimes consent or the lack of consent is an essential ingredient of the *actus reus*. Thus s 375(b) of the Penal Code defines rape as having sexual intercourse with a woman *without her consent*. Also, s 378 of the Penal Code defines theft as intending to take dishonestly any movable property out of the possession of any person without that person's consent. So in a charge of rape when an accused pleads that the victim consented he is not claiming the defence of consent. The *actus reus* of the offence, non-consensual intercourse, is not made out. Where the victim consented, the prosecution has to prove the lack of consent. (As to the *mens rea* of rape, see ch 3.)

Where consent or lack of consent is not part of the definition of an offence, the accused who has committed the *actus reus* of the offence may set up the consent of the victim as a defence. For instance, an accused who is charged with voluntarily causing hurt to a person under s 323 of the Penal Code can set up the defence of consent under s 87 of the Penal Code, if that person had consented to suffer the harm.

1.   The defence

(a)   Penal Code, s 87

Nothing, which in not intended to cause death or grievous hurt, and which is not known by the doer to be likely to cause death or grievous hurt, is an offence by reason of any harm which it may cause, or be intended by the doer to cause, to any person above 18 years of age, who has given consent, whether express or implied, to suffer that harm; or by reason of any harm which it may be known by the doer to be likely to cause to any such person who has consented to take the risk of that harm.

Illustration

A and Z agree to fence with each other for amusement. This agreement implies the consent of each to suffer any harm which, in the course of such fencing, may be caused without foul play; and if A, while playing fairly, hurts Z, A commits no offence.

The scope of s 87 is as follows:

If the doer *intends* or *knows* that death or grievous hurt would be caused, consent is no defence. If he *intends* or *knows* that the act from its nature would cause harm *less* than grievous hurt, consent is a defence.

Where death or grievous hurt is *not intended* or *known* by the doer to be caused, the fact that such harm resulted is immaterial, if done by consent of the person to suffer or to take the *risk* of that harm. It is important that the act is not from its *nature* one that would cause death or grievous hurt.

The age of consent is above 18 years.

The kinds of activities that are covered by s 87 are, eg sports and pastimes, and operations (see also s 88 below).

(i) Sports and pastimes

Sporting activities are encouraged; they are "manly diversions, they intend to give strength, skill and activity, and may fit people for defence, public as well as personal, in time of need" (Sir M Foster).

If a game is unlawful consent is no defence. Bearing in mind the scope of s 87, a game may be considered unlawful if by its nature it is intended or likely to cause death or grievous hurt. So if two persons play a game of Russian roulette until one of them is shot dead, consent is no defence. Some guidance may be obtained from the dictum of Bramwell LJ in *Bradshaw* (1878) in determining what games are lawful:

> No rules or practice of any game whatever can make that lawful which is unlawful by the law of the land; and the law of the land says you shall not do that which is likely to cause the death of another. For instance, no persons can by agreement go out to fight with deadly weapons, doing by agreement what the law says shall not be done, and thus shelter themselves from the consequences of their acts. Therefore, in one way you need not concern yourselves with the rules of football. But, on the other hand, if a man is playing according to the rules and practice of the game and not going beyond it, it may be reasonable to infer that he is not actuated by any malicious motive or intention, and that he is not acting in a manner which he knows will be likely to be productive of death or injury. But, independent of the rules, if the prisoner intended to cause serious hurt to the deceased, if he knew that, in charging as he did, he might produce serious injury and was indifferent and reckless as to whether he would produce serious injury or not, then the act would be unlawful. In either case he would be guilty of a criminal act and you must find him guilty; if you are of a contrary opinion you will acquit him. His Lordship carefully reviewed the evidence, stating that no doubt the game was, in any circumstances, a rough one; but he was unwilling to decry the manly sports of this country, all of which were no doubt attended with more or less danger.

Even if a game is lawful, it does not necessarily follow that consent is a defence. For instance, if two persons decide to have a boxing game until one of them falls dead, consent is no defence. However, if in the course of a lawful game of cricket, one of the players accidentally hits a player with a cricket bat and causes hurt, consent to play the game will be a defence.

(ii) Voluntary sterilization

The Voluntary Sterilization Act (Singapore) (Cap 347) was passed in Singapore to sanction treatment for sexual sterilization on a voluntary basis, ie consent must be obtained. Section 9 of the Act provides:

> For the avoidance of doubt it is hereby declared that any treatment for sexual sterilization authorized by a registered medical practitioner shall not constitute grievous hurt under ss 87 and 320 of the Penal Code.

There is no legislation sanctioning voluntary sterilization in Malaysia but there is no law against it. Sterilization on therapeutic grounds, eg to prevent a hereditary disease, would satisfy the requirement of "benefit" under s 88 of the FMS Penal Code and there is no need to rely on s 87. However, what about sterilization on contraceptive grounds? Sterilization for contraceptive reasons may be for economic reasons as it may be intended not to worsen the economic position of the family. This would not be "benefit" within the meaning of s 88 which excludes "mere pecuniary benefit" (see s 92 explanation). However, would s 87, which does not require "benefit", apply? If sterilization does not amount to grievous hurt (s 320; see ch 22) it can come within s 87, provided the other aspects of the section are satisfied (see above).

Sterilization is different from emasculation (castration), which is one of the categories of grievous hurt under s 320. Sterilization only deprives the patient of the faculty of procreation. On the part of males, vasectomy is performed (tying the vas above the testes); on the females, salpigectomy (making a break in the fallopian tube) which will block the passage between the ovary and the uterus. The operation does not impair the bodily vigour of the male, nor does it affect his power of consummation, unlike castration.

The next limb of s 320 of the Penal Code to consider is the fifth limb, ie destruction or permanent impairment of the powers of any member or joint. It has been medically proven that sterilization does not impair the bodily vigour of the person. The final limb under s 320 of the Penal Code which has to be considered is the eighth limb; sterilization is a relatively simple and minor operation and would not, within the meaning of grievous hurt, involve a patient in 20 days' severe bodily pain or prevent him from performing his ordinary pursuits.

It is submitted that a surgeon performing a sterilization operation in Malaysia would be able to raise the defence of consent under s 87 or s 88 of the FMS Penal Code.

(b) Penal Code, s 88

Nothing, which is not intended to cause death, is an offence by reason of any harm which it may cause, or be intended by the doer to cause, or be known by the doer to be likely to cause, to any person for whose benefit it is done in good faith, and who has given a consent, whether express or implied, to suffer that harm, or to take the risk of that harm.

Illustration

A, a surgeon, knowing that a particular operation is likely to cause the death of Z, who suffers under a painful complaint, but not intending to cause Z's death, and intending, in good faith, Z's benefit, performs that operation on Z, with Z's consent. A has committed no offence.

Section 88 is narrower in scope than s 87. Under s 88, provided the doer does not *intend* to cause death he is covered even though he *knows* that he is likely to cause death, if the act is done in good faith for the *benefit* of the person with his (ie the person's) consent (see illustration to the section).

(i) Surgical operations

Under s 88 a patient cannot consent to an operation which is intended to cause his death. If the doctor intended and the patient consented (eg mercy killing) the doctor may plead s 300 Exception 5. However, if the operation is a dangerous one and the doctor *knows* that he is likely to cause death but does not so intend, the patient's consent would be a defence even if death ensued, provided the operation is performed for the benefit of the patient. "Benefit" is not defined but s 92 states that "Mere pecuniary benefit is not benefit within the meaning of s 88...". Gour (1984, Vol 1, p 732) notes that this "implies that it *may be* a pecuniary benefit if it is also a benefit of some other kind, as, for instance, it may be for the benefit of his life, health or body. He may expect a legacy if he lives up to a certain age. It may then be also for his pecuniary benefit. But if the harm caused only a pecuniary benefit, it is not a benefit within the comprehension of the rule." Thus if a person were to have his cornea removed in order to sell it to another, consent under s 88 would be no defence as the purpose of the operation was to obtain a pecuniary benefit. As the removal of the cornea constitutes a permanent privation of the sight of an eye, it is grievous hurt under s 320(b). This being the case, s 87 also would not apply. Section 87 would only apply to an operation which, though not for the benefit of the patient, was not intended or known to cause grievous hurt.

What about cosmetic surgery? Can a surgeon who performs such surgery on a patient's face or body and causes permanent disfigurement under s 320 (f) of the Penal Code raise the defence of consent under s 88? Is such an operation for the benefit of the patient? There seems no reason to deny that such surgery is for the benefit of a person as he or she may feel a general sense of well-being from having a good appearance, although the social value may be rather vague. Certainly, there is no reason of public policy against it.

Under s 88 a surgeon must act in good faith (ie with due care and attention, s 52). On the question of unqualified persons performing an operation, the Law Commissioners said (1st Rep s 123, p 221):

> We apprehend that "an unqualified and ignorant quack" could hardly be excused, for it is not to be conceived that such a one could obtain the free and intelligent consent of any person to his performing upon him an operation dangerous to life but by misrepresentation, and such a one could hardly satisfy a Court of Justice that he had undertaken the operation in good faith under cl 72 (this section), for good faith must surely be construed here to mean a conscientious belief that he had skill to perform the operation and by it to benefit the party, while the supposition is that he was unskilled and ignorant.

In *Sukaroo Kobiraj* (1887) the appellant who was unskilled in surgery operated on a man for internal piles and the man died from haemorrhage. On a charge under s 304A for causing death by doing a rash and negligent act, the Calcutta High Court held that the element of good faith under s 88 was not satisfied as he "experimented" without any knowledge of the subject, even though he had performed at least two such operations previously. Also, the deceased could not be said to have accepted a risk he was unaware of.

Section 89 covers operations done in good faith for the benefit of a child under 12 years of age (see below) or of an insane person. In such situations the guardian should act in good faith for the benefit of the child or insane person. Certain restrictions are laid down in the section, which reads:

> Nothing, which is done in good faith for the benefit of a person under 12 years of age, or of unsound mind, by or by consent, either express or implied, of the guardian or other person having lawful charge of that person, is an offence by reason of any harm which it may cause, or be intended by the doer to cause, or be known by the doer to be likely to cause, to that person:
> Provided that this exception shall not extend to–
>
> (a) the intentional causing of death, or to the attempting to cause death;
> (b) the doing of anything which the person doing it knows to be likely to cause death for any purpose other than the preventing of death or grievous hurt, or the curing of any grievous disease or infirmity;
> (c) the voluntary causing of grievous hurt, or to the attempting to cause grievous hurt, unless it be for the purpose of preventing death or grievous hurt, or the curing of any grievous disease or infirmity.
> (d) the abetment of any offence, to the committing of which offence it would not extend.
>
> *Illustration*
> A, in good faith, for the benefit of his child, being under 12 years of age, without his child's consent, has his child cut for the stone by a surgeon, knowing it to be likely that the operation will cause the child's death, but not intending to cause the child's death. A is within the exception, inasmuch as his object was the cure of the child.

(ii) Corporal punishment by guardians and school teachers

A guardian or a person having lawful charge of a child under 12 years of age has the right under s 89 of the Penal Code to administer reasonable punishment on a child for the purpose of discipline. It may be argued that such punishment is for the "benefit" of the child as part of his welfare and upbringing. Where the child is above 12 years but under 18 years of age, it may be argued that there is implied consent given by the child to his guardian or a person having lawful charge of him to administer corporal punishment to him for his "benefit" (s 88).

In Singapore the position regarding corporal punishment by school teachers is governed by the School Regulations 1957 (S2/1958) made pursuant to the Education Ordinance 1957 (Ord 45 of 1957, now Cap 87). The position in Malaysia is governed by the Education (School) Discipline Regulations 1959 (LN 61/59, s 5(K)) which are similar to the regulations in Singapore.

One of the regulations contained in the School Regulations 1957 (Singapore) reads: "No corporal punishment shall be administered to girl pupils" (reg 88(1)). In the Singapore case of *Lam Kwok Weng* v *Noor Ahmad b Ibrahim* (1983, Unreported), the accused, a schoolteacher, was charged with voluntarily causing hurt (under s 323 of the Penal Code) to an eight-year-old female pupil by inflicting corporal punishment on her.

Having regard to the prohibition on corporal punishment of female pupils, the magistrate considered whether it was still open to the defence to establish that there was implied consent under s 89 of the Penal Code, on the part of the parents, to inflict the punishment in question. He held, obiter, that s 89 applied, provided the punishment was not excessive and unreasonable. He approved the English case of *Mansell* v *Griffin* (1908) which held that a teacher in a public elementary school had authority to inflict corporal punishment on a pupil. Walton J said:

> There is no evidence in this case that the parents of the plaintiff had any knowledge of the regulations of the school, and therefore it must be taken that the parents gave to the authorities of the school that ordinary authority which is presumed from the fact of a parent sending a child to school. It seems to me that the authority to administer moderate and reasonable corporal punishment, which any parent who sends a child to school is presumed to give the authorities, extends to the mistress occupying the position which the defendant occupied in this school.

The learned magistrate in *Lam Kwok Weng* (1983) did not consider whether the regulations on corporal punishment were merely ministerial directives or rules of law. These regulations are in fact subsidiary legislation. The question arises, having regard to the law on the prohibition of corporal punishment on female pupils, whether the defence of consent (including implied consent) under s 89 of the Penal Code applies? While s 89 could be construed to provide a defence of implied consent to corporal punishment meted out to pupils, it is arguable that the element of "benefit" in s 89 would not be satisfied in the case of the corporal punishment of female pupils. The Minister for Education, in his wisdom, has thought it undesirable that female pupils should be subject to corporal punishment. Such punishment may have an adverse psychological effect on the female child and no purpose may be served. If this view were accepted, reg 88(1) would have the effect not only of subjecting the teacher who inflicted the corporal punishment to disciplinary action by the Ministry of Education, but he could also be charged with causing hurt or grievous hurt, as the case may be, under s 323 or s 325 respectively of the Penal Code.

The position regarding male pupils is different. In the case of a male pupil under 12 years of age, implied consent of the parents may be deemed to be given under s 89. What is the position of a male pupil above 12 years of age?

Emperor v GB Ghatage (1948) 51 Bom LR 103, (HC, Bombay, India)

A school principal was convicted under s 323 of the Indian Penal Code for voluntarily causing hurt to the complainant, a 15-year-old pupil by administering corporal punishment on him. One of the points raised was the age of the complainant.

Chainan J: The material question in this case, however, is whether the applicant is guilty of any criminal offence. There is no doubt that in English law it is recognized that a schoolmaster may inflict corporal punishment on a pupil for purposes of correction or enforcing school discipline. In *Hopley* (1860), Cockburn CJ has observed (p 206):

> "By the law of England, a parent or a school master (who for this purpose represents the parent and has the parental authority delegated to him), may for the purpose of correcting what is evil in the child inflict moderate and reasonable corporal punishment, always, however, with this condition, that it is moderate and reasonable."

In *Mansell* v *Griffin* (1908) it has been held that a teacher in a public elementary school has authority to inflict corporal punishment on a pupil, if the punishment inflicted is moderate, is not dictated by any bad motive, is such as is usual in the school, and such as the parent of the child might expect that the child would receive if it did wrong. See also *Newport (Salop) Justices: Wright*, ex parte (1929) and *Cleary* v *Booth*   (1893).

In India, the question must be decided by reference to the provisions of the Indian Penal Code. Section 89 of the Code states that nothing which is done in good faith for the benefit of a person under twelve years of age, or of unsound mind, by or by consent, either express or implied, of the guardian or other person having lawful charge of that person, is an offence by reason of any harm which it may cause, or be intended by the doer to cause or be known by the doer to be likely to cause to that person....

When a child is sent by its parent or its guardian to a school, the parent or guardian must be held to have given an implied consent to its being under the discipline and control of the school authorities and to the infliction of such reasonable punishment as may be necessary for the purposes of school discipline or for correcting the child. This principle has been accepted by the Rangoon High Court in *Maung Ba Thaung* (1925). In that case a schoolmaster was prosecuted under s 323, Indian Penal Code, for caning a school boy under his charge. It was not suggested that the schoolmaster was actuated by improper motives or that he was not acting bona fide in the interest of the school discipline or that the punishment was unduly excessive. It was held that the schoolmaster had committed no offence, in view of the provisions of s 89, Indian Penal Code.

Section 89, Indian Penal Code, however, applies in the case of children under 12 years of age. The complainant is 15 years old. The relevant section applicable in this case is s 88, which provides, *inter alia*, that nothing, which is not intended to cause death, is an offence by reason of any harm which it may cause to any person for whose benefit it is done in good faith, and who has given consent, whether express or implied, to suffer that harm, or to take the risk of that harm. The principle referred to in the previous paragraph in respect of children under 12 will also apply in the case of children over 12, and when a child over 12 years of age goes to a school, it may be assumed that the child gives an implied consent to subject itself to the discipline and control of the school authorities and to receiving such reasonable and moderate corporal punishment as may be necessary for its correction or for maintaining school discipline. Under the Penal Code, a valid consent to suffer harm may be given by a person over 12 years of age, see s 90.

We have been referred to a circular issued by the Educational authorities, which states:

> "Corporal punishment shall not be inflicted, except by the Head-master, and by him only, in the case of serious and repeated misconduct. Only a light cane should be used when corporal punishment is considered absolutely necessary and the caning should be restricted to the palms of the hand. When corporal punishment is inflicted, reasons in writing should be recorded by the Head-master."

This circular shows that the Educational authorities in this Province also recognize that in certain circumstances it is necessary for the welfare of students to administer corporal punishment to them. The Madras High Court has taken a similar view in *Sankunni* v *Swaminatha Pattar* (1922). It is true that the case before the Madras High Court was an appeal from a suit for damages, but the principle of law enunciated is the same, viz that a schoolmaster as delegate of the parent may for the purpose of correction inflict moderate and reasonable corporal punishment on the child.

In our opinion, therefore, the applicant's act in administering corporal punishment to the complainant is covered by s 88, Indian Penal Code. He is consequently not guilty of any criminal offence. It has been urged in the course of the arguments that the applicant is also protected by ss 79 and 92 of the Indian Penal Code. We are, however, of opinion that these sections have no application to the facts of this case....

Conviction set aside

(c) Penal Code, s 91

The exceptions in sections 87, 88 and 89 do not extend to acts which are offences independently of any harm which they may cause, or be intended to cause, or be known to be likely to cause, to the person giving the consent, or on whose behalf the consent is given.

Illustration

Causing miscarriage, unless it is authorized under the Termination of Pregnancy Act [Cap 324] is an offence independently of any harm which it may cause or be intended to cause to the woman. Therefore it is not an offence "by reason of such harm"; and the consent of the woman, or of her guardian, to the causing of such miscarriage does not justify the act.

The object of this section is to explain that the defence of consent in ss 87, 88 and 89 does not extend to cases which are offences, not by reason of any harm caused. Consent to such offences is no defence. Examples are acts which affect the public tranquillity such as affrays (s 160) and riots (s 146). Consent to an affray or riot is no defence.

The illustration to s 91 concerns causing miscarriage. It is interesting to compare the position in Singapore on the scope of the defence of consent in this area with that in Malaysia.

The Termination of Pregnancy Act (Singapore) (Cap 324) provides for abortion by an authorized medical practitioner at the request of a pregnant woman with her written consent, provided certain conditions are satisfied. For example, the pregnant woman must, under s 3(3) of the Act be a citizen of Singapore, be the holder, or the wife of a holder, of an employment pass or a work permit pass issued under the Immigration Act (Singapore) (Cap 133); or be resident in Singapore for a period of at least four months immediately preceding the date on which such treatment is to be carried out. However, these requirements need not be complied with in any treatment to terminate pregnancy which is immediately necessary to save the life of the pregnant woman.

Under the Act no treatment for the termination of pregnancy is to be carried out if the pregnancy is of more than a certain duration unless there are special circumstances, viz where the treatment is immediately necessary to save the life or to prevent grave permanent injury to the physical or mental health of the pregnant woman (s 4).

Where abortion is not carried out within the scope of the Act as indicated above, a person who causes a woman with child to miscarry may be liable under ss 312, 313, 314 and 315 of the Penal Code (s 3 of the Act). Consent of the woman is no defence (see s 91 of the Penal Code), and if the woman does not consent, the punishment of the accused is heavier.

Malaysia does not have the above legislation on termination of pregnancy: the position is governed by the FMS Penal Code. The illustration to s 91 of the FMS Penal Code reads:

> Causing miscarriage, unless caused in good faith for the purpose of *saving the life* of the woman is an offence independently of any harm which it may cause or be intended to cause to the woman. Therefore it is not an offence "by reason of such harm"; and the consent of the woman or of her guardian, to the causing of such miscarriage does not justify the act. (Emphasis added.)

Causing miscarriage is governed by ss 312–316 of the FMS Penal Code. Under ss 313 and 314, consent is irrelevant, but if the act is done without the woman's consent the punishment is heavier. Under s 312 a woman who causes herself to miscarry would also be liable.

The defence of consent of the woman under s 91 is only recognized where the abortion is performed for the purpose of saving her life. The scope of the defence seems narrow—it would appear not to extend to a miscarriage to prevent grave permanent injury to the physical or mental health of the pregnant woman (compare the position in Singapore under the Termination of Pregnancy Act, see above). However, the English case of *Bourne* (1939) shows that there is no difference between, saving life and preserving her mental health. In *Bourne* (1939), a doctor was charged with using an instrument with intent to procure an abortion of a 14-year-old girl under s 58 of the (English) Offences Against the Person Act 1861, which reads:

> Whoever, with intent to procure the miscarriage of any woman, whether she be not with child, shall unlawfully administer to her or cause to be taken by her any poison or other noxious thing, or shall unlawfully use any instrument or other means whatsoever with the like intent, shall be guilty of felony.

Section 4(1) is to be read with s 58:

> ... Provided that no person shall be found guilty under this section unless it is proved that the act which caused the death of the child was not done in good faith for the purpose of preserving the life of the mother.

The girl was the victim of violent rape and he performed the operation with her parents' consent. His defence was that the operation was not "unlawful" as, if the operation had not been performed, she would have suffered a complete mental collapse. MacNaghten J was of the view that not only was there a right but a duty to perform the operation:

> ... if a case arose where the life of a woman could be saved by performing the operation and the doctor refused to perform it because of his religious opinions and the woman died, he would be in grave peril of being brought before this court in a charge of manslaughter by negligence. He would have no better defence than a person who, again for some religious reason, refused to call in a doctor to attend his sick child, where a doctor could have been called in and the life of the child could have been saved.

The learned judge acquitted the defendant and held that to preserve a woman's mental health was, in effect, to preserve her life. *Bourne* (1939) was considered in the only case in Malaysia under s 312 of the FMS Penal Code (see below).

PP v Dr Nadason Kanagalingam [1985] 2 MLJ 122 (HC, Kota Kinabalu, Malaysia)

The accused was charged under s 312 of the FMS Penal Code for causing a woman with child to miscarry. The evidence showed that the accused had not given reasonable consideration and neither had he come to a reasonable conclusion that he had to cause the woman to miscarry in order to save her life. There was no indication that her life was or would be in danger if pregnancy was allowed to continue.

Wan Mohamed J: [Counsel for the accused cited *R v Bourne*, 1939, see above.] Section 312 of the Penal Code:

> "[I]f the miscarriage be not caused in good faith for the purpose of saving the life of the woman ...".

The counsel for the defence submitted that the accused being an obstetrician and gynaecologist himself should be taken as a proper person with authority to decide whether a miscarriage should be procured or otherwise in the circumstances of this case where the woman was suffering from bad or enlarged varicose veins. This proposition was supported by DW2, Prof Sinnathuray, whose specialized field is also in obstetrics and gynaecology. He is also the Dean of the Faculty of Medicine, University of Malaya. With due respect to his qualifications and high office, I find that his support and approval for the abortion performed by the accused was not supported by reasonable explanation and having observed his demeanour and from the circumstances of the matter, I find that he (DW2) is not free from a motivation to help a friend (the accused) out of trouble. I am of the opinion that no reasonable person whether a qualified surgeon or not would perform or procure abortion in the circumstances of this case without infringing the law as it stands. Procuring an abortion is a serious matter and it should only be done as a last resort to save the life of a woman or to save a woman from becoming a mental wreck. In this case, although it is argued that accused had performed the abortion on the woman in good faith in order to save her life or to save her from becoming a mental wreck, I find that the argument cannot hold water because from evidence adduced before me the accused had not given reasonable thought and had not taken enough steps to examine the woman further. His finding that the woman had enlarged or bad varicose veins is no other than the result of his mere clinical examination.

For reasons stated above, I come to the conclusion that the accused has failed to rebut or throw any reasonable doubt into the case for the prosecution and I therefore find the accused guilty of the charge ....

Sentence accordingly

(d) Penal Code, s 92

Nothing is an offence by reason of any harm which it may cause to a person for whose benefit it is done in good faith, even without that person's consent, if the circumstances are such that it is impossible for that person to signify consent, or if that person is incapable of giving consent, and has no guardian or other person in lawful charge of him from whom it is possible to obtain consent in time for the thing to be done with benefit:

Provided that this exception shall not extend to–

(a) the intentional causing of death, or the attempting to cause death;

(b) the doing of anything which the person doing it knows to be likely to cause death, for any purpose other than the preventing of death or grievous hurt, or the curing of any grievous disease or infirmity;

(c) the voluntary causing of hurt, or to the attempting to cause hurt, for any purpose other than the preventing of death or hurt;

(d) the abetment of any offence, to the committing of which offence it would not extend.

Illustrations

(a) Z is thrown from his horse, and is insensible. A, a surgeon, finds that Z requires to be trepanned. A, not intending Z's death, but in good faith, for Z's benefit, performs the trepan before Z recovers his power of judging for himself. A has committed no offence.

(b) Z is carried off by a tiger. A fires at the tiger, knowing it to be likely that the shot may kill Z, but not intending to kill Z, and in good faith intending Z's benefit. A's ball gives Z a mortal wound. A has committed no offence.

(c) A, a surgeon, sees a child suffer an accident which is likely to prove fatal unless an operation is immediately performed. There is not time to apply to the child's guardian. A performs the operation in spite of the entreaties of the child, intending, in good faith, the child's benefit. A has committed no offence.

(d) A is in a house which is on fire, with Z, a child. People below hold out a blanket. A drops the child from the house-top, knowing it to be likely that the fall may kill the child, but not intending to kill the child, and intending in good faith, the child's benefit. Here, even if the child is killed by the fall, A has committed no offence.

Explanation–Mere pecuniary benefit is not benefit within the meaning of sections 88, 89 and 92.

The circumstances in s 92 where consent can be dispensed with are those where it is impossible to obtain consent from the person or where there is no one at hand to give consent on his behalf. The same limitations pertain to s 89.

2.   Reality of consent

Penal Code, s 90

A consent is not such a consent as is intended by any section of this Code–
(a) if the consent is given by a person under fear of injury, or under a misconception of fact, and if the person doing the act knows, or has reason to believe, that the consent was given in consequence of such fear or misconception;
(b) if the consent is given by a person who, from unsoundness of mind or intoxication, is unable to understand the nature and consequence of that to which he gives his consent; or
(c) unless the contrary appears from the context, if the consent is given by a person who is under 12 years of age.

Consent must be distinguished from submission; consent involves a positive action of the mind in agreement whereas submission is a yielding to the will of others. No doubt, every consent involves a submission but the converse is not necessarily true (Koh, 1968). Section 90 lays down the circumstances where there is no reality of consent.

(a) "Misconception of fact"

A misconception of fact may arise from fraudulent or innocent misrepresentation. Obvious examples where a misconception of fact will vitiate consent is where there is fraud as to the nature of the act (*Flattery*, 1877, see below, p150), or as to the identity of the person who does an act (eg a man has sexual intercourse with a woman in the dark representing to her that he is her husband when he is not). Another example where consent is vitiated by a misconception of fact is seen in *Poonai Fattemah* (1869), where the accused persons, who were snake charmers, induced the deceased persons to allow themselves to be bitten by a poisonous snake, inducing them to believe that they had the power to protect them from harm. The accused knew that consent was given in consequence of the misconception that they had such power. It was held that the consent was vitiated by the misconception and the accused persons were liable for the death of the deceased.

However, not all misconceptions of fact will vitiate consent. Suppose a man who is suffering from venereal disease or AIDS conceals this fact from his sexual partner, would her consent to the sexual intercourse be vitiated? Let it be supposed that she would not have consented had she known about it. In the English case of *Clarence* (1882) it was held, obiter, that consent was *not* vitiated by the fraud of a husband who had connection with his wife, he concealing the fact from her that he was suffering from gonorrhoea. On the question of the extent to which fraud vitiates consent in the context of criminal law, Stephen J said:

> It seems to me that the proposition that fraud vitiates consent in criminal matters is not true if taken to apply in the fullest sense of the words, and without qualification. It is too short to be true, as a mathematical formula is true. If we apply it in that sense to the present case, it is difficult to say that the prisoner was not guilty of rape, for the definition of rape is having connection with a woman without her consent; and if fraud vitiates consent, every case in which a man infects a woman or commits bigamy, the second wife being ignorant of the first marriage, is also a case of rape. Many seductions would be rapes, and so might acts of prostitution procured by fraud, as for instance by promises not intended to be fulfilled. These illustrations appear to shew clearly that the maxim that fraud vitiates consent is too general to be applied to these matters as if it were absolutely true ... the only sorts of fraud which so far destroy the effect of a woman's consent as to convert a connection consented to in fact into a rape are frauds as to the nature of the act itself, or as to the identity of the person who does the act.

[Is the position the same under s 90? See also Wills J, ibid.]

Ngwa Shwe Kin v Emperor (1915) 30 IC 133, (Lower Burma Chief Court, Burma)

Mr Justice Twomey: The deceased Pan Zan, a middle-aged man, was a believer in charms and apparently believed that he had rendered himself *da*-proof. In the course of an ordinary conversation he said to the appellant, Shwe Kin, "I am *da*-proof. I am not afraid of *da* or stick" and he told Shwe Kin to "test and see". Uttering the words of some charm he put out his right arm and Shwe Kin cut the arm with his *da*. It then appeared that Pan Zan was not invulnerable after all. Pan Zan did not reproach the appellant with having given too vigorous a cut, but only said "I made a mistake. I ought to have taken my coat, then the [da] could not have cut my arm." Unfortunately arteries were cut and Pan Zan's companions being ignorant of the proper method of checking arterial bleeding, he bled to death....

The case is governed by sections 87 and 90, Indian Penal Code. The deceased gave his consent under a misconception of fact, erroneously believing that he was proof against *da* cuts. But it cannot be said that the appellant knew of this misconception or had reason to believe that the deceased was mistaken in thinking himself invulnerable. He is a youth of 19 and the probability is that he really believed in the pretence of the deceased, a much elder man than himself.... The appellant certainly had no intention of causing death or grievous hurt, and I think it is highly doubtful whether he can properly be said to have known that his act was likely to cause any such result. In the *first* place, he did not use great force, *secondly*, he had Pan Zan's assurance that he was invulnerable and the appellant was too ignorant to see the absurdity of it, *lastly*, he inflicted the cut on the part of the body specially presented for the purpose by the deceased and this, moreover, was a part not ordinarily regarded as a vital part.

Conviction set aside

R v Flattery (1877) 13 Cox CC 388 (CCA, England)

The prosecutrix, who was 19 years of age, together with her mother went to see the "prisoner" for medical advice to cure her fits. Having examined the prosecutrix he told her mother that it was "nature's string wanted breaking", and asked if he might break it. The mother replied that she did not know what he meant, but that she did not mind, if it would do her daughter any good. At that moment the prosecutrix had a fit and fainted. When the prosecutrix recovered from her fainting, he repeated what he had said in the prosecutrix's hearing.

The prosecutrix then went with the "prisoner" to an adjoining room and there had sexual connection with her, she making feeble resistance, believing that he was treating her medically, and performing a surgical operation.

Kelly, CB: I am of opinion that the conviction should be affirmed. The prosecutrix, by the fraud and false representations of the prisoner, was induced and persuaded to allow him to touch and approach her person. There was not only no evidence of consent on the part of the prosecutrix, but the case states that she submitted to his treatment solely because she believed that he was treating her medically and performing a surgical operation, as he had advised, to cure her of her illness, and that, unless such submission in law constitutes consent, there was no consent to the prisoner having connection with the prosecutrix. We are now asked to say, because the prosecutrix was nineteen years of age, that she knew what was going on and consented to a violation of her person. It would be straining the language of the case to hold that there was any consent to what took place under the circumstances. It was contended that it lay on the part of the prosecution to show that the woman did not know what the nature of sexual connection was. I know of no principle of law on which that contention rests, and I am not prepared to say that, if she did know the nature of sexual intercourse it would have been any evidence of consent. But here it is consistent with her evidence that the prosecutrix may have been under the impression that the prisoner was performing the operation by some instrument or with his fingers. I lament that it has ever been decided, to be the law of England that where a man obtains possession of a woman's person by fraud that it does not amount to rape. In this case, however, there is no evidence to show that the prosecutrix knew that the prisoner was about to violate her person, on the contrary, it appears that she submitted to what was done under the belief that the prisoner was performing a surgical operation to cure her of her illness. I am clearly of opinion that the prisoner was guilty of the crime of rape and that the conviction should be affirmed.

Conviction affirmed

(b) "Unsoundness of mind"

KL Koh and Myint Soe, *The Penal Codes of Singapore and States of Malaya* (1976, Vol I) 74

Generally, a person suffering from unsoundness of mind cannot give consent except through his guardian or other person having lawful charge of him....

What is the position if, at lucid intervals, the guardian or person having lawful charge of him exercises consent? Section 90(b) provides, *inter alia*, that consent is not such a consent if given by a person who, from unsoundness of mind, is *unable to understand the nature and consequence* of that to which he gives his consent. It would seem that such a person could still consent if he understands the nature and consequence of the act, as when consent is given during lucid intervals. On the other hand, s 89 empowers a guardian or a person having lawful charge of the person to consent on his behalf. It is submitted that there is nothing in s 90(b) to delimit this power of the guardian or the person having lawful charge of him.

(c) Consent of child between 12 and 18 years of age

Can a child between 12 and 18 years of age consent?

KL Koh "Doctrine of consent in criminal law" (1967) 9 Mal LR 188, 200–201

The combined effect of ss 90 and 89, would seem to render a surgeon open to a criminal prosecution should he operate on a child under twelve without the guardian's consent even though the consent of the child is given.

The difficulty however arises in the case of a child above the age of twelve but below the age of eighteen. For under s 87, a person must be over the age of eighteen before he can consent to the infliction upon himself of injury not amounting to grievous hurt. This seems to render the position of a person between twelve to eighteen uncertain. If a boy of seventeen wishes to have an operation to improve his voice would the surgeon be liable? Where the operation is for the "benefit" of the person, the position would be covered by s 88 which does not mention anything about the age of consent. The real problem arises in an operation which is not performed for the benefit of the person.

Under s 87, ... the position remains uncertain. However, it is submitted that the maxim *exclusio unius alterius est* need not be applied. Thus, even though the operation were not for the benefit of the infant, so as to bring it within the exception of s 88, nevertheless, it does not follow that consent to say, simple hurt cannot be given, by a person under eighteen merely because s 87 is so limited in its application.

Chapter 7

Necessity

By CMV Clarkson

A. Introduction

Penal Code, s 81

Nothing is an offence merely by reason of its being done with the knowledge that it is likely to cause harm, if it be done without any criminal intention to cause harm, and in good faith for the purpose of preventing or avoiding other harm to person or property.

Explanation–It is a question of fact in such a case whether the harm to be prevented or avoided was of such a nature and so imminent as to justify or excuse the risk of doing the act with the knowledge that it was likely to cause harm.

Illustrations

(a) A, the captain of a steam vessel, suddenly and without any fault or negligence on his part, finds himself in such a position that, before he can stop his vessel, he must inevitably run down a boat B, with 20 or 30 passengers on board, unless he changes the course of his vessel, and that, by changing his course he must incur risk of running down a boat C, with only two passengers on board, which he may possibly clear. Here, if A alters his course without any intention to run down the boat C, and in good faith for the purposes of avoiding the danger to the passengers in the boat B, he is not guilty of an offence, though he may run down the boat C, by doing an act which he knew was likely to cause that effect, if it be found as a matter of fact that the danger which he intended to avoid was such as to excuse him in incurring the risk of running down the boat C.

(b) A in a great fire pulls down houses in order to prevent the conflagration from spreading. He does this with the intention, in good faith, of saving human life or property. Here, if it be found that the harm to be prevented was of such a nature and so imminent as to excuse A's act, A is not guilty of the offence.

The defence of necessity arises when an accused deliberately breaks the law but claims that it was necessary for him to do so in order to avert some greater evil. The defence and its scope is well illustrated by the following two cases. As the first is an English and the second a Pennsylvania decision, neither legal system having a counterpart to s 81, the decisions will be dealt with cursorily. What is important is how these two cases would be resolved in Singapore and Malaysia using s 81.

R v Dudley and Stephens (1884) 14 QBD 273 (Queens Bench Division, England)

The two accused, with a third man and a 17-year-old boy, were cast away on the high seas in an open boat, 1,600 miles from land. They drifted in the boat for 20 days. When they had been eight days without food and six days without water, and fearing they would all soon die without some sustenance, the defendants killed the boy who was likely to die first. The men ate his flesh and drank his blood for four days. They were then rescued by a passing vessel and were subsequently charged with murder. After referring the case to the Queen's Bench Division for its decision the accused were convicted of murder and sentenced to death, a sentence which was later commuted to six months' imprisonment. The ratio of this decision is controversial. One commonly accepted interpretation is that it is based on a denial of the existence of the defence of necessity in English law.

US v Holmes 26 Fed Cas 360 (1842) (Circuit Court, Eastern District, Pennsylvania, USA)

The accused along with eight other seamen and 32 passengers were in an overcrowded lifeboat. Fearing that the boat would sink he threw 16 passengers overboard. The crew were directed "not to part man and wife, and not to throw over any women. There was no other principle of selection." The next morning the survivors in the boat were all rescued.

Baldwin CJ (directing jury): [M]an, in taking away the life of a fellow being, assumes an awful responsibility to God, and to society; and that the administrators of public justice do themselves assume that responsibility if, when called on to pass judicially upon the act, they yield to the indulgence of misapplied humanity. It is one thing to give a favourable interpretation to evidence in order to mitigate an offence. It is a different thing, when we are asked, not to extenuate, but to justify, the act.... [T]he case does not become "a case of necessity", unless all ordinary means of self-preservation have been exhausted. The peril must be instant, over-whelming, leaving no alternative but to lose our own life, or to take the life of another person....

[He then held that the seamen should have been sacrificed first as they were not in an equal position with the passengers as "the sailor is bound ... to undergo whatever hazard is necessary to preserve the boat and the passengers". As between equals the decision as to who should be sacrificed should be made by drawing lots].

When the solution has been made by lots, the victim yields of course to his fate, or, if he resists, force may be employed to coerce submission. Whether or not "a case of necessity" has arisen, or whether the law under which death has been inflicted have been so exercised as to hold the executioner harmless, cannot depend on his own opinion; for no man may pass upon his own conduct when it concerns the rights and especially, when it affects the lives, of others.... [H]omicide is sometimes justifiable; and the law defines the occasions in which it is so. The transaction must, therefore, be justified to the law....

[The jury returned a verdict of guilty. The accused who had already been confined in jail for several months was sentenced to six months' imprisonment with hard labour and fined $20. The penalty was subsequently remitted.]

There is only one local case in which the defence of necessity has been raised:

PP v Ali b Umar [1982] 2 MLJ 51 (HC, Johore, Malaysia).

The respondents had been charged under s 49(1) of the Customs Act 1967 for carrying tin-ore in a local craft without the permission of the Director-General of Customs. They claimed as a defence that their boat, which was destined elsewhere, had a broken rudder forcing them in distress to enter Malaysian waters. The magistrate accepted this evidence and held that as the boat was in transit the offence had not been committed. The Public Prosecutor appealed.

Yusoff Mohamed J: ... In his judgment, the learned Magistrate accepted the evidence of the respondents that the rudder of the boat was broken while the boat was in International waters and that the boat drifted into Malaysian waters, but he held that in those circumstances, the boat was in transit and therefore the offence under s 49(1) was not committed. There was no argument before him whether the boat was in fact on transit. The defence of necessity raised by the respondents was not considered though the Magistrate acquitted and discharged all the respondents in consequence....

Most interesting is the case of *Germaine Larsonneur* (1933) also raised by the learned Senior Federal Counsel in support of his contention that *mens rea* is not relevant in cases of strict liability. In that case the facts are:

> "A French subject was permitted to land in the United Kingdom subject to certain conditions endorsed on her passport. These conditions were subsequently varied by a condition requiring her to depart from the United Kingdom not later than a certain date. On that date she went to the Irish Free State. An order for her deportation from the Irish Free State was made by the executive authorities of that country, and *she was subsequently brought back to Holyhead in the custody of the Irish Free State police, who there handed her over to the police of the United Kingdom*, by whom she was detained. She was convicted on a charge that she 'being an alien to whom leave to land in the United Kingdom has been refused was found in the United Kingdom', contrary to arts 1(3)(g) and 18(1)(b) of the Aliens Order 1920, as amended (a) ...." (my italics).

It was held there that the circumstances in which she (Larsonneur) returned to the United Kingdom being immaterial, although she had done no voluntary act but was brought into the United Kingdom in the custody of the police.

Larsonneur's case (1933) was decided on the peculiarity of the statute under which she was charged and some writers were confident that such an unjust result could hardly arise under any of other statutes.

[His Lordship then discussed whether the offence before him involved any mental element.]

The defence of necessity on the other hand, is very controversial in nature and there are conflicting views on its applicability. The decision in *Larsonneur*'s case (1933) is against the raising of necessity as a general defence. It was generally thought that the law ought not to afford a defence in such a case.

However, in certain circumstances, where a person is able to choose between two courses, one of which involves breaking the criminal law and the other some evil to himself or others of such magnitude that it may be thought to justify the infraction of the criminal law, the court would temper such situation with justice.

Instances of these are:

In a storm at sea, the cargo may be jettisoned for the safety of passengers.–See *Mouse*'s case (1608). There is a right to land on the shore (even where it would otherwise be a trespass) in cases of peril or necessity. –See *Halsbury*'s Laws of England, 3rd edition xxxix 564. Specifically the defence of necessity can be recognized during emergency, so specific in character that the acceptance of the defence does not imperil the general rule,–See Glanville Williams (1978). In an American case, the master of a ship was held not guilty of violating an embargo act by illegal entry into a Port when, as the result of storms, this course was "necessary" for the preservation of the vessel and the cargo and lives of those on board.–See *William Gray.*

In the present case, I am of the view that out of necessity it justified the respondents to enter the Malaysian waters on specific reasons that the boat in which they were travelling was in distress due to the fact that the rudder of the boat was broken in International waters. In those circumstances it would be necessary for the respondents to seek shelter for the safety of the boat and to preserve the lives of the crew during such distress. In that situation it would be far fetched to imagine that the respondents would have to obtain permission of the Director-General under s 49(1) and (2) of the Customs Act for carrying the tin-ores which were not destined nor intended for export from Malaysia....

[His Lordship then concluded that the same result would be reached on the ground of lack of requisite mental element.]

In this event, the appeal is dismissed and for different reasons, the Magistrate's order in respect of the boat and the goods is confirmed.

Appeal dismissed

It should be noted that it is in fact a moot point whether this case did actually raise a defence of necessity at all. The magistrate found that the boat *drifted* into Malaysian waters. If the accused had no control over the boat and could not have prevented it entering Malaysian waters then his actions were "involuntary" and his only defence would have to have been based on such grounds. The English case of *Larsonneur* (1933) was similarly not a case involving necessity–the defence was not and could not have been raised. The defence of necessity only applies to those who have *chosen* to break the law to avert some greater evil. Miss Larsonneur certainly never made such a choice.

However, it is possible to read *Ali b Umar* (1982) as a case involving necessity if one accepts Yusoff Mohamed J's interpretation of the facts that the accused *sought* shelter for the safety of the boat and to preserve the lives of the crew during such distress. On this interpretation they *chose* to enter Malaysian waters. The remainder of this chapter will proceed on the assumption that this latter view is correct and that the case does indeed raise the issue of necessity.

B. Rationale

The rationale of the general defence of necessity is similar to that of the defence of duress (see below, p 199). In moral terms we cannot blame the accused in *Ali b Umar* (1982) for entering Malaysian waters in order to save the lives of the crew. Any reasonable person would have done the same; the moral condemnation of the criminal law is thus clearly inappropriate. Further, there are no utilitarian reasons for imposing criminal liability in such cases. If the lives of the crew were at stake it can hardly be supposed that the accused in *Ali b Umar* (1982) would have been deterred from entering Malaysian waters by the knowledge that they were committing an offence under s 49(1) of the Customs Act 1967. Similarly, such persons acting in an exemplary manner in the best interests of their crew are clearly not in need of incapacitation or rehabilitation. In short, criminal liability would be unfair and pointless; the defence of necessity prevents such injustice.

Similar arguments may be adduced in relation to the accused in the two shipwreck cases above. Faced with impending death most persons would have acted in a similar manner. Only heroes or martyrs would lie back and stoically allow themselves to die. Laws, and particularly the criminal law, are made to regulate the affairs of ordinary people–not gods. Accordingly, a defence of necessity must be used to avoid the imposition of criminal liability.

Such thinking, particularly in the USA, has led to the view that since the greater evil has been averted the accused's conduct is *justified* in much the same way as private defence justifies otherwise criminal conduct. There is, however, a critical difference between the two defences. With private defence there is an aggressor–someone who by his original attack has forfeited his right to the protection of the criminal law. With necessity there is no blameworthy aggressor–only an innocent victim. If the boy in *Dudley and Stevens* (1884) had attacked the accused and tried to kill them we would have little difficulty in justifying their killing him in private defence. However, the boy did no such thing. He was an innocent who was killed and eaten not because of any wrongdoing on his part but simply because he was the weakest. Accordingly, it has been argued (Clarkson and Keating, 1984) that it would be better to view necessity as an *excuse*; the accused have done wrong–but because of their appalling plight we can excuse them from criminal liability.

C. The law

The parameters of necessity as a general defence are exceedingly ill-defined. Section 81 is highly ambiguous in its terms and the paucity of cases from other jurisdictions *in pari materia* with Singapore and Malaysia has not assisted in resolving the various interpretive problems.

An analysis of s 81 raises the following issues:

1. Necessity is a defence to all crimes

Necessity is a defence to any crime, including murder. This is provided for by s 81 which states that "*nothing* is an offence" if committed under circumstances of necessity. (This is in contrast to the defence of duress which specifically excludes murder from its ambit.) However, before necessity could be successfully pleaded in such a case an accused would have to be faced by an extreme and immediate harm–and would need to establish that he did not act with "criminal intention" (see below, p 160).

2. Seriousness of threatened harm

Section 81 merely states that it is permissible to cause "harm" in order to avoid "other harm" to person or property. The Explanation and Illustrations to s 81 refer to the harm being avoided as having to be "of such a nature and so imminent" as to excuse the accused's acts. However, what does this mean? Suppose four mountaineers are roped together in a situation of peril; all will certainly slip to their death; however, if the first mountaineer cuts the rope he can be saved even though this will mean the other three fall to an instant death. This can be viewed in one of two ways: either that he has killed three persons to save the life of only one, or, alternatively, that rather than four die he has at least saved the life of one person. Would such an accused be entitled to exemption from criminal liability under s 81?

The most commonly adopted solution to the problem is the "balancing of evils" approach (Nigam, 1965). This means that one is permitted to commit a lesser evil in order to prevent a greater evil. For instance, the accused in *Ali b Umar* (1982) by committing the lesser evil of entering Malaysian waters without the requisite customs permission averted the greater threatened evil of the crew losing their lives. If this reasoning were employed it would follow that one would never be justified in killing in order to save property–as the taking of human life must always be regarded as a greater evil than the destruction of property.

The other main approach that can be employed is that advocated by the English Law Commission Working Paper (1974) that "the harm to be avoided must, judged objectively, be found to be out of all proportion to that actually caused by the defendant's conduct". Thus, again, the harm avoided in *Ali b Umar* (1982) was out of all proportion to the harm actually caused by entering Malaysian waters and, accordingly, a defence under s 81 would be available under this approach. However, the application of this principle to the facts of *Dudley and Stevens* (1884) is less certain. Was avoiding the death of three persons avoiding a harm that was out of all proportion to the death of the boy?

The "balancing of evils" approach finds some support in the illustrations to s 81. The first illustration permits the lives of two persons to be sacrificed to save the lives of "20 or 30 passengers". The second Illustration permits houses to be pulled down in order to save "human life or property". At least in relation to the saving of human life a lesser evil is being committed to avert a greater evil. However, in relation to "property" it appears that it can be permissible to destroy some property to save other property. While this can conceivably be interpreted as allowing one evil to be committed to avert another "equal" evil, such a result is unlikely. The Penal Code has deliberately ensured flexibility by the Explanation to s 81 spelling out that it is a *question of fact* whether the threatened harm is sufficient to justify the commission of the crime. Being a question of fact means that no hard and fast rule can be laid down, but clearly where property is destroyed to save other property it is inevitable that the trier of fact would take into account factors such as the quality and value of the respective properties.

However, while most cases will be resolved in such a manner, the fact remains that in not expressly adopting the principle of proportionality in which human life is valued higher than property, the courts have been given enormous flexibility. In the following case it was even suggested (albeit obiter) that s 81 may permit the infliction of personal injuries (and perhaps even death) upon other persons in order to avert threatened harm to property.

Muhammad Sarwar v State PLD (1979) Lahore 711(2) (Lahore, Pakistan)

In order to prevent their houses from imminent danger of being washed away or getting submerged by flood water, the accused and others erected a *banna/bund* (a type of wall). The victims started trying to demolish the *banna/bund* whereupon the accused and others attacked the victims with bamboo sticks causing injuries to them.

RS Sidhwa J: But assuming, though not admitting, for a matter of argument, that the land on which the *banna/bund* was constructed by the accused party did not belong to them ... the question whether the accused party, in view of the heavy downpour, had the right of maintaining the *banna/bund* temporarily for protecting their houses and/or for passing over it to reach the street till the necessity continued, and repelling an attack launched by the complainant party to dismantle or demolish the same, requires legal consideration....

The immediate necessity for the accused party, therefore, to prevent their houses from imminent and pressing danger of being washed away or getting submerged by erecting a *banna*, which could also be used by them to pass over it so as to reach the street, could not be denied to them. Till such time that this imminent danger to their homes continued, the accused party had the right under s 81 of the Pakistan Penal Code in taking all such actions, which in normal circumstances would otherwise have been illegal, to prevent their houses being washed away or getting submerged due to accumulated rain water and for purpose of providing access to refuge, not only by building a temporary *banna/bund* in order to keep the excess water out and to provide a right of way to the street, but also in protecting and maintaining the same and preventing any third person from demolishing or destroying it. As the complainant party admittedly tried to demolish the *banna/bund* in question, the accused party had the right of inflicting harm to them in order to prevent them from doing so. This right extended to causing such harm as was reasonable in the circumstances.

3. Objectivity v subjectivity

At first sight the Explanation to s 81 seems to support an objective approach in that it makes it a *"question of fact* whether the harm to be prevented or avoided was of such a nature ..." to justify committing the crime.

However, such a view is not sustainable as s 81 itself expressly states that there is no liability if the accused acts "in good faith" for the purpose of averting other harm. "Good faith" is negatively defined in s 52:

> Nothing is said to be done or believed in good faith which is done or believed without due care and attention.

This means that a defence under s 81 will only be available if an accused acting with due care and attention concludes that it is necessary to act in a certain way. Such an approach is sensible. A defence of necessity could lead to horrendous results if one were permitted to injure innocent persons and property because one thought, on totally irrational grounds, that it was necessary so to act.

On this basis it follows that a defence of necessity will be available if the accused believes in good faith (ie with due care and attention) that:

(1) that there is a situation of necessity, ie that there is a threatened harm to person or property;
(2) that it is of such a nature as to justify his actions; and
(3) that it is so imminent as to justify his actions.

4. Criminal intention

The most difficult problem associated with the interpretation of s 81 is that of ascertaining the meaning of "criminal intention".

If "criminal intention" means an intention to cause a harm that is prohibited by the criminal law then the defence of necessity is in fact a very narrow one and only covers those accused persons who do not mean to cause harm but act in a certain way knowing that they are likely to cause harm. Gour (1982 Vol 1) places this interpretation upon the phrase:

> The section requires that the act done should be without "criminal intention", but the word "intention" is here evidently used in a somewhat narrower sense and as distinguished from "knowledge". Its primary meaning is the aim or resolution of the mind to produce an effect .... Its secondary meaning is the presumption which the law makes of such a resolution from action accompanied by knowledge of the consequence. The section only requires that "criminal intention" in the first sense shall be absent ....

This interpretation is borne out by the following Indian decision.

Paryaq v State of Allahabad (1967) 37 AWR 572 (Allahabad HC, India)

The accused dug a three-foot wide channel on a public road. They did this in order to prevent their fields being damaged by heavy rains and accumulated waters thereon. They were convicted under s 431 (mischief by injury to a public road) and applied for revision against the conviction.

Mahesh Chandra J: The contention of the learned counsel for the applicants is that no offence was committed because the applicants had no alternative but to create a breach on the road in view of the fact that water had accumulated in their fields. For this contention he relied on s 81 of the Indian Penal Code....

It will be evident from the wordings of the section that it applies only to those acts which are offences merely by reason of their being done with the knowledge that they are likely to cause harm. The offence with which the applicants were charged is not an act of this nature being an offence covered by s 431, IPC....

It is contended by the learned counsel for the applicants that in the present case there was no intention to cause harm. This contention is without force. If a man knows that a certain consequence will follow from his act it must be presumed in law that he intended that consequence to take place although he may have had some quite different ulterior motive for performing the act (vide *Mir Chitten* (1936). That was a case in which this court held that the person had a right to kill the cow, but if he wanted to kill it in a public place he should have done it in a manner so as not to injure the feelings of others. Applying this principle that a man intends the consequence to take place when he knows that a certain consequence will follow from his act, this court upheld the conviction although this court held that the person had a legal right to kill the cow. Under no circumstances can a person be justified in intentionally causing harm. The justification is only in a case where he has merely the knowledge that his act is likely to injure others or cause harm. The difference is between the knowledge that it is a mere likelihood and the knowledge that the consequence must necessarily follow.

In the present case when the applicants dug the road there was no question of there being a mere likelihood of causing damage to the public property. The road which was public property was being damaged by the act itself. It was, therefore, an act done with that intent in law and not merely with the knowledge that it would cause harm. Section 81 IPC cannot, therefore, help the applicants in the present case.

They had, therefore, clearly committed an offence under s 431 IPC by cutting the public road and making it impossible or at any rate less safe for travelling or conveying property. The conviction cannot, therefore, be said to be unjustified.

In view of the fact, however, that the fields of the applicants were also likely to be damaged by heavy rains and the accumulation of water I consider it proper to reduce the sentence of imprisonment to the period already undergone.

Revision dismissed

This is an exceedingly narrow and literal approach which if followed would mean that the defence of necessity would not be available in any of the cases so far discussed. The accused in *Muhammed Sarwar* (1979) *intended* to attack the men trying to pull down their *banna/bund*. The accused in *Ali b Umar* (1982) intended to seek protection within Malaysian waters. In short, under this view, s 81 will only apply to an accused, like the one in Illustration (a), who merely takes a risk of causing harm to others. Such an interpretation of course makes it more understandable why necessity is a broader defence than duress under the Penal Code in that it applies to murder (or, at least those murders that have been committed without intention).

Under this approach the defence would be so narrow as to be virtually useless. The classic situations of necessity are those where the accused chooses (ie *intends*) to cause a harm in order to avert some impending disaster. Under the narrow interpretation s 81 simply cannot apply to such cases. The necessity under which the accused acted can at most be taken into consideration as a mitigating factor in sentencing as was done in *Paryaq* (1967).

Fortunately, however, one is not bound to accept this literal interpretation of s 81 which would render the word "criminal" in "criminal intention" otiose. Illustration (b) to s 81 permits the defence of necessity to be available to an accused who "pulls down houses in order to prevent the conflagration from spreading". One does not "pull down houses" merely knowing that they are likely to come down. The process of "pulling down" necessarily involves an *intention* to pull down. Yet Illustration (b) makes it plain that there is no criminal liability in such cases. So what does "*criminal* intention" mean?

Ratanlal and Dhirajlal (1987, Vol 1) state that "'criminal intention' simply means the purpose or design of doing an act forbidden by the criminal law *without just cause or excuse*" (emphasis added). Koh and Myint Soe (1974) are to similar effect when they state in relation to Illustration (b) that "the intention is not criminal because it was done in good faith for the purpose of saving human life or property, and the harm to be prevented was of such a nature and was so imminent as to excuse it". Following this view, the word "criminal" adds nothing. If an accused can satisfy the court that he is acting within the scope of the defence of necessity as defined by s 81 then he is not acting with *criminal* intention.

Perhaps the best view and one that does give effect to the phrase "criminal intention" (although a view unsupported by authority) is that the phrase refers to *motive*. A motive is a reason for acting. It is an emotion or desire that causes one to form a particular intention. Illustration (b) describes a person pulling down houses to prevent fire spreading. He does this "with the *intention, in good faith, of saving human life or property*". Here, in reality, the accused has the motive of saving life or property. This motive inspired him to act. In acting it was his intention to pull down the houses (he did not merely foresee that they might fall down). He also had a further intention of halting the spread of the fire. However, all this was initiated by his original motive. Such a person acts with intention but because he is acting with a motive specifically provided for in s 81, he is not acting with a "criminal intention" and is accordingly exempted from liability.

If, however, his motive in pulling down the houses is not to save life or property, but rather to obtain vengeance upon his enemy, he is not acting with the appropriate motive specified in Illustration (b); he is thus acting with a "criminal intention". The fact that there was indeed a serious and imminent risk to human life or property is irrelevant. He has a blameworthy state of mind. The whole point of justifications and excuses is that they exempt from liability those who are not blameworthy even though they might have caused a harm. Accordingly, the blameworthy must not be allowed to shelter behind the protection of s 81.

Chapter 8

Superior orders

By CMV Clarkson

A. Introduction

What is the position if a soldier (or policeman) is ordered by his superior to commit certain actions that may amount to a crime? For instance, in *US* v *Calley* (1973) Lieutenant Calley alleged that he was ordered by his commanding officer to kill all persons (including women, children and old men) in Vietnamese villages as the US Forces were sweeping out the enemy in part of Vietnam. Calley and others killed 22 such persons.

The central dilemma here is how to balance two competing interests. On the one hand, there is the view that the army (and the police) depend on discipline and instant obedience to orders for their efficient operation. Lives could be lost or the security of the state threatened if soldiers were free to ignore orders while they debated the legality of such commands and whether to comply with them. In the interests of maintaining discipline such soldiers should be protected from criminal liability when they are simply obeying orders. Additionally, it can be argued that persons such as Lieutenant Calley are in an analogous position to those who commit crimes subject to duress. If they do not obey they will be subjected to military punishment–and in actual war situations, such as those in *US* v *Calley* (1973), disobedience could result in instant death. Accordingly, all the same arguments used in support of the defence of duress can be advanced here to support the view that soldiers in such situations are fully justified in their actions and deserve to be exempted from criminal liability.

On the other hand, there is a powerful argument that those responsible for the murder of innocent persons, such as in *US* v *Calley* (1973), should not be able to shield themselves behind the protection of a defence of superior orders. This view was dramatically stated by Lord Simon in the English case of *Abbott* (1976):

> In the trials of those responsible for war time atrocities such as mass killings of men, women and children, inhuman experiments on human beings, often resulting in death, and like crimes, it was invariably argued for the defence that these atrocities should be excused on the ground that they resulted from superior orders and duress: if the accused had refused to do these dreadful things, they would have been shot and therefore they should be acquitted and allowed to go free. This argument has always been rejected. Their Lordships would be sorry indeed to see it accepted....

164

If a defence of superior orders were to be admitted horrendous atrocities could be committed on millions of innocent persons with the perpetrators all the way up the military hierarchy claiming they were simply acting under orders. In the hope of emphasizing that such conduct is utterly wrong and that there is no escaping liability in such cases the defence of superior orders should not be admitted into the criminal law.

B. The law

Generally, most jurisdictions have adopted a compromise between these two extreme positions and allowed a defence of superior orders provided the orders were not manifestly illegal (*Keighley* v *Bell*, 1876). Those who committed the awful atrocities exposed in the Nuremberg trials were obeying manifestly illegal orders–any person of "ordinary sense and understanding" (*US* v *Calley*, 1973) would have recognized them as such. Accordingly, no defence based upon superior orders could be available in such cases.

What is the position in Singapore and Malaysia? Would the same results be reached here as in most other common law countries?

Because of the structure of the Penal Code it is necessary to distinguish between the following somewhat different situations. First, the order of the superior officer might be lawful or unlawful. Second, if unlawful, the inferior might have committed the harm either because he mistakenly believed the order was lawful or, alternatively, he might have been well aware of the illegality of the order but obeyed it out of fear of the consequences should he disobey. These different situations are covered by two provisions in the Penal Code, the duress exception of s 94 and the following directly relevant provision.

Penal Code, s 76

Nothing is an offence which is done by a person who is, or who, by reason of a mistake of fact and not by reason of a mistake of law, in good faith believes himself to be bound by law to do it.

Illustrations
(a) A, a soldier, fires on a mob by the order of his superior officer, in conformity with the commands of the law. A has committed no offence.
(b) A, an officer of a court of justice, being ordered by that court to arrest Y, and, after due enquiry, believing Z to be Y, arrests Z. A has committed no offence.

1. Lawful orders

If the order by the superior is in fact justified and lawful, those obeying such orders are fully protected even if charged with murder.

State of West Bengal v Shew Mangal Singh (1981) 4 SCC (Cri) 782
(SC, India)

During a civil disturbance attacks were made upon a police party. The
Deputy Commissioner of Police thereupon ordered the accused, members of the police group, to open fire. In obeying these orders two persons
were killed. At their trial the accused persons were convicted under
s 302 read with s 34 of the Penal Code. On appeal they were acquitted
by the High Court on the ground that the Deputy Commissioner's orders
were justified and the accused were bound to obey the lawful orders of
their superior officer. The State of West Bengal filed a petition for
leave to appeal against the judgment of the High Court.

Chandrachud CJ: A very interesting and important question was raised in the
High Court as to whether the command of a superior officer to open fire affords a complete defence to a subordinate officer if, while acting in the execution of that command he causes injury or death....

It is unnecessary for us to go into that question for the simple reason that
we are of the view that the High Court was justified in coming to the conclusion that the particular situation warranted and justified the order issued by the
Deputy Commissioner of Police to open fire. If that order was justified and is
therefore lawful, no further question can arise as to whether the respondents,
who acted in obedience to that order, believed or did not believe that order to
be lawful. Such an enquiry becomes necessary only when the order of the
superior officer, which is pleaded as a defence, is found not to be in conformity with the commands of the law....

The occasion to apply the provisions of s 76 does not arise in the instant
case since the question as to whether the accused believed in good faith on
account of a mistake of fact that he was bound by law to do the act which is
alleged to constitute an offence, would arise only if, to the extent relevant in
this case, the order or command of the superior officer is not justified or is
otherwise unlawful. Since the situation prevailing at the scene of the offence
was such as to justify the order given by the Deputy Commissioner of Police
to open fire, the respondents can seek the protection of that order and plead in
defence that they acted in obedience to that order and therefore they cannot be
held guilty of the offence of which they are charged. That is the purport of the
Illustration to s 76....

Special leave petition dismissed

2. Unlawful orders

A more difficult situation arises when the orders of the superior officer
are not in fact lawful. In such cases it is necessary to draw a further
distinction.

(a) Mistake

The accused might have obeyed an order not realizing that it was illegal.

An absurdly narrow interpretation of s 76 was adopted in *Nunn* (1935)
where a policeman exceeded the limits of the instructions given by his

superior officer when he killed a man whom he shot out of a coconut tree in order to effect an arrest. The defence argued that as he had a mistaken belief that his actions were lawful he should be excused liability by virtue of s 76. The court, however, rejected this contention and adopted the extraordinary stance that Illustration (a) refers only to the first branch of s 76, namely, that "nothing is an offence which is done by a person who is bound by law to do it". This means that obedience to an order is only justified if the order is lawful. According to this view, Illustration (a) has no application to cases such as the present one where there is a mistake of fact. The court held that s 76 contains two distinct propositions:

(1)   "nothing is an offence which is done by a person who is ... bound by law to do it"; and
(2)   "nothing is an offence which is done by a person who, by reason of a mistake of fact and not by reason of a mistake of law believes himself to be, bound by law to do it".

Illustration (a) illustrates the first proposition *only*. Illustration (b) illustrates the second one only.

This distinction, which, it is submitted, is not in accordance with the natural meaning of s 76 and its illustrations, has found no support in the Indian texts and can perhaps be safely disregarded with the following cases being more authoritative.

R v SAH Alsagoff [1946] 2 MC 191 (Assizes, Singapore)

The accused persons were working as police officers during the Japanese occupation of Singapore.

They were charged with acts of causing hurt for the purpose of extorting a confession contrary to s 330 of the Penal Code. In their defence they claimed, inter alia, that they were under a duty to obey orders given to them by the Japanese authorities.

Worley J: In my view there is no rule of International Law or rule of war which imposes on a local inhabitant the duty of obeying orders which are contrary to the criminal law of the territory at the time the acts are committed and if he does commit such acts he does so at the risk of being held accountable for those acts as soon as the Courts of the rightful Sovereign are re-established and, then, it is only if he can show that he comes within the scope of s 94 of the Penal Code that he can escape the ordinary consequences of a criminal act....

I think it only remains for me to refer to Alsagoff's belief that his Japanese superiors were within their legal rights in ordering him to beat Hay and what, I think, might be fairly stated as the consequent belief of the other two accused that Alsagoff was within his rights in ordering them to beat Hay. It is true that an honest and reasonable belief in the existence of circumstance of fact, which, if true, would make the act complained of an innocent one, would be a good defence, but, as I see it, the question whether the superiors of these accused were lawfully empowered to order beatings is not a question of fact but a question of law and it is a legal principle that a mistake of law is no defence.

Everybody is presumed to know the law. The 2nd and 3rd accused were in Straits Settlements Police before the fall of Singapore and continued to serve under the Japanese. The 1st accused joined the Police Force at the request of the Japanese and it seems to me that they put themselves in much the same position as a soldier who is under discipline and required to carry out the orders of a superior officer. The soldier's position is this: the Penal Code does not recognize the mere duty of blind obedience to the commands of a superior as sufficient to protect a soldier from the penal consequences of his act. Difficult as the position may appear to be, the law requires that the soldier should exercise his own judgment, and unless the actual circumstances are of such a character that he may have reasonably entertained the belief that the order was one which he was bound to obey, he will be responsible like any other sane person for his act, although he may have committed it under the erroneous supposition that his superior was by law authorized to issue the order. His mistake in short must be a mistake entertained in good faith on a question of fact. Such a construction of the law may indeed subject the soldier to military penalties and, in certain cases, place him in the serious dilemma of either refusing to obey an order which he believed to be unjustifiable in fact, thereby rendering himself liable to military law, or, by obeying it, subjecting himself to the general criminal law of the land. That is very much the position the accused say they were in. They allege that if they did not obey these orders they themselves would have been punished. That, as I see it, was their responsibility as it is the responsibility of the soldier. A mistake of law in either case would afford no protection, though it might go in mitigation of punishment, and thus military discipline, while it regulates the conduct of the soldier in military matters, is made subject to a higher law in favour of public safety, when the act which the military discipline attempts to enforce or to justify is one which affects the person or property of another. In such a case the civil law looks to the surrounding circumstances to see whether they are of such a character as would lead a man of ordinary intelligence to entertain a reasonable belief that he is bound by law to obey the commands of his superior. The principle generally appears to me to apply equally to the position of the accused in this case.

I do not think it is relevant to consider whether the accused could or could not have resigned. There is evidence that others have resigned. It does not appear to me to affect their legal position because the soldier is in a position where he cannot resign when he receives orders as to the legality of which he is doubtful but that does not excuse him from exercising his judgment as to the legality of the orders. The only point is, as stated in the extract I read to you, the difficult position of the soldier might well go to mitigate that punishment and it is open to you, should your verdict be one of guilty and should you think that the accused were in a position of difficulty or in an awkward dilemma when they had to choose between carrying out unlawful orders and running the risk of incurring punishment themselves, to make a recommendation for mercy.

Shew Mangal Singh v State of Calcutta (1981) Cri LJ 84 (HC, Calcutta, India)

(The facts of this case are cited above.)

PC Borooah J: It was urged on behalf of the appellants that they were members of a police party acting under the orders of the DC North ... (and that) the firing order not being manifestly illegal, none of the members of the police party can be deemed to have committed any offence under the Penal Code.... [Counsel for the State] has contended that the appellants are not entitled to any protection even if they had acted under the orders of their superior officer, as the firing ... is manifestly illegal....

The defence of acting under superior orders has an important bearing on the morale and discipline of the police force, which undoubtedly plays a vital role in the maintenance of law and order in any State. Like the armed forces the police force is a disciplined force; if the discipline goes, the force disintegrates. Acting in strict accordance with the order of a superior is a part of discipline. If an order to fire is given and there are casualties, can the policeman who opened fire be prosecuted for a criminal offence? If the order is not necessarily and on the face of it illegal, such as, an order to shoot an innocent passerby or to torture a person, the policeman carrying out the order is certainly entitled to protection under the law. Political considerations should have no bearing whatsoever....

In Glanville Williams' *Textbook of Criminal Law* (1978) the following passage appears:

> "The authorities are sparse and in conflict. In the old case of *Thomas* (1816) a naval sentinel who, being ordered to keep off all boats, fired at a boat and killed a man in it, was convicted of murder, notwithstanding that the jury found that he fired under a mistaken impression that it was his duty. A contrary view was taken by the Supreme Court of the Cape of Good Hope in *Smith* (1900), which is widely approved by commentators. The facts were that, during the South African War, a soldier was ordered by his officer to shoot a Boer civilian if he did not fetch a bridle, and obeyed the command by killing the Boer. He was acquitted of murder although the command was unlawful. Soleman J said: If a soldier honestly believes he is doing his duty in obeying the commands of his superior, and if the orders are not manifestly illegal that he must or ought to have known that they are unlawful, the private soldier would be protected by the orders of his superior officer."...

As regards the Australian law on this aspect there is a text book by Colin Howard on *Criminal Law* and in p 424 of the third Edition under the caption "Superior Orders" the following comments appear:

> "The rule is stated in the Queensland and Western Australian Codes, s 31 (2), that a person is not criminally responsible for an act or omission, if he does or omits to do the act... (in) obedience to the order of a competent authority which he is bound by law to obey, unless the order is manifestly unlawful."
>
> It is added that whether an order is manifestly unlawful is a question of law. To this the gloss must also no doubt be added that the section does dot exculpate D if he obeys an order which he knows to be unlawful merely because it is not manifestly so. The assumption must be made that D either does not know of the unlawfulness of the order or does know but obeys nevertheless. If this is correct the effect is that s 31 (2) lays down a rule that D is excused for obeying an order which he reasonably believes to be lawful, the test of reasonableness being the comparatively lenient criterion that the order must not be manifestly unlawful; and this may be the law in Australia generally."...

As far as the Calcutta Police is concerned there is a specific provision which requires obedience to an order passed by a superior officer. This requirement will be found in rule 25 of Chapter IV Part II of the Police Regulations, Calcutta, 1968, Vol I. The rule reads thus: "Every police officer shall be subordinate to and shall be bound to carry out any order given by, any police officer superior to him in rank."

On this aspect s 76 of the IPC and the first illustration appended thereto are also material....

It thus appears that the incident at Shyampukur Street on the night in question did not occur in the manner as sought to be brought out by the prosecution through its witnesses....

The situation prevailing at that place must have been such that the superior officer in charge of the force considered it necessary to give an order to fire. After such an order had been given were the members of the force expected to hold a discussion amongst themselves as to whether the order was legal and whether they should carry it out? Or is it expected that they would obey it promptly, as was their duty, if the order was not on the face of it illegal? It must also be remembered that Shyampukur was a troublesome area and, as stated earlier, in the year 1970–71 a number of policemen had been attacked. In such circumstances we have no other option but to hold that the order passed by Bibhuti Chakraborty cannot be deemed to be necessarily and manifestly illegal, and the police officers acting under him were bound by rule 25 of the Police Regulations, Calcutta to carry out the order. As such, if the appellants actually fired leading to the unfortunate deaths of Ranjit and Samir, they are fully protected by the superior order passed by Bibhuti Chakraborty and they cannot be deemed to have committed any offence. On this ground alone the appellants are entitled to succeed.

Appeal allowed

Section 76 allows a defence to a person who because of a mistake of fact in *good faith* believes himself bound to obey. As has already been examined, "good faith" requires an act or belief to be with "due care and attention" (s 52). Thus s 76 seems only to exempt from liability those who have made a mistake *on reasonable grounds* and consequently believe the order is lawful. This approach is confirmed by *Alsagoff* (1946). However, the Indian case of *Shew Mangal Singh* (1981) represents an expansion of the defence of superior orders. Instead of the accused's mistake having to be based on reasonable grounds, he is afforded a defence provided the order is not manifestly illegal. Clearly, it is possible to make a mistake "without due care and attention" (s 52) and obey an unreasonable order–yet one that does not come within the category of manifest illegality. Section 76 has thus been given a robust interpretation so as to bring it in line with the general common law position discussed above (see above, p 165). Bearing in mind the policy considerations discussed in the introduction to this section, is this broader interpretation adopted in *Shew Mangal Singh* (1981) to be welcomed?

(b) No mistake

Finally, what is the position where the accused knows the order is unlawful, but obeys because of fear to his life? There is only one possible route to escaping liability in such a case and that is by using the defence of duress under s 94 (*Alsagoff*, 1946). However, this can only be of limited application: the person obeying the orders must fear instant death if he does not obey, and he will have no defence to a charge of murder. (It should be borne in mind that most cases on superior orders from other jurisdictions have involved murder charges. The scope for the defence of duress in such situations is thus exceedingly narrow.

Excuses

Chapter 9

Mistake

By KL Koh

A. The law

Penal Code, ss 76 and 79

76. Nothing is an offence which is done by a person who is, or who by reason of a mistake of fact and not by reason of a mistake of law in good faith believes himself to be, bound by law to do it.

Illustrations

(a) A, a soldier, fires on a mob by the order of his superior officer, in conformity with the commands of the law. A has committed no offence.

(b) A, an officer of a court of justice, being ordered by that court to arrest Y, and, after due enquiry, believing Z to be Y, arrests Z. A has committed no offence.

79. Nothing is an offence which is done by any person who is justified by law, or who by reason of a mistake of fact and not by reason of a mistake of law in good faith believes himself to be justified by law in doing it.

Illustration

A sees Z commit what appears to A to be a murder. A, in the exercise, to the best of his judgment exerted in good faith, of the power which the law gives to all persons of apprehending murderers in the act, seizes Z, in order to bring Z before the proper authorities. A has committed no offence, though it may turn out that Z was acting in self-defence.

1. Distinction between ss 76 and 79

Both ss 76 and 79 of the Penal Code deal with mistake of fact and not mistake of law. Section 76 concerns a situation where a person under a mistake of fact thinks he is *bound by law* to do an act (see s 76 Illustration (b)), whereas s 79 deals with the case of a person who, under a mistake of fact, thinks he is *justified by law* to do it (s 79 Illustration).

The term "justified by law" is wide enough to cover "bound by law" which is a narrower concept and is limited to a situation where a person is under a legal obligation to do an act. It would therefore require some authority supported by law, for example, in Illustration(b) to s 76 the authority to arrest emanated from the court. There are very few cases on s 76 and most of the cases on the defence of mistake of fact would fall for consideration under s 79.

2.   Mistake of fact

Mistake of fact is not defined in the Penal Code. A mistake of fact is an error as to the existence of any state of things. It may arise from inadequate or wrong information, forgetfulness, negligence or superstition. Obvious examples are where A mistakes his son to be a tiger, or where B believes her husband is dead and remarries (see *Tolson*, 1889):

Jerome Hall, "Ignorance and Mistake in Criminal Law" 33 (1957) Ind LJ 1, 2–3

The meaning of "factual error", as defined in the criminal law, represents a common sense version of the philosopher's definition: "All error consists in taking for real what is mere appearance." For example, a person looks at a far-off object and believes he sees a man; later, on closer approach, he decides it is a tree. The first opinion is then recognized as error. But the object may not actually be a tree; perhaps it is a dead stump or a bit of sculpture. Indeed, on examining it the next morning by aid of daylight and a clear head, our actor decides that he was mistaken in both judgments the night before. In this view he will be supported by all normal persons who, viewing the object under "adequate" conditions, agree: "It is a tree stump"; moreover, they would not concede the possibility of the slightest error in this opinion. Thus, an opinion (judgment or belief) is erroneous by reference to another opinion which corresponds to the facts. In sum, "error" implies:

(1) That facts exist;
(2) That sense *impressions* of facts, "sensa", are different from the facts;
(3) That the sensa fit (correspond to, are congruent with) or do not fit the facts;
(4) That erroneous sensa (those that do not fit the facts) are for a time accepted as true, ie they are believed to be congruent with the facts; and
(5) That this is later recognized as erroneous, ie certain opinions become error when they are subjected to a broader experience, especially when relatively adequate conditions of correct perception obtain.

All mistakes of fact can be reduced to the above elements which are frequently directly applicable to the cases. There is, eg a mistake in identity, in believing that a pocket or drawer contains things, that a person is being attacked, that a dangerous weapon is in an assailant's hand, and so on. But while every case of mistake of fact can be stated in terms of the above criteria, it is also true that many such mistakes involve much more than perception. For example, in situations relevant to libel, perjury, or bigamy, the defendant may never have sensed the phenomena which he erroneously interpreted. Someone may have told him that X served a term in the penitentiary for forgery; he may have heard X's employer discharge him, and read in the newspaper that forged checks had been found in the possession of a certain employee of that firm; or someone may have informed a woman that he had learned "on good authority" of the death of her husband. Thus, mistakes of fact often result not only from faulty perception but also from erroneous higher types of cognitive experience, eg the ideas already in the interpreter's mind, including his bias. In the case of an inventor who makes certain mistakes of fact, these ideas may include invalid theories of physics.

Chirangi v State of Nagpur AIR (1952) Nagpur 282 (HC, Nagpur, India) (Hemeon and Sen JJ)

Chirangi killed his son Ghudsai by mistake thinking he was a tiger. He was suffering from bilateral cataract. There was also evidence that he had an abscess in his leg which would have produced a temperature which might have caused a temporary delirium. This might have created a secondary delusion affecting his vision. He was charged with murder under s 302 of the Indian Penal Code (1860).

Judgment of court: Chirangi, Lohar, 45 years, a widower, his unmarried daughter, only son Ghudsai, 12 years, and nephew Khotla (PW 2) lived together at Idnar, Narayanpur Tahsil, Bastar district. Their relations were cordial, and Ghudsai was attentive and considerate to his father who had an abscess in his leg for some time prior to the 3 April 1951. During that afternoon, while Khotla was working in his field, Chirangi took an axe and went with Ghudsai to a nearby hillock, known as Budra Meta, in order to gather "Siadi" leaves. When Khotla returned to his house in the evening, Ghudsai was not there and he found Chirangi asleep with the blood-stained axe beside him. Chirangi woke up at midnight, and when Khotla questioned him concerning his son's whereabouts he replied:

> "I had become insane. I have killed my son in Budra Meta. It occurred to me that a tiger come to me. I then dealt blows with the axe"....

[I]t was possible for Chirangi, who was suffering from bilateral cataract prior to the relevant date, to have because of this disability mistaken "bona fide" this son for a tiger. Dr Dube also opined that the abscess in his leg would have produced temperature which might well have been responsible after the fall for a temporary delirium which might have created a secondary delusion to magnify the image created by the defect in vision. Chirangi in all probability, he added, suffered from cardio-vascular disease which would have resulted in temporary confusion; and the injury to his eyebrow could have caused a state of confusion during which he might have inflicted the injuries on his son without being conscious of his actions. No symptoms of psychosis or insanity were present when Dr Dube examined him on the 11th February 1952, ie about 10 months after the occurrence.

The evidence ... showed clearly enough that Chirangi's fall combined with his existing physical ailments could have produced a state of mind in which he in good faith thought that the object of his attack was a tiger and was not his son. The appellant's conduct after the occurrence was in consonance with that estimate, and it was manifest that he had had no intention of doing wrong or of committing any offence. In *Waryam Singh* (1926), a Division Bench, acting under s 79 of the Indian Penal Code, held that an accused who killed a man with several blows from a stick was not liable under s 302, s 304 or s 304A ibid because he believed in good faith at the time of the attack that the object of his assault was not a living human being but a ghost or some object other than a living human being. The Division Bench made it clear that the ground for their opinion was that *mens rea* or an intention to do wrong or to commit an offence did not exist in the case and that the object of culpable homicide could only be a living human being.

This view was followed in *Bonda Kui* (1943) a case in which a woman in the middle of the night, saw a form, apparently human, dancing in a state of complete nudity with a broomstick tied on one side and a torn mat around the waist. The woman taking the form to be that on an evil spirit or a thing which consumes human beings, removed her own clothes and with repeated blows by a hatchet felled the thing to the ground. Examination showed, however, that she had killed a human being who was the wife of her husband's brother. The conviction and sentence of the accused woman under s 304 of the Indian Penal Code were set aside, on the ground that she was fully protected by the provisons of s 79 ibid, inasmuch as the statements made by her from time to time which constituted the only evidence in the case, demonstrated conclusively that she thought that she was by a mistake of fact, justified in killing the deceased who she did not consider to be a human being, but a thing which devoured human beings.

We are in respectful agreement with these two rulings the facts in which are largely *in pari materia* with those in the poignant case before us. It is abundantly clear that if Chirangi had for a single moment thought that the object of his attack was his son, he would have desisted forthwith. There was no reason of any kind why he should have attacked him and, as shown, they were mutually devoted. In short, all that happened was that the appellant in a moment of delusion had considered that his target was a tiger and he accordingly assailed it with his axe. He thought that by reason of a mistake of fact he was justified in destroying the deceased whom he did not regard to be a human being but who, as he thought, was a dangerous animal. He was in the circumstances protected by the provisions of s 79 of the Indian Penal Code....

Conviction set aside

The liability of the accused would be judged by the facts as he supposed them to be in his mistaken belief. If, for example, A intends to commit housebreaking of house No 10 but went instead to house No 12, his mistake is immaterial as all the *actus reus* and *mens rea* of the offence of housebreaking under s 441 of the Penal Code would be satisfied even in the circumstances supposed. It is irrelevant which house he enters for the purpose of committing the offence. However, if he wished to avoid the aggravated offence of housebreaking by night under s 446 of the Penal Code and decided to enter the house at 6 pm instead of 7 pm, his mistake as to time would be a defence to housebreaking by night but not for housebreaking as he would be liable on the facts as he supposed. If one were to ask, would the accused have done what he did if he were not mistaken, the answer would have been in the positive. He would still have committed housebreaking.

3. Mistake of law and ignorance of law

Mistake of law is expressly excluded from ss 76 and 79 of the Penal Code. Mistake of law is not defined. In *Tustipada Mandal* (1951) Ray CJ said:

Mistake of law ordinarily means mistake as to existence or otherwise of any law on a relevant subject as well as mistake as to what the law is.

There are two aspects to the maxim, *ignorantia juris non excusat*, ie ignorance of the law is no excuse. The first relates to ignorance as to the *existence* of the law; the second, as to the interpretation of what the law actually is. Strictly speaking, so far as the former is concerned, there cannot be a mistake as to something whose existence one does not know as one does not apply one's reasoning to a non-existent state of things. With regard to the latter, a mistake of law can arise from a process of reasoning as to what the law is. Thus, a mistake of law could arise as to a wrong interpretation of the law.

Let us now examine two categories of mistake of law:

(a) Ignorance as to existence or non-existence of law

Courts and writers have often regarded the question of ignorance as to the existence of the law as a mistake of law under s 76 or s 79 of the Penal Code. A more recent example is *Koo Cheh Yew* (1980), where Chang Min Tat FJ simply assumed, without argument, that the general rule that ignorance as to the existence of the law is no defence is found in s 79 of the Penal Code.

The distinction between ignorance and mistake was well noted by Bertram CJ in the Ceylon case of *Weerakoon v Ranhamy* (1921):

Now, in the view I take of the effect of s 72 [ie s 79 of the Singapore Penal Code], ignorance is not the same as mistake. Mistake, to my mind, implies a positive and conscious conception which is, in fact, a misconception. Thus, to take the case of the man who was convicted of selling a medicine containing a "trace of ganja", ... it does not seem to me that this man made a bona fide mistake about this trace of ganja. He did not know that it was there. He simply did not think about it, and cannot be said to have made a mistake on the subject. As I understand the matter, therefore, the English doctrine [ie *ignorance* or mistake] covers both ignorance and mistake, our own formula only includes mistake.

A contrary view was taken by Schneider AJ (p 58) when he said:

The word "mistake" in s 72 must be taken to include ignorance. Sections 69 and 72 are a paraphrase of the English Common Law maxim in its application to criminal law. *Ignorantia facti excusat; ignorantia juris non excusat.*

Failure to distinguish the maxim, ignorance as to the *existence* of the law is no excuse on the one hand and mistake of law under s 79 of the Penal Code on the other hand, has led to complications. In *Koo Cheh Yew* (1980), the Federal Court of Malaysia incorporated one of the exceptions to the maxim into s 79 of the Penal Code, namely, an accused can escape liability if he could not possibly have known of the existence of the law he had offended against. Chang Min Tat FJ in *Koo Cheh Yew* (1980) said he found "confirmation" of this exception to the maxim in s 79 of the Penal Code. The question which has been raised in *Koo Cheh Yew* (1980) is, as pointed out by Yeo (1985), whether the drafters of the Penal Code meant, by the wording of ss 76 and 79, to adopt only the maxim and not its exception, namely, where an accused could not possibly have known of the existence of the law he had breached the maxim would still apply and the accused be held liable.

The Federal Court in *Koo Cheh Yew* (1980) embodied both the maxim and its exception into "mistake of law" in s 79. Yeo (1985) criticizes the incorporation of the exception to the maxim:

> Given the exhaustive nature of the Code, it is submitted that the courts should have dealt at length with s 79 to determine if an adoption of the common law maxim would be consistent with that section and, if so, whether the maxim should accordingly be applied. Had this been done, it would have been observed that, by excluding "mistake of law" as a defence, the section clearly embodied the general proposition that ignorance of the law is no excuse. It would, however, have been much more difficult to see how s 79 also embodied the exception to the maxim. The section provides that an accused *in good faith* believed himself to be justified by law in doing an act. The words "in good faith" require the act in question to have been "done or believed with due care and attention". Is not this requirement basically what is envisaged by the exception to the English maxim? If this is so, then a plain reading of s 79 would be that a mistake or ignorance of the law is no defence even though the accused believed in good faith that he was justified by law in doing an act. The section is accordingly available only when there has been a mistake of fact. Thus it would appear that the Code does not embrace this common law defence and the courts in *Lim Chin Aik* (1963) and *Koo Cheh Yew* (1980) were wrong in adopting it.

The Penal Code is an exhaustive code; it can therefore be argued that there is no room for the reception of English criminal law under the Second Charter of Justice 1826. However, the maxim *ignorantia juris non excusat* is not a specific principle or rule of criminal law as such. As a maxim it forms part of the general corpus of English common law which was received under the Second Charter of Justice 1826 (see ch 1). It is a maxim that is so fundamental that it should be taken into consideration in applying the law generally, including the criminal law. A maxim is on a higher level than the law as embodied in legislation. However, courts can concretize a maxim and can also delimit its scope. Thus a maxim can eventually become a rule of law. Since the Penal Code is silent on the maxim *ignorantia juris non excusat*, it may be presumed that the intention of the legislature was not to depart from well-known common law maxims such as the one under consideration. Courts are also free to place exceptions on any maxim. The Privy Council in *Lim Chin Aik* (1963), in an appeal from Singapore, was of the view, obiter, that the maxim, ignorance of the law is no excuse, was not applicable where there was no provision designed to enable a man by appropriate enquiry to find out what the law was. Thus the Privy Council recognized the maxim as applicable in Singapore and made an exception to it. It is submitted that the Privy Council, quite rightly, did not make any reference to s 79 as it fell outside its scope. This approach is contrasted with the *Koo Cheh Yew* (1980) approach in Malaysia (see above).

(b) Mistake as to interpretation of law

A mistake based on a misconception of some general principle of law or a wrong interpretation of the law is a mistake of law. The mistaken belief may arise from a process of reasoning based on facts. An erroneous conclusion may be reached. A common example is a mistaken belief as to one's marital status. Is it a mistake of fact or a mistake of law? Suppose A went through what she thought was a wedding ceremony when in fact it was an engagement ceremony. She was therefore mistaken as to the performance of a marriage ceremony. This might be considered a mistake of fact. However, if a mistake as to marital status springs from the fact that she was mistaken that a divorce had been granted when in fact the court had no jurisdiction to grant the divorce, this is a mistake of law.

Thus, an erroneous conclusion reached on a knowledge of a state of things would be a mistake of law. Similarly, a belief that a book is not obscene based on a knowledge of the contents of a book is a mistake of law. In the Australian case of *Sancoff* v *Holford, ex p Holford* (1973), the appellant was charged with having in his possession certain obscene publications for the purpose of sale. The appellant's defence was that he did not believe that the contents of the books were obscene, though he knew its contents. Hanger CJ said:

> The position may be contrasted with that arising if a person has in his possession a book which he has not opened which is marked "Electrical Engineering" but which contains inside nothing but pornographic pictures. Here a plea that the possessor believed the contents of the book to relate only to electrical engineering would establish a belief in a state of things–the contents of the book. But the belief–if it existed–of the appellant in the instant case, based on a knowledge of the contents of the books is a very different thing. Knowing all the primary facts of the matter, the appellant claims to have reached a mistaken conclusion as to the result of the facts–that the books were not obscene and that he was entitled to sell them within the law. I think this was an error in law which was no excuse.

As noted in a different context but applicable in the context of criminal law, Dickinson (1927) observed:

> [Q]uestions of fact and questions of law are not two mutually exclusive kinds of questions based upon a difference of subject matter. Matters of law grow downward into roots of fact, and matters of fact reach upward without a break, into matters of law.

Even legal advice given by an expert lawyer would be no defence if it turned out that it was a mistaken view of the law. It seems harsh to deny an accused the right of defence of a mistaken view of the law when judges themselves may have different views of it as when an appeal on the law is allowed. Of course, one view is to say that the latter decision is simply a declaration as to what has always been the law–Bentham has called this a "childish fiction". (See Brett, (1966).)

Mistake of law can be divided into two categories: mistake of the criminal law and mistake of the civil law. The latter would include mistake as to the law of property, contract, tort and family law.

Under English law, a mistake as to the civil law may negative the *mens rea* required in a crime. It is to be noted that ss 76 and 79 of the Penal Code do not make a distinction between mistake as to criminal law and mistake as to civil law. Rather, the distinction is made between mistake of fact and mistake of law, the latter being no defence. However, a mistake as to the civil law may arise in a bona fide claim of title or right (see chs 23 and 26). Under the Penal Code, such a claim of right may negative the *mens rea* in a crime.

Mat Salleh v Sarah (1883) 3 Kyshe 167 (SC, Straits Settlements)

The appellant was convicted of criminal trespass under s 447 of the Penal Code in respect of the respondent's house. The appellant entered the house and attempted to pull it down because he thought he had purchased the house from one Samat. When the respondent protested, the appellant threw out the apparel and crockery, breaking and smashing them, released the goats, and tore the house completely down and carried away the materials. There was a dispute as to whether the appellant had the right to do what he did.

Wood J: The law being clear to me that the act is not criminal within s 441 of the Penal Code, if the appellant in this case acted as he did, on a *bona fide* belief of right, and it not being clear to me that the Magistrate in the Court below, had this view of the law clearly before him, I think I must remit the matter to him for a rehearing, leaving him to find, whether the appellant [the defendant] did as a matter of fact, do the several acts complained of, viz, the entry on the first occasion and the entry on the second occasion, and scattering the crockery and fowls, with the primary intent to annoy, or merely as incidents to a *bona fide* claim of title, and belief in his right to do so. Both parties will have liberty to call further witnesses.

Case remitted accordingly

18th February 1884
The case being now remitted with further evidence, I observe that though the case was sent back for the Magistrate to hear and determine anew, he has not in fact found anything, but has heard and not determined. But assuming that the original finding of the Magistrate is supported by his present return, I am of opinion that the Magistrate has leant too much to a criminal view, in his dealing with this case. Although some of the acts of the defendant might have been the cause of injury and annoyance to the complainant, yet I think, he may reasonably be taken to have done what he did, in pursuance of a right. The evidence is not sufficient in my opinion, to support a criminal charge. The conviction will therefore be quashed.

Conviction quashed

Compare *Mat Salleh* (1883) with *Swaine* (1935) below, where a bona fide mistake of legal powers to enforce a contract was held to be outside the scope of s 79 of the Penal Code. (See also the Ceylon case of *Weerakoon*, 1921, below, p 182.)

R v ALB Swaine (1935) 4 MLJ 276 (HC, Singapore)

(The facts appear in the judgment.)

Burton AG CJ: The appellant was convicted of the offence of mischief under s 426 of the Penal Code and sentenced to a fine of $50.

The complainant Ng Hock Su was a squatter on some land belonging to the Singapore United Rubber Plantations Ltd; he occupied a piece of land at a rental of $1 a month. This he paid regularly till in July 1934 the rent was increased and a sum of $1.50 demanded. This led to an affray and Ng Hock Su was convicted of causing hurt to the Mandor who attempted to collect the rent....

When Ng Hock Su caused hurt to the Mandor, the Manager sent for the Police and he was arrested. While he was in custody, and without notice to him the Manager caused his house to be demolished by sawing through the uprights embedded in the ground, with the result that the house collapsed and some poulty escaped and was lost.

It is here that I think the Manager was wrong. Though Ng Hock Su had given the estate just grounds to expel him, and though he was probably no more than a tenant at will, he was nevertheless entitled to notice of the Estate's intention to expel him and a reasonable time to demolish his ouse and remove his goods, which is as Willis, J said in *Cornish* v *Stubbs* (1870) a right annexed by law in the case of a tenant at will. It was not seriously argued that the house is not moveable property. I think it is generally conceded that such houses are. But whether they are or not, is not essential to this conviction because mischief was committed to the live-stock. However the act of mischief is laid in the charge as "pulling down an attap dwelling house and poultry shed" and I think that correctly represents the offence.

The appellant cannot plead that he did this *bona fide*, because he has made a mistake not of fact but of what his legal powers are to enforce the contract and is not within the protection of s 79 of the Penal Code....

Appeal dismissed

His Lordship regarded the appellant's bona fide mistake as to his legal powers to enforce the contract as a mistake of law and not of fact, and hence outside the scope of s 79. Can such a mistake as to the civil law negative the *mens rea* in mischief under s 425 (punishable under s 426)? One aspect of *mens rea* in mischief is the *intent* to cause wrongful loss or damage to any person. The complainant was a squatter of an estate and there were just grounds for his expulsion from the estate. However, no notice had been given to expel him. If the appellant mistakenly thought he was exercising his legal powers in demolishing the complainant's attap house and poultry shed (despite the lack of notice), he would lack the *intention* to cause damage to the property of the complainant. The situation is analogous to a bona fide claim of right in theft which negatives the intention to take dishonestly (see ch 23). It has nothing to do with the defence of mistake under s 79, which comes within the general exceptions of the Penal Code.

The burden of proving the general exceptions of the Penal Code is on the accused. Where a mistake as to the civil law negatives the *mens rea* of a crime, the prosecution has to prove the *mens rea*, taking this mistake into consideration.

Weerakoon v Ranhamy (1921) NLR 33 (Full Bench, Ceylon)

The accused was charged with clearing Crown land without a permit. He was acting under a mistaken belief that it was possible for him to acquire a good title to lands in the Kandyan Provinces merely by notarial deeds and posssession.

Bertram CJ: The Court may have to determine, first, whether the accused had title; and secondly, whether, if he had not, he acted upon a mistake of fact.

This brings me to the decisive question in the case, namely, whether a person who has inherited or acquired chena land in the Kandyan Provinces, and has cleared the growth upon it in the belief that it is private land and that he is the proprietor of it, but is not able to show any Crown grant or sannas, has acted under a mistake of fact or under a mistake of law. The question is a question of some difficulty. Mr Jayawardene cited a *dictum of* Lord Westbury in *Cooper v Phibbs*, (1867) repeated and adopted by Hall VC in *Jones v Clifford*, (1876) which is as follows:

> "It is said: *Ignorantia juris haud excusat*, but in that maxim the word *jus* is used in the sense of denoting general law, the ordinary law of the country. But when the word *jus* is used in the sense of denoting a private right, that maxim has no application. Private right of ownership is a matter of fact; it may be the result also of matter of law; but if parties contract under a mutual mistake and misapprehension as to their relative and respective rights, the result is that the agreement is liable to be set aside as having proceeded upon a common mistake."

In the first place, I would observe that, even if this *dictum* be accepted as authoritative for the present purpose, it does not carry Mr Jayawardene home. Lord Westbury says: "Private right of ownership is a matter of fact; it may be the result also of a matter of law", but to come within s 72 a person must show that he acted "by reason of a mistake of fact, and not by reason of a mistake of law". A person, therefore, who acts by reason of a mistake of fact, which is "the result of a matter of law", does not seem to me necessarily to come within the section. I cannot follow the reasoning of Dr Gour (2nd edn), that a mistake of mixed fact and law is, for the purpose of this section, to be treated as a mistake of fact. The passage which he cites as his authority is concerned with the law of larceny and the meaning of *animus furandi,* which is governed by wholly different considerations.

The observations of Lord Westbury, however, are not concerned with criminal responsibility, but with the equitable doctrine of relief against common mistakes. The question of the extent to which equity could give relief in such circumstances does not seem to me to be necessarily governed by the same principles as those which relate to criminal responsibility. A Court of Equity may well give relief in a contract where the parties act under a common mistake as to their rights, though the plea of such a mistake by one of the parties might not be an answer to a criminal charge where he had committed an offence by reason of that mistake.

My brother Ennis appears to hold that a mistaken belief that the land in question was private land is, in all cases, a mistake of fact. I very respectfully differ from that conclusion. It seems to me that it cannot be affirmed in all cases that a mistake as to one's title to property is a mistake of fact. The

Question requires further analysis. In some cases the mistake may be a mistake of fact, in others it may be a mistake of law. Thus, to take the case decided by my brother Ennis, *Cumberland* v *Dewarakkita Unnanse* (supra), in that case, it seems to me, the mistake was a mistake of fact. In that case the accused cut timber from Crown land, because he believed that the land from which he cut the timber was within his boundaries. His belief was based upon a survey and a path cut along what was believed to be the western boundary; it was proved that the survey and the boundary cut in accordance therewith was erroneous. Because of this mistake the defendant believed that the place where the trees were cut was not Crown property, but was private land. In this case, it seems to me, the mistake was a mistake of fact. Other instances of such a mistake, in the class of cases we are now considering, might be a mistake as to the boundary line of the Kandyan Provinces; a mistake as to the genuineness of a sannas which was in fact forged, or, in other cases, a mistake as to the fact of a marriage which was a necessary element in the title; a mistake as to a death or a birth or as to the date of the length of possession where prescription is in issue.

On the other hand, where the mistake as to a man's private rights is based upon a misconception of some general principle of law or the ignorance of some statutory enactment, then, it seems to me, his mistake is a mistake of law. Thus, to take an extreme case, supposing that a man in the maritime provinces knew that his brother-in-law had chenaed a land three times in succession in the course of ten years without interference by the Crown or anybody else, and supposing that he had the mistaken idea that a prescriptive title against the Crown should be acquired by ten years' possession and thereupon bought the land and chenaed it himself, such a man, in terms of s 72, by reason of a mistake, would in good faith believe himself to be justified by law in so doing, but surely there can be no doubt that his mistake would be a mistake not of fact but of law. So in the class of cases which we are now considering, for what reason do men, like the accused in the present case, who many years ago bought chena land on the basis of possession and notarial deeds, proceed to treat it as their own and clear it for cultivation? It is because they mistakenly imagine that ownership of such lands can be acquired by such a title. They do it because they have not realized that the decisions of this Court, taken in conjunction with s 6 of Ordinance No 12 of 1840, have converted their deeds into waste paper. Had they known the law, they would neither have paid money for the transfer nor chenaed the land. Owing to a mistake of law, namely, a mistaken opinion that title to such lands can be based on deeds and possession alone, they in good faith believe themselves to be justified by law in clearing it.

Conviction affirmed;
Sentence varied

4. Good faith

"Good faith" is defined in s 52:

> Nothing is said to be done or believed in good faith which is done or believed without due care and attention.

The definition is expressed in negative terms and is not very useful but in essence "good faith" means something which is done with due care and attention.

The question of good faith must be considered with reference to the position of the accused and the circumstances under which he acted, and also his capacity and intelligence. Even though there may not be a complete basis of fact to justify the action taken by the accused, he might still, in the circumstances, have acted in good faith. The question of good faith is one of fact.

In the recent Brunei case of *Zainal Abidin b Ismail* (1987), Dato Sir Denys Roberts applied the famous English case of *Morgan* (1976) in determining the question of mistake in rape under s 375 of the Brunei Penal Code (*in pari materia* with the local Penal Codes). There the House of Lords, by a majority of three to two, held that if an accused in fact believed that the woman had consented he could not be found guilty of rape whether or not that belief was based on reasonable grounds. To adopt the *Morgan* (1976) approach would involve a recognition of honest though unreasonable mistake as negating liability. This would fly in the face of the requirement of "good faith" (s 52 of the Penal Code) in the defence of mistake of fact in s 79 of the Penal Code. *Zainal Abidin b Ismail* (1987) is yet another example of slavish application of English criminal law without due regard to the position under the Penal Code. In contrast, in a similar case in *Teo Eng Chan* (1988), P Coomaraswamy J of the High Court of Singapore departed from the *Zainal* and *Morgan* approach and proceeded on the defence of mistake of fact under s 79 of the Penal Code which requires the element of "good faith". (For a fuller discussion see ch 3; see also Clarkson (1987).)

Bha'woo Jiva'ji v Mulji Daya'l (1888) 12 Bom 377 (HC, Bombay, India)

The accused, a police constable, was on duty when he saw the complainant carrying under his arm three pieces of cloth. Suspecting that the cloth was stolen property, he went up to the complainant and questioned him. The complainant said that the cloth was made in England. The accused, noticing that each piece bore Gujara'thi characters and not knowing that such marks are placed on English-made goods, concluded that this statement was false and that the cloth had been stolen. He took hold of one of the pieces of cloth in order to examine it more closely. The complianant objected to this; a scuffle followed and the complainant assaulted the accused, who then arrested him. The complainant charged the accused with wrongful restraint and wrongful confinement under ss 341 and 342 respectively of the Indian Penal Code (1860).

The magistrate held that there was no justification for the suspicion (see s 79 of the Indian Penal Code) which the accused professed to entertain and that there were no reasonable grounds for questioning the complainant about the cloth in his possession. The accused was convicted. On appeal:

Birdwood J: We think that, in dealing with the case, the Magistrate has been led to a wrong decision from failing to consider aright the question whether the accused acted in good faith in questioning the complainant and putting his hand on his bundle of cloth....

Assuming, then, that the complainant did not strike the accused, but merely struggled with him in order to free his property, the arrest of the complainant would be an offence against the section if the complainant was, in law, justified in resisting the action of the accused in putting his hand upon his property. That the complainant was justified in resenting the questions put to him, we cannot for a moment hold; for it is quite clear to us that the questions were put, not for the purpose of annoying the complainant, or from mere idle and officious curiosity, but in order to remove an honest suspicion in the mind of the constable that the bundle might be stolen property. The accused did not know the complainant, and could not, we think, have acted from any malicious motive. He was at his post, where he was required to be from 4 am to 7 am, his special duty being to prevent the removal of stolen property by thieves attempting to evade the police. He saw the complainant, who was waiting for a tram-car, with the cloth under his arm, at about half-past six o'clock, or perhaps a little later, on the morning of the 29th December, ie apparently about sunrise. We cannot say that the contention of the counsel for the accused in the Court below that that was an unusual time for persons to be carrying bundles is without weight. The accused himself said in his examination that he suspected the complainant, because he was dressed in dirty clothes, and because the uppermost of the three pieces of cloth was dirty. If he had an honest suspicion, as we think he had, then, even though the same facts might not have raised any suspicion in the mind of a police officer of higher grade, still he acted, we think, with due care in putting questions the answers to which might clear away his suspicions. The putting of questions under these circumstances was in itself an indication of good faith, as defined in s 52 of the Penal Code. He said at the trial that he received no answers to his questions....

He certainly obtained answers to his questions, and was evidently not satisfied with those answers, and then he seems to have put his hand on the bundle and was resisted by the complainant. He may have shown a want of intelligence in not accepting as satisfactory the complainant's answer that the cloth was of English manufacture, though it bore a name stamped in Gujarathi characters; but we do not doubt that this answer did not satisfy him as to the honesty of the complainant. He himself, as we think, believed that he was legally justified in detaining the cloth; and though he was entirely mistaken as to the character of the complainant, we think that his belief as to his legal right was a *bona-fide* belief, and that he is protected by s 79 of the Penal Code (Act XLV of 1860).

We also think that, under the first paragraph of s 99, the complainant had no right to resist the accused when he tried to detain the cloth. The decision of the case really turns upon the question whether the accused acted in good faith; and that question must be considered with reference to the position of the accused and the circumstances under which he acted. If he acted with due care and attention such as ought to be expected from a constable in his position, in the circumstances in which he was placed, then he acted in good faith; and even though his act might not have been "strictly justifiable by law",–that is, even though there might not have been a complete basis of fact to justify a reasonable suspicion that the cloth was stolen property,–still the complainant had no right of private defence, as the accused was a public servant acting under colour of his office, and his act was not one which caused the apprehension of death or of grievous hurt: see *Venkatrao* (1922). The question of good faith, as far as it is one of fact, we are prepared in this case to deal with ourselves. We think, as we have already said, that the accused was justified in questioning the complainant; and we think further that he is not liable to be dealt with as a criminal, because, after endeavouring to satisfy himself whether his suspicions were well founded or not, he was not satisfied by such answers as he received, though such answers might have satisfied a more intelligent man, or one in a higher position, and because he, thereupon, proceeded to put his hand on the property which he believed to be stolen, whether he did so with the intention of further inspecting it, or of arresting the accused for being in possession of it. We cannot hold that the law exacts the same care and attention from all public servants regardless of the position they occupy. If the same intelligence were required from a constable as from a Commissioner of Police, it would be impossible to obtain the services of constables on the salaries which the State gives them for such duties as are performed by the accused. We are forced, therefore, to consider whether there was some ground for suspicion, and whether the accused, in the circumstances in which he was placed, acted with such care as is sufficient to shield him from a criminal prosecution. Though we think that there was very little ground, indeed, to justify a reasonable suspicion that the cloth was stolen property, yet we think that there was some ground which gave rise to an honest belief on the part of the accused, after such inquiry as he was able to make, that such a state of facts existed as would justify his action. We think, therefore, that the Magistrate ought to have found in this case that the accused acted in good faith, and that even though his act might not be strictly justifiable by law, the complainant had no right to resist him.

Conviction and sentence reversed

5.   Mistake of fact justified by law

The essence of s 79 is that the accused, because of his bona fide mistake of fact, "believes himself to be justified by law" in acting as he does. What does "justified by law" mean? Something which is justified by law must be in conformity with the law. In other words, it must not be illegal. The word "illegal" is defined in s 43 of the Penal Code (see ch 3).

Abdullah v R (1954) 20 MLJ 195 (CCA, Singapore)

(The facts appear in the judgment.)

Murray-Aynsley CJ (with whom Whitton J agreed): This case turns on the construction of s 79 of the Penal Code. The appellant was charged with rape. It was clear at the trial that the offence, if committed, was only within the scope of s 376 by reason of the fact that the complainant was under 14 years of age. There was no doubt that appellant had carnal knowledge of the complainant and that her age was under 14. The appellant contended that he thought she was over 16. At the trial the learned Judge ruled that this belief, if it existed, was immaterial and refused to leave the matter to the consideration of the jury. He was convicted and now appeals on this point of law.

There is no equivalent to s 79 in English law. This section applies to all offences whether under the Penal Code or otherwise (s 40 PC). It is clear that if the appellant believed "in good faith" that the complainant was over 16 it would be a case of mistake of fact. In this case what he did would not be an offence had the facts been as he supposed them to be; would he be "justified by law"? If on this supposition he would have committed some other offence, eg, if he had thought the girl to be over 14 but under 16, he would clearly not have been justified by law. I think that if the act would have been a tort though not an offence, he would not have been "justified by law". On the other hand, in the present case, if his belief had been correct he would have committed neither a crime nor a tort. Is such an act always "justifiable by law"? In my opinion this is so. According to modern ideas, as embodied in the Penal Code, an act only acquires its criminal character by being forbidden by law. What the law does not forbid it allows, and what a law allows is I think justified by law. I do not think that it is possible to have an intermediate area that is not forbidden but not justifiable. I think that the question should have been left to the jury and I should order a new trial.

Pretheroe Ag CJ (FM): In arguing the appeal Counsel submitted that appellant was "justified by law" because he believed "in good faith" that the girl was over fourteen years of age. By reason of the view I have formed it is not necessary for me to consider this submission in detail. Section 375 of the Penal Code is a definition section and the sentence "with or without her consent, when she is under fourteen years of age" is part of the definition and consequently a provision of law. Mistakes of law are specifically excluded from the operation of s 79 of the Penal Code.

I am fortified in this opinion by certain provisions contained in s 300 of the Penal Code. The fifth exception to the definition in that section provides:

> "Culpable homicide is not murder when the person whose death is caused, being above the age of eighteen years, suffers death, or takes the risk of death with his own consent."

Then follows this explanation:

> "A, by instigation, voluntarily causes Z, a person under eighteen years of age, to commit suicide. Here, on account of Z's youth, he was incapable of giving consent to his own death. A has therefore abetted murder."

Likewise in this appeal I am of the opinion that the girl was "incapable of giving her consent" and that the appellant was therefore guilty of rape.

It seems that this construction must have always been adopted in India because I have been unable to trace a single case where a submission similar to that made in this appeal has been made there.

As far as I have been able to ascertain, all commentators on the Indian Penal Code express the emphatic view that intercourse with a girl under the age of fourteen years (subject only to the provisions of the exception) is rape in any circumstances, Thus, Gour in his *Penal Code of India* states:

> "The clause simply declares that an act even though committed with the consent of a child then under fourteen years of age would be rape, her consent and precocity being both immaterial. The fact that such a girl can discriminate between right and wrong and had invited the accused to the act are both wholly irrelevant, for the policy of the law is to protect children of such immature age against sexual intercourse."

I can find no direct authority on the point under present consideration, but

Ghose J, in *Mohiuddin* (1930) approaches it very closely. In his judgment in that case he said:

> "On the charge (sic) under ss 366 and 376 as indicated above the question of Sovana's age was very relevant. If in fact Sovana was less than 14 years of age although she had been love smitten and could write the letters referred to above, her consent to the acts referred to in ss 366 and 376, Indian Penal Code, was in law immaterial".

The words to which I invite attention are "if in fact" and "was in law immaterial".

For the reason stated earlier in this judgment, I am of opinion that the direction of the learned trial Judge was correct and consequently I would dismiss this appeal.

New trial ordered

In *Abdullah* (1954), Murray-Aynsley CJ said that if the appellant in good faith believed that the complainant was over 16 it would be a mistake of fact; he would not have committed a crime as what he did would have been justified by law. However, his Lordship stated that the position would be otherwise had the complainant thought the girl to be over 14 but under 16 years of age as he would "clearly not have been justified by law". It would appear that what his Lordship had in mind was the offence of carnal connection with a girl under the age of 16 (except by way of marriage) under the former Women and Girls Protection Ordinance (Cap 126, 1955 Rev Ed) (Singapore). This Ordinance has since been repealed and re-enacted in the Women's Charter (Singapore) (Cap 353), s 140(1)(i).

It is noted that the Women's Charter (s 140(1)(i)) contains a specific defence to a charge of carnal connection where a man (under 24 years and who has not previously been charged for carnal connection), has reasonable cause to believe that a girl was above the age of 16 years. Is this test the same as the defence of mistake under s 79?

Compare *Prince* (1875); *Prem Narain* (1929); *Kesar Mal* (1932); *Chathan Kunjukunju* (1959). Is rape a strict liability offence or is *mens rea* required? See ch 3.

6. Mistake in possession offences

The extent to which mistake under s 79 is relevant to strict liability offences depends on the interpretation of the statute concerned, as *mens rea* may still be required in relation to one of the elements of the *actus reus*. (See ch 3.)

Section 40 of the Penal Code provides for the application of the General Exceptions (Chapter IV) to offences both under the Penal Code as well as under any other written law. The question arises as to whether the defence of mistake applies to possession offences which are considered strict liability offences.

(a) Mistake in possession of arms

Sulong bin Nain v PP (1947) 13 MLJ 138 (CA, Malayan Union)

The appellant was found carrying a bag which contained two hand grenades.... The appellant was charged with carrying arms under s 3(1) of the Public Order and Safety Proclamation. At the trial he stated that when he was arrested he was carrying the grenades with the intention of handing them over to the police.

Willan CJ: We are fully aware of the number of crimes of violence committed in which firearms are used, and therefore have no doubt that the Public Order and Safety Proclamation, which repealed the Explosives and Firearms Proclamation, was promulgated to reduce crimes of violence by prescribing deterrent penalties in respect of all persons carrying arms. Hence we have no doubt that this was an attempt by the British Military Administration to reduce the state of lawlessness which existed throughout the country. Therefore, bearing in mind:

(a) That all persons had had adequate notice by the Explosives and Firearms Proclamation that they must surrender any firearms and explosives in their possession to the proper authorities by a certain date;

(b) The state of unlawfulness which existed in the country at the time the Public Order and Safety Proclamation was promulgated;

(c) That the Malayan Union Government, by s 87 of the Malayan Union Order in Council and by the Transfer of Powers and Interpretation Ordinance 1946, continued that Proclamation in force unaltered, except for an amendment to s 5(1) thereof (that amendment does not relate to the offence of carrying arms);

(d) The strict wording of s 3(I), when compared with other parts of the same Proclamation, we hold that s 3(I) of the Public Order and Safety Proclamation prohibits absolutely the carrying of arms and that it is not necessary to prove any ulterior intention to establish that offence.

Having held that s 3(I) of the Public Order and Safety Proclamation prohibits absolutely the carrying of arms, we are now required to answer question (3) set out above, ie whether a person carrying arms with a view to handing them to the police is guilty under that section.

As to this Mr Shearn argued that if the answer to that question is in the affirmative, then a person, who picks up a revolver which he finds lying on the road-side and takes it to the police station to surrender it, will be guilty of an offence. He gave other examples, but the one just mentioned suffices to show that unless a person who is found carrying arms with a good conscience is exempt under any provision of law excepting him from criminal liability, he would be committing an offence under s 3(1) of the Public Order and Safety Proclamation.

Regarding exemption from criminal liability, Mr Shearn relied on ss 76 and 79 of the Penal Code....

At the trial the appellant, as already stated, said that he was taking the two hand grenades to hand them over to the police, and he gave as his reason for this that there was a circular to the effect that if any person delivered arms to the police he would be rewarded. No evidence was adduced at the trial to prove that such a circular had ever been issued.

Mr Shearn argued that if this evidence was believed then, even though s 3(I) of the Public Order and Safety Proclamation is held to prohibit absolutely the carrying of arms, the appellant could not be guilty thereunder because he had acted in good faith in the belief that he was bound by law to carry the two hand grenades to surrender them to the police. Mr Shearn went further and argued that even if such a circular had never been issued the appellant would still not be liable, if his defence that he was carrying the arms to surrender them to the police was believed, as it was by the Assessors, because he would come under either of the exceptions contained in s 76 or s 79 of the Penal Code, particularly the latter.

It is clear from the wording of ss 76 and 79 that either of these sections only applies when there is a mistake of fact. A mistake of law does not excuse. Now mistake, as this term is understood in jurisprudence, is used in the sense of misconception or error of judgment not intended to produce the result attained. As stated in the Penal Law of British India by Gour, 5th edition, page 265:

> "Such a mistake may or may not be due to forgetfulness, ignorance, imperfect information, or faulty ratiocination. It may be due to chance, negligence, stupidity or even superstition, but it must not be due to design, pre-arrangement or pre-concert."

If a person is deliberately carrying arms to the police station there is no mistake as that term is used in jurisprudence. He knows what he is carrying and he is intentionally carrying those arms. Accordingly he cannot claim the protection of either s 76 or s 79 of the Penal Code.

Therefore our answer to question (3) set out above–ie whether a person carrying arms with a view to handing them to the police is guilty of an offence against s 3(I) of the Public Order and Safety Proclamation–is in the affirmative.

Having so decided we add that in our view the Legislature should seriously consider the advisability of amending the Proclamation so that persons who can prove they are carrying arms with the intention of surrendering them to the proper authorities should not be criminally liable. Until such an amendment is made, persons who do so must rely on the Public Prosecutor not to prosecute them.

Appeal dismissed

Bron McKillop "Strict liability offences in Singapore and Malaysia" (1967) 9 Mal LR 118, 119–120

The court [in *Sulong b Nain*, 1947] rejected this argument [ie defence of mistake under ss 76 and 79 of the Penal Code] on the ground that there had been no mistake of fact as these sections required. It said: "If a person is deliberately carrying arms to the police station there is no mistake as that term is used in jurisprudence. He knows that he is carrying and he is intentionally carrying those arms." Now the court is here suggesting that if the accused had been mistaken as to what he was carrying–if for instance he had believed he was carrying mangoes instead of hand grenades–he would have been entitled to the defence of mistake. But this is inconsistent with the court's earlier ruling that carrying arms was absolutely prohibited. If carrying arms is absolutely prohibited then if a person carries what are in fact arms he is liable, no matter what he thought he was carrying or how unintentional his carrying was. The offence is either one of absolute liability or lack of *mens rea* will prevent a conviction. The error here seems to lie in a failure to appreciate that mistake as a defence negatives *mens rea*. If *mens rea* is held not necessary for liability then there can be no scope for the defence of mistake.

There is the possibility that the court in *Sulong* used the notion of absolute prohibition in a different sense. After ruling that the offence of carrying arms was one of absolute prohibition, the court continued that it was "not necessary to prove any ulterior intention to establish the offence." This seems to suggest that the offence is being described as absolute in the sense that an intention to use the arms in a way prejudicial to public order and safety is not necessary for liability. This could still leave a measure of *mens rea* required for proof of "carrying", eg knowledge that it is arms that are being carried. Then mistake as to the nature of what is being carried could be a defence. It is submitted, however, that this possible second sense of "absolute prohibition" is quite untenable. As the offence of carrying arms was not defined to include an intent to use the arms in a prejudicial way, this intention could only be regarded as a motive for the offence. Whatever else it may mean, absolute prohibition can hardly be used to signify no more than the irrelevance of motive.

(b) Mistake in possession of drugs

The Misuse of Drugs Act (Singapore) (Cap 185) provides for certain offences involving possession of controlled drugs. Section 18(1) contains a number of presumptions relating to possession, custody or control of a controlled drug. Section 18(2) provides that any person who is proved or presumed to have had a controlled drug in his possession is presumed to have known the *nature* of such drug. The burden is on an accused to prove, on a balance of probabilities, that he does not know the nature of the controlled drug. A person may be able to rebut the presumption under s 18(2) on the ground that he is mistaken as to the nature of the drug. A similar provision in Malaysia is contained in s 37(d) of the Dangerous Drugs Act 1952 (Act 234). (This Act was extended to Sabah and Sarawak by PU(A) 157/78 Modification of Laws (Dangerous Drugs and Poisons) (Extension and Modification) Order 1978.)

In *Tan Ah Tee* (1980) the Court of Criminal Appeal, Singapore, considered the sort of explanation required to rebut the presumption under s 18(2) of the Misuse of Drugs Act. The court approved the approach taken by Lord Pearce in the English House of Lords decision in *Warner v Metropolitan Police Commissioner* (1969). Lord Pearce examined the meaning of the word "possess" and inquired how much knowledge is needed. He said:

> If we go to the extreme length of requiring the prosecution to prove that "possession" implies a full knowledge of the name and nature of the drug concerned, the efficacy of the Act is seriously impaired, since many drug pedlars may in truth be unaware of this. I think that the term "possession" is satisfied by a knowledge only of the existence of the thing itself and not its qualities, and that ignorance or mistake as to its qualities is not an excuse.

The kinds of mistake that could arise in possession of drugs as considered in the *Warner* court were:

(1)   A is under a mistaken belief that he possesses aspirins but they turn out to be heroin tablets. He is liable as he is in possession of heroin tablets.

(2)   A believes that the above heroin tablets are sweets. He is also liable as he is in possession of heroin tablets.

In (1) and (2) above, the physical characteristics of heroin may well be similar to aspirins or sweets. His Lordship made a distinction between mistake as to quality and mistake as to something "wholly different in nature". While the former could not provide an excuse, the latter could. For example, if A were to think that what he possessed were biscuits and not heroin that would satisfy his Lordship's test of mistake as to something wholly different in nature, unlike sweets (which can resemble heroin tablets) and the accused could escape liability.

The Misuse of Drugs Act (Singapore) may be considered a statute creating strict liability offences. Its objective is to stamp out the grave social evil of drug abuse (See ch 3; Koh, 1973). However, in view of the grave penalties imposed, including the death penalty, provision is made (eg in s 18(2)) for the accused to prove, on a balance of probabilities, that he was not in possession and *did not know the nature of the controlled drug*, eg if he made a mistake. The English Drugs (Prevention of Misuse) Act 1964 does not contain an equivalent of s 18(2). The House of Lords in *Warner* (1969) proceeded on the knowledge required in the word "possession" itself in order to draw the distinction between a mistake as to nature or kind and as to quality.

Yeo (1985) criticized the Court of Criminal Appeal in *Tan Ah Tee* (1980) for relying on Lord Pearce's judgment in *Warner* (1969) which spelt out when and how an accused could rebut an allegation of drug possession. He said:

> Instead of relying on this common law defence, the court in *Tan Ah Tee* should have dealt with s 79 of the Code which, applies equally to penal statutes. This is especially so when there is no provision in the Misuse of Drugs Act which ousts the application of this section.

It is submitted that the special provision in s 18(2) of the Misuse of Drugs Act, being narrower in scope, overrides s 79 of the Penal Code should the two provisions be inconsistent. Thus, as we have seen, a mistake between aspirins/heroin or sweets/heroin may not be considered a mistake as to "nature" under s 18(2) of the Misuse of Drugs Act and, hence, would not absolve the drug trafficker. If the defence of mistake under s 79 of the Penal Code were to apply, it would absolve an accused because a mistaken belief that heroin tablets are either aspirins or sweets is a mistake of fact. They are different things. However, it is submitted that s 79 of the Penal Code is superseded by the express provision relating to mistake as to the "nature" of a drug under s 18(2) of the Misuse of Drugs Act–the rule of statutory interpretation, ie *generalia specialibus non derogant* (general words do not derogate from special provisions, or special provisions will control general provisions) should apply.

Following *Warner* (1969), Singapore courts could draw the distinction between quality and nature. On this basis, the aspirin/heroin mistake would not absolve an accused: both are drugs. It could be regarded a mistake as to quality. However, would a mistake between sweets and heroin be regarded as a distinction wholly different in nature in the Singapore context? In England it is quite common knowledge what heroin looks like and what form it may take. The position in Singapore may well be different as it is not common knowledge that heroin can look like sweets. A Singapore court interpreting s 18(2) on mistake as to the nature of the controlled drug could depart from this aspect of the *Warner* (1969) approach. A Singapore court could hold that a sweets/heroin mistake is one regarding the nature of a thing as the physical characteristics of the two may not be appreciated by the public at large.

Chapter 10

Accident

By KL Koh

Penal Code, s 80

Nothing is an offence which is done by accident or misfortune, and without any criminal intention or knowledge, in the doing of a lawful act in a lawful manner, by lawful means, and with proper care and caution.

Illustration

A is at work with a hatchet; the head flies off and kills a man who is standing by. Here, if there was no want of proper caution on the part of A, his act is excusable and not an offence.

"Accident" is not defined in the Penal Code. Its scope is thus uncertain. For instance, it has been argued that it is wide enough to cover cases of automatism (see ch 3, above). In *Ong Choon* (1938), the Court of Criminal Appeal in Singapore approved the definition given by Stephen (1883):

> ... an effect is said to be accidental when the act by which it is caused is not done with the intention of causing it, and when its occurrence as a consequence of such act is not so probable that a person of ordinary prudence ought, under the circumstances in which it is done, to take reasonable precautions against it.

The act must be unintentional and a pure accident. (See *Ratnam*, 1937.) Where an accused intentionally causes harm or does an act with the knowledge that it is likely to cause harm there can be no "accident" under s 80. For the meaning of "criminal intention", see ch 7, above, pp 160-163.

A. Lawful act

The act must be a lawful one done in a lawful manner by lawful means. In *Timmappa* (1901) the victim and the accused were hunting porcupines in the jungle. They took up different positions to lie in wait for the game. At nightfall the accused heard a rustle and believing it was a porcupine, fired a shot which went into the victim's heart and he died immediately. He was convicted under s 304(A) of the Indian Penal Code. On appeal, the Division Bench of Bombay held that the defence of accident under s 80 of the Indian Penal Code applied.

Problems arise with regard to the requirement that the accused's act be "lawful". Suppose A is in possession of an unlicensed gun which he uses to go hunting. Would the shooting with an unlicensed gun preclude him from relying on the defence of accident? Would the common law distinction between *malum in se* and *malum prohibitum* determine whether shooting with an unlicensed gun is merely a technical offence (ie *malum prohibitum*)? If so, then the shooting could be regarded a "lawful act" under s 80 of the Penal Code. However, Mayne (1901) pointed out that this distinction must be applied with caution:

> Where the injury is purely accidental, but results from doing an act which is not *malum in se* but *malum prohibitum*, as being forbidden by statute under a penalty, it is stated by some of the highest authorities that this illegality does not render the accidental act criminal. Sir James Stephen says he thinks this distinction can no longer be regarded as law. Probably the decision would depend upon the further question whether the harm resulting from the accident was the sort of harm the statute had intended to prevent. Suppose, for instance, that a statute forbade under a penalty the sale of poisons, except in coloured and ribbed bottles, and that a chemist sold laudanum in a plain bottle, and that in consequence it was swallowed by accident as a harmless draught. There his act was perfectly innocent before the statute, but, from disregard of its provisions, the very death which the statutes intended to prevent, naturally resulted. I think he would certainly not be protected by s 80. The case put by Lord Hale is that of a man who accidentally kills another, while he is shooting without a game licence. Here it is evident the statute was intended to protect the King's Revenue, and not his subjects. On the same principle it has been frequently decided, that where a statute directs, or forbids, a particular act, in order to secure some special purpose, no action can be brought for the breach of it, by a person who has been injured in a way which the statute never contemplated.

An example where the accused was not doing a lawful act in a lawful manner by lawful means is *Jageshar* (1923) where the accused was beating a person with his fists when the latter's wife, with a baby on her shoulder, interfered. The accused hit the woman but the blow "accidentally" struck the baby and two days later it died from the effects of the blow. The Oudh High Court held that s 80 of the Indian Penal Code did not apply as he was doing an unlawful act.

This case can be distinguished from *Ong Choon* (1938), where the Singapore Court of Criminal Appeal quashed a conviction for murder on the ground that the defence of accident under s 80 was not put before the jury. During a fight the deceased was trying to push a knife into the appellant's chest. The appellant who was holding the deceased's hand (which had the knife) was trying to get away from him and was asking him to throw away the knife. The deceased refused and the appellant released the deceased's hand. The impact of the release was such that the deceased inflicted injuries on his own neck from which he died. It is noted that although the fight itself was an unlawful act, the "accident" occurred while the appellant was doing a lawful act of trying to release himself so as to stop the fighting.

Another case where the defence of accident might have succeeded is the Malaysian case of *Kong Poh Ing* (1977). The accused told her boyfriend that she wanted to commit suicide as he had betrayed her. When she showed him the knife, he hugged her and told her not to die. He then attempted to wrench the knife from her. They fell and he was "accidentally" stabbed in the stomach. The Federal Court allowed the appeal against her conviction for murder on the ground that the defence of accident was not adequately put to the assessors. (See *Ratnam*, 1937.)

It is noted that when the deceased intervened she was not in the act of committing suicide but had only expressed an intention to do so. Was she doing an unlawful act? If not, what was the lawful act? If she had done an act towards killing herself and the deceased had wrenched the knife from her in the course of which he was "accidentally" stabbed, then the defence of accident would not apply as she was doing an unlawful act, ie attempting suicide under s 309 of the Penal Code.

B. Proper care and caution

In *Hori Lal* (1983), a free fight occurred in the house of the accused. He aimed a lathi blow on "N" who had caused an injury to his father and suddenly the deceased came in between them to pacify the parties. The lathi blow which was aimed at "N" landed on the head of the deceased causing the fatal injury. What could have happened was that when the accused's father fell down on receiving the head injury, the accused aimed the lathi blow in defence of his father. The High Court of Uttar Pradesh held that the accused was exercising the right of private defence and was doing a lawful act in a lawful manner. On the evidence the court held that the facts did not disclose the absence of proper care and caution. Misra J stated:

> The caution which the law requires is not the utmost that can be used. It is sufficient if it is reasonable, such as is usual in ordinary and similar cases. The amount of care and caution must be such as a prudent and reasonable man would consider to be adequate upon all the circumstances of the case.

Another case which also demonstrates that care and caution had been exercised is *Ramgaswami Narsimha Naidu* (1952). The respondent fired at the deceased under the impression that it was the hyena which had been seen in the vicinity of his quarters on the previous day. His companions also shared the impression. At the time of the shooting it was raining, the sky was over-cast and visibility was poor. The respondent said that he had not expected a human being to be there and that the object at which he aimed had a brown covering. The deceased was wearing a gunny bag at that time. The court acquitted the respondent in respect of a charge under s 304A of the Indian Penal Code. On the facts, the court held that the care and circumspection taken by the respondent was such that a prudent and reasonable man would consider to be adequate upon all the circumstances of the case. The defence of accident under s 80 of the Indian Penal Code was available to him.

Chapter 11

Duress

By CMV Clarkson

A. Introduction

Penal Code, s 94

Except murder and offences against the State punishable with death, nothing is an offence which is done by a person who is compelled to do it by threats, which, at the time of doing it, reasonably cause the apprehension that instant death to that person will otherwise be the consequence:

Provided that the person doing the act did not of his own accord, or from a reasonable apprehension of harm to himself short of instant death, place himself in the situation by which he became subject to such constraint.

[FMS Penal Code, s 94 exempts murder and "offences included in Chapter VI punishable with death".]

Explanation 1–A person who, of his own accord, or by reason of a threat of being beaten, joins gang-robbers knowing their character, is not entitled to the benefit of this exception on the ground of his having been compelled by his associates to do anything that is an offence by law.

Explanation 2–A person seized by gang-robbers, and forced by threat of instant death to do a thing which is an offence by law–for example, a smith compelled to take his tools and to force the door of a house for the gang-robbers to enter and plunder it–is entitled to the benefit of this exception.

Mohamed Yusof b Haji Ahmad v PP [1983] 2 MLJ 167 (HC, Kedah, Malaysia)

The appellant was convicted of trafficking in dangerous drugs (cannabis). He claimed that he had been forced to do so by a Thai man who had threatened him with a pistol and told him to carry two bags of cannabis across the border into Malaysia. If he obeyed he would be paid M$400; if he disobeyed he would be shot. He was convicted and he appealed.

Syed Agil Barakbah J: The appellant was found guilty of trafficking on his own behalf of dangerous drugs to wit 2,700 grammes of cannabis, an offence under s 39B(1)(a) of the Dangerous Drugs Ordinance 1952, on December 27 1977 at about 1.45 pm at the Railway Station, Padang Besar, Perlis and was sentenced to life imprisonment and with four strokes of the rotan. He has now appealed against both the conviction and sentence....

In his defence the appellant admitted that he carried the two bags containing cannabis but maintained that he did so under threat from a male Thai, a Malaysian Citizen named Peri bin Safar, whom he met by chance in a hotel in Sadau. The man threatened him with a pistol and told him to carry the two bags across the border to the railway station, Padang Besar and if he did so the Thai promised to pay him M$400 but if he did not do so he would be shot. He was also warned not to go through the customs check point otherwise he would be shot. From Sadau the man gave him a lift on his motorcycle to Pekan Siam and from there he walked across the border and the railway lines to the railway station carrying the bags. The man he said followed him on foot up to the railway station and was about 20 feet or so away when he was arrested by the police. In his grounds of judgment the learned President discussed the provisions of section 94 of the Penal Code quite in detail and concluded that the appellant had failed to bring himself under the protection of that section.... He found the appellant guilty as charged....

Under this section there must be reasonable fear, at the very time, of instant death. Persons who do criminal acts from fear of anything but instant death do them at their peril. If an offence is completed when all danger of instant death has been removed the person committing the offence is not protected under this section. Further if the accused on his own accord places himself in a situation by which he became subject to the threats of another person, whatever threats may have been used towards him, the provisions of this section do not apply.

In *Tan Seng Ann* (1949) Willan CJ, delivering the judgment in the Court of Appeal in Kuala Lumpur held that duress in order to be pleaded successfully must be imminent, extreme and persistent. The facts in that case were that the appellant and 4 other Chinese were stopped while travelling in a motorcar and detained. As a result of the finding of a house key on his person, the appellant led the police to his house, unlocked the door with the key and pointed to the police inspector a revolver which was lying concealed in a cupboard. At the trial he made a statement from the dock stating that two men brought a small parcel requesting him to keep it in the house for the night. On being told that it contained a revolver he objected and requested them to take it away to avoid any trouble with the authorities. In spite of his non-cooperation they left the parcel in his house, took him in the car to Selayang where they were stopped by the police and arrested. The Court of Appeal in supporting the conviction concluded that there was nothing on the record in that case to suggest that duress was present or continued when the appellant went out in the car with the other Chinese.

Applying the principle stated above it is apparent that the illustration at Explanation 2 of section 94, the threat of instant death to the smith who was forced to open the door of the house for the gang-robbers to enter and plunder it, is imminent, extreme and persistent as to entitle him to the benefit of the exception even though he had committed an offence under the law which is not punishable with death. In the presence of the robbers it was reasonable for him to have the apprehension of being killed instantly if he refused to carry out their threat. With respect I do not agree with the trial President that since the accused mentioned about being shot rather than being killed there was no threat of instant death. A pistol shot at or near the vital part of the body normally results in instant death. Each case of course depends on the facts and surrounding circumstances. In the present case apart from being threatened by the Thai of being shot the man also followed him on foot by keeping a distance of about 20 feet or so away. However, from the appellant's own version he had complied with the request to carry the two bags to the railway station and had successfully eluded the customs check point. He had reached the station, placed the bags on the platform and had gone to purchase a ticket all indicating that he was leaving Padang Besar. He had been carrying the drug for about one and a half hours and had made no attempt to approach any member of the public or police authorities for help. In short he had already completed his mission except for the handing over the drugs to the Thai who was according to him also at the station platform and collect the $400 from him. In the circumstances it is my considered judgment that there is nothing to suggest that when the appellant placed the bags on the platform and went to purchase the ticket such duress was present or continued to be present.

Secondly, although according to the appellant the Thai was about 20 ft away on the platform when he last saw him, the presence of some people there, not to mention the four police personnel (then not known to the appellant), considered with the facts, stated above, rendered the duress no longer imminent, extreme or persistent. I find that there are no merits in this appeal and accordingly dismiss it.

As regards the sentence, in view of the seriousness of the offence the imposition of life imprisonment is therefore justified. However in the light of the extenuating circumstances which led him to commit the offence, he should be spared the rotan. He is a first offender.

Conviction affirmed;
Sentence to life imprisonment affirmed;
Sentence of whipping quashed

B. Rationale

The main rationale of the defence of duress is that a person forced to commit crimes through appalling threats has had no opportunity for effective choice; his actions are in effect "morally involuntary" and as such he deserves no blame. The law does not demand heroism of people, nor can it expect martyrdom. In the words of Lord Morris in *Lynch* (1975):

> For the law to understand not only how the timid but also the stalwart may in a moment of crisis behave is not to make the law weak but to make it just. ...[M]ust the law not remember that the instinct and perhaps the duty of self-preservation is powerful and natural?

Accordingly, duress can perhaps best be viewed as an *excuse*. The accused has done wrong but is exempted from blame on the basis that we can excuse his conduct given the overwhelming evil with which he was threatened.

It is further argued that criminal liability is inappropriate in such cases as none of the law's utilitarian objectives can be achieved in such cases. The law cannot hope to have a deterrent impact on persons committing crimes through sheer terror. Such persons are also clearly not dangerous, nor in need of rehabilitation.

On the other hand, it has been argued that a general defence of duress could provide a "charter for terrorists, gang leaders and kidnappers". In the famous words of Stephen (1883):

> Surely it is the moment when temptation to crime is strongest that the law should speak most clearly and emphatically to the contrary. It is, of course, a misfortune for a man that he should be placed between two fires, but it would be a much greater misfortune for society at large if criminals could confer immunity upon their agents by threatening them with death or violence.

It could further be argued that there are sound reasons for denying a general defence of duress. Particularly in doubtful situations it could help encourage threatened persons to try and resist their aggressors or seek help in other ways. For instance, complete denial of a defence of duress could have encouraged the accused in *Mohamed Yusof b Haji Ahmad* (1983) either to try and seek assistance or to escape from the Thai man.

The Penal Code, s 94, has opted for a general exception of duress. However, as will be revealed, there is an implicit recognition of the above competing arguments in that this general exception is so narrowly defined as to be available only in the most extreme situations.

C. The law

It is clear from s 94 and cases interpreting it that it is not necessary for the duress to induce such a state of fear that *mens rea* is negated. Indeed, were such an extreme terror induced, the accused would lack the necessary *mens rea* for a prima facie case of liability. The crucial point is that the accused is not blameworthy and therefore liability is inappropriate. The presence or absence of *mens rea* is only one factor (admittedly an important one) indicating whether the requisite degree of blameworthiness is established.

An analysis of s 94 reveals the following essential characteristics of the defence of duress under the Penal Code:

1. Threat must be one of death

No threat of extreme torture or serious injury short of death will suffice. This seems unduly strict and inconsistent with the rationale of the defence of duress as a concession to human infirmity. When faced with the threat of having one's fingernails torn out, one's eyes gouged out or one's home burnt to the ground the Penal Code clearly expects stoic valour!

There are two main alternatives that could be employed if seeking to effect a reform of the Penal Code on this point. Under English law the threat can be one of either death or serious bodily injury (*Lynch*, 1975;

Hudson and Taylor, 1971; *Valderrama-Vega*, 1985). Only in the presence of such overwhelming threats can the accused be said to be excused from blame on commission of a crime. Alternatively, one could adopt the approach adopted in the USA which involves a "balancing of harms" (Model Penal Code, 1962). Broadly speaking, one is permitted to commit a lesser harm to avoid a greater harm. If one stole a necklace in the face of a threat to destroy one's house, the defence of duress would be available.

2. Threat must be one of instant death

Threats of future violence will not generate the defence of duress. In *Tan Seng Ann* (1949) it was held that the threat must be "imminent, extreme and persistent". It was on this basis that the accused in *Mohamed Yusof b Haji Ahmad* (1983) failed in establishing his defence of duress. While there might have been an initial threat of instant death, by the time he reached the railway station, where there were several other people (including four policemen–albeit unknown to the accused as such) after having carried the drugs for one and a half hours without having made any attempt to approach any member of the public for help, the threat was no longer "imminent, extreme and persistent".

This is yet again an extremely narrow approach bearing in mind that all the time, including at the station, the Thai man was armed and only 20 feet away from the accused. Contrast this approach with that adopted by the Privy Council in *Subramaniam* (1956) and by the English Court of Appeal in *Hudson* and *Taylor* (1971). Which approach would be more consistent with the underlying rationale of the defence of duress?

Subramaniam v PP (1956) 22 MLJ 220 (PC, appeal from Malaya)

The appellant was convicted of being in possession of 20 rounds of ammunition contrary to reg 4(1)(b) of the Emergency Regulations 1951. He claimed he had been captured by Chinese communist terrorists and forced to go through a terrorist training programme during which time he was compelled to carry the ammunition.

Mr LMD de Silva: This is an appeal by special leave from a judgment of the Supreme Court of the Federation of Malaya (Mathew CJ, Wilson and Abbott JJ) dismissing an appeal against a conviction in the High Court of Johore Bahru (Storr J, sitting with two assessors) whereby the appellant was found guilty of being in possession on the 29th April 1955, of 20 rounds of ammunition contrary to regulation 4(1)(b) of the Emergency Regulations 1951, and sentenced to death....

The defence put forward on behalf of the appellant was that he had been captured by terrorists, that at material times he was acting under duress, and that at the time of his capture by the security forces he had formed the intention to surrender with which intention he had come to the place where he was found....

The members of the security forces deposed *inter alia* that on the 29th April a patrol went out to search a terrorist camp where an engagement had occurred earlier on the same day between another patrol and some terrorists. The patrol found the camp deserted. On searching the surrounding area they found the appellant wounded on the head, back, neck, right arm and right hand, with a belt containing twenty rounds of ammunition upon him. It was in respect of this ammunition that the appellant was charged.

The police inspector produced a statement which, after due caution, he had obtained, with the aid of the interpreter, from the appellant while he was lying in hospital in a wounded condition. In this statement he appellant said, among other things, that while walking along a certain road he was accosted by three Chinese terrorists armed with pistols and made to follow them, one walking in front and two behind him. He said that he was taken to a place where there were about a hundred terrorists, all armed, where he stayed about a month and was given training, and that after this training he was given a rifle and ammunition. He said he left the camp with twelve others to collect food and that after some days they camped at the spot where they were attacked by security forces....

It does not appear that he was asked whether the carrying of the ammunition, and his conduct generally, was voluntary or the result of duress, and there is nothing in the statement to the effect that duress had been exercised except what might be gathered remotely from the fact that the terrorists were armed.

The appellant gave evidence in defence. He called witnesses to give evidence as to his character and to support his story as to how he had been occupied for some months before his capture by the terrorists.

The appellant described his capture thus:

"... when I was just walking down a small hill, where there was lallang at the sides, a Chinese came out and asked me to halt; I did not know then that he was a communist; he came from behind me. I asked him why are you stopping me? I want to return home. He spoke in Malay and I replied in Malay. He then asked me: Do you know who I am? and so saying he drew out a revolver from behind him; to all appearance he was a civilian; he pointed that pistol at me and said 'I am a communist' and it was then I knew that he was one. He asked me to produce my Identity Card; when he looked at my Identity Card he spoke something in his own language and 2 others came out; the 3 then surrounded me; of the other 2 one had a pistol and the other had a rifle about a yard long; they told me I could not return home; two of them had knives like sickles."

He then described how he was forced to accompany the terrorists, one of whom walked in front and two behind, who told him he was being taken to their leader....

In the course of his evidence the appellant stated that he was given the ammunition belt to wear but no weapon, the object, according to him, being that others could use the ammunition. The evidence of the appellant, such as it was, suggested generally that he was in fear, that he planned unsuccessfully to escape, and that he had no alternative but to do as the terrorists asked him to do. He said amongst other things, "I could not refuse wearing the belt; if I had refused they would have done anything to me." Those words, in the context in which they occur, may well have been used by the appellant to indicate, as best as he could, that owing to what the terrorists said and did he was in reasonable fear of instant death if he refused to do what the terrorists demanded of him....

On the question of duress the following passage appears in ... [the trial judge's] judgment, "The question of duress was raised by the learned Counsel for the defence. Although I cannot find any evidence of duress, I put to the Gentlemen Assessors a question on that point." He then stated what the question was and what the answers were and went on to say, "With these answers I am unable to agree. I can find no evidence from which duress can be said to have been proved by the defence."

Their Lordships cannot agree with the statement made by the learned trial Judge to the assessors and repeated in his judgment that there was no evidence of duress in the evidence recorded, if by that statement he meant that as a matter of law there was no evidence of duress to be considered by a jury or, as in this case, by a Judge and assessors. The evidence may, after due consideration, have failed on grounds of credibility or other grounds, to establish the existence of duress but it would be incorrect to say that there was no evidence.

It is possible, though it is not clear, that in saying what he did the learned Judge did not intend to say that there was no evidence of duress but was saying (as he was entitled to do) that the evidence was unacceptable. The last sentence in the passage from his judgment quoted above would appear to support this view.

It is also possible, though in their Lordships' view, improbable, that the learned trial Judge directed himself and the assessors that there was no evidence of duress because at the actual moment of capture the terrorists had left and the learned Judge thought that duress, if it had existed, had then ceased to exist. But threats previously made could have been a continuing menace at the moment the appellant was captured, and this possibility was at least a matter for consideration by a jury or by a Judge and assessors. The terrorists or some of them may have come back at any moment.

Whatever may be said of the evidence of duress on the record it is only fair to the appellant to assume that the evidence which the appellant was in the course of, but was wrongly prevented from, giving would have borne upon the vital issues of duress, and their Lordships have to consider whether in the circumstances of this case this exclusion of admissible evidence affords sufficient reason for allowing this appeal....

Their Lordships feel unable to hold with any confidence that had the excluded evidence, which goes to the very root of the defence of duress, been admitted, the result of the trial would probably have been the same.

For the reasons which have been given their Lordships have humbly advised Her Majesty that the appeal be allowed.

Appeal allowed

R v Hudson and Taylor [1971] 2 QB 202 (CA, Criminal Division, England)

The appellants, two girls, told lies in court in an unlawful wounding case in which they were the principal prosecution witnesses. When charged with perjury they claimed that they had been threatened that they would be "cut up" unless they committed perjury; they were so frightened that they duly told the lies in court. They were convicted of perjury and they appealed.

Widgery LJ: This appeal raises two main questions: first, as to the nature of the necessary threat and, in particular, whether it must be "present and immediate"; secondly, as to the extent to which a right to plead duress may be lost if the accused has failed to take steps to remove the threat as, for example, by seeking police protection.

It is essential to the defence of duress that the threat shall be effective at the moment when the crime is committed. The threat must be a "present" threat in the sense that it is effective to neutralize the will of the accused at that time. Hence an accused who joins a rebellion under the compulsion of threats cannot plead duress if he remains with the rebels after the threats have lost their effect and his own will has had a chance to re-assert itself.... Similarly a threat of future violence may be so remote as to be insufficient to overpower the will at the moment when the offence was committed, or the accused may have elected to commit the offence in order to rid himself of a threat hanging over him and not because he was driven to act by immediate and unavoidable pressure. In none of these cases is the defence of duress available because a person cannot justify the commission of a crime merely to secure his own peace of mind.

When, however, there is no opportunity for delaying tactics, and the person threatened must make up his mind whether he is to commit the criminal act or not, the existence at that moment of threats sufficient to destroy his will ought to provide him with a defence even though the threatened injury may not follow instantly, but after an interval. This principle is illustrated by *Subramaniam* (1956) when the appellant was charged in Malaya with unlawful possession of ammunition and was held by the Privy Council to have a defence of duress, fit to go to the jury, on his plea that he had been compelled by terrorists to accept the ammunition and feared for his safety if the terrorists returned.

In the present case the threats of Farrell were likely to be no less compelling, because their execution could not be effected in the court room, if they could be carried out in the streets of Salford the same night. Insofar, therefore, as the recorder ruled as a matter of law that the threats were not sufficiently present and immediate to support the defence of duress we think that he was in error. He should have left the jury to decide whether the threats had overborne the will of the appellants at the time when they gave the false evidence.

Counsel for the Crown, however, contends that the recorder's ruling can be supported on another ground, namely, that the appellants should have taken steps to neutralize the threats by seeking police protection either when they came to court to give evidence, or beforehand. He submits on grounds of public policy that an accused should not be able to plead duress if he had the opportunity to ask for protection from the police before committing the offence and failed to do so. The argument does not distinguish cases in which the police would be able to provide effective protection, from those when they would not, and it would, in effect, restrict the defence of duress to cases where the person threatened had been kept in custody by the maker of the threats, or where the time interval between the making of the threats and the commission of the offence had made recourse to the police impossible. We recognize the need to keep the defence of duress within reasonable bounds but cannot accept so severe a restriction on it. The duty, of the person threatened, to take steps to remove the threat does not seem to have arisen in an English case but in a full review of the defence of duress in the Supreme Court of Victoria (*Harley Murray* (1967)), a condition of raising the defence was said to be that the accused "had no means, with safety to himself, of preventing the execution of the threat".

In the opinion of this court it is always open to the Crown to prove that the accused failed to avail himself of some opportunity which was reasonably open to him to render the threat ineffective, and that on this being established the threat in question can no longer be relied on by the defence. In deciding whether such an opportunity was reasonably open to the accused the jury should have regard to his age and circumstances, and to any risks to him which may be involved in the course of action relied on.

In our judgment the defence of duress should have been left to the jury in the present case, as should any issue raised by the Crown and arising out of the appellants' failure to seek police protection. The appeals will, therefore, be allowed and the convictions quashed.

Appeals allowed

3. Threat is objective in character

The accused must *reasonably* apprehend instant death. The fear must be well founded by the sort of threat that would also make the reasonable man apprehend death. In *Mohamed Yusof b Haji Ahmad (1983)* there was no express threat of *death* but rather to "shoot at" the accused. It was held that "a pistol shot at or near the vital part of the body normally results in instant death". The accused had reasonably apprehended death.

4. Threat must be directed at accused himself

Threats to kill one's wife, children, parents and so on will not suffice. Again this seems out of touch with the rationale of the law of duress. Many persons might indeed be heroic when faced with only harm to themselves but will give in to the pressure of death to those nearest to them. Laws that are made to regulate the affairs of men as opposed to gods should recognize this. Of course, once it is accepted that one can commit crimes to protect other persons it becomes difficult to determine how far the category should be extended. The English Law Commission (1974) has even suggested that the defence should be available when one acts to protect a complete stranger.

5. Voluntary exposure to threats

The defence is not available to those who voluntarily placed themselves in a situation by which they became subject to the threats. This is made clear by the proviso to s 94 and by Explanation 1 thereto. For instance, in the English case of *Lynch* (1975) it was made clear that if one chose to join an organization such as the IRA, known to use violence, one could not at a later date shelter behind a defence of duress should other members of the organization compel one to commit crimes. One could be blamed for joining the terrorist organization and this blame would infect one's subsequent actions. There are many unresolved problems in this regard–for instance, must the accused know that he is likely to be exposed to threats of death? What if he did not know but ought to have known?

6.   Restrictions on use of the defence

Offences against the state are mainly contained in Chapter VI of the Penal Code with the offences in s 121 (waging war against the government) and s 121A (imagining the death of the President) carrying the death penalty. Any other "offence against the State" punishable with death would be included even though not included within Chapter VI. In Malaysia the exception is slightly narrower with s 94 reading "Except murder and offences included in Chapter VI punishable with death...".

This exclusion of murder and offences against the state punishable by death from the ambit of the defence of duress is highly controversial. In the light of the following views is such an approach justifiable?

Abbott v R (1976) 3 All ER 140 (PC)

Lord Salmon: Counsel for the appellant has argued that the law presupposes a degree of heroism of which the ordinary man is incapable and which therefore should not be expected of him and that modern conditions and concepts of humanity have rendered obsolete the rule that the actual killer cannot rely on duress as a defence. Their Lordships do not agree. In the trials of those responsible for wartime atrocities such as mass killings of men, women or children, inhuman experiments on human beings, often resulting in death, and like crimes, it was invariably argued for the defence that these atrocities should be excused on the grounds that they resulted from superior orders and duress: if the accused had refused to do these dreadful things, they would have been shot and therefore they should be acquitted and allowed to go free. This argument has always been universally rejected. Their Lordships would be sorry indeed to see it accepted by the common law of England.

It seems incredible to their Lordships that in any civilized society, acts such as the appellant's, whatever threats may have been made to him, could be regarded as excusable or within the law. We are not living in a dream world in which the mounting wave of violence and terrorism can be contained by strict logic and intellectual niceties alone. Common sense surely reveals the added dangers to which in this modern world the public would be exposed, if the change in the law proposed on behalf of the appellant were effected. It might well, as Lord Simon of Glaisdale said in *Lynch* (1975), prove to be a charter for terrorists, gang leaders and kidnappers. A terrorist of notorious violence might, eg threaten death to A and his family unless A obeys his instructions to put a bomb with a time fuse set by A in a certain passenger aircraft and/or in a thronged market, railway station or the like. A, under duress, does obey his instructions and as a result, hundreds of men, women and children are killed or mangled. Should the contentions made on behalf of the appellant be correct, A would have a complete defence and, if charged, would be bound to be acquitted and set at liberty. Having now gained some real experience and expertise, he might again be approached by the terrorist who would make the same threats and exercise the same duress under which A would then give a repeat performance, killing even more men, women and children. Is there any limit to the number of people you may kill to save your own life and that of your family?

S v Goliath (1972) 3 SA 1 (South Africa)

Rumpff J: It is generally accepted ... that for the ordinary person in general his life is more valuable than that of another. Only they who possess the quality of heroism will intentionally offer their lives for another. Should the criminal law then state that compulsion could never be a defence to a charge of murder, it would demand that a person who killed another under duress, whatever the circumstances, would have to comply with a higher standard than that demanded of the average person. I do not think that such an exception to the general rule which applies in criminal law, is justified.

For a decade English law introduced some flexibility in this regard with the House of Lords decision in *Lynch* (1975) that duress is a defence to a secondary party to murder, albeit not to the actual killer (*Abbott*, 1977). However, fearing the increase of terrorism with its potential for forcing innocent persons to commit crimes, the House of Lords in *Howe* (1986) has resiled from this position and denied the defence of duress both to the actual killer and those assisting him.

If a reform of s 94 were being contemplated, the central issue would be whether duress should be a defence to all crimes. Perhaps it might be politically more acceptable to effect reforms to s 94 if murder remained exempted. There is, however, a strong argument that while duress ought not to be a complete defence to murder, persons who kill in such circumstances are clearly less blameworthy than those who kill in "cold blood" and, accordingly, a new exception to s 300 ought to be introduced whereby those who kill under duress are convicted of culpable homicide not amounting to murder.

Peter English, "The Defence of Duress under the Penal Code" (1983) 25 Mal LR 404, 414

In some legal systems the narrowness of the scope of the duress defence might be of little practical consequence. The musings of theorists, interesting though they might be in terms of criminal law principles, need not be of great social significance. If there are no death penalties and no mandatory sentences matters which amounted to duress in the ordinary sense, albeit not within the legal sense, can be taken into account when it comes to sentence. The defence may fail, in law, but the sentencer can take account of it, even perhaps to the extent of imposing a nominal penalty. In addition, there are the powers of the Executive to commute sentences and there is prosecutorial discretion not to press charges. The prosecutor can take account of the very real threats which compelled the accused to act in deciding whether to drop charges even though those threats did not amount, in law, to duress. This indeed is comforting and serves in some countries to assuage concern about the limited scope of the duress defence–and other defences. The question still remains whether it should be left to judicial or executive *discretion* to temper the severity of the law. If it is thought that a person who acted under threats which no ordinary person would have been capable of resisting should not be punished, then he ought not to be *liable to be punished.*

In some countries capital punishment is mandatory for a range of offences, and not just murder and treason. Other offences carry mandatory penalties–minimum sentences for drug trafficking, for example. If such is the case one cannot, with regard to those offences, rely on judicial discretion, in the sentencing process, to mitigate the effects of a too narrowly defined duress defence. There remains only the executive discretion in prosecution and commutation and remission of sentences to temper the law's strictness. The need for the legal definition of duress to be realistic, in terms of what can be expected of ordinary people, is strong. "[T]he criminal law should not be applied as if it were a blue print for saintliness, but rather in a manner in which it can be obeyed by the reasonable man." (*Goliath*, 1972).

Section 94, as it stands, demands quite enough saintliness. Let it be hoped that in its interpretation and application it will not appear that even more saintliness is being demanded of ordinary mortals.

Chapter 12

Unsoundness of mind

By KL Koh

A. Introduction

Penal Code, s 84

Nothing is an offence which is done by a person who, at the time of doing it, by reason of unsoundness of mind, is incapable of knowing the nature of the act, or that he is doing what is either wrong or contrary to law.

Courts have tended to refer to s 84 as dealing with "insanity" though the phrase used is "unsoundness of mind". The reason why such reference has been made is because s 84 drew its inspiration from the English McNaghten Rules (1843) on legal insanity, named after the famous House of Lords decision of *McNaghten* (1843). However, there are significant differences between the defence of unsoundness of mind and the defence of insanity as laid down in *McNaghten* (1843).

It is unfortunate that in the recent Malaysian case of *Tsung Tzee Chang* (1982, Unreported), the High Court in Malaya failed to appreciate that s 84 does not embody the legal test of insanity established in *McNaghten* (1843). Consequently, after referring to s 84 of the FMS Penal Code, the court proceeded to apply the McNaghten test of insanity:

> To establish a defence on the ground of insanity, it must be clearly proved that at the time of the committing of the act, the party accused was labouring under such a defect of reason, from disease of the mind, as not to know the nature and quality of the act he was doing, or if he did know it, that he did not know he was doing what was wrong.

To avoid confusion and to emphasize that "unsoundness of mind" is not the equivalent of "disease of mind", the terminology "unsoundness of mind" will be used to describe the defence under s 84, and "insanity" when reference is made to the McNaghten Rules (unless the context otherwise indicates, as when "insanity" is used by courts or academic writers to refer to s 84).

The original provisions contained in the draft Indian Penal Code (1837) dealt with persons who were idiots, mad or delirious. Section 66 of the draft Indian Penal Code (1837) reads: "Nothing is an offence which is done by a person in a state of idiocy."

Section 67 of the same draft reads:

> Nothing is an offence which is done by a person in consequence of being mad or delirious at the time of doing it.

In 1849 the Legislative Council of India enacted Act No IV and introduced the defence of unsoundness of mind in s 1 which reads:

> No person can be acquitted for unsoundness of mind, unless it can be proved that, by reason of unsoundness of mind, not wilfully caused by himself, he was unconscious and incapable of knowing, in doing the act, that he was doing an act forbidden by the law of the land.

This formulation, with some amendments, was subsequently incorporated in s 84 of the present Indian Penal Code which is *in pari materia* with s 84 of the Singapore and the FMS Penal Codes.

In contrast to s 84, s 85(2)(b) uses the word "insane" in cases of intoxication resulting in insanity (see ch 13).

B. The law

Before comparing s 84 with the legal test of insanity under the McNaghten rules, it is appropriate to consider that case.

In *McNaghten* (1843), Daniel McNaghten was charged with the murder of Edward Drummond, the private secretary of Sir Robert Peel who was then Prime Minister of England. McNaghten was suffering from delusions of persecution that Sir Robert Peel had injured him. He had intended to kill Sir Robert Peel but shot and killed Drummond instead, mistaking him for the former. He was acquitted on the ground of insanity. His acquittal raised a controversy in the House of Lords as a result of which a number of questions were put for the judges to answer. The answers to questions 2 and 3 form the legal test of insanity under the McNaghten Rules (1843):

> ... to establish a defence on the ground of insanity, it must be clearly proved that, at the time of the committing of the act, the party accused was labouring under such a defect of reason, from disease of the mind, as not to know the nature and quality of the act he was doing; or, if he did know it, that he did not know he was doing what was wrong.

Penal Code, s 84	*McNaghten Rules (1843)*
(1) ... at the time of doing it	... at the time of the committing of the act
(2) ... by reason of unsoundness of mind	... the party accused was labouring under such a defect of reason
(3) ——	... from
(4) ——	... disease of the mind
(5) ... is incapable of knowing	... as not to know

| (6) | ... the nature of the act | ... the nature and quality of the act he was doing |
| (7) | ... or that he is doing what is either wrong or contrary to law. | ... or, if he did know it, that he did not know he was doing what was wrong. |

There are two main limbs in s 84 of the Penal Code under which the accused is entitled to an acquittal. He can be acquitted if at the time of doing the act by reason of unsoundness of mind (1) he did not know the nature of the act, or (2) if he knew the nature of the act he did not know that it was either wrong or contrary to law.

1. Ingredients of the defence

(a) "At the time of doing it"

The crucial time that the accused is said to be suffering from unsoundness of mind, whether temporary or permanent, is the time of the commission of the offence. It is irrelevant if he was suffering from the alleged condition before or after the act.

(b) "By reason of unsoundness of mind"

The Penal Code does not define "unsoundness of mind". Trivedi (1981) states:

> Unsoundness of mine is a state when the mind does not function properly. It may manifest in so many ways eg idiocy, lunacy, imbecility, delusions, derangements, fits, etc. Then soundness or unsoundness is also a relative concept. It is matter of degrees. There is no hard and fast rule or limit within which a man can be said to be of sound mind. Normally a man can be said to be of unsound mind if he cannot understand others, cannot express himself, cannot judge the consequences of his acts or distinguish between good and bad, right and wrong. In other words, a person is of unsound mind whose mental faculties have been impaired and has become destitute of reason, intelligibility and coherence of thought. That is to say he has lost his mental balance or equilibrium. The unsoundness of mind may occur due to varied reasons and may be of varied degrees. It is not every degree of mental disease or disequilibrium that can avoid responsibility.

What is the difference between unsoundness of mind (s 84) and disease of the mind (McNaghten Rules)? To what extent do they over-lap?

Under the McNaghten Rules the disease of the mind must give rise to a defect of reason. There must be an impairment of the mind. In the English case of *Kemp* (1956), Devlin J held that legal insanity within the McNaghten Rules means malfunctioning of the mind–the mental faculties of reasoning, memory and understanding–caused by disease. The disease may be physical (organic) or functional in origin. There are two main categories of psychotic state–organic psychoses and functional psychoses.

HJ Wily and KR Stallworthy, *Mental Abnormality and the Law* **(1962), 26–27**

The psychoses fall into two great groups:

(a) *The organic psychoses,* in which there is some underlying physical cause for the mental derangement, such as the effect of some poison or of some other chemical derangement of the brain, or a degeneration or destruction of the brain such as may result from a tumour or loss of blood supply or a number of other diseases.

(b) *The functional psychoses,* which in medical terminology are equivalent to the various forms of insanity and in which there is no evidence of any physical disturbance of or damage to the brain.

The concept of "unsoundness of mind" is wider than "disease of the mind" causing a defect of reason. Section 84 would include not only diseases of the mind but, arguably, could also include mental deficiency not resulting from disease of the mind (see McKillop, 1966; Cheang, 1986). It could, for example, cover "brutish stupidity without rational power", which is excluded under the McNaghten test by the limiting effect of the words "defect of reason". These words ensure that unless the defect is due to a diseased mind, and not simply to an untrained one, there is no insanity within the meaning of the Rules. The words "defect of reason" are absent in s 84 (see *Kemp,* 1956).

As in the insanity rules in *McNaghten* (1843), "unsoundness of mind" under s 84 is a legal and not a medical concept, though the two may overlap. The lawyer is concerned with the question of the accused's *responsibility* for his actions, whereas the doctor is concerned with the medical treatment of a patient suffering from medical insanity who is unable to look after himself. The law is thus concerned with the cognitive or "knowingness" of the accused who pleads unsoundness of mind. To the psychiatrist "affect" (the psychological experience which determines behaviour) and conation (the psychological experience that determines desires and urges) are as important as cognition, if not more so. Thus even an uncontrollable impulse driving a man to kill would be considered by psychiatrists as medical insanity but would not be "unsoundness of mind" under s 84 or disease of the mind under the McNaghten Rules. However, what may be considered by lawyers as unsoundness of mind or disease of the mind may not be considered medical insanity. For example, a person who is grossly defective in intelligence or suffers from psychomotor epilepsy may fall within the scope of unsoundness of mind under s 84 though he may not be medically insane. Moreover, there are other conditions to be satisfied before the defence of unsoundness of mind can succeed (see below, pp 225–231).

However, the legal and the medical concept of insanity may overlap. Thus, for example, mental diseases such as schizophrenia, paranoia or lunacy are classified as medical insanity and can also come under the defence of unsoundness of mind, provided the other conditions in s 84 are satisfied.

(i) Insane delusions, hallucinations and illusions

Taylor, *Principles and Practice of Medical Jurisprudence* **(11th edn, 1956) Vol 1, 549–550**

Delusions, hallucinations, and illusions may all occur as symptoms of dementia or other psychotic illness. A delusion may be defined as a mistaken belief which has for the patient the force of conviction, and is firmly held despite all evidence to the contrary. A hallucination is a sensory perception which does not correspond to any stimulus from the outside world; whereas an illusion is a sensory perception, which although produced by external stimulus, is misinterpreted by the patient in purely subjective terms.

Examples will make these three descriptive terms clear. If a man believes that he has lost all his money, and is suffering from a fatal illness, despite the production of concrete evidence that he is still solvent, and has no demonstrable physical disease, then he is suffering from delusions. If he hears voices or sees visions which no one-else can hear or see, and which are in fact projections of his own fantasy, then he is hallucinated; while if he mistakes his physician or nurse for his father or mother, or for the devil come to take him away, then he is suffering from illusions, which are grafted on to the normal experience of seeing the people whose identity he misconstrues.

All these symptoms will be seen to have in common that severance of the patient's subjective experience from external reality which we have seen is characteristic of insanity. Under the influence of such severance from reality the patient's conduct is naturally disordered, and in this way his insanity may be made manifest. It remains important to realize that some forms of insane behaviour may be the outcome of purely temporary, acute, and short-lived confusion or delirium; for example in delirium tremens from the toxic confusional state produced after long addiction to alcohol: or from any of the other acute illnesses which may be accompanied by toxic confusional episodes. The importance to the patient and to the doctor of this recognition derives from the fact that it is never necessary to certify as of unsound mind the patient whose insanity is as short-lived and incidental to an acute physical illness as delirium or toxic confusional states of any kind.   .

Finally, the category of *moral insanity* has been put forward as a diagnostic entity, which has been called a disturbance of the upper levels of feeling and thought, not affecting the highest levels of intelligence. It is exemplified by the concept of the psychopathic personality. In fact careful examinatin of this proposition in practice leads to the conclusion that the individual's conduct, no matter how disturbed, does not in fact spring from a distortion of his subjective experience of reality. Such people are therefore not certifiable, and at present they remain to be dealt with by the law as responsible individuals, under the criteria at present existing for the recognition and definition of insanity in legal terms. Nevertheless the provision of special penal institutions for their care, after conviction, has now been proposed.

One of the most common situations in which s 84 can be invoked is where a person kills under some insane delusion. It may be noted that in the *McNaghten* case (1843) itself, the accused was suffering from morbid insane delusions of persecution by Sir Robert Peel. He wanted to shoot Sir Robert Peel but by mistake, shot Drummond, the secretary of Sir Robert Peel. There are also many Indian decisions under s 84 of the Indian Penal Code (1860) in which the accused killed while suffering from an insane delusion. For example, in *Lemos E* (1970), the accused who was suffering from schizophrenia was under a delusion and hallucination when he killed the deceased. (See also *Jai Lal*, 1969; *Ahmadulla*, 1961; *Dahyabhai*, 1964; *Ashiruddin Ahmed*, 1948; *Kanbi Kurji*, 1960.) In these cases, either the accused persons were under such delusion that they did not know the nature of the act, ie physical nature, or that it was wrong or contrary to law.

What about a person who suffers from partial delusion that affects part of the mind, leaving the other parts unaffected? One of the questions which the House of Lords in *McNaghten* (1843) put to the judges was:

> If a person under an insane delusion as to existing facts commits an offence in consequence thereof, is he thereby excused?

The reply was:

> ... the answer must, of course, depend on the nature of the delusion: but making the same assumption as we did before, namely, that he labours under such partial delusion only, and is not in other respects insane, we think he must be considered in the same situation as to responsibility as if the facts with respect to which the delusion exists were real. For example, if under the influence of his delusion he supposes another man to be in the act of attempting to take away his life, he would be exempt from punishment. If his delusion was that the deceased had inflicted a serious injury to his character and fortune, and he killed him in revenge for such supposed injury, he would be liable for punishment.

Under the Penal Code such a person who kills another thinking he is acting in self defence would be completely acquitted on the ground of private defence under s 100 (see ch 5).

It has been pointed out by Cheang (1986) that according to some medical opinions (see Report of the Royal Commission on the Law of Insanity as a Defence in Criminal Cases, Ottawa, 1956) it is erroneous to speak of partial delusion.

(ii) Mania

Jusoh v PP (1963) 29 MLJ 84 (CCA, KL, Malaya)

The appellant was convicted of murder under s 302 of the Penal Code. He ran amok for no apparent reason, and slashed his sister-in-law (inflicting 12 wounds) and her two children to death. He then killed a man who was a complete stranger to him and inflicted severe injuries on two young men who led the villagers to secure him. A medical officer who was with the appellant two hours after his arrest described him as "in a daze" and "overwhelmed with woe". He relied on the defence of unsoundness of mind under s 84.

Thomson CJ: The defence case was that there were four killings in circumstances of very great atrocity for which there was no motive at all, in short that the facts were such that an ordinary man might well be prompted to say "this is the work of a madman", that the uncontradicted evidence of a medical man with long experience in diseases of the mind who had had the appellant under observation for about three months was that at the time of the killings the accused was suffering from mania which would produce in him an irresistible impulse to do what he did, and that although irresistible impulse is no defence, the type of mania from which it springs generally produces the consequence that the sufferer does not know what he is doing is wrong. If the defence had been put to the jury in that way and if they then did not think that insanity was made out in terms of section 84 of the Penal Code the appellant would have had no ground of complaint.

But they were not directed in that way. There was no mention of the circumstance that the killings were apparently without motive, there was no mention of the complete absence of rebutting medical evidence. They were not invited to consider the question of whether on studying the story of the appellant's acts they did not think that that story lent support to the medical evidence. They were only told that "being from this country" (the suggestion clearly being that the medical witness was not from this country although he had had long experience in it) and having "studied" the appellant for two days they were in a better position to judge as to the appellant's mental condition at the time of the killing than anybody else including the medical witness who had had him under observation for three months.

In the circumstances we were compelled to the conclusion that the appellant had been deprived of a chance of being acquitted which he would have had had the jury been adequately directed and we accordingly quashed the conviction.

Appeal allowed

(iii) Insane automatism

English law recognizes two species of automatism, non-insane and insane automatism. Only the latter category comes within the McNaghten Rules. The important distinction under English law between the two categories is that a successful plea under the first category will lead to a complete acquittal whereas a successful plea under the second category will result in a special verdict of "not guilty by reason of insanity" and a detention in a mental institution at "Her Majesty's pleasure". One of the factors which English law has taken into consideration in determining whether automatism is non-insane or insane is whether the automatism is caused by an external or internal factor, the former resulting in non-insane and the latter, insane automatism.

Violence, drugs, the administration of anaesthetics causing a malfunctioning of the mind are considered external factors. In England insane automatism, arising from an internal condition, either organic or functional, which has been held to be within the McNaghten Rules, includes arteriosclerosis and psychomotor epilepsy.

The categories which are excluded from insanity but classified as non-insane automatism under English law are uncertain but probably include concussion, all reflex actions of external origin, somnambulism, hypnotism and hypoglycaemia (see ch 3). The position under s 84 of the Penal Code is considered below, pp 219–220.

Arteriosclerosis

In the English case of *Kemp* (1956), the accused, during a period of unconsciousness arising from arteriosclerosis (hardening of the arteries), attacked his wife with a hammer. Medical opinions given were that whereas arteriosclerosis can cause degeneration of the brain cells, which over time can result in a disease of the mind, this stage had not been reached. According to the medical evidence given, the accused at the time he committed the act suffered from a congestion of blood in the brain (due to arteriosclerosis) which caused a temporary loss of consciousness as a result of which he acted irrationally and irresponsibly. The accused pleaded that although he did not know the nature and quality of his act, he was not suffering from a *disease of the mind* and was not insane within the McNaghten Rules. He raised the defence of automatism and not insanity. Devlin J held that the accused was suffering from a disease of the mind.

Devlin J: It does not matter, for the purposes of the law, whether the defect of reason is due to a degeneration of the brain or to some other form of mental derangement. That may be a matter of importance medically, but it is of no importance to the law, which merely has to consider the state of mind in which the accused is, not how he got there.

The distinction that emerges from the evidence of Dr Gibson, and which has been argued by Mr Skelhorn, is a different one. It is that this is something which is capable of becoming a mental disease but has not yet become one. It has not yet created any degeneration of the brain and the argument is that it is merely interfering temporarily with the working of the brain by cutting off the supply of blood in the same way as concussion might, or something of that sort. I am invited to say that this disease at this stage is purely physical; when it interferes with the brain cells so that they degenerate, it then becomes a disease of the mind. This would be a very difficult test to apply for the purposes of the law. I should think it would be a matter of great difficulty medically to determine precisely at what point degeneration of the brain sets in, and it would mean that the verdict depended upon a doubtful medical borderline.

The law is not concerned with the brain but with the mind, in the sense that "mind" is ordinarily used, the mental faculties of reason, memory and understanding. If one read for "disease of the mind" "disease of the brain", it would follow that in many cases pleas of insanity would not be established because it could not be proved that the brain had been affected in any way, either by degeneration of the cells or in any other way. In my judgment the condition of the brain is irrelevant and so is the question of whether the condition of the mind is curable or incurable, transitory or permanent. There is no warranty for introducing those considerations into the definition in the McNaghten Rules. Temporary insanity is sufficient to satisfy them. It does not matter whether it is incurable and permanent or not.

Devlin J pointed to the difference between the legal and the medical concept of insanity when he said that for the purposes of law it did not matter whether the defect of reasoning was due to a degeneration of the brain or some other form of mental derangement. He said that while this "may be a matter of importance medically" what was important for the purpose of the law was the state of the mind and "not how he got there".

In *Quick* (1973) Lawton LJ, criticized Devlin J for ignoring the origin of the disease of the mind. He said:

> Applied without qualification of any kind, Devlin J's statement of the law would have some surprising consequences. Take the not uncommon cases of the rugby player who gets a kick on the head early in the game and plays on to the end in a state of automatism. If, whilst he was in that state, he assaulted the referee it is difficult to envisage any court adjudging that he was not guilty by reason of insanity. Another type of case which could occur is that of the dental patient who kicks out whilst coming round from an anaesthetic. The law would be in a defective state if a patient accused of assaulting a dental nurse by kicking her whilst regaining consciousness could only excuse himself by raising the defence of insanity.

These are examples of non-insane automatism and they fall outside the scope of s 84. (See ch 3 and Yeo, 1985.)

Psychomotor epilepsy

The question whether psychomotor epilepsy would be regarded as unsoundness of mind has not arisen in the local courts (compare *Sinnasamy* (1956), see ch 3).

R v Sullivan [1983] 3 WLR 123 (HL, England)

The appellant suffered from epilepsy and during the final stage of an epileptic fit, known as psychomotor epilepsy he kicked his friend, Payne, causing severe injuries on his head and body. He was charged with causing grievous body harm under s 20 of the Offences Against the Person Act 1861. The trial judge held that this amounted to insanity; consequently the appellant changed his plea to guilty to the lesser offence of assault occasioning actual bodily harm. He then appealed against conviction on the basis that he should have been allowed to raise the defence of automatism.

Lord Diplock (the other Law Lords agreeing): First, it is submitted the medical evidence in the instant case shows that psychomotor epilepsy is not a disease of the mind, whereas in *Bratty*'s case it was accepted by all the doctors that it was. The only evidential basis for this submission is that Dr Fenwick said that in medical terms to constitute a "disease of the mind" or "mental illness", which he appeared to regard as interchangeable descriptions, a disorder of brain functions (which undoubtedly occurs during a seizure in psychomotor epilepsy) must be prolonged for a period of time usually more than a day, while Dr Taylor would have it that the disorder must continue for a minimum of a month to qualify for the description "a disease of the mind".

The nomenclature adopted by the medical profession may change from time to time; Bratty was tried in 1961. But the meaning of the expression "disease of the mind" as the cause of "a defect of reason" remains unchanged for the purposes of the application of the M'Naghten Rules. I agree with what was said by Devlin J in *Kemp* (1956) that "mind" in the M'Naghten Rules is used in the ordinary sense of the mental faculties of reason, memory and understanding. If the effect of a disease is to impair these faculties so severely as to have either of the consequences referred to in the latter part of the rules, it matters not whether the aetiology of the impairment is organic, as in epilepsy, or functional, or whether the impairment itself is permanent or is transient and intermittent, provided that it subsisted at the time of commission of the act. The purpose of the legislation relating to the defence of insanity, ever since its origin in 1880, has been to protect society against recurrence of the dangerous conduct. The duration of a temporary suspension of the mental faculties of reason, memory and understanding, particularly if, as in the appellant's case, it is recurrent, cannot on any rational ground be relevant to the application by the courts of the M'Naghten Rules, though it may be relevant to the course adopted by the Secretary of State, to whom the responsibility for how the defendant is to be dealt with passes after the return of the special verdict of not guilty by reason of insanity.

To avoid misunderstanding I ought perhaps to add that in expressing my agreement with what was said by Devlin J in *Kemp* (1956), where the disease that caused the temporary and intermittent impairment of the mental faculties was arteriosclerosis, I do not regard that judge as excluding the possibility of non-insane automatism, for which the proper verdict would be a verdict of not guilty, in cases where temporary impairment not being self-induced by consuming drink or drugs, results from some external physical factor such as a blow on the head causing concussion or the administration of an anaesthetic for therapeutic purposes. I mention this because in *Quick* (1973) Lawton LJ appears to have regarded the ruling in *Kemp* (1956) as going as far as this. If it had done, it would have been inconsistent with the speeches in this House in *Bratty's* case, where *Kemp* was alluded to without disapproval by Viscount Kilmuir LC and received the express approval of Lord Denning. The instant case, however, does not in my view afford an appropriate occasion for exploring possible causes of non-insane automatism.

The only other submission in support of the appellant's appeal which I think it necessary to mention is that, because the expert evidence was to the effect that the appellant's acts in kicking Mr Payne were unconscious and thus "involuntary" in the legal sense of that term, his state of mind was not one dealt with by the M'Naghten Rules at all, since it was not covered by the phrase "as not to know the nature and quality of the act he was doing". Quite apart from being contrary to all three speeches in this House in *Bratty's* case, the submission appears to me, with all respect to counsel, to be quite unarguable. Dr Fenwick himself accepted it as an accurate description of the appellant's mental state in the post-ictal stage of a seizure. The audience to whom the phrase in the M'Naghten Rules was addressed consisted of peers of the realm in the 1840s when a certain orotundity of diction had not yet fallen out of fashion. Addressed to an audience of jurors in the 1980s it might more aptly be expressed as: he did not know what he was doing.

My Lords, it is natural to feel reluctant to attach the label of insanity to a sufferer from psychomotor epilepsy of the kind to which the appellant was subject, even though the expression in the context of a special verdict of not guilty by reason of insanity is a technical one which includes a purely temporary and intermittent suspension of the mental faculties of reason, memory and understanding resulting from the occurrence of an epileptic fit. But the label is contained in the current statute, it has appeared in this statute's predecessors ever since 1800. It does not lie within the power of the courts to alter it. Only Parliament can do that. It has done so twice; it could do so once again....

Appeal dismissed

CMV Clarkson and HM Keating, *Criminal Law: Text and Materials* (1984), 277–279

Whilst at one level this case [ie *Sullivan*, 1983] merely "confirm[s]" the status quo", in the sense that it has long been recognized that psychomotor epilepsy is a "disease of the mind", and judges before Lord Diplock have referred to the test of dangerousness that is thought to be able to illuminate the "grey area between insanity and automatism," this case is, nevertheless, highly significant.

It reveals not only that a *temporary* absence of reasoning powers of *very* limited duration may amount to a "disease of the mind", but that the distinction drawn between external and internal factors is of crucial importance. Epileptic fits are regarded as arising from an internal condition; hypoglycaemic states, arising from the combination of diabetes, insulin, food (or lack of it) and possibly alcohol, would seem not to be. As pointed out earlier, sleepwalking commonly occurs because of an internal condition. Are all epileptics (0.5 per cent of the population) and all sleepwalkers now at risk of an insanity verdict? Lord Diplock cannot circumvent his relutance in attaching the label of insanity to defendants such as Sullivan by saying that the label is merely a "technical" one. What his misgivings demonstrate is a two-fold problem.

First, if Lord Diplock is right in saying that the purpose of the insanity test is, and always has been, to identify the dangerous from the non-dangerous (who may safely be acquitted on the basis of sane automatism), then is it the case that epileptics are any more dangerous than diabetics? The internal/external factor distinction does not seem well-designed to constitute a test of dangerousness.

Secondly, faced with the prospect of an insanity verdict, defendants will change their pleas, just as Sullivan did, to guilty. Not only does this place unacceptable pressure upon them, but, if the isolation of the dangerous is our main concern, it is questionable whether they should be allowed to do so– conviction for some lesser offence may not lead to a sentence of imprisonment.

Both of these flaws highlight not only the failure of the internal/external factor distinction, but also what many commentators have perceived to be a more fundamental failure of the insanity test (and perhaps, any insanity test) to come to terms with the issue of the responsibility of the individual defendant on the one hand, and the protection of the public (and the defendant himself) against harm on the other. We shall return to this question later, once the remaining elements of the test of insanity, and proposed reform thereof, have been considered.

Is the distinction between internal/external factor applicable under s 84? In the Indian case of *Satwant Singh* (1975), the appellant, who had attacked the deceased with a Kassi without any motive and under the influence of a fit of "major" epilepsy, was held entitled to the defence of unsoundness of mind under s 84. So also in an earlier case of *Nga Ant Bwe* (1937), where an accused murdered his mother and wounded his stepfather in a fit of epilepsy without any apparent cause. After the murder he hid in a ravine. Medical evidence showed that he was subject to epileptic fits. The Rangoon High Court held that he was entitled to the defence of insanity under s 84 of the Indian Penal Code (1860). The court stated that "... probably he would not know what he was doing at all, much less be able to distinguish between right and wrong".

In their book, *Mental Abnormality and the Law*, Wily and Stallworthy (1962) state that "in medical language the offender who is ... subject to epileptic derangements of consciousness ... is not insane". They further state: "Yet if such a patient is tried on a criminal charge, he may very well be acquitted on the ground of insanity."

Somnambulism (sleepwalking)

The line between an internal and external cause in determining non-insane and insane automatism is not always clear-cut. In England, somnambulism (sleepwalking) could be regarded as insane automatism as it could be the result of some mental impairment. However, in the recent English case of *Lilienfield* (1985), a sleepwalker who stabbed his friend 20 times was acquitted on the ground of non-insane automatism.

The problem of sleepwalking was examined in ch 3. It will be recalled that the prevailing view there, as seen, for instance, in the Indian case of *Re Pappathi Ammal* (1959) was that somnambulism could come within the scope of s 84 of the Indian Penal Code. It was, however, argued in ch 3 that somnambulism would be better classified as *non-insane* automatism.

Hypnotism

It is clear that hypnotism is caused by an external factor and should not be considered as unsoundness of mind even if it causes somnambulism. Under English law hypnotism is classified as non-insane automatism (see ch 3). Although *Re Pappathi Ammal* (1959) suggested that hypnotism is allied to somnambulism and therefore within the scope of s 84, it is submitted that the better view is to consider it outside the scope of the section (see ch 3).

(iv) Mental deficiency

Mental deficiency like idiocy, imbecility and feeble-mindedness could be regarded as unsoundness of mind (Indian Law Commissioners (42nd Report, 1971), part 1, para 4.31).

HJ Wily and KR Stallworthy, *Mental Abnormality and the Law* (1962), 46–49

Idiocy

The idiot, as the term is accepted to-day, has an IQ of zero or near to it; he has no useful speech or understanding of speech, he can seldom feed himself, he cannot dress himself or keep himself clean; he has no capacity for thought, let alone guilty thought, he can never commit a crime, and seldom has either the wit or the physical capacity to perform an act which in another person would be a crime.

Imbecility

A lesser degree of severe intellectual subnormality, traditionally called imbecility.... The IQ of the imbecile is below fifty, which implies that at best he will be six before he is able to do the things an average child can do at three, that as an adult he will have, at least, a mental age near eight, and the average adult imbecile has a much lower mental age....

Feeble-mindedness
The feeble-minded, or morons ... or the subnormal are much the commonest and most important of the intellectual defectives; .... Subnormality merges imperceptibly into dull normal intelligence, and precisely where to draw the line between them is a matter of difficulty. The upper limit for the IQ of the subnormal is variously stated; some put it at 65, others as high as 80. The subnormal may be handicapped in ways other than lack of intelligence....

(v) Irresistible impulse

In *Sinnasamy* (1956), the Court of Appeal of Malaya held, obiter, that irresistible impulse per se is no defence, and that it can only be a defence when it is proved to have been the "result of *insanity* in law" (see ch 3).

Under s 84 the unsoundness of mind must affect the cognitive and not conative faculties as the phrases "incapable of knowing ..." and "by reason of unsoundness of mind" point to cognition. A person who is suffering from irresistible impulse per se may be in full possession of his cognitive faculties but he is unable to control his will-power. In India the position is the same. A person who is subject to insane impulses but whose cognitive faculties are unimpaired is not entitled to the defence in s 84 of the Indian Penal Code.

Queen-Express v Kader Nasyer Shah (1896) ILR 23 Cal 604 (HC, Calcutta, India) (O'Kinealy and Banerjee JJ)

The appellant was charged with the murder of a boy under s 302 of the Indian Penal Code. His plea was that he "was mad when he strangled the boy".

Judgment of court: Two questions arise for determination in this appeal: First, whether the appellant killed the boy; and, second, whether, if he did so, he is guilty of murder, or is entitled to be acquitted on the ground of unsoundness of mind....

The answer to the second question, however, is not equally easy. It is no doubt clear from the evidence that the accused had been suffering from mental derangement for some months previous to the date of the occurrence and since the destruction of his house and property by fire; that on one occasion he was seen eating potsherds; and that he often complained of pain in the head. It also appears that when the enquiry preliminary to the commitment was taken up, he was found not to be in a fit state of mind to be able to make his defence; and the enquiry was not resumed, until somewhat more than a year after when he was pronounced fit to be able to take his trial. The murder, moreover, was committed without any apparent sane motive. The evidence shows that the accused was fond of the boy, and he had no quarrel with the boy's father. On the other hand, however, it must be borne in mind that the accused observed some secrecy in committing the murder. He tried to conceal the corpse, and he hid himself in a jungle....

It might be said of our law as it has been said of the law of England by Sir J Stephen (see his *History of the Criminal Law of England*, Vol II, ch XIX, p 795) that even as it stands, the law extends the exemption as well to cases where insanity affects the offender's will and emotions as to those where it affects his cognitive faculties, because where the will and emotions are affected by the offender being subjected to insane impulses, it is difficult to say that his cognitive faculties are not affected. In extreme cases that may be true; but we are not prepared to accept the view as generally correct that a person is entitled to exemption from criminal liability under our law in cases in which it is only shown that he is subject to insane impulses, notwithstanding that it may appear clear that his cognitive faculties, so far as we can judge from his acts and words, are left unimpaired. To take such a view as this would be to go against the plain language of section 84 of the Indian Penal Code, and the received interpretation of that section. See the cases of *Lakshman Dagdu* (1886), *Tenkatasami* (1889) and *Razai Mia* (1895).

Applying then the law as we understand it to the facts of this case, we must say we are unable to hold that it has been shown that the accused, at the time he killed the child, was, by reason of unsoundness of mind, incapable of knowing the nature of his act, or that he was doing what was either wrong or contrary to law. The circumstances attending the murder go to show that he could not have been devoid of such knowledge, though they go to show that he must at that time have been suffering from mental derangement of some sort.

Appeal dismissed

The position is the same under English law. In *Burton* (1863), the defendant killed a boy without any motive other than that he wanted to be hanged. At the trial evidence that he was suffering from "moral insanity" was tended. Wightman J said:

> It was not mere eccentricity of conduct which made a man legally irresponsible for his acts. The medical man ... described moral insanity as a state of mind under which a man, perfectly aware that it was wrong to do so, killed another under an uncontrollable impulse.

It was held that despite his morbid state of mind he knew what he was doing was wrong and hence was not entitled to the defence of insanity.

In *Kopsch* (1925), Lord Hewart CJ said:

> It is the fantastic theory of uncontrollable impulse which, if it were to become part of our criminal law, would be merely subversive. It is not yet part of the criminal law; and it is to be hoped that the time is far distant when it will be made.

In *Brown* (1960) the Privy Council, in an appeal from Australia, said that evidence of irresistible impulse may be symptomatic of a particular disease of the mind (within the McNaghten Rules) as it may affect the accused's ability to know the nature and quality of his act or that it is wrong.

Since the introduction of diminished responsibility into the criminal law in Singapore and in England irresistible impulse could be a mitigating circumstance reducing liability for murder to one for culpable homicide not amounting to murder, if it arises from arrested or retarded development of the mind (s 300 Exception 7, see ch 20).

Swaminadhan S (ed), *Mayne's Criminal Law of India* (4th edn, 1914) pp 172–173

It is certainly conceivable that there might be a state of mental disease, which would deprive the sufferer of all capacity to resist a particular impulse, while it left him the perception of the nature and consequences of the act to which he was impelled. The insuperable difficulty in the way of giving legal effect to such a defence would be, that it would be impossible to establish it. We can tell that a man has not resisted an impulse, but how can we tell that he could not have resisted it, or why he could not? It is a matter of everyday experience that persons who are subject to no mental disease yield to apparently uncontrollable fits of passion, and commit crimes for which they are hanged. It may be that they could not control their passion, but we hang them all the more on that account ....

If a man who is mentally diseased acts in a similar way, how are we to know that his want of control is due to his mental disease, or that his mental disease did more than supply him with a motive for his act, while not depriving him of the power to refrain from it, if he had chosen? Even in a lunatic asylum some sort of discipline is maintained by pains and discomforts inflicted upon the patients, and they learn to exercise some self-restraint in order to avoid the infliction, *2 Steph Crim L, 181*. If a case arose in which it appeared to be made out that mental disease had absolutely destroyed the capacity to govern the will, the case would probably fall under one or other of the two grounds of exemption stated in the Penal Code. If it did not, the conflict between law and mercy would have to be solved by the dispensing power of the Executive, not by the exempting power of the judge. See the remarks of Sir James Stephen on the medical evidence in *Dove's* case, *3 Steph Crim L, pp 429–437*. It might only affect the question of the quantum of punishment.

(c) "Incapable of knowing"

Courts interpreting s 84 do not always address the question of *incapacity*. The difference between the capacity to know a thing and knowing it has been pointed out in the Indian case of *Lakshimi* (1959) where Beg J said:

The significant word in the above section is "incapable". The fallacy of the above view lies in the fact that it ignores that what s 84 lays down is not that the accused claiming protection under it should not know an act to be right or wrong, but that the accused should be "incapable" of knowing whether the act done by him is right or wrong. The capacity to know a thing is quite different from what a person knows. The former is a potentiality, the latter is the result of it. If a person possesses the former, he cannot be protected in law, whatever might be the result of his potentiality. In other words, what is protected is an inherent or organic incapacity, and not a wrong or erroneous belief which might be the result of a perverted potentiality.

A person might believe so many things. His beliefs can never protect him once it is found that he possessed the capacity to distinguish between right and wrong. If his potentialities lead him to a wrong conclusion, he takes the risk and law will hold him responsible for the deed which emanated from him. What the law protects is the case of a man in whom the guiding light that enables a man to distinguish between right and wrong and between legality and illegality is completely extinguished. Where such light is found to be still flickering, a man cannot be heard to plead that he should be protected because he was misled by his own misguided intuition or by any fancied delusion which had been haunting him and which he mistook to be a reality. Our beliefs are primarily the offsprings of the faculty of intuition. On the other hand the content of our knowledge and our realization of its nature is borne out of the facilities of cognition and reason.

In the Malaysian case of *Lee Ah Chye* (1963), Thomson CJ, in interpreting s 84 said:

> In other words, there must be a certain state of mind–incapacity of knowing the nature of the act or incapacity of knowing it is wrong–but in every case that must exist by reason of unsoundness of the mind.

However, no attempt was made to consider the implications of the word "incapacity".

Under the McNaghten Rules no mention is made of incapacity, and the question is simply whether the accused knew what he was doing. The test under s 84 appears stricter than the McNaghten test as it presupposes that it is possible not to know a thing but still not be incapable of knowing it. Under s 84 the accused must be *incapable* of knowing that he is doing what is either wrong or contrary to law. Canagarayar (1985) observes:

> "Incapacity" cannot relate to one form of "wrong" to the exclusion of the other. One simply cannot say that the accused does not have the capacity to know that his act was morally wrong and yet have the capacity to know that it is legally wrong. The same state of mind that would have affected the accused's rationalizing ability in regard to the reasons that made him believe that the act is not morally wrong would have also affected his thinking in regard to the issue of whether the act is contrary to law.

[See also, McKillop, 1966.]

Indian courts, taking a disjunctive view of wrong or contrary to law (see, eg *Ashiruddin Ahmed*, 1949, below, p 229) have held that a person suffering from delusion may think it is morally right to sacrifice his son because he is commanded by God even though he knows it is contrary to law. Either the element of "incapacity" is ignored or it is premised on his incapacity to know that it is contrary to morals because of the command although, at the same time, he has capacity to know that it is contrary to law.

There are various gradations of unsoundness of mind. A person's mind may be so unsound that he may not even know the physical nature of his act, let alone the moral character and legality of his act. However, a person of unsound mind may suffer from dissociation of ideas such that it may be possible for him to know one thing and not another.

Hence, his capacity to know that his killing, say, the president of a country is contrary to law but not that it is morally wrong because he firmly believes the killing is necessary to save the country from civil war or ruination. The term unsoundness of mind can accommodate this "twilight zone". However, the legal condition of "incapacity" for exculpation in criminal law may differ widely from the psychiatrist's view. Glanville Williams (1978) notes:

> The particular problem of dissociation is one example of the perpetual tension between law and psychiatry. Some psychiatrists, particularly those who do not believe in punishment, feel their function is to assist the "patient", or at least not to worsen his position; and they try to give the evidence that they think will help him. Others, however, object to being pressed to say whether the defendant was "responsible", at the time of the deed, and are no happier to be asked whether he was "insane" or "mentally diseased" or had the "*capacity to conform*" (emphasis added). They fear that such formulations involve them too directly in a moral question, and so tend to turn psychiatry into a system of ethics.

(d) "Nature of the act"

Under the McNaghten Rules the phrase is "nature and quality of his act"; this means the physical nature and quality of the act and not its moral or legal aspects (see *Codere*, 1916 and *Dickie*, 1984). For example, A is suffering from an insane delusion and cuts off B's head thinking that he is chopping a piece of wood. The omission of "quality" in s 84 does not appear to detract from the meaning that "nature" refers to the physical nature of the act.

(e) "That he is doing what is either wrong or contrary to law"

Even if the accused knows the nature of the act, ie that he is killing somebody, he can claim the defence under s 84 if, at the time of doing it, by reason of unsoundness of mind he does not know that the act is either wrong or contrary to law. In *Geron Ali* (1941) the High Court of Calcutta said:

> Section 84, IPC is quite clear on the point. It says that if a person does an act and at the time of doing the act by reason of insanity does not know that the act is either wrong or contrary to law then also he would be protected even though he knew the nature of the act. This is perfectly clear from the section and it is nothing but sound common sense. A person may be under the insane delusion that he is an executioner and under that delusion he beheads his son thinking that he has been ordered to do so by the king. He knows the nature of his act but obviously he cannot be held criminally liable in as much as he did not know that what he was doing was either wrong or contrary to law.

(i) "Wrong"

One view is that "wrong" in s 84 cannot mean contrary to law (as in the McNaghten Rules) since the alternative phrase "contrary to law" is given in the section. In *Shivraj Singh* (1975) the High Court of the State of Madhya Pradesh stated:

> The word "wrong" here [ie s 84] cannot be taken to mean contrary to law. The very fact that the framers of the Indian Penal Code used both the words "wrong or contrary to law" indicates that the word "wrong" does not mean contrary to law. This is a concluded position in law that Legislature would not use a word which is redundant. In case the word "wrong" is interpreted to mean contrary to law, those words already being in the section the word "wrong" becomes redundant. Hence, we are of the firm view that the word "wrong" means morally wrong.

However, what is not so clear is whether "moral wrong" should be viewed objectively or subjectively. If an objective view were to be taken of moral wrong the standard adopted could be "wrong according to the ordinary standards adopted by reasonable men" (see the Australian case of *Stapleton*, 1952). On the other hand, under a subjective view, the moral standard of the accused would have to be taken.

Bron McKillop, "Insanity under the Penal Code" (1966) 7 Me Judice 65, 71

This interpretation of "wrong" should be coupled with the High Court's [in *Stapleton*, 1952] interpretation of "know" in the same case so that for an accused to know he was doing what was wrong it is sufficient if he was incapable of reasoning moderately calmly about whether, according to the ordinary standards of reasonable men, he was doing wrong. It does not matter that the accused might have at the back of his mind an awareness that the act he proposes to do is punishable by law. It seems that the *Stapleton* type of "knowing" is only appropriate to moral wrongness and not to contrariness to law. Of course the result of a case would usually be the same whether the test was knowing the act to be wrong or knowing that it was contrary to law. The *Stapleton* test would appear to be more closely related to the realities of mental disorder. It will also more readily result in an acquittal and immediate confinement in a mental institution.

[See Canagarayar (1985) for the view that "contrary to law" in s 84 is "exegetical" of the term "wrong".]

(ii) "Either wrong or contrary to law"

The phrase "either wrong or contrary to law" is disjunctive in formula. Nevertheless, in the context of s 84 it could be read conjunctively. A disjunctive approach would mean that only one of the conditions need be satisfied for an acquittal. Thus if the accused knew that his act was contrary to law but did not know that it was morally wrong because of his unsoundness of mind he would succeed in the defence (even assuming he knew the nature of his act). On a conjunctive approach the accused must satisfy both the requirements that he did not know that the act was morally wrong and that it was contrary to law. Cases have supported both views.

Conjunctive view

Geron Ali v Emperor AIR (1941) Cal 129 (HC, Calcutta, India) (Sen and Boxburgh JJ)

(The facts appear in the judgment.)

Judgment of court: The appellant has been convicted of murder.... The case against him is as follows: One Khoaz Ali was known to be a Pir or holy man in the village of the appellant. He had a mistress Tayeba who used to be known as Pirani. The appellant was a disciple of the Pir and called him father and the Pirani mother. The Pir had become unpopular in the village because of the irregular relationship between him and Tayeba. The appellant was however loyal to them and on 14th October 1939 complained to them about the attitude of the villagers. The Pir said to him "Take the head of those who dissuade you and come to your doors." The Pir also gave him a dao. In the evening the Pir gave the appellant some substance to swallow which the latter did. At this time the Pirani said to the appellant that he would go to heaven if he offered a human head in sacrifice. She also told him that the day was auspicious as it was the first day of Ramzan. Geron armed himself with a dao and severed the head of one Shaz Ali. He carried the head to his house. He saw his young daughter, aged about three years, and he cut off her head also. Taking these two heads he approached Khoaz Ali and Tayeba Bibi and said: "Father, you asked me for one human head, I present you with two." He gave Khoaz Ali the head of Shaz Ali and the head of his daughter to Tayeba Bibi....

We are satisfied that the appellant knew the nature of his act; what we have to see is whether he knew that what he was doing was either wrong or contrary to law. If he knew that what he was doing was wrong then he will not be protected even if he did not know that it was contrary to law. If he knew that what he was doing was contrary to law then also he would not be protected even though he did not know that what he was doing is wrong. The law will punish a man for doing something which he knows to be contrary to the law whatever his private opinion may be regarding its ethics. Again if an act is contrary to law ignorance of the law will not protect a man from punishment when it is shown that the man knew that what he was doing is wrong. In our opinion, the appellant did not know that what he was doing was wrong. The evidence showed that he considered that he was doing a meritorious act which qualified him for heaven.

We also find that he did not know that what he was doing was contrary to law. His conduct establishes this. He killed these persons without any effort at concealment and he did not try to escape after doing this. We have also no doubt that this frame of mind was brought about by insanity. This is proved by his behaviour both prior to and subsequent to this act. In our opinion the appellant is entitled to the protection of s 84, IPC. We find that the appellant killed Shaz Ali and his daughter Shazda Banu, but that he was incapable of knowing that what he was doing was either wrong or contrary to law by reason of unsoundness of mind at the time of the occurrence...

Appeal allowed

Azro v PP (1962) 28 MLJ 321 (CA, Penang, Malaya)

(The facts appear in the judgment.)

Thomson CJ: This appellant was convicted at Muar for murder in contravention of s 302 of the Penal Code....

It is unnecessary to discuss the facts at any great length because it was proved up to the hilt, and indeed never denied that the appellant killed a man named Mir Afzalshah by stabbing him to death. It is clear that there was some sort of business arrangement between the parties. The appellant who had been in Singapore had just come back from there and was staying with the deceased and that at one o'clock in the morning he was found sitting astride the deceased and stabbing him to death. From the medical evidence it would seem that he inflicted some 20 stab wounds. The only other fact of which anything has been made is that when neighbours attempted to intervene the appellant bit one of them.

As has been said the killing was never denied. The only defence that was put forward at the trial was the defence of insanity and the only grounds of his appeal to this Court deal with the way that defence was dealt with at the trial.

Such medical evidence as there was, the evidence of a medical functionary in the asylum to which the appellant was sent after his arrest, did not support that defence. It was argued, however, that that witness was speaking to a time about a month after the killing and that on the actual facts of the case the conduct of the appellant made out or at least could have made out the defence of insanity. There was no evidence of motive; there was the very brutal and savage nature of the actual stabbing; and there was the act of the appellant, who was no doubt in a very excited state of mind at that time, in biting one of the people who tried to intervene. It may well be that these circumstances would justify one, speaking loosely and colloquially, in saying that the appellant behaved like a mad man....

That, however, was not the question before the Court. The question was whether the case came within section 84 of the Penal Code which reads as follows:....

In other words that section requires that there must be unsoundness of mind and that it must lead to one of two consequences, either that the accused person is incapable of knowing the nature of his act or that he is incapable of knowing that what he is doing is either wrong or contrary to law.

Appeal dismissed

As the appeal was dismissed the opinion expressed on s 84 is obiter. The court stated that for the defence of unsoundness of mind to apply it must lead to one of two consequences. One consequence is that he is incapable of knowing the nature of the act, ie the physical nature. The other is that he is "incapable of knowing that what he is doing is either wrong or contrary to law." Although the conjunctive view is not expressly stated by the court, the case has generally been regarded by academic writers as favouring a conjunctive view (McKillop, 1966; Canagarayar, 1985; Cheang, 1986).

It does not seem altogether clear whether the court was taking a conjunctive view. The court did not allude to the problem and no Indian authorities were cited. In any case as the appellant was not of unsound mind it was unnecessary to interpret the latter part of s 84. Regarding the phrase "either wrong or contrary to law" as one of two "consequences" may simply mean the whole *question* of either wrong or contrary to law (whether conjunctive or disjunctive), or it may mean the *effect* if both the requirements of wrong and contrary to law are satisfied. The court's statement is at most ambivalent.

Disjunctive view

Ashiruddin Ahmed v King (1949) 50 Cri LJ 255 (HC, Calcutta, India) (Boxburgh and Blank JJ)

The appellant was convicted under s 302 of the Indian Penal Code for the murder of his five-year-old son. He dreamt that he had been directed by someone in paradise to sacrifice his son by killing him as his previous sacrifices (korbani) had been "no good".

Judgment of court: Of the three elements necessary to be established under s 84, any one of which must be established by an accused to obtain the benefit of the provisions, it appears that first, the nature of the act, was clearly known to the accused; secondly, that he knew that the act was contrary to law, or we have said this was probably known to him. But the third element on which the case really turned is whether the accused knew that the act was wrong. This point has not been properly put to the jury, nor indeed was it apparent to the Judge himself. In our opinion, he clearly misunderstood the law on the point....

We find that the accused committed the act alleged, namely, the act of causing the death of his son by cutting his throat but by reason of unsoundness of mind he was incapable of knowing that his act was wrong. The accused is therefore acquitted of the charge under s 302 Penal Code.

Conviction set aside

It is noted that Boxburgh J sat in both *Geron Ali* (1941) and *Ashiruddin Ahmed* (1949). It may well have been that he changed his mind about the conjunctive view in *Ashiruddin Ahmed* (1949).

In *Jusoh* (1963), Thomson CJ stated that if it could be proved that the appellant did not know that what he was doing was *wrong* s 84 would have protected him. No mention was made of the other element "contrary to law". It would appear that it is sufficient if either one or the other element is established.

If the disjunctive view is preferred, it would widen the scope of s 84. It could include, for example, the English case of *Windle* (1952) which was held to fall outside the McNaghten Rules.

R v Windle [1952] 2 QB 826 (CCA, England)

The appellant was convicted of the murder of his wife who was insane. He had administered 100 aspirins to her. He pleaded insanity under the McNaghten Rules.

Lord Goddard CJ: There was some evidence that the appellant suffered from some defect of reason or, as it might be called, disease of the mind. The doctor who was called for him said that it was a form of communicated insanity known

as folie à deux. In such cases, it is said that if a person is in constant attendance on someone of unsound mind, in some way or another the insanity is, or
may be communicated to the attendant, so that, for a time at any rate, the
attendant has a defect of reason or disease of the mind.

The argument before us has really been on what is the meaning of the word
"wrong".... [T]he appellant knew, when administering this poison, for such it
was, to his wife, that he was doing an act which the law forbade.

It may well be that, ... with this nagging and tiresome wife who constantly
expressed the desire to commit suicide, he thought that she would be better out
of this world than in it. He may have thought that it would be a kindly act to
release her from what she was suffering from–or thought she was suffering
from–but that the law does not permit.... Mr Shawcross, in the course of his
very careful argument, suggested that the word "wrong", as it was used in the
McNaghten rules, did not mean contrary to law but had some kind of qualified
meaning, such as morally wrong, and that if a person was in such a state of
mind through a defect of reason that, although he knew that what he was doing
was wrong in law, he thought that it was beneficial or kind or praiseworthy,
that would excuse him.

Appeal dismissed

The question whether the appellant knew that what he was doing was
morally wrong was not raised as it was not necessary–under the
McNaghten Rules "wrong" means contrary to law. The appellant knew
his act was contrary to law. If the case had arisen in Singapore or Malaysia and a disjunctive view is accepted under s 84, the question whether
the appellant knew his act was immoral would be significant. On the
facts, the appellant might have thought that he was morally right in
killing his wife. As Goddard CJ stated: "He may have thought it was
a kindly act to put her out of her sufferings or imagined sufferings ...".
Thus the position may well be different under s 84.

Conjunctive or disjunctive view: a matter of justice and policy

**Bron McKillop "Insanity under the Penal Code" (1966) 7 Me Judice 65,
77–79**

Finally, what solution, if any, do considerations of justice (or policy, perhaps)
indicate for our problem. Both solutions, disjunctive and conjunctive, could be
supported from such considerations.... [A] retributive approach to punishment
could provide another argument for a conjunctive (or less available) as against
a disjunctive solution. Such an argument must remain weak while the retributive theory of punishment remains out of fashion. The current emphasis on the
reform, cure and rehabilitation of offenders would invite, rather, a disjunctive
solution so that more appropriate treatment (in a mental institution) would be
more readily available. A special argument for a conjunctive interpretation of
the words "either wrong or contrary to law" could be made as a result of a
particular kind of case that not infrequently arises in India. This kind of case
is that in which the accused acts under divine instruction or as a result of
having been possessed by spirits. The accused in these cases will very often
know that what he was doing was contrary to law but he will contend that, so
far from knowing he was doing wrong, he believed he was actually doing

something right because he had been instructed by God so to do or was simply the vehicle for a spirit....

The main argument from a justice or policy point of view for a disjunctive solution to our problem would probably be found in the contention that, if there is any doubt as to the interpretation of S 84, it should be resolved in favour of the accused. In other words, if an accused will be acquitted more readily on a disjunctive interpretation of "either wrong or contrary to law", that interpretation should be adopted. This argument is based on the policy of interpreting penal statutes strictly (against the prosecution) and, by implication, provisions exempting from liability liberally. Further, the result of such an interpretation would be that an accused who had a mental incapacity as to either the wrongness or contrariness to law of his act, even though not as to both of these things, would go immediately to a mental institution for needed treatment and not, in the first instance at least, to prison, or to execution....

The net result of the "either ... or ..." problem seems to be that a disjunctive solution is to be preferred. That is, the accused is entitled to the defence if he is incapable of knowing that his act is wrong even if he knows that it is contrary to law, and he is similarly entitled if he is incapable of knowing that his act is contrary to law even if he knows that it is wrong. This conclusion is tolerably clearly indicated by both our linguistic and our justice arguments. The case law is equivocal on the point but is inclined perhaps to an accused-favouring, disjunctive position also.

2.   Acquittal on ground of unsoundness of mind

The defence of unsoundness of mind differs from other defences under the Penal Code in its consequences. Under s 314 of the Criminal Procedure Code (Singapore) (Cap 68), (FMS Criminal Procedure Code (Cap 6)), the verdict is not guilty by reason of "unsoundness of mind" (s 84 of the Penal Code). However, while the accused is acquitted he is kept in safe custody, usually in a mental hospital or prison at the "President's pleasure" (in Singapore), or at the pleasure of the ruler of the state in the case of Malaysia.

3.   Procedure when accused is suspected to be of unsound mind

The Criminal Procedure Code of Singapore (the position in Malaysia is identical) contains provisions governing the position of a person of unsound mind who is charged with an offence. If such a person is incapable of making a defence because of his unsoundness of mind, his trial can be postponed by one month, or a further two months while he is detained for observation in a medical hospital.

Chapter 13

Intoxication

By KL Koh

A. Introduction

Penal Code, ss 85 and 86

85.–(1)   Except as provided in this section and in section 86, intoxication shall not constitute a defence to any criminal charge.

(2)   Intoxication shall be a defence to any criminal charge if by reason thereof the person charged at the time of the act or omission complained of did not know that such act or omission was wrong or did not know what he was doing and–

(a) the state of intoxication was caused without his consent by the malicious or negligent act of another person; or

(b) the person charged was, by reason of intoxication, insane, temporarily or otherwise, at the time of such act or omission.

86.–(1)   Where the defence under section 85 is established, then in a case falling under section 85 (2) (a) the accused person shall be acquitted, and in a case falling under section 85 (2) (b), section 84 of this Code and sections 314 and 315 of the Criminal Procedure Code shall apply.

(2)   Intoxication shall be taken into account for the purpose of determining whether the person charged had formed any intention, specific or otherwise, in the absence of which he would not be guilty of the offence.

(3)   For the purposes of this section and section 85 "intoxication" shall be deemed to include a state produced by narcotics or drugs.

[The law in s 85 and s 86 of the FMS Penal Code is *in pari materia*, though the subsections are designated (i) and (ii), etc. instead of (1) and (2) as in the Singapore version.]

From the viewpoint of criminal responsibility a person who commits a crime when involuntarily intoxicated should not be blameworthy while one who voluntarily gets into a state of intoxication should be responsible for his acts. The rationale for punishing the latter under English common law was stated by Sir Matthew Hale (1736):

> This "vice" (drunkenness) doth deprive men of the use of reason, and puts many men into a perfect, but temporary frenzy; ... such a person shall have no privilege by this voluntary contracted madness, but shall have the same judgment as if he were in his right senses.

The rigours of the common law in England have been relaxed. Drunkenness is a "defence" to crimes of "specific intent" and operates as a

232

mitigating circumstance (eg reducing murder to manslaughter). In some instances, eg theft, where there is no lesser offence, drunkenness can be a *complete* defence in England.

Under the Penal Code, the defence of intoxication operates as a complete defence and not as a mitigating circumstance (however, see *Tan Hung Song*, 1951, and *Suba Singh*, 1962, below p 242). It must be noted that the scope of the defence is narrow as the law does not generally countenance intoxication as a defence. Driving while under the influence of drinks or drugs is punishable under s 67 of the Road Traffic Act (Singapore) (Cap 276), as well as under its Malaysian counterpart (Road Traffic Ordinance 1958 (Ord 49 of 1958), s 37).

The original provisions of the defence of intoxication under ss 85 and 86 were amended in the light of the English case of *Beard* (1920) which laid down a number of propositions on the law of intoxication in England. However, as will be noted, these sections did not incorporate in toto the law as laid down in *Beard* (1920).

Intoxication includes a state produced by narcotics and drugs (s 86(3)).

B. The law

1. Involuntary intoxication caused by malicious or negligent act of another person

To succeed under s 85(2)(a) an accused must prove that his state of intoxication was caused without his consent by the malicious or negligent act of a person, and that he did not know the act or omission was wrong, or did not know what he was doing. This section differs from its Indian counterpart which reads:

> Nothing is an offence which is done by a person who, at the time of doing it, is, by reason of intoxication, incapable of knowing the nature of the act, or that he is doing what is either *wrong*, or *contrary to law*: provided that the thing which intoxicated him was administered to him *without his knowledge or against his will* (emphasis added).

The scope of the defence of involuntary intoxication is narrower compared to that under s 85 of the Indian Penal Code. The intoxicant must be administered to the accused by the malicious and negligent act of a third person. In India it is sufficient if it is administered without his knowledge or against his will. Under the local Penal Codes an accused who did not know that he was given a heavily-laced drink by a friend on his birthday would not be able to succeed under s 85(2)(a) if he became intoxicated and committed an assault. Nor would he be able to rely on the section where he became intoxicated by taking some wrong drugs given by a doctor by mistake, unless it can be proved that the doctor was negligent. However, s 86(2) may apply as it is wide enough to cover involuntary intoxication, apart from voluntary intoxication (see below, p 236).

(a) "Wrong"

The word used in s 85(2) is "wrong". In contrast, the phrase used in s 84 (unsoundness of mind) is "wrong or contrary to law". In ch 12, it was noted that the word "wrong" in the context of s 84 can be interpreted to mean (1) wrong according to the ordinary principles of reasonable men or (2) morally wrong as perceived by the accused. (However, see Canagarayar, 1985.)

Should "wrong" in s 85(2) be construed in accordance with the meaning in s 84, whether objectively or subjectively? According to the general rule of statutory interpretation the same word should be given the same meaning in a statute, unless there are compelling reasons to assign it a different meaning. It is suggested that there is good reason for departing from the meaning given to "wrong" under s 84. While the law is concerned with morals, the extent to which it will enforce a moral principle per se is open to doubt. It is submitted that wrong in s 85(2)(b) should mean contrary to law. (Such a view would accord with that in *Beard* (1920), see below.)

(b) "Did not know what he was doing"

It was noted in ch 12 that the phrase used in s 84 is "incapable of knowing the *nature* of the act" and this means the physical nature of the act. In s 85(2) the phrase is "did not know what he was doing". Despite the difference in wording, this phrase should also mean the physical nature of the act.

2. Voluntary intoxication giving rise to defence

Voluntary or self-induced intoxication is not defined in the Penal Code. It involves the deliberate or intentional taking of drinks or drugs to an amount that can produce a state of intoxication.

Before examining the position under the Penal Code, the law of intoxication as laid down in *Beard* (1920) should be noted.

DPP v Beard [1920] AC 479 (HL, England)

Arthur Beard was indicted for murder having ravished a 13-year-old girl and in furtherance of the act of rape placed his hand upon her mouth and his thumb upon her throat, thereby causing death by suffocation. The defence was drunkenness.

The following rules were drawn from the cases considered by the House of Lords. (On the facts, there was a no evidence that he was too drunk to form the intention of committing rape.)

Lord Birkenhead LC: (1) That insanity, whether produced by drunkenness or otherwise, is a defence to the crime charged. The distinction between the defence of insanity in the true sense caused by excessive drinking, and the defence of drunkenness which produces a condition such that the drunken man's mind becomes incapable of forming a specific intention, has been preserved throughout the cases. The insane person cannot be convicted of a crime: *Felstead* (1914); but, upon a verdict of insanity, is ordered to be detained during His Majesty's pleasure. The law takes no note of the cause of the insanity. If actual insanity in fact supervenes, as the result of alcoholic excess, it furnishes as complete an answer to a criminal charge as insanity induced by any other cause. In the early cases of *Burrow* (1823) and *Rennie* (1825), Holroyd J refused to regard drunkenness as an excuse unless it had induced a continuing and lasting condition of insanity. But in *Davis* (1881), where the prisoner was charged with wounding with intent to murder, Stephen J thought (and I agree with him) that insanity, even though temporary, was an answer. The defence was that the prisoner was of unsound mind at the time of the commission of the act, and the evidence established that he was suffering from delirium tremens resulting from over-indulgence in drink. Stephen J said:

> "But drunkenness is one thing and the diseases to which drunkenness leads are different things; and if a man by drunkenness brings on a state of disease which causes such a degree of madness, even for a time, which would have relieved him from responsibility if it had been caused in any other way, then he would not be criminally responsible. In my opinion, in such a case the man is a madman, and is to be treated as such, although his madness is only temporary.... If you think there was a distinct disease caused by drinking, but differing from drunkenness, and that by reason thereof he did not know that the act was wrong, you will find a verdict of not guilty on the ground of insanity."

To the same effect is a decision of Day J in *Baines* (unreported, 1886). The defence was that the prisoner was insane when the murder was committed. The evidence proved that the prisoner had on several occasions been under treatment for delirium tremens. He had one attack a week before, and another two days after, committing the crime. Day J held that it was immaterial whether the insanity was permanent or temporary. The question was whether there was insanity or not; and the learned judge ruled that if a man were in such a state of intoxication that he did not know the nature of his act or that his act was wrongful, his act would be excusable on the ground of insanity.

(2) That evidence of drunkenness which renders the accused incapable of forming the specific intent essential to constitute the crime should be taken into consideration with the other facts proved in order to determine whether or not he had this intent.

(3) That evidence of drunkenness falling short of a proved incapacity in the accused to form the intent necessary to constitute the crime, and merely establishing that his mind was affected by drink so that he more readily gave way to some violent passion, does not rebut the presumption that a man intends the natural consequences of his acts.

(a) Intoxication causing insanity

Under the Penal Code a distinction is made between insanity produced by intoxication (s 85(2)(b)) on the one hand and unsoundness of mind (s 84) on the other (see ch 12). It should also be noted that the word used in s 85(2)(b) is "insane" and not "unsoundness of mind". In contrast, in England under the McNaghten Rules no distinction is drawn between insanity arising from intoxication or other causes so long as it results in a "disease of the mind". As Lord Birkenhead LC in *Beard* (1920) said "insanity, whether produced by drunkenness or otherwise is a defence [ie under the McNaghten Rules] to a crime charged".

Should the test in s 85(2)(b) be the same as that in the McNaghten Rules in so far as the element of "disease of mind" is concerned? It may be argued that since s 85(2)(b) is an attempt to incorporate rule 1 of *Beard* (1920, see above, p 234), the test of "insanity" in this section should be the same as that under English law, ie it must result in a disease of the mind and not unsoundness of mind.

However, s 86(1) provides that where a person is by reason of intoxication insane under s 85(2)(b) "section 84 of this Code and ss 314 and 315 of the Criminal Procedure Code shall apply". What is the effect of the reference to s 84? Does it mean that the test of unsoundness of mind in s 84 is to apply, ie "insane' meaning "unsoundness of mind"? It is submitted that the effect is procedural and not substantive in that it does not incorporate the test of unsoundness of mind under s 84. (However, see *Tan Ho Teck*, 1987, below.) It provides for the procedure to be followed upon a successful plea under s 85(2)(b). As in s 84, the accused is acquitted on the ground of insanity but may be ordered to be confined in a mental hospital, prison or other suitable place of safe custody.

In what circumstances can intoxication bring about insanity, ie "a state of disease which causes a degree of madness" (see *Davis*, 1881)? The most obvious example is where excessive drinking causes an attack of *delirium tremens*. In *Tan Ho Teck* (1987), the accused was charged with the murder of his brother. At the time of the killing, he was suffering from *delirium tremens* due to acute alcoholic intoxication, and as a result was incapable of knowing the nature of his act or what he was doing. The Singapore High Court did not refer to s 85(2)(b). It said:

> [P]ursuant to s 313 of the Criminal Procedure Code [now s 314], we find that the Accused did stab and cause the death of his brother but he was, by reason of *unsoundness of mind at the time, incapable of knowing the nature of the act or that what he was doing was either wrong or contrary to law.* We order that the Accused, be kept in safe custody pending the order of the Minister under s 314 of the Criminal Procedure Code [now s 315] (emphasis added).

The language used is that of s 84. On the facts of this case the accused may well have satisfied both s 84 and s 85(2)(b). However, as s 85(2)(b) deals specifically with insanity caused by intoxication, the court should have referred to this section rather than s 84.

(b)　Intoxication and crimes of "intention, specific or otherwise"

Section 86(2) draws its inspiration from rule 2 of *Beard* (1920) (see above, p 235) but there are some differences in wording. The differences are summarized below:

Section 86(2)	Beard, rule 2
(1) Intoxication shall be taken into account.	Evidence of drunkenness should be taken into consideration.
(2) Whether person charged had formed an intention, specific or otherwise, in the absence of which he would not be guilty of the offence.	Whether person charged was incapable of forming the specific intent essential to constitute the crime.

(i) Relevance of incapacity to form intent

There is no mention of "incapacity" to form an intent in s 86(2) whereas the word appears in the corresponding proposition in rule 2 of *Beard* (1920). *Beard* (1920) itself has since undergone refinements in England and, today, there is no requirement that there must be *incapacity* due to intoxication to negative the intention to commit a crime. In the Privy Council case of *Broadhurst* (1964), Lord Devlin explained why it was thought necessary to require the element of incapacity in *Beard* (1920). This was because of the presumption in England at that time that a man intended the natural consequences of his acts. He pointed out that in a case in which the intent of an accused was to be ascertained solely by inference, and the effect of drink on him was at issue, nothing short of incapacity need be considered, for if he could not himself give evidence about his state of mind he could not say what intent he in fact formed or did not form. However, if there were material to suggest that by reason of intoxication he *could* not have formed a guilty intent, then the inference which would otherwise naturally be drawn from the circumstances could be questioned. His Lordship concluded that "the sort of approach that is contemplated in *Beard* (1920) is that there must be proof (or at least some suggestion) of incapacity in order to rebut the presumption that a man intends the natural consequences of his acts." The question to be asked in *Beard* (1920) is whether the accused was capable of forming an intention. Proof of incapacity will of course negative the *mens rea*. However, today English law is not so rigorous.

The prosecution has only to establish that the accused had the intent despite his intoxication. An intoxicated man may be capable of forming an intent but may not have done so in the particular alleged offence. In *Sheehan and Moore* (1975), the English Court of Appeal (Criminal Division) quashed a conviction for murder and substituted a conviction for manslaughter. The court held that the onus of proof was on the Crown to establish that, notwithstanding the alleged intoxication, the accused did form an intent. (See *Pordage*, 1975, *Garlick*, 1980.)

Despite the absence of the word "incapacity" in the Penal Code, Singapore and Malaysian courts have sometimes considered whether the accused was so intoxicated as to be *incapable* of forming the intention to kill even though they have not elaborated on the question (*Seah Eng Joo* 1961; *Ismail b Abdul Rahman*, 1974; see ch 12, p 223).

The law on intoxication contained in s 35(4) of the Criminal Code of Malta is *in pari materia* with s 86(2) of the Penal Code. It also makes no mention of incapacity. In *Broadhurst* (1964), the Privy Council, in an appeal from Malta, compared s 35(4) of the Criminal Code of Malta with the corresponding proposition in rule 2 of *Beard* (1920). It stated:

> It may be ... that there is no substantial difference between the two propositions. Or it may be that the law as laid down in *Beard* (1920) must now be interpreted in the light of later decisions on the proof of guilty intent. But superficially at any rate s 35(4) of the Code and *Beard* approach differently the problem of proving intent. One way of approaching the problem is to say that it is always for the Crown to prove that the accused actually had the intent necessary to constitute the crime: and that that proof may emerge from evidence or statements made by the accused about his own state of mind or may be made by way of inference from the totality of the circumstances. *Prima facie*, intoxication is one of the circumstances to be taken into account and on this view all that s 35(4) is doing is to make it plain that intoxication is not to be excluded. On the other hand, the sort of approach that is contemplated in *Beard* (1920) is that there must be proof (or at least some suggestion) of incapacity in order to rebut the presumption that a man intends the natural consequences of his acts.

Section 86(2) is also *in pari materia* with its counterpart under s 13 of the Zambian Penal Code. In *Musole* (1963), Convoy CJ said:

> It is not a question of whether the appellant was capable of forming the necessary intent, but of considering his intoxication as one of the circumstances on which to reach a decision as to whether he had in fact formed the intent.... *Beard*'s case proceeded on the principle that drunkenness which renders the necessary intent should be taken into account in deciding whether he has that intent. As Lord Delvin said (in *Broadhurst*, 1964), it is not a question of incapacity under the Code.

Earlier in the judgment, Convoy CJ was at pains to point out that:

> ... the section was intended to contain as far as possible a full and complete statement of the law of intoxication as it affects the criminal law in Zambia. It must therefore be construed in its application ... free from glosses and interpolations derived from any expositions, however authoritive, of the law of England.

The above remarks are equally applicable to s 86(2) (see ch 1 on the exhaustiveness of the Penal Code of Singapore and the FMS Penal Code). It is submitted that the question of incapacity of the accused is itself irrelevant in determining his intent. However, Hatchard (1983) pointed out that the question of incapacity is still relevant in determining whether the accused was or was not sufficiently intoxicated. In considering the position under s 13(4) of the Zambian Penal Code (which is *in pari materia* with the local Penal Codes), Hatchard (1983) states:

> ... the prosecution [is] required to negate the argument that the accused person did not have the intent necessary for the commission of the crime due to intoxication. However, there must be evidence that the accused was so

intoxicated and if this is not available by means of direct evidence, the accused person has the onus of producing evidence that he was incapable of forming the necessary intention due to intoxication.

(See Cheang, 1986.)

(ii) "Intention, specific or otherwise"

Rule 2 of *Beard* (1920) established that self-induced intoxication can provide a defence only to crimes of specific intent. This was intended to circumscribe the defence of intoxication. *Beard* (1920) has undergone some development in England in relation to the category of crimes of specific intent and crimes of basic intent. The dichotomy between the two categories is not very clear and is largely functional being based on "a compromise between the rigors of denying the relevance of intoxication and allowing it to undercut all liability" (Fletcher, 1978). Some refinements were made in *Majewski* (1976) and *Caldwell* (1981). The combined effect of the two cases seems to point to the following: crimes of specific intent are those that can only be committed intentionally and in which the *mens rea* goes further than the *actus reus*. In Singapore, an example is assault with intent to outrage modesty under s 354 of the Penal Code. The accused must intend to cause not only the assault (s 351), ie the apprehension of the use of criminal force, but he must also intend to outrage his victim's modesty. In crimes of basic intent the *mens rea* does not extend further than the *actus reus* as in simple assault under s 351 of the Penal Code.

In contrast to the position in England, s 86(2) covers both crimes of specific as well as basic intent. The section speaks of taking intoxication into account for the purpose of determining whether the person charged had formed any "intention, specific or otherwise". The word "otherwise" means an intention other than specific intention, ie basic intention. Thus the defence of intoxication avails for all crimes which require as a mental element an intention to commit them.

Section 86(2) speaks only of intention and not other mental elements such as knowledge, recklessness, negligence or wantonness. As noted above, the word "otherwise" in the context of s 86(2) refers to non-specific or basic intention and not to other mental elements (see Mooney, 1961; Koh, 1974; Cheang, 1986). Thus, a curious result arises in charges for murder under s 300 or culpable homicide not amounting to murder under s 299 of the Penal Code, as both sections contain the *mens rea* of intention and knowledge. While intention can include knowledge the converse may not be true. The effect is, for example, that if an accused is charged with intentional killing under s 300(a)(b) and (c), intoxication is a defence but if he is charged under s 300(d) where the *mens rea* element is knowledge and not intention, intoxication is not a defence (except where s 85 applies). From the viewpoint of punishment all the four limbs of s 300 carry the death penalty. It is anomalous to provide the defence of intoxication for s 300(a)(b) and (c) but not for s 300(d). It may well be that in practice the line between s 300(d) and s 300(a)(b) and (c) is so fine that no problem will arise (see ch 19). An intoxicated accused may have no knowledge and intention under s 300. For example, in the English case of *Lipman* (1970) the accused took some drugs and was on an "LSD trip". He was then under the illusion of descending to the centre of the earth and being attacked by snakes. In attempting to fight off the snakes he killed the victim who suffered two blows on the head, but died of asphyxia as a result of bedsheets being crammed into her mouth. He said he had no *knowledge* of what he was doing and no *intention* to kill or do grievous bodily harm.

3. Voluntary intoxication not giving rise to defence

(a) "Dutch courage" and inflamed passions

If a person has formed an intention to commit an offence and he drinks in order to give himself "Dutch courage" to do it, can he plead intoxication as a defence? This situation falls outside the scope of s 86(2) as he had formed the intention before taking the drink. Further, s 85(1) provides that voluntary intoxication does not constitute a defence to a criminal charge, other than those expressly provided for in ss 85 and 86. Another example where voluntary intoxication will not be a defence under the Penal Code is where a person drinks so that he will more readily give way to some violent passion.

The position in England is similar (see rules 2 and 3 of *Beard*, 1920). Regarding the example of "Dutch courage", Lord Denning in *Gallagher* (1963) said:

> If a man, whilst sane and sober, forms an intention to kill... and then get himself drunk so as to give himself Dutch courage to do the killing ... he cannot rely on this self-induced drunkenness as a defence to a charge of murder, not even as reducing it to manslaughter ... the wickedness of his mind before he got drunk is enough to condemn him, coupled with the act which he intended to do and did do.

(b) Intoxication and automatism

As noted in ch 3, the Penal Code does not expressly provide a defence of automatism. However, non-insane automatism may be introduced either within the framework of the defence of accident in s 80 of the Penal Code or it may go to the question whether the *actus reus* of an offence has been committed by a person. In a situation where the accused voluntarily gets himself into a state of intoxication through alcohol and/or drugs and becomes an automaton, it is unlikely that the "defence" of automatism will apply if he had already formed the intent before getting intoxicated. However, if there was no preceding fault and he did not realize that he would get into a state of automatism, s 86(2) might apply.

4. Intoxication and mistake

Suppose A while being voluntarily intoxicated after drinking some whisky mistook Y for Z, her twin sister who is his girlfriend. He proceeds to kiss Y thinking she is Z and tries to make love to her. Y, who detests A, runs away. If A is charged with using criminal force under s 352, can he plead the defence of mistake? Let it be supposed that this is the first time that A has ever had whisky and did not realize that he would get intoxicated with only two glasses. The mistake of fact in s 79 of the Penal Code must be made in good faith by one who because of the mistake believes himself to be justified by law. This raises difficult questions of fact whether due care and attention had been exercised by A in taking two glasses of whisky. A more likely view would be that a reasonable person, especially if he had never consumed alcohol before, should avoid drinking such quantities on a first occasion. Accordingly, it is submitted that A did not display "due care and attention" and thus no defence under s 79 would be available to him.

5. Intoxication and murder: a mitigating circumstance

The distinction between murder under s 300 and culpable homicide not amounting to murder under s 299 is thin. Intoxication could be a *complete* defence to a charge under each of these sections. Thus a successful plea of intoxication for murder under s 300 could lead to a complete acquittal and not merely to a reduction to culpable homicide not amounting to murder under s 299 unless it can be proved that whilst the intoxication negatived the intention required in s 300, nonetheless, it did not negative the lesser degree of intention required under s 299. It may well be possible to draw such a line of distinction in respect of intention under s 300 and s 299 in respect of the mental element of an intoxicated person. Unfortunately, local courts have never alluded to this question.

In *Tan Hung Song* (1951) the Singapore Court of Criminal Appeal reduced a verdict of murder under s 300 to one of culpable homicide not amounting to murder under s 299 on a successful plea of intoxication. The court pointed out that if evidence of the accused's intoxication had been admitted and put in evidence, "it is impossible to say that the jury must have reached the conclusion they did, (ie verdict of murder)". This suggests that the intoxication would have negatived the *mens rea* of intention in s 300. There should therefore have been a complete acquittal, unless there was sufficient intention under s 299. The court did not consider this question when it reduced the murder charge.

Similarly, in *Suba Singh* (1962) below, the Court of Appeal of Malaya also regarded the defence of intoxication not as a complete defence but only as a mitigating circumstance reducing a charge of murder to one of culpable homicide not amounting to murder.

Suba Singh v PP (1962) 28 MLJ 122 (CA, Ipoh, Malaya)

The appellant was convicted of murder under s 302 of the FMS Penal Code. He pleaded the defence of intoxication.

Thomson CJ: [The trial judge dealt] with the question of the drink which the appellant had taken and here unfortunately we find ourselves unable to agree with what he said.

"It is no defence for the accused to say that he has no recollection of what happened because he was drunk. Where an accused person gets into a state of drunkenness of his own free will, the Court will not attach any importance to the fact that he was drunk and will draw the natural inferences from his acts. So if you are satisfied and sure in your minds that the accused did in fact stab the deceased, the fact that he was drunk is no defence."

and again at a later stage:

"You must put the questions of drunkenness out of your minds when you come to consider your verdict, for, as I have already told you, voluntary drunkenness is no defence."

Now, no doubt these passages correctly state the effect of the Penal Code as it was before it was amended in 1936 and no doubt they correctly state the relevant provisions today of the Indian Penal Code, although I am not sure that they correctly state the law as it is in fact applied in India today. That, however, is beside the point, because in 1936 the Penal Code was amended and there is very little doubt that it was so amended in the light of the decision of the House of Lords in the case of *Beard* (1920), where the late Lord Birkenhead reviewed very extensively the English law relating to drunkenness which by that time had fallen into a certain amount of confusion. [His Lordship quoted the FMS Penal Code, s 86(ii) and continued.] That is the same as the English law and an example of how it has been put to a jury is to be found in the words of Lord Coleridge in *Meade*'s case (1909). Lord Coleridge's words were:

"Where it is part of the essence of a crime that a motive, a particular motive, shall exist in the mind of the man who does the act, the law declares this–that if the mind at that time is so obscured by drink, if the reason is dethroned and the man is incapable therefore of forming that intent, it justifies the reduction of the charge from murder to manslaughter."

Had some such words been used to the jury in the present case and had their attention been directed in the light of them to the evidence, regarding drunkenness we find it quite impossible to say whether or not they would have brought in a verdict of murder. After all it was a case where the prosecution were relying on a presumption to make out the intention which is a necessary ingredient of murder and the jury should have been invited to consider the evidence, such as it was, of drunkenness as something which might have the effect of rebutting that presumption.

Conviction for culpable homicide not amounting to murder substituted

In *Suba Singh* (1962) the confusion over the consequence of a success-ful plea of intoxication appears to have been based on a total reliance of English law without due regard to the actual position under the Penal Code. The court stated that "some such words" as those used in the English case of *Meade* (1909) should have been used to direct the jury. The direction given to the jury by Lord Coleridge in *Meade* was "that if the mind at that time is so obscured by drink, if the reason is de-throned and the man in incapable therefore of forming the intent, it justifies the *reduction of the charge from murder to manslaughter*". The court in *Suba Singh* (1962) overlooked the point that under the Penal Code intoxication is a complete defence and not merely a miti-gating circumstance, unlike the "defence" of intoxication in a murder case in England.

6. Sections 85(1) and 86(2): not a defence

JM Brabyn, "Intoxication in Singapore: An Alternative to *Majewski*" (1986) Lawasia, 60, pp 75–76

... [I]f, as Mooney (1961) suggests, intent [under s 86(2)] cannot be construed so as to include knowledge, and section 85(1) prohibits any return to general principles governing proof of *mens rea*, intoxication cannot be taken into account when determining the presence of the requisite knowledge even with respect to the offence of murder. Mooney concludes that:

> "[a]lthough it may be clear on general principles that manslaughter is the offence which has been committed, the alternatives before the Court would seem to be a conviction of murder or acquittal, depending upon the view taken of the meaning of the subsection."

With respect, this is not necessarily so. The error is in the interpretation of s 85(1). That subsection merely provides that intoxication may not amount to a defence except in certain stipulated circumstances. But to construe the sub-section in the manner which he suggests is to make intoxication a separate ground for liability, which is a very different thing. Why should the prosecu-tion be relieved of its duty to prove the requisite *mens rea* for an offence, eg the knowledge required under two of the limbs of s 300, merely because there is some evidence of intoxication? With respect to knowledge at least, that is not even the law in England.

Suppose a person commits the *actus reus* of murder. Since there is no evi-dence that the defendant intended to kill the victim or to cause any bodily injury of any kind, the prosecution rely upon s 300(d). Ordinarily, the prosecu-tion would be required to prove that the defendant actually knew, *at the time of doing the act complained of*, that the act was so imminently dangerous that it must in all probability cause death or such bodily injury as is likely to cause death. It is not sufficient that the act is in fact so imminently dangerous. The defendant must subjectively have appreciated this at the time of doing the act. However, suppose there is evidence that the defendant had consumed a consid-erable quantity of alcohol before doing the act complained of. The prosecution may be able to prove that at the time of doing the act the defendant still had the requisite knowledge. But suppose the evidence is unclear? There are at least three different answers which it has been suggested the prosecution might make:

(i)   Well, never mind. The defendant was intoxicated, and therefore s 85(1) applies. Intoxication cannot be a defence, so we are entitled to assume that the defendant knew what an ordinary sober person in the position of the defendant would probably have known. Such a person would have known that the defendant's act was imminently dangerous as required. Therefore, the defendant is guilty of murder.

(ii) Well, the defendant was intoxicated. Therefore s 85(1) applies and the intoxication cannot be a defence. We must then ask ourselves the hypothetical question: what would we have said was the defendant's state of knowledge considering all the evidence, except the evidence of intoxication? If we are satisfied that we would have said that the defendant knew of the danger, the defendant is guilty of murder.

(iii) Since the defendant's intoxication is no defence, it is not the defendant's actual knowledge at the time of doing the act complained of which is relevant, but what the defendant's state of knowledge would have been had the defendant been sober. If when sober, this particular defendant would have known, had he thought about it, that the act complained of was so imminently dangerous that it must in all probability cause death, the defendant is guilty of murder.

The first possibility adopts the approach suggested by Smith and Hogan as the rule for offences of basic intent, potentially applicable to s 300 in Singapore because of paragraph (d). It would impose a totally objective test for the *mens rea* of the capital crime of murder. The second uses the formulation Professor Williams suggests would be required for basic intention in England today. The third adopts Lord Diplock's interpretation of *Majewski* (1976) when applied to offences for which recklessness provides sufficient *mens rea* in *Caldwell* (1982). Each is inconsistent with at least one of the general principles of liability under the Penal Code. The first is totally inconsistent with the principle of subjective *mens rea*. It also effectively creates a special offence of drunken homicide not justified by the Code. The second and third involve consideration of purely hypothetical and artificial questions which at least partially ignore the principle of subjective *mens rea*.

If any of the three alternative answers listed above is accepted, there would be a further question as to how intoxicated a defendant would have to be before these special rules would apply. Would any evidence that a defendant's mental faculties had been impaired due to the consumption of an intoxicant suffice, or would the special rules only apply where the defendant was shown to have been grossly or totally intoxicated?

It is submitted that the least problematic interpretation of ss 85(1) and 86(2) is as follows. Section 85(1) simply states what has never been denied, that voluntary intoxication alone does not provide a true defence to a criminal charge. If an accused is proved to have had the *mens rea* required for a criminal charge, it does not matter that the accused was also drunk or otherwise intoxicated at the time. However, the general principle that the prosecution has the legal onus of establishing all the elements of a criminal offence, including the *mens rea*, still applies. The defendant's intoxication does not relieve the prosecution of this duty. On the contrary, intoxication is merely part of the evidence which a court would have to consider when deciding whether the prosecution have discharged their duty. Section 86(2) is for the purpose of clarification only, stating that the ordinary principles apply even in circumstances where for historical reasons there may otherwise have been some doubt.

Brabyn's interpretation of ss 85(1) and 86(2) of the Penal Code is that voluntary intoxication is neither a defence nor a special basis for liability. She suggests that where an accused was intoxicated at the time he committed the *actus reus* of the offence the ordinary principle that the prosecution must prove the requisite *mens rea* applies.

Section 85(1) clearly speaks of the "defence" of intoxication (including voluntary intoxication) as provided in ss 85(2)(b) and 86(2). Voluntary intoxication falling within the scope of these two sections constitutes a complete defence. Moreover, the two sections fall within Chapter IV, General Exceptions of the Penal Code, which deals with defences. The Evidence Act in Singapore (Cap 97) and that in Malaysia (Rev 1971, Act 56) provide that the burden of proving the existence of circumstances bringing a case within any of the General Exceptions in the Penal Codes is on the accused (see, eg *Jayasena*, 1970; *Govindasamy*, 1976; *Teo Eng Chan*, 1988, and ch 3). With respect, Brabyn's view cannot be supported.

Where an offence requires a mental element other than intention, it falls outside the scope of s 86(2). The prosecution then has to prove *beyond reasonable doubt* that the accused, despite his intoxication, had the requisite *mens rea* for the offence, eg knowledge. In other words, the accused's knowledge or other *mens rea* is viewed as though he were sober.

Part III

Inchoate offences

Chapter 14

Attempt

By CMV Clarkson

A. Rationale

No system of criminal law can afford to limit punishment to those who have actually caused a specified forbidden harm, such as killing another. The law needs to prevent persons from *trying* to kill. Punishment in such cases serves as appropriate deterrent notice both to the individual concerned and the public at large of the consequences of such acts and helps underwrite their moral reprehensibility. One who tries to kill another or to cause other harm is in as much need of incapacitation and rehabilitation as one who succeeds. Further, if there were no liability for trying to commit crimes the task of the police in preventing crime would be severely restricted. Intervention would not be possible until the crime had actually been committed.

Further, from a retributivist standpoint the person who tries to commit a crime is just as blameworthy as he who succeeds. The difference between success and failure could be mere chance and the criminal law is not a lottery with liability dependent on "the invisible hand of Fate" (Schulhofer, 1974).

For these reasons all systems of criminal law have provisions punishing attempts to commit a crime. However, while the existence of such crimes is readily explicable, the level of seriousness attached to attempts, as compared with completed offences, is highly controversial. These arguments have been fully debated elsewhere (Clarkson and Keating, 1984). Suffice it to point out that the general stance adopted by the Penal Code under s 511 is that an attempt to commit a crime is only punishable to a maximum of one-half the maximum term of imprisonment available for the completed crime. This approach stands in sharp contrast to that of English law where under s 4(1) of the Criminal Attempts Act 1981 an attempt can be punished to the same extent as the completed offence.

B. Structure of liability

Attempts in Singapore and Malaysia are provided for and punishable in one of three ways:

1. Section 511: general provision on attempt

Penal Code, s 511

Whoever attempts to commit an offence punishable by this Code or by any other written law with imprisonment or fine or with a combination of such punishments, or attempts to cause such an offence to be committed, and in such attempt does any act towards the commission of the offence, shall, where no express provision is made by this Code or by such other written law, as the case may be, for the punishment of such attempt, be punished with such punishment as is provided for the offence:

Provided that any term of imprisonment imposed shall not exceed one-half of the longest term provided for the offence.

This is an extremely broad provision. One can be liable for attempting to commit *any offence*, whether under the Penal Code or any other statute. This of course means that all offences of strict liability can be attempted. It should be noted in this context that s 511 here differs from its counterpart in the Indian Penal Code under which one can only be liable for attempting to commit crimes punishable by imprisonment; such crimes are generally the more serious ones.

It has been suggested (Wright, 1984) that one cannot attempt to commit an offence under s 511 if that offence carries a punishment of caning as an alternative, or as an additional punishment, to imprisonment. The only offences that can be attempted are those punishable with imprisonment or a fine or a combination of "such punishments", ie imprisonment and fine.

There is no authority on the point but such an interpretation is most unlikely to be accepted. It would lead to the remarkable conclusion that while trivial strict liability offences could be attempted, there could be no liability for serious offences, such as attempted rape. Such a narrow view has not been adopted in India where s 511 provides that "whoever attempts to commit an offence punishable by this Code with imprisonment for life or imprisonment...". As will be seen later, Indian courts have not limited this to attempts to commit offences punishable *only* by imprisonment. They have freely held that there can be liability to commit any offence carrying any type of punishment as long as imprisonment is one of the listed alternative punishments. Section 511 will almost certainly be read in the same way as simply requiring that the full offence be punishable, inter alia, by either imprisonment or a fine. The fact that other alternative punishments such as caning are also available is irrelevant.

2. Specific attempts

There are a few specific provisions in the Penal Code penalizing particular types of attempt.

Penal Code, s 307, attempted murder

(1) Whoever does any act with such intention or knowledge and under such circumstances that if he by that act caused death he would be guilty of murder, shall be punished with imprisonment for a term which may extend to 10 years, and shall also be liable to fine; and if hurt is caused to any person by such act, the offender shall be liable either to imprisonment for life, or to such punishment as is hereinbefore mentioned and shall also be liable to caning.

[The FMS Penal Code provides that if hurt is caused "the offender shall be liable to imprisonment for a term which may extend to twenty years"; no provision is made for caning as an alternative punishment.]

(2) When any person offending under this section is under sentence of imprisonment for life (Malaysia Penal Code: or for a term of twenty years), he may, if hurt is caused, be punished with death.

Penal Code, s 308: attempted culpable homicide

Whoever does any act with such intention or knowledge and under such circumstances that if he by that act caused death he would be guilty of culpable homicide not amounting to murder, shall be punished with imprisonment for a term which may extend to 3 years, or with fine, or with both; and if hurt is caused to any person by such act, shall be punished with imprisonment for a term which may extend to 7 years, or with fine, or with both.

Illustration
A, on grave and sudden provocation, fires a pistol at Z, under such circumstances that if he thereby caused death he would be guilty of culpable homicide not amounting to murder. A has committed the offence defined in this section.

Penal Code, s 309: attempted suicide

Whoever attempts to commit suicide, and does any act towards the commission of such offence, shall be punished with imprisonment for a term which may extend to one year, or with fine, or with both.

Penal Code, s 393: attempted robbery

Whoever attempts to commit robbery shall be punished with imprisonment for a term of not less than 2 years and not more than 7 years and shall also be punished with caning with not less than 6 strokes.

[Under the FMS Penal Code the punishment is "imprisonment for a term which may extend to seven years, and shall also be liable to fine."]

Some of these independent provisions can be rationalized: s 511 can not be applied to attempted murder as murder is not a crime punishable with imprisonment; s 511 can not be applied to attempted suicide as there is no crime of suicide–special provision therefore needed to be made otherwise there would have been no offence. The existence of some of the other provisions is, however, more difficult to explain.

Perhaps, there is a perceived need to have a special provision for the punishment of attempted robbery as the maximum punishment for such attempt is more than half that available for the completed offence.

Perhaps the real explanation for the existence of all these particular provisions and certainly the only explanation for the inclusion of s 308, attempted culpable homicide, is a historical one. Lord Macaulay drafted his original Penal Code in 1837. These proposals were used as a model but significant alterations were made to them by Sir Barnes Peacock who drafted the final version of the Indian Penal Code (1860). In Lord Macaulay's Draft Code (1837) there was no general attempt provision. Instead certain particular attempt provisions were provided. In his *Notes on the Indian Penal Code* (1837) Lord Macaulay makes a case for the inclusion of ss 307 and 308 on the ground that otherwise there would be no liability in clear cases of attempted murder and attempted culpable homicide and therefore these provisions were "absolutely necessary to the completeness of the code" (Macaulay, 1837). Between 1837 and 1860 the law of attempt, which was only in an embryonic state in English law, made great strides in its development and impact, for example, the leading case of *Eagleton* was decided in 1855. When the final version of the Indian Penal Code was amended by Sir Barnes Peacock all Lord Macaulay's original specific attempt provisions were retained but in addition a general attempt provision, s 511, was added. Whether this decision was simply an oversight or not is not revealed by the records.

3.   Definition of crime includes attempt

Certain crimes are defined in such a manner that the full crime is committed either by a successful completion thereof or by an attempt there at. For instance, s 121 of the Singapore Penal Code provides that "whoever wages war against the Government, or attempts to wage such war, ... shall be punished ..." (s 121 of the FMS Penal Code is to similar effect). Section 377A provides that it is an offence if any male person "commits ... or attempts to procure the commission by any male person of any act of gross indecency with another male person". The special offence of gang-robbery is defined in s 391 as being where "five or more persons conjointly commit or attempt a robbery".

The significant point about this category of attempts is that, unlike the former two categories, completed offences and attempts here carry the same potential maximum punishments. Again, some rationalization of this approach is possible–at least with regard to some of these offences. For example, it could be argued that the real harm sought to be prevented by s 377A is the threat to the common morality. This harm occurs whenever there is an attempt to commit an act of gross indecency, it being irrelevant whether there is ever any actual indecency. Accordingly, the harm being the same, attempts ought to be subjected to the same punishment as the completed offence.

Such rationalization across the board is, however, impossible. For instance, s 130 makes it an offence to "rescue or attempt to rescue" a prisoner. Bearing in mind that attempts are generally only punishable to half the extent of the completed offence, it is difficult to see what policy considerations dictate that an attempt to rescue a prisoner is "as bad as" or at least deserving of the same punishment as actually rescuing the prisoner.

Again, the truth probably lies in the same historical explanation as canvassed above–but while this might explain how these provisions came to exist alongside s 511, it cannot explain why attempted robbery should be punished to a lesser extent than robbery, but attempted rescue of a prisoner should be capable of punishment to the same extent as actual rescue of a prisoner (Penal Code, s 130).

It is clear then that much of the structure of the law of attempts in the Penal Code is haphazard. If a substantial overhaul and reform of the Penal Code were ever to be undertaken, this three-fold classification of attempts would need to be reconsidered and only retained if there were found to be sound policy reasons for treating any particular type of attempt differently. Historical oversights should not be perpetuated. It is thus a matter of regret that the Indian Law Commissioners in their proposed reformulation of the Indian Penal Code, simply assumed that ss 307, 308 and 511 should all continue, albeit in an amended form. If the inherent structure of a code is deficient, no amount of tinkering with detail will ever solve the problem.

C. A mutually exclusive classification?

Are these three different methods of punishing attempts mutually exclusive? If one tried to kill or rob another, would one *have* to be charged under s 307 or s 393–or could one alternatively be charged under s 511?

There is no problem with regard to attempted murder. A charge may only be brought under s 307. Section 511 only applies to attempts to commit offences punishable *with imprisonment or fine*. Murder, being punishable with death, is not an offence that can be attempted under s 511.

With other attempts the answer appears at first sight equally obvious. Section 511 only applies "where no express provision is made by this Code or by such other written law, as the case may be, for the punishment of such attempt". Sections 308 and 393, etc are precisely such express provisions dealing with specific attempts. Accordingly, s 511 cannot be used.

However, what if the test of an attempt in, say, s 308 were narrower than the test of an attempt in s 511? This would mean that it could be possible that on the facts of a particular case it *would not* amount to an attempt under s 308–but *would* amount to an attempt under s 511. It can therefore be argued that as there is no express provision elsewhere "for the punishment of *such attempt*" (ie this particular attempt), it is permissible to charge under s 511. Such an approach was adopted in *Francis Cassidy* (1867) where the Bombay High Court held that s 511 could be used in a case not covered by s 307. The court observed that s 307 was not intended to exhaust all attempts to commit murder.

The better view is, however, adopted in the following case.

Queen-Empress v Niddha (1891) XIV All 38 (HC, Allahabad, India)

Straight J: ...[It] is necessary for me to consider whether, having regard to the language of the Indian Penal Code, it is competent for me, as the learned Judges who decided that case held it was competent for them, to convict of attempted murder upon s 511 taken in connection with ss 299 and 300 of the Indian Penal Code. It will be convenient to consider that portion of the judgments of the Bombay Court (in *Francis Cassidy*) which deals with that matter first. I am of opinion that s 307, Indian Penal Code, is exhaustive and that within the four corners of that section are to be found the whole provisions of the law relating to attempts to murder. I am led to this conclusion by an examination of the terms of s 511, Indian Penal Code. They are as follows:

> "Whoever attempts to commit an offence punishable by this Code with transportation or imprisonment, or to cause such an offence to be committed, and in such attempt does any act towards, the commission of the offence."

Now it appears to me that the attempts which are limited by s 511 are attempts to commit offences, which by the Code itself are punishable either with "transportation or imprisonment". It cannot properly be said that the offence of murder is punishable with either of those things. In my opinion, if murder, as mentioned in ss 299 and 300, was intended to be included, the Legislature would before the word transportation have inserted the word "death". But, again, the section goes on and says that, certain things being done, the person who does those acts shall, "where no express provision is made for the punishment of such attempt", be punished in a particular way. As I have pointed out, by s 307, Indian Penal Code, there is express provision made in the Code itself for the punishment of an attempt to murder. It seems therefore to me that when the framers of s 511 drew it up in the terms that they have drawn it up, they especially meant to exclude those attempts to commit offences which in the various preceding sections of the Code were specifically and deliberately provided for with punishments enacted in the sections themselves. I have therefore for these reasons come to the conclusion that s 307 is exhaustive and that no Court has any right to resort to the provisions of ss 299 and 300 read with s 511 for the purpose of convicting a person of the offence of attempted murder, which, according to the view of the Court, does not come within the provision of s 307, Indian Penal Code. I need only add that the maxim *expressio unius, &c, &c*, should be applied in construing a penal statute of this kind, and, apart from that, it is obvious that any other view would introduce the greatest possible inconvenience and a vast conflict of opinion as to what would constitute an attempt to commit murder within the meaning of the Penal Code.

Argument on this point now looks to be placed beyond all doubt. In *Om Prakash* (1961) the Supreme Court of India ruled that the test for attempt under ss 307 and 308 was the same as the test under s 511. The whole argument about the sections being mutually exclusive is based on the premise that the test in s 511 is broader than that in ss 308 and 307. Accordingly, if the two tests are the same the argument collapses and s 511 cannot be used for such attempts.

Theoretically, problem areas do still remain with, first, those specific attempt provisions, such as s 393, that do not contain their own definitions and, second, with those undefined attempt provisions included within the definition of the full offence (the third category above). All these cases can presumably be dealt with in the same manner as an "attempt" is not defined in any of them. Thus s 393 makes it an offence to attempt to commit robbery. Unlike ss 307 and 308 no definition of attempt is provided. Accordingly, it *could* be that the test of an attempt under s 393 (which would have to be the common law test of attempt) is different from that of s 511 thus raising the same possibility that a particular case of attempted robbery might not be covered by s 393 but might be covered by the broader s 511. It is, however, submitted that this approach will never be adopted. First, if it were to be held that the two tests were different it would appear that in fact s 511 would be the narrower test. There would thus never be a case that did not fall within the specific attempt provisions but did fall within s 511. However, the second and more overwhelming reason is that it is simply inconceivable that judges in Singapore or Malaysia (or India for that matter) would suddenly abandon the practice of a century and start to manufacture two separate tests of attempt. Even where the wording is totally different, as it is with ss 307 and 308 on the one hand and s 511 on the other hand, the courts have held that the test is the same. They will certainly hold the same for sections where no definition of attempt is given. The test contained in s 511 will be held to be applicable.

We are thus left in the reasonably tolerable position (given that there are three categories) that each category of attempt is mutually exclusive. If one attempts robbery one can only be charged under s 393. If one attempts culpable homicide not amounting to murder one can only be charged under s 308. If one attempts to commit a crime and there is no express provision elsewhere for that *type* of attempted crime, one can only be charged with the provision punishing the full offence *as read with s 511*. For example, with attempted rape one would charge an accused with committing an offence contrary to s 376 as read with s 511.

D. The law

1. Mens rea

The widely accepted common law position is that one can only be liable for attempting to commit a crime if one has the *intention* to commit the complete offence. Even if the full offence can be committed knowingly or recklessly, only intention will suffice for the attempt to commit such an offence.

Merrit v Commonwealth 180 SE 395 (1935) (Supreme Court of Appeals, Virginia, USA)

[W]hile a person may be guilty of murder though there was no actual intent to kill, he cannot be guilty of an attempt to commit murder unless he has a specific intent to kill.... A common example, illustrating this principle is: "If one from a house-top recklessly throw a billet of wood upon the sidewalk where persons are constantly passing, and it fall upon a person passing by and kill him, this would be by the common law murder. But if, instead of killing, it inflicts only a slight injury, the party could not be convicted of an assault with intent to commit murder." (*Moore*) ....

When we say that a man attempted to do a given wrong, we mean that he intended to do it specifically; and proceeded a certain way in the doing. The intent in the mind covers the thing in full; the act covers it only in part....

To commit murder, one need not intend to take life; but to be guilty of an attempt to murder, he must so intend. It is not sufficient that his act, had it proved fatal, would have been murder.

R v Mohan [1976] QB 1 (CA, Criminal Division, England)

The accused, in response to a police officer's signal to stop, slowed his car down, but then accelerated and drove the car at the police officer. The police officer jumped aside and the accused continued on his journey. He was charged with the offence, *inter alia*, of an attempt by wanton driving to cause bodily harm to the police officer. The judge, in his final direction to the jury, said that it had to be proved that the accused deliberately drove wantonly, realizing that such wanton driving would be likely to cause, unless interrupted for some reason, bodily harm to the police officer or that the accused was reckless as to whether such bodily harm would be caused by his wanton driving. It was not necessary to prove an intention actually to cause bodily harm. The accused was convicted. He appealed against conviction.

James LJ: In our judgment it is well-established law that intent (*mens rea*) is an essential ingredient of the offence of attempt.... Insofar as the judge directed the jury that it was not necessary to prove any intent in relation to count 2 he fell into error.

That does not, however, dispose of this appeal.... It has been necessary, therefore, to consider whether taken as a whole the directions did, by the words:

> "he must have realized ... that such driving, unless it were to stop, ... was likely to cause bodily harm if he went on, or he was reckless as to whether bodily harm was caused."

include the need for proof of the element of *mens rea*. The first question we have to answer is: what is the meaning of "intention" when that word is used to describe the *mens rea* in attempt? It is to be distinguished from "motive" in the sense of an emotion leading to action: it has never been suggested that such a meaning is appropriate to "intention" in this context. It is equally clear that the word means what is often referred to as "specific intent" and can be defined as "a decision to bring about a certain consequence" or as the "aim."...

We do not find in the speeches of their Lordships in *Hyam* (1975) anything which binds us to hold that *mens rea* in the offence of attempt is proved by establishing beyond reasonable doubt that the accused knew or correctly foresaw that the consequences of his act unless interrupted would "as a high degree of probability", or would be "likely" to, be the commission of the complete offence. Nor do we find authority in that case for the proposition that a reckless state of mind is sufficient to constitute the *mens rea* in the offence of attempt.

In our judgment, evidence of knowledge of likely consequences, or from which knowledge of likely consequences can be inferred, is evidence by which intent may be established but it is not, in relation to the offence of attempt, to be equated with intent. If the jury find such knowledge established they may and, using common sense, they probably will find intent proved, but it is not the case that they must do so.

An attempt to commit crime is itself an offence. Often it is a grave offence. Often it is as morally culpable as the completed offence which is attempted but not in fact committed. Nevertheless it falls within the class of conduct which is preparatory to the commission of a crime and is one step removed from the offence which is attempted. The court must not strain to bring within the offence of attempt, conduct which does not fall within the well-established bounds of the offence. On the contrary, the court must safeguard against extension of those bounds save by the authority of Parliament. The bounds are presently set requiring proof of specific intent, a decision to bring about, in so far as it lies within the accused's power, the commission of the offence which it is alleged the accused attempted to commit, no matter whether the accused desired that consequence of his act or not.

In the present case the final direction was bad in law. Not only did the judge maintain the exclusion of "intent" as an ingredient of the offence in count 2, but he introduced an alternative basis for a conviction which did not and could not constitute the necessary *mens rea*.

Appeal against conviction on count 2 allowed

It is of course possible to argue that the *mens rea* of an attempt and that of the completed crime ought to be the same: after all, it could be pure chance whether the crime was successfully completed or not. If knowledge, or recklessness suffices for the full offence, why should a more stringent degree of *mens rea* be required for an attempt? (See Stuart, 1968.) However, despite such arguments, the traditional common law position is clearly more acceptable. It is semantic nonsense to speak of someone attempting to commit a crime unless he is *trying* to commit the crime. However, there is a more important reason for defending the common law position. With attempts one is punishing an accused who has caused no direct harm. This can only be justifiable if that accused possessed the highest degree of blameworthiness, namely, intention. Attempt is essentially a crime of *mens rea*, with the *actus reus* performing only a secondary or subsidiary role; accordingly, only the clearest form of *mens rea*, intention, should suffice.

What is the position in Singapore and Malaysia? It is necessary here to draw a distinction between the following attempts:

(1) an attempt under s 511 (and the other sections of the Penal Code) which simply require an "attempt" without defining that term; it

was argued above (see p 255) that the definition of "attempt" in such sections must be the same as in s 511), and

(2)   an attempt under ss 307 or 308 of the Penal Code.

(a) Section 511

Section 511 is silent as to the species of *mens rea* required. It simply says that "whoever attempts to commit an offence ..." and then adds a provision relating to the *actus reus* and the punishments of attempts. Great confusion was injected into the law by the Indian Supreme Court decision of *Om Prakash* (1961) where Raghabar Dayal J stated:

> The intention to commit an offence is different from the intention or knowledge requisite for constituting the act as that offence. The expression "whoever attempts to commit an offence" in s 511 can only mean "whoever intends to do a certain act with the intent or knowledge necessary for the commission of that offence."

The ambiguities inherent in this passage need not, however, detain us as it has been made clear by two other Indian Supreme Court decisions, *Abhayanand Mishra* (1961, see below, p 267), and *Mohd Yakub* (1980, see below, p 271), that there must be an *intention* to commit the complete offence. In the latter case the point was made expressly:

> In order to constitute "an attempt", first, there must be an intention to commit a particular offence ....

This approach was confirmed, albeit without discussion, in the Singapore case of *Oi Bee Kee* (1983, see below, p 274) and is to be welcomed. It is permissible to turn to the English common law and to follow developments there in interpreting words or concepts when the structure of the relevant section of the Penal Code does not dictate a particular meaning. With regard to the *mens rea* requirement, the phrase "whoever attempts" in s 511 is just such a concept.

For the same reasons it seems clear that specific attempt provisions in the Penal Code where no indication as to the requisite *mens rea* is given will be interpreted in the same way. Thus, for example, s 393 simply provides that "whoever attempts to commit robbery" is guilty of an offence. For this offence it will be necessary to prove that the accused *intended* to commit the offence of robbery.

(b) Sections 307 and 308

Unlike the above sections, the provisions on attempted murder (s 307) and attempted culpable homicide (s 308) do specify the appropriate degree of *mens rea* required. Thus s 307 provides that:

> Whoever does any act *with such intention or knowledge* and under such circumstances that if he by that act caused death he *would be guilty of murder* ... (Emphasis added.)

Section 308 is to similar effect. A literal interpretation of the italicized words would seem to indicate that the *mens rea* of attempted murder is the same as that of murder itself. This means that as murder can be committed *without an intention to kill* (as long as the accused has the requisite intention to cause a bodily injury which is objectively suffi-cient in the ordinary course of nature to cause death–s 300(c), or simply has the requisite degree of knowledge under s 300(d)) so too can at-tempted murder be committed without any intention to kill–provided of course that the accused has the specified degree of *mens rea* in order to satisfy one of the subsections of s 300.

Mohan Rathor v State of Madhya Pradesh (1986) Cri LJ 1280 (Madhya Pradesh HC, India)

Ram Pal Singh J: It has to be examined whether this act committed by the appellant comes within the scope and orbit of s 307 or s 308 of the Penal Code. If an accused does any act with such intention or knowledge, and under such circumstances that, if he, by that act, caused death, he would be guilty of murder, he shall be guilty of committing an offence punishable under s 307, but if an accused did any act that he would be guilty of culpable homicide not amounting to murder, he shall be guilty of committing an act punishable under s 308 of the Penal Code. Culpable homicide does not amount to murder (a) if the act is done with the intention or knowledge referred to in s 300 of the Penal Code but under circumstances which would bring the case within one of the Exceptions mentioned in that section or (b) if the act is done with the intention or knowledge referred to in s 299 but not falling under clauses (2), (3) and (4) of s 300 of the Penal Code. Thus, if an accused does not intend to cause death or any bodily injury, which he knows to be likely to cause death or even to cause such bodily injury as is sufficient, in the ordinary course of nature, to cause death, s 308 of the Penal Code would apply even if the case in not covered by any of the exceptions mentioned in s 300 of the Penal Code.

But before an act can be said to have been committed under s 308 of the Penal Code, it is essential to examine the *mens rea* of the appellant at the time of the incident, because *mens rea* is one of the two essential elements of the offence of an attempt of murder. To constitute an offence of attempt to murder, there must be an act coupled with *mens rea*. What inspired the appellant to commit the alleged crime? Had he intention to kill? Intention has been defined to consist of a desire that certain consequence shall follow from the act or omission of the accused. If there is no such intention or knowledge, as is necessary to constitute murder? there can be no attempt to commit it. The intention may be proved by res gestae, by acts or events, previous or subse-quent to the incident or occurrence. Various relevant circumstances from which the intention may be gathered are: nature of the weapon used, part of the body where injury was caused, nature of injury and opportunity available to accused.

In this case, it is apparent that there was no enmity between the appellant and the victim. There was also no premeditation or planning before the act. The appellant in a sudden flash of anger pierced the sharp edged weapon which was at the time in his hand. He had not gone anywhere to pick up the instru-ment of assault. Prior to the incident, he was not quarrelling with the injured. As the victim intervened in the quarrel, the appellant gave two quick blows with the sharp edged instrument, ie screw driver. But the part of the body which he chose to hit, was a vital part of the body, ie the chest. The force he used was not very strong so as to penetrate the lungs. Thus, the intention and knowledge of the appellant seems to be to cause such bodily injury to Ravindra Kumar that he would be guilty of culpable homicide not amounting to murder, if the injured had died. His act, therefore, comes within the orbit of s 308 and not s 307 of the Penal Code.

Not all the authorities, however, have adopted this literal interpretation unreservedly. Indeed, the Illustrations to s 307 (below, p 277) all specify that the accused must intend to kill (Illustrations (a) and (b) or "intend to murder" (Illustrations (c) and (d)). As the following extracts indicate, many of the authorites clearly favour this latter view that the accused must *intend to kill* but in trying to achieve this result while paying lip-service to the wording of s 307, the result is confusion.

Kalu Ram Brahma v State of Assam (1977) Cri LJ 98 (Guahati HC, India)

K Lahiri J: It may be stated here that the accused person was at all rele-vant time aged about 55 years, ... belonged to a backward class or community, (and)....

The injured PW 2 Rupsing Brahma sustained 4 simple injuries caused by "sharp weapon" and the expert evidence disclosed that not a bone was cut, nor the injured lost his senses after receiving the blows in question....

[It was] submitted before me that it is not a case covered by s 307 of the IPC inasmuch as the essential constituents or ingredients of the offence are conspicuously absent,.... The learned counsel submitted that it is a case in which the appellant is liable to be convicted under s 323 of the IPC...

The essential ingredients of the offence under s 307, IPC are the following:

(1) That the death of human being was attempted;
(2) That such death was attempted to be caused by, or in consequence of, the act of the accused;
(3) That such act was done with the intention of causing death; or
     that it was done with the intention of causing such bodily injury as—
     (i) the accused knew to be likely to cause death; or
     (ii) was sufficient in the ordinary course of nature to cause death; or
          that the accused attempted to cause such death by doing an act known to him to be so imminently dangerous that it must in all probability cause (1) death, or (2) such bodily injury as is likely to cause death, the accused having no excuse for incurring the risk of causing such death or injury.

The word "intent" is derived from the word archery or aim. The "act" attempted to must be with "intention" of killing a man.

Intention, which is a state of mind, can never be precisely proved by direct evidence as a fact; it can only be deduced or inferred from other facts which are proved. The intention may be proved by res gestae, by acts or events previous or subsequent to the incident or occurrence, on admission. Intention of a person can't be proved by direct evidence but is to be deduced from the facts and circumstances of a case.

There are various relevant circumstances from which the intention can be gathered. Some relevant considerations are the following:
(1) The nature of the weapon used.

(2) The place where the injuries were inflicted.
(3) The nature of the injuries caused.
(4) The opportunity available which the accused gets.

In the instant case, it is worthwhile to mention that the evidence of the doctor clearly shows and indicates that all injuries which were sustained by the injured were simple in nature and they were caused by sharp weapons. The nature of the injuries is indicative of the fact that no heavy weapon was used. No bone was cut. The injuries are such that even the injured did not lose his consciousness. Even the doctor does not say that any "blow" was given by any weapon whatsoever. His only evidence was to the effect that a "sharp weapon" was used. It was not even attempted to be elicited from the expert witness that from the nature of the injuries it could be inferred by him that the injuries were caused by any "dangerous weapon" or that the injuries were such from which the intent of the accused person could be gathered to cause death of the injured. Therefore, it is apparent that the prosecution has clearly failed to establish from evidence of the expert witness, namely, the doctor that the injuries were of grievous nature or that the weapon said to have been used by the accused person was "dangerous" or that from the injuries itself the intention could be inferred or gathered that the accused person had the intention of doing away with the life of the injured person. In the instant case, from the nature of the injuries, I find that it was nothing but graze or scrapes made by a sharp weapon on the injured. The nature of the injuries do not show that even "blows" were given by a "sharp weapon". If the accused person had the intention of killing the injured with a so-called dangerous weapon, the injuries would not have been so innocuous, simple and superficial....

In the instant case it is apparent that the injured person was completely at the mercy of the person causing the injury (the appellant) and that, according to the prosecution allegation a weapon like dao was available to the accused yet he did not make use of that in a cruel or brutal or merciless manner but inflicts only some scrapes, grazes and superficial injuries under such circumstances no offence under s 307 of the IPC can be sustained....

There is not the least doubt about the fact that the injuries were caused by the accused person and it has been established beyond all reasonable doubt that pork vendor was assaulted and injured and that he must have sustained pain and injuries and in fact the action of the accused person was an offence under s 323 IPC.

Om Prakash v State of Punjab AIR (1961) SC 1782 (SC, India)

Raghubar Dayal J: A person commits an offence under s 307 when he has an intention to commit murder and, in pursuance of that intention, does an act towards its commission irrespective of the fact whether that act is the penultimate act or not. It is to be clearly understood, however, that the intention to commit the offence of murder means that the person concerned has the intention to do certain act with the necessary intention or knowledge mentioned in s 300. The intention to commit an offence is different from the intention or knowledge requisite for constituting the act as that offence. The expression "whoever attempts to commit an offence" in s 511, can only mean "whoever intends to do a certain act with the intent or knowledge necessary for the commission of that offence". The same is meant by the expression "whoever does an act with such intention or knowledge and under such circumstances that if he, by that act, caused death, he would be guilty of murder" in s 307.

This simply means that the act must be done with the intent or knowledge requisite for the commission of the offence of murder. The expression "by that act" does not mean that the immediate effect of the act committed must be death. Such a result must be the result of that act whether immediately or after a lapse of time.

State of Maharashtra v Balram Bama Patil (1983) 2 SCC (Cri) 320 (SC, India)

Misra J: To justify a conviction under this s 307 it is not essential that bodily injury capable of causing death should have been inflicted. Although the nature of injury actually caused may often give considerable assistance in coming to a finding as to the intention of the accused, such intention may also be deduced from other circumstances, and may even, in some cases, be ascertained without any reference at all to actual wounds. The section makes a distinction between an act of the accused and its result, if any. Such an act may not be attended by any result so far as the person assaulted is concerned, but still there may be cases in which the culprit would be liable under this section. It is not necessary that the injury actually caused to the victim of the assault should be sufficient under ordinary circumstances to cause the death of the person assaulted. What the Court has to see is whether the act, irrespective of its result, was done with the intention or knowledge and under circumstances mentioned in this section. An attempt in order to be criminal need not be the penultimate act. It is sufficient in law, if there is present an intent coupled with some overt act in execution thereof.

10. The High Court, in our opinion, was not correct in acquitting the accused of the charge under s 307, IPC merely because the injuries inflicted on the victims were in the nature of a simple hurt.

Mohib v State PLD (1977) Karachi 726 (Pakistan)

Mushtak Ali Kazi J: The only point that has been urged by the appellants is that simple injuries were caused to Head Constable Eid Mohammad for which the two appellants have been held constructively liable under s 307 read with s 34, PPC. That the intention to cause death on the part of the two appellants cannot, therefore, be inferred and the mere fact that gunshot injuries were caused would not necessarily show that the intention of the culprits was to kill any of the police officers....

An act which falls within the purview of s 307 is an act which by itself must be ordinarily capable of causing death in the natural and ordinary course of events. A case of firing of pistol under some circumstances has been discussed in *Dhani Bux* (1964) by Faruqui J. It was observed in that case that:

> "from the mere fact that the pistol shot was fired it cannot be said that the only inference which follows is that the intention was to kill. We cannot, from the nature of the injuries themselves, reach the only conclusion, namely, that there was an intention to kill. It is possible that the accused had intended to cause the injuries which he in fact caused. One cannot upon the basis of the evidence reach a conclusion beyond a reasonable doubt that Dhani Bux had intended to cause death of Majid. The injuries in this case were simple. The offence would, therefore fall under s 324, PPC. I would, therefore, alter his conviction under 307, to one under s 324, PPC."

Thus the essence of offence under s 307, PPC is the doing of an act which by itself must be ordinarily sufficient to cause death and the presence of the necessary intention or knowledge that death should be caused by that act. The burden of intention could be proved by inference from the circumstances. Where the circumstances are such that but for some intervening fact death would have resulted in natural course of events, then the offence would be one under s 307. In the present case gunshots appear to have been fired from a distance and only 3 stray pellets have caused simple injuries to PW Head Constable Eid Mohammad. The party was armed with rifle also. If they had intended to cause death they could not have missed the target, as the dacoits in this part of the country are considered good-shots. Possibly these shots were fired at random to create terror in the minds of the pursuers in order to facilitate their escape. Therefore, from the nature of the injuries actually caused under the circumstances, it cannot be definitely stated, that the object of the person firing the gunshots was to cause death. In a similar case *Mansuri Nizamuddin* (1955), where the accused was shooting at random for the purpose of frightening his pursuers and would be captors, it was observed that it was not possible to hold that he had the *mens rea*, that is, he had intended to cause death, or knew that, in the circumstances, his act of firing was going to cause death, to any of his pur-suers. In another case where the accused fired a small pellet shot on the victim from a distance of 100 yards and caused fracture of his index finger, it was held that his intention was to be deduced from his choice of the cartridge, and the distance from which the gun was fired, that he could not have intended to kill by a small shot fired from such distance. *Abdul Rahman* (1964). Thus no hard and fast rule can be laid down and the intention is to be judged from the act itself and the attending circumstances. If from circumstances the intention to cause death can be inferred then accused can be held guilty under s 307; but where there is no evidence of surrounding circumstances or motive then the intention is to be gathered from the nature of the injury actually caused and the probability of such injury ordinarily causing death of the victim. Where the conclusion regarding intention to cause death cannot be reached, then the conviction can be one under s 324 and not under s 307, PPC. The nature of the injuries and the probability of the object to cause death can be considered as indications of the intention. The benefit of doubt in this respect would go to the accused rather than to prosecution.

There are a number of decisions covering cases of firing from guns or pistols, and in order to reach the right conclusion, it would not be out of place to quote some of these contrary decisions in order to bring out certain fine distinctions regarding the question of *mens rea* so as to bring the case under s 307, PPC. For constituting an attempt to murder, there must be some overt act combined with evidence of *mens rea*. The burden is always on the prosecution to prove, first, the *actus reus*, ie the accused had done something which in point of law marked the commission of the offence, and second, the *mens rea*, that is, in taking this step he was inspired by the intention to go on to reach a definite object which would constitute a specific offence....

Considering all the facts and circumstances of this case, in the light of the above reasoning, I am of opinion that the person who fired these shots with small pellets, from a distance, must have done so to frighten the police party and to effect his escape and the intention to kill cannot be inferred from the nature of the injuries which were simple and of no consequence. The offence would, therefore, fall not under s 307 but under s 324, PPC. The appellants however, deserve the maximum punishment prescribed for offence under that section.

2. Actus reus

The problem here is one of determining *how much* action is needed before one can be said to be attempting a crime. How close must the accused get to completion of the offence before he can be held liable?

The position at common law is that an accused must have proceeded beyond the stage of preparation; his actions must be sufficiently close to the completed offence to be described as "proximate" to that offence. In the famous words of Baron Parke in *Eagleton* (1855):

> Acts remotely leading towards the commission of the offence are not to be considered as attempts to commit it; but acts immediately connected with it are....

CMV Clarkson, *Understanding Criminal Law* (1987), 28–29

We have examined why the law demands some conduct. But why does it insist on so much conduct? Why does the law not punish purely preparatory acts? After all, when a person has started preparing for his crime we are able to overcome the evidential problem of not being able to prove "mere intentions"; his actions now demonstrate some firmness of purpose; arguments concerning invasion of liberty and privacy become less plausible when a person has actually committed physical actions directed towards the commission of a crime; and, of course, imposing liability for preparatory acts would allow the police to intervene at an earlier stage to prevent the commission of crimes. Such reasoning led the Law Commission in 1973 to propose that liability for attempt should be imposed at the much earlier stage when the defendant had merely taken a "substantial step" towards the commission of his crime (Law Commission, 1973). For example, a person "reconnoitring the place contemplated for the commission of the intended offence" or "preparing or acting a falsehood for the purpose of an offence of fraud or deception", ... would be liable for attempt under such a proposal.

Such thinking reflects what can be described as a "subjectivist" approach to the law of attempt. This approach, while insisting on *some* conduct as corroboration of the defendant's purpose, nevertheless stresses the mental element of the defendant. He intended to commit a crime; he is dangerous and needs restraining; he also needs rehabilitation and punishment to deter him and others from attempting to commit crimes. Criminal liability can thus justifiably be imposed at a much earlier stage.

However, while English law has embraced a subjectivist approach in many other areas of the criminal law (including impossible attempts), it has here preferred the view that liability in such cases would involve too serious an invasion of personal liberty; it would open the door to the possibility of abuse by the police and "goes much too far in making guilty intention overshadow guilty conduct" (Law Commission, 1980). Also, the mere preparer is regarded as relatively non-dangerous. Only when he has got sufficiently near to committing the crime that he can be said to have "broken through the psychological barrier to crime" (Glanville Williams, 1978) or to have "crossed the Rubicon and burnt his boats" (*Stonehouse*, 1978) can he be regarded as sufficiently dangerous to warrant restraining. In short, English law can be said to have adopted an "objectivist" approach to defining the contours of this aspect of the law of attempt. An objectivist approach focuses on the *actions* of the defendant; these actions must "conform to objective criteria defined in advance. The act must evidence attributes subject to determination independently of the actor's intent" (Fletcher, 1978). In the law of attempt the defendant's actions must bring him 'within striking distance' of committing the crime. Only at this point does his conduct generate apprehension; only then does it present a clear threat of harm justifying the imposition of criminal liability.

English law used to translate this requirement as one of "proximity"–the defendant's actions must be proximate to the complete crime.

Which of these two approaches is adopted in Singapore and Malaysia? In order to answer this question and examine the elements required for the *actus reus* of an attempt under the Penal Code it is necessary to distinguish the general attempt provision of s 511 from the specific attempt provisions such as ss 307 and 308.

(a) Section 511

Section 511 does not provide a full definition of the ingredients of an attempt. It merely provides:

> Whoever attempts to commit an offence ..., or attempts to cause such an offence to be committed, and in such attempt does any act towards the commission of the offence, shall, ... be punished....

Abhayanand Mishra v State of Bihar AIR (1961) SC 1698 (SC, India)

Raghubar Dayal J: These provisions require that it is only when one, firstly, attempts to commit an offence and, secondly, in such attempt, does any act towards the commission of the offence, that he is punishable for that attempt to commit the offence.

Before examining the authorities on the meaning of this, it is necessary to make two preliminary points.

First, while earlier cases such as *Abhayanand Mishra* (1961) held that the question whether certain acts amount to an attempt was a *question of fact* (an approach also adopted by English law in *Stonehouse*, 1978), the latest Indian Supreme Court decision, *Mohd Yakub* (1980, see below, p 271) makes it clear that it is a *"mixed question of law and fact, depending largely on the circumstances of the particular case"* (emphasis added). It is difficult to know quite how, and in what proportions, this "mix" of law and fact operates. It is submitted that this should be taken to mean that it is a question of law whether the given acts of the accused are capable of amounting to an attempt and thereafter it is a question of fact whether such facts actually do amount to an attempt. (This is the "mix" adopted by the English Criminal Attempts Act 1981, s 4(3).) Of course, such a distinction will be difficult to draw in Singapore where the same judge is trier of both fact and law–but it is a distinction that is important to draw, most importantly, because findings of law generate precedents for the future while findings of fact do not.

Second, s 511 does not define "attempt" other than to provide that "in such attempt" (whatever that means) there must be "any act towards the commission of the offence". The better view is that this does not mean that there must be "an attempt" *plus* an "act towards the commission of the offence" but rather that before an act can be classified as "an attempt" there must be, inter alia, an act towards the commission of the crime. In other words "an attempt" is partially defined. Whatever comprises "an attempt" it must include, among other things, an act towards the commission of the offence.

This point has particular importance with regard to the permissible sources of law in the interpretation of s 511. If the notion of "an attempt" in s 511 were completely undefined, reference to the English common law on the meaning of "an attempt" would be acceptable. However, because of the partial definition, reference to English law is only permissible to ascertain *what else* is required for an attempt–apart from the "act towards the commission of the offence". Such reference can only be a partial one. Whatever is found in the English common law on the meaning of attempt has to be modified or adapted to fit in with the particular wording of s 511 requiring that the attempt must also encompass the specified "act towards the commission of the offence". This point seems to have been implicitly understood in the leading Indian Supreme Court decision of *Mohd Yakub* (1980) where some effort is made to examine the meaning of "attempt" as found in the English common law and then, drawing on Indian authorities, this is adapted to the particular wording of s 511. This approach stands in sharp contrast to the leading local decision of the Johore Bahru High Court *Kee Ah Bah* (1979) where, in ascertaining the meaning of "attempt", *total* reliance was placed on English authorities and no cognizance taken at all of s 511!

Having disposed of these preliminary points one is still left with the central problem: how much action is necessary before the *actus reus* of attempt can be said to be committed? How close must the accused come to his objective before he is regarded as having attempted to commit the crime?

Arjan Singh v PP (1948) 14 MLJ 73 (CCA, Malayan Union)

The accused was charged with attempted extortion in that a letter demanding money and containing threats was found in a locked wooden chest at his house; two further extortionate letters were discovered at another house also occupied by the accused.

Willan CJ: [T]he letters addressed to the two Chettiars were found in the drawer of a writing table and there was no evidence of any attempt to transfer them by any means to the addressees. The mere act of writing and detaining a letter is not an attempt to commit extortion but at the most a preparatory step towards the commission of that offence. The gist of the offence of extortion is putting another person in fear of an injury and similarly to support a conviction for attempted extortion the intending extortioner must have done some act with this intention. For this reason the conviction on the second charge is also quashed and the appeal of Arjan Singh allowed.

Appeal allowed

Abhayanand Mishra v State of Bihar AIR (1961) SC 1698 (SC, India)

The appellant was convicted of an attempt to cheat contrary to s 420 read with s 511 of the Indian Penal Code. He had applied to the Patna University for permission to sit the MA Examination in English as a private candidate, representing falsely that he was a graduate with a BA degree and that he had been teaching in a certain school. In support of his application he attached forged certificates purporting to be from the headmaster of the school and the inspector of schools. The university authorities accepted the appellant's statements and gave permission and wrote to him asking for the remission of the fees and two copies of his photograph. He furnished these and an admission card for him was dispatched. When the untruth of his representations was discovered he was prosecuted. He appealed against his conviction.

Raghubar Dayal J: Another contention for the appellant is that the facts proved do not go beyond the stage of preparation for the commission of the offence of "cheating", and do not make out the offence of attempting to cheat. There is a thin line between the preparation for and an attempt to commit an offence. Undoubtedly, a culprit first intends to commit the offence, then makes preparation for committing it and thereafter attempts to commit the offence. If the attempt succeeds, he has committed the offence; if it fails due to reasons beyond his control, he is said to have attempted to commit the offence. Attempt to commit an offence, therefore, can be said to begin when the preparations are complete and the culprit commences to do something with the intention of committing the offence and which is a step towards the commission of the offence. The moment he commences to do an act with the necessary intention, he commences his attempt to commit the offence. This is clear from the general expression "attempt to commit an offence" and is exactly what the provisions of s 511, IPC, require....

These provisions require that it is only when one, firstly, attempts to commit an offence and, secondly, in such attempt, does any act towards the commission of the offence, that he is punishable for that attempt to commit the offence. It follows, therefore, that the act which would make the culprits attempt to commit an offence punishable, must be an act which, by itself or in combination with other acts, leads to the commission of the offence. The first step in the commission of the offence of cheating, therefore, must be an act which would lead to the deception of the person sought to be cheated. The moment a person takes some step to deceive the person sought to be cheated, he has embarked on a course of conduct which is nothing less than an attempt to commit the offence, as contemplated by s 511. He does the act with the intention to commit the offence and the act is a step towards the commission of the offence....

We do not agree that the "act towards the commission of such offence" must be "an act which leads immediately to the commission of the offence". The purpose of the illustration is not to indicate such a construction of the section, but to point out that the culprit has done all that be necessary for the commission of the offence even though he may not actually succeed in his object and commit the offence....

In *Re R MacCrea*, (1893) it was held ... that s 511 was not meant to cover only the penultimate act towards the completion of an offence and not acts precedent, if those acts are done in the course of the attempt to commit the offence, and were done with the intent to commit it and done towards its commission. Knox J, said at page 179:

> "Many offences can easily be conceived where, with all necessary preparations made, a long interval will still elapse between the hour when the attempt to commit the offence commences and the hour when it is completed. The offence of cheating and inducing delivery is an offence in point. The time that may elapse between the moment when the preparations made for committing the fraud are brought to bear upon the mind of the person to be deceived and the moment when he yields to the deception practised upon him may be a very considerable interval of time.... [A]nd yet the first act after preparations completed will, if criminal in itself, be beyond all doubt, equally an attempt with the ninety and ninth act in the series.
>
> Again, the attempt once begun and a criminal act done in pursuance of it towards the commission of the act attempted, does not cease to be a criminal attempt, in my opinion, because the person committing the offence does or may repent before the attempt is completed."

Blair J, said at page 181:

> "It seems to me that that section (s 511) uses the word "attempt" in a very large sense; it seems to imply that such an attempt may be made up of a series of acts, and that any one of those acts done towards the commission of the offence, that is, conducive to its commission, is itself punishable, and though the act does not use the words, it can mean nothing but punishable as an attempt. It does not say that the last act which would form the final part of an attempt in the larger sense is the only act punishable under the section. It says expressly that whosoever in such attempt, obviously using the word in the larger sense, does any act, &c, shall be punishable. The term "any act" excludes the notion that the final act short of actual commission is alone punishable."

We fully approve of the decision and the reasons therefor.

In *Peterson* (1876) the publication of banns of marriage was not held to amount to an attempt to commit the offence of bigamy under s 494, IPC. It was observed at page 317:

> "The publication of banns may, or may not be, in cases in which a special license is not obtained, a condition essential to the validity of a marriage, but common sense forbids us to regard either the publication of the banns or the procuring of the license as a part of the marriage ceremony."

In *Padala Venkatasami,* (1881) the preparation of a copy of an intended false document together with the purchase of stamped paper for the purpose of writing that false document and the securing of information about the facts to be inserted in the document, were held not to amount to an attempt to commit forgery, because the accused had not, in doing these acts, proceeded to do an act towards the commission of the offence of forgery.... We may summarize our views about the construction of s 511, IPC., thus: A person commits the offence of "attempt to commit a particular offence" when (i) he intends to commit that particular offence; and (ii) he, having made preparations and with the intention to commit the offence, does an act towards its commission: such an act need not be the penultimate act towards the commission of that offence but must be an act during the course of committing that offence.

In the present case, the appellant intended to deceive the University and obtain the necessary permission and the admission card and, not only sent an application for permission to sit at the University examination, but also followed it up, on getting the necessary permission, by remitting the necessary fees and sending the copies of his photograph, on the receipt of which the University did issue the admission card. There is therefore hardly any scope for saying that what the appellant had actually done did not amount to his attempting to commit the offence and had not gone beyond the stage of preparation. The preparation was complete when he had prepared the application for the purpose of submission to the University. The moment he despatched it, he entered the realm of attempting to commit the offence of "cheating". He did succeed in deceiving the University and inducing it to issue the admission card. He just failed to get it and sit for the examination because something beyond his control took place inasmuch as the University was informed about his being neither a graduate nor a teacher.

We therefore hold that the appellant has been rightly convicted of the offence under s 420, read with s 511, IPC, and accordingly dismiss the appeal.

Appeal dismissed

PP v Kee Ah Bah [1979] 1 MLJ 26 (HC, Johore Bahru, Malaysia)

The appellant was acquitted on a charge of having been knowingly concerned in an attempt at fraudulent evasion of export duty on 21 bags of tin-ore contrary to s 135(1)(e) of the Customs Act 1967. He had hidden the tin-ore in his car. He left the immigration check point at Johore Bahru causeway and approached the customs check point. When the car was about ten yards from the check point, with two cars ahead of it, a customs officer signalled to the appellant to stop. The appellant reversed and made a U turn and escaped back into Johore Bahru. The car was discovered shortly afterwards still containing the tin-ore. The prosecution appealed against the acquittal.

Syed Othman J: From his grounds of judgment, the learned President seemed to be of the mind that since the respondent was still within the Malaysian territory, before there could be an attempt at fraudulent evasion of export duty there must have been 2 ingredients (1) an irrevocable intention to leave the country; (2) what I would describe as a further step by the respondent to commit the completed offence.

As regards (1) irrevocable intention to leave the country, he said there would have been such intention if the respondent had reached the customs check point. By way of fortifying his findings he said:

> "[A]n innocent traveller carrying dutiable goods could drive right to the check point either to declare his goods and pay duty ... or he could drive up to the check point to enquire from the officers where to pay the duty. It is clear therefore that the intention of the motorist whether lawful or unlawful cannot be determined until he has actually reached the check point itself."

I fail to see the necessity for dividing an intention into irrevocable and, impliedly, revocable. On the learned President's finding there is nothing to prevent a person from turning back even after leaving the customs check point, as the boundary is much further ahead. Under ordinary circumstances, a person must be said to have the intention to leave the country when he reaches the immigration check point and presents his travel documents, and if there is no immigration check point, when he is seen heading towards the border. The fact that he may change his mind about leaving the country later on, does not detract from his original intention. It is not for the court to speculate on what an innocent traveller would have done. The purpose of the customs check point after the immigration point, as the very name itself signifies, is merely to check whether any exporter of goods has complied with s 80 of the Act, ie whether he has paid duty to the proper officer at the appropriate place after making a declaration in the prescribed form. Considering the requirements of law, I am of the opinion that when the goods are being taken to the customs check point, the exporter is in fact in the course of exporting the goods....

As regards (2)–further step–the learned President was of the mind that there must be evidence that the respondent had dashed on without stopping at the customs check point. Now the evidence shows there were 2 cars ahead of the respondent's and the customs had also closed the emergency gate. If indeed the respondent could have got over the cars ahead of him or through the closed emergency gate, he could have easily got to the other end of the causeway. Then the question of attempt does not arise. The offence of fraudulent evasion would have been completed....

On the evidence, he must have had the intention to leave the country, when he presented his travel documents at the immigration check point he came into the area of customs check point. To my mind, the customs have the right to examine a vehicle after it leaves the immigration point, because after this point the traveller must be said to be in the course of leaving the country, and if he has goods, then they are in the course of being exported....

In the present case, the remote acts ..., ie preparatory to or as showing intention to commit the offence, would be the making of the secret compartments in the car, the obtaining and loading of the tin ore into the car, and the driving up to the immigration check point to present his travel documents. After the immigration, the goods were at law in the course of being exported. As indicated earlier, the offence in the present case must be assessed in a different light. *Hope v Brown* (1954) spoke of immediate acts or acts immediatley connected with attempt. In the context of the present case, regard must be had to the prevailing circumstances, ie the nature of the goods, the nature of the conveyance or vehicle, and the location of the goods on the person or in the conveyance. In the present case, these were the prevailing circumstances; when the respondent left the immigration point, he had in the car tin ore which was later found mostly in secret compartments in a vehicle not intended to carry tin ore; (perhaps it would have been another matter if he had goods which could have been seen by the customs easily on cursory examination); the car was a Volkswagon designed to carry 4 passengers, not a load of 9.45 piculs of tin ore, equivalent to the weight of not less than 10 Asian passengers; he had no documents to show that he was permittted to export tin ore; he had no documents to show that duty on the tin ore had been paid. The immediate acts were: He was within the area of the customs check point; he failed to stop when called upon to do so; then he reversed the car and drove off. The very fact that he had the tin ore in secret compartments in a small car goes to show that he expected the customs officers to believe that he was carrying no goods in the car. If in fact he ever had the intention to pay duty or to make enquiries where to pay duty, as suggested in the grounds of judgment, then it was all the more reason for him to have stopped. The respondent's acts in reversing the car, not heeding the signal and the call of the customs officer for him to stop, in getting the car into the gap and then in continuing to drive the car in spite of the adventurous feat of the customs officer to stop him, were to retrieve himself from the immediate acts. They also show that the respondent knew that he could not complete the commission of the offence, ie of fraudulent evasion of the duty, as the customs men were ready for him. All the evidence, the immediate acts and the prevailing circumstances, considered as a whole, to my mind constitute the offence of attempt at fraudulent evasion of export duty.

As to the gap which lies between the immigration check point and the customs check point, I should think that it is meant to facilitate those travellers in vehicles who in good faith change their mind about leaving the country after the immigration check point, or who have no proper travel documents and are ordered by the immigration officers not to leave the country. It is a notorious fact that vehicles get into the immigration point in lanes, and ordinarily it is not possible for a vehicle which has got into a lane to reverse because of vehicles. It is not intended to provide an escape route for a prospective smuggler, who has a change of heart on finding that he cannot dodge the customs at the check point.

The very finding of the learned President that the respondent should have taken a further step, ie dashing on without stopping at the customs check point shows that the prosecution's evidence as it stood falls within principle (a) in *Haughton*'s case (1975) indicated above. If the further step had been accomplished, the question of attempt does not arise as the offence of fraudulent evasion would have been completed, whether or not the offender reaches the border, as in this event the respondent would have got over the customs without declaring the goods....

I hereby order that the acquittal be set aside and the case be tried before another President.

Acquittal set aside

State of Maharashtra v Mohd Yakub (1980) SCC (Cri) 513 (SC, India)

Customs officers arrested the accused at midnight when he stopped his jeep near a bridge at a creek and started removing silver ingots from the vehicle. At the same time the sound of the engine of a mechanized sea-craft from the side of the creek was heard by the officers. The accused gave a false name and address. He was convicted at his trial of attempting to smuggle out of India silver ingots contrary to s 135(1)(a) read with s 135(2) of the Customs Act. However, the Additional Sessions Judge acquitted him on the ground that the facts fell short of establishing that the accused had "attempted" to export silver in contravention of the law. The High Court upheld the acquittal. The prosecution appealed to the Supreme Court.

Sakaria J: The question, therefore, is whether from the facts and circumstances, enumerated above, it could be inferred beyond reasonable doubt that the respondents had attempted to export the silver in contravention of law from India?...

Well then, what is an "attempt"? Kenny in his *Outlines of Criminal Law* defined "attempt" to commit a crime as the "last proximate act which a person does towards the commission of an offence, the consummation of the offence being hindered by circumstances beyond his control". This definition is too narrow. What constitutes an "attempt" is a mixed question of law and fact, depending largely on the circumstances of the particular case. "Attempt" defies a precise and exact definition. Broadly speaking, all crimes which consist of the commission of affirmative acts are preceded by some covert or overt conduct which may be divided into three stages. The first stage exists when the culprit first entertains the idea or intention to commit an offence. In the second stage, he makes preparations to commit it. The third stage is reached when the culprit takes deliberate overt steps to commit the offence. Such overt act or step in order to be "criminal" need not be the penultimate act towards the commission of the offence. It is sufficient if such act or acts were deliberately done, and manifest a clear intention to commit the offence aimed, being reasonably proximate to the consummation of the offence. As pointed out in *Abhayanand Mishra* (1961) there is a distinction between "preparation" and "attempt". Attempt begins where preparation ends. In sum, a person commits the offence of "attempt to commit a particular offence" when (i) he *intends* to commit that particular offence; and (ii) he, having made preparations and with the intention to commit the offence, does an act towards its commission; such an act need not be the penultimate act towards the commission of that offence *but must be an act during the course of committing that offence.*

Now, let us apply the above principles to the facts of the case in hand. The intention of the accused to export the silver from India by sea was clear from the circumstances enumerated above. They were taking the silver ingots concealed in the two vehicles under cover of darkness. They had reached close to the sea-shore and had started unloading the silver there near a creek from which the sound of the engine of a sea-craft was also heard. Beyond the stage of preparation, most of the steps necessary in the course of export by sea had been taken. The only step that remained to be taken towards the export of the silver was to load it on a sea-craft for moving out of the territorial waters of India. But for the intervention of the officers of law, the unlawful export of silver would have been consummated. The clandestine disappearance of the sea-craft when the officers intercepted and rounded up the vehicles and the accused at the creek, reinforces the inference that the accused had deliberately attempted to export silver by sea in contravention of law.

It is important to bear in mind that the penal provisions with which we are concerned have been enacted to suppress the evil of smuggling precious metal out of India. Smuggling is an anti-social activity which adversely affects the public revenues, the earning of foreign exchange, the financial stability and the economy of the country. A narrow interpretation of the word "attempt" therefore, in these penal provisions which will impair their efficacy as instruments for combating this baneful activity has to be eschewed. These provisions should be construed in a manner which would suppress the mischief, promote their object, prevent their subtle evasion and foil their artful circumvention. Thus construed, the expression "attempt" within the meaning of these penal provisions is wide enough to take in its fold any one or series of acts committed, beyond the stage of preparation in moving the contraband goods deliberately to the place of embarkation, such act or acts being reasonably proximate to the completion of the unlawful export. The inference arising out of the facts and circumstances established by the prosecution, unerringly pointed to the conclusion, that the accused had committed the offence of *attempting* to export silver out of India by sea, in contravention of law....

Chinnappa Reddy J (concurring)–I concur in the conclusion of my brother Sarkaria J.... I wish to add a few paragraphs on the nature of the *actus reus* to be proved on a charge of an attempt to commit an offence.

The question is what is the difference between preparation and perpetration? An attempt to define "attempt" has to be a frustrating exercise....

In England Parke B, described the characteristics of an "attempt" in *Eagleton* (1855), as follows:

"The mere intention to commit a misdemeanour is not criminal. Some act is required, and we do not think that all acts towards committing a misdemeanour indictable. Acts remotely leading towards the commission of the offence are not to be considered as attempts to commit it, but acts immediately connected with it are ...".

The dictum of Parke B is considered as the locus classicus on the subject and the test of "proximity" suggested by it has been accepted and applied by English courts....

Parke B, himself appeared to have thought that the last possible act before the achievement of the end constituted the attempt....

As a general principle the test of "the last possible act before the achievement of the end" would be entirely unacceptable. If that principle be correct, a person who has cocked his gun at another and is about to pull the trigger but is prevented from doing so by the intervention of someone or something cannot be convicted of attempt to murder....

Another attempt at definition was made by Professor Turner (1934), and this was substantially reproduced in Archbold (1966). Archbold's reproduction was quoted with approval in *Davey* v *Lee* and was as follows:

"... the *actus reus* necessary to constitute an attempt is complete if the prisoner does an act which is a step towards the commission of a specific crime, which is immediately and not merely remotely connected with the commission of it, and the doing of which cannot reasonably be regarded as having any other purpose than the commission of the specific crime."

... Turner was himself not satisfied with the definition propounded by him and felt compelled to modify it, as he thought that to require that the act could not reasonably be regarded as having any other purpose than the commission of the specific crime went too far and it should be sufficient "to show prime facie, the offender's intention to commit the crime which he is charged with attempting".

Editing ... 18th edition of Kenny's *Outlines of Criminal Law* (1962), Professor Turner explained his modified definition as follows:

"It is therefore suggested that a practical test for *actus reus* in attempt is that the prosecution must prove that the steps taken by the accused must have reached the point when they themselves clearly indicate what was the end towards which they were directed. In other words the steps taken must themselves be sufficient to show, prima facie, the offender's intention to commit the crime which he is charged with attempting. That there may be abundant other evidence to establish his *mens rea* (such as a confession) is irrelevant to the question of whether he had done enough to constitute the *actus reus*."

We must say here that we are unable to see any justification for excluding evidence aliunde on the question of *mens rea* in considering what constitutes the *actus reus*. That would be placing the *actus reus* in too narrow a pigeon-hole.

In *Haughton* v *Smith* (1975), Hailsham, LC quoted Parke B from the *Eagleton* case (1855) and Lord Parker CJ from *Davey* v *Lee* and proceeded to mention three propositions as emerging from the two definitions:

"(1) There is a distinction between the intention to commit a crime and an attempt to commit it .... (2) In addition to the intention, or *mens rea*, there must be an overt act of such a kind that it is intended to form and does form part of a series of acts which would constitute the actual commission of the offence if it were not interrupted .... (3) The act relied on as constituting the attempt must not be an act merely preparatory to commit the completed offence, but must bear a relationship to the completion of the offence referred to in *Eagleton* (1855), as being 'proximate' to the completion of the offence in *Davey* v *Lee* as being 'immediately and not merely remotely connected' with the completed offence ...".

In India, while attempts to commit certain specified offences have themselves been made specific offences (eg ss 307, 308, Indian Penal Code, etc), an attempt to commit an offence punishable under the Penal Code, generally, is dealt with under s 511, Indian Penal Code. But the expression "attempt" has not been defined anywhere.

In *Abhayanand Mishra* (1961), Raghubar Dayal and Subba Rao JJ, disapproved of the test of "last act which if uninterrupted and successful would constitute a criminal offence"....

Let me now state the result of the search and research: In order to constitute "an attempt", first, there must be an intention to commit a particular offence, second, some act must have been done which would necessarily have to be done towards the commission of the offence, and, third, such act must be "proximate" to the intended result. The measure of proximity is not in relation to time and action but in relation to intention. In other words, the act must reveal, with reasonable certainty, in conjunction with other facts and circumstances and not necessarily in isolation, an intention, as distinguished from a mere desire or object, to commit the particular offence, though the act by itself may be merely suggestive or indicative of such intention; but, that it must be, that is, it must be indicative or suggestive of the intention. For instance, in the instant case, had the truck been stopped and searched at the very commencement of the journey or even at Shirsat Naka, the discovery of silver ingots in the truck might at the worst lead to the inference that the accused had prepared or were preparing for the commission of the offence. It could be said that the accused were transporting or attempting to transport silver somewhere but it would not necessarily suggest or indicate that the intention was to export silver. The fact that the truck was driven up to a lonely creek from where the silver could be transferred into a sea-faring vessel was suggestive or indicative though not conclusive, that the accused wanted to export the silver. It might have been open to the accused to plead that the silver was not to be exported but only to be transported in the course of inter-coastal trade. But, the circumstance that all this was done in a clandestine fashion, at dead of night, revealed, with reasonable certainty, the intention of the accused that the silver was to be exported.

In the result I agree with the order proposed by Sarkaria J.

Appeal allowed

Oi Bee Kee v PP (Unreported, Magistrate's Appeal No 175 of 1983, Subordinate Courts, Singapore)

The accused was charged with attempted theft punishable under s 379 read with s 511 of the Penal Code. The facts appear in the judgment.

Ng Peng Hong, Magistrate: (P)olice officers spotted the accused tampering with a motor car.... The accused was seen trying to open the vehicle's nearside door, with a piece of cloth and a bunch of keys. At the same time, the accused was looking round, presumably to ensure no one was around. After a short while, the party of police officers stopped him....

[L]earned counsel submitted that in law, the facts did not disclose any offence–that the acts done by the accused were mere preparation to commit the offence. In support of this submission, learned counsel referred to Ratanlal (1966). With due respect, I disagreed with her contention. It was beyond doubt that the accused had the intention of committing the said offence; otherwise, he would not have confessed to attempting to steal in his statement (Exhibit P7). The fact that he had in his possession Exhibits P3 and P4, indicated that he had completed his preparation to steal the car. This conclusion was irresistible in view of the fact that he had with him Exhibit P3–a piece of cloth which an ordinary person would not ordinarily carry it with him. Accordingly, I was of the view that the insertion of the key(s) into the key slot of the car was a direct act done towards the commission of the offence. As pointed out by Ratanlal (1966), "the moment he commences to do an act with the necessary intention, he commences his attempt to commit the offence. This is exactly what the provisions of this section require".

Accused convicted

From the above cases the following general propositions seem to emerge:

(1) The accused's actions must be proximate to the completed offence; he must be beyond the stage of mere preparation.

(2) The accused must do some act towards the commission of the offence. This act must be committed in the stage of proximity, or can itself be the act taking the accused into the realms of proximity.

(3) Actions are proximate to a completed offence when they are reasonably close to the commission of the offence–but

   (a) the accused's act need not be the penultimate act towards the commission of the offence; he may still have further acts to do before the crime can be successfully completed;

   (b) it is irrelevant that the accused still has time to change his mind; his actions can be proximate even though he still has an opportunity of repenting and withdrawing from the criminal enterprise.

(4) In *Mohd Yakub* (1980) it was held that actions were proximate when they revealed, with reasonable certainty, the intention of the accused to commit the crime. This is similar to, but not identical with, the "equivocality test" formerly adopted by English law under which the accused would only be liable if his objective actions unequivocally indicated his purpose. Under the *Mohd Yakub* (1980) test such actions need not unequivocally indicate the accused's purpose but, taken in conjunction with all the facts and circumstances including any confession of the accused, they must be suggestive or indicative of the intention to commit the crime.

These four propositions are at most loose indicators of the elements required for an attempt. Further, while *Mohd Yakub* (1980) with its watered-down equivocality test is the leading Indian Supreme Court decision, it remains to be seen to what extent local cases will follow this approach, as opposed to relying, as in *Kee Ah Bah* (1979), on English authorities which have long since rejected any form of equivocality test.

As the above cases reveal, it is extremely difficult to apply any principles consistently to determine in concrete cases whether an accused has committed the *actus reus* of attempt. As whether there is an attempt is a mixed question of fact and law, decisions have to be made on a case-by-case basis with much depending on the definition of the crime attempted. Even when dealing with attempts to commit the same crime, uniformity of decision will be almost impossible to achieve as the following two cases on attempted rape reveal.

PP v Zainal Abidin b Ismail [1987] 2 MLJ 741 (HC, Brunei)

The accused was charged with attempted rape. He lay on top of the complainant with the intention of penetrating her but abandoned his plan when he was unable to obtain an erection. He did not remove his trousers.

Roberts CJ: [T]he act relied on as constituting the offence must be more than an act preparatory to the offence, but must be proximate to and not merely remotely connected with the offence–see *Haughton* v *Smith* (1975).... Applying this test, I find that, notwithstanding that he failed to penetrate the girl by reason of his inability to obtain any erection, D4 did attempt to penetrate the girl, and that the acts which he took preparatory to the offence, namely by lying on top of the girl, with his expressed intention of having intercourse are sufficient in law to constitute an attempt of rape.

Harishchandra Narayah Khardape v State of Maharashtra (1983) 2 Crimes 98 (HC, Bombay, India)

The accused was spending the night with the complainant and her family. He entered the kitchen where the complainant and her children were sleeping, bolted the kitchen door from the inside, extinguished the lamp and made advances to the woman. He denuded himself below the waist and attempted to remove her blouse and sari. A scuffle ensued; the complainant shouted for help and was rescued by neighbours.

Held: The accused was in the stage of preparation and had not gone beyond the stage of preparation and as such the accused cannot be said to have attempted to commit rape.... This was, therefore, a case of indecent assault punishable under s 354 of the Indian Penal Code.

These two decisions are not easily reconciled. It seems difficult to see how lying on top of a woman with one's trousers on and without an erection as in *Zainal Abidin b Ismail* (1987) can constitute an attempt, yet bolting a door, extinguishing a light and removing one's clothes and then trying to remove the woman's clothes as in *Harishchandra* (1983) are still only preparatory acts! Surely, applying the test in *Mohd*

Yakub (1980) the accused's actions in the latter case more than clearly indicated his purpose!

(b) Sections 307 and 308

Taken literally, the wording of ss 307 and 308 suggests a different test. Whereas s 511 requires that "in such attempt (he) does any act towards the commission of the offence", s 307 requires "any act ... that *if he by that act caused death* he would be guilty of murder" (s 308 is to the same effect). This is somewhat obscure. The italicized words could be read as suggesting that the accused must have done the *last act* necessary for him to achieve his objective. If yet further action were required, then there would be no question of his having committed the requisite "act" that "if (it) caused death" because that act, without more, could not cause death.

Nelson, *The Indian Penal Code* (7th edn, 1983), 1166

(A)s a rule, it is the last proximate act, done in the execution of the crime, the completion of the offence being prevented only by some cause, independent of the offender's volition. In other words, an attempt to commit an offence is an act, or series of acts, which leads inevitably to the commission of the offence unless something, which the doer of the act or acts neither foresaw nor intended, happens to prevent this. An act done towards the commission of an offence, which does not inevitably lead to the commission of the offence unless it is followed or, perhaps, preceded by other acts, is merely an act of preparation.

This interpretation is borne out by the four illustrations to s 307. In each, the accused has done everything necessary for the commission of the crime. He has committed the last act dependent on himself.

Penal Code, s 307 (1)

Illustrations

(a) A shoots at Z with intention to kill him, under such circumstances that, if death ensued, A would be guilty of murder. A is liable to punishment under this section.

(b) A, with the intention of causing the death of a child of tender years, exposes it in a desert place. A has committed the offence defined by this section, though the death of the child does not ensue.

(c) A, intending to murder Z, buys a gun and loads it. A has not yet committed the offence. A fires the gun at Z. He has committed the offence defined in this section; and if by such firing he wounds Z, he is liable to the punishment provided by the latter part of this section.

(d) A, intending to murder Z by poison, purchases poison and mixes the same with food which remains in A's keeping; A has not yet committed the offence defined in this section. A places the food on Z's table or delivers it to Z's servants to place it on Z's table. A has committed the offence defined in this section.

On the other hand, leading Indian decisions have rejected this rigorous "last act" approach:

Om Prakash v State of Punjab AIR (1961) SC 1782 (SC, India)

The accused ill treated and deliberately undernourished his wife causing her health to deteriorate. He then starved her and prevented her leaving the house. "She was denied food for days altogether and used to be given gram husk mixed in water after five or six days." Once she nearly escaped but was caught, dragged back inside the house and severely beaten. Thereafter she was kept locked in a room. Two months later she did manage to escape and obtain help. The accused was convicted of attempted murder contrary to s 307 of the Indian Penal Code and appealed against his conviction.

Raghubar Dayal J: The next contention for the appellant is that the ingredients of an offence under s 307 are materially different from the ingredients of an offence under s 511, IPC. The difference is that for an act to amount to the commission of the offence of attempting to commit an offence, it need not be the last act and can be the first act towards the commission of the offence, while for an offence under s 307, it is the last act which if effective to cause death, would constitute the offence of an attempt to commit murder. The contention really is that even if Bimla Devi had been deprived of food for a certain period, the act of so depriving her does not come under s 307, IPC, as that act could not, by itself, have caused her death, it being necessary for the period of starvation to continue for a longer period to cause death.

We do not agree with this contention....

[T]he ingredients of an offence of attempt to commit culpable homicide not amounting to murder should be the same as the ingredients of an offence of attempt to commit that offence under s 511. We have held this day in *Abhayanand Mishra* (1961), that a person commits the offence of attempting to commit a particular offence, when he intends to commit that particular offence and, having made preparations and with the intention to commit that offence does an act towards its commission and that such act need not be penultimate act towards the commission of that offence, but must be an act during the course of committing such offence. It follows therefore that a person commits an offence under s 308 when he has an intention to commit culpable homicide not amounting to murder and in pursuance of that intention does an act towards the commission of that offence whether that act be the penultimate act or not. On a parity of reasoning, a person commits an offence under s 307 when he has an intention to commit murder and, in pursuance of that intention, does an act towards its commission irrespective of the fact whether that act is the penultimate act or not....

The word "act" again, does not mean only any particular, specific, instantaneous act of a person, but denotes, according to s 33 of the Code, as well, a series of acts. The course of conduct adopted by the appellant in regularly starving Bimla Devi comprised a series of acts and therefore acts falling short of completing the series, and would therefore come within the purview of s 307 of the Code....

In *Vasudeo Balvant Gogte* (1932) a person fired several shots at another. No injury was in fact occasioned due to certain obstruction. The culprit was convicted of an offence under s 307, IPC Beaumont CJ, said:

"I think that what s 307 really means is that the accused must do an act with such a guilty intention and knowledge and in such circumstances that but for some intervening fact the act would have amounted to murder in the normal course of events."

This is correct. In the present case, the intervening fact which thwarted the attempt of the appellant to commit the murder of Bimla Devi was her happening to escape from the house and succeeding in reaching the hospital and thereafter securing good medical treatment.

It may, however, be mentioned that in cases of attempt to commit murder by firearm, the act amounting to an attempt to commit murder is bound to be the only and the last act to be done by the culprit. Till he fires, he does not do any act towards the commission of the offence and once he fires, and something happens to prevent the shot taking effect, the offence under s 307 is made out. Expressions, in such cases, indicate that one commits an attempt to murder only when one has committed the last act necessary to commit murder. Such expressions, however, are not to be taken as precise exposition of the law, though the statements in the context of the cases are correct....

We may now refer to *White* (1910–12). In that case, the accused, who was indicted for the murder of his mother, was convicted of attempt to murder her. It was held that the accused had put two grains of cyanide of potassium in the wine glass with the intent to murder her. It was, however, argued that there was no attempt at murder because "the act of which he was guilty, namely, the putting the poison in the wine glass, was a completed act and could not be and was not intended by the appellant to have the effect of killing her at once; it could not kill unless it were followed by other acts which he might never have done". This contention was repelled and it was said:

"There seems no doubt that the learned judge in effect did tell the jury that if this was a case of slow poisoning the appellant would be guilty of the attempt to murder. We are of opinion that this direction was right, and that the completion or attempted completion of one of a series of acts intended by a man to result in killing is an attempt to murder even although this completed act would not, unless followed by the other acts, result in killing. It might be the beginning of the attempt, but would nonetheless be an attempt."

This supports our view.

Appeal dismissed

This approach with regard to firearms was approved in *Awadhesh Mahto* (1979) where it was held that in cases of attempted murder by firearms no attempt is committed until the firearm is actually fired. Until then pointing a loaded gun at someone "could only be termed an attempt to discharge a loaded gun". With firearms the position appears to be as follows:

the act amounting to an attempt to commit murder is bound to be the only and the last act to be done by the culprit. Till he fires he does not do any act towards the commission of the offence and once he fires, and something happens to prevent the shot from taking effect, the offence under s 307 is made out.

It was held that in other cases such as trying to starve someone to death (see *Om Prakash* (1961)) the accused need not commit his "last act which if effective would cause death".

A more emphatic rejection of the "last act test" came in the Indian Supreme Court decision of *Balram Bama Patil* (1983) (see above, p 262) where it was stated:

> An attempt in order to be criminal need not be the penultimate act. It is sufficient in law, if there is present an intent coupled with *some overt act* in execution thereof.

According to this somewhat ambiguous case what is necessary is that the act of the accused be done with the requisite *mens rea* for murder. If the accused thinks his act will kill that is sufficient, even though in fact it could never do so, or even if objectively further actions by him would be necessary. Further, as stated in *Om Prakash* (1961), it must be recalled that under s 33 "the word 'act' denotes as well a series of acts". Accordingly, if the accused is planning a series of acts, such as starving his wife to death over a period of time, each individual act is accompanied by the requisite *mens rea* and the accused can be liable at a relatively early stage despite his not having committed the penultimate act.

From this it follows that it is possible to argue, contrary to what was held in *Om Prakash* (1961), that liability can be imposed at an earlier stage for attempted murder than for attempts contrary to s 511 where even under *Mohamed Yakub* (1980) a more rigorous and objective test would need to be satisfied. All that would be required under this view is that the accused do some overt act which *he thinks* will be sufficient to kill, or some overt act, forming part of a series of acts committed with this same *mens rea*.

It is submitted that such an interpretation, given the wording of s 307 and the Illustrations thereto, is quite unacceptable. Accordingly, it is more likely that the view put forward in *Om Prakash* (1961) will be the one accepted in Singapore and Malaysia. According to this the test for the *actus reus* of an attempt is the same whether the accused is being charged under s 511 or under s 307 or s 308. However, it must be remembered that the test under s 511 is now the test in *Mohamed Yakub* (1980). Applying this to s 307 might well satisfy those primarily interested in law enforcement, but it would be a travesty and distortion of the wording of s 307 and its Illustrations.

If both these above tests are rejected one is left only with the "last act" test under which the accused will only be liable for attempted murder if he has done the last act dependent on himself. This may seem unduly restrictive but there are strong arguments for such an approach. First, it is the only interpretation that is consistent with the wording of s 307 and its Illustrations. Second, it is a view consistent with the "second order harm" theory espoused above. Only when an accused has come *very near* to committing his crime can his actions be said to generate the necessary alarm and apprehension for there to be a second order harm justifying the imposition of criminal liability. Third, it must be recalled that the penalty for conviction under s 307 is severe–particularly in comparison with s 511. With such a potentially heavy sentence it is perhaps not unreasonable to insist that the accused come extremely close to committing the full offence before such a punishment be imposed upon him.

3. Impossible attempts

In understanding the law on this it will be useful to employ the following common law classification–bearing in mind that this is a classification of convenience and *not* one expressly drawn by the Penal Code.

(i) Physical impossibility

This is where it is physically impossible for the accused to commit the crime, whatever means he adopts. For example, he intends to steal from a safe; he breaks into the safe, but it is empty; there is nothing for him to steal.

(ii) Legal impossibility

This is where the accused has done everything he means to do but in fact, and unknown to him, what he has done does not amount to a crime. For example, he intends to steal an umbrella but unknown to him, the umbrella he takes turns out to be his own.

(iii) Impossibility through ineptitude

This is where the crime is impossible in the circumstances because of the accused's ineptitude, inefficiency or his adoption of insufficient means. For example, he tries to break open a safe with a jemmy, but the jemmy is too weak ever to open the safe.

The position under the English common law was that there could be no criminal liability for impossible attempts in either of the first two categories above. There could, however, be liability for an attempt that was only impossible because of the ineptitude of the accused (*Haughton* v *Smith*, 1975). The rationale of this approach is that when a crime is physically or legally impossible to commit the accused can never get close enough to *the crime* to satisfy the *actus reus* of attempt. One cannot get proximate to nothing! Further, imposing criminal liability in such cases is basing liability purely on guilty intentions. Believing that an umbrella is stolen, for instance, does not make it a stolen umbrella. A law that recoils from "thought crime" (see above, p 36) must recoil from liability in such cases. With impossibility through ineptitude, on the other hand, the crime is not actually "impossible": the accused *can* break into the safe; he simply needs to fetch and use a stronger jemmy.

This whole common law approach was open to severe criticism. First, when is a crime really "impossible'? If a pocket contains a dirty handkerchief or, say, a broken match (both "movable property" capable of being stolen–see s 378), is the pickpocket who places his hand into that pocket in the hope of finding money attempting the impossible or not? Second, how does one distinguish between physical impossibility and impossibility through ineptitude? If a believer in black magic sticks pins into a doll in an effort thereby to cause the death of his victim, is this impossibility by ineptitude or physical impossibility?

The most fundamental criticisms, however, were those of principle. It was argued that those who try and commit crimes are just as blameworthy and in need of incapacitation as those who succeed. Punishment is just as much needed in such cases to deter them and others from attempting such crimes in the future. It is "sheer chance" whether a pocket is empty or not. The pickpocket who slips his hand in that pocket deserves punishment irrespective of the contents of the pocket. The criminal law is not a lottery with liability dependent on chance, ie whether the pocket contains money or not. (For a contrary argument, see Clarkson, 1987).

These latter arguments won the day in England and resulted in the enactment of the Criminal Attempts Act 1981 which imposes liability in all situations of attempting the impossible. An assessment of the position in Singapore and Malaysia necessitates distinguishing again the general attempt provision of s 511 from the specific provisions such as s 307.

(a) Section 511

It is clear that there can be no liability for attempting the physically impossible.

Penal Code, s 511

Illustrations

(a) A makes an attempt to steal some jewels by breaking open a box, and finds after so opening the box that there is no jewel in it. He has done an act towards the commission of theft, and therefore is guilty under this section.

(b) A makes an attempt to pick the pocket of Z by thrusting his hand into Z's pocket. A fails in the attempt in consequence of Z's having nothing in his pocket; A is guilty under this section.

While these are both examples of attempted theft it was made clear in *Munah b Ali* (1958) that they are of "general application" extending to all attempts to commit the physically impossible under s 511. Unfortunately, however, both illustrations are clearly confined to attempting the physically impossible–leaving wide open the question as to what the law is on the other two categories of impossible attempts.

Munah b Ali v PP (1958) 24 MLJ 159 (CA, Malaya)

The accused, trying to procure an illegal abortion, inserted an instrument into a woman's vagina with a view to thereby causing a miscarriage. Unknown to the parties the woman was not in fact pregnant and thus it was "impossible" to cause her to have a miscarriage.

Thomson CJ (dissenting): My own views on the point involved can be stated very shortly.
    Section 312 of the Penal Code reads as follows:

> "Whoever voluntarily causes a woman with child to miscarry shall, if such miscarriage be not caused in good faith for the purpose of saving the life of the woman be punished with imprisonment of ...".

The only observation I would make regarding [that section] is that it is quite clear that the expression "causes a woman with child to miscarry" means to cause her to lose from the womb prematurely the products of conception and that therefore there can be no offence under the section unless there are products of conception....
    The question of attempts to commit offences is dealt with by section 511 of the Penal Code...
    The argument for the prosecution here was that what the present appellant did was punishable as an offence by reason of the provisions of this section. It was said that there was a very close analogy between the illustration appended to the section and the facts of the present case....
    The analogy between the present case and the illustrations to s 511 is attractive. An analogy, however, is not an argument and in any event this analogy is a bad one. There may be a notional similarity between attempting to remove a non-existent coin from a woman's handbag and attempting to remove non-existent products of conception from her womb. But there is all the difference in the world between something which is in fact impossible but which if possible would be an offence and something which cannot possibly be an offence in any circumstance whatsoever.
    It will be observed that s 511 does not define an attempt. It only states what attempts are themselves offences. It says in effect that before an attempt is itself an offence it must satisfy two conditions. The first of these is that it must be an attempt to commit an offence punishable by the Code or by any other written law. The other is that there must be an act towards the commission of the offence.
    In other words, before an offence is punishable it must be an attempt to do something which is an offence punishable under the Code or some other written law. It follows that an attempt to do something which is not an offence is not punishable. As was said by Birkett J, in the case of *Percy Dalton* (1949)

> "Steps on the way to the doing of something, which is thereafter done, and which is no crime, cannot be regarded as attempts to commit a crime."

The present case seems to come fairly and squarely within these words. What the appellant did was to pass an instrument and thereby cause the woman in the case to have a haemorrhage but did not amount to causing her to miscarry because she was not with child.
    The matter was dealt with in much the same way in the case of the *Mangesh Jiva'ji* (1887) in which the facts were strikingly similar to those in the

present case. The accused was charged with criminal intimidation in contravention of s 507 of the Code, the allegation against him being that he had sent a letter to the Revenue Commissioner containing a threat that if a certain forest officer who was said to be a person in whom the Commissioner was interested was not removed elsewhere he could be killed. The Sessions Judge found that the letter was in fact sent but that the forest officer was not a person in whom the Commissioner was interested. He accordingly acquitted the accused of the offence of criminal intimidation but convicted him of an attempt to commit that offence. The conviction was quashed and Birdwood J, in the course of his judgment made the following observations (at page 331):

> "It appears, therefore, that the act intended and done by the accused lacked an essential element of the offence of committing criminal intimidation....But it does not follow that the accused could still be legally convicted of an attempt to commit that offence. It is possible to attempt to commit an impossible theft, and so offend against the Code, because theft is itself an offence against the Code, and may, therefore, be attempted within the meaning of the Code. But no criminal liability can be incurred under the Code by an attempt to do an act, which, if done, would not be an offence against the Code. In the present case, therefore, if the accused was not guilty of committing criminal intimidation, because the act intended and done by him lacked an ingredient of that offence, he could not be guilty of the attempt of which he has been convicted."

I would add that there would appear to be no English case directly bearing on the point although in the case of the *Whitechurch* (1890) Lord Coleridge CJ, expressed doubt as to whether a woman who was not in fact with child could be indicted for an attempt to procure abortion on herself. In Scotland, however, while as in England it may be an offence to attempt to steal where there is nothing to steal (*Lamont* v *Strathearn* (1933)) it has been held that a woman must be pregnant before the crime of attempting to procure abortion can be committed (*Peggy Anderson* (1928); and *Semple* (1937)) ....

For the foregoing reasons I would have allowed the appeal.

Whyatt CJ (S): If this question depended solely upon the laws of logic, there would be much to be said for the view that a person cannot attempt to commit an offence if the offence itself cannot be committed but it is in the provisions of the Penal Code and in the judicial decisions interpreting those provisions, rather than in simple logic, that the answer is to be found.

It appears to me that the analogy between the two illustrations, [to section 511] in particular Illustration (b), and the present case is exact for if it be an offence to thrust a hand into a person's pocket with intent to steal, notwithstanding that the pocket is empty, it is equally an offence, in my view, to insert an instrument into a vagina with intent to cause a miscarriage, notwithstanding that the uterus is empty. Moreover the Courts in India, construing precisely similar provisions in the Indian Penal Code, have interpreted them in this wide sense. As long ago as 1887, in the case of the *Jiva'ji* Birdword J said:

> "No doubt an attempt, within the meaning of section 511 of the Indian Penal Code, is possible, even when the offence attempted cannot be committed; as when a person, intending to pick another person's pocket, thrust his hand into the pocket but finds it empty. That such an act would amount to a criminal attempt, appears from the illustration to section 511. But in doing such an act, the offender's intention is to commit a complete offence and his act only falls short of the offence by reason of an accidental circumstance which has prevented the completion of the offence."

So in the present case, the offender's intention was to commit the complete offence of causing a woman to have a miscarriage but her act fell short of the offence by reason of the accidental circumstance that the woman was not pregnant....

I would add that the case of *Asgaralli Pradhanin* (1933) is also of importance since it removes any doubt (if indeed there is room for doubt) that s 511 and the Illustrations are general in their application and apply to an attempt to cause a miscarriage under s 312. It is true that Lort-Williams J held in that case that there was no attempt to cause miscarriage because the drug which was administered was harmless but it is implicit throughout the judgment that s 511 and the principles embodied in the Illustrations are wide enough to cover a case where an act is done towards the commission of an offence against s 312, notwithstanding that the complete offence cannot be committed by reason of some fact unknown to and independent of the person who seeks to commit the offence....

The question to be decided in this reference depends in my view, not upon the English cases, but upon the interpretation to be placed on ss 312 and 511 of the Penal Code and the Illustrations thereto, such interpretation being assisted by the decisions of the courts of India on precisely similar provisions of the Indian Penal Code. For the reasons given earlier in this judgment I am of the opinion that s 511 and the principles embodied in the Illustrations apply to the present case and I would, therefore, answer the question referred to this Court by stating that, in my view, in a charge of attempting to cause a woman to have a miscarriage it is not necessary for the Court to be satisfied that the woman is with child before the Court proceeds to convict.

Good J: It is perhaps unfortunate that both these illustrations [to section 511] deal with cases of attempted theft, but I see no reason for supposing that the principle which they set out is related to the offence of attempted theft alone. If this was so, they would be *ad hoc* illustrations and useless as statements of principle. In my view, they must be construed as being of general application although the examples chosen happened to be examples of cases of attempted theft....

In an Indian case in 1887 *Mangesh Jiva'ji* (1887) [facts above, p 284]... from the judgment of Birdwood J:

> "No doubt, an attempt, within the meaning of s 511 of the Indian Penal Code (Act XLV of 1860), is possible, even when the offence attempted cannot be committed; as when a person, intending to pick another person's pocket, thrusts his hand into the pocket, but finds it empty. That such an act would amount to a criminal attempt, appears from the illustrations to s 511. But in doing such an act, the offender's intention is to commit a complete offence, and his act only falls short of the offence by reason of an accidental circumstance which has prevented the completion of the offence. In the present case, it cannot be said that the accused intended to do more than he actually did. He intended to send a fabricated petition to the Commissioner, containing a threat directed against Mr MacGregor. And that intention,–assuming the facts to be as found by the Sessions Judge,–he carried out completely. If, therefore, he committed an offence at all, he committed the offence which he intended to commit;–not an attempt, but the offence attempted. The Sessions Judge has, however, found that the offence attempted was not, as a matter fact and law, committed, because the person to whom the petition was sent by the accused was not himself threatened, and was not "interested" in the person threatened."...

For the purposes of the present case, I think it is important to emphasize the words: "It is possible to attempt to commit an impossible theft, and so offend against the Code, because theft is itself an offence against the Code, and may, therefore be attempted within the meaning of the Code." On the analogy of this proposition, with which I am respectfully in complete agreement, it seems to me to be possible to attempt to cause an impossible miscarriage and still offend against the Code because the voluntary causing of a miscarriage is itself an offence against the Code and may, therefore, be attempted within the meaning of the Code.

The vital operative words of section 511 in my view are the words: "and in such attempt does any act towards the commission of such offence." In *Luzman Naryan Joshi* (1899), Sir Lawrence Jenkins CJ, defined "attempt" as "an intentionally preparatory action which failed in its object through circumstances independent of the person who seeks its accomplishment". And the same Judge in *Vinayek Narayen Bhatye* (1899) defined "attempt" as "when a man does an intentional act with a view to attain a certain end, and fails in his object through some circumstance independent of his own will". These two definitions were referred to by Lort-Williams J, in his judgment in *Asgaralli Pradhanin* (1933). In *Asgaralli*'s case, which was concerned with a charge of attempting to cause a miscarriage, the accused was proved to have attempted to administer to the complainant two chemicals, a liquid and a powder, for the purpose of procuring a miscarriage but there was no evidence to show that either of the chemicals was capable of operating an an abortifacient; and on appeal against conviction, the appellate Court held that on the facts the appellant could not be convicted of an attempt to cause a miscarriage because what he did was not an "act done towards the commission of the offence" of causing miscarriage.

"Neither the liquid nor the powder being harmful, they could not have caused a miscarriage. The appellant's failure was not due to a factor independent of himself."

In the present case, the circumstances are different. The evidence clearly showed that it was the intention of the appellant to bring about a miscarriage and she could not have made the attempt unless she believed the complainant to be pregnant. If the complainant was not pregnant, then the failure of the attempt was due to a factor independent of the appellant herself. Her attempt was prevented or frustrated by the non-existence of a circumstance which she believed to exist. As I see it, she is in exactly the same position as the would-be pickpocket who, believing that there is or may be something capable of being stolen in the pocket which he decides to pick, attempts to steal it and finds his attempt foiled by a circumstance independent of himself, namely, the non-existence of anything capable of being stolen. The circumstances of the present case seem to me to be exactly covered by the illustrations to s 511 of the Penal Code, even though these illustrations speak of attempts to commit a different type of offence.

Appeal dismissed

From this decison and from the Indian case of *Mangesh Jiva'ji* (1887) it appears safe to conclude that while there can be liability for attempting the physically impossible, there can be no liability for attempting the legally impossible. This was a conclusion favoured by many commentators in England, but ultimately rejected because of the difficulty of distinguishing the two categories of impossibility, a difficulty manifest in *Munah b Ali* (1958).

What is the position with regard to those attempts that are "impossible' because of the ineptitude of the accused?

It is implicit in the decision of *Munah b Ali* (1958) that there will be no liability in such cases. The majority approved the Indian decision of *Asgaralli Pradhanin* (1933) where it had been held that there was no liability for attempting a miscarriage when harmless drugs were administered as this was not "an act towards the commission of an offence". The majority stated that there would only be liability if the failure to commit the crime was due to a factor independent of the accused, such as a pocket being empty. If, however, the failure is due to the accused himself (say, on account of his inefficiency), then if the crime is not possible he has not done the requisite "act towards the commission of the offence" and must escape liability.

Such an approach is, it is submitted, highly undesirable and ought to be rejected. Apart from the immense difficulty of distinguishing such cases from physical impossibility, it would appear that every policy reason suggests that if there is to be liability for attempting the physically impossible there ought to be liability here. An accused trying to open a safe with a jemmy too weak is causing just as much of a "second order harm", is just as blameworthy, dangerous and in need of rehabilitation and deterrence as the accused who manages to open the safe only to find it empty. It seems absurd to suggest liability in one case but not the other.

Indeed, the following two recent local cases have clearly stated that there will be liability in cases where the accused has only failed to commit the crime because of his own ineptitude.

PP v Zainal Abidin b Ismail [1987] 2 MLJ 741 (HC, Brunei)

(For the facts, see above, p 70.)

Roberts CJ: [T]he act ... must be proximate ... with the offence see *Haughton v Smith* (1975) ... There can be an attempt where the failure to convict the offence is due to "ineptitude, inefficiency or insufficient means on the part of the defendant".

Applying this test, I find that, notwithstanding that he failed to penetrate the girl by reason of his inability to obtain any erection, D4 did attempt to penetrate the girl ... (and he is guilty of) an attempt of rape.

Oi Bee Kee v PP (Unreported, Magistrate's Appeal No 175 of 1983, Subordinate Courts, Singapore)

(For the facts, see above, p 274.)

Ng Peng Hong, Magistrate: The accused was seen trying to open the vehicle's nearside door, with a piece of cloth and a bunch of keys....

The next defence submitted by learned counsel was that as the accused could not unlock the car's door in any event, the accused should not be found guilty of attempted theft. This led me to examine s 511 of the Penal Code. All that is required under the said s 511 is that there must be an attempt and "in such attempt does any act towards the commission of the offence". In my opinion, these requirements are satisfied by the insertion of the key(s) into the key slot by the accused. I therefore rejected this submission.

(b)　Sections 307 and 308

R v Francis Cassidy (1867) 4 Bom HCR (Cr Ca) 17 (Bombay HC, India)

The accused pointed a loaded uncapped gun (believing it was capped) at his superior officer with the intention of murdering him. He was about to pull the trigger when the gun was pushed up and he was prevented from doing so.

Couch CJ: [L]ooking, at the terms of this s [307], as well as the illustrations to it, it is necessary, in order to constitute an offence under it, that there must be an act done under such circumstances that death might be caused if the act took effect. The act must be capable of causing death in the natural and ordinary course of things; and if the act complained of is not of that description, a prisoner cannot be convicted of an attempt to murder under this section.

　The illustrations given bear out this view. One is that of a man firing a loaded gun; and another is that of a man placing food mixed with poison on another's table. Both these acts are capable of causing death: but in the present case, although the act was done with the intention of causing death, and was likely in the belief of the prisoner to cause death; yet in point of fact it could not have caused death, and it, therefore, does not come within that section.

Queen-Empress v Niddha (1891) XIV 14 All 38 (HC, Allahabad, India)

Straight J: The appellant was an absconding criminal in the company of another absconding criminal.... [H]e was determined in conjunction with that person to resist his lawful apprehension, and that for the purpose of doing so he was armed with a loaded blunderbuss, and that in the directions of the person who was seeking to arrest him, he presented the weapon, pulled the trigger, the hammer fell on the nipple, and it was only owing to the circumstance that the cap did not explode, that the gun failed to go off and consequently no harm was done....

　It seems to me that ... (such a person) is not entitled to pray in his aid an obstacle intervening not known to himself.... I do not think he can escape criminal responsibility ... (because) a fact unknown to him and at variance with his own belief intervened to prevent the consequences of that act which he expected to ensue, ensuing.

　In the present case ... the failure to discharge the weapon was wholly independent of any action of (the accused) ....

　I direct that the conviction be recorded under s 307....

This latter case seems to be following the same approach as that adopted by the Indian decisions on s 511, namely, that while there can be liability for attempting the physically impossible (caused by factors independent of the accused), there can be no liability for impossibility due to ineptitude (eg failing to load a gun). Such an approach is consistent with the view taken in *Om Prakash* (1961) that the tests in ss 511 and 307 are the same. This was indeed the approach adopted by the Indian cases: there could be liability for attempting the physically impossible but not for the other two categories of impossibility.

However, as seen above, two recent local cases have departed from this view and held that there can be liability for impossibility due to ineptitude. It is likely that this will be the approach adopted in Singapore and Malaysia–and support can be found in the Indian authorities.

Awadhesh Mahto v State of Bihar (1979) Cri LJ 1275 (Patna HC, India)

The accused drew a loaded pistol and pointed it at P but before he had time to shoot the pistol, it was snatched from his hand and he was arrested.

MP Singh J: It is quite clear that act which is punishable under s 307 must be an act which is itself capable of causing death.... In the present case A-1 had not fired the pistol. It was not a case of misfire .... It was also not a case where A-1 pulled the trigger and due to some mechanical defect in the pistol the bullet could not pass.... Till he fires he does not do any act towards the commission of the offence and once he fires, and something happens to prevent the shot from taking effect, the offence under s 307 is made out.

From this it seems relatively clear that once the gun is fired, liability will follow. A fired gun is capable of causing death. It is irrelevant that in the circumstances death would not actually have resulted, or indeed, was impossible.

Chapter 15

Conspiracy

By CMV Clarkson

A. Introduction

Penal Code, ss 120A and 120B

120A. When two or more persons agree to do, or cause to be done–
(a) an illegal act; or
(b) an act, which is not illegal, by illegal means, such an agreement is designated a criminal conspiracy:

Provided, that no agreement except an agreement to commit an offence shall amount to a criminal conspiracy unless some act besides the agreement is done by one or more parties to such agreement in pursuance thereof.

Explanation–It is immaterial whether the illegal act is the ultimate object of such agreement, or is merely incidental to that object.

120B.–(1) Whoever is a party to a criminal conspiracy to commit an offence punishable with death or imprisonment for a term of 2 years or upwards shall, where no express provision is made in this Code for the punishment of such a conspiracy, be punished in the same manner as if he had abetted such offence.

(2) Whoever is a party to a criminal conspiracy other than a criminal conspiracy to commit an offence punishable as aforesaid shall be punished with imprisonment for a term not exceeding 6 months, or with fine, or with both.

It is often thought that a combination of persons is more dangerous than a single actor. This is because such a combination is capable of doing more harm than the single actor–particularly when there is an agreement to commit a series of offences. Also, when there is a collaboration between persons there is less chance of abandonment of the criminal enterprise; the shared commitment to perpetrate the crime makes it more likely that the crime will actually be committed by at least one of the parties. And, of course, it is more difficult for society to protect itself against collective criminal organizations, say, organized crime, than against the anti-social designs of the individual. Accordingly, the criminal laws of most countries have special provisions dealing with such group criminality and permitting the imposition of criminal liability and punishment even though the ultimate planned harm has not been caused. In the Penal Code there are a few particularized provisions striking at such criminal combinations. For instance, s 400 makes it a criminal offence simply to belong to a gang of persons associated for the purpose of habitually committing gang-robbery. No actual robbery need take place. The essence of the criminal liability is simply being a member of such a gang–membership itself being perceived as dangerous for the above reasons.

Apart from such specific prohibitions, when the Penal Code was enacted it contained a general provision aimed at criminal combinations and agreements. This was s 107(b) which provided that one of the ways in which one could abet an offence was by "engag(ing) with one or more person or persons in any conspiracy for the doing of that thing". Section 107(b), however, contained the important qualification that one would only be liable for abetting an offence if "an act or illegal omission takes place in pursuance of that conspiracy, and in order to the doing of that thing". This meant that the law of consiracy under Indian and Singapore law was a good deal more narrow than under English law in two important respects. First, under English law all that was required was a mere agreement to commit an offence; no act pursuant to that agreement was necessary. Second, in England the law of conspiracy had come to be regarded as a valuable weapon in striking at any combination that posed a threat to vested interests even if no actual crime was being committed by the group as long as there was an agreement "to do an unlawful act, or do to a lawful act by unlawful means" (*Mulcahy*, 1868). Under s 107(b) (as is made clear by s 108), on the other hand, liability for abetting is restricted to the abetting of offences.

Having to satisfy the more rigorous criteria of conspiracy by abetment was perceived as a gap under the Penal Code and so ss 120A and 120B were inserted into the Indian Penal Code by amendment in 1913. The Penal Codes of Singapore and Malaysia were similarly amended. Under s 120A it is not necessary to establish that any act was done pursuant to the agreement. Further, there can now be a criminal conspiracy even where the object of the agreement is not the commission of the crime, but simply the doing of something "illegal" (as defined in s 43, see above, p 44), or even something legal, by illegal means. The main activity caught by this loose provision is agreements to commit torts. Similarly, in England in *Kamara* (1974) an agreement to commit the tort of trespass to land, if accompanied by an intention to commit more than nominal damage, was once held to be a criminal conspiracy. Such an approach is difficult to justify. If an activity is not regarded as being "bad" enough to be a crime when actually done why should a mere agreement to commit that same activity be a criminal offence? English law eventually recognized that there was no satisfactory answer to such a question and accordingly the Criminal Law Act 1977 limited criminal conspiracy to agreements to commit crimes (subject to one exception, designed as a temporary stop-gap measure, relating to conspiracy to defraud). It is strongly submitted that Singapore law should follow this example and limit the offence of criminal conspiracy to agreements to. commit crimes.

The punishment of conspiracy is laid down by s 120B. A distinction is drawn between two classes of criminal conspiracy.

First, if there is a conspiracy to commit an offence punishable with death or imprisonment for a term of two years or more, the accused shall be punished as if he abetted the offence. The punishment provisions for abetting offences are complex (see ss 109–117, below pp 333–337), but broadly provide as follows:

(1)   If the ultimate offence is actually committed, the punishment for abetment is the same as for that ultimate offence.

(2)   If the ultimate offence is not committed:

    (a)   where that offence is punishable with death or life imprisonment, the abettor shall be liable to a maximum of seven years' imprisonment (or 14 years if harm is caused to any person);

    (b)   where that offence is punishable with a lesser term of imprisonment, the abettor shall be liable to a maximum of imprisonment for one-quarter of the term prescribed for the ultimate offence. For example, theft is punishable with a maximum of three years' imprisonment (s 379). This means that conspiracy to commit theft is punishable with a maximum of nine months' imprisonment.

Second, if the conspiracy is to commit an offence punishable by a maximum of less than two years' imprisonment or is a criminal conspiracy to commit a non-criminal act, the maximum penalty shall be six months' imprisonment.

It can thus be seen that as a general rule the Penal Code is adopting the logical view that an agreement to commit a crime is less serious than the actual commission of the crime and therefore deserving of a lesser punishment. However, this logic collapses with regard to conspiracies to commit minor offences (or non-offences) where the six-month maximum can be higher than the maximum available for the completed offence (and of course is "higher" than no punishment for non-offences!). It is true of course that this is the maximum possible penalty and with conspiracies to commit minor offences it is unlikely that a prosecution would ever be brought and, if it were, it is even more unlikely that a punishment in excess of that available for the completed offence would be imposed. Nevertheless, the fact that greater punishment for a conspiracy than for the completed ultimate offence is a possibility raises grave questions of principle. It is submitted that such an option be foreclosed by the insertion of an amendment to the effect that the punishment for a conspiracy shall never exceed that available for the completed offence.

B. The law

1. Actus reus

The ingredients of the *actus reus* of conspiracy depend on whether there is an agreement to commit an offence or not:

(1) With conspiracies to commit crimes, the *actus reus* of the offence is the agreement to commit the offence.
(2) With conspiracies to commit non-criminal illegal acts or legal acts by illegal means, the *actus reus* of the offence is the agreement to commit such a prohibited act and in addition one of the parties to the agreement must have committed "some act" in pursuance of the agreement.

The essence of the offence is thus the agreement:

EG Barsay v State of Bombay (1962) 2 SCR 195 (SC, India)

The gist of the offence is an agreement to break the law. The parties to such an agreement will be guilty of criminal conspiracy, though the illegal act agreed to be done has not been done. So too, it is not an ingredient of the offence that all the parties should agree to do a single illegal act. It may comprise the commission of a number of acts.

Lennart Schussler v Director of Enforcement AIR (1970) SC 549 (SC, India)

There must be a meeting of minds in the doing of the illegal act or the doing of a legal act by illegal means. If in the furtherance of the conspiracy certain persons are induced to do an unlawful act without the knowledge of the conspiracy or the plot they cannot be held to be conspirators, though they may be guilty of an offence pertaining to the specific unlawful act. The offence of conspiracy is complete when two or more conspirators have agreed to do or cause to be done an act which is itself an offence, in which case no overt act need be established. It is also clear that an agreement to do an illegal act which amounts to a conspiracy will continue as long as the members of the conspiracy remain in agreement and as long as they are acting in accord and in furtherance of the object for which they entered into the agreement.

Yash Pal v State of Punjab (1978) Cri LJ 189 (SC, India)

Goswami J: The very agreement, concert or league is the ingredient of the offence. It is not necessary that all the conspirators must know each and every detail of the conspiracy as long as they are co-conspirators in the main object of the conspiracy. There may be so many devices and techniques adopted to achieve the common goal of the conspiracy and there may be division of performances in the chain of actions....

Saleem-Un-Din v State of Delhi ILR (1971) I Delhi 432 (Delhi HC, India)

The accused and others agreed in Pakistan to commit the offence of spying in India. When charged with s 120B read with s 3 of the Indian Official Secrets Act 1923 the question arose as to whether the Indian courts would have jurisdiction as the crime was committed in Pakistan.

Hardayal Hardy J: There is a fallacy in the learned Judge's view which is opposed to the very language of ss 120A and 120B of the Indian Penal Code.

It is true that a mere agreement may bring the conspiracy into existence and since the offence of criminal conspiracy is a substantive offence a mere agreement would render the persons taking part in that agreement liable for being prosecuted on the charge of conspiracy. But it has no where been said in the Code that as soon as an agreement is entered into between the persons concerned the offence no longer exists. Criminal conspiracy may come into existence and may persist and will persist so long as persons constituting the conspiracy remain in agreement and so long as they are acting in accord, in furtherance of the object for which they had entered into the agreement. This was the view taken by a Division Bench of Calcutta High Court in *Abdul Rahman* (1935).

The same view was also taken by the Supreme Court in *Mohd Hussain Umar Kochra etc* v *KS Dalipsinghji* (1970) where it was said that the agreement is the gist of the offence but in order to constitute a single general conspiracy there must be a common design and a common intention of all to work in furtherance of the common design. Each conspirator plays separate part in one integrated and united effort to achieve the common purpose. Each one is aware that he has a part to play in a general conspiracy though he may not know all its secrets or the means by which the common purpose is to be accomplished. The evil scheme may be promoted by a few, some may drop out and some may join at a later stage, but the conspiracy continues until it is broken up. A general conspiracy must be distinguished from a number of separate conspiracies having a similar general purpose. Where different groups of persons co-operate towards their separate ends without any privity with each other, each combination constitutes a separate conspiracy.

In another case it was said that the conspiracy is like a running stream. Some persons join it in the beginning while others join it later. But they are all parties to the same general conspiracy, leaving aside certain other-unrelated conspiracies or separate conspiracies among some of the members who co-operate towards their separate ends.

R v Chew Chong Jin (1956) 22 MLJ 185 (HC, Singapore)

The accused was charged with abetting by conspiracy in the illegal importation of gold into Singapore contrary to the Prohibition of Imports Order 1950. The accused wearing a special white waistcoat with a number of pockets entered a plane shortly after it landed in Singapore and made several trips to a hanger where he hid parcels containing gold. At his trial he was acquitted on the ground, inter alia, that the prosecution had failed to establish a prima facie case that the accused was engaged in a conspiracy (as opposed to acting alone) for the importation of gold into Singapore.

Whitton J: I now turn to the second part of the Appeal. This involves the issue whether the facts established by the Crown *prima facie* proved the respondent was a conspirator in the illegal importation of the gold. The first observation I would make in this connection is that I think it is clear there must have existed a conspiracy between one or more persons at the place the gold was put on the plane, or, alternatively some person travelling on the plane either as passenger or member of the crew, on the one hand, and one or more persons in Singapore who were to receive the gold on arrival. The only other possible theory does not seem to me at all tenable; that is an illegal importer on the plane trusting to luck came across the respondent and forthwith arranged with him to take charge of the gold.

The learned District Judge held there was no evidence the respondent had engaged with any other person or persons in any conspiracy for the importing of gold into the Colony. True there is no direct evidence, but as *Kenny* remarks (1936) "it rarely happens that the actual fact of the conspiracy can be proved by direct evidence; since such agreements are usually entered into both swiftly and secretly". Now it does not appear that to constitute a conspiracy it is essential a person must have been a party to the wrongful agreement from the start, provided that at some stage before the unlawful act is carried out he joins in the agreement to carry it out. Again it is clear that there need not be communication between each conspirer and every other, provided that there be a design common to them all (*Meyrick and Ribuffi*, (1929)). So the issue, as I see it, resolves itself thus: having regard to all the circumstances does the evidence for the Crown raise the *prima facie* inference that at some time before the gold was imported, ie carried inside territorial limits, the respondent had become a party to the conspiracy for its illegal importation, or is it also consistent with the respondent being a "stooge" who merely took over the gold on his principal's instructions? To my mind when due weight is given to such circumstances as (1) the nature of the respondent's employment at the Airport; (2) the value of the gold–in the region of $80,000–being such that the illegal importers were very likely to make sure that it only passed into–from their point of view–trusted hands; (3) the preparedness of the respondent for receiving the slabs of gold as evidenced by the special waistcoat he was wearing under his singlet and his conduct just before he was apprehended, there were adequate grounds for the District Judge to hold there was a case to meet....

The order of acquittal is set aside and I direct that the District Judge should proceed to call upon the respondent for his defence.

Order accordingly

The essence of the offence being the agreement, the following points are clear:

(1) There must be a real "agreement". This means that there must have been a meeting of minds. The parties must be beyond the stage of negotiation or exhortation. A decision to commit the crime (or other prohibited objective) must have been reached. While each of the parties need not be in direct communication with each other, the decision to commit the crime (or other prohibited objective) must have been communicated between the parties (see, Orchard, 1974).

(2) An agreement necessarily involves at least two parties. This means that where several persons are charged with conspiracy and there is no evidence implicating anyone else, if all are acquitted except one, that one must also be acquitted as he is now the sole alleged conspirator (*Bhagat Ram*, 1972). One person alone may be convicted of conspiracy but only if evidence emerges implicating other persons or if he has been charged with other persons who have not been acquitted. Such other persons need not be expressly named in the charges (*Bimbadhar Pradhna*, 1956).

It is submitted that these Indian authorities should not be followed on this point. One is here simply interpreting the concept of an agreement and the word "agree" in s 120A. One is not interpreting the structure of s 120A which would have necessitated reference to other legal systems *in pari materia* with Singapore and Malaysian law. Reliance on Indian authorities on this point could lead to unfortunate results. An accused could be charged with conspiring with two other persons. It might be clear that he conspired with one of them but the evidence might not establish which one, with the result that they both had to be acquitted. It seems odd that the accused who has been proved to have conspired with one of them should have to be acquitted. In England the House of Lords in *Shannon* (1975) had indicated obiter that in exceptional circumstances an accused in a joint trial could be convicted of conspiracy despite the only other alleged conspirator being acquitted. This approach was not followed in the subsequent case of *Coughlan* (1977) but the *Shannon* (1975) principle has subsequently been enshrined by statute (Criminal Law Act 1977, s 5(8)). It is hoped that this approach will be followed locally if and when the point arises.

(3) As clearly emerges from *Saleem-Un-Din* (1971) the Singapore or Malaysian courts would have jurisdiction in respect of conspiracies entered into in foreign countries provided the object of the conspiracy was to commit an offence in Singapore or Malaysia and provided some overt act in pursuance of the conspiracy was committed within the jurisdiction. This is also clearly the position in England (*Doot*, 1973). Thus in *Khoo Ban Hock* (1987) an agreement was entered into in Singapore to defraud the National Bank of Brunei. Various acts pursuant to this agreement were committed in Brunei. The Brunei court held, relying on both the Indian and English authorities cited above, that it had jurisdiction to hear the case.

(4) The Singapore decision of *Chew Chong Jin* (1956) emphasizes the important point that in most cases agreements take place behind closed doors and therefore, in the absence of a confession, have to be inferred from the subsequent actions of the accused. This means that while in theory all that is needed for the *actus reus* of conspiracy is an agreement, in practice there will almost always be subsequent conduct towards the commission of the crime. While this may help allay the fears of those concerned that conspiracy is getting rather too near to the punishment of thought-crime, it nevertheless raises yet further questions in relation to the justifiability of the crime of conspiracy. For instance, one concern is that while *mens rea* must generally be inferred for all offences, with conspiracy the *actus reus* also has to be inferred making the entire offence one of inference–hardly a satisfactory state of affairs. Second, if in practice overt acts towards the commission of the offence are required, why not insist that those overt acts be such as to come within the definition of attempt–or if necessary even expand the definition of attempt to catch many such overt acts; the result could be the abolition of the offence of conspiracy.

(a) Overt act

Where the agreement is to commit an act which is not an offence it is necessary to establish that "some act" was committed by one or more parties to the agreement in pursuance thereof.

Marsi Balayya v State of Orissa (1976) 42 Cut LT 374 (Orissa HC, India)

KB Panda J: Naxalite leaders came ... to ... Orissa. They arranged meetings at 9 different places on different dates and it is alleged that they exerted [sic] the people to join their party. Accordingly, these appellants associated themselves with theses Naxalites whose object was to commit docoity in the house of the rich....

The substance of [the speech at the meetings] .. was that a Government of the poor people should be established after over-throwing the present Government; that the rich Sahukars should be robbed and if necessary may be killed and their riches and lands distributed amongst the poor. In case the police would intervene, they would be destroyed with bombs.

With the money so obtained, communist schools should be established in which children of the poor should be given free education, wells would be dug, roads laid and the like. (The appellants thereupon joined the party)....

[T]he Police had been alerted. A joint raid was made. In that from the house of accused ... the Police recovered some Naxalite literature .... (Other articles were discovered but in circumstances described as "suspicious"–and can therefore be discounted.)...

[E]ven on facts I do not think the prosecution has a formidable case. The charge under criminal conspiracy appears shaky. It is not the case of the prosecution that the conspiracy was about doing of any illegal act to come under s 120A(1), but it comes under s 120A(2), for, from the literature seized, there is no direct exhortation for committing dacoity but for distribution of the riches of the rich to the poor. The object, therefore, is noble, though the method proposed, namely, by robbing the rich, is illegal. Under the proviso to s 120A(2) besides the agreement, there must be some act done by one or some such party to such agreement, in pursuance of conspiracy, to constitute an offence but here no such allegation is there. That apart, ... the nine meetings referred to by the prosecution are either exhortations to join the camp of the Naxalites and that too under threat and coercion [sic]. It has been held in the case of *Jagannath Misra* (1974) that mere exhortation to take the Naxalite methods without anything more, may not satisfy the requirements of s 120A of the Code....

Appeals allowed

The ultimate result reached in this case is correct in that mere exhortation, or the joining of a party cannot in themselves amount to the necessary agreement. However, it is submitted that the dicta in the above extract adopt fallacious reasoning. Assuming there were an agreement, what would be the object of this agreement? Surely, it would be, inter alia, to commit robbery, a crime under the Penal Code. Accordingly, no overt act should be required. The fact that the reason or motive for the robbery may be non-criminal is irrelevant if an agreement to commit a *crime* can be proved. If this view were accepted, s 120A(2) and the requirement of an overt act would be restricted to agreements to commit lawful acts adopting means which in themselves would give rise to civil liability (ie "illegal" as defined by s 43 but not criminal); in all probability this would refer to adopting means that gave rise to tortious liability.

2.   Mens rea

The parties must have intended that their agreement be carried out.

Churchill v Walton [1967] 1 All ER 497 (HL)

Viscount Dilhorne: [M]ens rea] is only an essential ingredient in conspiracy insofar as there must be an intention to be a party to an agreement to do an unlawful act; .... [I]t is desirable to ... concentrate on the terms or effect of the agreement made by the alleged conspirators. The question is "What did they agree to do?" If what they agreed to do was, on the facts known to them, an unlawful act, they are guilty of conspiracy ....

Yash Pal Mital v State of Punjab AIR (1977) Punjab 189 (SC, India)

[T]he conspirators must act with one object to achieve the real end of which every collaborator must be aware and in which each one of them must be interested. There must be unity of object or purpose ....

This rule that the accused must have *mens rea* applies equally to conspiracies to commit offences of strict liability (*Churchill* v *Walton*, 1967).

Finally, it is important to note that the requirement that the conspirators intend to commit the offence does *not* mean that each conspirator must intend to do those acts that would constitute the complete offence. What is necessary here is that at the time of agreement each conspirator should intend that the crime be committed and that he will fulfil *his* role in that agreement, even if that role be no more than agreeing that the crime be committed by another.

3.   Conspiracy to commit the impossible

Emperor v Hiremath AIR (1940) Bom 365 (HC, Bombay, India)

The accused was charged, inter alia, with conspiracy to murder one Muchkandappa. (Further charges included the actual murder of Muchkandappa by drowning.)

Beaumont CJ: The first attempt to murder was between January and August 1938, by means of witchcraft. There is, I think, abundant evidence that all the accused ... did conspire together at the instance of accused 1 to murder Muchkandappa by means of a form of witchcraft known as *bhanumati*. I think that was the effect of the jury's verdict of guilty under s 120B. The learned Judge, as I understand him, did not doubt that there was plenty of evidence of a conspiracy to murder Muchkandappa by means of witchcraft, but he thought that such a conspiracy was not a criminal offence and did not fall within s 120B.

It is plain that an agreement to commit murder being an agreement to commit an offence, falls within s 120B, and nonetheless so, in my opinion, because the means by which the murder is to be perpetrated are not agreed upon, or the means which are agreed upon are such as are not likely to prove, and do not in fact prove, effective. If once there is a conspiracy to commit murder, the case falls within s 120B, the offence under that section being the conspiracy, and not the acts by which the subject matter of the conspiracy is to be carried into effect. But if the conspiracy is merely to do an act which is not illegal, though in the hope and belief that that act may result in the death of or injury to some person, in my opinion that does not amount to a conspiracy to do an illegal act. To take an example: "if A and B agree that they will induce 'Y' to point his finger at X, believing that 'Y' is endowed with some special power which will enable him to kill X by so doing, there is no agreement to do an illegal act, and no conspiracy to commit an offence." But if the agreement is to commit the murder of X, and the first means to that end is to be to induce Y to point his finger at X, then I think the agreement being in its essence to cause the death of X and the means being subsidiary there is a conspiracy to commit an offence.

Now, it is argued here that the agreement between the parties was to cause the death of Muchkandappa by means of *bhanumati*, and by no other means. The actual *bhanumati*, which was practised by the witness Machendra as a result of this conspiracy, was certainly not witchcraft which could in the ordinary course of nature cause death. It consisted of acquiring a pig's leg, some earth wetted by his urine and a piece of cloth worn by the threatened boy, burying them in front of his house, and reciting incantations over the concoction. I agree that if the only agreement between the accused was to perform this curious act, the mere act that accused 1 and possibly some of the others, might have anticipated that the death of Muchkandappa would ensue, would not constitute an offence under s 120B. But I think there was ample evidence on which the jury could find, and that they in fact did find, that the real agreement was to cause the death of Muchkandappa, the means to be tried in the first instance being a form of witchcraft, the nature of which, as the evidence makes clear, none of the accused understood, when they entered into this conspiracy. As I think that the jury were entitled to find that there was a conspiracy to murder Muchkandappa....

Order accordingly

DPP v Nock [1978] 2 All ER 654 (HL, England)

The accused persons agreed to extract cocaine from a powder in their possession which they believed to be a mixture of cocaine and lignocaine. In fact, the powder was lignocaine hydrochloride which contained no cocaine. It was thus impossible to extract cocaine from the powder. They were nevertheless convicted of the offence of conspiracy to produce a controlled drug contrary to s 4(2) of the Misuse of Drugs Act 1971.

Lord Scarman: [The question on appeal is] better put as follows: when two or more persons agree on a course of conduct with the object of committing a criminal offence, but, unknown to them, it is not possible to achieve their object by the course of conduct agreed on, do they commit the crime of conspiracy? The question falls to be considered at common law.

... The trial judge described it simply as an agreement to produce cocaine. The Court of Appeal thought it enough that the prosecution had proved "an agreement to do an act which was forbidden by s 4 of the Misuse of Drugs Act 1971". Both descriptions are accurate, as far as they go. But neither contains any reference to the limited nature of the agreement proved: it was an agreement on a specific course of conduct with the object of producing cocaine, and limited to that course of conduct. Since it would not result in the production of cocaine, the two appellants by pursuing it could not commit the statutory offence of producing a controlled drug. The appellants, who did get a chemist to take on the impossible job of extracting cocaine from the powder, may perhaps be treated as having completed their agreed course of conduct; if so, they completed it without committing the statutory offence. Perhaps, however, it would be more accurate to treat them as having desisted before they had completed all that they had agreed to do; but it makes no difference because, had they completed all that they had agreed to do, no cocaine would have been produced.

If, therefore, their agreement, limited as it was to a specific course of conduct which could not result in the commission of the statutory offence, constituted (as the Court of Appeal held) a criminal conspiracy, the strange consequence ensues, that by agreeing on a course of conduct which was not criminal (or unlawful) the appellants were guilty of conspiring to commit a crime.

On these facts the appellants submit that the evidence reveals no "conspiracy at large", by which they mean an agreement in general terms to produce cocaine if and when they could find a suitable raw material, but only the limited agreement, to which I have referred. Counsel for the appellants concedes that, if two or more persons decide to go into business as cocaine producers, or, to take another example, as assassins for hire (eg "Murder Incorporated"), the mere fact that in the course of performing their agreement they attempt to produce cocaine from a raw material which could not possibly yield it or, in the second example, stab a corpse, believing it to be the body of a living man, would not avail them as a defence: for the performance of their general agreement would not be rendered impossible by such transient frustrations. But performance of the limited agreement proved in this case could not in any circumstances have involved the commission of the offence created by the statute....

[T]here is no logical difficulty in applying a rule that an agreement is a conspiracy to commit a statutory offence only if it is an agreement to do that which Parliament has forbidden. It is no more than the application of the principle that an *actus reus* as well as *mens rea* must be established. And in the present case there was no *actus reus*, because there was no agreement on a course of conduct forbidden by the statute. Secondly, the application of such a rule is consistent with principle. Unless the law requires the *actus reus* as well as *mens rea* to be proved, men, whether they be accused of conspiracy or attempt, will be punished for their guilty intentions alone....

The second ground of decision, the common law principle, can be summarized in words which commended themselves to all the noble and learned Lords concerned with the case. In *Percy Dalton (London) Ltd* (1949) Birkett J giving the judgment of the Court of Criminal Appeal said:

"Steps on the way to the commission of what would be a crime, if the acts were completed, may amount to attempts to commit that crime, to which, unless interrupted, they would have led; but steps on the way to the doing of something, which is thereafter done, and which is no crime, cannot be regarded as attempts to commit a crime."

In his speech Lord Hailsham LC added the rider (a logical one) to the effect "that equally steps on the way to do something which is thereafter *not* completed, but which if· done would not constitute a crime cannot be indicted as attempts to commit that crime". As in the case of the statutory ground, there is no logical difficulty in the way of applying this principle to the law relating to conspiracy provided it is recognized that conspiracy is a "preliminary" or "auxiliary" crime. And again, as with the statutory ground, common sense and justice combine to require of the law that no man should be punished criminally for the intention with which he enters an agreement unless it can also be shown that what he has agreed to do is unlawful.

The Crown's argument, as developed before your Lordships, rests, in my judgment, on a misconception of the nature of the agreement proved. This is a case not of an agreement to commit a crime capable of being committed in the way agreed on, but frustrated by a supervening event making its completion impossible, which was the Crown's submission, but of an agreement on a course of conduct which could not in any circumstances result in the statutory offence alleged, ie the offence of producing the controlled drug, cocaine.

I conclude therefore that the two parallel lines of reasoning on which this House decided *Haughton* v *Smith* (1975) apply equally to criminal conspiracy as they do to attempted crime.

Appeal allowed

With Indian law and English common law thus being broadly in accord it is likely that this is the approach that will be followed in Singapore and Malaysia. The result is that in every case there will need to be a detailed examination of the exact scope of the agreement in order to ascertain its "essence" (*Hiremath*, 1940) or the "course of conduct" (*Nock*, 1978) agreed upon. Thus, if the parties agreed to do certain acts of witchcraft, there is no conspiracy to murder, whereas if they agree to kill, using whatever means are at their disposal including witchcraft, there is a conspiracy to murder. This is little more than a semantic distinction. We agree to do certain acts of witchcraft (assuming we believe in their efficacy) because we think they will kill the victim–just as surely as if we plan to plant a bomb and thereby cause his death. Either way, we plan to kill and it is absurd to allow the ascertainment of criminal liability to depend upon the way in which we choose linguistically to formulate the nature of the agreement.

The House of Lords decision in *Nock* (1978) is similarly flawed in its reasoning. The accused in that case agreed to produce cocaine. Thus they have committed the *actus reus* of the offence and ought to have been held liable. It is simply not good enough to assert that the scope of their agreement was the narrow one of separating two substances in a powder. Why were they doing this? Were they scientists engaged in research? No. They were illicit drug producers who had agreed to produce cocaine and were doing everything in their power to achieve success in their project. Under s 120A the question would be: have they agreed to do an illegal act? Such a question has surely to be answered affirmatively. The decision in *Nock* (1978) has now been replaced in England by the Criminal Law Act 1977 which makes it clear that there will be criminal liability in such circumstances despite the alleged impossibility of the agreed objective. While this statute has no application in Singapore or Malaysia it is to be hoped that if and when this controversy raises itself in a local case the judges will focus on the wording of s 120A and interpret the provision literally. The essence of the crime is the agreement. What did the parties agree to do? Is that object of their agreement an illegal act? If so, they are clearly liable. The accused in *Nock* (1978) agreed to produce cocaine. That is an illegal act. Criminal liability for conspiracy must necessarily follow.

Part IV

Parties to crime

Chapter 16

Abetment

By KL Koh

A. Introduction

Many crimes would not be committed but for the support and encouragement of others. The law punishes an abettor in order to prevent the commission of the principal offence. Abetment involves the complicity of an abettor towards the commission of an offence, but it may not necessarily involve the actual commission of the crime abetted. It is a crime by itself (see *Barendra Kumar Ghosh*, 1925; s 108 Explanation 4). This means, for example, that the offence of abetment of murder, say, by instigation, may be complete even though the killing is not carried out. There can also be an attempted abetment, and an abetment of an abetment (s 108 Explanation 4, see below, p 318).

B. The law

1. Types of abetment

Penal Code, s 107

107. A person abets the doing of a thing who—
(a) instigates any person to do that thing;
(b) engages with one or more other person or persons in any conspiracy for the doing of that thing, if an act or illegal omission takes place in pursuance of that conspiracy, and in order to the doing of that thing; or
(c) intentionally aids, by any act or illegal omission, the doing of that thing.

Explanation 1–A person who, by wilful misrepresentation, or by wilful concealment of a material fact which he is bound to disclose, voluntarily causes or procures, or attempts to cause or procure, a thing to be done, is said to instigate the doing of that thing.

Illustration

A, a public officer, is authorised by a warrant from a court of justice to apprehend Z. B, knowing that fact and also that C is not Z, wilfully represents to A that C is Z, and thereby intentionally causes A to apprehend C. Here B abets by instigation the apprehension of C.

Explanation 2–Whoever, either prior to or at the time of the commission of an act, does anything in order to facilitate the commission of that act, and thereby facilitates the commission thereof, is said to aid the doing of that act.

Abetment may take place by instigation, conspiracy or intentional aid.

(a) Abetment by instigation

The *Shorter Oxford English Dictionary on Historical Principles* (1984) defines instigation as "[t]he action of instigating or goading; incitement, stimulation, an incentive, stimulus, spur."

In *Haji Abdul Ghani b Ishak* (1981), Raja Azlan Shah CJ, in considering abetment by instigation, said:

> It is of the essence of the offence of abetment that the abettor should substantially assist the principal offender towards the commission of the principal offence. In fact it is an essential ingredient in a prosecution for abetment that there must be some evidence to show that the abettor actively suggested or stimulated the principal offender to the act by any means of language, direct or indirect in the form of "hints, insinuations or encouragement".... The word "instigates" in s 107 of the Penal Code does not merely mean placing of temptation to do a forbidden thing but actively stimulating a person to do it....

In abetment by instigation under s 107(a), it is not necessary that the abettor should *assist* the principal offender *towards* the commission of the principal offence. In *Datuk Haji Harun b Haji Idris* (1977), Abdoolcader J said:

> Instigation consists of acts which amount to active suggestion or support or stimulation for the commission of the main act or offence. Advice can also become instigation if that advice is meant to actively suggest or stimulate the commission of an offence.

The element of active suggestion, support or stimulation on the part of the abettor in the instigation is important (see *Tee Tean Siong*, 1983, below, p 312). Raja Azlan Shah CJ in *Haji Abdul Ghani b Ishak* (1981) did mention this aspect in his judgment. Passivity either by mere acquiescence or silence does not constitute instigation. If A tells B that he wants to steal C's car and B says: "Do as you please" or simply keeps quiet, and A steals C's car, B cannot be said to have instigated A. In *Etim Ali Majumdar* (1899), it was held that influential persons, who were aware of the object of an unlawful assembly and thereby deliberately kept away from the venue in order to sympathize with the object of the assembly, were held not to be abettors.

The *actus reus* of abetment by instigation is complete as soon as the abettor has instigated the person abetted to commit the crime whether the latter consents or not, or whether, having consented, he commits the crime or not. This is clear from s 108 Explanation 2 (see below, p 318).

(i) Communication of instigation

When is instigation deemed to take effect in communication by a letter which is posted or given to a person to be handed over to the person abetted?

Isaac Paul Ratnam v The Law Society [1976] 1 MLJ 195 (PC, appeal from Singapore)

The appellant, a lawyer in Singapore, was charged with abetment by instigation in the dishonest or fraudulent removal or concealment of property under s 424 of the Penal Code. On behalf of his client he wrote to Kumuran, the general manager of Germini's branch office in KL, Malaysia instructing him to remove dishonestly five cars and other movable properties belonging to the company. The letter was sent "by hand for personal delivery".

The case concerned disciplinary proceedings under the Legal Profession Act, s 84(2)(a) (conviction implying a defect of character). One of the points raised was whether there could be instigation when the communication did not take place in Singapore but in KL, Malaysia. Section 108A of the Penal Code reads:

A person abets an offence within the meaning of this Code who, in Singapore, abets the commission of any act without and beyond Singapore which would constitute an offence if committed in Singapore.

Illustration

A, in Singapore, instigates B, a foreigner in Java, to commit murder in Java. A is guilty of abetting murder.

Lord Simon of Glaisdale: First it was said that "instigates" implies communication; there was no communication in Singapore, communication only took place when the letter was received in Kuala Lumpur: See Ranchhoddas and Thakore, *The law of Crimes* (21st edn, 1966) p 251 commenting on the similar provision of the Indian Penal Code; in consequence no criminal offence was committed within the jurisdiction of the Singapore Court....

The word "instigates" no doubt often, perhaps generally, connotes communication. But it can also be used more loosely to look at from the point of view of the alleged instigator. In this respect it is like the word "demand" in the English Theft Act 1968 s 21(1) which was considered in *Treacy* (1971). There the Court of Appeal and the majority of the House of Lords held that a demand was made when a letter of demand was written in England and that there was no requirement that it should be communicated to the person of whom the demand was made (who was abroad). This sense of "instigates" in s 107 of the Penal Code is borne out by the Illustration to s 108A: ss 107 and 108A must be construed together. The relevance of Illustrations in such a Penal Code was indicated in *Mahomed Syedol Ariffin v Yeoh Ooi Gark* (1962) where a provision of a Straits Settlements Ordinance fell for construction. At page 581 it was said:

"It is the duty of a court of law to accept, if that can be done, the illustrations given as being both of relevance and value in the construction of the text. The illustrations should in no case be rejected because they do not square with ideas possibly derived from another system of jurisprudence as to the law with which they or the sections deal. And it would require a very special case to warrant their rejection on the ground of their assumed repugnancy to the sections themselves. It would be the very last resort of construction to make any such assumption."

The Illustration to s 108A in the light of this passage in their Lordships view also completely disposes of the argument on behalf of the appellant based on *Cox v Army Council* (1963).

Appeal dismissed

In *Isaac Paul Ratnam* (1976), the Privy Council viewed the question of communication under s 107(a) read with s 108A "loosely" from the viewpoint of the instigator. It drew an analogy from the word "demand" in the English offence of blackmail (English Theft Act 1968, s 21(1)). In *Treacy* (1971), the House of Lords held that the gist of the offence of blackmail is the making of an unwarranted demand. It was held that communication of the letter of demand took place when it was posted. Applying this analogy, the offence of abetment in *Isaac Paul Ratnam* (1976) was held to be committed in Singapore when the appellant handed the letter to a person (in Singapore) to be personally delivered to Kumuran in KL, Malaysia.

The Privy Council also relied on the illustration to s 108A which states:

"A, in Singapore, instigates B, a foreigner in Java, to commit murder in Java. A is guilty of abetting murder."

The illustration is ambivalent and does not conclusively answer the question whether if a letter of instigation is personally handed by Y to Z in Singapore to be delivered to X outside Singapore, the abetment is to be regarded as having taken place in Singapore. Or, whether the abetment takes place only when the actual contents of the letter are known to X. In the illustration, the foreigner, B, could have been in Singapore when he was instigated by A in Singapore to commit murder in Java. This would clearly fall within the scope of s 108A. Whether the *actus reus* is complete the moment the letter is handed to a person to be delivered to the person abetted or whether the contents must be actually known to the person abetted is, it is submitted, one of policy. It is submitted that from the policy viewpoint the former is preferable. Section 108A is designed to prevent crimes from being committed abroad. So far as the abettor in *Isaac Paul Ratnam* was concerned, there was nothing more to be done after the letter was handed over to the person in Singapore.

(ii)   Instigation with reference to thing done

An instigation must refer directly to the thing done and not to the thing that was likely to have been done by the person instigated.

Baby John v State of Travancore-Cochin (1953) Cri LJ 1273 (HC, Travancore, Cochin, India)(Kunhi Raman CJ and Subramonia Iyer J)

The 1st accused was convicted, inter alia, of abetment of offences under ss 307, 324, 333 and 427 of the Travancore Penal Code (*in pari materia* with the Penal Codes of Singapore and of Malaysia). He had exhorted to the members of an unlawful assembly to use violence to overcome any resistence offered by the Army or the Police.

Judgment of court: In interpreting the meaning of the word "instigate" in the case that is reported in–*Amruddin Salebhoy Tyabjee*, (1923), the learned Chief Justice Macleod CJ in the course of his judgment quotes an extract from *Russell on Crimes*....

> "A person is said to instigate another to an act when he actively suggests or stimu-
> lates him to the act by any means or language direct or indirect, whether it takes
> [the] form of express solicitation or of hints, insinuation or encouragement." (at page
> 46 of the report).

Applying the meaning of the word "instigate" as explained in *Russell on Crimes* it is not necessary that express and direct words should be used to instigate what exactly should be done by the persons to whom directions were given by a person in the position of the 1st accused. In the evidence in this case of PWs 75, 43 and 78 who have taken to the idea conveyed in the directions given by the 1st accused to his audience, there is sufficient material for drawing the inference that there was instigation on the part of the 1st accused to the members of the procession and to the leaders of the procession that they must resist any opposition that may be offered by the Police or by the Army and see that the procession goes from the point where it was to start and reaches Quilon. When there was a prohibitory order issued by the District Magistrate, Quilon it is rea-sonable to presume that the 1st accused would have realized that so long as law and order were maintained in the State, the authorities concerned would not permit the ban to be ignored and processions taken which were expressly prohibited by the District Magistrate. It is easy to infer that the meaning con-veyed by the exhortation made by the 1st accused was that there must be force used for resisting any obstacles placed in their way by the Police or by the Army. In other words he was instigating the assembly to use force if they found that there was opposition to their progress towards Quilon.

We are here concerned with abetment by instigation and the wording of the definition has to be carefully noted. It says: "A person abets the doing of a thing, who instigates any person to do that thing". Considering this definition strictly, the instigation must have reference to the thing that was done and not to the thing that was likely to have been done by the person who is instigated. It is only if this condition is fulfilled that a person can be guilty of abetment by instigation. In the present case there is no evidence to support a finding that the throwing of stones at PW 5 and other members of the Police party at the point at which the unlawful assembly launched a joint attack upon the Police was specifically instigated by the 1st accused. Therefore, the finding that the 1st accused is liable for abetment of all the acts of violence or of the individual acts of violence done by the unlawful assembly at the place at which the Police Inspector (PW 5) was brutally assaulted by the members of the mob, cannot be upheld. But there is sufficient evidence to support a finding that as active suggestion of resistance by violence was made and the members and leaders of the unlawful assembly were called upon to indulge in such violence at the stage at which the 1st accused made his exhortation to his followers. If that conclusion is established by the evidence in this case (and we have doubt that the evidence is sufficient for establishing this) then the result is the 1st accused has become liable for abetment of the offence of rioting under ss 138 and 139, Travancore PC. According to s 138:

"Whenever force or violence is used by an unlawful assembly or by any member thereof, in prosecution of common object of such assembly, every member of such assembly is guilty of the offence of rioting."

According to s 139:

"Whoever is guilty of rioting shall be punished with imprisonment of either description for a term which may extend to two years, or with fine or with both."

In the present case, the common object of the assembly was to march in a Jatha or procession from the office of the Union from the vicinity of which the procession started, and proceed without stopping up to Quilon breaking the conditions imposed upon the residents of the locality in the proclamation that was promulgated by the District Magistrate, Quilon. The abetment of which the 1st accused is guilty consisted in his instigating the members of the unlawful assembly to use force or violence for overcoming any resistance offered by the Army or by the Police with the object of making them break up and desist. This is a natural inference that can be gathered from the evidence of the witnesses who have been believed by the learned trial Judge. The offence committed by the 1st accused is therefore abetment by instigation of rioting. Since there is no specific punishment provided for such abetment according to the Travancore Penal Code, the punishment under s 139 for the offence of rioting can be awarded to the abettor. In these circumstances we set aside the conviction for abetment of the offence under ss 307, 324, 332, 333 and 427 and find that what has been made out in the evidence called for the prosecution is abetment of the offence of rioting and not abetment of the specific acts of violence which were actually done by the members of the unlawful assembly when they become liable for rioting at the point at which PW 5 was brutally assaulted. There cannot be any doubt that he did walk with the members of the assembly after it had become an unlawful assembly up to Sankaramangalam junction and he has incurred liability for the offence. We also find that he has become liable for abetting the offence of rioting. He is accordingly convicted for this offence 99/39 and we direct that he shall undergo a sentence of rigorous imprisonment for one year and pay a fine of Rs 300 (three hundred rupees)....
   The appeal is allowed to this extent.

Order accordingly

The court in *Baby John* (1953) acquitted the 1st accused of the specific acts of violence committed by the members of the unlawful assembly, viz s 307 (attempt to murder), s 324 (voluntarily causing hurt by dangerous weapons or means), s 332 (voluntarily causing hurt to deter a public servant from his duty), s 333 (voluntarily causing grievous hurt to deter public servant from his duty) and s 427 (committing mischief and thereby causing damage). Unfortunately the court overlooked s 111 (see below, p 324) which deals with the liability of an abettor when an act is abetted and a different act is done, and s 113 (see below, p 325) concerning the liability of an abettor for an offence which is different from that intended by the abettor, provided he knew such offence is likely to be caused.

(iii) Mens rea of abettor and of person abetted

The mental elements of intention or knowledge are required for abetment by instigation. The offence of abetment by instigation depends on the *mens rea* of the abettor and not on the knowledge or intention of the person abetted. It is therefore not necessary that the person abetted should have the same guilty intention or knowledge as the abettor or should have any guilty intention or knowledge in committing the act. Indeed it is irrelevant whether the person abetted should be capable by law of committing an offence (s 108 Explanation 3). The abettor is liable for the abetment.

(b) Abetment by conspiracy

Until 1941 conspiracy under the Penal Code was governed by s 107(b). By the Straits Settlements Penal Code (Amendment) Ordinance 1941 (Ord 12 of 1941) the substantive offence of criminal conspiracy under ss 120A and 120B, based on the Indian Penal Code, was incorporated into the SS Penal Code. Consequently, s 107(b) was amended by deletion of the words "[s]econdly–Conspires with any other person to do that thing; or," and substituting the present wording in s 107(b). (For the position in Malaysia, see the FMS Penal Code.) The Indian Law Commission (42nd Report, 1971) recommended the repeal of s 107(b) of the Indian Penal Code.

(i) Distinction between criminal conspiracy and abetment by conspiracy

The law on criminal conspiracy under ss 120A and 120B is discussed in ch 15. The distinction between criminal conspiracy under s 120A and abetment by conspiracy under s 107 was pointed out by the Supreme Court in India in *NMMY Momin* (1971):

> Criminal conspiracy postulates an agreement between two or more persons to do, or cause to be done, an illegal act or an act which is not illegal, by illegal means. It differs from other offences in that mere agreement is made an offence even if no step is taken to carry out that agreement. Though there is close association of conspiracy with incitement and abetment the substantive offence of criminal conspiracy is somewhat wider in amplitude than abetment by conspiracy as contemplated by s 107, IPC.

Abetment by conspiracy is confined to conspiracies to commit an offence. Unlike criminal conspiracy under s 120A abetment by conspiracy requires some further act done pursuant to the conspiracy. (See s 108 Explanation 5, below, p 318.)

The following are the essential elements of abetment by conspiracy:

(1) the person abetting must engage, with one or more other persons in a conspiracy;

(2)   the conspiracy must be for doing the thing abetted; and
(3)   an act or illegal omission must take place in pursuance of the con-
      spiracy in order to the doing of that thing.

(ii) Mens rea of abettor

Abetment by conspiracy postulates a knowledge of the abettor that he
is "engaged" in a conspiracy to do a thing by an act or illegal omission.
Gour (1982, Vol 1) points out that it is not necessary that all co-conspirators should be equally informed as to the details of the conspiracy,
but they must be aware of the general purpose of the plot and also that
it is unlawful.

(c) Abetment by intentional aid

This is dealt with by s 107(c) and Explanation 2 of s 107 (see above,
pp 305–306).

The *actus reus* of abetment by intentional aid may consist of assisting the commission of an offence either by doing an act or illegally
omitting to do it. There can also be intentional aid by facilitating the
commission of an act either prior to or at the time of commission (see
s 107 Explanation 2).

(i) Mere attendance at show

Is mere attendance at a show an "act"?

PP v Tee Tean Siong (1963) 29 MLJ 201 (HC, Kota Bahru, Malaya)

The accused persons were attending a "blue film" show. They were
charged under s 109 (ie punishment for abetment, see below, p 323)
and s 292(a) of the Penal Code for exhibiting "blue films".

Hashim J: I should say *prima facie* mere attendance at the show, assuming
there was an actual filming at the time of the raid, cannot amount to abetment
which is defined in terms as an act in relation to the thing which is charged.
If the charge is of exhibition one fails to see how the audience can be regarded
as abetting the exhibition. They participate in the exhibition but that is not
abetting. Of course, it might be said that without an audience there can be no
exhibition, but it is possible to have a picture exhibited to an empty house.
That is why, in the normal case, it is a member of the audience who provides
the best evidence against one who is charged with exhibition. If, on the other
hand, there is any cogent evidence that a few persons got together and incited
or encouraged the possessor of the film to give a show by actually offering
him payment in circumstances in which but for such incitement or encouragement there would have been no show, or where he provides knowingly the
accommodation for such exhibition, such act will be caught by section 109 of
the Penal Code and not otherwise. Moreover, it has got to be a *public* exhibition and without that ingredient there is no offence at all.

In my view, therefore "blue films" should not be charged under s 292(a), or s 109 and s 292(a)....

> *Finding and sentence reversed;*
> *Accused discharged*

(ii) Aiding by illegal omission

Where abetment is by omission, the omission must be an illegal one. The word "illegal" is defined in s 43 of the Penal Code (see ch 3).

Chuan Keat Chan Ltd v PP [1972] 2 MLJ 57 (HC, Ipoh, Malaysia)

The first appellant was charged under s 120(2) of the Road Traffic Ordinance for failing to comply with condition No 6 of a "C" carrier licence which requires an attendant at the rear of the vehicle, so placed that he can signal to over-taking traffic. The second appellant, the driver of the vehicle, was charged with abetting the offence of failing to carry an attendant at the rear of the vehicle, punishable under s 120(2) of the Road Traffic Ordinance, read with s 109 of the Penal Code.

Sharma J: I will deal with the charge against the second appellant first as it is the simpler of the two charges to deal with....

There was no evidence of any instigation by the second appellant nor of any conspiracy between the two appellants. The only part of s 107 which could if at all apply would be the third clause thereof. In order however to constitute an offence of abetment by omission, the omission must be an illegal one. In other words, there must be a duty to act. The words "illegal omission" in the third clause of s 107 have reference to an intention of "aiding the doing of a thing". There seems nothing in our legislation which casts a duty on the driver of a goods vehicle not to drive the said vehicle without an attendant. There was consequently no evidence of abetment against the second appellant. The learned magistrate failed to consider what was required of the prosecution to prove a charge under s 109 of the Penal Code. The charge was not for using a goods vehicle without there being an attendant on it as required by one of the conditions of the licence granted to the first appellant but was a charge for abetment. The appeal of the second appellant is consequently allowed and the order of the learned magistrate set aside and conviction quashed. The fine, if paid, is to be refunded to him.

> *Order accordingly*

An illegal omission may involve a breach of a *legal obligation*. In *Latifkhan* (1895), it was held that as every police officer is bound to shelter persons in custody and to arrest persons committing assaults which are likely to cause grievous bodily hurt, an omission to perform this duty would result in an abetment by omission. To prove abetment by illegal omission, it must be shown that the accused intentionally aided the commission of an act by not doing it. In *Latifkhan* (1895) the abetment was the non-arrest. In *Chuan Keat Chan* (1972), the second appellant was *only* the driver; it was the first appellant who was granted a "C" carrier's licence and it was he who was under a legal obligation to comply with condition 6. As the court pointed out there was nothing in the Road Traffic Ordinance which obliged the *driver* of a goods vehicle to drive with an attendant. Hence there can be no abetment by illegal omission. (See also *Tan Poh Keah*, 1883.)

(iii)   Contemporaneous or prior act

Explanation 2 to s 107 requires that the facilitation of the commission of an act by aiding must occur prior to or at the time of the commission of the act.

Varatharajalu v PP (1960) 26 MLJ 158 (HC, Raub, Malaya)

The appellant was a clerk in the Bentong Sub-Treasury and he received certain cheques issued by the 1st accused in payment of royalties for the extraction of timber. The cheques were dishonoured. Contrary to his duty, the appellant failed to inform the District Officer until nine months later. If the appellant had informed the District Officer at the due time, the latter could have prevented the further extraction of timber until payment was made.

Hepworth J: But the most pertinent objection of all was that the action of the appellant in not returning these dishonoured cheques to the District Forest Officer as soon as they were received was an action which had taken place at a point of time after and not contemporaneously with or before that at which Toh Wai Teng had done the acts which were alleged in the charges to constitute the offences which the appellant was supposed to have abetted. It could not accordingly be said that the actions of the appellant whatever their motive, in the absence of any evidence of contemporaneous or prior complicity, were actions abetting the actions of the 1st accused which were alleged to justify the charges of cheating the District Forest Officer. The offence of abetment corresponds as nearly as one word can be said to correspond to another to the offence which is known in England of being an "accessory before the fact". It has no reference to "accessories after the fact".

(iv)   Liability of abettor dependent on liability of person abetted

In abetment by instigation it is clearly not necessary that the offence abetted be committed. However, in abetment by intentional aid, must the person abetted be guilty of the offence charged, before the alleged abettor can be liable for the abetment of the offence?

Faguna Kanta Nath v State of Assam AIR (1959) SC 673 (SC, India)

The complainant was taking paddy to the market when he was stopped by a paddy checking inspector, Khalilur Rahman, who was accompanied by the appellant, Faguna Kanta Nath and three others. Khalilur Rahman demanded a sum of money as bribe threatening that he would otherwise confiscate the paddy.

The Special Judge convicted Khalilur Rahman under s 161 of the Indian Penal Code, and the appellant for abetment of that offence. On appeal to the High Court, it was held that the evidence was not strong enough to prove payment to Khalilur Rahman. His conviction was set aside. So far as the appellant was concerned, the court held that money was taken by him for payment to Khalilur Rahman and whether he actually paid it to him or not the offence fell under s 165A of the Indian Penal Code and the appellant was guilty under that section. The appellant appealed.

JL Kapur J: The main argument raised on behalf of the appellant is that as Khalilur Rahman has been acquitted, on the facts and circumstances of this case the conviction of the appellant for abetment cannot be sustained....

Under the Indian law for an offence of abetment it is not necessary that the offence should have been committed. A man may be guilty as an abettor whether the offence is committed or not. Section 165A is as follows:

> "S 165A. Whoever abets any offence punishable under section 161 or section 165, whether or not that offence is committed in consequence of the abetment, shall be punished with imprisonment of either description for a term which may extend to three years or with fine or with both."

Therefore for a person to be guilty of abetment of an offence under s 161, it is not necessary that the offence should have been committed.... It is not suggested that there was any instigation by the appellant for the commission of the offence. Further the circumstances proved against the appellant did not bring the case under the second part of s 107 because it is not alleged that there was any conspiracy and a charge of conspiracy must necessarily fail if the other alleged conspirator is acquitted: See *Plummer* (1902) which has received the approval of this Court in *Topandas* (1955).

In either of these cases it is immaterial whether the person instigated commits the offence or not or the persons conspiring together actually carry out the object of conspiracy.

There then remains the third part of s 107 that is abetment by aid. A person abets by aiding when by the commission of an act he intends to facilitate and does facilitate the commisssion thereof. By the acquittal of Khalilur Rahman the High Court must be deemed to have held that there was no offence under s 161....

In the present case the person who demanded the illegal gratification for allowing the carts to proceed was Khalilur Rahman who had the authority to do or not to do a particular act and all that the appellant is alleged to have done was to receive the money at the instance of Khalilur Rahman for counting and then paid the money to him. It is not the prosecution case that the appellant abetted the offence by instigating Khalilur Rahman to demand the illegal gratification; nor has the prosecution set up or proved a case of conspiracy between the appellant and Khalilur Rahman for the commission of an offence under s 161. On the findings of the Court the appellant received the money for and on behalf of Khalilur Rahman and the evidence of the complainant is that Khalilur Rahman had asked him to hand over the money to the appellant. If Khalilur Rahman is acquitted and therefore the offence under s 161 is held not to have been committed, then in this case no question of intentionally aiding by any act or omission the commission of the offence arises....

We are of the opinion that on the facts found and circumstances established in this case and as Khalilur Rahman has been acquitted the appellant's conviction cannot be upheld. We therefore allow this appeal and set aside the order of conviction. The bail bonds shall also stand discharged.

Appeal allowed

Shelly Wright, "Attempt and Abandonment where there are Several Participants in the Commission of a Crime" (unpublished)

One difficulty with abetment by aiding is whether or not it is necessary that the principal offence be successfully completed before a charge of aiding can succeed. Explanation 2 under s 107 says that aiding occurs whenever anyone does anything to facilitate the commission of an act "and thereby facilitates the commission thereof". Cases in both India and Malaysia state that before a person can be convicted of abetment by aiding, there must be an offence to which the abetment can attach. Section 108, Explanation 2 however provides:

> "To constitute the offence of abetment it is not necessary that the act abetted should be committed, or that the effect requisite to constitute the offence should be caused."

The two illustrations which follow refer to instigation only. Nevertheless it has been stated that abetment by conspiracy as well as by instigation may occur where the offence has not been committed. It has also been stated that "the commission of an offence is a prerequisite [to aiding] otherwise the question of aiding by an act or illegal omission does not arise". It is not clear from the literal wording of ss 107 to 109 of the Penal Code and the accompanying explanations and illustrations that in order for aiding to occur an offence must have been committed. Section 107 defines aiding of "the doing of that thing". Explanation 2 which follows talks about facilitating the commission of "that act". Sections 108 and 109 however speak directly of the abetment of an offence. Are the words "thing" or "act" synonymous with "offence"? It seems to the author that it is not necessary that an offence has been completed for a charge of aiding to arise so long as the aider has intentionally, by some act or illegal omission, facilitated the commission of an act towards the commission of an offence. Section 108, including Explanation 2, does not distinguish between the different types of abetment in determining when abetment may occur. In the Malaysian High Court decision of *Datuk Tan Cheng Swee* (1979) Justice Ajaib Singh in defining aiding quotes the English decision of *National Coal Board* v *Gamble* (1958) where it is stated that before a person could be said to aid "it must be shown that the unlawful act has been committed". This may be good law in England, however, the Penal Code was drafted at least partly to simplify the criminal law and remove some of the complications which have developed in English law. Aiding, despite authority to the contrary, does not appear to depend, by a strict reading of the Penal Code, on the commission of an offence. Nevertheless, although there does not appear to be any local decisions on the point, the Malaysian and Indian (and English) position would most likely be followed in Singapore.

(v) Mens rea of abettor

The *mens rea* in abetment by intentional aid is more complicated than that of abetment by instigation or conspiracy. Such abetment requires the abettor to assist either by an act, omission or facilitation the doing of a thing towards the commission of an offence or the offence itself.

The initiation of aiding could come from the actual offender. Must the abettor who is aiding know the offender's *mens rea*? If so, to what extent?

In *Datuk Tan Cheng Swee* (1979) Ajaib J, in considering the *mens rea* under s 107(c), ie intentional aid, stated:

> Briefly to constitute the offence of aiding and abetting the prosecution must prove intention on the part of the abettor to aid and he must be shown to have known the circumstances constituting the crime at the time when he voluntarily does a positive act of assistance.

In *Ramabatar Agarwalla* (1983), a dealer in high-speed diesel oil who had been served with a notice under cl 3 of the Orissa Petroleum Products (Sale by Dealers) Order 1979, requiring him to maintain a specified quantity as minimum reserve, failed to maintain the minimum reserve by selling off oil in excess to consumers. Thus he committed an offence under s 7 of the Essential Commodities Act. The accused, a consumer, was charged with abetment of the offence by purchasing the diesel oil. There was no allegation against the accused (consumer) that he was aware of the notice alleged to have been issued to the dealer nor was there any allegation of intentional aid by the consumer. The Orissa High Court held that the consumer could not be guilty of abetment of the offence under s 7 of the Act as the consumer was not expected to have any knowledge of the notice served on the dealer or about the stock position. The law imposed no obligation on the accused to enquire and ascertain. Accordingly, it was held that compliance with the notice was a duty imposed solely on the dealer and not the consumer, Patnaik J stated:

> [M]ere giving of an aid will not make the act an abetment of an offence, if the person who gave the aid *did not know* or has *no reason* to *believe* that an offence was being committed or contemplated.

Hence, if the abettor does not know that what he is aiding is towards the commission of an offence, he is not liable as an abettor. Mere knowledge of surrounding circumstances may also be insufficient for abetment by intentional aid. (See *Datuk Tan Cheng Swee*, 1979.)

2. Definition of "abettor"

Penal Code, s 108

108. A person abets an offence who abets either the commission of an offence, or the commission of an act which would be an offence, if committed by a person capable by law of committing an offence with the same intention or knowledge as that of the abettor.

Explanation 1–The abetment of the illegal omission of an act may amount to an offence, although the abettor may not himself be bound to do that act.

Explanation 2–To constitute the offence of abetment, it is not necessary that the act abetted should be committed, or that the effect requisite to constitute the offence should be caused.

Illustrations

(a) A instigates B to murder C. B refuses to do so. A is guilty of abetting B to commit murder.

(b) A instigates B to murder D. B, in pursuance of the instigation, stabs D. D recovers from the wound. A is guilty of instigating B to commit murder.

Explanation 3–It is not necessary that the person abetted should be capable by law of commiting an offence, or that he should have the same guilty intention or knowledge as that of the abettor, or any guilty intention or knowledge.

Illustrations

(a) A, with a guilty intention, abets a child or a lunatic to commit an act which would be an offence if committed by a person capable by law of committing an offence, and having the same intention as A. Here A, whether the act is committed or not, is guilty of abetting an offence.

(b) A, with the intention of murdering Z, instigates B, a child under 7 years of age, to do an act which causes Z's death. B, in consequence of the abetment, does the act, and thereby causes Z's death. Here, though B was not capable by law of committing an offence, A is liable to be punished in the same manner as if B had been capable by law of committing an offence and had committed murder, and he is therefore subject to the punishment of death.

(c) A instigates B to set fire to a dwelling-house. B, in consequence of the unsoundness of his mind, being incapable of knowing the nature of the act, or that he is doing what is wrong or contrary to law, sets fire to the house in consequence of A's instigation. B has committed no offence, but A is guilty of abetting the offence of setting fire to a dwelling-house, and is liable to the punishment provided for that offence.

(d) A, intending to cause a theft to be committed, instigates B to take property belonging to Z out of Z's possession. A induces B to believe that the property belongs to A. B takes the property out of Z's possession, in good faith believing it to be A's property. B, acting under this misconception, does not take dishonestly, and therefore does not commit theft. But A is guilty of abetting theft, and is liable to the same punishment as if B had committed theft.

Explanation 4–The abetment of an offence being an offence, the abetment of such an abetment is also an offence.

Illustration

A instigates B to instigate C to murder Z. B accordingly instigates C to murder Z, and C commits that offence in consequence of B's instigation. B is liable to be punished for his offence with the punishment for murder; and as A instigated B to commit the offence A is also liable to the same punishment.

Explanation 5–It is not necessary to the commission of the offence of abetment by conspiracy that the abettor should concert the offence with the person who commits it. It is sufficient if he engages in the conspiracy in pursuance of which the offence is committed.

Illustration

A concerts with B a plan for poisoning Z. It is agreed that A shall administer the poison. B then explains the plan to C, mentioning that a third person is to administer the poison, but without mentioning A's name. C agrees to procure the poison, and procures and delivers it to B for the purpose of its being used in the manner explained. A administers the poison; Z dies in consequence. Here, though A and C have not conspired together, yet C has been engaged in the conspiracy in pursuance of which Z has been murdered. C has therefore committed the offence defined in this section, and is liable to the punishment for murder.

(a) Scope of ss 108 and 109

The scope of ss 108 and 109 (see below, p 323) read with s 40 of the Penal Code was considered in *Mirza Khan* (1947).

PP v Mirza Khan (1947) 13 MLJ 526 (HC, Malayan Union)

(The facts appear in the judgment.)

Spenser-Wilkinson J: In this case the accused, a member of the Armed Forces within the meaning of the exception in the definition of "person" in s 2 of the Proclamation 50, is charged *inter alia* with having abetted the act of carrying arms committed by a detective in the Police Force. The charge is laid under s 109 of the Penal Code and s 3(1) of the Public Order and Safety Proclamation.

A preliminary objection has been raised to this charge upon two main grounds. The first is that the abetment of an offence under the Proclamation is made an offence by s 6 of the same Proclamation and that this provision impliedly repeals the provisions of the Penal Code relating to abetment so far as those provisions refer to offences under the Proclamation. It is argued that s 6, having provided for abetment of offences under the Proclamation, no other provisions can be used; and as this section does not apply to members of the Armed Forces the accused in this case cannot be liable thereunder. The second ground of objection to the charge is that the person abetted in this case being a member of the Police Force and therefore also exempt from the provisions of the Proclamation, the carrying of arms by him was no offence, so that there was no offence which could be abetted and the accused cannot be liable.

Dealing with the first objection, I am of opinion that s 6 of the Public Order and Safety Proclamation does not effect a repeal of any part of the Penal Code. There does not seem to me to be any inconsistency between the provisions of this Proclamation and the provisions of the Penal Code relating to abetment, and I can see nothing in the Proclamation as a whole to indicate any intention to repeal or override any of the existing provisions of the criminal law. The section in question is more drastic than was the law before the Proclamation was passed and not only deals with attempts and abetment but also makes it punishable for any person having knowledge of an offence to fail to report it. I think the intention was to give special facilities to deal with accessories of all kinds in respect of the special offences dealt with by the Proclamation. It is quite common in the criminal law to find that an act or omission is punishable in different ways under different provisions of the law and I see no reason why the provisions of s 6 of the Proclamation and the provisions relating to abetment in the Penal Code should not stand side by side.

The result is that a member of the Forces, although not himself liable under s 6 of the Proclamation, may be liable for abetment or an attempt under the Penal Code. This objection therefore fails.

The second point turns upon the construction of ss 108, 109 and 40 of the Penal Code. Section 108 reads as follows:

> "A person abets an offence who abets either the commission of an offence, or the commission of an act which would be an offence, if committed by a person capable by law of committing an offence with the same intention or knowledge as that of the abettor."

It is clear that the act of the accused could not amount to abetting the commission of an offence within the meaning of the first part of this section because the carrying of arms by a detective, who is a member of the Police Force, is not an offence. The next question therefore is whether the case falls within the second branch of s 108. Was the act of the detective in carrying this arm an "act which would be an offence if committed by a person capable by law of committing an offence with the same intention or knowledge as that of the abettor?" Were it not for the provisions of s 40 of the Penal Code I would be prepared to hold that it was such an act. Illustration (d) to Explanation 3 to s 108 is an example of an act which would have been an offence but for circumstances peculiar to the person who committed the act, in the same way that a detective who carried arms would be guilty of an offence but for the particular fact that he is a member of the Police Force....

By reason of s 40 of the Penal Code, however, the expression "offence" in s 108 denotes only an offence punishable under the Code. And it is only by virtue of s 108 that the abetment of an act which is not itself punishable can be made punishable under s 109. The latter section punishes anyone who abets any "offence", which here means an offence against the Penal Code or any other law. Section 108 has the effect of extending the meaning of the expression "abetting an offence" by including in that expression the abetment of acts which are not, but which in certain circumstances would be, offences under the Penal Code itself. It does not extend it to include the abetment of acts which are not offences but which might in certain circumstances be offences against laws other than the Penal Code.

The results which flow from s 40 giving a different meaning to the word "offence" in ss 108 and 109 seem at first sight somewhat peculiar. I must assume, however, that the difference is intentional.

The result in my opinion is that a member of the Armed Forces or of the Police Force may be liable for abetting the offence of carrying arms if the person abetted is not a member of the Armed Forces or the Police but cannot be made liable for abetting the act of carrying arms by any person who is a member of the Armed Forces or of the Police.

The charge against the accused in this case under s 109 of the Penal Code and s 3(1) of the Public Order and Safety Proclamation is therefore bad.

Preliminary objection upheld

Dealing with the second objection in the case, Spencer-Wilkinson J pointed out that the word "offence" in s 40(1) of the Penal Code denotes only an offence punishable under the Code, unlike s 40(2) which provides that "offence" denotes a thing punishable under the Code or under *any other law*. As s 109 (but not s 108) is expressly mentioned in s 40(2), the learned judge came to the conclusion that s 108 has no application in determining whether or not the act of the detective in carrying the arms was an "act which would be an offence if committed by a person capable by law of committing an offence with the same intention or knowledge of the abettor". Consequently, the accused was held not liable for abetting the carrying of arms by the detective as under the Public Order and Safety Proclamation he (the detective) was within an exempted class of persons who were permitted to carry arms.

It is to be noted that s 109 deals only with the question of punishment of an abettor and is not a "substantive" section. The phrase "[w]hoever abets any offence" in s 109 must refer back to the definition of an abettor in s 108. It is submitted that s 108 applies to an offence not only under the Code but also *under any other law* via s 109 read with s 40(2) of the Penal Code.

Section 108 provides for abetment of an act which would be an offence, if committed by a person capable by law of committing an offence. The accompanying Explanation 3 and Illustrations deal with persons abetted who are incapable of committing an offence by reason of infancy (s 82) or unsound mind (s 84) under the General Exceptions in the Penal Code. Here, the abettor is liable for the full offence even though the person abetted is not liable. What would be the position of an abettor if the person abetted could plead the special exceptions under s 300 Exceptions 1 to 7, thereby reducing the offence from murder to culpable homicide not amounting to murder? Would the abettor be liable for murder or culpable homicide not amounting to murder?

BJ Brown "Diminished Responsibility" (1961) 3 Mal LR 331, 334–335

"What," it may be asked, "would be the position under the Singapore Penal Code if X abets Y in the perpetration of what, had not Y been found to have been suffering from diminished responsibility, would have amounted to murder?"

The clear terms of s 109 of the Penal Code render X (despite his murderous intention) guilty of no more than culpable homicide not amounting to murder–the offence of Y, the actual killer; for "whoever abets any offence shall, if the act abetted is committed in consequence of the abetment, and no express provision is made by this Code for the punishment of such abetment, be punished with the punishment provided *for the offence*."

Against this it can be argued that where X, manifests eg a murderous intentions, abets a child, a lunatic or any other "innocent agent" to kill on his behalf, he is clearly guilty of murder [s 10 and the Illustrations (a), (b), (c) and (d) to Explanation 3 thereof]. But it would be stretching the doctrine of diminished responsibility too far in favour of the killer and his abettor to regard the former as an "innocent agent" in the same sense as a person who would qualify for the operation of, for instance, ss 82, 83, 84, 85 and 86 of the Penal Code. For a person suffering from "substantial impairment of mind" may avail himself of the palliative defence of diminished responsibility even though he has committed an offence *prima facie* within one of the four descriptions of murder under s 300, and was at the time of the commission a sober adult capable of understanding the nature of the act, that it was wrong or contrary to law and that it was not done under any misconception of fact. In no sense of the term can such a person be described as an "innocent agent".

Illustration (f) to Exception 1 to s 300 may also be invoked to support the case against X's conviction for the less serious offence, under s 109. This illustration refers to the defence of provocation:

Z strikes B. B is by this provocation excited to violent rage. A, a bystander, intending to take advantage of B's rage, and to cause him to kill Z, puts a knife into B's hand for that purpose. B kills Z with the knife. *Here B may have committed only culpable homicide, but A is guilty of murder.*

However, despite the several ways in which diminished responsibility resembles provocation, there is some support (in the maxim *expressio unius est exclusio alterius*) for the claim that the application of Illustration (f) should not be extended to cases falling outside Exception 1.

The possibility of such a conflict arising before the courts of Singapore could have been avoided by the simple expedient of adopting the words of the fourth subsection to s 2 of the English provision as a Proviso to Exception 7 to s 300 of the Penal Code:—*abundans cautela non nocet.*

[See Gillian Douglas, 1983, below, ch 17, p 348.]

(b) Abetment of an abetment

Under s 108 Explanation 4, the phrase "abetment of an offence being an offence" does not mean that the offence abetted must be actually committed. It means that when the abetment of an offence is by definition or description an offence, then the abetment of such abetment is also an offence.

Srilal Chamaria v Emperor AIR (1919) Cal 654 (HC, Calcutta, India)

One Srilal, an agent or partner of one B, was charged under ss 448, 453 and 430 of the Indian Penal Code. Srilal approached Karuna, the bench clerk of a Presidency Magistrate, to incite him to instigate the Magistrate to take a bribe and to acquit B. Karuna then approached the Magistrate and informed him of the matter. Karuna subsequently acted as a spy of the police and received such gratification to entrap Srilal to get him arrested. When Srilal handed over the bribe to Karuna to be handed to the Magistrate, a Police Inspector, who was concealed behind a curtain, seized the money. Srilal was then charged under s 161 (offence relating to a public servant taking a gratification) and s 109 of the Indian Penal Code (ie punishment for abetment).

One of the issues was whether for s 108 Explanation 4 to apply the abetment of an offence must be actually committed, as no bribe was actually offered to the Magistrate.

Fletcher J: There seems to have been a clear incitement by Srilal of Karuna to instigate the Magistrate to accept a bribe, which Srilal then handed over to Karuna. The question is whether on these facts the conviction of Srilal can be supported. The answer depends on the meaning of ss 107, 108, 109 and 116 of the Penal Code. No bribe was actually offered to the Magistrate. It was argued on behalf of the defence that the Code does not make it an offence for a man to instigate another to instigate the commission of bribery unless the second abetment is actually committed. Under s 107 a person abets the doing of a thing who instigates any person to do that thing. Section 108 defines what is meant by the abetment of an offence. There are five explanations to this section. The second explanation provides that to constitute the offence of abetment, it is not necessary that the act abetted should be committed or that the effect requisite to constitute the offence should be caused.

Expl 4 is in the following terms:

"The abetment of an offence being an offence, the abetment of such an abetment is also an offence."

The prosecution read the explanation as follows:

"When the abetment of an offence is an offence, the abetment of such an abetment is also an offence."

Both Richardson and Shamsul Huda, JJ, adopted this view. On consideration I am of the same opinion. As Richardson, J, points out in his judgment, the words "when the abetment of an offence is an offence" do not mean "when an abetment of an offence is actually committed." They mean when the abetment of an offence is by definition or description an offence under the Code, that is when an abetment of an offence is punishable under s 109 or s 116 or some other provision of the Code, then the abetment of such abetment is also an offence.

Now, if that be the true reading of Expl 4, s 108, there can, to my mind, be no doubt about the correctness of the conviction of Srilal. Srilal, when he handed over on 5th February Rs 2,500 committed a distinct incitement of Karuna to instigate the Magistrate to accept a bribe. It makes no difference in the guilt of the abettor if the agent

"falls in with the plans of the abettor, knowing his criminal purpose, but intending to cause its detection."

[Mayne's *Criminal Law* (2nd edn, 1901) p 469, *Troylukho Nath Chowdhry* (1878)]. In the circumstances, I hold that the appellant Srilal was rightly convicted and accordingly dismiss his appeal. The appellant must surrender and serve out his sentence.

Appeal dismissed

[See ch 23 below, p 540.]

C. Punishment of abettor

Penal Code, ss 109–114

109. Whoever abets any offence shall, if the act abetted is committed in consequence of the abetment, and no express provision is made by this Code for the punishment of such abetment, be punished with the punishment provided for the offence.

Explanation–An act or offence is said to be committed in consequence of abetment, when it is committed in consequence of the instigation, or in pursuance of the conspiracy, or with the aid which constitutes the abetment.

Illustrations

(a) A offers a bribe to B, a public servant, as a reward for showing A some favour in the exercise of B's official functions. B accepts the bribe. A has abetted the offence defined in section 161.

(b) A instigates B to give false evidence. B, in consequence of the instigation, commits that offence. A is guilty of abetting that offence, and is liable to the same punishment as B.

(c) A and B conspire to poison Z. A, in pursuance of the conspiracy, procures the poison and delivers it to B, in order that he may administer it to Z. B, in pursuance of the conspiracy, administers the poison to Z, in A's absence and thereby causes Z's death. Here B is guilty of murder. A is guilty of abetting that offence by conspiracy, and is liable to the punishment for murder.

110.   Whoever abets the commission of an offence shall, if the person abetted does the act with a different intention or knowledge from that of the abettor, be punished with the punishment provided for the offence which would have been committed if the act had been done with the intention or knowledge of the abettor and with no other.

111.   When an act is abetted and a different act is done, the abettor is liable for the act done, in the same manner, and to the same extent, as if he had directly abetted it:

Provided the act done was a probable consequence of the abetment, and was committed under influence of the instigation, or with the aid or in pursuance of the conspiracy which constituted the abetment.

Illustrations

(a) A instigates a child to put poison into the food of Z, and gives him poison for that purpose. The child, in consequence of the instigation, by mistake puts the poison into the food of Y, which is by the side of that of Z. Here, if the child was acting under the influence of A's instigation, and the act done was under the circumstances a probable consequence of the abetment, A is liable in the same manner, and to the same extent, as if he had instigated the child to put the poison into the food of Y.

(b) A instigates B to burn Z's house. B sets fire to the house, and at the same time commits theft of property there. A, though guilty of abetting the burning of the house, is not guilty of abetting the theft; for the theft was a distinct act, and not a probable consequence of the burning.

(c) A instigates B and C to break into an inhabited house at midnight for the purpose of robbery, and provides them with arms for that purpose. B and C break into the house, and being resisted by Z, one of the inmates, murder Z. Here, if that murder was the probable consequence of the abetment, A is liable to the punishment provided for murder.

112.   If the act for which the abettor is liable under section 111 is committed in addition to the act abetted, and constitutes a distinct offence, the abettor is liable to punishment for each of the offences.

Illustration

A instigates B to resist by force a distress made by a public servant, B, in consequence, resists that distress. In offering the resistance, B voluntarily caused grievous hurt to the officer executing the distress. As B has committed both the offence of resisting the distress, and the offence of voluntarily causing grievous hurt, B is liable to punishment for both these offences, and if A knew that B was likely voluntarily to cause grievous hurt in resisting the distress, A will also be liable to punishment for each of the offences.

113. When an act is abetted with the intention on the part of the abettor of causing a particular effect, and an act for which the abettor is liable in consequence of the abetment causes a different effect from that intended by the abettor, the abettor is liable for the effect caused, in the same manner, and to the same extent, as if he had abetted the act with the intention of causing that effect, provided he knew that the act abetted was likely to cause that effect.

Illustration

A instigates B to cause grievous hurt to Z. B, in consequence of the instigation, causes grievous hurt to Z. Z dies in consequence. Here, if A knew that the grievous hurt abetted was likely to cause death, A is liable to be punished with the punishment provided for murder.

114. Whenever any person who, if absent, would be liable to be punished as an abettor, is present when the act or offence for which he would be punishable in consequence of the abetment is committed, he shall be deemed to have committed such act or offence.

Punishment of abettor

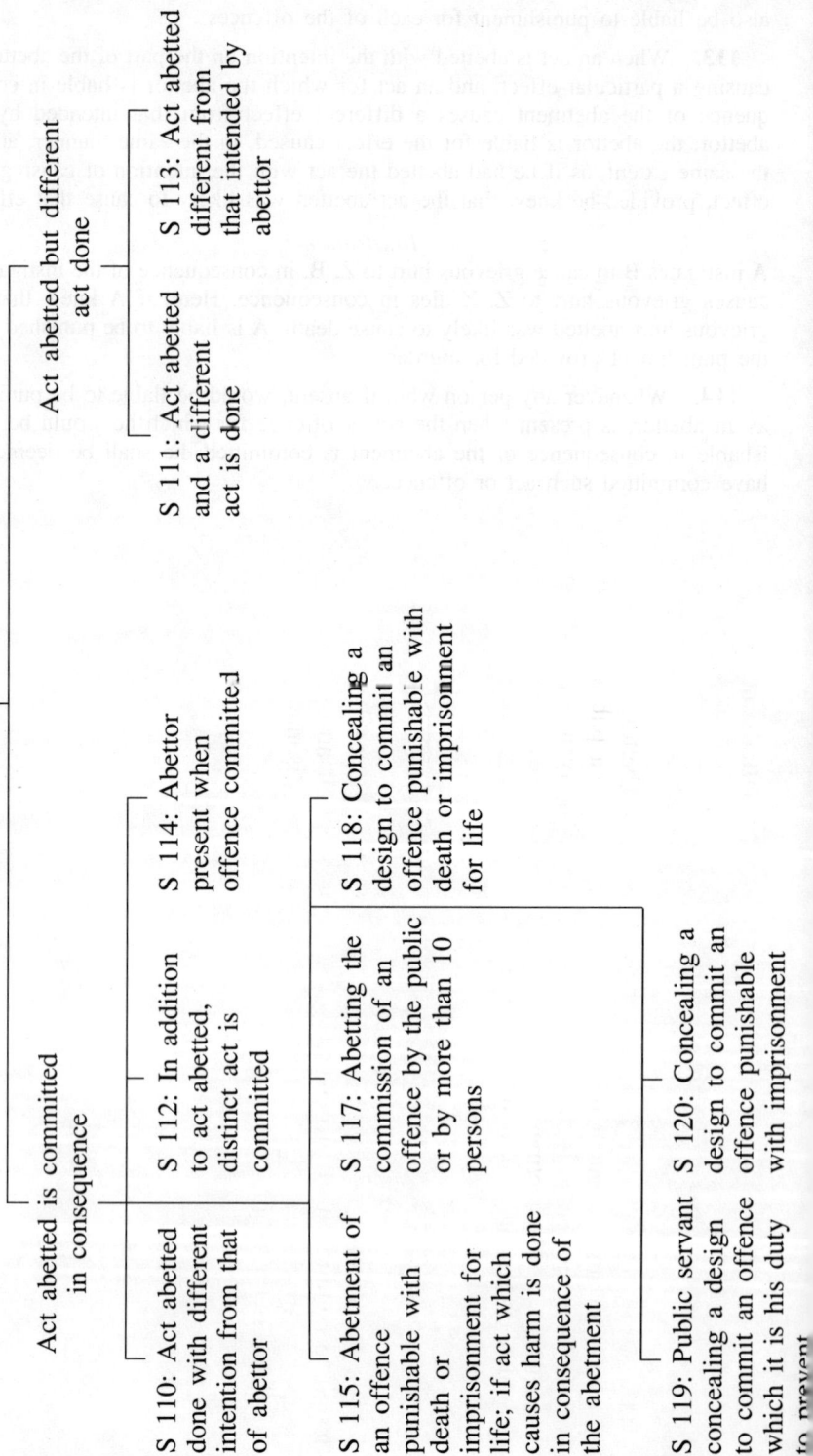

- Act abetted is committed in consequence
  - S 110: Act abetted done with different intention from that of abettor
  - S 112: In addition to act abetted, distinct act is committed
  - S 114: Abettor present when offence committed
  - S 115: Abetment of an offence punishable with death or imprisonment for life; if act which causes harm is done in consequence of the abetment
  - S 117: Abetting the commission of an offence by the public or by more than 10 persons
  - S 118: Concealing a design to commit an offence punishable with death or imprisonment for life
  - S 119: Public servant concealing a design to commit an offence which it is his duty to prevent
  - S 120: Concealing a design to commit an offence punishable with imprisonment

- Act abetted but different act done
  - S 111: Act abetted and a different act is done
  - S 113: Act abetted different from that intended by abettor

Act abetted not committed

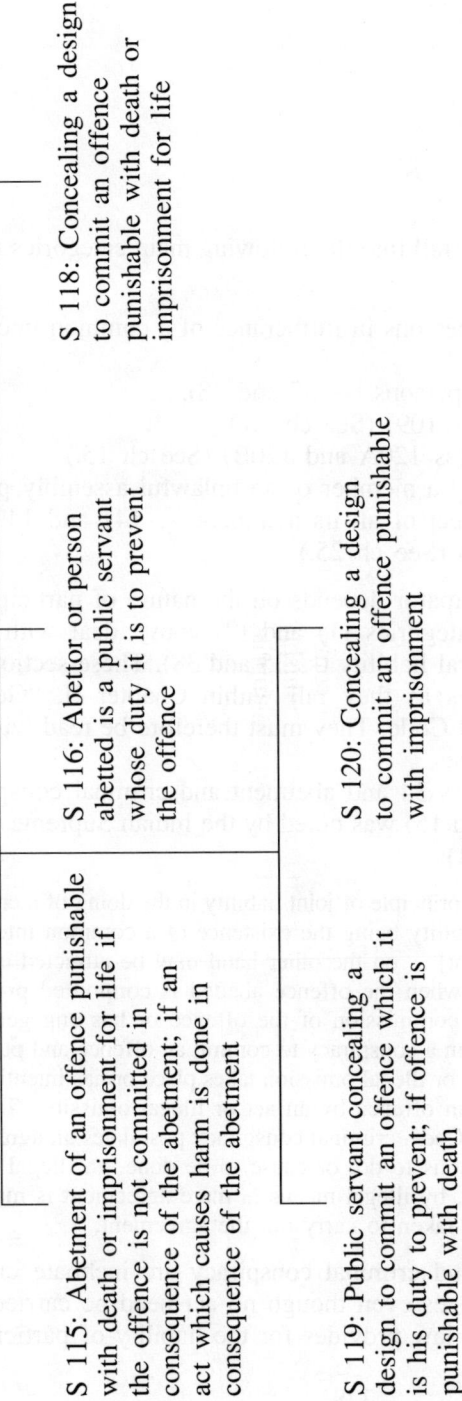

S 115: Abetment of an offence punishable with death or imprisonment for life if the offence is not committed in consequence of the abetment; if an act which causes harm is done in consequence of the abetment

S 116: Abettor or person abetted is a public servant whose duty it is to prevent the offence

S 118: Concealing a design to commit an offence punishable with death or imprisonment for life

S 119: Public servant concealing a design to commit an offence which it is his duty to prevent; if offence is punishable with death

S 120: Concealing a design to commit an offence punishable with imprisonment

Chapter 17

Participation

By KL Koh

A. Introduction

Participation in crimes may fall into the following main categories under the Penal Code:

(1) Act done by several persons in furtherance of a common intention (s 34).
(2) Act done by several persons (ss 35 and 38).
(3) Abetment of an act (s 109) (See ch 16.)
(4) Criminal conspiracy (ss 120A and 120B) (See ch 15.)
(5) Offence committed by a member of an unlawful assembly pursuant to a common object of all its members (ss 141 and 149).
(6) Gang-robbery (s 391) (See ch 25.)

The liability of each participator depends on the nature of participation and the circumstances. Categories (1) and (2) above deal with joint liability (s 34) and/or several liability (ss 35 and 38). These sections do not create distinct offences as they fall within Chapter II, "General Explanations", of the Penal Code. They must therefore be read with the relevant substantive offences.

The distinction between s 34 and abetment and criminal conspiracy respectively (see chs 16 and 15) was noted by the Indian Supreme Court in *Noor Mohammad* (1971):

> Section 34 ... embodies the principle of joint liability in the doing of a criminal act, the essence of that liability being the existence of a common intention. ... Section 109 [ie abetment] ... on the other hand may be attracted even if the abettor is not present when the offence abetted is committed provided that he has instigated the commission of the offence or has engaged with one or more other persons in a conspiracy to commit an offence and pursuant to that conspiracy some act or illegal omission takes place or has intentionally aided the commission of an offence by an act or illegal omission. Turning to ... s 120B, Indian Penal Code, criminal conspiracy postulates an agreement between two or more persons to do, or cause to be done, an illegal act or an act which is not illegal, by illegal means ... mere agreement is made an offence even if no step is taken to carry out the agreement.

Abetment by instigation and criminal conspiracy are inchoate crimes. They are substantive offences even though no act need be carried out. Other examples where the law provides for the liability of participants in crimes, without having to resort to s 34 "common intention", are being a member of an unlawful assembly (s 141) or of a gang of robbers (s 400).

The relevance or otherwise of English cases on "common intention" was considered in some cases below.

R v Vincent Banka (1936) 5 MLJ 66 (CCA, Singapore, Straits Settlements)

Huggard CJ: In the course of the arguments on this appeal this Court was referred to a number of English cases where the question of "common intent" or "common design" has been considered. The more important of these cases were:

> *Jackson* (1857)
> *Harrington* (1851)
> *Bridmore* 6 Cr AR 195
> *Short* (1932)
> *Betts and Ridley* (1930)

In considering these English cases, however, it is necessary to remember that there is a very important difference between the law as enacted in section 34 of our Penal Code and the Common Law of England as to the evidence necessary to establish a common intention. Under our Code it is essential that there should be evidence of a common intention, or evidence from which such a common intention can properly be inferred, *to commit the act actually committed.* In England that is not essential. The result of the English decided cases on this question is summed up in *Halsbury*'s Laws of England (Second Edition), Vol IX, at page 435, as follows:

> "Where several persons are engaged in a common design and another person is killed, whether intentionally or unintentionally, by an act of one of them done in prosecution of the common design, the others present are guilty of murder, if the common design was to commit murder, or to inflict felonious violence, or to commit any breach of the peace and violently to resist all opposers."

It is clear from this summary that the decisions in England have gone further than decisions in India or in this Colony, under the more restricted provisions of section 34 of the Penal Code, could possibly go. Obviously, therefore, authoritative decisions of the Courts of India and of Burma are a safer guide for the Courts of this Colony to follow in dealing with cases in which this difficult question of "common intention" arises.

The observations in *Vincent Banka* (1936) were approved in *Lee Yoon Chong* (1948–49). (Note: *Vincent Banka* is no longer good law, see below, p 335.)

In India some courts have expressed the view that resort may be had to the English common law on some of the expressions used in s 34. For example, Khundakar J in *Ibra Akanda* (1944) said:

> It will now be clear that the phrase "common intention" in s 34 is not free from ambiguity, and therefore in order to ascertain its real meaning it is permissible and indeed necessary, to consider what are the principles of joint criminal liability in the English common law.

And, in *Bashir* (1953), the court stated:

> Section 34 has to be interpreted in conformity with the English law .... The interpretation that we have placed on the various expressions used in the section is in conformity with the English law.

B. The law

1. Common intention

Penal Code, s 34

When a criminal act is done by several persons, in furtherance of the common intention of all, each of such persons is liable for that act in the same manner as if the act were done by him alone.

The original draft of the Indian Penal Code did not contain the phrase "in furtherance of the common intention of all". The words were inserted by s 1 of Act xxvii of 1870 (India). When the Indian Penal Code was introduced into the Straits Settlements in 1872 and the Federated and unfederated Malay States, the section as amended was also received.

In the administration of criminal law, experience has shown that it is often difficult, if not impossible, to prove which of several participants inflicted, say, the fatal injury or struck the blow. Section 34 is in effect a rule of evidence: where no direct evidence is available, common intention is to be inferred from the facts and circumstances of the case. Section 34 operates where the participant cannot be proved to have committed the *actus reus* himself, although his participation contributed to the result; he is liable for it.

(a) "Criminal act"

Section 34 has had a chequered interpretation because of the words "criminal act" and "common intention" contained in it. We shall consider the interpretation given by two Singapore courts of the same hierachy, ie the former Court of Criminal Appeal of the Straits Settlements in *Vincent Banka* (1936) and the present Singapore Court of Criminal Appeal in *Mimi Wong* (1972, below, pp 332, 334-336); and *Neoh Bean Chye* (1975, below, pp 335-336). Each court took a different interpretation of s 34.

(i) Identical with "crime actually committed"

R v Vincent Banka (1936) 5 MLJ 66 (CCA, Singapore, Straits Settlements)

The two appellants were charged with committing robbery and murder in the course of robbery. Evidence was inconclusive as to which of the two appellants carried a knife or inflicted the fatal wound. They were convicted by the Assizes on both charges. They appealed against their convictions for murder.

Huggard CJ: The learned Judge should have told the Jury, in effect, that they had first to be satisfied as to the identity of the robbers; that then, if so satisfied, they had to consider the further question whether on the evidence placed before them they were satisfied as to the existence of a common intention between the robbers not merely to commit robbery but, if necessary, to kill the deceased; that for the purpose of coming to a decision they must consider the evidence against each of the Accused separately; and that they could not properly convict either of the Accused of murder by reason of s 34 of the Code unless they were satisfied that this common intention existed....

In our opinion the omission to direct the Jury on the lines indicated above constitutes a fatal defect in an otherwise unexceptionable summing-up. It would, of course, be quite unsafe to assume that the Jury, if correctly directed, would have arrived at the same conclusion, and accordingly this Court has no option but to quash the convictions for murder. The convictions and sentences for robbery will stand.

We think it desirable to add a few words regarding the learned trial Judge's paraphrase of s 34 of the Code which has already been quoted in this Judgment but which, for convenience, may here be set out again. It is as follows:

"I would propose to paraphrase s 34 as follows: Where there is unity of criminal behaviour among several persons in the furtherance of a common intention which results in something being done by one of those persons for which that one would be punished, then all who so took part in the criminal behaviour are responsible for the act of that one individual." [See *Barendra Kumar Ghosh*, 1925.]

If this is intended to be in the nature of a proposition of general application, then in the view of this Court it is much too wide. It may find some measure of support in the English decisions based on Common Law which were cited to us, but it cannot be supported in such general terms by any decision which has been given under the express and more restricted terms of s 34 of the Penal Code. Under the terms of that section, as has already been pointed out, there must exist a common intention to commit the crime actually committed, and it is not sufficient that there should be merely a common intention to "behave criminally". We would add further that, as indicated in the Rangoon case already referred to, it is impossible to lay down a general proposition of law which could be applied to all cases, since the existence of a common intention must be a question of fact to be determined upon the evidence in each individual case.

Appeal allowed

The two offences considered were murder and robbery. It was clear that the two accused had set out to commit robbery. However, regarding the murder, evidence was inconclusive as to who inflicted the fatal wound or who carried the knife. The issue before the court was whether both the accused persons could be convicted of murder under s 302 read with s 34. Was the murder committed in furtherance of a common intention? The court held that the requirement under s 34 was that "there must exist a common intention to commit the crime actually committed, and that it is not sufficient that there should be merely a common intention to 'behave criminally'". Applying this test, the court held that before common intention could be found there must be evidence that there was "a common intention between the robbers not merely to commit robbery but, if necessary, to *kill* the deceased". Since there was no evidence of any express agreement between the two accused persons that a knife should be carried or that the victim should be stabbed, the court convicted them only of robbery but acquitted them of murder.

The requirement that the common intention under s 34 should refer to the "crime actually committed" is narrow. It would mean, for example, that if A and B had agreed that A would carry a knife only to frighten the victim or to cause him simple hurt, if necessary, in the course of the robbery, B would not be guilty of murder should A kill the victim.

(ii)   Distinguished from "crime actually committed"

In *Nazia* (1948), the Allahabad High Court, after examining *Barendra Kumar Ghosh* (1925) and *Mahboob Shah* (1945) said:

> [The Privy Council] have not expressed in any of these cases their opinion that the common intention of all must be to commit the particular offence which is the result of the criminal act.

This is a wider view of "criminal act". This view was endorsed by *Mimi Wong* (1972) and *Neoh Bean Chye* (1975). The difference between the two views appears to lie in the *mens rea* required before there can be joint liability under s 34.

Must the actual doer and the participants have the same *mens rea* before there can be joint liability under s 34? Alternatively, is it suffficient if only the *mens rea* of the perpetrator is proved to determine the charge and the other participants are vicariously liable for the offence charged, provided the criminal act was done in furtherance of the "common intention"? The phrase "common intention" refers to a more general intention of committing an act to which a further act is done to achieve the act.

In *Vincent Banka* (1936), the Court of Criminal Appeal of the Straits Settlements was of the view that before s 34 of the Penal Code could apply there must exist between the two men a common intention not only to rob but also, if necessary, to kill the deceased. This coupled with the view that common intention refers to the intention to commit the crime actually committed would appear to require the participators to have the *mens rea* for the actual offence charged.

In view of the fact that where it is not possible to determine the actual doer and the participators, the requirement to prove the *mens rea* of each participant for the offence charged leans in favour of the accused persons. However, the necessity for a provision on joint liability seems to be obviated.

In *Chhui Yi* (1936), Whitley AG CJ, in clarifying and elaborating the test of "crime actually committed" used in *Vincent Banka* (1936), said:

That does not, of course, mean that, in the case of murder, there need have been a common intention actually to kill; but there must have been a common intention to do any of the acts which are described in ss 299 and 300 of the Penal Code and the doing of which, if death in fact results, amounts to murder.

This view somewhat widens the scope of common intention as it includes the knowledge in ss 299 and 300. Thus even though the participator did not intend the consequence he would, nonetheless, be liable if he knew the likely consequence. His Lordship regarded common intention as the intention or knowledge which is an ingredient of the offence.

Bashir v State of Allahabad (1953) Cri LJ 1505 (HC, Allahabad, India)

Desai J: "Common intention" should not be confused with the intention that is an ingredient of many of the offences defined in the Penal Code. The intention, that is an ingredient of many of the offences, is the intention formed by a person himself committing the offence; it is a personal matter. It is the intention immediately behind the act done by the doer. On the other hand, "common intention" is the common design or common intent of two or more persons acting together. It is, more akin to motive or object. It is remoter than the intention with which each act included in the criminal act is done; it is what the persons jointly decide to achieve. It is the reason or object for doing all the acts forming the criminal act. In some cases, the intention which is an ingredient of an offence, may be identical with the common intention of the conspirators but it would still be separate from, or in addition to the common intention and not merge in it. If the common intention is to do a simple act, which can be done with only one intention, the intention with which that act is done by the doer will be identical with the common intention. But when the common intention is to do an act which can be done with different intentions, the intention of the doer may be different from the common intention. Even when it is identical, it is distinct from the common intention, being the intention of the doer....

Therefore it is quite wrong to stake everything upon whether the common intention is to do the criminal act actually done or not. The words, "in furtherance of the common intention" are not enacted for nothing. They are not to be treated as non-existent or mere surplusage. If the common intention contemplated by the section were the intention to do the criminal act actually done, then that by itself would mean that the criminal act done was done in furtherance of the common intention and the words "in furtherance of the common intention would be without any content. These words were added by the legislature in 1870 and must have been added for a purpose. That purpose could be none other than to make persons, acting in concert, liable for an act, which is not exactly the act jointly intended by them, but has been done in furtherance of their common intention. The words would not have been required at all if the common intention implied an intention to do the very criminal act done....

[I]t is not essential in every case to find out the exact nature of the common intention. If the common intention was formed by conduct or is to be inferred from conduct, the Court can infer only a general outline of the common intention and cannot infer its details. Another warning that is necessary to be given is that, the common intention should be inferred from the whole conduct of all the persons concerned and not only from an individual act actually done. As the criminal act done is not to be assumed to be in furtherance of the common intention it follows that the common intention is not to be inferred exclusively from the criminal act done. The criminal act done will certainly be one of the factors to be taken into consideration but should not be taken to be the sole factor. Besides proving that a certain criminal act was done, the prosecution has to prove the existence of common intention and that the criminal act was done in furtherance of it, these two are independent facts and one is not to be assumed or inferred exclusively from the other....

A slight variation will not prevent the act from being in furtherance of the common intention; what is required to prevent that is altogether departing from the agreement or direction....

If the conditions mentioned in s 34 are fulfilled, then each of the persons or conspirators is responsible for the whole criminal act done by all of them. If A and B do a criminal act in furtherance of their common intention, each of them is guilty of that offence of which he would have been guilty if he alone had done the whole criminal act. The law makes no distinction between them or between the parts played by them in doing the criminal act; each is guilty of the same offence. If s 34 applies, it is impossible to convict the conspirators of different offences....

All that remains to do is to find out the offence constituted by the whole criminal act (done by all the conspirators); each conspirator is to be convicted of it. If the nature of the offence depends on a particular intention or knowledge, the intention or knowledge of the actual doer of the criminal act is to be taken into account. What intention or knowledge will decide the nature of the offence committed by him and the others will be convicted of the same offence because, as pointed out above, they cannot be convicted of a different offence. The intention of the actual doer must be distinguished from the common intention as already pointed out. It is an ingredient of the offence said to be constituted by the criminal act. It is a personal matter. When an offence requires a particular intention that intention must be harboured by the person doing the physical act. That the intention must be of the person doing the act is laid down in the definitions of the offences themselves. When A is made responsible for an act done by B, the nature of the offence must necessarily depend upon the intention of B, when A himself has not done an act there cannot arise any question of his intention for that act. Though the intention of the actual doer is to be distinguished from the common intention, the intention must not be foreign to or inconsistent with the common intention. It must be consistent with the carrying out of the common intention, otherwise the criminal act done will not be in furtherance of the common intention....

Section 34 makes it quite clear that the liability of all the conspirators is for the criminal act actually done and not for the common intention, eg the act jointly intended by them. Nothing can be clearer than this and one has only to read s 34 to know it. What the common intention was, is therefore not to be considered at all in deciding for what the conspirators are liable. The section does not punish the conspirators for the act jointly intended by them; it punishes them for the act actually done. Even if A and B formed a common intention to cause simple or grievous hurt and the simple or grievous hurt caused by them resulted in death, they will be liable for causing the death....

In *Mimi Wong* (1972), the Singapore Court of Criminal Appeal held that only the *mens rea* of the actual doer is necessary to establish the offence charged for which all the participators would be vicariously liable. Wee Chong Jin CJ said:

> It is clear from the Privy Council's (*Mahboob Shah*, 1945) interpretation of the words "criminal act", that it is the result of a criminal act which is a criminal offence. It then remains, in any particular case, to find out the actual offence constituted by the "criminal act". If the nature of the offence depends on a particular intention the intention of the actual doer of the criminal act has to be considered. What this intention is will decide the offence committed by him and then s 34 applies to make the others vicariously or collectively liable for the same offence. The intention that is an ingredient of the offence constituted by the criminal act is the intention of the actual doer and must be distinguished from the common intention of the doer and his confederates. It may be identical with the common intention or it may not. Where it is not identical with the common intention, it must nevertheless be consistent with the carrying out of the common intention, otherwise the criminal act done by the actual doer would not be in furtherance of the common intention. Thus if A and B form a common intention to cause injury to C with a knife and A holds C while B stabs C deliberately in the region of the heart and the stab wound is sufficient in the ordinary course of nature to cause death, B is clearly guilty of murder. Applying s 34 it is also clear that B's act in stabbing C is in furtherance of the common intention to cause injury to C with a knife because B's act is clearly consistent with the carrying out of that common intention and as their "criminal act", ie that unity of criminal behaviour, resulted in the criminal offence of murder punishable under s 302, A is also guilty of murder.

This view was endorsed by *Neoh Bean Chye* (1975) where the trial judge, Choor Singh J, pointed out that *Vincent Banka* (1936) was wrongly decided. He said:

> In our judgment the head note of the report of the decision in *Vincent Banka* (1936) does not contain a correct statement of the law. In a criminal prosecution where s 34 of the Penal Code is invoked, it is not incumbent on the prosecution, to prove that there existed between the participants a common intention to commit the crime actually committed. For s 34 to apply it is sufficient if the prosecution prove that there was in existence a common intention between all the persons who committed the criminal act and that the act which constituted the offence charged was done in furtherance of that common intention. This is clear from the decisions of the Privy Council in *Barendra Kumar Ghosh* (1925), *Mahboob Shah* (1945) and also from the recent decision of the Court of Criminal Appeal of Singapore in *Mimi Wong* (1972).

In *Neoh Bean Chye* (1975), the first appellant knew that the second appellant carried a loaded revolver and that it would be used, if necessary, during the course of the robbery. He himself had loaded the gun and handed it to the second appellant who shot the deceased when he offered resistance during the robbery. The first appellant's conviction for murder under s 34 read with s 302 was upheld by the Court of Criminal Appeal.

The effect of both *Mimi Wong* (1972) and *Neoh Bean Chye* (1975) is that it is not necessary to require a common intention to commit the crime charged. All that is required is a common intention to do a criminal act (physical act as distinguished from the result of it) which ultimately leads to an offence.

However, the accused must have a knowledge that some act may be committed which is consistent with the carrying out of the common intention. In *Mimi Wong* (1972), the court stated that the intention of the "actual doer" must first be determined in order to decide the offence committed by him. Section 34 will then apply to make the others vicariously liable. However, Douglas (1983, below) has considered the problem which arises where it is not clear which of several actors was the perpetrator.

Gillian Douglas, "Joint Liability in the Penal Code" (1983) 25 Mal LR 259, 267

It is submitted that this statement [the statement of Wee Chong Jin CJ, see above] raises certain problems. First, what is the position where it is not possible to prove which of several actors was the perpetrator? The Court says that it is the "intention of the actual doer" which determines the offence committed, but how does the Court know what this intention was if it cannot identify the doer? The Court seems to be ruling out the possibility of presuming an intention based on the "lowest common denominator" of all the actors. This would anyway come close to equating the intention required for the offence with the "common intention" which the Court clearly rejected. This problem did not arise in *Mimi Wong* (1972) where the evidence showed which of the accused was the perpetrator. It is submitted that the difficulty of proving which accused was the perpetrator justifies the argument presented above, that the court must consider the knowledge or intention of the *accomplice* under s 35 before holding him liable under s 34. It is precisely because the *mens rea* of the perpetrator may be unknown, that it is necessary to have regard to the *mens rea* of the accomplice.

Secondly, the Court implies that an act which is inconsistent with the common intention cannot be in furtherance of it. This need not be so. Suppose that two men plan to steal jewels from a house. While one opens the safe, the other keeps a look out. He sees the householder coming to investigate the noise, and hits him on the head with a chair to avoid detection. As a result, the two make a successful getaway with the jewels. The householder dies. The safecracker argues that the plan worked out beforehand was that the lookout would simply warn him that someone was coming so that he could hide, and that no violence had ever been suggested. While perhaps *not consistent* with the common intention, the attack undoubtedly *furthered* its achievement.

Clearly, the Court was not envisaging liability based on such "objective" furtherance of the common intention, and it is submitted that the Court should accordingly be understood to have meant that the act must be both consistent with *and* in furtherance of the common intention. Certainly, other courts seem to have assumed that both requirements must be fulfilled. For example, in *Neoh Bean Chye* (1975), while the trial judges cited that case with approval, they seem to have been concerned, in their review of the evidence, to be satisfied that both accused knew of the likelihood of the victim of the robbery being shot. Their judgment was upheld on appeal.

(b) Furtherance of common intention

The "criminal act" that is done by one of the accused must be in *furtherance* of the common intention of all confederates. (See, eg *Barendra Kumar Ghosh*, 1925, below; *Mimi Wong*, 1972; *Neoh Bean Chye*, 1975; and *Sim Min Teck*, 1987 and above, pp 333–336). The common intention must precede the criminal act. Such act may, first, be directly intended by all confederates; second, it may be inferred from the circumstances; third, the act may be committed so as to carry out the common intention, eg to overcome resistance. This third type of act may cause difficulties as the act of the accused may not be the one intended by the others.

Common intention must be distinguished from *same* or *similar* intention. In the Privy Council case of *Mahboob Shah* (1945) (an appeal from India), the appellant, Mahboob Shah, and one Wali Shah were out on a shooting game when they heard shouts for help from one Ghulam Quasim Shah who was being attacked by the deceased, Alla Dad. (Ghulam had tried to get back from Alla Dad the reeds which had been unlawfully taken from the lands of Ghulam's uncle.) Wali Shah in trying to rescue Ghulam shot and killed Alla Dad while the appellant injured one Hamidullah Khan. Both the appellant and Wali Shah were convicted under s 302 read with s 34. The Privy Council, in allowing the appeal, said that while the appellant and Wali Shah had the *same* or *similar* intention to rescue Ghulam by using their guns, if necessary, there was no evidence that the killing of Alla Dad was in *furtherance of a common* intention.

Barendra Kumar Ghosh v Emperor Air 1925 PC 1 (Privy Council)

The appellant, together with a few others, went to a Post Office in Bengal to demand money from the sub-postmaster. All of them fired at him with their pistols. He was arrested while the others fled. The trial judge directed the jury that the appellant might be the man who fired the fatal shot and that if the jury were satisfied that the sub-postmaster was killed in furtherance of the common intention of all, the appellant was guilty of murder whether he fired the fatal shot or not. The appellant was convicted of murder by the jury.

Lord Sumner: The appellant's argument is, in brief, that in S. 34, "a criminal act," in so far as murder is concerned, means an act which takes life criminally within S.302, ... It follows from the appellant's argument that the section only applies to cases where several persons (acting in furtherance of a common intention) do some fatal act, which one could do by himself....

Suppose two men tie a rope round the neck of a third and pull opposite ends of the rope till he is strangled.... Obviously each is pulling his own end of the rope, with his own strength, standing in the position that he chooses to take up, and exerting himself in the way that is natural to him, in a word in a way that is his. Let it be that in effect each pulls as hard as the other and at the same time and that both equally contribute to the result. Still the act, for which either would be liable, is done by himself alone, is precisely not the act done by the other person.

There are two acts, for which both actors ought to suffer death, separately done by two persons but identically similar... if it is read as the appellant reads it, then,... if both men are charged together but each is to be made liable for his act only and as if he had done it by himself, each can say that the prosecution has not discharged the onus, for no more is proved against him than an attempt, which might not have succeeded in the absence of the other party charged. Thus both will be acquitted of murder, and will only be convicted of an attempt, although the victim is and remains a murdered man....

If the appellant's argument were to be adopted, the Code, during its early years, before the words "in furtherance of the common intention of all" were added to S. 34, really enacted that each person is liable criminally for what he does himself, as if he had done it by himself, even though others did something at the same time as he did. This actually negatives participation altogether and the amendment was needless, for the original words expressed all that the appellant contends that the amended section expresses....

Instead of enacting in effect that participation as such might be ignored, which is what the argument amounts to, the amended section said that, if there was action in furtherance of a common intention, the individual came under a special liability thereby, a change altogether repugnant to the suggested view of the original section. [See above, p 334.]

Really the amendment is an amendment, in any true sense of the word, only if the original object was to punish participants by making one man answerable for what another does, provided what is done is done in furtherance of a common intention, and if the amendment then defines more precisely the conditions under which this vicarious or collective liability arises. In other words, "a criminal act" means that unity of criminal behaviour, which results in something, for which an individual would be punishable, if it were all done by himself alone, that is, in a criminal offence.

Appeal dismissed

In *Gui Hoi Cham* (1970) the appellants were convicted of culpable homicide not amounting to murder under s 34 read with s 304 of the Penal Code. Evidence was that there was a fight between two factions. Although the appellants together with the combatants from the deceased's party might have gone to the scene of the fight for a "common purpose", the appellants had gone unarmed. When fighting erupted each one armed himself only with the weapon close at hand from the same stack of firewood. The court came to the conclusion that as they were not armed when they went there for a "common purpose" (meaning "common intention"), ie to fight, the killing was not done in furtherance of the common intention. The court convicted them under s 326 for voluntarily causing grievous hurt by dangerous weapons. Can common intention be developed on the spot? (See below.)

(c) Common intention and prearranged plan

Section 34 does not use the phrase "prearranged plan". Courts have on occasions considered whether or not there was a need to find à prearranged plan in determining whether the "criminal act" was done "in furtherance of a common intention." In *Barendra Kumar Ghosh* (1924) the direction to the jury was:

> If you come to the conclusion that these three or four persons came into the Post Office with that intention to rob and, if necessary to kill, and death resulted from their acts, if that be so, you are bound to find a verdict of guilty.

Similarly, in *Mahboob Shah* (1945), the Privy Council said:

> It is clear to their Lordships that common intention within the meaning of the section implies a pre-arranged plan, and to convict the accused of an offence applying the section it should be proved that the criminal act was done in concert pursuant to the pre-arranged plan. As has been often observed, it is difficult if not impossible to procure direct evidence to prove the intention of an individual; in most cases it has to be inferred from his act or conduct or other relevant circumstances of the case.

However, the difficulty of proving a prearranged plan was noted by the Rangoon case of *Nga Aung Thein* (1935). Baguley J did not think it was an essential precondition:

> It seems that the condition precedent suggested in the question, namely, a pre-arranged intention to commit murder, a pre-arrangement which from the nature of things in the vast majority of cases it would be absolutely impossible to prove, is not essential ....

In *Bashir* (1953), the Privy Council clarified the statement in *Mahboob Shah* (1945):

> In *Mahboob Shah* (1945) "common intention" was held to imply a "pre-arranged plan." This does not mean either that there should be confabulation, discussion and agreement in writing or by word, nor that the plan should be arranged for a considerable time before the doing of the criminal act. The Judicial Committee in the case of Mahboob Shah (*D*), did not lay down that a certain interval should elapse between the formation of a pre-arranged plan and the doing of the criminal act and did not negative the formation of a pre-arranged plan just a moment before the doing of the criminal act....

Some more recent Indian decisions seem to insist on a prearrangement in the sense of a prior plan before convicting the accused of an offence with the aid of s 34. In *Ram Prasad* (1976), Untwalia J, in setting aside the convictions of two of the appellants under s 302 read with s 34 stated that on the evidence "[t]here is nothing to indicate the appellants had arrived at the scene with a preplanned common intention of causing the death of the deceased".

The Straits Settlements Court of Appeal in *Vincent Banka* (1936) agreed with the observations in *Nga Aung Thein* (1935) that prearrangement was not necessary. Of course, where there is evidence of a prearranged plan, it is easier to conclude that there is a joint liability.

Kee Ah Tee v PP [1971] 2 MLJ 242 (CCA, Singapore)

The first appellant and the second appellant were convicted of murder under s 302 of the Penal Code for causing the death of two deceased in circumstances which amounted to murder read with s 34 of the Penal Code. Both of them had gone to a factory to commit robbery together with one Ah Choon.

Wee Chong Jin CJ: By their own admissions they were at the scene of the killings; they had gone there to commit robbery together with Ah Choon; they knew two knives were carried; they knew that these knives were necessary to carry out their planned object. Two persons were seen running from the scene of the killings and one of whom, having regard to the evidence of the discarding of the blood stained shirt was the first appellant and these facts were also admitted by them. The second appellant had a recently caused incised cut on his right index finger. The injuries on the victims were caused by two knives and could not all have been inflicted by one assailant only. The first appellant led the police to the place where the knife with the jagged sides was found and the fatal wound on the body of the male deceased was consistent with it having been caused by this knife....

There was clearly more than sufficient independent evidence connecting each of the appellants with the two killings and implicating each of them and which confirms in some material particular not only the evidence that the crimes have been committed but also that the appellants committed them.

It was also argued on behalf of the second appellant that there was insufficient evidence to prove beyond a reasonable doubt that the criminal acts which resulted in the deaths of the two deceased persons were committed by him and the first appellant in furtherance of a pre-arranged plan to carry out those criminal acts. In our opinion this ground is also without substance. There were two of three persons who set out that afternoon to commit robbery at the feathers factory armed with two knives knowing it was necessary to be so armed to carry out their planned object. The trial judges found on the evidence that they entered the factory building each armed with a knife. These facts coupled with the number and extent of the injuries which were inflicted on the two victims by two knives constituted in our view sufficient evidence on which the trial judges could properly find, as they did, that the appellants entered the factory building with the common intention to rob and with the common intention to use the knife each of them carried, if necessary, to inflict such bodily injury on any person offering resistance as would be sufficient in the ordinary course of nature to cause death.

Appeal dismissed

Lee Choh Pet v PP (No 2) [1972] 1 MLJ 187 (CCA, Singapore)

The three appellants were charged as follows:

> You are charged that you ... together with two other persons ... in furtherance of the common intention of you all committed extortion by putting one Ong

Yew Kee in fear of grievous hurt being caused to Ong Beang Leck and thereby dishonestly induced the said Ong Yew Kee to deliver to you $20,000 an offence punishable under s 386 of the Penal Code ... read with s 34 of the said Code.

Choor Singh J: The evidence led by the prosecution was that ... the deceased was taken in a car ... and ... sat in the front seat .... In the back seat of the car were three other persons. ... As the car travelled along this unlit road the deceased was attacked from behind with a weapon or weapons by one or more of the persons in the back seat of the car. The deceased resisted the attack and the car pulled up. The deceased opened the door of the car and ran out but he was chased and attacked again until he collapsed on the road. He was carried into the car which was then driven to a sewerage manhole in Jurong where the deceased's body was dumped into the manhole. The manhole cover which consisted of two heavy cement slabs was then replaced. The deceased's abductors then commenced negotiations with the father of the deceased who did not know that his son had been killed. These negotiations resulted in $20,000 being paid on the 5th June 1968 to the abductors for the promised release of the deceased....

It was argued on behalf of the appellants that there was insufficient evidence to prove beyond a reasonable doubt that the criminal acts which resulted in the death of the deceased were committed in furtherance of a pre-arranged plan to carry out those criminal acts. In our opinion this ground is without substance. The trial judges found on the evidence that all the three appellants were in the back seat of the car; that weapons with which the deceased was to be attacked and killed were carried on the floor-board of the rear compartment of the car; and that levers for lifting the heavy covers of the sewerage manhole in which the deceased's body was to be dumped were also carried in the car. There facts coupled with the character of the assault on the deceased and the number and extent of the injuries which were inflicted on him with the weapons available in the car constituted in our view sufficient evidence on which the trial judges could properly find, as they did, that the three appellants had the common intention to abduct the deceased in order that he may be murdered and the common intention to murder him.

Appeal against convictions under ss 364 and 302 dismissed
Conviction under s 386 quashed

Prearrangement need not exist in the sense of a prior plan. The plan could develop on the spot. In *Mimi Wong* (1972), the first appellant, Mimi Wong, was convicted of murder of one Mrs Watanabe (whose husband she had an affair with). The second appellant (the husband of the first appellant) was also convicted of murder under s 302 read with s 34.

When the first appellant went to the house of the deceased, she brought with her a knife which she subsequently used to inflict the fatal injury. So far as the part played by the second appellant was concerned, the court accepted the following findings of the trial judges:

 ... that the idea of throwing detergent came from him; that he brought the glucolin tin containing the detergent; that he requested the first appellant to lure the deceased to the bathroom on the pretext of inspecting the broken wash basin; that he mixed water with the detergent; that he wrapped a towel round the glucolin tin to prevent his leaving finger prints on it; that he threw the detergent into the eyes of the deceased after he saw the first appellant had taken a knife and was ready to stab the deceased and that he was clearly a party to the stabbing of the deceased.

It is not surprising that the court did not mention a "pre-arranged" plan to commit murder as in most cases it is virtually impossible to prove. Failure to prove an express prearrangement is not essential. In *Nga Aung Thein* (1935), Baguley J said that:

> ... it is sufficient if the Court is of opinion that from all the facts proved, the way in which the robbery is carried out, the weapons with which the robbers were armed, and their knowledge of the way in which their robbers were armed, the characters of the robbers themselves, and so on, a legitimate inference can be drawn that the robbers went out "to commit robbery and, if necessary, to kill," and that death resulted in consequence of what they, as a band did.

That was in the context of robbery and murder. The same sort of considerations ought to apply in *Mimi Wong* (1972). The manner in which the killing was done, should be taken into consideration. Certainly the part played by the second appellant showed some strategy which was not inconsistent with the killing. The throwing of the detergent in Mrs Watanabe's eyes at the critical moment when the first appellant was about to stab her was to prevent any resistance on her part.

Similarly, in *Lee Choh Pet* (1972) the Court of Criminal Appeal considered the weapons used, including the levers found in the car (apparently known to all three appellants as knowledge was not denied) which were intended to lift the heavy covers of the sewerage manhole in which the deceased's body was to be dumped. It came to the conclusion that there was sufficient evidence that the criminal acts which resulted in the death were committed in furtherance of a prearranged plan. In *Kee Ah Tee* (1971) the Court of Criminal Appeal held that the appellants had the knowledge that the knives which they were armed with would be used to carry out their common intention to rob–their "planned object". There was sufficient evidence to show that they would use the knives, if necessary, to inflict such bodily injury on any person offering resistance as would be sufficient in the ordinary course of nature to cause death.

Malaysian courts have also considered the question of prearranged plan in interpreting s 34. In *Abu Bakar b Iman Idris* (1947), Court of Appeal of the Federation of Malaya approved the test in *Mahboob Shah* (1945) that common intention under s 34 implies a prearranged plan, and to convict an accused of an offence applying the section it should be proved that the criminal act was done according to the prearranged plan (see also *Chan Chun Ling*, 1956; *Lee Fook Sam*, 1963).

In all the cases in Singapore and Malaysia where the question of a prearranged plan was considered there was no direct evidence of a prior plan regarding the furtherance of the common intention to kill. Inference of the prearranged plan was gathered from indirect evidence such as the weapons or instruments used, the nature of the wounds inflicted and the common intention itself. Perhaps the expression "prearranged" is rather misleading if it gives the impression of a deliberate arrangement made before setting out to commit the criminal act. The expression "prearranged plan" was clarified in *Bashir* (1953, see above, p 337).

In a more recent Malaysian case of *Namasiyiam* (1987), the Supreme Court of Malaysia stated that:

> Direct evidence of a prior plan to commit an offence is not necessary in every case because common intention may develop on the spot and without any long interval of time between it and the doing of the act commonly intended. In such a case, common intention may be inferred from the facts and circumstances of the case.

(d) Participation and mere presence

Section 34 requires the criminal act to be "done by several persons". Section 33 defines "act" to mean a single act as well as a series of acts and to include omissions. There must be actual participation, whether active or passive. Regarding passive participation, Lord Sumner in *Barendra Kumar Ghosh* (1925) said, obiter, "... it is to be remembered that in crimes as in other things they also serve who only stand and wait". However, in what circumstances would a person be liable under s 34 (read with a substantive offence) if he is merely present and does not even raise a finger throughout the criminal act. Whitton J in *Chew Cheng Lye* (1956) stated that once common intention, say, to kill, has been formed mere presence at the subsequent killing constitutes participation in the criminal act as it is reasonable to presume that such presence is in furtherance of the common intention. Does this suggest a prearranged plan? (See above, p 337.) According to the learned judge, this is to be distinguished from mere presence in a situation where one does not assist in any way, such as keeping watch. What if the person who keeps watch takes fright and does not give the warning at the appropriate time? Would his mere presence be sufficient to satisfy passive participation? (See s 114 in ch 16.)

(e) "Common intention" and crimes imputing knowledge

The question has been raised as to whether common intention under s 34 can be read with offences requiring knowledge. For example, whether s 300(d) can be read with s 34.

If it is accepted that "common intention" is different from the *mens rea* of the actual doer of the offence, then s 34 can be read with offences of various types of *mens rea*. This is the view of *Bashir* (1953). After distinguishing "common intention" in s 34 with the "intention that is the *ingredient*" of an offence, Desai J said:

> All that remains to do is to find out the offence constituted by the whole criminal act (done by all the conspirators); each conspirator is to be convicted

of it. If the nature of the offence depends on a particular intention or knowledge, the intention or knowledge of the actual doer of the criminal act is to be taken into account. What intention or knowledge will decide the nature of the offence committed by him and the others will be convicted of the same offence because, as pointed out above, they cannot be convicted of a different offence. The intention of the actual doer must be distinguished from the common intention as already pointed out. It is an ingredient of the offence said to be constituted by the criminal act. It is a personal matter. When an offence requires a particular intention that intention must be harboured by the person doing the physical act. That the intention must be of the person doing the act is laid down in the definitions of the offences themselves. When A is made responsible for an act done by B, the nature of the offence must necessarily depend upon the intention of B. When A himself has not done an act there cannot arise any question of his intention for that act. Though the intention of the actual doer is to be distinguished from the common intention, the intention must not be foreign to or inconsistent with the common intention. It must be consistent with the carrying out of the common intention, otherwise the criminal act done will not be in furtherance of the common intention....

(f)   Section 34 and strict liability offences

Ibra Akanda v Emperor AIR (1944) Cal 339 (HC, Calcutta, India)

Khundkar J: Section 34 begins by speaking of "a criminal act"; it starts with the assumption that a criminal act has been committed. Now a criminal act may be an offence of one of two kinds: (a) one which is punishable even if there is no *mens rea* ...; (b) one which requires the *mens rea* ... As regards class (a), there is no difficulty, for it is per se an offence, and, by the operation of what s 34 goes on to enact, each and every person who performs a fractional part of the act is to be regarded as the performers of the whole of it.

(g)   Relationship between ss 34, 35 and 38

For s 34, see above, p 330.

Penal Code, ss 35 and 38

35.   Whenever an act, which is criminal only by reason of its being done with a criminal knowledge or intention, is done by several persons, each of such persons who joins in the act with such knowledge or intention, is liable for the act in the same manner as if the act were done by him alone with that knowledge or intention.

38.   Where several persons are engaged or concerned in the commission of a criminal act, they may be guilty of different offences by means of that act.

Illustration

A attacks Z under such circumstances of grave provocation that his killing of Z would be only cuplable homicide not amounting to murder. B, having ill-will towards Z, and intending to kill him, and not having been subject to the provocation, assists A in killing Z. Here, though A and B are both engaged in causing Z's death, B is guilty of murder, and A is guilty only of culpable homicide.

Section 34 is concerned with joint liability. The question under s 34 is whether the act is done in *furtherance* of the common intention. Section 35 is intended to deal with the question whether the persons who did the act had the same knowledge or intention, if the act is criminal by reason only if its being done with a criminal knowledge or intention. Each person would only be liable for the act to the extent of his knowledge or intention. The following example given in *Abdul Gaffur Panchayat* (1926) illustrates the operation of s 35: A and B beat C who died as a result. A intended to murder C and knew that the act would cause death. B only intended to cause grievous hurt and did not know that his act would cause death or such bodily injury as was likely to result in death. A is guilty of murder and B of causing grievous hurt. The two sections may overlap. Thus, where several persons beat the victim and there is a common intention with regard to the criminal act, that is, the act of beating, if each of the assailants possesses knowledge that death is the likely consequence of the criminal act and death of the victim results from the beating, each of the assailants will be liable under s 304 read with s 34 or 35 of the Penal Code (*Afrahim Sheikh*, 1964).

As section 35 is not intended to cover "common intention" of the participants, it would apply, for example, where the participants were strangers to one another and each dealt with his victim with a different intention or knowledge. As such the *mens rea* of each wrongdoer might be different and each would be liable accordingly. It would, for example, cover the following situation: A waylaid B, his enemy, on a lonely road. He proceeded to beat B intending to kill him. C came along and thought it would be fun to give B a kick in his stomach. B died as a result of the beating from A. A could be liable for murder, while C, who had no intention or knowledge to kill B but only to cause hurt, would be liable for voluntarily causing hurt or grievous hurt.

Where furtherance of a common intention cannot be established under s 34, the participants may be liable under s 35. Thus the two sections are complementary (see Indian Law Commission, 42nd Report, 1971). Balasubrahmanyam (1962) posed the question "whether s 34 has necessarily got to be read with s 35 or can be applied independently". The answer seems obvious that the two sections, though complementary, are independent.

Section 38 deals with a situation, as the illustration to the section shows, where several persons are engaged or concerned in the commission of a criminal act. Each may be guilty of different offences. It also takes into consideration the defences available to the wrongdoer, although this aspect will be generally covered by the general exceptions in Chapter IV or the exceptions to s 300. It is unnecessary to deal with this question in s 38. However, as s 38 is contained in "General Explanations" in Chapter II of the Penal Code, it simply explains that although a person may commit a "criminal act", he may not have committed an offence in view of certain exceptions provided in the law. The section also makes clear the position that a defence which is available to a participant does not necessarily avail the others who may have committed the criminal act with the same intention or knowledge.

Section 38 is supplementary to s 34. The inter-relationship between the two sections is brought out by a comparison between *Mimi Wong* (1972) and *Bhaba Nanda Sharma* (1977).

In *Mimi Wong* (1972), Wee Chong Jin CJ, gave the following illustration showing that the intention of the actual doer is to be distinguished from the common intention of the doer and his confederates:

> [I]f A and B form a common intention to cause injury to C with a knife and A holds C while B stabs C deliberately in the region of the heart and the stab wound is sufficient in the ordinary course of nature to cause death, B is clearly guilty of murder. Applying s 34 it is also clear that B's act in stabbing C is in furtherance of the common intention to cause injury to C with a knife because B's act is clearly consistent with the carrying out of that common intention and as their criminal act", ie that unity of criminal behaviour, resulted in the criminal offence of murder punishable under s 302, A is also guilty of murder.

A different view is taken in *Bhaba Nanda Sharma* (1977). The accused B, P and II armed with different weapons chased the deceased. B caught hold of the hands of the deceased from behind and P gave the deceased a blow on the head with a *dolibari*. H gave further blows on the deceased's head and other parts of his body after he fell down. The Assam High Court convicted all the three accused of the offence of murder read with s 34 and also s 323 read with s 34. On appeal to the Indian Supreme Court, it was held that so far as B was concerned since he merely caught hold of the hands of the deceased it was difficult to hold that he shared the common intention of the other two accused in causing the death of the deceased. The court held that B's intention was to join in the commission of the acts by the other two who had intended to get the deceased severely assaulted with the knowledge that such an assault in all probability and likelihood might result in his death. He was not liable for murder read with s 34 but under s 38 read with s 304, Part II.

Gillian Douglas "Joint Liability in the Penal Code" (1983) 25 Mal LR 259, pp 260–263

Section 34 as originally drafted would have provided for the *actus reus*, if one may call it that, of joint liability, since it dealt with the doing of the criminal act. It would certainly appear to be too wide in isolation. However, s 35 could be said to provide the *mens rea* element of the rule, by stipulating that where a criminal act requires a particular knowledge or intention in order to attract criminal liability, each accomplice must be proved to have had such knowledge or intention before being held liable. Where the criminal act may be done negligently, and no knowledge or intention need be proved, then s 35 would not apply, and liability would attach simply by virtue of s 34. Such a construction would bring the Code broadly into line with English law, which would be consistent with what has been assumed to have been the draftsman's intention. Also, the reference to knowledge as well as intention would fit the circumstances of much group participation in crime, where it may be difficult to prove that an accomplice had the same intention as the perpetrator, but much easier to show that he did have knowledge of the likely events.

While s 34 is not expressly stated to be read subject to s 35, the similarity of language and of structure of the two sections certainly admits of the possibility of the construction being suggested here. VB Raju points out that the marginal note to s 35 states: "When *such* an act is criminal by reason of its being done with a criminal knowledge or intention."

The only act to which this can refer is the criminal act outlined in s 34. Of course, one cannot put much empahsis on the marginal note as an aid to construction, though it perhaps may help to tip the balance further in favour of a particular interpretation. Rather, it is suggested that without the interpretation offered here, it is hard to see when s 35 could operate, and it must surely have been drafted with some purpose in mind. Gour suggests that s 34:

"is limited to offences which are independent of intention or knowledge, that is, those in which intention or knowledge is presumed, while ... [s 35] is limited to those in which intention or knowledge cannot be presumed but must be expressly proved."

It is submitted that this view should not be supported. Gour apparently accepts that s 34 is applicable to cases of murder, for example, but murder is an offence where intention or knowledge must be proved by the prosecution and is not presumed.

One argument against the suggested interpretation is that in s 35, the act is stated to be criminal "*only* by reason of its being done with a criminal knowledge or intention". It could be argued that an act may be criminal by reason of a particular circumstance or consequence *as well as* by reason of a particular knowledge or intention, in which case s 35 would not apply and s 34 would stand by itself. However, it is submitted that, for most offences under the Code, what makes an act criminal is the existence of the requisite knowledge or intention. For example, under the Code, even if not under the common law at the time when the Code was drafted, a killing is not culpable homicide *unless* it is done with the knowledge or intention specified in s 299. Acts may be *unlawful* independently of knowledge or intention, but not, it is suggested, criminal, except in the instance where the Code itself makes an offence one of negligence.

(ii) *Section 38*

"Where several persons are engaged or concerned in the commission of a criminal act, they may be guilty of different offences by means of that act."

It may be noted that s 38, like ss 34 and 35, uses the term "criminal act", and it is convenient to deal with this section before considering ss 36 and 37.

The illustration to the section demonstrates that where a perpetrator would have a limited defence, such as provocation, to a charge of murder, the accomplice who has no such defence may be convicted of murder even though the former is convicted of culpable homicide only. The question arises as to whether this section applies to s 34, or whether all accomplices liable by virtue of that section must be held guilty of the same offence. While the Indian Law Commission saw no difficulty in the working of s 38, it seems that different courts and commentators do take different views on this question.

Various arguments may be put forward to suggest that s 38 *does* apply to s 34 read with s 35. First, it has been noted that this section refers to a "criminal act", just as s 34 does, suggesting that the similarity of wording was intended to point out a connection between the two sections. Secondly, s 34 provides that each accomplice is liable for the criminal act "in the same manner as if the act were done by him alone". This may imply that if the accused had acted alone and would have had a particular *mens rea* or partial defence, he should be dealt with on the same basis when acting in concert. Thirdly, the illustration to s 38 seems to raise circumstances which would fit within s 34, for the two accused both do the criminal act and both have *mens rea* (which, on the suggested interpretation, is required by virtue of s 35).

On the other hand, it may be argued that s 38 is intended to apply when the requirements of ss 34 and 35 are not satisfied, that is, when the accomplice does *not* have the same knowledge or intention as the perpetrator and so cannot be convicted of the same offence. This view would seem to do less violence to the argument that s 35 is intended to qualify s 34 and result in conviction for the offence actually committed, only of those with the *mens rea* for that offence. It would also seem to fit with judicial practice, which has certainly operated on the basis that use of s 34 results in conviction for the same offence. It may be that the working of s 34, stating that the accused is liable "in the same manner as if the act were done by him alone", simply explains that the accomplice is to be treated as if he were a perpetrator and not in some other way. This view also has the merit of making the scheme of the sections coherent. Sections 34 and 35 apply where the accomplice joins in the criminal act and has *mens rea*. Section 38 applies where he joins in but does *not* have the same *mens rea*.

There are two difficulties with this view. First, the illustration to s 38 may be taken as a case where *both* parties have the same *mens rea*, so that surely ss 34 and 35 should operate? However, the illustration may have been based on the assumption current in the nineteenth century, that an accused who has limited defence such as provocation, must *necessarily* have lacked *mens rea* for murder. This is not in fact invariably so. Yet, the application of s 38 to such a situation makes good sense for there is no reason why we should allow the more blameworthy accomplice to escape liability for the *mens rea which he actually had*–the *mens rea* for murder–whereas there is a reason, in order to do justice, to allow a less blameworthy accomplice to avoid liability for *mens rea* which he lacked. Secondly, it could be argued that if ss 34 and 35 require that each accomplice has *mens rea* for the actual offence committed, then the ambit of s 34 is unduly narrowed. It will be shown later that this has been a concern of the courts in their interpretation of s 34. However, it is submitted that so long as one remembers that s 38 is available as a back-up if liability under ss 34 and 35 cannot be sustained, there is no problem.

This interpretation may also help to settle an issue concerning the defence of diminished responsibility under Exception 7 to s 300. It has been argued that it is doubtful whether an accomplice who *abets* a perpetrator suffering from diminished responsibility, could be convicted of murder while the perpetrator is convicted of culpable homicide, because the wording of s 109 would seem to exclude this possibility. However, the same restriction does not arise in relation to s 38, so that if the accomplice actually engages or is concerned in the commission of the criminal act, he could be convicted of murder even though the perpetrator could rely on diminished responsibility. Is it possible to arrive at different results simply depending on whether the accomplice participates in the criminal act or only abets it? The answer would be yes in English law, which distinguishes between the liability of an aider and abettor (participant in the criminal act) and an accessary before the fact (abettor under the Code) holding that the former can be convicted of a higher offence than the perpetrator, while the latter cannot. It would be a shame if the Code perpetuated such an illogical and undesirable distinction, and it is submitted that it need not be interpreted as doing so. Section 110 provides that:

"Whoever abets the commission of an offence shall, if the person abetted does the act with a different intention or knowledge from that of the abettor, be punished with the punishment provided for the offence which would have been committed if the act had been done with the intention or knowledge of the abettor and with no other."

In other words, the abettor may be punished according to his own *mens rea*, just as in s 38 which is the corresponding section governing participants. Of course, as was pointed out in relation to s 38, a limited defence does not necessarily mean that the accused lacks *mens rea*. The language of s 110 is not as wide as that of s 38, but it could be applied in *some* cases of diminished responsibility or some other limited defence, to help obviate this problem.

2. Common object: unlawful assembly

Penal Code, ss 149, 141, 142 and 143

149. If an offence is committed by any member of an unlawful assembly in prosecution of the common object of that assembly, or such as the members of that assembly knew to be likely to be committed in prosecution of that object, every person who, at the time of the committing of that offence, is a member of the same assembly, is guilty of that offence.

141. An assembly of 5 or more persons is designated an "unlawful assembly", if the common object of the persons composing that assembly is —
(a) to overawe by criminal force, or show of criminal force, the Legislative or Executive Government, or any public servant in the exercise of the lawful power of such public servant;
(b) to resist the execution of any law, or of any legal process;
(c) to commit any mischief or criminal trespass, or other offence;
(d) by means of criminal force, or show of criminal force, to any person, to take or obtain possession of any property, or to deprive any person of the enjoyment of a right of way, or of the use of water or other incorporeal right of which he is in possession or enjoyment, or to enforce any right or supposed right; or
(e) by means of criminal force, or show of criminal force, to compel any person to do what he is not legally bound to do, or to omit to do what he is legally entitled to do.

 Explanation–An assembly which was not unlawful when it assembled may subsequently become an unlawful assembly.

142. Whoever, being aware of facts which render any assembly an unlawful assembly, intentionally joins that assembly, or continues in it, is said to be a member of an unlawful assembly.

143.   Whoever is a member of an unlawful assembly, shall be punished with imprisonment for a term which may extend to 6 months, or with fine, or with both.

[For other forms of unlawful assembly, see ss 144–148 and 150–151.]

When a crime is committed by the concerted action of a number of persons the question may arise as to whether they should be liable under s 34 read with a substantive offence or whether s 149 should apply. The line between s 34 and s 149 could be a thin one.

Sepai Bhaimiya Nathu v State of Gujarat (1960) 61 Cri LJ 1329 (HC, India)

Raju J: But although there is a distinction between s 34 which deals with common intention and s 149 which deals with constructive liability based on common object, there may not be much difference between intention and object, because if there is common intention to commit an offence it must also be assumed that the common object was to commit that offence. Similarly if the common object of a group of persons be to do an act that would be a case of the group of persons having a common intention to do that act although the act may be such that s 141 [definition of unlawful assembly] would apply to an assembly of five or more persons with the common object of doing that act, but s 34 would not apply. That is so because for the application of s 34, the common intention must be to do a criminal act whereas the common object falling under s 141 need not necessarily be a criminal act. For instance, the common object of an unlawful assembly may be to take or obtain possession of any property or to deprive any person of the enjoyment of right of way or of the use of water of which he is in possession or enjoyment although in such cases the common object must be to do so by means of criminal force or show of criminal force. But if the common object of a group of persons be to do a criminal act, their common intention would also be to do that criminal act. But if some members of an assembly share a common intention to commit an offence, it can also be assumed that their common object was to commit that offence. In this view, it may be possible to make a distinction between similar object and common object just as a distinction has been drawn between similar intention and common intention.

Appeal dismissed

(a) Distinctions between s 149 and s 34

Section 149	*Section 34*
(1) This section creates a specific offence and deals with the punishment of that offence alone. (*Barendra Kumar Ghosh*, 1925; *Francis*, 1960.)	The section does not create an offence–the section comes under Chapter II, "General Explanations" of the Code. It has to be read with a specific offence.

(2) There must be a "common object" among the accused persons: "... though their object is common, the intentions of the several members may differ and indeed may be similar only in respect that they are all unlawful". (*Barendra Kumar Ghosh*, 1925.)	"Common intention": the leading feature is the element of participation in a criminal act. (*Barendra Kumar Ghosh*, 1925.)
(3) This section postulates an assembly of five or more persons having a common object, viz one of those objects named in s 141.	There must be at least two persons but need not be five.
(4) Common object need not necessarily be a criminal act (s 141(d)).	Common intention must be to do a criminal act.
(5) Liability of every member of an unlawful assembly is not limited to acts done in prosecution of the common object of the assembly but extends to acts which the members of the assembly knew to be likely to be committed in prosecution of the common object (s 149).	Liability depends on participation in furtherance of a common intention.

(b) Overlap between ss 149 and 34

Despite the distinctions noted above there is an overlap between the two sections. In *Barendra Kumar Ghosh* (1925), the Privy Council observed that both sections deal with combinations of persons, who become punishable as sharers in an offence. Indeed, courts have substituted s 34 for s 149.

Francis v PP (1960) 26 MLJ 40 (CA, KL, Malaya)

Nine persons, viz the four appellants together with five others, assembled together with the common object of causing hurt to one Kuda Baksh, his wife and the deceased. In carrying out their common object another person was killed by one or more persons of the group of nine. The nine were charged under ss 149 and 304 of the Penal Code.

At the close of the case for the prosecution the trial judge was of the opinion that there was no evidence against three of the accused and they were accordingly found not guilty. Of the remaining six, the jury found the four appellants "guilty of unlawful assembly and manslaughter [sic]"; another of the accused "not guilty of murder or manslaughter [sic] but guilty of unlawful assembly" and the remainder not guilty of any offence.

The question before the Court of Criminal Appeal was that since four persons could not constitute an "unlawful assembly" under s 141 (which requires at least five persons) could they be guilty of "manslaughter" [sic] in pursuance of their common object; or could s 34 be applied?

Thomson CJ: Before us the convictions of the four appellants have been attacked on the sole ground that they were convictions under ss 149 and 304 of the Penal Code and that as such they were bad in law because it was clear from the jury's verdict as elucidated by the Judge's questions that there was a finding of fact by the jury that only four persons were involved in the attack on the dead man and that as a matter of law four persons cannot constitute an unlawful assembly as defined by s 141 of the Penal Code.

Although based to some extent on the English Criminal Law as it was about 1860, the Penal Code differs from the English Law in some very fundamental respects. In particular it ignores the division of criminal offences into felonies and misdemeanours nor does it regard participators in crime as principals in the first or second degree as does the law of England in relation to felonies only. Instead, apart from questions of conspiracy and abetment with which we are not concerned here, it deals with what may be called constructive liability for crime in ss 34 and 149 and it is important to note just how these sections deal with that question.

Section 34 says that when a criminal act is done by several persons, in furtherance of the common intention of all, each of such persons is liable for that act in the same manner as if the act were done by him alone. Here, the conditions are some overt act, not necessarily the full criminal act itself, and a common intention.

Section 149 has to be read in the light of ss 141 and 143. Section 141 defines an unlawful assembly as an assembly of five or more persons having any one of a number of specified common objects one of which is to commit any offence. Section 143 creates the specific offence of being a member of an unlawful assembly. Section 149 provides that if an offence is committed by a member of an unlawful assembly then every member of the same assembly is guilty of that offence if either it is committed in prosecution of the common object of the assembly or it is such as the members of the assembly know to be likely to be committed in prosecution of the common object. Here the conditions are that there must be a common object, for without a common object there can be no assembly, and then either that common object must be to commit the offence which is in question or where the common object is not to commit it there must be knowledge that the offence is likely to be committed in prosecution of the common object.

The first point to be observed here is that although s 34 does not like s 149 create a specific offence both sections have this in common that each prescribes conditions in which a person may be convicted for something that is constituted a substantive offence by the other provisions of the Code. Where, for example, the offence in question is murder in contravention of s 302, s 34 provides that if its conditions are fulfilled each of the persons who has fulfilled them is liable for the murder as if he had committed it alone. Again, s 149 provides that if its conditions are fulfilled then any person who fulfils them is by reason of it guilty of the offence of murder.

The second point to be observed is that although s 34 uses the expression "common intention" and s 149 uses the expression "common object" these expressions may or may not mean different things according to the facts of the case. Object and purpose mean the same thing and it may well be as was pointed out by Viscount Simon LC, in another connection in the case of *Crofter Hand Woven Harris Tweed Co, Ltd* v *Veitch* (1942):

> "The test is not what is the natural result to the plaintiffs of such combined action, or what is the resulting damage which the defendants realize or should realize will follow, but what is in truth the object in the minds of the combiners when they acted as they did. It is not consequence that matters, but purpose; the relevant conjunction is not ὥστε, 'so that ...' but 'ἵνα 'in order that'."

In other words it can be argued that the effect of the use of the word "object" in s 149 is to exclude any sort of constructive intention such as might arise from the presumption that a man must be held to intend the natural and probable consequences of his acts.

Again, it may well be in the case of an unlawful assembly that certain members of it have in addition to the common object which they share with its other members private intentions of their own which only have the quality of being unlawful in common with the common object.

On the other hand there may well be circumstances in which object and intention are the same where parties act not only "so that" but also "in order that" a particular result may follow.

The position is summarized in the following passage from the judgment of Lord Sumner in the case of *Barendra Kumar Ghosh* (1925) in which their Lordships were primarily concerned with the interpretation of s 34:

> "Section 149,...creates a specific offence and deals with the punishment of that offence alone. It postulates an assembly of five or more persons having a common object— namely, one of those named in s 141 ... and then the doing of acts by members of it in prosecution of that object. There is a difference between object and intention, for, though their object is common, the intentions of the several members may differ and indeed may be similar only in respect that they are all unlawful, while the element of participation in action, which is the leading feature of s 34, is replaced in s 149 by membership of the assembly at the time of the committing of the offence. Both sections deal with combinations of persons who become punishable as sharers in an offence. Thus they have a certain resemblance and may to some extent overlap."

Having reached these conclusions it is clear that in the present case any of the accused could as a matter of law have been convicted for murder or for manslaughter by reason of s 34, although the charge against them alleged their guilt by reason of s 149 if it was proved that they acted together in causing the death of the deceased and each of them shared in a common intention to cause his death within the meaning of s 299 or s 300. That is clear from the provisions of ss 166 and 167 of the Criminal Procedure Code, the combined effect of which was thus stated by Viscount Haldane in the case of *Begu* (1925):

> "A man may be convicted of an offence, although there has been no charge in respect of it, if the evidence is such as to establish a charge that might have been made."

We find support for this view in certain decisions of the Courts in India.

In the case of *Sheo Ram* (1948) the Allahabad Court considered the effect of the decision of the Privy Council in the case of *Barendra Kumar Ghosh* (1925) on certain previous Indian decisions and concluded by holding (at p 165) that:

> "A person can be convicted of an offence read with s 34, Penal Code, if the facts of the case justify it and if the accused has not been misled in his defence and if there has been no failure of justice, irrespective of the fact whether the charge framed against him mentioned s 34, Penal Code, or not, or the charge framed against him was a charge of an offence read with s 149, Penal Code."

That is an Allahabad case but the same conclusions have been reached in two recent decisions of the Supreme Court of India....

In the present case, having regard to the whole tenor of the trial, to the Judge's summing-up and to his subsequent questioning of the jury as read in the light of that summing-up we are of the opinion that so far as the appellants are concerned the intention of the jury and their true verdict was that each of the appellants was guilty of culpable homicide not amounting to murder in contravention of s 304.

The jury had in effect been told that if they were satisfied that there was an unlawful assembly of five or more persons having the common object of causing hurt and that these persons knew that murder was likely to be committed and that murder was committed, then it was open to them to convict each of the persons concerned of murder or manslaughter as the case might be because of the provisions of s 149. They were then told that if there was an assembly which was not unlawful only by reason of its consisting of less than five persons then it was open to them on the evidence to convict the persons concerned of murder or manslaughter as the case might be by reason of s 34 if they were satisfied that each of these persons took part in the killing in prosecution of a common intention to kill, an expression which was explained to them at great length....

As regards the four appellants, they clearly reconsidered the position in the light of the consideration which had already been fully explained, that being only four in number they did not constitute an unlawful assembly. They were asked if the appellants or one of them killed but did not murder the deceased Mohamed Ali. The terms of that question considered in isolation were not happy but in view of all that had been said by the Judge in his summing-up and in view of what the jury had already said to the effect that each of the appellants was guilty of manslaughter and unlawful assembly they could only interpret that question by the Judge as being whether they meant that, having regard to the provisions of s 34, they were still of the opinion that these appellants were guilty of manslaughter. And the answer to that question was "yes."

In the circumstances we are compelled to dismiss the appeal but in pursuance of our powers under s 29(1) of the Courts Ordinance we vary the judgment of the High Court by substituting in the case of each of the appellants a judgment of culpable homicide not amounting to murder in contravention of s 304 for the judgment entered under ss 304 and 149.

Appeal dismissed

However, even though the number of convicted persons is less than five, the court can still convict under s 149 if the convicted persons together with unidentified persons make up the number of five or more. (See Myint Soe, 1972.)

Tan Kheng Ann v PP [1965] 2 MLJ 108 (FC, Singapore)

This case concerns the attack on Pulau Senang, the hitherto model penal island of Singapore, by criminal detainees there. The appellants and 63 others were charged with being members of an unlawful assembly under s 149 and also for the murder of a number of persons and the destruction of property in the island.

The overlap between ss 34 and 149 was considered.

Thomson LJ: In the first place it was said that if constructive liability was to be imputed to the accused it should have been by reason of s 34 and not s 149 of the Penal Code. It is not necessary here to quote at length what was said by the former Court of Appeal of the Federation regarding ss 34 and 149 in the case of *Francis* (1960) beyond repeating that the "common intention" of s 34 and the "common object" of s 149 may or may not mean different things according to the facts of the individual case. As was said by Lord Sumner in the case of *Barendra Kumar Ghosh* (1925) the two sections "have a certain resemblance and may to some extent overlap".

Here it was the case for the prosecution that the common object of the alleged unlawful assembly and the common intention of its members were the same, that is to say to kill and to destroy, and in the circumstances it was open to the prosecution to proceed either by virtue of s 34 or by virtue of s 149. The consideration that in the event they proceeded under the latter section cannot in itself be said to have prejudiced the accused in any way or to vitiate the convictions.

Then it was said that each of the charges was "bad in law" because "it averred the murder of one person in two different sets of circumstances". This arises in this way. Section 149 says that a member of an unlawful assembly is guilty of any offence that is committed by any member of the assembly in prosecution of the common object of the assembly *or* is such that he knew to be likely to be committed in prosecution of the common object. Here in each of the charges the allegation was that each of the accused was a member of an unlawful assembly whose common objects were to cause death and destruction *and* that in the prosecution of these common objects murder was committed which was an offence which the members of the assembly knew to be likely to be committed in prosecution of their common objects. It is thus clear that circumstances which in the section are alternative were in the charges alleged conjunctively. There was, however, no reason why this should not be done....

At this stage it will be convenient to deal with one other matter regarding the charges of which complaint has been made. Each of the charges alleged that the common objects of the unlawful assembly were to cause the deaths of five named persons "and others".

With regard to the presentation of the case as a whole the complaints made can be summed up in the proposition that the case was put to the jury on the basis that there was a single assembly with a single combination of common objects as averred in the charges. And that this was wrong....

Each of those who took part in the events of 12th July may have had different thoughts in his heart, though none of them told the court what they were. Notionally, there may have been many assemblies in the sense of groups of people who had the same thoughts as each other but different thoughts from those of the members of other groups. The composition of those notional groups may have varied from time to time, even from minute to minute, as changes in the hearts of their members took place. The thoughts of one group may have had something but not everything in common with those of any other group. Some individuals may have been inspired with animus against Dutton [one of the deceased], some may have felt a general resentment against the fact and the conditions of their detention. Some may have premeditated the outbreak. Others may have been in ignorance of its likelihood and only adhered to it when it started or may for some reason or other lost taste for what was happening and at some stage or other dissociated themselves from it, a possibility that was in fact put to the jury by the judge.

As regards premeditation there was no doubt that there was some premeditation; Dutton himself knew at the latest on the morning of 12th July that something was afoot and he sent a telephone message to the mainland and had the serviceable boats removed to a neighbouring island. It is to be observed in parenthesis, however, that the evidence as to the persons who took part in this premeditation, if it was believed, only implicated a few of the accused, and in any event this evidence, even is so far as it did implicate them, was not of great importance because there was no question of any charge of conspiracy.

As regards the general question of objects, the court was not concerned wth motives and any philosophical discussion of motives and how far they are capable of being shared would have been out of place and would only have served to confuse the mind of the jury. What the court was concerned with was the alleged common object of a number of persons. And if a number of persons do the same acts voluntarily and consciously then, in the absence of anything which suggests that these acts are not done consciously and voluntarily, these acts must be regarded as evidence of the common object of the individuals who do them and, so far as the doing of these acts is concerned, these individuals, must be regarded as a single assembly.

It was said by the Supreme Court of India in the case of *Sukha* (1956):

> "a common object is different from a common intention in that it does not require prior concert and a common meeting of minds before the attack, and an unlawful object can develop after the people get there."

And in that connection we would adopt the following passage from Gour's (1961):

> "The purpose for which the members of assembly set out or which they desired to achieve is the object. Each member may have an object in view and may also have his own idea of the means with which that object is to be achieved and the extent to which he is prepared to go for attaining it. If the object desired by all the members is the same, the knowledge that that is the object which is being pursued is shared by all the members and they are in general agreement as to how it is to be achieved; the object then becomes the common object of the assembly. Normally, a determination to achieve an object includes a resolve to meet with force any resistance to its attainment. A common object may be found by express agreement after mutual consultations but that is not necessary. It may be formed at any stage by all or some members of the assembly and the other members may join and accept it. It may be modified or altered or abandoned at any stage. What the common object of the unlawful assembly is at a particular stage of the incident is essentially a question of fact to be determined by keeping in view the nature of the assembly, the arms it carries and the behaviour of its members at or near the scene of the incident."

In the present case, having regard to the evidence, it was clearly in the interests of justice that the jury should have been asked to consider the whole affair on the basis of it being a single transaction. It was for them to say (and it was left to them to say) whether there was an assembly with the common unlawful objects averred by the prosecution. If there was not that was then the end of the matter. If they were satisfied there was such an unlawful assembly it was then for them to say in the case of each of the accused whether they were satisfied that at the material time he was a member of it....

Appeals dismissed

(c) Unlawful assembly

Section 141 lays down what constitutes an "unlawful assembly". An assembly becomes "unlawful" only if its members consist of five or more persons and if the "common object" is to do one of the things specified in s 141. It is not necessary for the assembly to have had a common object prior to the time they assemble together–the common object can be formed at the meeting. The explanation to s 141 states that an assembly which was not unlawful when it assembled may subsequently become an unlawful assembly. It is sufficient that each person in the assembly has the same object in view and that they assemble to achieve the object.

(i) Common object

R v Abdulrahman (1874) 3 Kyshe 61 (SC, Straits Settlements)

The appellants were convicted ... of rioting under s 147 of the Penal Code.... From the evidence, it appeared that some of the appellants were members of the red flag Society, and the others of the white; and in consequence of a dispute between two members of the respective Kongsees, the appellants, as members of these respective Kongsees, turned out at Ayer Etam and had a free fight among themselves. The members of the one Society opposing and trying to do as much harm as they could to the members of the other. The appellants were all arrested on the spot by the Police, who charged all appellants jointly, with rioting and they were convicted by the Magistrate, as above stated. The appellants now appealed against this decision.

CW Rodyk, for some of the appellants, members of the white flag Society, contended that the conviction was bad, as the appellants were members of two opposite factions and had not a common object in view. The object of the members of the one Society being, to do as much harm as possible to the members of the other. He referred to ss 141, 146 & 147 of the Penal Code, and cited *Sheik Bazu* (1867) and *Surroop Chundra Paul* (1869).

DC Presgrave, for the respondent, contended that the Court could amend the conviction by charging and convicting the members of the respective Kongsees separately; that the appellants had, in fact a common object within the meaning of s 141, viz to fight and commit a breach of the peace, which was an "offence", s 141, cl 3; that the cases cited were Indian decisions, and not binding on this Court.

Sidgreaves CJ, held that the appellants had not a common object within the meaning of s 141; that the Indian decisions, though not binding on this Court, nevertheless were useful as precedents, and as they supported his view of the meaning to be put on the section, he looked upon them as authorities. The conviction would therefore be quashed.

Conviction quashed

The two Indian cases, viz *Sheikh Bazu* (1867) and *Surroop Chundra Paul* (1869) relied on by the appellants were accepted by his Lordship in quashing the conviction. With respect, it is submitted that the two cases were misapplied: while both *Sheikh Bazu* (1867) and *Surroop Chundra Paul* (1869) held that the common object of one faction would be the very opposite of the common object of the other faction, this does not mean that there cannot be *two* unlawful assemblies. The courts in these two cases simply held that the two opposing factions in each of these cases should not be lumped together as constituting *one* unlawful assembly.

In the recent case of *Sikhar Behera* (1982) (see below, p 362), the Orissa High Court held that when members of two opposing groups went to a meeting place together with a number of people to defeat the other group, the assemblies on both sides were unlawful assemblies and it was immaterial which party began the attack.

There must be clear evidence as to the object of the assembly. In *Khoo See Hee* (1884), the six appellants were members of a secret society and were found standing in front of the *Kongsee* (ie society) House in which several others were assembled. They fled on the approach of the police, who went there on information that the members of that society were gathered there with a view to attacking another society. The appellants were arrested and the police found in the *Kongsee* House a number of clubs, or poles, apparently intended as weapons of offence. The Supreme Court of the Straits Settlements, in quashing the conviction under s 149, held that there was no "reasonable proof that the appellants had formed part of any such assembly"; also while there was suspicion, the evidence did not reasonably show any common object of committing a breach of peace. The court held it was not sufficient that they were contemplating a breach of the peace.

Section 141 does not require the actual commission of an offence for the purpose of determining an unlawful assembly: the consensus of the "common object" is itself an offence. Being a member of an unlawful assembly is punishable under s 143. This must be distinguished from s 149 which provides for vicarious liability of the members of an unlawful society for an offence committed in prosecution of that assembly. The common object contemplated by s 141 can be gathered from the facts and circumstances, for example, the nature of the assembly and behaviour of the members. The six appellants in *Khoo See Hee* (1884) were members of a secret society standing outside the society's premises. It may be significant to note their behaviour when the police arrived. They fled. There was information that they gathered there with the object of attacking another society, and clubs were found inside the premises of the society. It could therefore be reasonably inferred that there was a common object to commit a breach of the peace. Although the court did not raise the point, it may be that they were waiting for the members of another society to arrive. It was unfortunate that they were charged under s 149 rather than s 143.

(ii) Section 141 (c): "to commit any mischief or criminal trespass, or other offence"

The question has arisen as to whether the phrase "or other offence" under s 141(c) is to be read *ejusdem generis* with "mischief or criminal trespass" or whether it has a wider import.

Ong Chin Seng v R (1960) 26 MLJ 34 (CCA, Singapore)

The appellants were convicted of being members of an unlawful assembly whose common object was to cause hurt by dangerous weapons and of the murder of one Ong Hock Soon, an offence which the members of the assembly knew likely to be committed in the prosecution of the common object of the assembly. They were convicted under ss 149 and 302 of the Penal Code.

Rose CJ: In the charge the common object alleged was to cause hurt by dangerous weapons. It is contended that this common object is not expressly mentioned in s 141 of the Code and that the only words under which it could possibly be caught up are "or other offence" contained in the third head in that section.

Learned Counsel for the first appellant, with whose submission learned Counsel for the second appellant associates himself, contends that the *ejusdem generis* rule should apply and that causing hurt with dangerous weapons is not *ejusdem generis* with mischief of criminal trespass.

It seems to us, however, that this is putting too narrow a construction upon the section. Chapter VIII of the Code, within which s 141 falls, relates to "offences against the public tranquillity". The commission of an offence by five or more persons whose common object was to cause hurt by dangerous weapons would seem eminently to fall within the ambit of the Chapter. It is, moreover, of interest, perhaps, to note the comment of Dr Gour ...: "This clause is not free from avoidable ambiguity. It says that an assembly is unlawful, if its common object is 'to commit any mischief or criminal trespass, or other offence'. Now, strictly speaking, the other offence must be *ejusdem generis*; otherwise the preceding enumeration was unnecessary. But the clause is intended to include all offences both against person and property, and not only mischief, criminal trespass and *ejusdem generis*." He proceeds to cite some Indian authorities for his proposition.

We therefore consider that there is no substance in the point. We would add, although this is not the reason for our conclusion, that there have been other cases before the Courts of Singapore in which, (although admittedly the point was not taken) convictions have been recorded in the Assize Courts and upheld on appeal where the common object of the alleged unlawful assembly was similar to that in the current case.

Appeal dismissed

Fung Yin Ching v PP [1965] 1 MLJ 49 (FC, Singapore)

(The facts appear in the judgment.)

Thomson LP: These appellants were tried on charges of ... being members of an unlawful assembly whose common object was to overawe the Government and in prosecution of such common object they used force and thereby committed rioting in contravention of s 147 of the Penal Code, or, alternatively, being members of an unlawful assembly whose common object was to resist the execution of law and in prosecution of such common object they used force and thereby committed rioting in contravention of s 147 of the Penal Code; thirdly, they were members of an unlawful assembly whose common object was to overawe by the show of criminal force the executive Government of the State in contravention of s 143 of the Penal Code, or, alternatively, they were members of an unlawful assembly whose common object was to resist the execution of law in contravention of s 143 of the Penal Code....

Against these convictions and sentences the appellants have now appealed....

Sometime in April they were apparently concerned with the treatment in prison of a number of persons who were detained under the local law relating to public security and they resolved to bring this matter to the notice of the local Government allegedly with a view to obtaining some alleviation of the conditions of these persons.

In pursuance of this object they got in touch with the relatives of the proposed objects of their benevolent activities, prepared petitions to the Government and, in the event, organized a procession of these relatives which was to proceed from the headquarters of the appellants' political party to the City Hall in Singapore which is the headquarters of the Government of the State of Singapore and where the Prime Minister of that State has his place of business....

[The procession, comprising about 100–200 people, was led by the appellants.]

[T]he police tried to prevent the crowd from going further into the Hall than the ground floor and that a large number of the crowd, including the appellants, then formed a common intention to go up to the floor on which the Prime Minister's room was situated in spite of the police and proceeded to use force in prosecution of that intention.

The Chief Justice regarded that intention as intention to resist the execution of the law....

Section 141 defines "unlawful assembly" as an assembly of five or more persons with a common object to do one of a number of things which are set out under five heads. It is only necessary to refer to the second and third heads. The second is to resist the execution of any law, or of any legal process, and the third is to commit any mischief or criminal trespass or other offence. The Chief Justice was of the opinion that the present case fell under the second of these heads. For reasons which I am about to state we are not prepared to quarrel with that conclusion, but it seems to us he could equally have held that it fell under the third head.

Regarding the second head, s 110 of the Criminal Procedure Code reads as follows:

> "Every police officer may interpose for the purpose of preventing and shall be to the best of his ability using all lawful means prevent the commission of any offence."

That places a duty upon the police and it confers upon them the power to carry out that duty.

In the present case all the appellants and a great number of other people commenced to commit an offence when the procession was formed and started on its way. It is true that that was not an offence in the sense that the word is used in the Penal Code; but it was an offence in the sense in which the word is used in the Criminal Procedure Code, it was an offence against the Minor Offences (Assemblies and Processions) Rules. And so long as the unauthorized procession continued in existence that offence continued to be committed and by reason of s 110 the police had the power, and were indeed obliged, to prevent it and to use lawful means to that end, that is to say to execute the law. It is immaterial in the present case that the police in their discretion did not intervene right at the beginning, that they did not intervene in the public streets but that they refrained from intervening until what they considered a suitable time. When they did so intervene, however, it is clear that the crowd, including the appellants, formed a common intention to resist what they were doing by way of execution of the law. In the circumstances everyone who was present and animated by that common intention was guilty of the offence of unlawful assembly and when that common intention was prosecuted and any degree of force was used in the prosecution of it then every other member of the unlawful assembly was also guilty of rioting irrespective of whether or not he himself individually used actual force.

On that the case clearly fell within the second head of s 141. But it also fell under the third head of s 141.

Appeals dismissed

(d) Section 149

(i) "In prosecution of the common object of that assembly"

"In prosecution of the common object of the unlawful assembly" means that the offence must be directly in connection with the common object.

Mizaji v State of Uttar Pradesh (1959) Cri LJ 177 (SC) (SC, Allahabad, India)

JL Kapur J: (6) This section [s 149] has been the subject matter of interpretation in the various High Courts of India, but every case has to be decided on its own facts. The first part of the section means that the offence committed in prosecution of the common object must be one which is committed with a view to accomplish the common object. It is not necessary that there should be a preconcert in the sense of a meeting of the members of the unlawful assembly as to the common object; it is enough if it is adopted by all the members and is shared by all of them. In order that the case may fall under the first part the offence committed must be connected immediately with the common object of the unlawful assembly of which the accused were members. Even if the offence committed is not in direct prosecution of the common object of the assembly, it may yet fall under s 149 if it can be held that the offence was such as the members knew was likely to be committed. The expression "know" does not mean a mere possibility, such as might or might not happen. For instance, it is a matter of common knowledge that when in a village a body of heavily armed men set out to take a woman by force, someone is likely to be killed and all the members of the unlawful assembly must be aware of that likelihood and would be guilty under the second part of s 149. Similarly, if a body of persons go armed to take forcible possession of the land, it would be equally right to say that they have the knowledge that murder is likely to be committed if the circumstances as to the weapons carried and other conduct of the members of the unlawful assembly clearly point to such knowledge on the part of them all. There is a great deal to be said for the opinion of Couch CJ in *Sabed Ali*'s case (1873) that when an offence is committed in prosecution of the common object, it would generally be an offence which the members of the unlawful assembly knew was likely to be committed in prosecution of the common object. That, however, does not make the converse proposition true: there may be cases which would come within the second part, but not within the first. The distinction between the two parts of s 149, Indian Penal Code cannot be ignored or obliterated. In every case it would be an issue to be determined whether the offence committed falls within the first part of s 149 as explained above or it was an offence such as the members of the assembly knew to be likely to be committed in prosecution of the common object and falls within the second part.

If the offence committed goes beyond the immediate prosecution of the common object it falls to be considered under the second limb of s 149 (see below).

(ii) "Acts which members of the assembly knew to be likely to be committed"

The essence of liability under this limb is the word "knew". It has been interpreted to imply the existence of facts from which a certain inference is so irresistibly drawn as to amount to a certainty. In *Lalman* (1973), the High Court of Madhya Pradesh stated:

> It could not be reasonably inferred from the circumstances of the case that the assembly which was animated with a common object to chastise could also be imputed with the knowledge that some of the members may give such fatal blows on the head or chest as would result in the death of the victims.... It could not be said that the assembly was of such a kind where the members knew what the other members were going to do. It could not be said that it was known to members the extent to which the other man was likely to act in achieving the common object. The word "knew" in s 149 of the Indian Penal Code has been interpreted by Supreme Court to imply the existence of facts from which a certain inference is so irresistible as to amount to a certainty. This knowledge must be shown to exist at the time of commission of the offence and not knowledge acquired in the light of subsequent events.

In *Sikhar Behera* (1982), there was a dispute between the appellants and members of the prosecution party regarding the possession of some land. The two parties were prepared for a fight. The appellants (16 of them) were jointly tried with 25 others and convicted of various offences, including being members of an unlawful assembly under s 149 of the Indian Penal Code.

PK Mohanti J said:

Section 149, IPC fixes vicarious liability of the members of an unlawful assembly for the acts done in prosecution of the common object of that assembly. But such liability is not limited to the acts done in prosecution of the common object of the assembly. It extends even to acts which the members of the assembly knew to be likely to be committed in prosecution of that common object. If an offence is committed by a member of an unlawful assembly and that offence is one which the members of the unlawful assembly know to be likely to be committed in prosecution of the common object, every member who had that knowledge will be guilty of the offence so committed. In the instant case, the members of the assembly came heavily armed with deadly weapons, some with Tentas, some with Bhalis and some with lathis in order to carry out their common object. If the members of the assembly knew that by using those weapons death would be caused they are guilty under s 302/149, IPC. In our opinion, the second part of s 149 is clearly established in this case. If the appellants were members of the unlawful assembly, they cannot escape their liability for the murders.

Part V

Causation

Chapter 18

Causation

By NA Morgan

A. Introduction

The *actus reus* of result crimes requires the accused not merely to have behaved in a particular manner but also to have caused a particular result or event. The most obvious examples are offences against the person such as hurt and grievous hurt and all forms of homicide. Criminal force (s 349) also requires causing of motion, cessation of motion, etc. Causing a particular result may also be an element in some property offences such as mischief (causing destruction of or damage to property, s 425).

Difficult problems have arisen in some cases, particularly involving offences against the person, in deciding whether the accused's conduct is to be regarded as a legal cause of the injury or death. Suppose, for example, that the victim of an attack refuses to have medical treatment which would certainly save his life; or that the treatment he is given turns out to be negligent in circumstances where he would have been saved by proper treatment. Consider the situation where a manufacturer fails to maintain his machinery to the official safety standards but the victim himself also does something "silly" such as falling asleep at his machine. It might be shown that his injuries would not have occurred if he had not fallen asleep but also that they would have been prevented if proper safety standards had been met. The law faces the problem of deciding who, if anybody, should be held legally responsible for such injuries or deaths.

The fundamental distinction traditionally drawn by the law is between a "factual" (or "but for" or "*sine qua non*") cause and a "legal" (or "imputable") cause (or the "causa causans"). Factual causes are wider than legal causes and, at least according to conventional wisdom, causation will only be established where the accused's conduct amounts not only to a factual but also to a legal cause. Sometimes the same general principle is expressed in negative terms; there must be no break in the chain of causation between the accused's conduct and the resulting injury.

Factual causes are those factors without which the result would not have occurred, and thus form a very broad category. However, establishing the accused's conduct as a factual cause is an important preliminary hurdle to liability. In *White* (1910) the accused attempted to poison his mother. She died with a glass containing poison by her side but she had apparently not drunk any and had died of a heart attack brought on by other causes. However blameworthy the accused's conduct, he could only be convicted of attempted murder. In *Chanan Das* (1934) the victim died from meningitis and compression of the brain; however, it was held that the prosecution had not established that this was attributable to head injuries received at the hands of the accused. Although the terminology was not adopted by the court, this was clearly a case where "but for" causation was not established. However, in most cases factual causation is not difficult to satisfy. To take the earlier examples, the victim of the attack would not have died but for the original injury. The machine operator would not have been injured if not for both the defective machinery and his falling asleep. However, the dividing line between causes which are merely factual and those which are also legal is in practice difficult to identify with precision and, as shown in the following analysis, differs between different offences.

B. Conceptual background

In their leading work on causation in civil and criminal law, Hart and Honoré (1985) identify three main positions which differ in the relative importance they attach to causation principles in establishing liability.

1. Causal minimalism

HLA Hart and AM Honoré, *Causation in the Law* (2nd edn, 1985), xxxiv

According to this [theory], genuine causal issues are of small importance in settling questions of legal responsibility. In most instances they are confined to the issue whether the harm would have occurred in the absence of the wrongful conduct, and even this factual-sounding question is often answered in a way which owes more to considerations of legal policy than to any genuine attempt to determine the facts of the case. It is true that courts appear to take seriously, as raising causal issues, such further questions as whether the defendant's conduct was the "proximate cause" of the harm or whether the harm was "too remote". They speak as if these presented issues of fact suitable, in an appropriate case, for submission to a jury. But the issues in question are not, according to causal minimalism, really either causal or factual and to treat them as such is to "overload" the causal issue. They are rather issues of legal policy in disguise, better answered by asking whether, all things considered, the defendant should be held liable for the harm which ensued....

Causal minimalists are therefore sceptical of the very notion of a legal cause and would confine themselves to questions of "but for" causation; once this is satisfied, despite any appearances to the contrary, the argument in reality shifts to the question of whether the accused should, as a matter of policy, be liable. In the criminal law, the causal minimalist position is exemplified by extreme versions of what has been termed the *mens rea* approach to causation. This is the view that once it is established that the accused's conduct was a "but for" cause, attention should shift to the *mens rea*; thus "all the 'real work' [in determining liability] is done by the doctrine of *mens rea*" (Clarkson and Keating, 1984, p 330).

2. Causal maximalism

The doctrine of causal maximalism has developed primarily in the law of tort and is "the doctrine that causing harm is a necessary and sufficient condition of tort liability" (Hart and Honoré, 1985, p lxxiv). Under this view, subject only perhaps to specific exceptions such as insanity and infancy, fault is generally not relevant to the defendant's liability. Some advocates of the rehabilitative ideal came close to the same doctrine for criminal law in the 1960s. For example, Lady Wootton (1981, p 46) wrote, in support of strict liability:

> If the law says that certain things are not to be done, it is illogical to confine this prohibition to occasions when they are done from malice aforethought; for at least the material consequences of an action, and the reasons for prohibiting it, are the same whether it is the result of sinister malicious plotting, of negligence or of sheer accident. A man is equally dead whether he was stabbed or run over by a drunken motorist or by an incompetent one....

With regard to result crimes, she would therefore have proposed that the fact that the accused caused a particular result would be sufficient grounds for the intervention of the law; his state of mind at the time of the offence would be irrelevant to the question of conviction and would simply be one of the factors relevant to deciding the appropriate form of treatment. However, although the concept of no fault liability in tort has many modern adherents, the demise of rehabilitative thinking means that causal maximalism is of little practical help in analysing contemporary causation problems in criminal law. An advocate of causal maximalism in the criminal law would also have to address–as Lady Wootton does not–the difficult question of what it means to "cause" a result; should the concept be widely defined so that "but for" causation suffices, or should causation principles be developed which restrict those for whom treatment is deemed necessary?

3. Commonsense notions of causation

Hart and Honoré (1985) analyse case law from numerous jurisdictions and, rejecting both of the previous views, come to a conclusion somewhere in the middle ground; they suggest that causation per se is, and should be, insufficient ground for liability. On the other hand, causation is not determined, as causal minimalists suggest, by vague general policy considerations on a purely ad hoc basis. Instead, they argue, decided cases indicate that causation plays more than a residual role and is determined according to certain identifiable principles founded on commonsense views of causation:

> [A]s in tort, so in criminal law courts have often limited responsibility by appealing to the causal distinctions embedded in ordinary thought with their emphasis on voluntary interventions and abnormal or coincidental events as factors negativing responsibility (1985, p 325).

C. Causation for homicide under the Penal Code

There appears to be a significant difference in the approach to causation between culpable homicide and murder (ss 299 and 300) and causing death by a rash or negligent act (s 304(A)), even though the Penal Code makes no reference to the possibility of different tests.

1. Section 304(A) causation

Under s 304(A) of the Penal Code, it is an offence punishable with up to two years' imprisonment to cause death by rash or negligent conduct. The local cases under this section have very significantly avoided reference to English law and have consistently followed a long line of Indian decisions. The test of causation is a strict one, as evidenced by the numerous reported decisions where the accused has been acquitted on causation grounds even though the court has accepted that he was either rash or negligent and his conduct was clearly a "but for" cause of death. These cases do not, therefore, accord with versions of causal minimalism where "but for" causation alone would suffice.

Lee Kim Leng v R (1964) 30 MLJ 285 (HC, Singapore)

The deceased was knocked down and killed as she crossed the road at a pedestrian crossing. The appellant's car had collided with a stationary taxi which consequently lurched forward into her. The taxi had stopped without giving hand signals.

Chua J: In the Indian case of *Omkar Ram Pratap* (1902) it was held that to impose criminal liability under s 304(A) ... it is necessary that the death should have been the direct result of a rash and negligent act of the accused and that act must have been the proximate and efficient cause without the intervention of another's negligence. It must have been the *causa causans*; it is not enough that it may have been *causa sine qua non*....

In the present case the death of the pedestrian was due to the collision between the appellant's car ... and the taxi and in order to impose a criminal liability on the appellant it must be found as a fact that the collision was entirely or at least mainly due to the act of the appellant.

[His Lordship seems to have held some doubts as to whether the accused was negligent on the facts of the case but was of the view that the taxi driver was. He concluded:]

[S]o far as the evidence goes it is not sufficient to establish that the appellant was wholly or mainly responsible for the collision.

Appeal allowed

In *Mills* (1971) Williams CJ said it was necessary that "the death was directly attributable to accused's act, ie that the 'rash or negligent' act was the immediate cause of death and not merely a remote cause of it". This was subsequently followed in *Lee Lai Siew* (1978, below, p 373).

Indian courts have consistently adopted the same approach. In *Suleman Rahiman Mulani* (1968) the Supreme Court held that "there must be proof that the rash or negligent act of the accused was the proximate cause of the death. There must be direct nexus between the death of a person and the rash or negligent act of the accused".

Kurban Hussein Mohamedalli Rangawalla v State of Maharashtra
AIR (1965) SC 1616 (SC, India)

The appellant was one of the owners of a factory used for the manufacture of paints and varnishes. The factory was licensed for the manufacture of dry paints by a cold process but the appellant converted to the manufacture of wet paints by a heating process. The process involved heating rosin and bitumen and then adding turpentine when the mixture had cooled. The process was carried on in a room where drums of turpentine and varnish were stored and on the day in question was under the control of Hatim. A fire broke out and spread rapidly. Seven workers lost their lives and seven others were seriously burned.

Wanchoo J: The mere fact that the appellant allowed the burners to be used in the same room in which varnish and turpentine were stored, even though it might be a negligent act, would not be enough to make the appellant responsible for the fire which broke out .... [s] 304(A) requires ... that death must be the direct or proximate result of the rash or negligent act. It appears that the direct or proximate cause of the fire which resulted in seven deaths was the act of Hatim. It seems to us clear that Hatim was apparently in a hurry and, therefore, he did not perhaps allow the rosin to cool down sufficiently and poured turpentine too quickly. The advice of the expert is that the process of adding turpentine to melted rosin is a hazardous process and the proportion of froth would depend upon the quantity of turpentine added. The expert also stated that if turpentine is not slowly added to bitumen and rosin before it is cooled down to a certain temperature, such fire is likely to break out.... Therefore, the mere fact that the fire would not have taken place if the appellant had not allowed burners to be put in the same room in which turpentine and varnish were stored, would not be enough to make him liable under s 304(A), for the fire would not have taken place, with the result that seven persons were burnt to death, without the negligence of Hatim. The death in this case was therefore

... not directly the result of a rash or negligent act on the part of the appellant and was not the proximate and efficient cause without the intervention of another's negligence. The appellant must therefore be acquitted of the offence under s 304(A).

[The appellant was, however, convicted under s 285 of negligently omitting to guard against the dangers posed by combustible material in his possession.]

This decision may be compared with *Balchandra* (1968) where an explosion took place in the appellants' firework factory. The explosion resulted in injuries and deaths. It was found that prohibited explosives were being stored on the premises and the appellants were held liable under s 304(A). Glover J distinguished *Kurban Hussein* (1965) on its facts; there was no direct evidence of the immediate cause of the explosion but he felt it must be attributed to the prohibited explosives which were being stored and used there and there was no evidence of any other's negligence.

AD Bhatt v State of Gujarat AIR (1972) SC 1150 (SC, India)

The appellant was a chemist in charge of a department which prepared a solution of glucose in saline. Under the Drugs Rules, made under the Drugs Act, a separate batch number was to be given to every lot of bottles. The appellant did not conform to these rules and gave the same batch number to four separate lots. One lot turned out to be heavily contaminated with lead nitrate and 12 people died. The state argued that if the appellant had not ignored the Rules, the chief analyst would have discovered the contamination.

P Jaganmohan Reddy J: [T]he mere fact that an accused contravenes certain rules or regulations in the doing of an act which causes death of another does not establish that the death was the result of a rash or negligent act or that any such act was the proximate and efficient cause of death ... we have to determine whether the appellant's act in giving only one batch number to all the four lots ... was the cause of deaths and whether those deaths were a direct consequence of the appellant's act, that is, whether the appellant's act ... was the proximate and efficient cause without the intervention of another's negligence....

[The appeal was allowed on the basis that the chief analyst had also been at fault in failing to detect the impurities and because the production superintendant appeared not to have carried out all the necessary checks.]

Causation therefore presents a significant hurdle under s 304(A); this is in marked contrast to the position under the accepted approach to causation under ss 299 and 300 (see below, p 387). The s 304(A) test is worded in such a manner that it may be difficult in cases where there are several causes, particularly involving other acts of negligence, to hold anybody criminally liable for the deaths. The problem is best demonstrated by posing a series of questions arising out of the facts of *Kurban Hussein* (1965). Hatim's negligence was held to have broken the chain of causation so the factory manager was not liable. Would Hatim himself have been liable if he had been prosecuted? Was his negligence the proximate and efficient cause without the intervention of another's negligence? His negligence may have been the closest in time to the fire, but it would surely be wrong to impose liability only on the most recent act of negligence where another is substantially, perhaps even more, to blame. Adopting the other terminology found in the cases, could it be said that the fire was "entirely or mainly" due to Hatim's negligence? If the problem is that both Hatim and the manager were to some extent to blame, should both of them have been held liable or neither? Consider, also, *Lee Kim Leng* (1964). The car driver was not liable on causation grounds; would the taxi driver, who was apparently considered negligent, have been liable? Would the taxi driver's liability depend (rather artificially) on whether the car driver was negligent too?

The s 304(A) cases provide a fascinating contrast with the US case of *Welansky* (1944; see Clarkson and Keating, 1984). Nearly 500 people died in a nightclub fire. A prankster had turned off a bulb in an artificial palm tree. A 16-year-old boy was ordered to replace it. In order to see what he was doing he lit a match; unfortunately, the flame ignited the tree and the fire spread rapidly. Welansky was the owner of the club and it was shown that in equipping the club he had used defective wiring and inflammable decorations. It was also shown that inspite of these defects, and even though there were inadequate fire escapes, the local Fire Department had approved the club as safe. Welansky was convicted of manslaughter and given a semi-determinate sentence of betweeen 12 and 15 years' imprisonment. He was subsequently pardoned by the Governor of Massachusetts after serving three years. His conviction has been criticized as an exercise in scapegoating; because of the appalling consequences of the fire, the people of Boston wanted to blame someone for the incident. Under the cases examined above, he would not have been liable under s 304(A) as there were numerous other acts of negligence or fault on the part of the Fire Department, the prankster and the 16-year-old boy. Indeed the s 304(A) test suggests that none of them would have been liable under that section.

A fundamental issue is therefore whether it is appropriate for those who have been negligent or rash to escape liability under s 304(A) on causation grounds. It may be possible, as in the following case, to convict of a lesser, possibly regulatory, offence but is the deterrent effect of the criminal law reduced by such a result?

Lee Lai Siew v PP, Voon Wee Hian v PP [1978] 1 MLJ 259 (HC, Kota Kinabalu, Malaysia)

A passenger ship, the *Nanukan Express*, sank whilst allegedly carrying passengers well in excess of the authorized number of 80 plus four crew. Lee Lai Siew was the master of the ship; he faced one charge under s 304(A) and further charges under the Merchant Shipping Ordinance. The other appellants, the shipowners, faced five charges under the Ordinance.

BTH Lee J: [I]t was in evidence that the ship sailed normally for about half an hour. In another 15 minutes the ship would have arrived at Sebatik Island. There was evidence of heavy waves which hit against the ship and which broke the window glasses. There can be no doubt in my view that those who drowned met with their deaths through drowning caused by the waves, the winds and swell at the rough patch referred to by the witnesses. There was also evidence that the waves resulted in creating confusion and panic seized the passengers on board the ship.

Overloading if there be, can only be a very remote fact in causing this tragedy....

[U]nder circumstances such as existed in the present case it would be wrong to attribute to the appellant, Lee Lai Siew, the alleged negligence of overloading resulting in the loss of lives.

[Although Lee Lai Siew's appeal under s 304(A) was allowed, all the appellants were fined in respect of offences under the Ordinance such as carrying excessive passengers.]

2.   Section 299/300 causation

Section 299 of the Penal Code defines the offence of culpable homicide and s 300 provides that murder is a type of culpable homicide. The only punishment for murder is death; for culpable homicide not amounting to murder, the maximum penalty is life imprisonment or ten years, depending on the *mens rea* of the accused (see ch 19). As in the case of s 304(A), the *actus reus* is causing the death of a human being. Local cases have not been called upon to discuss in detail the question of causation in culpable homicide and murder. In the absence of local cases, it is generally assumed that English law would be followed. This view is graphically shown in the following case.

Leong Siong Sun v PP [1985] 2 MCLJ 250 (HC, Seremban, Malaysia)

The deceased was admitted to hospital for treatment to a lacerated wound on the arm and swelling of the abdomen. It turned out that his intestines were ruptured. He left hospital of his own accord after treatment but without being operated on.

Peh Swee Chin J: The deceased had died of peritonitis, ie the infection and inflammation of the membrane which lines the cavity of the abdomen, brought about undoubtedly by the rupture of the intestine which was obviously not treated by surgery. In these circumstances, could the appellants be convicted of causing the death of the deceased as opposed to merely causing grievous bodily harm to him? Learned counsel has submitted for the appellants that the cause of death of the deceased was the failure for the deceased to be treated properly and the deceased's own negligence in discharging himself. I am fairly certain that if the deceased had been told that if he discharged himself without surgery to repair the rupture of the intestine he would have faced a very likely death, the deceased would have practically begged for the surgery and discarded any intention to discharge himself from the hospital.

To revert to learned counsel's submission that the cause of death was the failure on the part of the deceased to be treated properly, the case of *Smith* (1959), is pertinent ....

In the course of judgment, Lord Parker CJ laid down a test as follows :...

> "It seems to the Court that, if at the time of death the original wound is still an operating cause and a substantial cause, then the death can properly be said to be the result of the wound, albeit that some other cause of death is also operating. Only if it can be said that the original wounding is merely the setting in which another cause operates can it be said that the death does not result from the wound. Putting it another way, only if the second cause is so overwhelming as to make the original wound merely part of the history can it be said that the death does not flow from the wound."

Here in this case I am unable to say that the rupture of the intestine was not the operating and substantial cause of death, neither am I able to say that the failure to operate on the deceased was so overwhelming a cause of death as to make the rupture of the intestine merely a part of the history.

Appeal dismissed

R v Smith [1959] 2 QB 35 (Courts Martial Appeal Court, England)

The deceased received bayonet wounds during a fight with soldiers from a rival regiment. One pierced his lung and caused haemorrhage. A friend carried him to the medical station but tripped and dropped him twice. On arrival he was given a transfusion of saline and, when his breathing appeared impaired, oxygen and artificial respiration.

Parker LCJ: It is now known that, having regard to the injuries which the man had in fact suffered, his lung being pierced, the treatment that he was given was thoroughly bad and might well have affected his chances of recovery. There was evidence that there is a tendency for a wound of this sort to heal and for the haemorrhage to stop. No doubt his being dropped on the ground and having artificial respiration applied would halt or at any rate impede the chances of healing. Further, there were no facilities whatsoever for blood transfusion, which would have been the best possible treatment. There was evidence that, if he had received immediate and different treatment, he might not have died....

[The appellant contends that if] there was ... any other cause, whether resulting from negligence or not, or if, as he contends here, something happened which impeded the chance of the deceased recovering, then the death did not result from the wound. The court is quite unable to accept that contention.

[His Lordship then provided the test approved in *Leong Siong Sun*, 1985, and approved the following test provided by Lord Wright in *The Oropesa*, 1943.]

To break the chain of causation it must be shown that there is something which I will call ultroneous, something unwarrantable, a new cause which disturbs the sequence of events, something which can be described as either unreasonable or extraneous or extrinsic.

Appeal dismissed

The use of English law to consider the meaning of a common law concept such as "cause", which is left undetermined by the Penal Code, is permissible and often desirable (see ch 1, p 10). However, it should always be considered in the light of any local statutory provisions. Explanation 1 and especially Explanation 2 to s 299 are particularly important to the following analysis.

Penal Code, s 299

Explanation 1–A person who causes bodily injury to another who is labouring under a disorder, disease or bodily infirmity, and thereby accelerates the death of that other shall be deemed to have caused his death.

Explanation 2–Where death is caused by bodily injury, the person who causes such bodily injury shall be deemed to have caused the death, although by resorting to proper remedies and skilful treatment the death might have been prevented.

Explanation 1 embodies the fundamental general principle that you must take the victim as you find him or the "egg shell skull rule"; the accused will still be regarded as having caused death even if a person of ordinary health would not have died. The limits of this principle and the precise role of Explanation 2 are considered below, but two points about the decision in *Leong Siong Sun* (1985) should be noted here. First, it was unnecessary for the judge to resort to *Smith* (1959) given the broad and clear wording of Explanation 2. Second, there was no reference to the s 304(A) test even though it is couched in very different terms from *Smith* (1959); nor was there any consideration of the possible development of a local test different from English law.

It is notoriously difficult to categorize causation cases. Categorization is necessary for the purposes of exposition, but the cases must be read not simply in terms of their particular facts but also with regard to any general principles they adopt. With that fundamental caveat, the following discussion is grouped under two main headings. Cases giving rise to medical complications are considered first. These embody many of the general principles and also raise particular complications in the light of Explanation 2. The second broad heading deals with non-medical cases where the question is whether voluntary conduct of the victim or third parties has broken the chain of causation.

(a) Complications of medical treatment

It is not uncommon, particularly in older cases, to find that the official cause of death in homicide cases was not said to be the injury itself but, for example, pneumonia or gangrene. Numerous Indian cases show that such ordinary complications flowing from the original injury will not break the chain of causation (eg *Salebhai Kadarali*, 1949). This will be so even where a long time elapses between the original injury and the death.

D Yohannan v State of Kerala AIR (1958) Ker 207 (HC, Kerala, India)

The accused's wife left him in order to live with her parents. He went to their house one night and stabbed her. The court had no doubt that he had the intention to kill her, which was inferred from the nature of the injuries and the circumstances of the offence. The injury received by the victim was a stab wound in the spine from which she suffered paralysis of her lower body. She died several months later.

PT Raman Nayar J: [T]he comparatively long interval of seven months between the injury and the death might at first sight induce an element of doubt as to whether their relation as cause and effect is not too remote. For all causing of death by injury is but the hastening of an inevitable event, and, when that event is so long delayed, the mind is tempted to ask whether the cause of the death is not really to be found in something other than the injury ....

In the present case however we are satisfied that there is no room for any doubt that both factually and legally the injury was the cause of death ....

[According to PW 9] Death was due to syncope due to asthenia from cystitis and trophic changes which were caused by the injury to the spinal cord.... There is no surgical method for curing it when the spinal cord is cut. The time or period taken for death to ensue depends upon the depth of the injury on the spinal cord....

[O]ne would have liked to know whether any of these ... factors could be regarded as an unexpected complication breaking the chain of causation. These are matters which ought to have been clarified by counsel, and, failing counsel, by the court. But, the failure notwithstanding, we are ... satisfied that the death in this case is legally attributable to the injury....

There is no indication of any unexpected intervention, and as observed by Mayne (4th edn, 1914) "any act is said to cause death within the meaning of s 299 when the death results either from the act itself or from some consequences necessarily or naturally flowing from that act and reasonably contemplated as its result". Where without the intervention of any considerable change of circumstances the death is connected with the act of violence by a chain of causes and effects, the death must be regarded as a proximate and not too remote a consequence of the act of violence.

Appeal dismissed

More difficult problems arise where the victim has either not received any medical treatment or has received inadequate treatment in circumstances where his life might have been saved. Simple unavailability of treatment (eg because of the distance from a hospital) is a risk the accused must run by virtue of Explanation 2. Thus, in *Morcha* (1979) the Indian Supreme Court held that "The mere fact that if expert treatment had been available and the emergency operation had been performed, there were chances of survival of the deceased can be of no avail to the appellant."

However, suppose that medical treatment is available but for some reason the victim decides not to make use of it and consequently dies. Both the Penal Code and the English cases suggest that in these circumstances it will be very difficult, perhaps impossible, for the accused to argue that he did not cause the death. The key principle is that you must take the victim as you find him in a mental as well as a physical sense. Just as he may have an egg-shell skull, he may also have certain beliefs which lead him to refuse treatment.

R v Blaue [1975] 61 Cr App R 271 (CA, Criminal Division, England)

The victim, a Jehovah witness, refused a blood transfusion which might well have saved her life.

Lawton LJ: In *Holland* (1841) the defendant, in the course of a violent assault, had injuried one of his victim's fingers. A surgeon had advised amputation because of danger to life through complications developing. The advice was rejected. A fortnight later the victim died of lockjaw. "The real question is," said Maule J, "whether in the end the wound inflicted by the prisoner was the cause of death"....

[His Lordship approved the test in *Smith* (1959) and continued:]

[Counsel for the appellant submitted] that the jury should have been directed that, if they thought the girl's decision not to have a blood transfusion was an unreasonable one, then the chain of causation would have been broken. At once the question arises—reasonable by whose standards? Those of Jehovah's Witnesses? Humanists? Roman Catholics? Protestants of Anglo-Saxon descent? The man on the Clapham omnibus? But he might well be an admirer of Eleazar who suffered death rather than eat the flesh of swine (2 Maccabees, Ch 6, v 18–31) or of Sir Thomas More who, unlike nearly all of his contemporaries, was unwilling to accept Henry VIII as Head of the Church in England. Those brought up in the Hebraic and Christian traditions would probably be reluctant to accept that these martyrs caused their own deaths....

It has long been the policy of the law that those who use violence on other people must take their victims as they find them. This in our judgment means the whole man, not just the physical man. It does not lie in the mouth of the assailant to say that his victim's religious beliefs which inhibited him from accepting certain types of treatment was unreasonable. The question for decision is what caused her death. The answer is the stab wound. The fact that the victim refused to stop this end coming about did not break the causal connection between the act and death.

Appeal dismissed

Lawton LJ based his decision on the grounds that death flowed from the original wound and that the principle that the accused must take the victim as he finds him extends to the "whole man". Explanation 1 to s 299 clearly embodies the principle that you take the physical man as you find him. Explanation 1 does not cover such cases, except by analogy; however, the broad wording of Explanation 2 would appear to lead to the same result and, like *Blaue* (1975), does not admit consideration of the reasonable man.

Arguments can be made both ways on the reasoning in *Blaue* (1975). Explanation 1, dealing with the physical man, is not qualified by any test of reasonableness and it may be totally unreasonable to expect an accused to have realized that the victim was suffering from certain disorders. If no medical treatment had been available, the accused would also be liable. It would therefore seem strange to read in a reasonableness test under Explanation 2 for cases concerning a victim's beliefs. On the other hand, the Penal Code was drafted in the 19th Century and the court in *Blaue* (1975) makes reference to old cases and old textbook writers. Is such reasoning appropriate given the advances in medical science? The refusal of treatment in *Blaue* (1975) resulted from deeply held religious beliefs which in a free, and multi-cultural society should be respected; however, the absence of any reasonableness test in *Blaue* (1975) or in Explanation 2 may mean that no refusal to accept medical treatment, however bizarre or unreasonable, could ever break the chain of causation; eg if the deceased in *Leong Siong Sun* (1985) had refused treatment because he distrusted modern medicine or because he thought the doctors were simply out for his money (see *Smith*, 1979).

In discussing the scope of *Blaue* (1975) Hart and Honoré (1985, p 361) pose a further question:

> What if the victim had called for a blood transfusion and the doctor had refused to administer one, saying that he preferred to play a round of golf, so the the victim died?

If Explanation 2 were applied to these facts, it might lead to the result that the accused would still be liable; as in *Blaue*, the death would have flowed from the injury and it would therefore be difficult to argue that death was somehow "caused" by the doctor's callous omissions rather than the wound. *Roberts* (1971, below, p 386) suggests an alternative approach, leading perhaps to a different conclusion; where the victim–or presumably a third party–does something "daft" and unforeseeable this should break the chain of causation. However, this was decided before *Blaue* (1975) where Lawton LJ doubted the application in criminal law of a reasonable foresight test. It is also difficult to avoid the broad wording of Explanation 2 unless the word "resorting" is read as meaning "resorting *by the victim*". Under this interpretation, the chain of causation might be regarded as broken where the victim requested treatment but a third party refused to act.

Improper treatment, as opposed to the absence of treatment, can give rise to additional medical complications which lead to death. The interpretation of Explanation 2 again raises some questions.

Nga Ba Min v Emperor AIR (1935) Ran 418 (HC, Rangoon, Burma)

The deceased was struck on the head and arms by robbers. She was admitted to hospital approximately 36 hours later.

Dunkley J: Under ordinary circumstances she would have completely recovered from the effects of these injuries within about a fortnight. Her wounds were dressed and she remained in the hospital for two days and was then discharged at her own request, but was warned to attend daily as an out-patient to have the injuries dressed. She returned to her village and did not go back to the hospital. Owing to the unskilful attention which she received in her village the two wounds on the head became septic.... Post mortem examination showed that the sepsis had penetrated through the skull to the brain.... Death was due to abscess forming on the brain as a result of the injuries becoming septic....

[T]he appellant cannot be held responsible for causing [her] death. Her death was due to her own ignorance and the unskilful treatment which she received in her village, and the injuries on her head were only the remote cause of death. In order that a person should be convicted of culpable homicide it is indispensable that the death of the deceased should be connected with the act of violence or other primary cause, not merely by a chain of causes and effect, but by such direct influence as is calculated to produce the effect without the intervention of any considerable change of circumstances.

The injuries in *Nga Ba Min* (1935) were a "but for" cause of death but the court clearly regarded sepsis as having displaced the previous causes. It might be argued that the decision was *per incuriam* because there was no reference to Explanation 2 but they can be reconciled. The first clause of Explanation 2 provides that death must be "caused by the bodily injury". The original injuries were certainly a "but for cause" of death, but this is not enough to satisfy the first clause; on the facts, death was really "caused" by the bad care. Under this interpretation, proof that the injuries were a "but for" cause of death will not be sufficient to satisfy the first clause; it must be shown that death is legally attributable to the original injuries and not to some intervening cause. In cases like *Nga Ba Min* (1935) where the victim has been treated and released from hospital and then administers bad treatment to her wound, it will probably be easier to show a break in the chain of causation than where, as in the following cases, the original treatment was itself bad in some way.

R v Jordan (1956) 40 Cr App R 152 (CCA, England)

The victim was stabbed during a fight. The appellant was convicted of murder but new evidence became available on the cause of death. Medical witnesses stated that the administration of an antibiotic was proper. However, even though the victim proved to be allergic to the antibiotic, he continued to be treated with it. This was said to be "palpably wrong". Another step, described as wrong was the "intravenous introduction of wholly abnormal quantities" of liquid which clogged the lungs, leading to pulmonary oedema and broncho-pneumonia, from which the victim died.

Hallett J: We are disposed to accept it as the law that death resulting from any normal treatment employed to deal with a felonious injury may be regarded as caused by the felonious injury, but we do not think it necessary to examine the cases in detail or to formulate for the assistance of those who have to deal with such matters in the future the correct test which ought to be laid down with regard to what is necessary to be proved in order to establish the causal connection between the death and the felonious injury. It is sufficient to point out here that this was not normal treatment. Not only one feature, but two separate and independent features of treatment were, in the opinion of the doctors, palpably wrong and these produced the symptoms ... which were the direct and immediate cause of death, namely, the pneumonia resulting from the condition of oedema which was found.

Appeal allowed

Jordan (1956) is a rare example in English law where the accused has successfully argued that causation has not been established. The decision has been critically regarded in subsequent English cases (eg *Blaue*, 1975 and *Smith*, 1959); although regarded as a correct decision, it is explained and distinguished as based on its own particular facts. In the light of the broad language of Explanation 2, as interpreted by the following case, it is not clear whether, even on its own particular facts, *Jordan* (1956) would be decided the same way under the Penal Code.

Tajammal Hussein v Nasar Mehdi PLD (1976) SC 377 (SC, Pakistan.)

The deceased received medical treatment for a wound. He died 13 days after the fight. The cause of death was "cardio-respiratory failure", apparently resulting from a "blackened and gangrenous wound" on the thigh. There was some evidence that the gangrene could have been caused by negligence in treatment of the wound and the Lahore High Court held the accused not liable for culpable homicide but convicted him of attempted murder. The prosecutor appealed.

Dorab Patel J: [The respondent] relied on a judgment of a Division Bench of the West Pakistan High Court in *Said Amin* (1959) [where the] learned judges observed:

> "that evidence also reveals that the stab wound was fatal, in the ordinary course of nature, but as the wound was not necessarily fatal, if there had been no haemolysis, which followed blood transfusion, the deceased might have been still alive.... In the present case we do not know why haemolysis has set in. It might be that some foreign matter was injected in the body at the time of transfusion or it might be that the blood which was injected was of the wrong species or of a person from a wrong group."

In view of this possibility of negligence in the treatment of the victim, the learned judges altered the appellant's conviction to s 307, PPC. Whilst the judgment fully supports [the respondent's] contention, I regret my inability to agree with it, because even though the haemolysis to the deceased might have developed on account of negligence in the treatment of the wound, this negligence amounted to not "resorting to proper remedies and skilful treatment" within the meaning of the second explanation s 299....

[His Lordship then referred to the difficulty of reconciling the English cases of *Smith* (1959) and *Jordan* (1956) and concluded:]

[T]his illustrates the difficulty of determining the consequences of a felonious injury in a case in which there has been negligence in treating it. However, as that difficulty has been reduced, if not removed by the explanations to s 299, PPC, I am satisfied that *Jordan*'s Case is of no help to the ... respondent....

Appeal allowed; however, his Lordship agreed with the
High Court's sentence

This interpretation of Explanation 2 to s 299 virtually rules out the possibility of abnormal medical treatment ever breaking the chain of causation and suggests that *Jordan* (1956) would be decided differently under the Penal Code. Such an interpretation amounts in substance to the causal minimalist position that "but for" causation suffices. However, there are two reasons to doubt this reasoning. First, it is unclear how far the rest of the court agreed with Patel J; Md Akram J regarded the precise offence committed by the accused to be "altogether academic" because he agreed with the sentence. Md Yaqub Ali CJ merely said, "I agree"; with what or with whom is left unsaid. Furthermore, it is hard to reconcile the reasoning with the analysis of Explanation 2 suggested above in the context of *Nga Ba Min* (1935). It was argued there that the chain of causation should be considered broken in a case where the medical treatment is so dramatically wrong that, in the terms of Explanation 2, death was caused by the bad treatment and can no longer be regarded as "caused by the bodily injury"; the fact that the original injuries amount to a "but for" cause, does not satisfy the requirement that death is caused by the bodily injury. If this interpretation is followed, it is possible, though not certain, that *Jordan* (1956) would be decided the same way. It may also be noted that there are still decisions from the lower courts in Pakistan (eg *Allah Bachayo*, 1982) which do not appear as strict as *Tajammal Hussein* (1976).

A final problem in medical cases concerns the decision to discontinue treatment.

R v Malcherek; R v Steel (1981) 73 Cr App R 173 (CA, Criminal Division, England)

The appeals arose out of cases where the deceased had been placed on life support machines which were then turned off after tests indicated brain death.

Lord Lane CJ: This is not the occasion for any decision as to what constitutes death. Modern techniques have undoubtedly resulted in the blurring of many of the conventional and traditional concepts of death .... There is, it seems, a body of opinion in the medical profession that there is only one true test of death and this is the irreversible death of the brain stem, which controls the basic functions of the body such as breathing. When that occurs it is said the body has died, even though by mechanical means the lungs are being caused to operate and some circulation of blood is taking place.

We have had placed before us ... evidence that the medical men concerned did not comply with all the suggested criteria for establishing such brain death. Indeed, further evidence has been suggested ... that those criteria or tests are not in themselves stringent enough. However ... there is no doubt that whatever test is applied the victim died; that is to say, applying the traditional test, all body functions, breathing and heartbeat and brain function came to an end, at the latest, soon after the ventilator was disconnected.

[His Lordship turned to causation and approved the test in *Smith*, 1959.]

[I]f a choice has to be made between the decision in *Jordan* (1956) and that in *Smith* (1959) which we do not believe it does (*Jordan* (1956) being a very exceptional case) then the decision in *Smith* (1959) is to be preferred....

[After discussing *Blaue*, 1975, he continued:]

There is no evidence ... here that at the time of conventional death, after the life support machinery was disconnected, the original wound or injury was other than a continuing, operating and indeed substantial cause of the death of the victim, although it need hardly be added that it need not be substantial to render the assailant guilty. There may be occasions, although they will be rare, when the original injury has ceased to operate as a cause at all, but in the ordinary case if the treatment is given bona fide by competent and careful medical practitioners, then evidence will not be admissible to show that the treatment would not have been administered in the same way by other medical practitioners. In other words, the fact that the victim has died, despite or because of medical treatment for the initial injury given by careful and skilled medical practitioners, will not exonerate the original assailant from responsibility for the death....

Where a medical practitioner adopting methods which are generally accepted comes bona fide and conscientiously to the conclusion that the patient is for practical purposes dead, and that such vital functions as exist (for example, circulation) are being maintained solely by mechanical means, and therefore discontinues treatment, that does not prevent the person who inflicted the initial injury from being responsible for the victim's death. Putting it another way, the discontinuance of treatment in those circumstances does not break the chain of causation betweeen the initial injury and the death.

Appeal dismissed

Lord Lane's approval of the test in *Smith* (1959) which states that the injuries must be an operating and substantial cause, followed by his assertion that the cause need not be substantial is typical of the terminological confusion which afflicts causation cases. However, it seems clear that not much emphasis should be placed on the term "substantial"; it probably means simply that factors will not be sufficient where they are so trivial that they may be disregarded under the *de minimis* principle (see also *Hennigan*, 1971, below, p 392). Thus, administering a superficial scratch to a man who is almost dead from a serious bullet wound may be regarded as insignificant.

(b) Other voluntary interventions of victim or third parties

The medical cases have suggested that it is highly unlikely that either a victim's refusal of medical treatment or bad treatment by a third party will break the chain of causation. It is also difficult to find cases where the chain of causation is broken in other areas of third-party interventions.

R v Pagett (1983) 76 Cr App R 279 (CA, Criminal Division, England)

The police were attempting to arrest the appellant for certain serious offences. He fired at the police, using a girl as a shield to protect himself against police bullets. The girl died from three bullet wounds from police guns. The appellant was convicted of manslaughter but appealed mainly on causation grounds.

Robert Goff LJ: [I]t was pressed on us by Lord Gifford [counsel for appellant] that there either was or should be a ... rule ... whereby as a matter of policy, no man should be convicted of homicide (or, we imagine, any crime of violence to another person) unless he himself, or another person acting in concert with him, fired the shot (or, we imagine, struck the blow) which was the immediate cause of the victim's death (or injury).

No English authority was cited to us in support of any such proposition, and we know of none. So far as we are aware, there is no such rule in English law; and ... we can see no basis in principle for any such rule .... Lord Gifford urged upon us that, in a case where the accused did not, for example, fire the shot which was the immediate cause of the victim's death, he will inevitably have committed some lesser crime, and that it would be sufficient that he should be convicted of that lesser crime. So, on the facts of the present case, it would be enough that the appellant was convicted of the crime of attempted murder of the two police officers.... We see no force in this submission.... It is not difficult to imagine circumstances in which it would manifestly be inadequate for the accused merely to be convicted of a lesser offence; for example, a man beseiged by armed terrorists in a house might attempt to make his escape by forcing some other person to act as a shield, knowing full well that that person would in all probability be shot....

In our judgment, the question whether an accused person can be held guilty of homicide ... of a victim the immediate cause of whose death is the act of another person must be determined on the ordinary principles of causation, uninhibited by any such rule of policy as that for which Lord Gifford has contended....

Problems of causation have troubled philosophers and lawyers throughout the ages; and it would be rash in the extreme for us to trespass beyond the boundaries of our immediate problem. Our comments should therefore be understood to be confined not merely to the criminal law, but to cases of homicide (and possibly also other crimes of violence to the person)....

In cases of homicide, it is rarely necessary to give the jury any direction on causation.... Even where it is necessary ... it is usually enough to direct them simply that in law the accused's act need not be the sole cause, or even the main cause, of the victim's death, it being enough that his act contributed significantly to that result....

Occasionally, however, a specific issue of causation may arise. One such case is where, although an act of the accused constitutes a *causa sine qua non* of (or necessary condition for) the death of the victim, nevertheless the intervention of a third person may be regarded as the sole cause of the victim's death, thereby relieving the accused of criminal responsibility....

Professors Hart and Honoré, *Causation in the Law* (1985) ... consider the circumstances in which the intervention of a third person, not acting in concert with the accused, may have the effect of relieving the accused of criminal responsibility. The criterion which they suggest should be applied in such circumstances is whether the intervention is voluntary, ie whether it is "free, deliberate and informed". We resist the temptation of expressing the judicial opinion whether we find ourselves in complete agreement with that definition; though we certainly consider it to be broadly correct and supported by authority. Among the examples which the authors give of non-voluntary conduct, which is not effective to relieve the accused of responsibility, are two which are germane to the present case, viz a reasonable act performed for the purpose of self-preservation, and an act done in performance of a legal duty.

There can, we consider, be no doubt that a reasonable act performed for the purpose of self-preservation, being of course itself an act caused by the accused's own act, does not operate as a *novus actus interveniens*....

No English authority was cited to us ... in support of the proposition that an act done in the execution of a legal duty, again of course being an act itself caused by the act of the accused, does not operate as a *novus actus interveniens*.... [However] the proposition is sound in law, because as a matter of principle such an act cannot be regarded as a voluntary act independent of the wrongful act of the accused....

[G]enerally speaking causation is a question of fact .... But that does not mean that there are no principles of law relating to causation....

Appeal dismissed

With regard to the victim's own conduct, the Madras High Court in *Dorasamy Servai* (1944) approved the following general approach. Although it was derived from some early English cases, it is equally consistent with later cases:

> [I]f a man who has received a serious blow or hurt does not alter his ways on that account, but continues to go through the ordinary course of life he has been accustomed to pursue, that shall not exonerate the giver of the blow from his liability if such conduct has the effect of causing death. But if, on the other hand, his acts subsequent to the blow have been so far out of his ordinary course as to give rise to a distinct set of circumstances causing a new mischief, then the new mischief will be regarded as the *causa causanti* and not the original blow.

A number of cases have arisen concerning the accused's liability for injuries sustained by the victim whilst trying to escape.

R v Halliday (1889) 61 LT 701 (Court of Crown Cases Reserved, England)

Whilst drunk, the appellant threatened his wife. She attempted to escape through a window and broke her leg in the fall.

Lord Coleridge CJ: Here the woman came by her mischief by getting out of a window .... Now that might have been done accidentally or deliberately, in which case the prisoner would not have been guilty ... [however] if a man creates in another man's mind an immediate sense of danger which causes such person to try to escape, and in so doing he injures himself, the person who creates such a state of mind is responsible for the injuries which result.

Appeal dismissed

R v Roberts (1971) 56 Cr App R 95 (CA, Criminal Division, England)

The appellant made unwanted sexual advances towards the victim, a passenger in his car. She jumped from the moving car and the appellant was convicted of an assault occasioning actual bodily harm. One ground of appeal was causation.

Stephenson LJ: The test is: Was it the natural result of what the alleged assailant said and did, in the sense that it was something that could reasonably have been foreseen as the consequence of what he was saying or doing? As it was put in one of the old cases, it has got to be shown to be his act, and if of course the victim does something so "daft", in the words of the appellant in this case, or so unexpected, not that this particular assailant did not actually foresee it but that no reasonable man could be expected to foresee it, then it is only in a very remote and unreal sense a consequence of his assault, it is really occasioned by a voluntary act on the part of the victim which could not reasonably be foreseen and which breaks the chain of causation between the assault and the harm or injury.

Appeal dismissed

Roberts (1971) is an interesting case as it proposes a reasonable foresight test of causation in criminal law. This is very unusual and it is unclear how far such an approach survives the views subsequently expressed by Lawton LJ in *Blaue* (1975, above, p 378). Although causation was established on the facts of *Roberts* (1971), the approach might in some situations lead to a different result from the traditional approach. For example, the decision in *Halliday* (1889) coupled with the principle that one must take the victim as found, suggests that causation will be established even in circumstances where the victim is unusually timorous and a reasonable person would not have reacted in such a manner. Under *Roberts* (1971), the chain of causation might be broken in such cases. In *Roberts* (1971) and *Halliday* (1889) the victims had little choice in their methods of escape but a break in the chain of causation will be found more readily where the victim had a choice of options and can be regarded as having freely chosen the course of action which resulted in death. This is Hart and Honoré's explanation of the decision in the US case of *Hendrickson* (1877). A husband had a violent row with his wife who ran outside. He shut the door but there was no evidence that he prevented her from re-entering the house. She was found dead the following morning due to the cold; there was 18 inches of snow on the ground. The husband was held not liable as the wife was regarded as having chosen to remain outdoors. In such cases according to Fletcher (1978, p 365), "the self-destructive act appears to be more the choice of the wife than the product of the defendant's acts". The principle that voluntary acts of the victim may break the chain of causation was used in the following Indian case even though the victim apparently had very few options open to him in effecting his escape.

Joginder Singh v State of Punjab (1980) SCC (Cri) 255 (SC, India)

Chinnappa Reddy J: We will now deal with the death of Rupinder Singh. After Kuldip Singh was attacked [and killed], Rupinder Singh ran from his house towards the fields. He was followed, apparently chased by Joginder Singh and Balwinder Singh. According to PW 1, Rupinder Singh jumped into a well "in order to save himself". Joginder Singh and Balwinder Singh were about 15 to 20 feet from Rupinder Singh when he jumped into the well. It is not the case of the prosecution, nor is there any evidence to justify such a case, that the accused drove Rupinder Singh to jump into the well leaving him no option except to do so.... It is not the case of the prosecution that Rupinder Singh was beaten on the head and then thrown into the well .... Apparently when Rupinder Singh jumped into the well his head hit a hard substance with the result that he lost consciousness and thereafter died of asphyxia. In the circumstances of the case we are unable to say that the death of Rupinder Singh was homicidal, though we are conscious of the fact that what induced [him] to jump into the well was ... that Joginder Singh and Balwinder Singh were following him closely. If we were satisfied that [they] drove him to jump into the well without the option of pursuing any other course, the result might have been different.

Appeal allowed in respect of Rupinder Singh's death

D. Assessment of causation for homicide under the Penal Code

1. Extent of difference between ss 304(A) and 299/300

Under the strict approach to causation under s 304(A), liability has frequently not arisen even where the accused was rash or negligent. In its positive form the s 304(A) approach requires that the accused's conduct was the "proximate and efficient cause of death", that he was "wholly or mainly" responsible for the death or that it was "directly attributable" to his conduct. Expressed in negative terms, death must result "without the intervention of another's negligence". By contrast, the English approach to causation, exemplified by *Smith* (1959) and followed in *Leong Siong Sun* (1985) is couched in far less stringent terms which rarely relieve the accused of liability. The positive aspect of this approach is that the accused's conduct must be an operating cause although it need not, according to *Malcherek* (1981) be a substantial cause. In *Pagett* (1983) it was said–in stark contrast to the s 304(A) cases–that the accused's conduct need not be either the sole or the main cause of death. The negative aspect of this approach is that the chain of causation will not be broken unless the wound is "merely part of history" or the "setting in which another cause operates".

Neither of these approaches amounts either in its wording or in its application to the purest form of causal minimalism that "but for" causation alone is sufficient. Even under s 299, there have been cases where "but for" causation has proved insufficient (eg *Nga Ba Min*, 1935; *Jordan*, 1956; and *Joginder Singh*, 1980). However, it must be said that these cases are exceptional; the English test of causation, favoured for s 299, comes much closer to the causal minimalist position than the s 304(A) test. Hart and Honoré's (1985) view is that causation is a significant hurdle which is determined in accordance with identifiable, broad commonsense principles; the chain of causation is broken by voluntary interventions and coincidental or abnormal events. This approach is broadly reflected in the terminology adopted in the cases but Hart and Honoré's broad principles are not consistently applied to all offences; under s 304(A) the positive aspect is harder to satisfy and voluntary interventions and abnormal events appear more likely to break the chain of causation.

The terminology in this area is notoriously difficult and the tests are invariably couched in vague, open-ended language. Given this terminological confusion, we must consider whether, although the tests are differently expressed, they would nevertheless lead to the same results in practice. It seems clear that they would not. There is a striking disparity in the extent to which causation has been established under s 304(A) by contrast with s 299 and the English cases. If the tests are applied to the facts of some individual cases, the results would also appear to be different. In *Kurban Hussein* (1965) the storage of inflammable items in the factory was not the "immediate" cause of the fire; however, it would probably have satisfied the laxer definition of an operating cause and it would hardly be possible to say that such storage was so insignificant to the result that it was merely part of history or fell under the *de minimis* principle. Explanation 2–particularly as interpreted in *Tajammal Hussein* (1976)–also differs from the s 304(A) approach since the "immediate" or "main" cause of death may be improper medical treatment rather than the original wound. In *Pagett* (1983) the immediate cause of death might have been regarded as the police bullet. Finally, it is worth noting the contrasting attitudes of the courts in two cases. In *Lee Lai Siew* (1978) the appellants were convicted of lesser offences and the judge expressed no regret at such a result; by contrast in *Pagett* (1983) the court was at pains to point out that conviction for lesser offences might be inappropriate in some situations.

2.   Towards a single approach on existing authority

It is appropriate to consider at this stage whether it is possible to develop a uniform approach locally to the problem of causation. When homicide is considered this has the obvious logical attraction that for all forms of homicide the *actus reus* is the same and the Penal Code does not suggest any differences except that Explanations 1 and 2 to s 299 are absent from s 304(A). If a common approach can be derived it could also be applied to other offences such as the non-fatal offences against the person. The possibility of legislative action is considered below (p 393) but this section considers whether it is possible to achieve a common approach based on a reconciliation of the existing cases and statutory provisions.

One possibility would be to consider adopting the s 304(A) test more widely on the basis that it is the only test which has received the detailed consideration of the local courts. This would require that English cases are not followed. Such an approach might derive some support from the fact that the wording of some of the Indian cases on s 299 (eg *Yohannan*, 1958 and *Nga Ba Min*, 1935) appears stricter in form than the English cases and closer to the s 304(A) position. However, this approach is difficult; departing from the traditional blind reliance on English cases, exemplified by *Leong Siong Sun* (1985) is not a serious obstacle but, as we have seen, the s 304(A) test apppears incompatible not only with the English cases but also with the unqualified wording of Explanation 2 to s 299. The Indian cases are vague and do not either recognize or explore these complexities. Furthermore, many would be reluctant on policy grounds to adopt a more rigid test of causation under s 299/s 300 lest very blameworthy offenders escape the full rigour of the law on causation grounds; for example, where the accused's direct objective was to murder and, even though he did not immediately achieve his aim, the victim did ultimately die (see also *Thabo Meli*, 1954, discussed in ch 19). The authors of the Penal Code were extremely concerned by this prospect.

Macaulay and other Indian Law Commissioners, A Penal Code Prepared by the Indian Law Commissioners, Note M (1837), 116

There is undoubtedly a great difference between acts which cause death immediately and acts which cause death remotely; between acts which are almost certain to cause death, and acts which cause death only under very extraordinary circumstances. But that difference, we conceive, is a matter to be considered by the tribunals when estimating the effect of the evidence in a particular case, not by the legislature in framing the general law....

[One commentator] excepts from the definition of homicide the case of a person who dies of a slight wound, which, from neglect or from the application of improper remedies, has proved mortal. We see no reason for excepting such cases from the general rule.... It will, indeed, be more difficult to prove that death has been caused by a scratch than by a stab which has reached the heart; and it will in a still greater degree, be difficult to prove that a scratch was intended to cause death ... yet both these points might be fully established. Suppose ... that A inflicted a slight wound on Z, a child who stood between him and a large property. It is proved that the ignorant and superstitious servants about Z applied the most absurd remedies to the wound. It is proved that under their treatment the wound mortified and the child died .... A congratulates himself on his skill ... relates with exultation the mode of treatment followed by the people who have charge of Z, and boasts that he always foresaw that they would turn the slightest incision into a mortal wound.... In such cases there is no doubt whatever as to the intention.... [W]e are unable to perceive any good reason for not punishing A as a murderer.

It seems clear that this concern is incompatible with the strict test of causation under s 304(A) where the application of such absurd remedies would most certainly break the chain of causation.

The alternative route to a uniform approach using existing authorities might be to argue for a reconsideration of the s 304(A) cases on the grounds that the laxer test is more appropriate on policy grounds. This again seems unacceptable; the cases locally and in India have adopted such a consistent approach to s 304(A) that it is too late for judicial reconsideration. We are therefore faced with two causation tests and must attempt to explain their existence and consider their application to other offences.

3. Accounting for the double track system

Logically it is impossible to account for the existence of two approaches to causation in homicide offences where the *actus reus* is the same. However, the probable reason for this situation may be suggested. Fletcher (1978) outlines two broad ways to analyse homicide. Under the "harm oriented" analysis, the prima facie case of homicide is "simply killing another human being"; under the "act-oriented" analysis, the prima facie case is "*intentionally or negligently* causing death" (emphasis added). The act oriented analysis thus places greater emphasis on the *mens rea*. Later, using this distinction, he draws attention to a crucial tension in causation (p 370):

> Perhaps the most difficult issue in the theory of causation is whether the issues of causation and culpability should be kept rigidly distinct or whether the presence of a particularly heinous motive should influence the analysis of causation. The shift from a harm-oriented to an act-oriented mode of analysis would tend to support the interweaving of criteria of causation with criteria of culpability; this interweaving might lead to the view, for example, that those who intentionally cause harm should be liable for more remote consequences than those who negligently cause harm.

Such interweaving of issues of causation and culpability clearly goes against traditional wisdom under which causation, as part of the *actus reus*, is considered logically distinct from *mens rea*. Under the traditional analysis, the fact that the accused in, say, *Blaue* (1975) might have been intoxicated or insane at the time of his assault is relevant to his *mens rea* and the existence of a defence, but should not affect in any way the question of whether he caused the victim's death. Equally, if the court had decided that he had not caused her death, the fact that all along he intended to kill her is irrelevant, at least as far as a conviction for homicide is concerned. However, it is striking that the courts, not only in England but also in India, have been very reluctant to find a break in the chain of causation where the accused has been particularly blameworthy. Because *Jordan* (1956) is so exceptional, it perhaps serves to show the general rule. As we have seen, the authors of the Penal Code wanted a lax approach to causation because of cases where the accused clearly intended to kill. There are also numerous cases where the issues of causation and *mens rea* have not been clearly distinguished and which suggest that the courts are at least influenced by the *mens rea* when deciding causation. Thus in *Yohannan* (1958, above, p 377) we find the following passage:

> No doubt when death is ... caused by ... remote or indirect causes, it might be difficult to establish the *mens rea* necessary for the offence of murder.... But where, as in the present case, the intention to cause death is clearly made out, it seems to us that it does not matter that death was caused, not in the language of the medical books, directly but by a chain of consequences, each following upon the other in the processes of nature and not being an unexpected complication causing a new mischief.

The same is true in some s 304(A) cases. In *Balchandra* (1968, above, p 372), where causation was established, the judge made little attempt to conceal his disgust and annoyance at the appellants' blameworthiness in failing to take greater care given the nature of the work, the location of the factory near a residential area, etc.

This intermingling of causation and culpability provides a useful insight into the probable but hitherto unexplicated reasons for the existence of different tests under ss 299 and 304(A). Where the accused has acted with the necessary *mens rea* for ss 299/300, especially where he has the intention to kill, the court will be reluctant to find him not guilty on causation grounds; by contrast, if he was only rash or negligent, he is less morally blameworthy and the court may be less willing to find him guilty. This does not lead us to the strictest version of the causal minimalist position since there will be many cases under s 304(A) and at least a few cases under ss 299/300 where "but for" causation alone will not suffice. However, it clearly suggests that although legal causation remains a hurdle, *mens rea* is "doing most of the work" in determining liability; it is the different degrees of blameworthiness embodied in the different *mens rea* terms which explain the existence of two different tests.

Although we have provided the probable explanation of the dual track system of causation, we have not thereby justified this situation. Fletcher (1978) suggests that such "interweaving of issues ... seems dubious in assessing liability for homicide". In the context of homicide under the Penal Code it seems particularly inappropriate. The different degrees of culpability are already recognized in the enormous difference in penalties provided for the different offences. Under s 299 the maximum penalty is life or ten years, depending on the *mens rea* (see s 304, below, 400); under s 300 the only sentence is death; for s 304(A) the maximum is only two years. Since the differing degrees of culpability are so clearly recognized in the sentences, is it right that they apparently play a role at the conviction stage too? Are negligent and rash offenders enjoying unjust advantages? It could be argued that if different tests are adopted, the stricter test should in fact be applied to cases carrying the heavier penalties. This latter argument has particular force when it is borne in mind that murder, with the mandatory death penalty, may be committed without the intention to kill and in circumstances very different from the extreme example of a carefully premeditated murder postulated by the authors of the Penal Code.

E. Causation in other offences

The existence of two tests for homicide under the Penal Code makes it difficult to state with any certainty what test should be followed with regard to other offences. Staying with homicide, it is unclear which test should be followed for offences contained under separate road traffic legislation (see p 490) of causing death by dangerous or reckless driving (which carries a maximum penalty of five years' imprisonment). These provisions were imported directly from England where the same test of causation is adopted as for murder and manslaughter. In *Hennigan* (1971) the appellant had driven his car "dangerously fast". He crashed into a car, driven by Mrs Lowe, which emerged from a minor side road. Two of Mrs Lowe's passengers were killed. The Court of Appeal held that in a civil action Mrs Lowe might be held "substantially responsible because she was clearly at fault". The judge's direction to the jury indicated that the accused should only be convicted if he was more than one fifth to blame. In the Court of Appeal's view, this was unduly favourable to the appellant and his appeal was dismissed. Under the s 304(A) test adopted in *Lee Kim Leng* (1964) he would probably not have been liable.

There are strong reasons why the English causation cases should not be followed under the road traffic legislation, even though the local provisions are *in pari materia* with English law at the time of *Hennigan* (1971), and why the s 304(A) test should be adopted. Since dangerous and reckless driving under the road traffic legislation is not easily distinguishable in terms of blameworthiness from rash and negligent conduct under the Penal Code (see ch 21) it follows from the preceding analysis, which explains the two tests on the basis of *mens rea*, that the s 304(A) test should be adopted. Furthermore, to adopt the English approach would lead to absurd results. In driving cases, there is enormous overlap between s 304(A) and the road traffic legislation but, as judged by the penalties, the road traffic legislation provides the more serious offence. It would be absurd to hold in a case like *Hennigan* (1971) that the accused was liable for the more serious offence when he would clearly not be liable under s 304(A).

When the non-fatal offences against the person are considered, questions of causation may again hinge on the *mens rea*. Thus for offences where the *mens rea* is intention or knowledge (eg voluntarily causing hurt or grievous hurt, ss 321 and 322), the s 299 test would suffice; where it is rashness or negligence (eg causing hurt or grievous hurt by rash or negligent conduct, ss 337 and 338), the s 304(A) test would be appropriate.

F. Conclusions

The rules relating to causation in the criminal law of Singapore and Malaysia appear inconsistent and inadequately analysed. If the present inconsistencies are attributable, as suggested, to the different degrees of blameworthiness required by different offences, this should be explicitly recognized and debated. If they are attributable to some other factor, this should be identified and explained. Reconciliation of the different lines of authority into one test is impossible and in the interests of consistency it may be appropriate to consider legislative action. One possible approach would be to adopt the views of the English Law Commission (1985):

> 21.–(1) A person causes a result when–
> (a) his act makes a more than negligible contribution to its occurrence; or
> (b) in breach of duty, he fails to do what he might do to prevent it occurring,
>   unless in either case some other cause supervenes which is unforeseen,
>   extremely improbable and sufficient in itself to produce the result.

This formulation is vague and is open to judicial interpretation but it is intended to apply to all result crimes. It interestingly suggests a test of foreseeability but in all other respects is in line with the English cases. It produces very different results from the s 304(A) test, as evidenced by a comparison of *Lee Kim Leng* (1964) with the following proposed illustration (Illustration 21(ii)) to the draft English Code:

> It is made a code offence to cause death by "driving with criminal negligence". D drives on a main road at an excessive speed to impress his girlfriend P. E drives out of a side road in front of D's car without keeping a proper lookout. P is killed in the collision. Assuming D and E to have been negligent ... both are guilty of the offence ... provided that the manner of driving of each was a more than negligible contribution to P's death.

Part VI

Homicide and non-fatal offences

Chapter 19

Culpable homicide and murder

By NA Morgan

A. Structure of homicide offences

The Penal Code contains three homicide offences: murder, culpable homicide not amounting to murder and causing death by rash or negligent conduct. In both Singapore and Malaysia, separate road traffic legislation provides for offences of causing death by dangerous or reckless driving. Despite the adoption of different causation rules with regard to these offences (see ch 18) the *actus reus* common to all forms of homicide is "causing the death of a human being". The different homicide offences are therefore distinguished primarily by their different *mens rea* terms.

1. Culpable homicide and murder

Penal Code, ss 299 and 300

   299. Whoever causes death by doing an act with the intention of causing death, or with the intention of causing such bodily injury as is likely to cause death, or with the knowledge that he is likely by such act to cause death, commits the offence of culpable homicide.

Illustrations

(a) A lays sticks and turf over a pit, with the intention of thereby causing death, or with the knowledge that death is likely to be thereby caused. Z, believing the ground to be firm, treads on it, falls in and is killed. A has committed the offence of culpable homicide.

(b) A knows Z to be behind a bush. B does not know it. A, intending to cause, or knowing it to be likely to cause Z's death, induces B to fire at the bush. B fires and kills Z. Here B may be guilty of no offence; but A has committed the offence of culpable homicide.

(c) A, by shooting at a fowl with intent to kill and steal it kills B, who is behind a bush, A not knowing that he was there. Here, although A was doing an unlawful act, he was not guilty of culpable homicide, as he did not intend to kill B, or to cause death by doing an act that he knew was likely to cause death.

Explanation 1–A person who causes bodily injury to another who is labouring under a disorder, disease, or bodily infirmity, and thereby accelerates the death of that other, shall be deemed to have caused his death.

Explanation 2–Where death is caused by bodily injury, the person who causes such bodily injury shall be deemed to have caused the death, although by resorting to proper remedies and skilful treatment the death might have been prevented.

Explanation 3–The causing of the death of a child in the mother's womb is not homicide. But it may amount to culpable homicide to cause the death of a living child, if any part of that child has been brought forth, though the child may not have breathed or been completely born.

300.   Except in the cases hereinafter excepted culpable homicide is murder–
(a) if the act by which the death is caused is done with the intention of causing death; or
(b) if it is done with the intention of causing such bodily injury as the offender knows to be likely to cause the death of the person to whom the harm is caused; or
(c) if it is done with the intention of causing bodily injury to any person, and the bodily injury intended to be inflicted is sufficient in the ordinary course of nature to cause death; or
(d) if the person committing the act knows that it is so imminently dangerous that it must in all probability cause death, or such bodily injury as is likely to cause death, and commits such act without any excuse for incurring the risk of causing death, or such injury as aforesaid.

Illustrations

(a) A shoots Z with the intention of killing him. Z dies in consequence. A commits murder.
(b) A, knowing that Z is labouring under such a disease that a blow is likely to cause his death, strikes him with the intention of causing bodily injury. Z dies in consequence of the blow. A is guilty of murder, although the blow might not have been sufficient in the ordinary course of nature to cause the death of a person in a sound state of health. But if A, not knowing that Z is labouring under any disease, gives him such a blow as would not in the ordinary course of nature kill a person in a sound state of health, here A, although he may intend to cause bodily injury, is not guilty of murder, if he did not intend to cause death, or such bodily injury as in the ordinary course of nature would cause death.
(c) A intentionally gives Z a sword-cut or club-wound sufficient to cause the death of a man in the ordinary course of nature. Z dies in consequence. Here A is guilty of murder, although he may not have intended to cause Z's death.
(d) A, without any excuse, fires a loaded cannon into a crowd of persons and kills one of them. A is guilty of murder, although he may not have had a premeditated design to kill any particular individual.

(There are several exceptions to liability under s 300. These are set out in ch 20.)

The following table contrasts the different *mens rea* terms and its scheme will be adopted throughout the chapter.

Section 299	*Section 300*
1 Intention to cause death.	(a) Intention to cause death.
	(b) Intention to cause a bodily injury which the offender knows is likely to cause the death of the person to whom the harm is caused.
2 Intention to cause bodily injury which is likely to cause death.	(c) Intention to cause a bodily injury where the injury intended to be inflicted is sufficient in the ordinary course of nature to cause death.
3 Knowledge of the likelihood of death.	(d) Knowledge that the act is so imminently dangerous that it must in all probability cause either (i) death or (ii) such bodily injury as is likely to cause death and there is no excuse for incurring such a risk.

Sir James Stephen (1883, vol III) castigated ss 299 and 300 as "defined in terms so closely resembling each other that it is difficult to distinguish them". Culpable homicide under s 299 is defined as the generic offence of which murder under s 300 is one species. Despite a slight difference in wording, s 299.1 and s 300(a) are identical. There are two reasons for this repetition. First, all offences of murder under s 300 also fall, by definition, under s 299. Second, if the accused can establish one of the "special exceptions" to s 300, such as provocation, he will only be guilty of culpable homicide even if his intention was to kill. The special exceptions provide "formal" mitigation in that the offence category is reduced. This must be distinguished from "informal" mitigation where a judge may take account of factors such as youth, a guilty plea or cooperation with the police when considering what sentence to impose. It will be noted that despite the tendency in local cases to use the term "manslaughter" as shorthand for "culpable homicide not amounting to murder" (especially in the context of the special exceptions), the term is not used anywhere in the Penal Code. Given the existence of s 304(A), which overlaps with English manslaughter (see ch 21), and the absence of "constructive manslaughter" locally (see below, p 426), such usage is apt to confuse and should properly be avoided.

The structure proposed for homicide offences in the Indian Law Commission's original (1837) draft Code was far clearer; under their scheme, "voluntary culpable homicide" (causing death with the intention of causing death or with knowledge that death was likely) was to be murder unless the exceptions of provocation, exceeding private defence or consent were available. As it is now drafted, culpable homicide covers more than just those cases where the special exceptions apply. There are differences in wording between s 299.2 and 299.3 and s 300 (b),(c) and (d) (revolving around the probability of death resulting) and there are cases where the *mens rea* for s 299 alone is satisfied.

Tham Kai Yau v PP [1977] 1 MLJ 174 (FC, KL, Malaysia)

Raja Azlan Shah FJ: A comparison that frequently arises in the application of ss 299 and 300 is the tenuous contention that s 299 is not a substantive offence and therefore an offence is either murder or culpable homicide according to whether or not one of the exceptions to s 300 apply, and if by reason of the absence of the necessary degree of *mens rea* an offence does not fall within s 300, it cannot be one of culpable homicide not amounting to murder ... but would amount to causing grievous hurt. In our view, the correct approach to the application of the two sections is this. Section 299 clearly defines the offence of culpable homicide. Culpable homicide may not amount to murder (a) where the evidence is sufficient to constitute murder, but one or more of the exceptions to s 300 ... apply, and (b) where the necessary degree of *mens rea* specified in s 299 is present, but not the special degrees of *mens rea* referred to in s 300.... [A]ll cases falling within s 300 ... must necessarily fall within s 299, but all cases falling within s 299 do not necessarily fall within s 300.

[See also *Ramiah*, 1986.]

Not only do ss 299 and 300 overlap, so do the different limbs within each section. In *Chung Kum Moey* (1967) Viscount Dilhorne expressed this point in a Privy Council appeal from the Federal Court of Malaysia:

> The learned judge appears to have proceeded on the basis that the four limbs of s 300 are mutually exclusive. That would not appear to be the case. For instance, an act may be done with the intention of causing bodily injury sufficient in the ordinary course of nature to cause death and also with the knowledge that it is so imminently dangerous that it must in all probability cause death or such bodily injury as is likely to cause death.

Despite the overlap, it is important to distinguish the limbs of s 299 because different maximum penalties are provided according to whether the accused acted with intention or knowledge.

Penal Code, s 304

Whoever commits culpable homicide not amounting to murder shall be punished–
(a) with imprisonment for life, or imprisonment for a term which may extend to ten years and shall also be liable to fine, if the act by which death is caused is done with the intention of causing death, or of causing such bodily injury as is likely to cause death.
(b) with imprisonment for a term which may extend to ten years, or with fine, or with both, if the act is done with the knowledge that it is likely to cause death, but without any intention to cause death, or to cause such bodily injury as is likely to cause death.

[The FMS Penal Code also regards intention as more blameworthy than knowledge in the context of culpable homicide but has replaced the life sentence for intention cases with a fixed maximum of 20 years.]

In theory it is therefore possible for a person convicted of culpable homicide with knowledge to be punished simply with a fine, whereas a fine is only additional to imprisonment if he acted with intention. In practice it is highly unlikely that a person convicted of culpable homicide would be only fined, but it may be of practical significance that the knowledge limb carries a lower maximum. In *Gopalen* (1985) Wan Yahya J complained:

> In an offence of this nature, I consider the imposition of 14 years' imprisonment to be expedient with a view to the offender's reformation. Happily for him, the learned Public Prosecutor omitted to refer in the facts of the case [to] matters which would have placed the offence under the first limb of [s 304]. I am therefore compelled to convict the accused under the second limb of s 304 Penal Code and to impose a sentence of 7 years only.

Section 304 is unusual in that the Penal Code does not generally differentiate sentences according to *mens rea*. Thus s 304(A) does not distinguish sentences for rashness and negligence. For cases of hurt and grievous hurt (ss 323 and 325) acting with knowledge as opposed to intention could, at most, be an informal mitigating factor. In the case of murder, where the *mens rea* is also intention or knowledge, there is of course no scope for any form of mitigation.

Penal Code, s 302

Whoever commits murder shall be punished with death.

Section 304 also embodies a highly questionable view of blameworthiness. An assessment that knowledge is less blameworthy than intention should depend on what you intend or have knowledge of. An intention to kill is more blameworthy than knowledge of the likelihood of death, but intention under s 299.2 seems less culpable than knowledge under s 299.3. Under s 299.2 it is enough to prove that the accused intended a bodily injury which was *objectively* likely to cause death; it is not necessary also to prove that he *knew* it was likely to cause death (see below, p 407). Is an accused person not *more* blameworthy where he knows he is likely to cause *death* than where he simply intends a *bodily injury* which (whether he knows it or not) is likely to cause death?

A final difficulty with s 304 concerns the sentencing of cases falling under the special exceptions. In *Tham Kai Yau* (1977) Raja Azlan Shah FJ had this to say:

> The first part of s 304, Penal Code, covers cases which by reason of the exceptions are taken out of the purview of s 300, clauses (1), (2) and (3) but

otherwise would fall within it and also cases which fall within the second part of s 299, but not within s 300, clauses (2) and (3). The second part of s 304, Penal Code covers cases falling within the third part of s 299 not falling within s 300, clause (4).

Cases taken out of the purview of s 300(d) by virtue of the special exceptions were not expressly mentioned by his Lordship. In such cases the accused should be sentenced under s 304(b). Consequently, even if one of the special exceptions applies, the court should be satisfied before it sentences under s 304(a) that the accused acted with intention rather than knowledge. As suggested below, in the context of diminished responsibility, this may at times be problematic.

2.   Penal Code, s 304(A) and road traffic legislation

Where the accused acted with neither intention nor knowledge, he will not be liable for *culpable* homicide; however, he may still be liable for a homicide offence under s 304(A):

Penal Code, s 304(A)
Whoever causes the death of any person by doing a rash or negligent act not amounting to culpable homicide, shall be punished with imprisonment for a term which may extend to two years, or with fine, or with both

Section 304(A) is frequently invoked in cases involving drivers on the roads. Such cases may also give rise to charges under road traffic legislation of causing death by *reckless* or *dangerous* driving. The Penal Code and the road traffic legislation therefore adopt four different *mens rea* terms: rashness, negligence, recklessness and dangerousness. These terms are analysed in detail below; suffice it to say at this stage that it is impossible to distinguish them sensibly from each other and it is incoherent for the maximum penalties to be so different. The penalties, particularly under s 304(A), are also much lower than for any form of culpable homicide. The basic distinction between s 304(A) and culpable homicide was said in *Idu Beg* (1881) to be that s 304(A) does not extend to the intentional infliction of violence. This is only partially correct because s 299 covers cases of knowledge as well as intention and the distinction between knowledge and rashness (s 304(A)) or recklessness (road traffic legislation) is less clear-cut.

B. Actus reus of homicide

Although different causation tests have been adopted for s 299/300 and 304(A) (see ch 18), the *actus reus* rules ought in principle to be the same in other respects. Interestingly the Penal Code has departed from the common law view that death must occur within a year and a day (see *Yohannan*, 1958, above, p 377) and in its delineation of the point at which human life comes into existence for the purposes of homicide.

With regard to the latter point, culpable homicide (and by definition murder) can be committed on any living child "if any part of that child has been brought forth, though the child may not have breathed or been completely born" (Explanation 3 to s 299). In principle the same test should be applied to s 304(A). However, the Singapore provisions are in certain respects inconsistent. Prior to the point at which human life comes into being for the purposes of homicide, other offences may, of course, be committed (eg s 312, causing miscarriage). There is also the offence of child destruction.

Penal Code, s 315

Any person, other than a registered medical practitioner permitted by or authorised under the provisions of the Abortion Act 1969, to terminate a pregnancy to save the life or to prevent grave permanent injury to the physical or mental health of the pregnant woman, who, with intent to destroy the life of a child capable of being born alive, by any wilful act causes a child to die before it has an existence independent of its mother or by such act causes a child to die after its birth, shall be punished with imprisonment for a term not exceeding ten years or to a fine not exceeding five thousand dollars or to both such imprisonment and fine.

The wording of s 315 was imported from the English Infant Life (Preservation) Act 1929. It is based on the English test of when life comes into being for the purposes of homicide in England, namely, whether the child has an existence independent of its mother. An independent existence seems to mean that the child should have been *fully* expelled from the womb; however, culpable homicide may be committed before the child is fully expelled. Thus, the offences of child destruction and unlawful homicide appear to be based on different tests, with an unfortunate resultant overlap. The FMS Penal Code, having retained the original wording of s 315, does not give rise to the same difficulty; it talks simply of the child being "born"; this rather imprecise word could be interpreted in the light of Explanation 3.

Advances in medical science have made it increasingly difficult to say when human life ceases. As far as the criminal law is concerned, there is no clearly delineated point in the Penal Code or in English or local cases. However, it is generally accepted that the best test is "brain death" (see *Malcherek*, 1981, see above, p 382). The alternative test of "breathing and heartbeat" can lead to serious difficulties because it is possible by the use of machinery to keep such functions going artificially even when brain death has occurred. If, in these circumstances, a doctor eventually turned off the ventilator, it would be wrong for the accused to escape liability in respect of the victim's death or for the doctor to be regarded as causing the death. The brain death test is also in line with the test of death for organ transplants in Singapore.

Human Organ Transplant Act (Singapore), s 3(1):

> For the purposes of this Act, a person has died when there has occurred irreversible cessation of all functions of the brain of the person.

C.   Culpable homicide and murder: Mens rea terms compared

1.   Sections 299.1 and 300(a)

(a)   Proof of intention

Mens rea is inferred from the facts of the case, from what the accused now says and what he did and said earlier, as established by all the available evidence. In deciding whether the accused had the intention to kill it is particularly important to consider factors such as the nature, place and number of injuries inflicted, method of infliction, the use and nature of weapons, etc. If the accused carefully aims a gun, which he knows is loaded, at the victim's heart when standing a short distance away, and pulls the trigger, and he can provide no other explanation of his conduct, the only reasonable conclusion is that he intended to kill. The authorities are such that generalizations are difficult, but it seems that an intention to kill is more likely to be inferred where the weapon is one for cutting or firing rather than beating.

Tan Buck Tee v PP (1961) 27 MLJ 176 (CA, KL, Malaya)

Thomson CJ: [I]ntention is something the existence and nature of which are to be deduced from the evidence. In some cases the evidence may be such that it becomes necessary to consider with very great care whether or not the intention with which the act was done does or does not come within the definition of criminal intention set out in s 299 of the Code as being necessary to make the act out to be culpable homicide and whether it does or does not come within the definition of criminal intention set out in s 300 as being necessary to make the act out to be murder. In such cases it is necessary for the judge to spell out with the greatest possible care such portions of ss 299 and 300 as may be appropriate so that the jury may be in no doubt as to the question to which they have to give the answer.

The present, however, was not one of this class of case.

There was the body with five appalling wounds on it, wounds penetrating to the heart and liver, which must have been caused by violent blows with a heavy sharp instrument like an axe. In the absence of anything else, whoever inflicted those blows must have intended to kill the person on whom they were inflicted.

However, because ss 299 and 300 are defined in such closely related terms, it will frequently be extremely difficult to decide what precise inference is to be drawn or which particular limb of s 299 or s 300 is satisfied; for example, whether there was an intention to cause death or merely bodily injury and whether the injury was likely (s 299) or sufficient in the ordinary course of nature (s 300) to cause death (see, especially, *Tham Kai Yau*, 1977, below p 405).

Ismail b Hussain v PP (1953) 19 MLJ 48 (CA, KL, Malaya)

The appellant, a member of the Home Guard, was convicted of the murder of Omar, also a Home Guard, and the attempted murder of Rifin. He claimed to have mistaken them for terrorists. Omar died instantly from his wounds; Rifin was injured in the legs.

Taylor J: The evidence as a whole shows beyond doubt that the accused saw a man and shot him at close range. Obviously he intended to kill.

It may be that he did not recognize Omar. It is highly unlikely that he had any premeditated design to kill anyone or even to fire.... The most probable explanation is that the accused ... saw a man and fired at once–on impulse– without any conscious or reasoned thought. But however suddenly the intention was formed, the intention was to kill. That amounts to murder.

As regards the shooting of Rifin, it is not unusual to fire a shot gun at a man's legs, to prevent escape and the like, where there is a definite intention not to kill. The second conviction should therefore have been for causing grievous hurt and a sentence of three years would have sufficed.

At one time, English law adopted a highly objective approach to inferring *mens rea*, encapsulated in the discredited maxim that a person should be "deemed to intend the natural and probable consequences of his acts".

Glanville Williams, *Textbook of Criminal Law* (1983) 81:

The maxim gained some plausibility from the fact that it superficially resembled a common sense rule of evidence. Often one can judge whether a man intended a consequence only by asking whether anyone in his shoes would have realized that the consequence was likely and *whether there is any reasonable interpretation of his actions other than the hypothesis that he intended the consequence.* The maxim was erroneous because it omitted the italicized words .... [T]he House of Lords in *Smith* (1961) ... applied the probable consequence maxim even to the crime of murder. They held that not merely could intent be inferred from the probability of the consequence but that the presumption of intent in such circumstances was irrebuttable. In other words, the judge could say to the jury:

> "Members of the jury, in deciding whether the defendant intended this consequence you merely have to consider whether a reasonable man would have foreseen it as probable. Do not inquire whether the defendant foresaw it, or whether he intended it. You can find that he intended it although you are sure he did not."

The maxim should be avoided. First, on policy grounds it is unjust to impose liability according to such objective criteria; as Glanville Williams (1983) suggests, it can lead to the "preposterous result" of a person being convicted not according to how he viewed a situation but how somebody else, the hypothetical reasonable person, would have viewed it in the circumstances (see also *Elliott* v *C (A Minor)*, 1983, discussed in ch 3). Although some cases decided around the same time as *Smith* (1961) flirted with the maxim (eg *Tan Buck Tee*, 1961; *Suba Singh*, 1962), more recent cases indicate that it should not be followed. In *Yeo Ah Seng* (1967), the Malaysian Federal Court approved the Australian case of *Stapleton* (1952), where it was said that "the introduction of the maxim ... is seldom helpful and always dangerous", and concluded that "judges in this country should avoid using this maxim in their summings up to the jury when dealing with the question of intention in murder trials".

(b) Meaning of intention

It is clear from *Ismail b Hussein* (1953, see above, p 405) that intention may be formed on the spur of the moment and that whilst evidence of premeditation may support a conclusion that the accused intended to kill, it is not essential to that conclusion. However, the fundamental question of the meaning of intention under the Penal Code in general and under s 299/300 in particular is otherwise unclear. According to the English case of *Nedrick* (1986; see ch 3), two main meanings may be ascribed to "intention". First, the accused's direct or primary aim or objective (the narrow meaning), second, foresight that the prohibited result is, for all practical purposes, inevitable. It appears that intention under the Penal Code should carry only the narrow meaning. Sections 299.3 and 300(d) already provide for cases where the mental state is one of knowledge. There would be no merit in dealing with a case involving foresight of a "virtual certainty" as one of intention rather than knowledge. Neither would there be sense in attempting to draw a distinction between foreseeing a virtual certainty ("intention" under *Nedrick*, 1986) and the degree of knowledge required by s 300(d). Furthermore, unless intention is given its narrow meaning it is hard to see what role is played by s 300(b).

2. Sections 299.2, 299.3 and 300(b)

Section 300(b) combines the subjective requirements of intention and knowledge in the second and third limbs of s 299. Consequently, murder under s 300(b) is clearly narrower than the generic offence of culpable homicide. The accused must not only intend a bodily injury but must also know that the injury is likely to cause the victim's death. The situation which is most likely to be covered by s 300(b) is the so-called "pin-prick murder" where "the offender knows that the particular person injured is likely, either from peculiarity of constitution, or immature age, or other special circumstance, to be killed by an injury which would not ordinarily cause death" (*Govinda*, 1876; see also Illustration (b) to s 300). Under the principle that one takes the victim as one finds him, there is no difficulty establishing causation in such cases, and liability hinges on *mens rea*. Unless it can be inferred that the accused's direct objective was to cause death, he will not be liable under s 300(a). Furthermore, unless he was sufficiently aware of the victim's disorder to know death was likely, he will not fall under s 300(b). In cases where the accused causes the death of a particularly susceptible victim but lacks the degree of knowledge required for s 300(b), liability will depend on whether the case can be brought within ss 299.2 and 300(c).

3. Sections 299.2 and 300(c)

(a) Introduction

Section 299.2 differs from ss 299.1 and 300(a) and (b) in that it is not purely subjective but partly subjective and partly objective. It requires that the accused intended (subjective) to cause a bodily injury of a type which is objectively likely to cause death; it is *not* necessary that he should have realized or even considered the likely effects of the injuries. The likelihood clause in s 299.2 must be given this objective interpretation as a matter of statutory interpretation; to read it subjectively, requiring the accused not only to have intended a bodily injury but also to have realized that such an injury was likely to cause death, would make s 299.2 identical with s 300(b). Although there has been some confusion on this point (see below, p 409), the correct approach to s 300(c) is also to read only the first clause subjectively. The basic distinction between s 299.2 and s 300(c) lies in the likelihood of death resulting from the injuries; the greater the probability of death resulting, the more likely the case is to fall under s 300. Thus, an injury intentionally inflicted by the accused may be considered likely to cause death (s 299.2) but insufficient in the ordinary course of nature to do so (s 300(c)). The dividing line between the sections, being based on degrees of probability, is very fine and it will often be extremely difficult to decide on the inferences to be drawn in any given case.

Tham Kai Yau v PP [1977] 1 MLJ 174 (FC, KL, Malaysia)

The facts were disputed but it appears that the appellants had attacked the deceased with choppers, inflicting multiple deep incised wounds, two being serious head wounds. However, the pathologist was not asked–and this proved significant–for his opinion on the nature of the injuries and their probable effects.

Raja Azlan Shah FJ: It cannot be disputed that intention is a matter of inference. The deliberate use by some men of dangerous weapons at another leads to the irresistible inference that their intention is to cause death. This inference should therefore make it a simple matter to come to a decision in any case, such as the present, where the weapons used by the appellants were deadly weapons and where the person killed was struck more than one blow. In actual practice however it is frequently a matter of considerable difficulty to arrive at a conclusion by application of this principle in view of the close connection that the Penal Code makes between intention and knowledge. The provisions relating to murder and culpable homicide are probably the most tricky in the Code and are so technical as frequently to lead to confusion. Not only does the Code draw a distinction between intention and knowledge but subtle distinctions are drawn between the degrees of intention to inflict bodily injury....

In the present appeal we think that in view of the nature of the injuries sustained by the deceased and the time and place of the incident, there was evidence of an intention on the part of the appellants to cause bodily injury to the deceased. Therefore in those circumstances, the fine distinction between s 299 and s 300 is very important and that point should have been put clearly to the jury in such a way that they would be able to come to a correct conclusion. The forensic practice of reading s 299 and s 300 to juries is likely to confuse rather than help. In view of what we have stated above, a case such as the present must therefore fall within the second part of s 299 or the third clause of s 300. Speaking generally, if the act must in all probability cause death, the offence is within s 300, Penal Code, and if the act is only likely to cause death, the offence falls within s 299, Penal Code. None of the exceptions to s 300, Penal Code were established. In ordinary circumstances we should probably have had little difficulty in upholding the convictions of the appellants for murder but in view of the nature of the medical evidence ... we felt the case might not unreasonably be brought within the lesser offence of culpable homicide not amounting to murder, falling within the first part of s 304, Penal Code. We have thought it necessary to deal with this matter at some length to ensure if possible that our finding shall not be construed as a declaration that in all cases such as the present the offence is culpable homicide not amounting to murder.

Order accordingly

Chung Kum Moey v PP [1967] 1 MLJ 205 (PC, appeal from FC, Malaysia, on appeal from HC, Singapore)

The deceased suffered five bullet wounds, three to his body and two on his right arm. There was some dispute as to whether five bullets were fired or whether one or both of the shots which went through the arm may then have penetrated the body. The trial judge told the jury that in his view it was a "reasonable possibility" that in firing the shots the appellant was intending to intimidate the deceased and to prevent him phoning the police, by hitting him in the arm, and that he therefore did not intend to kill or to cause a bodily injury falling within s 300(c). However, he said, it was "impossible to believe" that the appellant did not have the requisite knowledge for s 300(d).

Viscount Dilhorne: If [the] direction with regard to the first and third parts of s 300 based on the hypothesis, unsupported by any evidence, that the shots were fired with the intention of only hitting the deceased in the forearm was unduly favourable to the accused, his direction with regard to the fourth part really amounted to taking the issue away from the jury.

In their Lordships' view it was unfortunate that the learned judge gave expression to his views in the way he did. Although he told the jury that it was for them to consider what was the accused's state of mind, he only gave them his own views as to that. He did not put before them other possible views for their consideration and expressed the conclusion that it was an irresistible inference that the accused had knowledge that shooting at the deceased's forearm was so imminently dangerous that it must in all probability cause death or bodily injury likely to cause death. The jury might have taken the view that shooting at the deceased's forearm was not of itself likely to cause death or such a bodily injury, or if it was, that the accused did not know it....

In their Lordships' view, this amounted to a misdirection of such a character that the conviction cannot be allowed to stand....

It was [also] argued that the learned judge was wrong in not leaving the offence of culpable homicide to the jury. If the act causing death is done with the intention of causing bodily injury sufficient in the ordinary course of nature to cause death, it comes within the third limb of s 300 and the offence is murder. If the act is done with the intention of causing bodily injury likely to cause death and it is not shown that the accused knew that was the likely consequence, it is culpable homicide. It is not possible to define with precision the meaning to be given to the word "likely" but the contrast between the use of that word in s 299 and the words in the third limb of s 300 indicates that a higher degree of certainty is required to justify conviction under that limb for murder. In this case although the judge did tell the jury that they had to consider the third part of s 300, his direction was such as to amount to a direction that that part of s 300 did not apply. Where the question whether a case comes within this part of s 300 is in reality left to the jury, it is difficult to envisage a case in which reference ought not to be made to s 299 and to the contrast between the word "likely" in that section and the words "sufficient in the ordinary course of nature" in s 300, and it would also be difficult to envisage a case in which it would not be right to leave the question of a verdict of culpable homicide to the jury.

Appeal allowed;
Sentence of life imprisonment substituted

(b) Section 300(c): subjective or objective

As a matter of interpretation, the likelihood clause of s 299.2 can only be read objectively. Logic and the following leading Indian case suggest the same approach to s 300(c).

Virsa Singh v State of Punjab AIR (1958) SC 465 (HC, Punjab, India)

The deceased suffered one injury and there was no dispute that it was caused by a spear thrust by the appellant. He died 21 hours after the injury after peritonitis intervened. The appellant appealed against his conviction under s 300(c).

V Bose J: (8) It was argued... that ... the prosecution has not proved that there was an intention to inflict a bodily injury that was sufficient to cause death in the ordinary course of nature....

It was said that the intention that the section requires must be related, not only to the bodily injury inflicted, but also to the clause, "and the bodily injury intended to be inflicted is sufficient in the ordinary course of nature to cause death".

(9) This is a favourite argument in this kind of case but is fallacious. If there is an intention to inflict an injury that is sufficient to cause death in the ordinary course of nature, then the intention is to kill and in that event, the "thirdly" would be unnecessary because the act would fall under the first part of the section, namely–

"If the act by which the death is caused is done with the intention of causing death."

In our opinion, the two clauses are disjunctive and separate. The first is subjective to the offender:

"If it is done with the intention of causing bodily injury to any person."

It must, of course, first be found that bodily injury was caused and the nature of the injury must be established, that is to say, whether the injury is on the leg or the arm or the stomach, how deep it penetrated, whether any vital organs were cut and so forth. These are purely objectives facts and leave no room for inference or deduction: to that extent the enquiry is objective; but when it comes to the question of intention, that is subjective to the offender and it must be proved that he had an intention to cause the bodily injury that is found to be present.

(10) Once that is found, the enquiry shifts to the next clause:

"and the bodily injury intended to be inflicted is sufficient in the ordinary course of nature to cause death".

The first part of this is descriptive of the earlier part of the section, namely, the infliction of bodily injury with the intention to inflict it that is to say, if the circumstances justify an inference that a man's intention was only to inflict a blow on the lower part of the leg, or some lesser blow, and it can be shown that the blow landed in the region of the heart by accident, then, though an injury to the heart is shown to be present, the intention to inflict an injury in that region, or of that nature is not proved. In that case, the first part of the clause does not come into play. But once it is proved that there was an intention to inflict the injury that is found to be present, then the earlier part of the clause we are now examining–

"and the bodily injury intended to be inflicted"

is merely descriptive. All it means is that it is not enough to prove that the injury found to be present is sufficient to cause death in the ordinary course of nature; it must in addition be shown that the injury is of the kind that falls within the earlier clause, namely, that the injury found to be present was the injury that was intended to be inflicted. Whether it was sufficient to cause death in the ordinary course of nature is a matter of inference or deduction from the proved facts about the nature of the injury and has nothing to do with the question of intention.

(11) In considering whether the intention was to inflict the injury found to have been inflicted, the enquiry necessarily proceeds on broad lines as, for example, whether there was an intention to strike at a vital or a dangerous spot and whether with sufficient force to cause the kind of injury found to have been inflicted. It is, of course, not necessary to enquire into every last detail as, for instance, whether the prisoner intended to have the bowels fall out, or whether he intended to penetrate the liver or the kidneys or the heart. Otherwise, a man who has no knowledge of anatomy could never be convicted, for, if he does

not know that there is a heart or a kidney or bowels, he cannot be said to have intended to injure them. Of course, that is not the kind of enquiry. It is broad-based and simple and based on commonsense: the kind of enquiry that "twelve good men and true" could readily appreciate and understand.

(12) To put it shortly, the prosecution must prove the following facts before it can bring a case under s 300 "thirdly";

First, it must establish, quite objectively, that a bodily injury is present;

Secondly, the nature of the injury must be proved; these are purely objective investigations.

Thirdly, it must be proved that there was an intention to inflict that particular bodily injury, that is to say, that it was not accident or unintentional, or that some other kind of injury was intended.

Once these three elements are proved to be present, the enquiry proceeds further and,

Fourthly, it must be proved that the injury of the type just described made up of the three elements set out above is sufficient to cause death in the ordinary course of nature. This part of the enquiry is purely objective and inferential and has nothing to do with the intention of the offender.

(13) Once these four elements are established by the prosecution (and, of course, the burden is on the prosecution throughout) the offence is murder under s 300 "thirdly". It does not matter that there was no intention to cause death. It does not matter that there was no intention even to cause an injury of a kind that is sufficient to cause death in the ordinary course of nature (not that there is any real distinction between the two). It does not even matter that there is no knowledge that an act of that kind will be likely to cause death. Once the intention to cause the bodily injury actually found to be present is proved, the rest of the enquiry is purely objective and the only question is whether, as a matter of purely objective inference, the injury is sufficient in the ordinary course of nature to cause death. No one has a licence to run around inflicting injuries that are sufficient to cause death in the ordinary course of nature and claim that they are not guilty of murder. If they inflict injuries of that kind, they must face the consequences; and they can only escape if it can be shown, or reasonably deduced, that the injury was accidental or otherwise unintentional....

(16) The learned counsel for the appellant referred us to *Sardarkhan Jaridkhan*, (1916) where Beaman J, says that:

"where death is caused by a single blow, it is always much more difficult to be absolutely certain what degree of bodily injury the offender intended".

With due respect to the learned Judge he has linked up the intent required with the seriousness of the injury, and that, as we have shown, is not what the section requires. The two matters are quite separate and distinct, though the evidence about them may sometimes overlap. The question is not whether the prisoner intended to inflict a serious injury or a trivial one but whether he intended to inflict the injury that is proved to be present....

(17) It is true that in a given case the enquiry may be linked up with the seriousness of the injury. For example, if it can be proved, or if the totality of the circumstances justify an inference that the prisoner only intended a superficial scratch and that by accident his victim stumbled and fell on the sword or spear that was used, then of course the offence is not murder. But that is not because the prisoner did not intend the injury that he intended to inflict to be as serious as it turned out to be but because he did not intend to inflict the injury in question at all. His intention in such a case would be to inflict a totally

different injury. The difference is not one of law but one of fact; and whether the conclusion should be one way or the other is a matter of proof, where necessary, by calling in aid all reasonable inferences of fact in the absence of direct testimony. It is not one for guess-work and fanciful conjecture.

Appeal dismissed

Virsa Singh (1958) has frequently been approved by the Indian Supreme Court (eg *Jagrup Singh*, 1981) and locally (eg *Mimi Wong*, 1972) and undoubtedly represents the law. However, the legal and policy aspects of the approach deserve careful analysis. The main legal basis of the decision (eg paras (9) and (13)) is that if s 300(c) was read purely subjectively, it would be otiose in view of s 300(a); in other words, if the prosecution had to prove not only an intention to cause a bodily injury but also knowledge that such bodily injury was sufficient in the ordinary course of nature to cause death, then an intention to kill would have been shown. This reasoning was expressly approved in the Singapore case of *Visuvanathan* (1978, see below, p 414). However, its validity depends on the meaning ascribed to s 300(a). It was suggested above that because of the structure of s 300 as a whole, intention must bear its narrow meaning of direct aim. Under this view, s 300(a) would be distinguishable from a purely subjective interpretation of s 300(c); on a subjective reading, s 300(c) would cover cases where the direct aim was not to kill but to cause a bodily injury which the accused himself recognized to be sufficient in the ordinary course of nature to cause death. This is close to but certainly not identical with an intention to kill; thus, a subjective reading of s 300(c) would not render s 300(a) otiose. The better reason for reading only the first clause of s 300(c) subjectively is the existence of s 300(b). If s 300(c) was read purely subjectively it would not only be otiose, it would be *narrower* than s 300(b) since it would require knowlege that the injury was *sufficient in the ordinary course of nature to cause death*; by contrast, s 300(b) only requires knowledge of the *likelihood* of death.

As a matter of interpretation, s 300(c) must therefore be read in the manner suggested in *Virsa Singh* (1958) but for different reasons. The general policy arguments in *Virsa Singh* (1958) are clearest in para (13): "No one has a licence to run around inflicting injuries that are sufficient to cause death in the ordinary course of nature and claim that they are not guilty of murder." This assertion raises a fundamental question; if a person has never intended more than bodily injury, and never knew it even likely to cause death, is it right that he should be convicted of murder if he causes death? How is this question influenced by the rules on causation for culpable homicide? Should the causation rules be more restrictive, so that intervening events are more likely to break the chain of causation?

An important limitation in *Virsa Singh* (1958) is that the accused must have intended the particular type of injury found present. Thus, even if death is caused by a bodily injury which is sufficient in the ordinary course of nature to cause death and it is shown that the injury was caused by the accused, he will not be liable under s 300(c) unless he intended that type of injury. This principle has proved very significant in a number of cases; it lay at the root of the judge's direction to the jury in *Chung Kum Moey* (1967, see above, p 408) and was dramatically emphasized in the following case.

Mohamed Yasin b Hussin v PP [1976] 1 MLJ 156 (PC, appeal from Singapore)

The appellant was convicted of murder. Along with another person he had gone to the victim's hut at night intending to burgle it. The accused grabbed the victim (a 58-year-old Chinese woman weighing 112 lbs) and threw her to the ground; during the struggle, her trousers apparently slipped off and the appellant, overcome with desire, raped her. When he finished, he discovered she was dead.

Lord Diplock: The evidence of the pathologist was that the victim had received a number of superficial injuries, ie bruises and abrasions, including bruises on both her knees consistent with her legs having been forced apart, and abrasions on the vaginal wall. None of these superficial injuries was sufficient in the ordinary course of nature to cause death. The fatal injuries, according to the pathologist, consisted of fractures of the second to fifth ribs on the left and of the second to sixth ribs on the right, in the front portion of her chest. These fractures that had caused congestion of the lungs, resulted in cardiac arrest. They were consistent with, and were most likely to have been caused by, someone sitting with force on her chest as she was lying on the floor on her back. In his opinion, which was accepted by the trial judges, they were sufficient in the ordinary course of nature to cause death....

The trial judges found that the injuries which resulted in the death of the victim were caused by the appellant's sitting forcibly on the victim's chest in the course of a violent struggle when she was resisting his attempt to rape her. Their reasons for finding him guilty of murder were expressed succinctly:

> "On the evidence before us we have no doubt at all that the aforesaid fatal injury was intentionally caused by the second accused and that it was not caused accidentally or otherwise unintentionally. Consequently the act of the second accused in causing the fatal injury was an act which clearly falls within the third limb of the definition of murder...."

In their Lordships' view, this fails to give effect to the distinction drawn in ss 299 and 300 of the Penal Code, in cases where the accused did not deliberately intend to kill, between the act by which death is caused and the bodily injury resulting from that act. In the instant case, the act of the appellant which caused the death, viz sitting forcibly on the victim's chest, was voluntary on his part. He knew what he was doing; he meant to do it; it was not accidental or unintentional. This, however, is only the first step towards proving an offence under s 300(c) of the Penal Code. Not only must the act of the accused which caused the death be voluntary in this sense; the prosecution must also prove that the accused intended, by doing it, to cause some bodily injury to the victim of a kind which is sufficient in the ordinary course of nature to cause death.

In the instant case, the bodily injury caused by the appellant's voluntary act was the fracture of the victim's ribs. It was established by the evidence of the pathologist that this injury was of a kind sufficient in the course of nature to cause death by cardiac arrest. The lacuna in the prosecution's case which the trial judges overlooked was the need to show that, when the accused sat forcibly on the victim's chest in order to subdue her struggles, he intended to inflict upon her the kind of bodily injury which, as a matter of scientific fact, was sufficiently grave to cause the death of a normal human being of the victim's apparent age and build even though he himself may not have had sufficient medical knowledge to be aware that its gravity was such as to make it likely to prove fatal.

There was no finding of fact by the trial judges that this was the appellant's intention; nor, in their Lordships' view, was there any evidence upon which an inference that such was his intention could have been based. There was no admission by the accused that he had sat on the victim's chest at all. The judges' finding that he did so was based upon the evidence of the pathologist, which they were entitled to accept, that this was the most probable way in which the internal injuries to the victim's ribs had been caused. But to fall on someone's chest, even forcibly, is something which occurs frequently in many ordinary sports, such as Rugby Football, and though it may cause temporary pain, it is most unusual for it to result in internal injuries at all, let alone fatal injuries.

To establish that an offence had been committed under s 300(c) or under s 299, it would not have been necessary for the trial judges in the instant case to enter into an enquiry whether the appellant intended to cause the precise injuries which in fact resulted or had sufficient knowledge of anatomy to know that the internal injury which might result from his act would take the form of fracture of the ribs, followed by cardiac arrest. As was said by the Supreme Court of India when dealing with the identical provisions of the Indian Penal Code in *Virsa Singh* (1958)....

> "that is not the kind of enquiry. It is broad-based and simple and based on common-sense".

It was, however, essential for the prosecution to prove, at very least, that the appellant did intend by sitting on the victim's chest to inflict upon her some internal, as distinct from mere superficial, injuries or temporary pain.

The trial judges did not find this to be proved. There was no evidence upon which such a finding could have been based, had they directed their minds to the question. It follows, therefore, that the appellant's conviction for murder must be set aside. For similar reasons a conviction for culpable homicide under s 299 cannot be substituted for the conviction under s 300(c), since an intention on the part of the accused to inflict such bodily injury as is likely to cause death is a necessary ingredient of an offence under the relevant part of s 299....

Appeal allowed

PP v Visuvanathan [1978] 1 MLJ 159 (HC, Singapore)

The accused stabbed the deceased in the chest with a knife. The deceased suffered a fatal stab wound; an 8 cm deep cut through the third and fourth ribs penetrated the left lung and produced a 2 cm cut at the anterior surface of the heart. The prosecution relied on s 300(c). The defence argued for a fully subjective approach to s 300(c) and relied on the passage of Lord Diplock's judgment in *Mohamed Yasin b Hussin* (1976) where he said:

> the prosecution must also prove that the accused intended ... to cause some bodily injury to the victim of a kind which is sufficient in the ordinary course of nature to cause death.

Choor Singh and Rajah JJ: [Their Lordships approved both the test and the reasoning in *Virsa Singh*, 1958, and continued:]

In our opinion there is a clear distinction between the intention to cause the bodily injury found to be present and the intention to cause "some bodily injury of a kind which is sufficient in the ordinary course of nature to cause death". The prosecution do not have to prove the latter intention.

In our judgment for the application of clause (c) of s 300 of the Penal Code, all that the prosecution need prove is–

(1) that the accused did an act which caused the death of the deceased;
(2) that the said act was done with the intention of causing bodily injury;
(3) that the injury caused–

    (a) was intended and was not accidental or otherwise unintentional; and
    (b) was sufficient in the ordinary course of nature to cause death.

There is no other requirement. In our opinion the submission of counsel for the defence based on Lord Diplock's dictum ... was untenable because such a requirement would make clause (c) otiose in view of the provisions of clause (a).

The language used by Lord Diplock in the passage already cited from his judgment is perhaps unfortunate as it has given rise to submissions by counsel in recent cases that the intention that clause (c) requires must be related, not only to the bodily injury inflicted, but also to the clause, "and the bodily injury intended to be inflicted is sufficient in the ordinary course of nature to cause death". We do not think that that was what Lord Diplock meant. Lord Diplock's speech must be read in full. Clearly, it has to be shown that the accused intended to cause bodily injury–that is subjective, but we do not think that Lord Diplock meant that the second limb of clause (c), the sufficiency to cause death, was also subjective....

The dictum of Lord Diplock relied upon by counsel for the defence was factually appropriate in *Mohamed Yasin*'s case (1976) but it is not, in our opinion, of universal application. When considered in isolation it gives a different meaning to the third limb of s 300 but it is clear from a reading of the whole judgment in *Mohamed Yasin*'s case (1976) that the Privy Council has not differed from the views of the Supreme Court of India in *Virsa Singh*'s case (1958).

In this case we had no doubt at all that the act of the accused in stabbing the deceased in the chest was an act which fell squarely within the provisions of clause (c) of s 300 of the Penal Code. The fatal injury was an intended injury and was not caused accidentally or otherwise unintentionally. It was also sufficient in the ordinary course of nature to cause death.

Even if the law is that for the application of clause (c) of s 300 of the Penal Code, the prosecution must prove that the accused intended to cause some bodily injury to the victim of a kind which is sufficient in the ordinary course of nature to cause death, there was sufficient evidence in this case to warrant that inference. Having regard to the weapon used, the force used in stabbing the deceased, and the fact that the deceased was stabbed in a very vulnerable part of his body, we had no doubt at all that the accused had such an intention. The accused had used a kitchen knife used for cutting vegetables and inflicted a fatal gaping stab wound below the left clavicle. He had used so much force that the wound was 8 cm deep and the blade of the knife had cut through the third and fourth ribs and left parasternal edge, had penetrated the left lung near the anterior margin of the left upper lobe and then produced a 2 cm cut at the anterior surface of the heart (right ventricle below pulmonary valve).... The medical evidence left us in no doubt at all that the accused, when he stabbed the deceased with the kitchen knife, intended to cause some bodily injury to the victim of a kind which is sufficient in the ordinary course of nature to cause death.

Accused convicted

Although it has given rise to some difficulty, the decision in *Mohamed Yasin b Hussin* (1976) is in line with *Virsa Singh* (1958). The key factor in the Privy Council's decision in *Mohamed Yasin b Hussin* (1976) was that it was not satisfied that the appellant intended the type of injuries which are sufficient in the ordinary course of nature to cause death. Lord Diplock clearly pointed out that the injuries he did intend ("bruises and abrasions ... and abrasions on the vaginal wall") were "superficial" and insufficient to cause death in the ordinary course of nature. Although he intended external injuries, it had not been proved that he intended the internal injuries which caused the victim's death. The only possible confusion in the case appeared in the passage cited by counsel in *Visuvanathan* (1978) and this is attributable to the inelegant wording of s 300(c) which Lord Diplock was restating. The principle that the accused must have intended injuries of the nature found present may prove particularly significant in cases where the injuries were indirectly inflicted. For example, if A throws a chopper or knife in V's direction, not intending to hit any particular part of the body, it may be difficult to prove the intention to inflict injuries of the particular nature found present.

(c) Escape cases

The principle that the accused must have intended the type of injuries found present also raises some unsolved questions in cases where the victim is killed in escaping from the accused. Suppose that A has inflicted knife injuries on V's body; V tries to escape by jumping from the window but is killed by injuries sustained by the fall. In such cases there is generally no difficulty establishing causation (see ch 18) and A's liability hinges on his *mens rea*. If the nature of the knife injuries justifies the inference that A intended to kill, he will presumably be held liable for murder under s 300(a); he caused V's death and intended all along to do so. There may also be cases where ss 299.3 and 300(d) become relevant; for example, if A knew that V was emotionally highly strung and likely to jump when attacked. However, suppose that A only intended bodily injuries and had no knowledge of the likelihood of death. Would he be liable under s 299.2 or s 300(c)? Since V died from the fall, it would be hard to infer that A intended the particular type of injuries from which V actually died. However, the wording of *Virsa Singh* (1958) suggests that A could still be liable, depending on the seriousness of the original wounds. The test does not specify that V must die directly from the injuries intentionally inflicted by A; it suggests that it is sufficient if the injuries intentionally inflicted by A are objectively likely (s 299) or sufficient in the ordinary course of nature (s 300) to cause death; this may be so even if the immediate cause of death was the other injuries.

(d) Egg-shell skull cases

Further problems arise where the victim suffers from an infirmity and dies from injuries which would not have killed an ordinary person. Section 300(b) only applies where the accused knows that death is likely. He will frequently not have this degree of knowledge; he may never have given any thought to the possibility of death or may have considered it less than "likely". For example, he may have known that the victim was generally not in good health but may not have known enough about the nature of his illness to have contemplated the possibility of death; or he may have considered death to be only an "outside chance". In such circumstances, it is far from clear what offence has been committed. Clearly such cases do not fall under s 299.3 because of the lack of knowledge and (subject to the interpretation of s 300(d)(ii), discussed below, p 421) cannot therefore fall under s 300(d). It is also debatable whether they fall under s 299.2; certainly the accused intended a bodily injury, but was it likely to cause death? Two possibilities come to mind. The first is to say that the accused *is* liable under s 299.2 because in judging the likelihood of death we must consider whether the *particular* victim was likely to die; in other words, we extend the causation principle that you take the victim as found to the question whether death was a likely result. Under this view, it would be no excuse to say that an ordinary person was not likely to die from the injuries; if satisfied that the case fell under s 299.2, the court would then have to consider whether the injuries were such that s 300(c) was also satisfied. The alternative view, which is generally supported by the Indian decisions, is to argue that since an ordinary person would not have died, the correct conviction in such cases is for voluntarily causing hurt or grievous hurt and *not* for culpable homicide. Under this view, s 299.2 would only be satisfied if the injuries were likely to cause the death not only of the particularly susceptible victim but also of an ordinary victim, presumably taking account of the size, age and sex of the deceased.

Bharat Singh v Emperor (1933) 34 Cri LJ 99 (Oudh Chief Court, India)

The deceased died several days after being attacked. The post mortem report stated the cause of death to be asphyxia and heart failure brought on by the injuries. The evidence disclosed that he was suffering from an enlarged heart which increased the probability of heart failure even from minor injuries. The appellant appealed against his conviction for culpable homicide not amounting to murder.

Bisheshwar Nath J: There is absolutely no evidence and there is no reason to suppose that the accused had any knowledge that [the deceased] was suffering from a badly enlarged heart. We have no evidence either about [the deceased] having been physically infirm. The mere fact that he was an old man of sixty would not be sufficient under the circumstances of the case to justify the inference that the offence was one of culpable homicide not amounting to murder.

Appeal allowed;
Conviction for voluntarily causing grievous hurt substituted

It was suggested in *Munni Lal* (1943) that it is unsatisfactory to convict merely of one of the non-fatal offences in cases where death is caused. Nevertheless, it does seem that the likelihood of death clause in s 299.2 should not be read by reference to the special characteristics of the particular victim. If it was read in that manner, the same approach should logically be taken to the parallel clause–"sufficient in the ordinary course of nature"–in s 300(c). If this was done, s 300(b) would be rendered otiose as pin-prick murders would fall under s 300(c) and there would be no need to prove knowledge of the victim's particular susceptibilities to convict of murder.

Another possibility would be to consider using s 304(A) in this type of case. However, since the decision in *Idu Beg* (1881, below, p 477), where it was held that the accused cannot be considered rash or negligent where he intentionally or knowingly inflicted injuries, this approach has not been adopted.

4.   Sections 299.3 and 300(d)

(a)   Sections 299.3 and 300(d)(i)

Section 299.3 requires knowledge of the likelihood of death; s 300(d)(i) is narrower as it requires the accused to know that his conduct is so imminently dangerous that it must in all probability cause death. Both clauses require the accused to have contemplated death; they are differentiated by the subjectively perceived risk of death ensuing. The cases have scarcely considered the meaning of knowledge but, following the analysis in ch 3, it will be taken to mean being aware that something exists or being almost certain that it exists or will exist or occur.

William Tan Cheng Eng v PP [1970] 2 MLJ 244 (CA, Singapore)

The appellant was charged with murder under s 300(d). He was driving his car when he saw his ex-girlfriend sitting in another man's car. He gave chase. The cars touched and the appellant's car zig-zagged across the road into a motor cyclist coming in the other direction. The rider died almost instantaneously.

Wee Chong Jin CJ: The prosecution said that ... the appellant by driving his car in an extremely reckless and dangerous manner with utter disregard for, or total indifference to other users of the road had committed murder within the meaning of the fourth clause of s 300 of the Penal Code. The law is clear. Knowledge on the part of an accused person of the consequences of his act which has resulted in death is an essential ingredient of the offence of murder under the fourth clause of s 300. In order to succeed the prosecution must prove beyond a reasonable doubt that the *appellant knew*, when he drove his car in such a manner as to come into contact first with the rear and then with the front off-side mudguard of the Morris car, that it was so imminently dangerous that it must in all probability cause death or such bodily injury as was likely to cause death.

The trial judge in a long and detailed summing-up to the jury however ... omitted the most vital ingredient which the prosecution had to prove, namely, that the appellant knew the consequences of his act. It is not sufficient to amount to murder under s 300 for an act to be so imminently dangerous that it must in all probability cause death. Such an act becomes murder only if the person who commits the act, and death results, knew, when committing the act, that it was so imminently dangerous that it would in all probability cause death, or such bodily injury as was likely to cause death.

Another ground on which we came to the conclusion that the murder conviction could not stand was that on the evidence no reasonable jury could have found beyond a reasonable doubt that the appellant at the material time knew that he was driving in a manner that was so imminently dangerous that it must in all probability cause death, or such bodily injury as was likely to result in death.... There was no other traffic between him and them. The picture then, according to the prosecution evidence, was of an angry, jilted young man, driving a 1954 model Ford Prefect along Bedok Road, overtaking and then being overtaken and finally overtaking another car in which his former "steady" girl friend was a passenger. When overtaking the Morris car on the final occasion, he drove his Ford car in such a manner as to first come into contact with the rear and then with the front off-side mudguard of the Morris car. Having regard to what had happened along Changi Road, but bearing in mind that there was no other traffic at the material time while both cars were proceeding along Bedok Road and that no harm was caused to the passengers or to the Morris car which stopped by the left hand side of the road, the most adverse inference that can be drawn from the appellant's manner of driving was that he intended to cause harm to the passengers of the Morris car.

In our judgment there was no sufficient evidence on which a reasonable jury could find the appellant guilty of murder under the fourth clause of s 300 of the Penal Code.

Conviction for murder set aside;
Conviction for causing death by dangerous/
reckless driving substituted therefor

In *William Tan Cheng Eng* (1970) the Singapore Court of Appeal stressed the importance of the accused's subjective knowledge of the risks of his conduct. In the following Indian case, the approach was more objective.

Emperor v Dhirajia [1940] All 647 (HC, Allahabad, India)

The appellant, aged 20, was frequently ill-treated by her husband. Late one night, after a quarrel, she slipped from the house. Hearing footsteps behind her, she panicked and jumped down a well with her baby in her arms. The baby died. At her trial she was convicted of murder but acquitted of attempted suicide.

Bajpai and Braund JJ: [W]e can say it at once that we do not, on the facts, attribute to Mst Dhirajia an intention to cause the death of her baby. We are satisfied that no such intention was ever present in her mind. Indeed, we think there was no room in her mind for any such intention having regard to the panic she was in. But we have to consider whether what she did, she did with the "knowledge" that she was likely by such act to cause death. It has been strongly ... argued ... that we cannot in this case, having regard to all the circumstances, attribute to this unfortunate woman the "knowledge" of anything at all at that particular moment.... We regret that we are unable to go as far as this. "Intention" appears to us to be one thing and "knowledge" ... a different thing. In order to possess and to form an intention there must be a capacity for reason. And when by some extraneous force the capacity for reason has been ousted, it seems to us that the capacity to form an intention must have been unseated too. But to our minds, knowledge stands upon a different footing.... Obviously the degree of knowledge which any particular person can be assumed to possess must vary. For instance, we cannot attribute the same degree of knowledge to an uneducated as to an educated person. But we think that to some extent knowledge must be attributed to everyone who is sane. And what we have to consider here is whether it is possible for us–treating Mst Dhirajia as a sane person, which we are bound to do–to conclude that she could possibly have been ignorant of the fact that the act of jumping into a well with a baby in her arms was likely to cause that baby's death. We do not think we can. We think that however primitive a man or woman may be and however frightened he or she may be, knowledge of the likely consequence of so imminently dangerous an act must be supposed to have remained with him or her.... The act of jumping into a well with a six-month-old baby on one's arms can, in our opinion, but for a miracle have only one conclusion, and we regret that we have to assume that that consequence must have been within the knowledge, but not within the intention, of Mst Dhirajia.

For these reasons we think this was a case of culpable homicide. We must now proceed to consider whether or not is was murder.... The first three cases in which culpable homicide is designated as murder are all cases in which there is found a positive "intention" in the doer of the act.... [W]e do not think that in the circumstances of this case it is possible to attribute to Mst Dhirajia any positive or active intention at all. The only case we need discuss is the fourth.... Mst Dhirajia must be taken to have known that what she did must in all probability cause the death of her baby.

[Her appeal was allowed on the basis that she had an "excuse" for jumping into the well under the last clause of s 300(d); see below, p 422.]

This approach to the question of knowledge is problematic; having decided on a subjective basis, without reference to any hypothetical ordinary person, that Mst Dhirajia could not have formed any "intention" because of her general state of panic, the court abruptly switched to a very objective stance to the question of knowledge. Both intention and knowledge should in principle be judged subjectively and although an ordinary person's reaction is relevant to assessing the accused's own state of mind, it should not be conclusive. In the English case of *Hudson* (1965), the accused was convicted of having unlawful sexual intercourse with a defective. His defence was that under the terms of the relevant statute he "did not know and had no reason to suspect her to be a defective". His appeal was allowed on the basis that the judge's direction to the jury had suggested an objective approach to the question of knowledge. Ashworth J argued:

> [I]n considering his state of mind, in the view of this court a jury is entitled and indeed bound to take into account the accused himself. There may be cases ... where there is evidence before the jury to show that the accused himself is a person of limited intelligence, or possibly suffering from some handicap which would prevent him from appreciating the state of affairs which an ordinary man might realize.

If Mst Dhirajia herself gave no thought to the risk because of her panic, her case would more appropriately have been considered under the negligence head of s 304(A) rather than the knowledge limbs of ss 299 and 300.

(b) Sections 299.3 and 300(d)(ii)

These provisions raise some fundamental difficulties. Under s 300(d)(ii), the accused must know that his conduct is so imminently dangerous that it must in all probability cause a *bodily injury which is likely to cause death*. Clearly the first part is subjective; the accused himself must know that he will in all probability cause a bodily injury. The more difficult question is whether the likelihood of death clause is an objective or a subjective requirement. On an objective reading, the prosecution simply has to establish that the accused knew his conduct was so imminently dangerous that it would in all probability cause a bodily injury; thereafter, the question whether the injury is likely to cause death is objective. This interpretation has a superficial attraction in that it would parallel the objective approach taken to similar wording in ss 299.3 and 300(c). However, to read it this way would lead to there being some cases of murder which do not amount to culpable homicide, contrary to the fundamental definition of murder as a subset of culpable homicide. The problem is that s 299.3 requires the accused to have contemplated the possibility of *death* whereas s 300(d)(ii) only requires contemplation of *bodily injury*. The accused may know that his conduct is so imminently dangerous that it must in all probability cause a bodily injury, but he may not contemplate death as a likely or even a possible consequence. He would therefore not fall under either s 299.3 (or s 300(d)(i)). However, such a case would fall under an objective interpretation of s 300(d)(ii), provided the bodily injury was assessed to be likely to cause death.

Since the objective view of s 300(d)(ii) must therefore be rejected in view of the structure of the Penal Code, we must adopt the subjective interpretation. The prosecution must prove not only that the accused knew his act was so imminently dangerous that it would in all probability cause a bodily injury, but also that he knew such a bodily injury was likely to cause death. This interpretation at least renders s 300(d)(ii)

no wider than s 299.3 since both sections now require knowledge of
the likelihood of death. However, s 300 should, as a species of culpable
homicide, be narrower than s 299 and not merely coextensive with it.
Are there, then, any cases which would fall under s 299.3 but not under
the subjective interpretation of s 300(d)(ii)? Clearly the subsections are
very close in scope but they may lead to different results on the facts
of some cases. Consider *Nedrick* (1986) again: A poured paraffin through
the letterbox of a woman's house and set it alight. His aim was revenge
and he did not aim to hurt or kill anyone. However, one of the woman's
children died in the ensuing fire. If such a case fell to be considered
under the Penal Code, each limb of ss 299 and 300 should be analysed.
In such an uncertain area of law it may be rash to predict the inferences
to be drawn and the outcome of such a case but certain observations
may be made. If intention means direct objective, A would not be liable
under s 299.1 and s 299.2 or s 300(a), (b) or (c) as he did not intend
or "aim at" causing either bodily injury or death. With regard to
ss 299.3 and 300(d), there might be three stages of analysis. The first
question would be whether the case fell under s 299.3; it would do so
only if A was regarded as having the knowledge that he was likely to
cause not merely a bodily injury, but death. If this first question was
answered in the affirmative, the second question would be whether the
case fell under s 300(d)(i). Although A might be regarded as having the
knowledge that he was *likely* to cause death, the court might infer that
he did not know that his conduct was so imminently dangerous that it
would *in all probability* cause death; in other words, his assessment of
the risk might fall short of the level required by s 300(d)(i). Finally, the
court should consider whether the subjective interpretation of s 300(d)(ii)
was satisfied. Again, A's assessment of the risk might fall short of that
required. Even though he saw death as likely, it might be inferred that
he did not know that any type of injury would *in all probability* result.

(c) Lack of excuse

The clause restricting liability to cases where there is no "excuse for
incurring the risk of causing death" appears otiose on first reading in
that it seems simply to affirm the application of the special exceptions.
However, it seems designed to attract a wider meaning so that culpable
homicide with knowledge will not amount to murder where the accused
has an excuse for incurring the risk even where, on the facts of the
case, none of the special exceptions would apply.

Emperor v Dhirajia [1940] All 647 (HC, Allahabad, India)

This case was also considered above (see p 419). Having decided that
the appellant possessed the requisite knowledge for s 300(d), the court
continued:

> But [s 300(d)] is qualified by the further requirement that "such act" must
> be "without any excuse for incurring the risk of causing death ...". The

construction of this particular passage of s 300 is well settled. It is well settled that it is not murder merely to cause death by doing an act with the knowledge that it is so imminently dangerous that it must in all probability cause death. In order that an act done with such knowledge should constitute murder it is necessary that it should be committed without any excuse for incurring the risk of causing the death or bodily injury. An act done with the knowledge of its consequence is not prima facie murder. It becomes murder only if it can be positively affirmed that there was no excuse. The requirements of the section are not satisfied by the act of homicide being one of extreme recklessness. It must in addition be wholly inexcusable. When a risk is incurred–even a risk of the gravest possible character which must normally result in death–the taking of that risk is not murder unless it was inexcusable to take it.... [W]e think that it is not possible to say that Mst Dhirajia in jumping into the well did so without excuse. We must consider in assessing what is excuse or is not excuse the state of mind she was in. She feared her husband and she had reason to fear her husband. She was endeavouring to escape from him at dawn and in the panic into which she was thrown when she saw him behind her she jumped into the well. We think she had excuse and that that excuse was panic or fright or whatever you like to call it. For these reasons we do not think Mst Dhirajia is guilty of murder ... [but] is guilty of culpable homicide not amounting to murder.

Appeal allowed

It is clear that none of the special exceptions to s 300 would have applied on the facts of the case but the court was nevertheless able to hold that the offence fell only under s 299 and thus to impose a lenient sentence (six months' imprisonment) to reflect the strong mitigating factors in the case. Further insight into the probable scope and rationale of the clause may be gleaned from the English Law Commission's (1978) reflections on the meaning of recklessness:

[A] person should not be regarded as reckless as to the result of his conduct unless at the time of that conduct he foresaw that that result might occur and, *in the judgment of a reasonable man with that person's appreciation of the degree of the risk involved, it would have been unreasonable to pursue that conduct* (para 56, emphasis added).

The Law Commission's views on the proper definition of recklessness in English law have been overtaken by events (see ch 3) but it would seem that the excuse clause of s 300(d) performs a similar role to that envisaged in the preceding passage; s 300(d) should not impose liability on those who take risks which society treats as "acceptable" or "reasonable" even though they have recognized the dangers in their conduct.

5.   Conclusions

In a famous passage in *Govinda* (1876) Melville J described the dividing line between the different limbs of ss 299 and 300 as "fine but appreciable". The preceding analysis has suggested that in theory there may be fine linguistic distinctions between the different sections. However, where the basic distinction revolves around words denoting vaguely differentiated degrees of probability of death resulting–around the difference between "likelihood" and "sufficiency in the ordinary course of nature" or "all probability"–it is extremely difficult to appreciate any practical distinction in borderline cases or to predict their outcome. In the niceties of academic debate on ss 299 and 300 it must be remembered that the consequences of falling on one side of the line as opposed to the other are very dramatic. In cases of murder the judge has no choice but to impose the death penalty; in cases falling under s 299, he has a broad discretion. When liability is being imposed for the most heinous offence in the criminal calendar, it is unacceptable that it is so difficult to state the difference between the sections even in abstract terms.

The thin dividing line between the sections and the consequences for the accused in terms of the penalties naturally renders prosecution decisions of the utmost significance to the outcome of the case. This is well illustrated by the following case.

Selvraj Subramaniam v PP [1985] 1 MLJ 190 (HC, Singapore)

The accused, a police inspector, was charged with culpable homicide not amounting to murder, punishable under s 304(b). The cause of death was asphyxia by smothering

Lai Kew Chai J: I was invited by counsel for the defence to find that if the accused had smothered his wife to death the act of smothering was a rash act punishable under s 304(A) of the Penal Code. Clearly this submission must fail. It was culpable homicide. I have no doubt that the accused knew that his act of smothering was likely to cause death. It was done in such a way and with such force that the deceased was totally deprived of any air so that death ensued within ten minutes or so. The evidence also suggests that the accused had effectively immobilized the deceased with the result that she could not put up any struggle.

I accordingly convict the accused as charged.

Addendum
This case is on that side of the scale which borders on murder. Having considered all that has been canvassed in mitigation on behalf of the accused, including the circumstances of the marriage, the good record of the accused as a police officer and the circumstances of the homicide I sentence the accused to 8 years' imprisonment .... But for the mitigating circumstances I have mentioned, I would have had no hesitation in imposing the maximum of 10 years imprisonment.

There are some interesting features in this case. First, the decision to charge only under s 299 in a case which the judge regarded as falling on the borderline between culpable homicide and murder; normally in borderline cases one would expect the heavier charge to be brought. As a result of the charge, the court was not called upon to decide the difficult question whether the accused's knowledge was such as to satisfy s 300(d). The second point of interest is the decision to charge under the knowledge limb, with its lower punishment. The accused was held to have known that he was likely to cause death; is it not possible that he could have been regarded as having the intention to inflict a bodily injury? If so, could his case not have fallen under s 299.2?

The existence of the mandatory death penalty for murder and the close relationship between ss 299 and 300 increases the likelihood of plea negotiation between defence and prosecution. The defendant in *Selvraj* (1985) did not plead guilty but there are many cases where the accused agrees to plead guilty to the lesser offence in return for the prosecution dropping the heavier charge. The role of prosecutorial discretion in this area has been dramatically illustrated by Yeo's (1985) study of homicide in Singapore. From 1973 to 1982 out of 157 offenders convicted of culpable homicide, over 75% faced charges of culpable homicide not amounting to murder. During the period 1979 to 1982, the proportion rose to 90%. From 1980 to 1982 there was only one murder charge and no murder convictions. Yeo concludes:

> This indicates prosecutorial discretion and plea-bargaining in operation, the lower charge under s 304 being preferred because of the interplay of factors such as the insufficiency of evidence, the accused's willingness to plead guilty and the presence of circumstances which could broadly constitute one of the special exceptions to s 300 of the Code .... It may be that this paucity of murder convictions is the result of an aversion to capital punishment by both the prosecution and the courts.

As far as reform is concerned, the Indian Law Commission (42nd Report, 1971, para 16.3) did not share the concerns expressed in this book and said that:

> Such obscurity as might have been initially felt in interpreting the definitions ... is hardly felt now after they have been expounded and clarified by dozens of authoritative judicial decisions.

It proposed minor changes to the drafting and structure of ss 299 and 300 but retained the existing terminology for the *mens rea*. This is too complacent. The time has come for an open discussion and clear definition of those states of mind which are regarded as so blameworthy that they should attract a conviction for the most serious offence on the penal calendar, and whether such offences should attract a mandatory penalty of any description.

D. Transferred malice and constructive mens rea

Penal Code, s 301

If a person, by doing anything which he intends or knows to be likely to cause death, commits culpable homicide by causing the death of any person whose death he neither intends nor knows himself to be likely to cause, the culpable homicide committed by the offender is of the description of which it would have been if he had caused the death of the person whose death he intended or knew himself to be likely to cause.

Section 301 seems designed to embrace the English doctrine of transferred malice. Suppose A shoots at P with the intention to kill, but in fact kills V; A's *mens rea* can be "transferred" from P to V. However, the scope of s 301 is problematic. It provides that *mens rea* may be "transferred" from the intended to the actual victim where the accused either intends death or knows death is likely; therefore, it does not cover the situation where he intended only a bodily injury under ss 299.2 or 300(c). In a case falling under these limbs, it might be possible to allow the transfer of *mens rea* under the broad wording of ss 299 and 300, under which it is not necessary to intend or know of the likelihood of a *particular* person's death (see also Illustration (d) to s 300). On the other hand, however, it could be argued that s 301 is conclusive of the circumstances in which there can be such a transfer.

In the Indian case of *Mushunooru Surayanarayana Moorty* (1912), the dissenting judge suggested that s 301 only applies where the intended victim does not die and does not apply where the intended victim also dies. This appears unduly restrictive and was rejected by the majority.

Transferred *mens rea* is to be distinguished from the common law doctrine of *constructive mens rea*, exemplified by the so-called "felony-murder" rule which once formed part of English law. A person who caused death while committing a violent felony such as rape or robbery, or while attempting to prevent arrest was considered under this rule to have sufficient *mens rea* for murder. Thus, where the victim was killed during the course of a rape, the *mens rea* for rape was regarded, artificially, as constituting the necessary *mens rea* for murder. This draconian doctrine has now been abolished. On the other hand, constructive *manslaughter* does still exist in English law. As Clarkson (1987, p 140) puts it:

> [I]f the accused is engaged in committing an *unlawful act* (for example, a common assault) from which death results, the law will readily impose liability [for manslaughter] insisting only that the unlawful act be slightly dangerous in that it must be [likely] (objectively) *to cause some physical harm.*

Gaur (1985) equates s 301 with the doctrine of constructive *mens rea*. This must be wrong. The wording of s 301 requires the offender to intend or know himself likely to cause death; ie to have the necessary *mens rea* for culpable homicide or murder. This is not automatically satisfied by, for example, a finding that he had the *mens rea* for rape (whatever that is; see ch 3). This interpretation is supported, though not fully argued, by Edwards (1959) and illustrated by *Ali b Haji Abdullah* (1948), where a girl aged ten died in consequence of being raped. The Court of Appeal of the Malayan Union held that where there was no indication of any intention other than to rape or of any violence other than that necessary to effect the rape, a conviction for murder could not stand. Murray Aynsley CJ approved the views of Bucknill J in *Shambu Khatri* (1924) where the appellant had been convicted of culpable homicide not amounting to murder in similar circumstances:

> In English law there is no doubt that the perpetrator could have been properly indicted for murder or manslaughter, but there is no reason to think for one moment nor is there any evidence to show that the person who had sexual intercourse with the deceased did anything which any reasonable person would contemplate as being likely to cause injury which would result in the girl's death. In the course of many cases in which I have prosecuted or which I have tried of this character, I cannot recollect one which has resulted in death; and in the medical textbooks there are but few instances (and those of extraordinary character)....

[See also *Mohamed Yasin b Hussin*, 1976, above, p 413 and *Woo Sing* (1954), below, p 482.]

Utilitarian considerations and a concern for individual justice led the authors of the Penal Code to the following conclusion.

Macaulay and other Indian Law Commissioners, A Penal Code Prepared by the Indian Law Commissioners, Note M (1837), 130

To punish as a murderer every man who, while committing a heinous offence, causes death by pure misadventure, is a course which evidently adds nothing to the security of human life.... For example, hundreds of persons in some great cities are in the habit of picking pockets. They know that they are guilty of a great offence .... Unhappily one of these hundred attempts to take the purse of a gentleman who has a loaded pistol in his pocket. The thief touches the trigger, the pistol goes off, the gentleman is shot dead. To treat the case of this pick-pocket differently from that of the numerous pick-pockets who steal under exactly the same circumstances, with exactly the same intentions, with no less risk of causing death ... appears to us an unreasonable course.

E. Killing a supposed corpse

1. The problem

The principle that the *actus reus* and the *mens rea* of offences should coincide in time generally presents no difficulty. However, particularly in the case of homicide, there have been cases where there appears to be no coincidence. The problem has usually arisen where the accused believed the victim of his initial assault to be dead but actually caused the death when attempting to hide his crime; eg, by disposing of the supposed corpse. The Penal Code is silent on these problems and there are no local cases in which the issue has been discussed. Consequently, decisions from other jurisdictions will be of persuasive authority. The general problem is dramatically illustrated by the US case of *Jackson* v *The Commonwealth* (1896). Jackson attempted to murder his victim in the state of Ohio by administering a large dose of cocaine. He loaded her into his car and drove into the neighbouring state of Kentucky. Believing her to be dead, he then cut off her head. She died from the decapitation and not from the drugs. It was argued that the Kentucky courts could not convict of murder as Jackson did not realize she was alive when he cut off her head. On the same argument he could not be convicted of murder in Ohio because the death was not caused there. Not surprisingly the Kentucky court rejected his argument. *Jackson* (1896) dramatically illustrates the fundamental problems in this area. The legal principle that the *actus reus* and the *mens rea* must coincide appears to conflict with policy arguments which strongly suggest that offenders such as Jackson should not escape liability for murder.

2.　The solutions

Two main paths to liability are available in this type of case, depending on the facts. In a minority of cases it will be possible to adopt the approach taken in the English case of *Fagan* v *MPC* (1969). When parking his car, Fagan accidentally drove onto a policeman's foot. This constituted the *actus reus* of battery but he had no *mens rea* at that stage. The policeman asked Fagan to remove his car but he colourfully declined. It was held that although Fagan had no *mens rea* when he drove onto the foot, he did have the necessary *mens rea* during the time that the car remained on the policeman's foot. The defence nevertheless argued that the *mens rea* and *actus reus* did not coincide as the *actus reus* consisted in driving onto the foot. However, the majority of the Court of Appeal held that the *actus reus* continued until Fagan drove off the foot. Thus, by "stretching" the *actus reus* to cover the refusal to move the car, the *actus reus* and *mens rea* did coincide.

However, the *Fagan* (1969) approach will frequently be unavailable; it is more common, as in *Jackson* (1896), for there to be a series of distinct acts resulting in death. The approach to liability in such a situation is shown in the following case.

Thabo Meli v R [1954] 1 All ER 373 (PC, appeal from Basutoland)

The appellants, in accordance with a prearranged plan, took the victim to a hut where they gave him beer. When he was partially intoxicated, they struck him over the head. Believing him to be dead, they rolled his body over the cliff to make his death appear accidental. He died of exposure when lying unconscious at the foot of the cliff.

Lord Reid: It is said that two acts were done: first the attack in the hut; and, secondly, the placing of the body outside afterwards—and that they were separate acts. It is said that, while the first act was accompanied by *mens rea*, it was not the cause of death; but that the second act, while it was the cause of death, was not accompanied by *mens rea*; and on that ground, it is said that the accused are not guilty of murder, though they may be guilty of culpable homicide. It is said that the *mens rea* necessary to establish murder is an intention to kill, and that there could be no intention to kill when the accused thought that the man was already dead, so their original intention to kill had ceased before they did the act which caused the man's death. It appears to their Lordships impossible to divide up what was really one series of acts in this way. There is no doubt that the accused set out to do all these acts in order to achieve their plan, and as parts of their plan; and it is much too refined a ground of judgment to say that, because they were under a misapprehension at one stage and thought that their guilty purpose had been achieved before, in fact, it was achieved, therefore they are to escape the penalties of the law.... Their crime is not reduced from murder to a lesser crime merely because the accused were under some misapprehension for a time during the completion of their criminal plot.

Appeal dismissed

Under this approach, a series of admittedly distinct acts may in some circumstances be regarded as forming part of a longer transaction; it will suffice if the accused had the necessary *mens rea* at some point in the transaction, even if it did not coincide precisely in time with the act which caused the death. However, the limits of this approach are unclear. It is often said (see, eg Koh and Myint Soe, 1974, p 179) that Indian cases follow a different approach. However, the position is more complicated. Many of the Indian cases, often predating *Thabo Meli* (1954), adopt the same reasoning, at least where there appears to have been a preconceived plan to kill the victim and to dispose of the body. In *Kaliappa Goundan* (1933) the appellants "decoyed" the victim under the pretence of taking her to visit a sick relative. They strangled her and placed her "body" on the railway track. She was decapitated by a passing train and there was evidence that this, rather than the strangulation, might have been the cause of death. The convictions for murder were upheld and the court stressed that the victim was killed "in pursuance of a deliberate plan". The same result was reached on similar facts in *Nehal Mehto* (1939) where "the intention of the accused was from the outset to cause the death of the victim in pursuance of a preconceived plan".

The language of a preconceived plan tends to obscure the fact that there may in fact be two plans; first, to kill; and, second, to dispose of the corpse. However, the cases seem to suggest that the *Thabo Meli* (1954) approach will apply provided that there is a plan to kill, even if the decision to dispose of the body in a particular manner is only decided later (see also *Lingraj Das*, 1944). In principle this is correct as there is little to choose in the blameworthiness of the accused in such cases.

Although the reports are unclear, the *Thabo Meli* (1954) approach also seems to have been used in some Indian cases where there was no preconceived plan to kill but there was nevertheless a clear intention to cause death. In *Thavamani* (1943), convictions for murder were upheld where the victim appeared to have died from being thrown into a well rather than from an earlier assault. Beyond that the facts are unclear from the report. Although the killing might have been in pursuance of a preconceived plan, such language was noticeably absent from the judgment. Instead, the court stated that the intention to cause death was made out. This is perhaps wider than *Thabo Meli* (1954) since an intention to kill does not require premeditation and may be formed on the spur of the moment.

The following cases are the main source of the view that Indian courts prefer the general principle that *actus reus* and *mens rea* must coincide to the approach in *Thabo Meli* (1954).

Queen-Empress v Khandu Valad Bhavani (1891) 15 Bom 194 (Division Bench, Bombay, India)

The accused struck his father-in-law three blows on the head. When he fell down senseless, the accused sought to cover his deeds by placing firewood under the father-in-law's head and setting fire to the hut.

Birdwood J: [T]he medical evidence ... is to the effect that the death of the deceased was not caused by the blows struck by the accused, and that those blows, moreover, were not likely to cause death. They probably, however, stunned the deceased. Death was really caused by the injuries from burning .... Reading the medical evidence with the accused's confession, I have no doubt that the accused believed the deceased to be already dead when he set fire to the shed.

The accused admits that he struck the deceased with the intention of killing him. In intention, therefore, he was a murderer. But on the evidence, such as it is, it must be found that the striking did not amount to murder. It was, however, an attempt to murder .... As I am of opinion that the accused thought, when he set fire to the house, that the deceased was already dead, I cannot hold that the act of setting fire to the shed by which death was caused was done with such intent or knowledge as is contemplated in s 299.... It is not as if the accused had intended, by setting fire to the shed, to make the deceased's death certain.

Parsons J: I am unable to agree with my learned colleague that the offence of which the accused is guilty is only an attempted murder. In my opinion it is murder .... [T]he intention of the accused [was] to cause death and there are two acts committed by him which together have caused death–acts so closely following upon and so intimately connected with each other that they cannot be separated and assigned the one to one intention and the other to another, but must both be ascribed to the original intention which prompted the commission of those acts and without which neither would have been done. In my opinion, the accused in committing those acts is guilty of murder.

In consequence of this difference of opinion, the case was referred to **Sargent CJ** (who agreed with Birdwood J):

Assuming that the deceased would not have died from the effect of the blows ... there would be difficulty in regarding what occurred from first to last as one continuous act done with the intention of killing the deceased.

Convicted of attempted murder

Palani Goundan v Emperor (1919) 42 Mad 547 (Full Bench, Madras, India)

The appellant struck his wife on the head with a ploughshare, knocking her senseless. Believing her dead, and hoping to fake suicide, he hung her from a beam by means of a rope. She died by hanging.

Wallis CJ: [A]ll three intentions [under s 299] must be directed either deliberately to putting an end to human life or to some act which to the knowledge of the accused is likely to eventuate in the putting an end to human life. The knowledge must have reference to the particular circumstances in which the accused is placed.... [T]he intention of the accused must be judged not in the light of the actual circumstances, but in the light of what he supposed to be the circumstances. It follows that a man is not guilty of culpable homicide if his intention was directed only to what he believed to be a lifeless body. Complications may arise when it is arguable that the two acts of the accused should be treated as being really one transaction ... or when the facts suggest a ... reckless indifference ... as to whether the body handled was alive or dead.

The case was referred back to the Division Bench which convicted the accused of grievous hurt under s 326

The judgments in *Palani Goundan* (1919) and *Khandu Valad Bhavani* (1891) therefore place significantly more emphasis on the general principle requiring coincidence of *actus reus* and *mens rea* than on the approach of regarding the distinct acts as part of a longer transaction. Both cases are technically distinguishable on their facts from *Thabo Meli* (1954) and from cases like *Kaliappa Goundan* (1933) since they did not apparently involve preconceived plans to kill. However, their general approach is nevertheless hard to reconcile with the other cases, particularly with those which assume that the *Thabo Meli* (1954) approach applies whenever there is an intention to cause death, even if there is no preplanning. In *Thavamani* (1943), *Palani Goundan* (1919) was distinguished as a case where "there was never at any time an intention to cause death. The original intention was only to cause injury". This is a debatable assessment of the facts in that case but, if correct, is an interesting approach. It suggests that the *Thabo Meli* (1954) reasoning depends on the particular *mens rea* of the accused; it will not apply to all the limbs of s 300 but only where there is a direct intention to cause death under s 300(a). Distinguishing the different limbs of s 300 in this manner is reminiscent of the *mens rea* approach to causation (see ch 18); where the *mens rea* is particularly blameworthy, the courts may prefer the *Thabo Meli* (1954) approach and where it is less blameworthy, they may prefer the general doctrine. It is unclear which approach would consequently be applied where there was an intention to kill but the offence was mitigated to culpable homicide not amounting to murder by virtue of the special exceptions; since the accused is regarded as less blameworthy in such cases, it would not be surprising to find the general doctrine being used. *Khandu Valad Bhavani* (1891) is more difficult to distinguish since the general doctrine was applied even though the appellant had intended to kill. However, it is worth noting that the intention to kill was based on a confession and the original

injuries were "not likely to cause death"; this seemed to play a significant part in the reasoning of the majority.

The state of the Indian authorities is such that it is dangerous to
draw concrete conclusions. However, it does appear that the *Thabo Meli*
(1954) approach will be applied where there is a preconceived plan and
where there is a clear intention to kill. On the other hand, it is not clear
whether it will be applied in other cases. In other jurisdictions it is also
difficult to state the law. In England, there is evidence of a willingness
to apply *Thabo Meli* (1954) more widely; in *Church* (1965) the Court
of Appeal suggested, probably obiter, that it should apply to cases of
manslaughter where there is no preconceived plan. On the other hand,
in New Zealand (*Ramsay*, 1967), the courts have been unwilling to
extend *Thabo Meli* (1954) beyond cases of preconceived plans.

3. Conclusions

Since the Penal Code is silent, it is not necessary for the courts in
Singapore and Malaysia to follow Indian decisions, nor, indeed, decisions from other jurisdictions. Consequently, it is unclear what rules
apply. However, on the basis of cases from other jurisdictions and
relevant policy questions, the following guidelines may be suggested.

(1) Where there is a preconceived plan not only to murder the deceased but also to dispose of the body, *Thabo Meli* (1954) should be
followed. The case was decided by the Privy Council and is generally
regarded as correct from the policy point of view. The same approach
should apply where there was a premeditated plan to kill, even though
the decision as to the method of disposing of the body was only determined later.

(2) The policy arguments are a little less clear in other situations.
However, there are Indian authorities which suggest that the *Thabo Meli*
(1954) approach should also be used where there is a clear intention to
kill, even if formed on the spur of the moment.

(3) Where there is only an intention to inflict bodily injury under ss
299.2 and 300(c), or knowledge under s 299.3 or 300(d), it is again unclear whether the *Thabo Meli* (1954) reasoning is appropriate. The
English case of *Church* (1965) suggests a broad application of *Thabo
Meli* (1954) but it is not perhaps as strong an authority as the Indian
cases. Too wide an application of *Thabo Meli* (1954) would deprive the
general doctrine of any significant force in such cases. It should not be
forgotten that the accused can always be convicted of another offence,
often carrying a heavy penalty. Thus, in *Palani Goundan* (1919), the
accused was convicted of grievous hurt and in *Khandu Valad Bhavani*
(1891) of attempted murder. Those who are most blameworthy, like
Jackson, will still be convicted of murder.

Chapter 20

Special exceptions

By NA Morgan

A. Introduction

The special exceptions to s 300 provide formal mitigation in that they reduce cases which would otherwise be murder to simple culpable homicide. They therefore allow reduced punishment where the death penalty is considered undeserved. Since the death penalty is mandatory for murder in Singapore and Malaysia, there is no scope for informal judicial mitigation. It is important at this stage to enter a caveat about the use of Indian decisions on the special exceptions. In India, the sentencer retains a residual discretion because the punishment for murder is either death or imprisonment for life. In a very large number of the Indian cases discussed here, the courts felt that even though the special exception in question was not satisfied, the death penalty was undeserved (see especially p 461). Since the Indian courts can avoid the "ultimate" penalty by virtue of their residual discretion, it is arguable that the courts in Singapore and Malaysia should in principle treat Indian decisions with reserve and interpret the special exceptions more generously. However, this point has not been taken in practice (and is very unlikely to be); the following discussion therefore draws widely on Indian decisions.

Some of the special exceptions, such as consent and exceeding private defence, build on the general exceptions to liability contained in Chapter IV of the Penal Code. Others, notably provocation and, in Singapore, diminished responsibility, stand on their own. In attempting to understand the structure and rationale of these exceptions, the distinction is again drawn between "justifications" and "excuses" (see ch 4). The basic distinction between these terms is that justifications deny the wrongfulness of the conduct, whereas excuses deny the individual actor's blameworthiness.

B. Provocation

Penal Code, s 300, Exception 1

Culpable homicide is not murder if the offender whilst deprived of the power of self-control by grave and sudden provocation, causes the death of the person

433

who gave the provocation, or causes the death of any other person by mistake or accident.

The above exception is subject to the following provisos:

(a) that the provocation is not sought or voluntarily provoked by the offender as an excuse for killing or doing harm to any person;
(b) that the provocation is not given by anything done in obedience to the law, or by a public servant in the lawful exercise of the powers of such public servant;
(c) that the provocation is not given by anything done in the lawful exercise of the right of private defence.

Explanation–Whether the provocation was grave and sudden enough to prevent the offence from amounting to murder, is a question of fact.

Illustrations

(a) A, under the influence of passion excited by a provocation given by Z, intentionally kills Y, Z's child. This is murder, inasmuch as the provocation was not given by the child, and the death of the child was not caused by accident or misfortune in doing an act caused by the provocation.
(b) Y gives grave and sudden provocation to A. A, on this provocation, fires a pistol at Y, neither intending nor knowing himself to be likely to kill Z, who is near him, but out of sight. A kills Z. Here A has not committed murder but merely culpable homicide.
(c) A is lawfully arrested by Z, a bailiff. A is excited to sudden and violent passion by the arrest, and kills Z. This is murder, inasmuch as the provocation was given by a thing done by a public servant in the exercise of his powers.
(d) A appears as a witness before Z, a Magistrate. Z says that he does not believe a word of A's deposition, and that A has perjured himself. A is moved to sudden passion by these words, and kills Z. This is murder.
(e) A attempts to pull Z's nose. Z, in the exercise of the right of private defence, lays hold of A to prevent him from doing so. A is moved to sudden and violent passion in consequence, and kills Z. This is murder, inasmuch as the provocation was given by a thing done in the exercise of the right of private defence.
(f) Z strikes B. B is by this provocation excited to violent rage, A, a by-stander, intending to take advantage of B's rage, and to cause him to kill Z, puts a knife into B's hand for that purpose. B kills Z with the knife. Here B may have committed only culpable homicide, but A is guilty of murder.

1.   Introduction

Provocation was originally developed by the common law as an indication of the law's "compassion to human infirmity" (*Hayward*, 1833). This rationale, which focuses on the accused's powers of self control, was recognized by the authors of the Penal Code who at the same time cautioned that provocation should not afford a complete defence.

Macaulay and Other Indian Law Commissioners, A Penal Code Prepared by the Indian Law Commissioners, Note M (1837), 120

We agree with the great mass of mankind, and with the majority of jurists, ancient and modern, in thinking that homicide committed in the heat of passion, on great provocation, ought to be punished; but that in general it ought not to be punished so severely as murder. It ought to be punished in order to give men a motive for accustoming themselves to govern their passions, and in some few cases ... with the utmost rigour. In general, however, we would not visit homicide committed in violent passion, which had been suddenly provoked, with the highest penalties of the law. We think that to treat a person guilty of such homicide, as we should treat a murderer, would be a highly inexpedient course–a course which would shock the universal feeling of mankind, and would engage the public sympathy on the side of the delinquent against the law.

Viewed from this perspective, which focuses on the offender and emphasizes his subjective loss of self control, provocation is in the nature of a partial excuse rather than a partial justification; the conduct has no objective justification but the offender is deemed in the particular circumstances to be less culpable.

However, it is also possible to make out a case for provocation to be treated as a partial justification. Modern empirical research into the circumstances surrounding murders and crimes of violence (eg West, 1965 and Yeo, 1985) has highlighted the involvement of victims in "precipitating" such crimes. When this is recognized, provocation assumes some of the characteristics of a partial justification; the response to the victim's precipitative conduct may be partly justified, in the same way that it is justifiable to respond to physical force by way of private defence. However, the case for provocation being an excuse is strengthened if the acts of third parties are capable of amounting to or contributing to the provocation or if the provocation does not have to be directed at the accused personally (see below, p 440). On balance, it seems better to regard provocation as a partial excuse.

The scope of provocation as a mitigating factor under the Penal Code is significantly wider than under the common law. In English law, provocation only has formal mitigating effect in the case of murder with its mandatory penalty of life imprisonment; in other circumstances, where the punishment is not mandatory, it has only an informal mitigating effect on sentence. It has been suggested that provocation could be abolished if the mandatory sentence was removed and the sentencer given a discretion as to sentence (see Criminal Law Revision Committee, 1980). By contrast, under the Penal Code provocation has a broader and more established role since it substantially reduces the maximum sentences for hurt (s 334), grievous hurt (s 335) and criminal force (s 358), offences which do not carry mandatory sentences (see ch 22).

2. Elements of the defence

Various conditions need to be satisfied under the wording of the Penal Code and as a result of judicial interpretation. Generally the same principles apply to the non-fatal offences (see ch 22).

(a) Link between provocation and killing

The accused must have killed whilst deprived of self-control and his loss of self-control must result from the provocation. Consequently, however extreme the provocation, there will be no defence if the accused actually retained self-control. Neither will the necessary link be established between the provocation and the killing in cases of "self-induced provocation" falling under proviso (a); if provocation is deliberately sought by the accused or used as an excuse for the killing, it cannot be said that the killing was attributable to the provocation.

Chong Teng v PP (1960) 26 MLJ 153 (CA, KL, Malaya)

The accused had gone to the Central Market in Seremban to fight with the deceased who had "taken away" his wife. He was convicted of murder and sentenced to death. The trial judge had summarized proviso (a) as saying "The law says the provocation must come to you. You should not go to the provocation."

Thomson CJ: In our view this statement of the law is not altogether accurate. Exception 1 ... is subject to [the proviso] that the provocation must not be sought 'as an excuse for killing' any person. In other words to bring a case within the proviso and so take it out of the exception it is not sufficient that the accused must go to the provocation, he must go to it as an excuse for killing.

Nevertheless, inspite of this defect in his reasoning the trial Judge's conclusion that in law a defence of provocation was not open to the appellant was in our judgment correct. As he pointed out, whatever happened in the way of taking away the appellant's wife happened a long time ago. As regards what happened in the market place ... even if it was thought that the appellant had then received some sort of provocation that provocation could not by any stretch of the English language be described as sudden. "Sudden" means unexpected and in view of the fact that the appellant on his own admission had gone to the market place with the intention of fighting with the deceased it did not lie in his mouth to say that any violence offered to him (if it was offered) by the deceased could be described as unexpected.

Appeal dismissed

(b) "Grave and sudden" provocation

Since it is a question of fact whether provocation is grave and sudden (explanation to Exception 1), much will depend on the facts of the case. However, the cases reveal several inter-related general points on the interpretation of the words.

(i)   Sudden and cumulative provocation

In *Chong Teng* (1960) Thomson CJ equated the words "sudden" and "unexpected". "Suddenness" also suggests that the provocation must be recent in time. It is clear that the necessary link between the provocation, the loss of self-control and the killing will not be satisfied where there has been a "cooling off period" between the provocation and the killing (*Nanavati*, 1967, see below, p 445). As Glanville Williams (1983) points out, this general principle of "immediacy" reflects the law's concern to distinguish between deliberate killing in cold blood and hot-blooded impulsive killings since only the latter should be mitigated. However, problems arise, particularly in domestic killings, where the latest affront may appear relatively trivial when viewed on its own but there is a long history behind it–where the latest insult is the proverbial "straw that breaks the camel's back". In England, the courts now appear willing in such cases of cumulative provocation to consider the entire history; although appellate decisions still emphasize the requirement for at least some immediate provocative act prior to the killing in order to ensure that cold-blooded revenge killings are not covered; this is not in practice a difficult requirement to satisfy, at least in domestic cases (Wasik, 1982). Furthermore, even when a plea of provocation fails the immediacy test, it must be noted that it may be possible in Singapore to adduce sufficient evidence for diminished responsibility (see below, p 472). Local cases have not addressed the more liberal trends in provocation as clearly as they might (see *Kuan Ted Fatt*, 1985; Sornarajah, 1985) and in *Chong Teng* (1960) acts which occurred several months earlier were discounted. However, there have been a number of cases involving longstanding domestic/family disputes in which earlier acts were treated as relevant without argument.

Mat Sawi b Bahodin v PP (1958) 24 MLJ 189 (CA, KL, Malaya)

There was some dispute as to the precise circumstances surrounding the killing itself but all the versions of the story agreed on the background.

Thomson CJ: [T]here was a long history of domestic unhappiness on the part of the appellant and his wife which had probably been aggravated by the attitude of the dead woman in siding with her daughter. It is clear that for some considerable time the appellant had taken exception to his wife going out to work and that the mother-in-law had supported her daughter against him. There was also evidence to show that the basis of his objecting his wife going out to work was that rightly or wrongly he was of the opinion that it conduced to her forming unsatisfactory relationships with other men....

[I]n his confession [h]e tells the story of previous domestic troubles and of his suspicions as to his wife's fidelity. Then he comes to the night of the material events:

> "About 7 pm I had stomach-ache. Up to 2 am I had been continuously waking my wife up telling her that I was having stomach-ache. She got up sometime after 2 am–and rubbed some oil over my abdomen, without looking at me. Her face was turned the other way. I asked her why she was not looking at me. I asked her if she did not like me or not. I asked her this gently but she gave no answer. I told her that

since she is not even looking at my face I was sure her heart was with someone else. I told her 'Don't you love the small children? How can you love someone else?' She did not reply. Then I spoke to my mother-in-law Karimah. I drew her attention to the behaviour of her daughter. I reminded her this was all due to my mother-in-law allowing my wife to go to work. Karimah began to scold me and accused me of treating her daughter in a rough way. I told my mother-in-law that I was speaking to my wife only in a gentle way. When my mother-in-law came towards me scolding me I picked up a knife which was in the room—the knife used for cutting fowls. When my mother-in-law came towards me scolding me I stabbed my mother-in-law."

[The trial judge] dealt with [provocation] as follows:

"I must tell you that in order to set up the defence of grave and sudden provocation it has to be shown that the provocation was grave, that it was sudden, and that it was such provocation as would cause a reasonable man to lose his self-control. There is only one point in this connection about which I would like to tell you, and that is about the question of suddenness. The only provocation here was a suspicion in the mind of the accused that his wife was unfaithful to him while she was working first on one estate and then on another, and that the deceased was responsible for her going to this work. That suspicion had arisen some time ago and there was no suddenness about it. Therefore in this case the defence of grave and sudden provocation does not arise."

In our opinion the ... summing up ... was a misdirection.... [T]he appellant was at the very lowest entitled to have what he had done considered in the light of his confession which after all, was part of the prosecution case against him.... [W]e are not satisfied that the view could not (as distinct from would not) fairly have been taken that the offence was not murder but culpable homicide not amounting to murder. As we see it the provocation of which there was evidence, if it was believed, was not "only ... a suspicion in the mind of the accused that his wife was unfaithful to him ... and that the deceased was responsible", about which of course there was no question of suddenness. There was evidence that the provocation was that the dead woman whom he regarded as partly responsible for his domestic trouble came towards him scolding him at a time when he was in pain and his wife's coldness in dealing with his pain had revived all his longstanding suspicions.

Appeal allowed

A similar approach may be seen in *Ikau Anak Mail* (1973) where the judge directed that "the mental background created by the [deceased's] previous acts" should be taken into account in deciding the strength of the provocation. In *Lasakke* (1964), the deceased verbally taunted the accused that he had interfered sexually with his wife. Although the accused felt ashamed, he did not retaliate. It seems that later on, after a meal, the accused tried to leave but was obstructed by the deceased; this was "the last of a series of undoubtedly grave provocations". The accused attacked and killed his provoker and was convicted of culpable homicide not amounting to murder. The leading Indian decision of *Nanavati* (1962, see below, p 445) also stressed that the "mental background created by the previous acts of the victim may be taken into consideration".

(ii) Verbal insults

The Penal Code is silent on the types of insult which are sufficiently grave to amount to provocation. Some English cases took the view that verbal insults and gestures could not in themselves amount to provocation except on a confession of adultery, and generally required that some degree of force had been used against the accused or that he had personally witnessed some provocative act. Since the English Homicide Act 1957 now provides specifically that verbal insults may suffice, English cases decided after the passing of the English Homicide Act 1957 on this point are not applicable. Although the issue has not been clearly resolved in Singapore and Malaysia, there are several reasons why the narrow English common law approach should not be applied. From the point of view of principle, it appears unduly restrictive to adopt any rule of law to the effect that words or particular types of conduct can never in themselves amount to provocation. This point was recognized, if also exaggerated, by the authors of the Penal Code:

Macaulay and Other Indian Law Commissioners, A Penal Code Prepared by the Indian Law Commissioners Note M, (1837), 121

It is an indisputable fact that gross insults by word or gesture have as great a tendency to move many persons to violent passion as dangerous or painful bodily injuries. Nor does it appear to us that the passion excited by insult is entitled to less indulgence than passion excited by pain. On the contrary, the circumstance that a man resents an insult more than a wound is any thing but a proof that he is a man of a peculiarly bad heart. It would be a fortunate thing for mankind if every person felt an outrage which left a stain upon his honour more acutely than an outrage which had fractured one of his limbs.

There is little danger of the defence becoming too broad if words can in principle amount to provocation because the other elements of the defence must also be satisfied. It could only be in extreme cases that it would be held that a reasonable person would have killed in reaction to verbal provocation. It will also be very unusual for killing to be reasonably proportionate to merely verbal provocation.

Furthermore, it is important to recognize that words can in principle be provocation in order to deal with cumulative provocation cases. If some immediate "provocation" is required, it could be words as much as deeds which "break the camel's back".

Admitting words as provocation also accords with the structure and wording of the exceptions to s 300 and the rather tentative observations in the cases. Exception 1 does not limit the defence to particular types of provocative act and in the absence of such a restriction should be interpreted in favour of the accused. Furthermore, Exception 2 provides for a separate but related exception of exceeding private defence. This has no parallel in English law but would be applicable locally in some cases involving the provocative use of force; one difference between excessive private defence and provocation under the Penal Code may therefore be that provocation covers verbal insults. Dicta from Indian and local cases support this. In *Nanavati* (1962, see below, p 445) it was strongly stated, although strictly obiter, that words can be sufficient provocation in certain cases. This was approved and followed by the Gujerat High Court in *Bhand Jusub Mamad* (1982). In the Malaysian case of *Lasakke* (1964, see above, p 438) the straw that broke the camel's back was physical provocation but verbal insults were regarded as prior acts of grave provocation.

Chan Tong v R (1960) 26 MLJ 250 (CA, Singapore)

The trial judge directed the jury, inter alia, that "mere words cannot in law ever amount to provocation".

Rose CJ: [T]he case as put forward by the defence, while primarily one of self-defence or, alternatively, of exceeding the right of self-defence, nonetheless contained the further element of provocation by a mixture of words and acts on the part of the deceased woman and the members of her family....

The Jury unhesitatingly rejected the fact of such assault in the context of the defences of self-defence, but we find ourselves unable to say positively that leaving aside the question of self-defence, the physical aggression alleged by the appellant to have taken place coupled with the scolding, which must be regarded in the context of the resentment engendered by the previous evening's episode, did not amount to material which would entitle the Jury, had they so wished, to bring in a verdict of culpable homicide not amounting to murder on the ground of provocation.

Appeal allowed

(iii)   Provocation moving from victim

The question whether acts of third parties or acts which are not directed against the accused personally can constitute or contribute to provocation may be regarded as an aspect of gravity. Exception 1 states that the accused must have caused the death of the *provoker* or *by accident* the death of someone else. It therefore appears that the provocation must have "moved from" the deceased personally. The more strictly this requirement is followed, the more provocation may be seen as a partial justification since the victim's conduct will be precipitative. The common law generally favoured the same narrow view and recent English cases which suggest that the acts of third parties can amount to sufficient provocation (eg *Davies*, 1975) are inapplicable because the English Homicide Act is worded more broadly. The extent to which third parties' acts may be taken into consideration remains undecided locally.

Othman Mat v PP (1964) 30 MLJ 118 (FC, Singapore)

Wee Chong Jin CJ: It was next contended by counsel for the appellant that the learned trial Judge misdirected the jury in so directing them as to restrict their consideration on the same issue to evidence of provocation emanating only from the deceased. Counsel's contention is that on the true construction of *Exception* 1 to s 300 provocation coming from the deceased includes provocation coming from another person with whom he is identified so that it can be said he adopted it.

Counsel referred us to the Hongkong case of *Ho Chun Yuen* (1961) where Hogan CJ, delivering the judgment of the Hongkong Supreme Court, after considering the number of English and Privy Council cases and a Canadian case, which were also cited before us, said:

"With such guidance as one can get from these cases and having regard to the essential element in provocation as defined in *Holmes* (1946) it seems reasonable to interpret any limitation of provocation to acts by the deceased, as including acts of others so closely associated with the deceased and the deceased's actions that the deceased can be considered, in effect, to have adopted and joined in those acts".

In the case before us counsel for the appellant submitted that the deceased's actions on the evening of the 28th April showed that he had adopted and joined in the provocative acts of his wife earlier that day relating to the use of the common bathroom. Having regard however to the appellant's own evidence that he was not angry when the deceased's wife called him swine and said when her husband returned she would tell her husband and he would teach the appellant, and having regard to the long lapse of time between the bathroom incident and the start of the deceased's incident with the appellant we are of the opinion, assuming the law on this point to be as stated by Hogan CJ in *Ho Chun Yuen* (1961), that there was no misdirection by the learned trial Judge.

The criminal law of Hongkong is however different from ours in that ours is codified. English law is again different from ours for the same reason and in England there are conflicting decisions as to whether or not provocation must be limited to acts of the deceased.

It is unnecessary in the present case for us to state the law on this point in general terms and we accordingly do not propose to do so.

In the majority of cases, the provocation not only emanates from the deceased but is also directed at the accused. However, this is not always so. In *Doughty* (1986) the English Court of Appeal held that the question of provocation should be left to the jury where the accused claimed he was provoked by the crying and restlessness of his 17-day-old baby. A baby's crying can hardly be said to be directed at anybody in particular. In such a case it is hardly conceivable that the accused would pass the reasonable man test (see below, p 443), but should such cases even be left to be decided according to the reasonable man test? Should there alternatively be a rule under the Penal Code that provocation cannot by definition be grave unless it is directed at the accused? On the other hand, would such a rule be too rigid if provocation were conceived as a partial *excuse*?

(iv) Proportionality

The words "grave and sudden" have been interpreted to embrace the important and frequently cited principle that the retaliation should not be out of proportion to the degree of provocation.

AG for Ceylon v Don John Perera [1953] AC 200 (PC, appeal from Ceylon)

Lord Goddard: Turning now to the facts, it is enough to say that the case made at the trial was that ill-feeling had long existed between the respondent and the family of the deceased, and that on the day in question he shot and killed the woman Kumarihamy and other members of her family, and it was sought to reduce the crime from murder to manslaughter by reason of certain provocation consisting of stone-throwing by the woman's family, and threats uttered by them, so that, the respondent said, he was suddenly provoked and at the same time felt serious danger to his life and that he did not know what happened as he had lost control over himself....

The Court of Criminal Appeal were at pains to consider whether the law in England relating to homicide and the reduction of a crime from murder to manslaughter was the same as in Ceylon, where the lesser crime is known as culpable homicide not amounting to murder. The court were of opinion that while it was undoubtedly the law in England that the act of retaliation must be reasonably commensurate with the provocation received this was not the law of Ceylon. The question that falls for decision is one which, in the opinion of their Lordships, depends entirely on the true construction of s 294 of the Penal Code. That code does not provide for any doctrines of English law to be imported into the criminal law of Ceylon. There is no provision similar to that which is found in the Code of Criminal Procedure whereby the English criminal law can be used to fill any gap which may be found to exist in that code....

To reduce the crime from murder to manslaughter the offender must show, first, that he was deprived of self-control, and secondly, that that deprivation was caused by provocation which in the opinion of a jury was both grave and sudden. In directing the jury that they must ask themselves whether the kind of provocation actually given was the kind of provocation which they as reasonable men would regard as sufficiently grave to mitigate the actual killing of the woman, in the opinion of their Lordships the judge was merely directing the jury as to how they should determine whether the provocation was grave. The words "grave" and "sudden" are both of them relative terms and must at least to a great extent be decided by comparing the nature of the provocation with that of the retaliatory act. It is impossible to determine whether the provocation was grave without at the same time considering the act which resulted from the provocation, otherwise some quite minor or trivial provocation might be thought to excuse the use of a deadly weapon. A blow with a fist or with the open hand is undoubtedly provocation, and provocation which may cause the sufferer to lose a degree of control, but will not excuse the use of a deadly weapon, and in the opinion of their Lordships it is quite wrong to say that because the code does not in so many words say that the retaliation must bear some relation to the provocation it is true to say that the contrary is the case.

Appeal dismissed

In *Vijayan* (1975, see below, p 446) and *Wo Yok Ling* (1979), this principle was accepted as binding and applied in Singapore (see also *Cheng Ka Leung, Edmond*, 1987). Clearly, it is an objective test, but its role must be further considered in the light of the objectivity also introduced by the reasonable man test.

(c)   The reasonable person test

(i)   Source and rationale

The Penal Code makes no mention of the reasonable man, but numerous cases have read in the requirement that the provocation must have been such that a reasonable person would have behaved in the same manner.

One of many examples of this can be seen in *Mat Sawi b Bahodin* (1958, see above, p 437) where the Federation of Malaya Court of Appeal did not reject the trial judge's reference to the reasonable man and cited with approval passages adopting such a test in the English case of *Holmes* (1946). The rationale for the reasonable man test is that concessions to human infirmity embodied by provocation must be subject to objective limits of reasonableness and should not involve a wholly subjective inquiry in which actual loss of self-control suffices. Thus, a common theme is that an unusually excitable or pugnacious temperament should be ignored (*Lesbini*, 1914 and *Ghulam Mustapha Ghano*, 1937). It is argued that to take such factors into account would be unduly favourable to those of excitable temperament and unfair to the more phlegmatic. However, the reasonable man has proved, as always, an illusive and chameleonic character and one who may not be well suited to the defence of provocation. A persistent problem has been the definition of the reasonable man. At one time, English law adopted a strict objective test, dramatically illustrated by the following decision.

Bedder v DPP [1954] 1 WLR 1119 (HL, England)

An impotent 18-year-old killed a prostitute who jeered at his efforts to prove his virility and then kicked him in the groin. The House of Lords held that the trial judge had correctly directed the jury that the accused should be judged by the standard of the reasonable man and that they should therefore ignore his youth and impotence.

Lord Simmonds LC explained:

> It would be plainly illogical not to recognize an unusually excitable or pugnacious temperament in the accused as a matter to be taken into account but yet to recognize for that purpose some unusual physical characteristic be it impotence or another.

However, despite Lord Simmonds' fear that it is illogical to recognize some but not all of an offender's characteristics, it has long been recognized that a single standard yardstick will lead to harsh and unfair results and *Bedder* (1954) is no longer good law in England where, since *Camplin* (1978) a more flexible approach has been adopted. Interestingly, the Indian courts recognized at a much earlier date that it was wholly inappropriate to apply a single standard test in a socially, culturally and racially diverse country. In defining the reasonable man the local courts have followed the Indian decisions (Yeo, 1987).

Ghulam Mustapha Ghano v Emperor (1939) 40 Cri LJ 778 (Sind Judicial Commissioners Court)

Davis JC: The grave and sudden provocation urged by the defence is said to lie in the fact that when the girl was reproved by her husband for her absence, she showed him a *booja* that is to say, made a gesture of contempt, and it is urged that among the Baluchis who are excitable people, a *booja* shown to them so enrages them as to deprive them of self-control....

[The learned judge referred to Lord Reading's judgment in the English case of *Lesbini* (1914) where a strict reasonable man test, ignoring different mental abilities of the accused was adopted.]

Lord Reading was dealing presumably with Englishmen or some people like them. He was not dealing with Baluchis nor do we think that judgment was intended to lay down that what is grave and sudden provocation to a Baluchi is grave and sudden provocation to an Englishman or *vice versa*. In short, the "reasonable man" always a somewhat ideal figure, is not a person of identical habits, manners and feelings wherever he may be. We think the generality of the words used in the judgment necessarily imply some qualification. The "reasonable man" is the normal man of the same class or community as that to which the accused belongs; and we think the judgment which refers however specifically to "mental ability" should be read in conjunction with Exception 1 to s 300, Indian Penal Code....

Now, it is to be noted that the Exception refers to the offender. The words are: "Culpable homicide is not murder if the offender, whilst deprived of the power of self-control ...;" it does not say "if the offender being a reasonable man", but we think it means so, bearing in mind the habits, manners and feelings of the class or community to which the offender belongs. We do not think it was intended that in deciding whether the provocation was grave and sudden, it is open to an accused person to show that he was a person of particular excitability or of a particular mental instability or of a particularly volatile temperament. It was not intended that the law should take into account the peculiar idiosyncracies of the offending individual, but it was intended that the Court should take into account the habits, manners and feelings of the class or community to which the accused belonged.... Therefore then the ordinary man, or, what we may call in the words of Lord Reading, the "reasonable man" comes in the interpretation of this Exception to s 300, Indian Penal Code in this way: that while it is the offender whom the Court regards when considering the question whether he was deprived of the power of self-control by grave and sudden provocation, it decides whether this was so by the test of the "reasonable man", the ordinary normal man, the ordinary normal Baluchi, when dealing with Baluchis and the ordinary normal Englishman when dealing with the English. Clearly, there rests with the Judge and there was intended to rest with the Judge, a judicial discretion. Each case must be dealt with on its own facts. The law against murder, however, is not lightly to be relaxed. So far as the Sessions Judge in the case now before us decides that what constitutes grave and sudden provocation does not vary among different peoples in different countries at different times, and that what is not grave and sudden provocation to one is not grave and sudden provocation to any, we think he must be wrong. But it is clear that the learned Judge on other grounds has come to a proper conclusion. The mere fact, as he says, that when the Baluchis are shown a *booja*, they get excited is not in itself sufficient to give them the benefit of the Exception. They must show that showing a *booja* is to Baluchis so grave and sudden a provocation as would deprive the ordinary normal Baluchi of the power of self-control, within the meaning of the Exception, and this, on the evidence, the accused clearly fails to do. When Morio, the uncle of the murdered girl, the complainant and a Baluchi was asked definitely whether if his wife showed *booja* to him, he would kill her, he said "No, if my wife shows *booja* to me, I would beat her but will not kill her."

Appeal dismissed

KM Nanavati v State of Maharashtra AIR (1962) SC 605 (SC, India)

The defendant, a naval officer, was frequently away from his wife Sylvia who remained in Bombay when he was on board ship. Illicit intimacy developed between Sylvia and a family friend, Ahuja.

Subba Rao J: Sylvia confessed to Nanavati of her illicit intimacy with Ahuja. Enraged at the conduct of Ahuja, Nanavati went to his ship, took from the stores of the ship a semi-automatic revolver and six cartridges on a false pretext, loaded the same, went to the flat of Ahuja entered his bedroom and shot him dead. Thereafter, the accused surrendered himself to the police....

The question that the court has to consider is whether a reasonable person placed in the same position as the accused was, would have reacted to the confession of adultery by his wife in the manner in which the accused did.

[The learned judge referred to some English cases, including *Mancini*, (1942), and continued:]

[I]ndian courts have not maintained the distinction between words and acts in the application of the doctrine of provocation in a given case (as is done in English law). The Indian law on the subject may be considered from two aspects, namely, (1) whether words or gestures unaccompanied by acts can amount to provocation, and (2) what is the effect of the time lag between the act of provocation and the commission of the offence.... [The Madras High Court] in *Boya Munigodu* (1881) upheld the plea of grave and sudden provocation in the following circumstances. The accused saw the deceased when she had cohabitation with his bitter enemy; that night he had no meals; next morning he went to the ryots to get his wages from them, and at that time he saw his wife eating food along with her paramour; he killed the paramour with a bill-hook. The learned judges held that the accused had sufficient provocation to bring the case within the first exception to s 300 of the Indian Penal Code....

The case illustrates that the state of mind of the accused, having regard to the earlier conduct of the deceased, may be taken into consideration in considering whether the subsequent act would be a sufficient provocation to bring the case within the exception....

Is there any standard of a reasonable man for the application of the doctrine of "grave and sudden" provocation? No abstract standard of reasonableness can be laid down. What a reasonable man will do in certain circumstances depends upon the customs, manners, way of life, traditional values, etc; in short, the cultural, social and emotional background of the society to which an accused belongs. In our vast country there are social groups ranging from the lowest to the highest state of civilization. It is neither possible nor desirable to lay down any standard with precision: it is for the court to decide in each case....

The Indian law, relevant to the present enquiry, may be stated thus: (1) The test of "grave and sudden" provocation is whether a reasonable man, belonging to the same class of society as the accused, placed in the situation in which the accused was placed would be so provoked as to lose his self-control. (2) In India, words and gestures may also, under certain circumstances, cause grave and sudden provocation to an accused so as to bring his act within the first Exception to s 300 of the Indian Penal Code. (3) The mental background created by the previous act of the victim may be taken into consideration in ascertaining whether the subsequent act caused grave and sudden provocation for committing the offence. (4) The fatal blow should be clearly traced to the influence of passion arising from that provocation and not after the passion had cooled down by lapse of time, or otherwise giving room and scope for premeditation and calculation.

[The learned judge concluded, however, that on the facts the case did not come within Exception 1.]

Appeal dismissed

Vijayan v PP [1975] 2 MLJ 8 (CA, Singapore)

The appellant, a Malaysian, stayed in Singapore on a social visit pass. His friend Velu was involved in a dispute with the room-mates of the deceased's friend Subramaniam. There were some inconclusive meetings to try to resolve the matter. The deceased agreed to try and meet again with the appellant. On the evening in question, the deceased was 'in a quarrelsome mood and expressed a desire to meet the appellant' and a fight ensued.

Choor Singh J: In the present case counsel for the appellant's main criticism is of what is now known as the "reasonable relationship" rule which he says has no validity....

Counsel submitted that the root principle of the doctrine of provocation is that a killing in the heat of blood did not deserve the supreme penalty and that a radical change of opinion has occurred since the judgment of the House of Lords in *Mancini* (1942). It was submitted that the requirement of a reasonable relationship between the act of provocation and the act of retaliation was illogical and unjust because if the provocation was in the circumstances of the case sufficiently grave and sudden to cause the appellant to lose self-control, it did not matter in what form or manner he retaliated. Having lost control of himself he could not be expected to control his retaliation. Counsel argued that the severity of the retaliation was merely evidence of the loss of self-control.

Finally, it was submitted that in any event, the "reasonable relationship" rule was illogical and contrary to modern thinking and should be rejected.

In our opinion although Exception 1 of s 300 of the Penal Code does not apparently state in full the common law as expounded in *Mancini* (1942) and *Lee Chun-Chuen* (1963) that does not mean that provocation under this Exception and common law provocation involve widely different concepts. They do not. In our opinion in enacting Exception 1 of s 300 the Legislature has not limited the common law meaning of provocation. The test to be applied to ascertain the sufficiency of provocation under our law is the same as that applied under the common law. In every case it depends on the effect of the provocative act on the ordinary man, that is, an ordinary reasonable man belonging to the same class of society as the accused.... Whether an act which caused death was done in the heat of passion caused by grave and sudden provocation depends in our opinion on whether the provocative act was such as was likely to cause a reasonable man to lose his self-control and to do the act in question.

It is true that Exception 1 of s 300 which defines provocation does not do so by reference to any comparison between the provocative act and the retaliatory act. But as the test of the sufficiency of the provocation, namely, whether or not the provocation offered would have induced a reasonable man to do what the accused did, cannot be applied without comparing the provocation with the retaliation, the element of "reasonable relationship" is an essential factor to be taken into consideration.

In our judgment, under our law, where an accused person charged with murder relies on provocation and claims the benefit of Exception 1 of s 300, the test to be applied is, would the act or acts alleged to constitute provocation have deprived a reasonable man of his self-control and induced him to do the act which caused the death of the deceased and in applying this test it is relevant to look at and compare the act of provocation with the act of retaliation.

To put it in another way, it must be shown distinctly not only that the act which caused death was done under the influence of some feeling which took away from the accused all control over his actions, but also that that feeling had an adequate cause and here again it is relevant to compare the provocative act with the act of retaliation. If it can reasonably be said that these two acts more or less balance each other in the sense that the proved provocation could have driven a reasonable person to do what the accused did, then he is entitled to the benefit of this Exception. On the other hand, if the act of retaliation is entirely out of proportion to the provocation offered, the plea of grave and sudden provocation fails....

In any event, whatever the law of England may be, the decision in *Perera*'s case (1953) is binding on this court. In our opinion it is also, with respect, entirely correct.

In the present case, counsel for the appellant submitted that the trial judges should have considered the issue of provocation in the light of the appellant's background, namely, that he was a Malaysian who had no right to live and work in Singapore; that he was living in fear that if this fact was discovered by the authorities he would be thrown out of Singapore; that on the night in question the deceased referred to this very sensitive subject when he asked aggressively, "Who has given houses to Malaysians?"; and that when he followed it up by challenging the appellant to a fight, the appellant completely lost his self-control and attacked the deceased. Counsel contended that all this closely following the previous ill-feeling between them, was sufficient provocation to reduce the offence from murder to culpable homicide not amounting to murder. It is pertinent to observe that the appellant, when giving evidence, did not say that he lost his self-control because of the abovementioned provocation by the deceased....

The provocative acts relied upon in this case to constitute grave and sudden provocation within the meaning of Exception 1 of s 300 were not capable of constituting provocation sufficient to reduce the appellant's crime from murder to culpable homicide not amounting to murder.

Appeal dismissed

Although frequently used to limit the scope of the defence, the reasonable man seems remarkably unsuited to provocation. Glanville Williams (1983, p 536) observed:

> The introduction of the reasonable man into the law of provocation is strange. Elsewhere the "reasonable man" test is used to indicate a standard of care required by law. The reasonable man is careful, moral, prudent, calculating, law-abiding. How absurd, then, to imagine that he is capable of losing all control of himself and committing a crime punishable with imprisonment for life!

Some fundamental questions arise. If a reasonable person of the same class and society as the accused would have killed.in the circumstances

of a particular case, why do we not afford the accused a *complete*
defence? Why do we still convict him of culpable homicide, a very
serious offence, when reasonable people in our society would have behaved in the same way?

George P Fletcher, *Rethinking Criminal Law* (1978), 246–247

The primary difficulty in the analysis of provocation derives from the failure of
the courts and commentators to face the underlying normative issue whether
the accused may be fairly expected to control an impulse to kill under the
circumstances. Obviously, there are some impulses such as anger ... that we do
expect people to control. If they fail to control these impulses and they kill
another intentionally, they are liable for unmitigated homicide or murder. The
basic moral question in the law of homicide is distinguishing between those
impulses to kill as to which we as a society demand self-control, and those as
to which we relax our inhibitions.

Courts and commentators seek to evade this moral issue by tying the partial
defense of provocation to the likely behavior of the "reasonable person".

(ii) Reasonable men and proportional responses

The relationship between the reasonable man test, as read into the Penal Code, and the concept of reasonable proportion is obscure and has
not been carefully considered by the courts. If the reasonable man is
wholly objective (as in *Bedder*, 1954) there is no difficulty incorporating an equally objective requirement that the retaliation must also be
reasonably in proportion with the degree of provocation. Thus when the
fully objective test was favoured in England, Viscount Simon LC laid
down in *Mancini* (1942):

> The test to be applied is that of the effect of the provocation upon a reasonable
> man.... In applying the test, it is of particular importance (i) to consider
> whether a sufficient interval has elapsed since the provocation to allow a
> reasonable man time to cool, and (ii) to take into account the instrument
> with which the homicide was effected, for to resort in the heat of passion
> induced by provocation by a single blow is a very different thing from making
> use of a deadly instrument like a concealed dagger. In short, the mode of
> resentment must bear a reasonable relationship to the provocation, if the
> offence is to be reduced to manslaughter.

Both *Mancini* (1942) and *Don John Perera* (1953), as approved in
Vijayan (1975) and *Wo Yok Ling* (1979), suggest that there are two
aspects to the reasonable proportion rule: it relates both to the fact of
killing and to the method. For example, even if the provocation was
such that it might justify a response with fists, it might not justify the
use of a weapon such as a chopper. However, it is unclear from the
judgment in *Don John Perera* (1953) whether, on the facts of the case,
killing by blows might have attracted the provocation defence when
blazing away with a gun did not.

The concept of reasonable proportion has been greatly criticized in
England; it is now rarely articulated by the courts and it is unclear

whether or how far it still applies. By contrast, it is frequently employed in local cases inspite of some major conceptual difficulties. The first problem is that it seems both over-refined and unduly restrictive to say that if the accused has lost self-control as a result of provocation, to the extent that a reasonable man would have been justified in killing, he may nevertheless be denied the defence because, after losing his self-control, he did not give rational consideration to the most proportionate mode of response. This is particularly true if provocation is conceived as a partial excuse where the primary focus is on the accused's lack of self-control. This point has been clearly recognized in some Indian decisions.

State of Gujerat v Bhand Jusub Mamad (1982) Cri LJ 1691 (Gujerat HC, India)

Bedarkar J: It was argued ... that if there would have been one or two blows, it would have been said that that was an act done under "grave and sudden" provocation; but ... when eight blows are given, it cannot be said that the "grave and sudden" provocation continued till then. This argument is without any merit.... It has been accepted by the Courts that when a person loses the self-control under "grave and sudden" provocation, he loses all faculties of calculation and balance of mind and the Court would not weigh in golden scales as to how many blows would be sufficient to convince a Court that the act done by the accused was under "grave and sudden" provocation.... When one loses the mental faculty by [being] gravely provoked, one would not go on calculating the blows.

The injection by the courts of an objective reasonable proportion test also contrasts with the related Exception 2, "exceeding private defence". There, the test of the response is primarily subjective; even if the accused exceeds the bounds of an objectively reasonable response so that the general right of private defence cannot apply (s 102), he will nevertheless be able to rely on Exception 2 provided he acted "without premeditation and without any *intention* of doing more harm than is necessary for the purpose of such defence" and provided he acted "in good faith" (see below, p 454).

Another fundamental problem is that although the courts have frequently employed a reasonable proportion test, they have failed to articulate with care either its source or status. In *Don John Perera* (1953) it was clearly based on the words "sudden and unexpected". In *Mancini* (1942, see above, p 448) Viscount Simon seemed to regard it as one of a number of questions to be considered in determining the response of the (wholly objective) reasonable man. In some cases it even appears to be seen as a separate rule of law operating independently of the reasonable man test; thus in *Lee Chun-Chuen* (1963), again dating from the time of the wholly objective reasonable man, Lord Devlin stated that the common law of provocation consisted of three elements: "the act of provocation, the loss of self control, both actual and reasonable, and the retaliation proportionate to the provocation". Consider the reasoning in *Vijayan* (1975). How was the "reasonable proportion" test conceptualized there? Did the courts treat it as an independent rule of law sufficient in itself to defeat the defence? If not, what was its role?

N Govindasamy v PP [1976] 2 MLJ 49 (CA, Singapore)

The appellant, a Hindu, killed his daughter's Muslim boyfriend. There was a long history of disagreement between the father and daughter which was exacerbated by her relationship with the deceased and by the father's perception of the life she was leading at University. On the night in question, the deceased had gone to see the girl's father. An argument apparently ensued.

Wee Chong Jin CJ: The trial judges rejected the defence of grave and sudden provocation. They found that the appellant inflicted the seven fatal wounds found on the head of the deceased with the intention of causing the death of the deceased. They disbelieved his version that he had acted under grave and sudden provocation. They also found that the provocative conduct of the deceased as related by the appellant in his unsworn statement from the dock did not entitle the appellant to the benefit of Exception 1 of s 300 of the Penal Code because the retaliation on his part was not commensurate with the degree of provocation given by the deceased. Their finding was that the medical evidence showed that the appellant acted with gross and savage violence on an unarmed man.

With these findings of fact we entirely agreed and accordingly we rejected the contention of the appellant that on all the evidence the retaliatory acts of the appellant were proportionate to the provocation given by the deceased which was of a character which affected the appellant's religion, his daughter's honour and his conduct as a father.

Appeal dismissed

If the rule about reasonable proportion is retained, it is submitted that its basis should be analysed with care by the courts and that it should be reduced in significance to, at most, one factor relevant to determining the reasonable man requirement. In some of the cases such as *Govindasamy* (1976), the test of reasonable proportion seems to operate virtually as an independent, objective rule of law which may in itself defeat the defence. Operating in this manner, it seems incompatible with a reasonable man test which is not wholly objective but recognizes the accused's class and background. The court may recognize that a person from the particular background of the accused would have reacted violently in the same circumstances, perhaps even to the extent of causing death, but may still deny the defence on the narrow grounds that the particular mode of retaliation was, according to some objective assessment, excessive.

Some comment must also be made on the reliance on English cases in some of the decisions. In *Vijayan* (1975) Choor Singh J argued that Exception 1 is "quite obviously based on the common law of England and ... it is desirable to examine English cases". After discussing several English decisions, he turned to *Don John Perera* (1953) and *Nanavati* (1962). He followed *Don John Perera* (1953) and suggested that it was not considered in *Nanavati* (1962) because the question there was the loss of self-control rather than proportionality; he then went on to cite *Mancini* (1942) with apparent approval. However, although the court in *Nanavati* (1962) did not consider *Don John Perera* (1953), it treated *Mancini* (1942) and other English cases with considerable reserve. It is also important to recognize that both *Mancini* (1942) and *Don John Perera* (1953) date from the time when the fully objective reasonable man was favoured in England (eg *Bedder*, 1954), a test which has, quite properly, not been adopted locally. Since the Privy Council in *Don John Perera* (1953) did not direct its attention to existing Indian cases such as *Ghulam Mustapha Ghano* (1939) which castigated this approach as unjust and unworkable outside England, it did not address the question of the inter-relationship between the reasonable man and the concept of reasonable proportion. Had it done so, it might have been less willing to superimpose the reasonable proportion test on the Penal Code.

(iii) Characteristics of a reasonable man

The test of the reasonable person from the class and background of the accused is intended to discount purely personal idiosyncracies. However, the dividing line between background factors and personal idiosyncracies is obscure. In *Ghulam Mustapha Ghano* (1939), the test was the provocative effect on a reasonable Baluchi of being showed a *booja* Suppose the facts of *Bedder* (1954) had arisen. Should the accused's impotence have been taken into account? Even if the reasonable Baluchi is inherently more excitable than other races, he is not, we may assume, generally impotent. Is impotence a purely personal idiosyncracy which should be ignored? What about such factors as age and sex? What exactly does it mean to talk of the "class and background" of the accused?

The problem of delimiting relevant characteristics also afflicts English law (see Glanville Williams, 1983; Clarkson and Keating, 1984). In *Camplin* (1978) the House of Lords made clear that it was wrong to adopt a purely objective approach and that account should be taken of the accused's age and other relevant characteristics. Their Lordships approved Lord Diplock's suggested direction to a jury that:

> [T]he reasonable man ... is a person having the power of self-control to be expected of an ordinary person of the sex and age of the accused but in other respects sharing such of the accused's characteristics as they think would affect the gravity of the provocation to him.

However, this direction is vague and their Lordships were not drawn into a detailed discussion of the factors to be taken into account. *Camplin* (1978) was further considered in *Newell* (1980) where the Court of Appeal held that "chronic alcoholism" was not a characteristic to be taken into account. In *Raven* (1982) the test was that of a "reasonable man who has lived the same type of life as the defendant for twenty-two years but who has the mental age of the defendant". In that case the defendant's mental age was nine. Is mental deficiency something which should be taken into account? If so, why not take account of chronic alcoholism? No doubt, such problems will continue to be dealt with in Singapore and Malaysia, as in England, on an ad hoc basis as and when cases reach the courts.

C. Exceeding private defence

Penal Code, s 300, Exception 2

Culpable homicide is not murder if the offender, in the exercise in good faith of the right of private defence of person or property, exceeds the power given to him by law, and causes the death of the person against whom he is exercising such right of defence, without premeditation and without any intention of doing more harm than is necessary for the purpose of such defence.

Illustration

Z attempts to horse-whip A, not in such a manner as to cause grievous hurt to A. A draws out a pistol. Z persists in the assault. A, believing in good faith that he can by no other means prevent himself from being horse-whipped, shoots Z dead. A has not committed murder, but only culpable homicide.

1.   Introduction

The purpose of Exception 2 is to provide formal mitigation in those cases where the accused was originally exercising the right of private defence but went beyond the powers contained in the general exceptions. It is an idea which as yet has no counterpart in English law and it may be observed that one difficulty with the local reliance on English provocation cases is that provocation there covers much of the ground covered in the Penal Code by exceeding private defence (see *McInnes*, 1971).

The general right of private defence is justificatory. Society not only tolerates but, to some degree at least, encourages the victim of an offence to take retaliatory action. However, the notion of excessive private defence appears to be a partial excuse. Exception 2 applies where the accused has gone beyond what was objectively necessary for the purposes of defence but was unable in the heat of the moment to judge that he had done enough by way of defence; the focus is therefore on partially excusing his inability to judge when to stop rather than on justifying (even in part) the retaliatory act.

2.   Elements of the defence

(a) Accused exercising right of private defence

Exception 2 is available only if the right of private defence of person or property has arisen. This is determined according to the criteria applied in the case of the general defence (see above, ch 5).

Bhagwan Munjaji Pawade v State of Maharashtra 1978 SCC (Cri) 428 (SC, India)

The deceased's mother became involved in an argument when her she-buffalo browsed her neighbours' vegetable creepers. When the deceased returned home he asked why the accused was arguing with his mother.

Sarkaria J: [The appellant] ... was armed with an axe.... [He] suddenly surged ahead and gave three blows to [the deceased] two with the blunt side and one with the sharp side of the weapon on the head....

[The High Court observed] "it is clear from the medical evidence and other evidence ... that he (appellant) has far exceeded the limits of his right of private defence". On the basis of this observation, it is urged that the case of the appellant was covered by Exception 2 to s 300....

We do not think much can be made out of the stray observation of the High Court "that the appellant had far exceeded his right of private defence". The circumstances of the case disclose that no right of private defence, either of person or property, had ever accrued to the appellant. The deceased was unarmed. Exception 2 can have no application.

Appeal dismissed

There are various reasons why the accused may originally have had the right of private defence but will not satisfy the general exception. It may be that the offence which occasions the exercise of the right does not justify causing death according to the categories stated in s 100; for example, as in the illustration to Exception 2 itself, the original assault by the victim may not reasonably have caused the apprehension of death or grievous hurt. Alternatively, the accused may not satisfy s 99. For example, even if the deceased's initial offence did reasonably cause the apprehension of grievous hurt, he may have inflicted more force than was (objectively) necessary for the purposes of defence (s 99(4)) or have failed to have resort to the protection of the authorities (s 99(3)). Exception 2, read with its illustration, clearly covers these situations.

Another reason the accused may not be entitled to the full defence is that he may have "gone too far" in the *duration* of his defensive response. The right of private defence of the body continues only as long as a reasonable apprehension of danger to the body continues (s 102). The right of private defence of property is also limited in duration (s 104). If the accused continues after that time, it might be argued that Exception 2 is not available; he is no longer "exercising" the right of private defence because the right has ceased. Although this argument may have a certain purely logical attraction, it should not be allowed to restrict the scope of Exception 2 as questions of the degree of force and the duration of the attack are generally quite inseparable. Furthermore, if it is wrong in principle to expect the accused to have exercised a rational decision as to when "enough force was enough", it would be equally wrong to expect a rational decision as to the precise time at which to stop. If a situation arose in which the accused clearly carried on too long in order to "teach the victim a lesson", Exception 2 should be denied to him on the basis of his mental attitude, not on technical grounds of the duration of the right of private defence.

(b) Accused's mental attitude

Exception 2 will not apply unless the accused acted in good faith, without premeditation and without the intention of doing more harm than was necessary for the purposes of private defence. These concluding words of Exception 2 clearly indicate a subjective test; even if the accused inflicted more harm than was objectively "necessary" for the purposes of defence (s 99(4)), he will be able to rely on the exception provided he did not *intend* to cause more harm than necessary. This subjectivity is of crucial importance since it is what clearly distinguishes Exception 2 from the general defence. It is also in sharp contrast to the objective requirement of reasonable proportion, read into provocation by local courts (see above, p 448).

Latchmi Koeri v State of Bihar AIR (1960) Pat 62 (HC, Patna, India)

The appellant was held to have the right of private defence against a havildar since the havildar was not in uniform and there was nothing to show that the appellant knew he was a public servant (s 99(2)). However, since the appellant could not have feared grievous hurt or death from the havildar, he was not entitled to the full defence (s 100). It was also held that he could not rely on Exception 2:

Sahai J: The question which arises is whether he can be held to have merely exceeded the right of private defence in committing murder.... [I]t cannot be held in the circumstances of this case that the appellant had no intention of doing more harm than was necessary for the purpose of this defence.... [I]n view of the injuries caused, I am perfectly satisfied that the appellant intended to cause very much more harm than was necessary for his defence, in fact, he appears to have inflicted most of the injuries including the fatal one at a time when the havildar was lying helpless under him. The counsel for the appellant argued that the appellant's right of private defence extended to the causing of all those injuries because he himself was found to have a number of injuries on his person and he received them at the time of his scuffle with the havildar.

[On the basis of the prison doctor's evidence, his Lordship concluded that the appellant had received most of the injuries after or at the time of his arrest.]

Hence, I am not prepared to accept [the] argument that the right of private defence available to the appellant extended to the causing of the injuries including the fatal injury which he caused to the havildar.

Appeal dismissed

Although there are passages in this decision which do not clearly distinguish the limits of the general and special exceptions, the appellant was clearly denied the benefit of Exception 2 because he failed the subjective test. In other Indian cases the reasoning has been less clear.

Gransham Dass v State of Delhi (1978) 3 SCC 391 (SC, India)

The appellant stabbed the victim to death when he came to his shop late at night in order to dissuade him from building a wall about which the appellant was in dispute with the victim's friend. He appealed against his conviction for murder.

Kailasam J: [A]s we have found that [the victim] was not armed and that he had no intention of causing any injury to the appellant ... the appellant far exceeded his right by using the dangerous weapon, *chhura*, with deadly effect and causing two injuries which cut the heart and the lung. On a consideration of all the circumstances, we feel it is very likely that the appellant caused the injuries when the deceased ... trespassed into the shop. But there could have been no apprehension that death or grievous hurt was likely to be caused to the accused. The conclusion is therefore irresistible that the appellant exceeded his right of private defence of property.... We find the appellant guilty of an offence under s 304(1) and sentence him to imprisonment for five years.

Appeal allowed

Does Kailasam J do anything more than state his conclusion? If the approach in *Latchmi Koeri* (1960) was applied to the facts of this case, would the court have inferred, from the nature of the injuries inflicted on an unarmed man, that the appellant had intended more harm than was necessary?

Since Exception 2 is distinguished from the general defence primarily by its subjectivity, it is not easy to see what role is performed by the injection of the requirement (objective) of good faith.

Penal Code, s 52

Nothing is said to be done or believed in good faith which is done or believed without due care and attention.

Gour (1983, Vol 2) suggests that good faith precludes the defence where the accused uses the opportunity to pursue a private grudge against the victim, but it is submitted that such a case would be covered by the subjective requirement that the accused acts without premeditation and without the intention of causing more harm than is necessary for the purposes of defence. The following case vaguely hints at a possible role for good faith.

Sabal Singh v State of Rajasthan 1979 SCC (Cri) 69 (SC, India)

A dispute arose over a piece of land of which the appellants were in possession. The deceased, who were armed and intoxicated, went along to remove crops from the land and a fight ensued.

Sarkaria J: The occurrence was not a one-sided affair ... blows were exchanged and both sides received injuries. But the injuries inflicted by the accused party on the deceased persons both in severity and number were far greater than those received by the accused party.

In view of these facts, it can be said that the accused had a right to defend their possession and property. But the force used by them was recklessly excessive, and as such, they were rightly not given the benefit of Exception II to s 300 IPC. Nevertheless, the circumstances showing that the appellants had a right of private defence of property, which they had exceeded, could be taken into consideration in extenuation of the extreme penalty. Accordingly, we allow this appeal and while maintaining the conviction of the appellants, commute the capital sentence of each of them to imprisonment for life.

Appeal dismissed

The description of the appellants' use of force as "recklessly excessive" is very interesting. Sarkaria J does not analyse the wording of Exception 2; neither does he explain the meaning of recklessness or how it operates in this context. Consequently, it is unclear whether on the facts the appellants were denied the defence because they *intended* more harm than was necessary or because, even though they did not intend excess harm, they were reckless as to whether excess harm was caused. However, the judgment raises the interesting possibility that even if an accused did not *intend* more harm than was necessary, he may be denied the defence if he was *reckless* because in such circumstances he will not be in good faith. Such an interpretation does afford a possible meaning to good faith (not being reckless) but requires more analysis and explanation before being used. The most obvious difficulty is that recklessness is essentially an English law concept (it is nowhere used or defined in the Penal Code) and one which has consistently defied precise definition (see ch 3). The higher the degree of fault necessary to constitute recklessness, the closer it approximates to intention (depending, of course, on the way in which intention is defined) and therefore the role of good faith as an independent limitation on the scope of Exception 2 becomes less clear. On the other hand, any definition of recklessness used in this context must not be so broad that it erodes the fundamental difference between the general defence and the Exception, which lies in the contrast between the pure objectivity of the general defence and the subjectivity of the words "without premeditation or the intention of doing more harm than necessary" in Exception 2. It is therefore incumbent on the courts to define with care the concepts of intention and recklessness in this context and also their relationship with the Penal Code's favoured word, "knowledge". Presumably good faith is not to be equated with lack of knowledge since this could easily have been specifically provided for in the Penal Code.

D. Sudden fight

Penal Code, s 300, Exception 4

Culpable homicide is not murder if it is committed without premeditation in a sudden fight in the heat of passion upon a sudden quarrel, and without the offender having taken undue advantage or acted in a cruel or unusual manner.

Explanation–It is immaterial in such cases which party offers the provocation or commits the first assault.

1. Introduction

It is interesting that this exception was included in the Penal Code even though its English progenitor, the common law defence of chance medley, had been abolished in 1828 (Brown, 1961) and even though it was not in Macaulay's original draft Code. The exception may arise on the same facts as some cases of provocation and exceeding private defence and it will therefore be considered before Exception 3, exceeding official powers. Like provocation and exceeding private defence, sudden fight is in the nature of a partial excuse; it is not justifiable to fight but the accused's conduct is less blameworthy as he was acting in the heat of passion, without premeditation, etc. The case for it being a partial excuse is strengthened by the fact that under the explanation to Exception 4, it is immaterial who was the aggressor.

2. Elements of the defence

(a) Sudden fight, heat of passion, sudden quarrel

These requirements are closely inter-related, dealing largely with the circumstances in which the offence occurred. Although any one of the elements may be missing, the most difficult element to satisfy has in practice proved to be that of a fight.

Sis v State of Punjab (1973) 75 Punj LR 25 (Punjab and Haryana HC, India)

AD Koshal J: The wordy duel between the deceased and the appellant can at best be termed "a sudden quarrel" but it never developed into a "sudden fight" because there was no use or attempted use of violence on the part of the deceased against the appellant and without such use or attempted use on both sides the affair could not be termed a "fight". Reference in this connection [may] be made with advantage to *Atma Singh* (1955) ... [where] the following observations ... appear to me, with all respect, to lay down the law ... correctly:

"The term 'fight' is not defined in the Code, but everyone knows what a fight is and that it takes two to make a fight. I would agree with the argument of the learned counsel for the appellant that it is not necessary that weapons should be used in a fight, and also that an affray can be a fight even if only one party in the fight is successful in landing a blow on his opponent.
I would however hold that in order to constitute a fight it is necessary that blows should be exchanged even if they do not find their target...."

In *Bhagwan Munjaji Pawade* (1978; see above, p 453) Sarkaria J argued:

The quarrel had broken out suddenly, but there was no sudden *fight* between the deceased and the appellant. "Fight" postulates a bilateral transaction in which blows are exchanged. The deceased was unarmed. He did not cause any injury to the appellant or his companions. Furthermore, no less than three fatal injuries were inflicted by the appellant with an axe which is a formidable weapon on the unarmed victim.

The requirement that blows are exchanged seems preferable to the laxer definition in *Jusab Usman* (1983) where a fight was defined as requiring at least the offer of violence on both sides. However, whichever definition is adopted, it is clear that a fight will be more easily implied when both parties suffer injuries.

Ram Karam v State of Uttar Pradesh 1982 SCC (Cri) 386 (SC, India)

There was a "chronic land dispute" between the parties who were exasperated by seemingly endless litigation.

Fazal Ali J: Suddenly at the spur of the moment there ensued a quarrel.... [A and B] on the side of the prosecution died and ... [C] on the side of the accused died and each of them met a homicidal death. On the side of the prosecution ... [D] was injured, on the side of the accused ... [E] was injured. From this an irresistible inference ensues that Exception 4 ... would be attracted. ... [A] and ... others came to protest to the house of accused 1 ... [D] amongst them was armed with a knife.... There is no evidence to show that anyone took undue advantage or acted in a cruel or unusual manner.

Since Exception 4 applies to killings in the course of a fight, it should not apply where the fighting parties have disengaged; however, some cases have taken a generous view of the scope of a "fight".

Amrithalinga Nadar v State of Tamil Nadu AIR (1976) SC 1133 (SC, India)

There was a village festival at which a fight broke out over the payment of a festival troupe. The deceased ran out with a knife to help one of the combatants. The accused grabbed the deceased but the latter inflicted injuries on them with his knife. The deceased then ran off and was chased by the appellant:

Bhagwati J: It is apparent that the fatal injury was caused by the appellant to the deceased without premeditation in a sudden fight in the heat of passion upon a sudden quarrel. It is not possible to say that the appellant took any undue advantage or acted in a cruel or unusual manner in chasing the deceased and inflicting the fatal injury on him. The deceased was armed with [a 9"] knife which he had freely and unhesitatingly used for the purpose of causing injuries ... and there is little doubt that he carried that knife with him when he ran for shelter....

Appeal allowed

It is clear that the defence should only be available where the fight involved the accused and the deceased; if A was fighting with X but killed Y who was not involved in the fight, the killing would not fall within the scope of a sudden fight (see *Narayan Nair Raghavan*, 1956, below, p 460).

The elements of Exception 4 have not been clearly discussed locally, perhaps because it is rarely pleaded. In *Soh Cheow Hor* (1960), the Singapore Court of Appeal allowed an appeal against a conviction for murder in a case where the evidence was "borderline" on the grounds that the trial judge had not properly directed the jury on the burden of proof. However, they did not disapprove of his direction which had not referred to the requirements of a quarrel and heat of passion. In *Vaeyapuri* (1966) the Malaysian Federal Court substituted a conviction for culpable homicide for one of murder on the grounds that the judge's direction had been in terms of "murder or nothing" whereas the evidence suggested that one of the exceptions might have been available. The court did not spell out with care which of the exceptions were potentially applicable but they may well have been thinking of sudden fight: "Whether or not the appellant was attacked, as he said, it is clear that whatever happened at the house was not altogether one-sided because the appellant was examined by a doctor about an hour and a half after the killing and was then found to have a wound on his head which required stitching and was still (to use the words of the doctor) 'spurting blood'." Similarly in *Haji Talib* (1969) the Federal Court held that the direction to the jury based on Exceptions 1 and 2 alone was defective in that it overlooked the possibility of Exception 4 even though that exception had not been raised by the accused.

The cases have not discussed the meaning of "sudden" but it may well be interpreted as synonymous with "unexpected" as in the case of provocation (see above, p 437).

(b) Absence of premeditation

It is clear that the requirements of a *sudden* fight and a *sudden* quarrel and the absence of premeditation mean that the exception will not cover prearranged fights. Premeditation has also been subject to fuller definition.

Kirpal Singh v State of Punjab AIR (1951) Punjab 137 (HC, Punjab, India)

Bhandari J: To constitute a premeditated killing it is necessary that the accused should have reflected with a view to determine whether he would kill or not; and that he should have determined to kill as the result of that reflection; that is to say, the killing should be a pre-determined killing upon consideration and not a sudden killing under the momentary excitement and impulse of passion.... Evidence of premeditation can be furnished by former grudges or previous threats and expressions of ill-feeling; by acts of preparation to kill, such as procuring a deadly weapon or selecting a dangerous weapon in preference to one less dangerous and by the manner in which the killing was committed. For example, repeated shots, blows or other acts of violence are sufficient evidence of premeditation.

The first part of this quotation seems correct and was approved by the Privy Council in *Mohamed Kunjo* (1978, below, p 461) where Lord Scarman said that "premeditation" involves an "element of design or prior planning"; on the other hand, it does not seem right that evidence of "repeated blows" may be regarded as "sufficient evidence of premeditation" as suggested in the latter part.

(c) No undue advantage or cruel or unusual acts

The cases suggest that this element of the defence will be assessed primarily by comparing the methods of fighting adopted by the parties to the fight; if the deceased was unarmed, the accused is unlikely to be allowed the defence if he resorted to the use of weapons or dangerous objects.

Narayan Nair Raghavan Wair v State of Travancore-Cochin AIR (1956) SC 99 (SC, India)

A dispute arose over the partition of property as a result of which the appellant became involved in a struggle with the deceased's son-in-law. The deceased stepped in and told his son-in-law not to fight as he would find a solution to the problem. The appellant then struck the deceased with a penknife and was convicted of murder under s 300(c). The Supreme Court held that he could not rely on Exception 4.

Bose J: It is impossible to say that there is no undue advantage when a man stabs an unarmed person who makes no threatening gestures and merely asks the accused's opponent to stop fighting. Then also, the fight must be with the person who is killed.... But we feel that on the question of sentence this is not the type of case where the death sentence is called for. There was no premeditation and the knife was not ready in the hand but was drawn from the waist after the appellant had been slapped and the quarrel ... had started. We therefore reduce the sentence to one of transportation for life.

Mohamed Kunjo v PP [1978] 1 MLJ 51 (PC, appeal from Singapore)

A fight broke out between two work colleagues who had been drinking. They argued, then fell to the floor, wrestled and exchanged punches. The appellant then ran towards a store-room and returned with an exhaust pipe. He struck the deceased one blow on the head and he fell to the ground. He then hit him three or four more times and walked off.

Lord Scarman: [His Lordship held that the Privy Council could consider Exception 4 even though it had not been raised in the courts below. He quoted from *Kirpal Singh* (1951, see above, p 460) and continued:]

In the present case there was evidence that suggested strongly the absence of any element of design or planning. There was also evidence that the blow, or blows, were struck "in a sudden fight in the heat of passion upon a sudden quarrel", though there was also evidence (ie going in search of the weapon, returning with it, and striking the deceased when he appeared to be neither aggressive nor on his guard) which suggested the contrary. But formidable difficulties face the appellant when he attempts to show that the act causing death was committed "without the offender having taken undue advantage or acted in a cruel or unusual manner". The appellant, who had been engaged in a fight with the deceased, ran to get a weapon and returned to attack the defenceless deceased with a truly murderous weapon, the exhaust pipe.... The evidence of the assault shows that the deceased was taken by surprise and attacked with a very unusual and unexpected weapon, a heavy blow on the head ... which could reasonably be expected to be lethal. In one of the Indian cases to which we were most helpfully referred, *Sarjug Prasad* (1959), K Sahai J commented that "undue advantage ... means unfair advantage". In the face of the evidence we do not see how the appellant could prove that he had not taken undue advantage or acted in a cruel or unusual manner....

It follows that the appeal must be dismissed. We would, however, respectfully wish to draw the attention of those whose duty it is to advise the President on the death sentence that the offence was committed over 2 years ago, and that there are mitigating factors worthy, it may be thought, of consideration before a decision is taken in regard to the sentence.

Appeal dismissed

The Privy Council's recommendation for clemency was accepted. *Mohamed Kunjo* (1978) provides an interesting contrast with the Indian cases; in both *Narayan Nair Raghavan* (1956) and *Sis* (1973), for example, the respective courts rejected the defence but argued that the "ultimate" penalty was not called for.

E. Exceeding public powers

Penal Code, s 300, Exception 3

Culpable homicide is not murder if the offender, being a public servant, or aiding a public servant acting for the advancement of public justice, exceeds the powers given to him by law and causes death by doing an act which he, in good faith, believes to be lawful and necessary for the due discharge of his duty as such public servant, and without ill-will towards the person whose death is caused.

The purpose of this exception is to allow greater latitude to those involved in law enforcement than is allowed under the general law. However, this broader power is subject to two restrictions which suggest that the exception is once again excusatory in nature. First, the defendant must in good faith believe that his acts were lawful and necessary for the discharge of his duties as a public servant; in other words, even if he acts outside his powers, the exception will be available if he believed he was acting within his powers. Second, he must not be motivated by ill will. The exception is rarely used and has not been interpreted locally. However, one illustration of its use in India may be given.

Dukhi Singh v State of Allahabad AIR (1955) All 379 (HC, Allahabad, India)

The appellant was convicted of murder and sentenced to death. He was a constable with the Railway Protection Police who was travelling on a train and noticed a man "standing near a goods wagon in suspicious circumstances"; there had been thefts from trains at this place in the past. He took the suspect back to his compartment for questioning but he jumped down and ran off. The appellant gave chase and got into an argument with the fireman whom he suspected of aiding the suspect. He shot the fireman dead. The court rejected defences founded on ss 76 and 79 but allowed him the benefit of Exception 3.

Roy J: From a consideration of the totality of circumstances and the evidence in the case we are inclined to think that after the arrested man had escaped from the running train the appellant pursued him with a view to effect his re-arrest and, when he was in a position to apprehend him, he fired at him and in that process he hit the deceased fireman.... We are of opinion that the case would be covered by Exception 3.... In the present case there was no ill-will between the appellant and the deceased. The appellant was a public servant and his object was the advancement of public justice. He no doubt exceeded the powers given to him by law, and he caused the death of the fireman by doing an act which he, in good faith, believed to be lawful and necessary for the due discharge of his duty. In such circumstances the offence that was committed was culpable homicide not amounting to murder punishable under s 304, Part II, Penal Code.

Appeal allowed

F. Consent

Penal Code, s 300, Exception 5

Culpable homicide is not murder when the person whose death is caused, being above the age of eighteen years, suffers death or takes the risk of death with his own consent.

Illustration

A, by instigation, voluntarily causes Z, a person under eighteen years of age, to commit suicide. Here, on account of Z's youth, he was incapable of giving consent to his own death. A has therefore abetted murder.

1. Introduction

This exception was highly innovative. The common law has always maintained that a person cannot consent to his own death. Under English law, if the accused has intentionally killed his terminally sick mother, this will be murder even if she voluntarily and genuinely consented, unless he can bring himself under another defence such as diminished responsibility. By contrast, the Indian Law Commissioners, on drafting the Code, sought, as with the other special exceptions, to temper respect for the principle of the sanctity of life with a degree of compassion. They argued that although "no consent ought to be a justification of the causing of death" (note B), such offences should not be punished as murder for reasons which reflect secular moral and utilitarian concerns.

Macaulay and other Indian Law Commissioners, A Penal Code Prepared by the Indian Law Commissioners Note M, (1837), 124–125

In the first place, the motives which prompt men to the commission of this offence are generally far more respectable than those which prompt men to the commission of murder. Sometimes it is the effect of a strong sense of religious duty, sometimes of a strong sense of honour, not infrequently of humanity. The soldier who, at the entreaty of a wounded comrade, puts that comrade out of pain, the friend who supplies laudanum to a person suffering the torment of a lingering disease, the freedman who in ancient times held out the sword that his master might fall on it, the high-born native of India who stabs the females of his family at their own entreaty in order to save them from the licentiousness of a band of marauders, would, except in Christian societies, scarcely be thought culpable, and even in Christian societies would not be regarded by the public, and ought not to be treated by the law as assassins.

Again, this crime is by no means productive of so much evil to the community as murder. One evil ingredient of the utmost importance is altogether wanting to the offence of voluntary culpable homicide by consent. It does not produce general insecurity. It does not spread terror through society. When we punish murder with such signal severity, we have two ends in view. One end is that people may not be murdered. Another end is that people may not live in constant dread of being murdered. This second end is perhaps the more important of the two. For if assassination were left unpunished, the number of persons assassinated would probably bear a very small proportion to the whole population; but the life of every human being would be passed in constant anxiety and alarm. This property of the offence of murder is not found in the offence of voluntary culpable homicide by consent. Every man who has not given his consent to be put to death is perfectly certain that this latter offence cannot at present be committed on him, and that it never will be committed unless he shall first be convinced that it is his interest to consent to it.

Exception 5 presents serious difficulties under the conceptualization of defences as justifications or excuses. The general defence of consent is a justification (see p 107); the consensual and intentional infliction of harm falling short of death or grievous hurt may be fully exculpated because society does not regard such conduct as wrong. Exception 5 has many of the trappings of a partial justification. In particular, as the Indian Law Commissioners (1837, see above) indicate, consensual homicide does not present the same threat to the rest of society as non-consensual homicide; consequently, we do not consider consensual killing to be as wrongful as "assassination". Furthermore, in Robinson's (1984) analysis (see above, p 105) excuses are founded on some *disability* on the part of the actor. In cases falling under Exception 5, there is generally no such disability and the accused's conduct may be perfectly rational and carefully planned. In the examples provided by the Indian Law Commissioners (1837), the actor was not deprived of self-control (as in provocation) and did not lack mental awareness of what he was doing (as in diminished responsibility). On the other hand, it is also possible to focus on the question of blame or attribution (see p 104) and to see Exception 5 as a partial excuse. This approach would emphasize that consensual killing is still wrong and that the accused is held liable for culpable homicide, a very serious offence. It remains wrong to kill even where the "victim" consents, and even though it would not be wrong to inflict a lesser degree of harm. Under this analysis, the accused is being partially excused by Exception 5; he is rendered less culpable by virtue of the victim's consent—we do not blame him to the extent that we blame the person who kills without consent. As the Indian Law Commissioners (1837) point out, the motives of those who kill with consent are "far more respectable" than those of "assassins".

2.   Elements of the defence

It is necessary to satisfy the requirements of a voluntary and genuine consent applicable to the general defence of consent (s 90). In *Poonai Fattemah* (1869) a snake charmer told his audience that if they were bitten, he possessed the necessary antidote; the deceased thereupon allowed himself to be bitten. In the circumstances this was the last thing he should have done. It turned out to be the last thing he ever did. The snake charmer was charged with murder. It was held that Exception 5 did not apply because the victim's consent was based on a misconception of fact. The Indian cases also make clear that the consent must be unequivocal and not an expression of a willingness to die as one possible option. In *Ambalathil Assainar* (1955) a wife refused to go back to her mother, saying that she would rather die. Thereupon her husband killed her. He was convicted of murder and was not allowed the benefit of Exception 5; his wife had not unequivocally consented to be killed.

3.   Suicide and suicide pacts

One situation in which Exception 5 imports a welcome flexibility into the law is where the accused has killed in pursuance of a "suicide pact". In *Dasrath Paswan* (1958) a student who had failed his exams for three successive years decided in desperation to end his life and informed his 19-year-old wife of his plans. Distraught, she asked him to kill her first and then to kill himself. He killed her but was arrested before he could kill himself. The court held that the exception was satisfied and rejected the tenuous submission of the prosecution that the consent was obtained by the accused pressurizing the deceased with fears of future widowhood.

If the accused in suicide pact cases actually does the killing, he will be convicted of culpable homicide not amounting to murder. However, there will be other suicide pact cases where the correct charge would be of abetting suicide under s 306, Penal Code. This would have been the case, for example, if the accused in *Dasrath Paswan* (1958) had given his wife a cup of poison which she herself proceeded to drink. The dividing line between killing a person with his consent and abetting suicide may be clear in theory but is extremely thin in practice; suppose A and B agreed to gas themselves and A turned on the gas tap. If B died but A survived, A might be regarded as having committed an offence of culpable homicide falling under Exception 5, with a potential maximum of life imprisonment. On the other hand, suppose B had turned on the tap; A's offence would, at most, have been one of abetment of B's suicide; this ordinarily carries a maximum of ten years (s 306). It may, of course, be a matter of pure (mis)fortune which of them survived and which turned the tap. Should there be a difference in the offences which have been committed and in the potential sentences? Is there any difference in the moral stigma of a conviction for culpable homicide and one for abetment of suicide? Is there any real difference in A's culpability in each case? Would it not be better to provide for a distinct offence of killing in pursuit of a suicide pact?

A further difficulty with suicide cases arises out of the illustration to Exception 5. It is clear from the wording to Exception 5 that if the accused himself kills a minor, then consent cannot operate even as a partial defence and the conviction will be for murder. However, the illustration to Exception 5 goes further. It suggests that if A *abets* Z, a minor, to commit suicide (eg by instigation) A is guilty of abetting *murder* on the grounds that Z cannot consent to his own death. The mandatory penalty for abetting murder is death (s 109 and Illustration (c) thereto). However, the better view is that such cases should be dealt with under the separate offence provided by s 305; abetment of *suicide* (as opposed to murder in the illustration to Exception 5) by a child, etc. Even though the deceased was a minor, he did kill himself. An obvious advantage with this approach is that the judge retains a broad discretion as to the sentence which can be adjusted to the circumstances of the offence.

Penal Code, s 305

If any person under eighteen years of age, any insane person, any delirious person, any idiot, or any person in a state of intoxication, commits suicide, whoever abets the commission of such suicide shall be punished with death or imprisonment for life, or with imprisonment for a term not exceeding ten years, and shall also be liable to fine.

4. Mercy killings

Exception 5 also covers some mercy killings; thus the Indian Law Commissioners (1837, see above, p 463) suggested that it should cover the soldier who puts a wounded comrade out of pain or the friend supplying poison to a person suffering from a lingering disease. However, it does not deal with all mercy killing cases, as for example, where the deceased is a minor or a comatose adult who is unable to give consent. Many of these cases may now be forced in Singapore to be considered under a generous interpretation of diminished responsibility (see below, p 472). It is not clear how they would be resolved in Malaysia, where there is no defence of diminished responsibility.

G. Infanticide

The FMS and Indian Penal Codes include only the first five exceptions to s 300. The Singapore Penal Code contains seven.

Penal Code, s 300, Exception 6

Culpable homicide is not murder if the offender being a woman voluntarily causes the death of her child being a child under the age of twelve months, and at the time of the offence the balance of her mind was disturbed by reason of her not having fully recovered from the effect of giving birth to the child or by reason of the effect of lactation consequent upon the birth of the child.

Infanticide is clearly an excuse rather than a justification, since its focus is the accused's disabilities. It is difficult to explain its existence in Singapore, given the existence of an independent offence of infanticide.

Penal Code, s 310

When any woman by any wilful act or omission causes the death of her child being a child under the age of twelve months, but at the time of the act or omission the balance of her mind was disturbed by reason of her not having fully recovered from the effect of giving birth to the child or by reason of the effect of lactation consequent upon the birth of the child, she shall notwithstanding that the circumstances were such that but for this section the offence would have amounted to murder, be guilty of the offence of infanticide.

[Section 309(A) of the Malaysian Code is in substantially the same language. The only differences are that the Malaysian Code refers to a "newly born child", without any specific age limit, and also omits the words "or by reason of the effect of lactation consequent upon the birth".]

H. Diminished responsibility

Penal Code, s 300, Exception 7

Culpable homicide is not murder if the offender was suffering from such abnormality of mind (whether arising from a condition of arrested or retarded development of mind or any inherent causes or induced by disease or injury) as substantially impaired his mental responsibility for his acts and omissions in causing the death or being a party to causing the death.

1. Introduction

Diminished responsibility was introduced into Singapore in 1961 and is *in pari materia* with s 2(1) of the English Homicide Act 1957. Since there is no corresponding provision in Malaysia or India, this exception must be interpreted by reference to English and Singapore cases. Diminished responsibility is clearly a partial excuse rather than a partial justification; the accused was in no way justified in acting as he did but, because his mental responsibility was substantially impaired, he is partially excused.

Since its introduction, the plea of diminished responsibility has proved more attractive than insanity to those accused of murder; it is easier to satisfy (see *Byrne*, 1960, see below, p 469) and, although insanity affords a complete defence, the accused will generally prefer the prospect of a conviction and a term of imprisonment rather than the greater uncertainty of a successful insanity plea. However, the close relationship between the two defences raises certain difficulties. In cases of insanity the accused is not regarded as responsible for his actions and is completely excused. Diminished responsibility is based on the assumption that a person can in certain cases be regarded as only partially responsible. In the words of Wee Chong Jin CJ in *Cheng Swee Hin* (1981, see below, p 474) diminished responsibility involves a "state of mind bordering on but not amounting to insanity". This notion is not easy to grasp and has sometimes been regarded sceptically; thus Lord Justice-General Normand criticized the similar Scottish doctrine of "impaired responsibility" as "somewhat inconsistent with the basic doctrine of our criminal law that a man, if sane, is responsible for his acts, and, if not sane, is not responsible" (*Kirkwood*, 1939).

Although the concept of partial responsibility is now clearly recognized, it presents certain sentencing problems under the Penal Code. There are a number of cases in which the Singapore courts have applied s 304(a) of the Penal Code in sentencing, and a sentence of life imprisonment is not infrequent in diminished responsibility cases (eg *Freddy Tan*, 1969 and *Mohamed b Jamal*, 1964). However, such sentences must be based on the assumption that the accused's *mens rea* was intention and not merely knowledge. In cases which "border on insanity", where the accused's mental responsibility was by definition "substantially impaired", it is not clear how the court is to determine whether the accused acted with intention or knowledge.

Another problem in Singapore is whether, if the accused pleads diminished responsibility, the prosecution can argue that he was in fact insane. Such an idea seems initially absurd; in the caustic words of Lawton J in *Price* (1963): "Prosecutors prosecute. They do not ask juries to return a verdict of acquittal." On the other hand, others would argue that public interest demands that the prosecution has this power to ensure that the accused receives the appropriate treatment. After a series of conflicting cases in England, the Criminal Procedure (Insanity) Act 1964 specifically empowered the prosecution to raise the question of insanity. Koh and Myint Soe (1974, p 211) argue that:

> It seems that though no statutory provisions exist regarding the right of the prosecution to prove insanity where diminished responsibility is pleaded, Singapore Courts would allow the prosecution to take such a course, as it is in the interests of the public that a really insane person should be in a mental institution instead of a prison.

This argument has some attraction, especially as the Singapore courts have no power to impose "hospital orders" on convicted persons who are thought to require treatment in secure hospitals. In England, such powers do exist and, as in *Price* (1963) itself, can be exercised in diminished responsibility cases provided the necessary medical evidence is forthcoming. On the other hand, if the prosecution successfully raises insanity and the accused is thereby acquitted, he will lose the right of appeal (see Criminal Procedure Code, s 245 and Supreme Court of Judicature Act, s 44). This loss of the right of appeal was a strong factor in Lawton J's decision in *Price* (1963) and the subsequent English legislation not only empowered the prosecution to raise insanity but also provided the accused with the safeguard of a right of appeal. This is an area where statutory clarification is needed in Singapore; if the prosecution is allowed to raise insanity, the defence must be allowed the right of appeal. It also seems right that if the prosecution is given this power, it should, in line with English cases, be required to prove insanity beyond reasonable doubt, and not merely on the balance of probabilities (*Grant*, 1960).

2.   Elements of the defence

Three closely inter-related questions arise for the defence to be satisfied. Although they are here treated under separate heads for the purposes of exposition, it will be clear from the cases and the discussion that they cannot always be easily separated. The first question is whether the accused was suffering from an abnormality of mind at the time of the offence. If he was, what were the causes of that abnormality? Finally, was the abnormality such as substantially to impair his mental responsibility?

(a) "Abnormality of mind"

No clear definition of the term "abnormality of mind" appears in the legislation or cases. The starting point must be the leading English case of *Byrne* (1960) in which the Court of Appeal suggests a broad commonsense approach.

R v Byrne [1960] 2 QB 396 (CCA, England)

The appellant admitted to strangling a young girl and thereafter to mutilating her body. The trial judge directed the jury to the effect that if he killed the girl under an abnormal sexual impulse or urge which was so strong that he found it difficult or impossible to resist it, but that otherwise he was normal, the plea of diminished responsibility would fail. He was convicted of murder.

Lord Parker CJ: [The] uncontradicted evidence was that the accused was a sexual psychopath, that he suffered from abnormality of mind which arose from a condition of arrested or retarded development of mind or inherent causes. The nature of the abnormality of mind of a sexual psychopath, according to the medical evidence, is that he suffers from violent perverted sexual desires which he finds difficult or impossible to control. Save when under the influence of his perverted desires he may be normal. All three doctors were of opinion that the killing was done under the influence of his perverted sexual desires, and although all three were of opinion that he was not insane in the technical sense of insanity laid down in the McNaughten Rules it was their view that his sexual psychopathy could properly be described as partial insanity....

"Abnormality of mind" means a state of mind so different from that of ordinary human beings that the reasonable man would term it abnormal. It appears to us to be wide enough to cover the mind's activities in all its aspects, not only the perception of physical acts and matters, and the ability to form a rational judgment as to whether an act is right or wrong, but also the ability to exercise will power to control physical acts in accordance with that rational judgment. The expression "mental responsibility for his acts" points to a consideration of the extent to which the accused's mind is answerable for his physical acts which must include a consideration of the extent of his ability to exercise will power to control his physical acts.

Whether the accused was at the time of the killing suffering from any "abnormality of mind" in the broad sense we have indicated above is a question for the jury. On this question medical evidence is no doubt of importance, but the jury are entitled to take into consideration all the evidence, including the acts or statements of the accused and his demeanour. They are not bound to accept the medical evidence if there is other material before them which, in their good judgment, conflicts with it and outweighs it.

The aetiology of the abnormality (namely, whether it arose from a condition of arrested or retarded development of mind or any inherent causes, or was induced by disease or injury) does, however, seem to be a matter to be determined on expert evidence.

Assuming that the jury are satisfied on the balance of probabilities that the accused was suffering from "abnormality of mind" from one of the causes specified in the parenthesis of the subsection, the crucial question nevertheless arises: was the abnormality such as substantially impaired his mental responsibility for his acts in doing or being a party to the killing? This is a question of degree and essentially one for the jury. Medical evidence is, of course, relevant, but the question involves a decision not merely as to whether there was some impairment of the mental responsibility of the accused for his acts but whether such impairment can properly be called "substantial", a matter upon which juries may quite legitimately differ from doctors....

Furthermore, in a case where the abnormality of mind is one which affects the accused's self-control the step between "he did not resist his impulse" and "he could not resist his impulse" is, as the evidence in this case shows, one which is incapable of scientific proof. A fortiori there is no scientific measurement of the degree of difficulty which an abnormal person finds in controlling his impulses. These problems which in the present state of medical knowledge are scientifically insoluble, the jury can only approach in a broad, common-sense way.

Inability to exercise will power to control physical acts, provided that it is due to abnormality of mind from one of the causes specified in the parenthesis in the subsection is, in our view, sufficient to entitle the accused to the benefit of the section; difficulty in controlling his physical acts, depending on the degree of difficulty, may be. It is for the jury to decide on the whole of the evidence whether such inability or difficulty has, not as a matter of scientific certainty but on the balance of probabilities, been established, and in the case of difficulty, whether the difficulty is so great as to amount in their view to a substantial impairment of the accused's mental responsibility for his acts....

[T]he medical evidence as to the appellant's ability to control his physical acts at the time of the killing was all one way. The evidence of the revolting circumstances of the killing and the subsequent mutilations, as of the previous sexual history of the appellant pointed, we think plainly, to the conclusion that the accused was what would be described in ordinary language as on the borderline of insanity or partially insane.

Appeal allowed

Byrne (1960) therefore establishes that abnormality of mind is to be given a commonsense meaning, broader than that given to insanity in English law under the McNaghten Rules. Although the wording, and therefore perhaps the scope, of s 84 differs from the McNaghten Rules (see ch 12), "unsoundness of mind" under s 84 is clearly narrower than "abnormality of mind".

In *Mohamed b Jamal* (1964), the first case of diminished responsibility in Singapore, the defence was not raised until the end of the trial because counsel was unaware of its existence. However, on appeal a witness testified that the appellant had an "abnormal brain structure as a result of which he suffered from a condition of arrested or retarded development of mind which was such as substantially to impair his mental responsibility for his acts". His convictions for murder were quashed; convictions for culpable homicide not amounting to murder were substituted with a sentence of life imprisonment. On the other hand, low intelligence and a particular sensitivity to provocation were not regarded as amounting to an 'abnormality of mind' in *Osman b Ali* (1972).

By not delineating strict categories of mental abnormality, the courts retain the flexibility to include new forms of abnormality which were not within the contemplation of the drafters. For example, the English courts have accepted premenstrual tension as an abnormality for the purposes of diminished responsibility (*Smith*, 1982; Edwards, 1982).

In considering the first and third questions in diminished responsibility it may be necessary to consider not only the nature of the accused's illness but also the age of its development:

Mimi Wong v PP [1972] 2 MLJ 75 (CA, Singapore)

Wee Chong Jin CJ: The defence case was that at the time of the commission of the offence she [first appellant] was suffering from encephalitis which had reached the stage where there would be impairment of the brain function to an extent as to have substantially impaired her mental responsibility for her acts. This defence was based primarily on the evidence of Dr Tan Bok Yang ... and Dr Wong Yip Cheong....

Dr Tan however admitted that he could not positively say she was suffering from encephalitis or a viral infection of the brain on 6th January (the date of the offence) and assuming she had a viral infection probably of the encephalitis strain on 6th January she would be very likely to be in the incubation or prodromal stage of her illness. He also said her actions on that day do not suggest to him that there was impairment of the function of her brain. It was common ground that in encephalitis there are three definite stages beginning with the incubation stage, then the prodromal stage and finally the frank stage but the period when one stage merges into the next is variable. It was also common ground that a person suffering from encephalitis may have that illness in a mild or moderate form.

Dr Wong ... said that upon the basis that she was suffering from encephalitis on 14th January and upon projection backwards he was of the opinion that she would still be suffering from encephalitis which was likely to be in a more severe form on 6th January. On that basis he was of the opinion that in the context of the circumstances governing the alleged offence, her mind had, by reason of this illness of the brain, been abnormally affected to such a substantial degree that her mental responsibility could reasonably be considered to be significantly diminished.

Dr Ngui ... said that assuming she was suffering from encephalitis on 6th January, the stage of development of the encephalitic illness is important from the point of her mental responsiblity at the time of the offence. If it was during the frank stage that she committed the offence alleged, where symptoms of the brain disfunction in the form of confusion, disorientation, stupor, sensory and speech disturbances are present then, depending on the severity of these symptoms, she is very likely to come under the purview of either the McNaughton rules of insanity or of diminished responsibility. If it was during the prodromal stage again depending on the nature and severity of the prodromal symptoms she could come under the purview of diminished responsibility. If it was during the incubation stage, it is very unlikely that there would be impairment of the brain function and therefore it is very unlikely that she would come under the purview of diminished responsibility. Based on the facts presented by the prosecution Dr Ngui's opinion was that it is improbable that she could have been suffering from the frank stage of encephalitis on 6th January and it is unlikely that she could have been suffering from the prodromal stage of encephalitis on that day and if she was suffering from encephalitis at the incubation stage, the fact that during this stage there were usually no symptoms would mean that the illness at that stage would not have adversely affected her mental responsibility at that time.

The trial judges, on the whole of the evidence, were not satisfied on the balance of probabilities, that at the time of the commission of the offence, the first appellant was suffering from any abnormality of the mind. They then went on to find, even assuming she was at the time suffering from encephalitis, that they were not satisfied on a balance of probabilities that the illness had caused impairment of the brain function so as to have substantially impaired her mental responsibility for her acts.

In our judgment there was ample evidence to support the trial judges' findings....

Appeals dismissed

(b) Cause of abnormality

The wording in the parentheses of Exception 7 places an important restriction on its operation. The abnormality of mind must be one which arises from "a condition of arrested or retarded development of mind or any inherent causes or induced by disease or injury". However, there have been a number of English cases where the courts have tended to gloss over the strict statutory requirements where the accused has been placed in such a distressing situation that a murder verdict with its mandatory sentence would be unjustly harsh. Although the Singapore courts have not yet faced such cases, they are of obvious importance. One example where the English courts have been lenient, has been in cases where the accused has been severely provoked but does not qualify for the provocation defence, perhaps because there has been a cooling off period (eg *Coles*, 1980 where the husband "slept on his wrath" before killing his wife). It is debatable whether diminished responsibility should be used in cases where provocation fails.

The most difficult area concerns certain "mercy killings". Under Exception 5, culpable homicide is not murder where the deceased, if over 18, consents (see above, p 466). However, there will be cases where this exception is not available, as in the case of minors or comatose adults who are unable to give consent. In one English case (*Gray*, 1965), a father killed his young son who was suffering from an incurable cancer and was in so much pain that he could not even stand the weight of sheets upon his body. He was convicted of manslaughter on grounds of diminished responsibility. However, was he suffering from any abnormality of mind? If so, how could it be regarded as arising from inherent causes, disease or injury? Was it right that he was convicted of manslaughter, a very serious offence?

Glanville Williams, *Textbook of Criminal Law* (2nd edn, 1983), 693

[T]he defence of diminished [responsibility] is interpreted in accordance with the morality of the case rather than as an application of psychiatric concepts.... One may question whether leniency has not sometimes gone too far; but there can be no doubt of the beneficial effect of the defence in mercy killing cases. Here it is invariably accepted by the jury on the flimsiest of medical evidence, and thankfully used by the judge as a reason for leniency.... Although the judges are to be warmly congratulated for humanity in mercy-killing cases, the invocation of the psychiatrist and the probation officer could not have been regarded as necessary for any of the purposes for which those persons are normally used. It was merely an attempt by the judge to render workable a law that is grossly out of accord with present thought, and to maintain, as is required by his office, an appearance of official disapproval towards an act that most people nowadays would regard as a normal reaction to an impossible situation.

Since there are no local cases on these difficult problems, it would be open to the Singapore courts either to develop their own principles or to follow the course favoured by the English courts. A degree of flexibility is especially important given the death penalty for murder; it is scarcely conceivable that anyone should believe that somebody like Mr Gray deserved the death penalty. Is it right that mercy killings should attract a conviction for culpable homicide or should there be a separate offence? At one time the English Criminal Law Revision Committee (1976) favoured a new offence to cover such cases but they dropped this proposal in view of the difficulty of delineating appropriate cases and public controversy (1980). However, it would be preferable to consider introducing a new offence rather than stretching diminished responsibility beyond its proper wording.

The requirement that the mental abnormality be traced to inherent causes, disease or injury clearly rules out any argument that intoxication in itself can attract the defence. However, there may be cases where there is evidence that the mental abnormality can be attributed to the combination of intoxication and inherent causes. In such situations the view of the English courts is that the intoxication must be ignored; the two questions for the jury are whether, if he had not been intoxicated, the accused would have killed and, if so, whether he would have been acting under diminished responsibility (*Atkinson*, 1985). It seems unrealistic to expect a jury or, in Singapore, a judge to discount one of the factors in this way but the approach recently received the approval of the English Law Commission (1985).

(c) Effect of abnormality

In both *Mimi Wong* (1972) and *Osman b Ali* (1972) it was held that the appellants were not suffering from an abnormality of mind at the time of the offence but that even if they had been, it was not such as substantially to impair their responsibility. However, there has been little effort in Singapore or England to delineate when impairment will be "substantial". *Byrne* (1960) emphasized that the defence was available where the accused found it impossible to control himself, ie irresistible impulse arising from the requisite causes (compare *Sinnasamy*, 1956, above, p 39). It was also made clear in *Byrne* (1960) that the defence is available in cases where the accused had difficulty controlling his actions; its availability in such circumstances depends on the degree of difficulty which is not a question capable of exact measurement nor a matter to be determined by scientific evidence. Beyond this the courts have not gone except in the occasional utterance of banal platitudes, as in *Lloyd* (1967) where Ashworth J said that juries should use their common sense; substantial meant something less than total impairment but something more than trivial or minimal. In Singapore, where the matter is one for the judge, the question is also approached on a commonsense basis.

Cheng Swee Hin v PP [1981] 1 MLJ 1 (CA, Singapore)

The appellant and the deceased were partners in a firm. Relations between them became very strained and the deceased told the appellant that he was no longer to be actively engaged in the business of the company. The trial court rejected pleas of provocation and diminished responsibility.

Wee Chong Jin CJ: The trial judges after reviewing the medical evidence found that the appellant was not suffering from an abnormality of mind when he shot the deceased. They went on to make another finding, on the assumption that the appellant was suffering from an abnormality of mind at the material time. We set out their further finding in the following passage ...:

> "[W]as the abnormality such as to have substantially impaired the mental responsi-
> bility for his act? Our finding was that the evidence ... confirmed our judgment that
> on the facts, on a balance of probabilities, the defence had not been proved....
>   The correct test ... is that laid down by Lord Parker in *Byrne* (1960) ... where the
> expression 'mental responsibility for his acts' was explained to mean a 'mental state
> which ... a jury would regard as amounting to partial insanity or being on the bor-
> derline of insanity"....

In a case where the accused is tried before a judge without a jury, where the defence of diminished responsibility is raised and the judge is satisfied on the balance of probabilities that the accused was suffering from "abnormality of mind" from one of the causes specified in Exception 7 ... the crucial question ... is whether or not the abnormality was such as substantially impaired the accused's mental responsibility.... Adopting the language of *Walton* (1978) the judge is to approach that task in a broad common sense way and he has essentially to decide whether at the time of the killing the accused was suffering from a state of mind bordering on but not amounting to insanity.

Appeal dismissed

3. Importance of medical evidence

Medical evidence plays a significant but not conclusive role in diminished responsibility cases. In *Byrne* (1960) Lord Parker regarded the second question of the aetiology of the abnormality to be a matter to be determined by expert evidence but the first and third questions to be matters for the jury (in Singapore, the judge) to consider; whilst medical evidence was relevant to these questions, it was not conclusive.

In some cases (eg *Mohamed b Jamal*, 1964) the evidence all points in one direction and, as Glanville Williams pointed out (1983, see above, p 472) there may be cases where even the flimsiest of evidence is accepted. However, this is not always the case; in many instances, the court must weigh up medical reports which are widely different (eg *Osman b Ali*, 1972; *Mimi Wong*, 1972 and *Cheng Swee Hin*, 1981). Even where there is no contradiction between the pieces of medical evidence, the court must assess the case as a whole.

Walton v The Queen [1978] 1 All ER 542 (PC, appeal from Barbados)

The provisions on diminished responsibility in Barbados are *in pari materia* with the English and Singapore provisions. The appellant appealed against his conviction for murder on the grounds that in the light of the medical evidence he satisfied the requirements of diminished responsibility.

Lord Keith of Kinkel: [The] cases make clear that on an issue of diminished responsibility the jury are entitled and indeed bound to consider not only the medical evidence but the evidence on the whole facts and circumstances of the case. These include the nature of the killing, the conduct of the accused before, at the time of and after it and any history of mental abnormality. It being recognized that the jury on occasion may properly refuse to accept medical evidence, it follows that they must be entitled to consider the quality and weight of that evidence....

In the present case their Lordships are of opinion that, insofar as they can judge of the medical evidence from the trial judge's notes, the jury were entitled to regard it as not entirely convincing. Dr Patricia Bannister, whose evidence was subjected to quite lengthy cross-examination, expressed an opinion as to the appellant's state of mind which in terms satisfied the statutory definition. The particular mental abnormality which she identified was that of an extremely immature personality. Mr Browne, the clinical psychologist, found the appellant to be of average intellectual ability with good observational ability and clear thinking. He supported Dr Patricia Bannister's evidence by describing the appellant as having an inadequate personality enhanced by emotional immaturity and a low tolerance level. The evidence of Dr Lawrence Bannister was merely to the effect that he treated the appellant for depression, with disappointing results.

[His Lordship concluded that the evidence here fell "a long way short" of that in other English cases where there was evidence of a history of prior mental disorder and/or clear agreement between the medical witnesses.]

Appeal dismissed

Chapter 21

Homicide by negligence

By NA Morgan

A. Introduction

Penal Code, s 304(A)

Whoever causes the death of any person by doing any rash or negligent act not amounting to culpable homicide, shall be punished with imprisonment for a term which may extend to two years, or with fine, or with both.

The causation rules (see ch 18) and *actus reus* (see p 402) for s 304(A) have already been discussed. It was argued that although the causation rules for s 304(A) are different from those for culpable homicide, the *actus reus* should in all other respects be the same. This section considers the terms "rashness" and "negligence" under s 304(A) and draws comparisons with related offences, contained in separate road traffic legislation in both Singapore and Malaysia, of careless, dangerous and reckless driving.

B. Causing death by rash or negligent conduct

1. Rashness

The classic definition of "rashness" in *Nidamarti Nagabhushanam* (1872, see above, p 61) requires the accused to have considered the possibility of "the mischievous consequences" occurring but to have decided to run that risk; "the imputability arises from acting despite the consciousness". This may be termed the "carry on regardless" state of mind. Rashness is generally considered to be more blameworthy than negligence which is objectively defined in terms which do not require the accused to have adverted to the risks of his conduct. However, by contrast with cases of culpable homicide not amounting to murder, where the punishments for intention and knowledge are differentiated, both rashness and negligence are subject to the same maximum penalty. Since there is no differentiation in penalty, and since borderline cases will invariably turn on the definition of the broader term "negligence", the definition of "rashness" has tended to be ignored or glossed over (eg *Ramlan b Salleh*, 1987).

476

The following leading Indian decision raises some interesting questions:

Empress of India v Idu Beg ILR (1881) 3 All 776 (HC, Allahabad, India)

The accused struck his wife a blow on her left side with great force. She died from a ruptured spleen. The spleen was slightly enlarged at the time of the blow. The trial judge held that culpable homicide had not been committed as the accused lacked the necessary *mens rea* for s 299 and convicted him under s 304(A).

Straight J: It appears to me impossible to hold that cases of direct violence, wilfully inflicted, can be regarded as either rash or negligent acts. There may be in the act an absence of intention to kill, to cause such bodily injury as is likely to cause death, or of knowledge that death will be the most probable result, or even of intention to cause grievous hurt or of knowledge that grievous hurt is likely to be caused. But the inference seems irresistible that hurt at the very least must be presumed to have been intended or to have been known to be likely to be caused. If such intention or knowledge is present, it is a misapplication of terms to say that the act itself, which is the real test of criminality, amounts to no more than rashness or negligence. In the present case the evidence is clear that the blow was wilfully and consciously given to the deceased woman by the accused, and he obviously therefore committed an assault at the very least. The consequences that resulted from it could not change a wilful and conscious act into a rash or negligent one, but their relevancy and importance, as indicating the amount of violence used, bore upon the question as to the character of the intention or knowledge to be presumed against the accused.

Conviction under s 304(A) quashed;
Conviction under s 325 substituted and sentence enhanced from four
months' to three years' rigorous imprisonment

The first issue raised by *Idu Beg* (1881) concerns the relationship between the *mens rea* terms in ss 299/300 and 304(A). The point at which these sections come closest is in the definitions of rashness (s 304(A)) and knowledge (s 299.3, see above, p 418). Rashness, being defined as the subjective recognition of the risk, amounts to the same as "subjective recklessness" in the English case of *Cunningham* (1957); it is necessary that the accused foresaw "that the particular kind of harm might be done, and yet has gone on to take the risk of it". *Cunningham* (1957) required the accused to have recognized a risk of the particular kind of harm forbidden by the offence definition. The cases on s 304(A) have not clearly discussed whether rashness requires recognition of the possibility of *death* as opposed to mere injury; however, the wording of *Nidamarti Nagabhushanam* (1872) ("consciousness that *the* mischievous and illegal consequences may follow") seems to suggest that death must be recognized as a possibility. Adopting this analysis, the distinction between ss 304(A) and 299.3 is, in theory, clear. Rashness requires *recognition* of a risk that death *may* ensue. Recognition of such a *possibility* falls well short of the degree of awareness contemplated by s 299.3; namely, *knowledge* that death is a *likely* consequence. However, although rashness and knowledge are distinguishable in principle, their borders blur when specific cases are considered. Return again to *Nedrick* (1986, see above, pp 57–58, 422); was Mr Nedrick sufficiently aware of the risks to be deemed to have knowledge of the likelihood of death? Alternatively, was he simply "rash"?

A second question is whether the court was right to hold that the appellant was not guilty under s 304(A) on the basis that acts done with intention or knowledge cannot be considered rash or negligent. This suggests that where an accused intentionally or knowingly causes injury, but does not fall under ss 299/300 (eg because the injury was not objectively likely to cause death under s 299.2, see above, p 407) then, even though the victim dies, he is not liable for a homicide offence but only for voluntarily causing hurt or, perhaps, as in *Idu Beg* (1881) itself, for causing grievous hurt. Could it not be argued, contra *Idu Beg* (1881), that intention and knowledge, being narrower *mens rea* terms, are embraced by the wider concepts of negligence and rashness? If so, could it not be that the correct conviction, when death has been caused, is generally for a homicide offence under s 304(A)? Is it not rather artificial to hold the accused liable for hurt or grievous hurt when, under the causation rules, he has satisfied the *actus reus* of homicide?

2. Negligence

Again the starting point is the classic definition in *Nidamarti Nagabhushanam* (1872). As defined there, negligence is disregarding a risk which the accused would have recognized if he had exercised proper caution: "the imputability arises from the neglect of the civic duty of circumspection". Negligence is thus an essentially objective question. However, this definition does contain a very important concession to subjectivity; it requires that the *accused himself* would have recognized the risk if he had exercised due care; this is not necessarily satisfied by proof that a reasonable man would have recognized the risk since the accused, through no fault of his own (eg mental capacity), might not have recognized the risk even if he had considered it (see p 61).

Since negligence involves a *failure* to consider risks, it is inappropriate to consider it a species of *mens rea* (compare *Adnan b Khamis*, 1972, see below, p 489). As Clarkson (1987, pp 68–69) puts it:

> Negligence is often classed as a species of *mens rea* on the basis that it is a state of mind: it is the failure to think about the consequences of one's actions. Not thinking refers to a state of mind, albeit a blank state of mind. However, such a view cannot be accepted for three reasons. First, it is semantic nonsense to describe a blank state of mind as a state of mind. Presumably, then, unconsciousness would need to be described as a state of mind! Second, a person can be negligent even if he does anticipate the consequences of his actions (ie does not have a blank state of mind). Such

a person would also be at least reckless [or rash under the Code] but that does not alter the fact that if his conduct fell below that of the reasonable man he is negligent. Finally, English law [and local courts have] long recognized ... degrees of negligence. There is simple negligence which is the same standard as that employed by the civil law and there is gross negligence which involves a major departure from the standards of the reasonable man. If negligence were an empty mind, how could there be degrees of emptiness and negligence? Accordingly, it is better to regard negligence not as a part of *mens rea* but as a separate factor indicating blameworthiness.

Although *Nidamarti Nagabhushanam* (1872) explains the fundamental difference between rashness and negligence, it does not consider what degree of negligence is required for s 304(A) or any other Penal Code offence. Numerous cases in Malaysia and Singapore have explored this vexed question. They are confusing, convoluted and contradictory. Discussion has generally centred around the two standards of negligence identified in the preceding quotation. First, there is the view that s 304(A) is a statutory equivalent of the English offence of manslaughter by "gross negligence". The nebulous concept of gross negligence seems to require a very high degree of negligence, going well beyond that required to establish a case in tort. At the other end of the scale is the view that the standard of negligence under s 304(A) is the same as the civil standard; ie that required for tort liability. There are also those who argue for an "intermediate standard" falling somewhere between the two. The attractions of each approach will be considered as they arise but it must be noted at this stage that although there can be degrees of negligence, the standard which is enunciated in the abstract may prove extremely difficult to apply in practice (see Canagarayar, 1981).

Lai Tin v PP (1939) 8 MLJ 248 (HC, Perak, FMS)

Murray-Aynsley J: [I]t appears to me to be dangerous to construe the Penal Code and similar Enactments by reference to similar provisions of English Law. Those responsible for the drafting of the Indian Penal Code deliberately departed from English Law in many important respects and I think one can only look at the Code as it stands and construe it as one would any other enactment. In English law there is for the purpose of the Criminal Law a double standard of negligence. In the judgment of Lord Atkin in *Andrews* (1937), it is held that negligence may be great enough to support a conviction for "driving without due care and attention" or for "driving recklessly or at a speed or in a manner which is dangerous to the public", but not great enough to support a conviction for manslaughter. That learned Lord says—"it is perfectly possible that a man may drive at a speed or in a manner dangerous to the public and cause death and yet not be guilty of manslaughter". I do not think that is possible here. The section contains the words "rash" and "negligent". The latter word is one in common usage, both as a legal term and otherwise. I do not consider that there is any reason for giving it a special meaning in this case.

I would not go as far as to say that the degree of negligence necessary to support a civil action should be applied without reservation. A criminal charge and a civil action should be approached in a different spirit. But English law has as I have said a double standard of negligence in criminal law, and I do not consider that s 304(A) gives any basis for the suggestion that such a double standard should be applied here.

In the present case the learned Magistrate has held that the Appellant was guilty of negligence but not of such negligence as would be considered sufficient for conviction for manslaughter in England. In my opinion the facts of the case disclose a substantial and serious degree of negligence. Whether or not in the present case it would be sufficient for a conviction for manslaughter, it is in my opinion sufficient for a conviction under s 304A....

Appeal dismissed

This analysis, which rejects English manslaughter cases and enunciates the principle that civil and criminal cases should be approached in a different spirit, led Murray-Aynsley J to suggest an intermediate standard of negligence. This has obvious attractions. To give rise to criminal liability, conduct should generally be more blameworthy than would be necessary to give rise to a claim in tort; it should be so blameworthy that it requires punishment by the state and can no longer be regarded as a matter of compensation between individuals. On the other hand, s 304(A) carries a maximum of only two years' imprisonment whereas English manslaughter carries a maximun of life imprisonment; it is arguable that s 304(A) was therefore intended to embrace cases with a lower degree of fault than gross negligence in English law. An intermediate standard was also favoured in the following case.

Dabholkar v King AIR (1948) PC 183 (PC, appeal from East Africa)

Section 222, Tangyanika Penal Code provides for a number of offences of causing harm short of death by rash or negligent conduct. The provisions are *in pari materia* with the Indian and local Penal Codes.

Lord Oaksey: The negligence charged in that section is not necessarily as grave, either in its nature or its consequences as in the offence of manslaughter. The analogy between this section and s 2, English Road Traffic Act 1930, is in their Lordships' view, a true analogy and just as in *Andrews* (1937) the House of Lords explained the different degrees of negligence which the prosecution must prove to establish the offences of manslaughter and dangerous driving, so in the case of s 222 the degree of negligence differs in cases of the felony of manslaughter and in cases of misdemeanour under s 222. The circumstances dealt with in the subsections of s 222 are all circumstances which in themselves involve danger and, although the negligence which constitutes the offence in these circumstances must be of a higher degree than the negligence which gives rise to a claim for compensation in a Civil Court, it is not, in their Lordships' opinion of so high a degree as that which is necessary to constitute the offence of manslaughter.

However, the courts in Malaysia and Singapore have generally been attracted to either the manslaughter standard or the civil standard rather than an intermediate position. *Lai Tin* (1939) has been over-ruled and *Dabholkar* (1948) generally ignored.

Cheow Keok v PP (1940) 9 MLJ 103 (CA, Selangor, FMS)

In the High Court, Aitken J refused to follow *Lai Tin* (1939). His judgment was upheld on appeal by Poyser CJ, McElwaine CJ (SS) and Gordon-Smith JA.

Judgment of court: We have no hesitation in coming to the conclusion that Aitken, J's interpretation of the law is the correct one. [It was] argued that English decisions on Common Law offences had no application to offences under the Penal Code; that as the Federated Malay States criminal law was codified we should only consider that Code and interpret negligence in its ordinary meaning and not interpret it as meaning "gross negligence".

If we were to adopt this argument, we should be putting an interpretation of this section which, as far as we know, with the exception of the case previously referred to, has never been placed on it before either in India, Malaya, or in other countries where a criminal code based on the Indian Penal Code is in force. Further, as Aitken J points out, s 304A is a codification of the English Common Law offence of manslaughter by negligence.

This section did not appear in the original Indian Penal Code; it was added thereto by an amending Act of 1870. *Gour* (5th ed, page 1044) states in regard to such amendment:

> "This supplied an omission providing for the offence of manslaughter by negligence which had been provided for by the two clauses in the draft code but which appear to have been unaccountably omitted from the code when it was finally enacted".

And at page 1045:

> "it (ie, a rash or negligent act) corresponds exactly to what is designated in English law as manslaughter by negligence"....

There are other reasons for treating the word "negligence" differently in civil and criminal proceedings. Take the word "prove" for instance. In all criminal cases in the British Empire such word used in regard to a criminal prosecution means "to prove beyond all reasonable doubt". In civil proceedings such strict proof is not necessary; it is only necessary to establish a balance of probabilities.

In view of the above we have no doubt that English authorities may be followed in considering whether an offence under s 304A is established, and that being the case, we have not the slightest hesitation in coming to the conclusion that Aitken J's statement of the law is correct.

He referred to the two leading cases on the point, viz: *Bateman*, (1925) and *Andrews* (1937) the latter a House of Lords decision. From those authorities it is plainly manifest, as Aitken J held that:

> "a very high degree of negligence must be proved before an accused person can properly be convicted in England on an indictment for manslaughter by negligence and the same very high degree of negligence is required to establish an offence under s 304A".

It is unnecessary that we should examine in detail these authorities. Aitken J, has done so, and we need only state that we entirely agree with the conclusions he arrived at.

The first attraction of the English manslaughter standard is that it clearly distinguishes civil and criminal liability. The second is that the provisions relating to culpable homicide, since they require subjective intention or knowledge, will not cover cases of negligence, however gross (see below, p 487); it may therefore be argued that s 304(A) was designed to fill this gap in the law. On the other hand, there are two major difficulties with this analysis. The first is the low sentence provided by s 304(A) by comparison with English manslaughter. The only response to this is the (rather unconvincing) argument that although English law provides a high maximum penalty for all forms of manslaughter, the judge's sentence will in practice reflect the accused's blameworthiness, in particular that he was only negligent; by contrast, the Penal Code is explicitly recognizing that rashness and negligence are less blameworthy rather than leaving this to the sentencer's discretion. A second difficulty with the gross negligence test is that the cases have accepted, in accordance with general principles of statutory interpretation, that negligence ought to be given the same meaning throughout the Penal Code. It can be argued that *gross* negligence is a concept developed in England in the context of the very serious offence of manslaughter, and that such a high degree of negligence should not be necessary for other negligence offences in the Penal Code (eg negligent handling of explosives, s 286 or negligent spreading of disease, s 269) which are less serious than manslaughter and carry much lower penalties. Consequently, if negligence is given the same meaning throughout the Penal Code, it should be lower than the manslaughter standard.

The manslaughter standard was adopted in numerous cases following *Cheow Keok* (1940) (eg *Kuan Choon Hin*, 1940, and *Lee Fong*, 1940). In *Lee Ah Chai* (1947) Murray-Aynsley CJ expressed the view that *Cheow Keok* (1940) was wrong, but nevertheless chose to follow it "on grounds of convenience". Doubts were also expressed as to the correctness of the decision in *Low Hiong Boon* (1948) but the court felt bound to follow it.

One of the arguments used in *Cheow Keok* (1940) was that the standard of negligence under s 304(A) should be higher than the civil standard because civil and criminal cases have different standards of proof. However, in the leading Singapore case, the better view was taken that the questions of the standard of negligence and the standard of proof were distinct and separate issues.

Woo Sing and Sim Ah Kow v R (1954) 20 MLJ 200 (Full Bench of HC, Singapore)

Murray-Aynsley CJ (with whom Pretheroe Ag CJ (FM) agreed): As regards interpretation, we are dealing with a code. In the first instance we study the words of the code itself. We are not justified in looking outside the code in order to give a special meaning to the words used in it.... The Penal Code is not a codification of English law. In numerous respects its provisions resemble the corresponding English law. In others, particularly as regards homicide, its provisions differ very greatly and deliberately so. In my opinion it is always dangerous to introduce English cases into the consideration of the Penal Code. The English law as to homicide remains unwritten and is still in a confused state, though of recent years there has been some clarification. But there still remains, in theory at least, constructive murder and constructive manslaughter. The Penal Code deliberately excluded the constructive offences and in ss 299-300 required certain specific intentions. In England involuntary manslaughter has always been very much tied up with the notion of constructive offences, in early times entirely so. It was the doing of an unlawful act, not the doing of a negligent act, that rendered a person guilty of manslaughter.

In these circumstances the English law of manslaughter has no relevance in the interpretation of s 304A. In England negligence in any ordinary sense of the word is not the criterium of manslaughter. In *Bateman's case* (1925) Lord Hewart CJ, said: "It is most desirable that in trials for manslaughter by negligence it should be impressed on the jury that the issue is not negligence or no negligence, but felony or no felony." I do not think that once this source of confusion is removed Courts need have any difficulty in the application of this section to particular cases. Different degrees of gravity can be treated by a suitable variation in the penalty, bearing in mind that s 304A involves offences of much less gravity than such as would come within the scope of manslaughter in England.

I do not think it is necessary to lay down a different standard of negligence in civil and criminal cases, although, of course, a higher standard of proof is required in the latter cases....

Whitton J: I have had the advantage of reading the judgment of the learned President, and am in agreement with it subject to saying I think a higher degree of negligence is necessary in order to establish a criminal offence than is sufficient to create civil liability.

Order accordingly

Murray-Aynsley CJ's views were significantly different from those he had expressed earlier in *Lai Tin* (1939) since he now expressly equated the civil and criminal standards of negligence and suggested that the only difference between negligence in civil and criminal cases was the standard of proof. Confusion still reigns.

PP v Mills [1971] 1 MLJ 4 (CA of Sarawak, North Borneo and Brunei, Kuching)

This case was decided in 1955 but was reported only in 1971, along with the Singapore case of *Mah Kah Yew* (1971). The respondent was charged under s 304(A). The trial judge ruled in favour of the manslaughter standard. The public prosecutor challenged the directions.

Williams CJ (President): Careful comparison of [manslaughter] with the crimes of murder, culpable homicide not amounting to murder and killing by a rash or negligent act (ss 299–304A of the Penal Code) shows that what would be charged as manslaughter under English law, is under the Penal Code spread over ss 299, 300 and 304A. It is apparent therefore that s 304A at best only embraces a small proportion of what might be called manslaughter cases–only that proportion in fact which would be designated as involuntary manslaughter or manslaughter by negligence under English law, and not necessarily all of that.

The next marked difference to note is that manslaughter whether it be voluntary or involuntary is a felony punishable with imprisonment for life whereas killing by a rash or negligent act under s 304A has always been punishable with no more than two years' rigorous imprisonment or with a fine or with both....

Speaking of manslaughter by negligence, that is involuntary manslaughter, Lord Hewart LCJ said in *Bateman* (1925): "It is, nevertheless, most desirable that in trials for manslaughter by negligence it should be impressed on the jury that the issue they have to try is not negligence or no negligence, but felony or no felony." I do not see how homicide under s 304A with its comparatively limited scale of punishment can be said to be the equivalent of a felony. It is more logical to equate the standard of negligence required in s 304A cases with that in offences of rashness and negligence carrying punishments of comparable severity; for instance, s 336 (rash or negligent act endangering safety), 279 (rash or negligent driving), 337 (causing hurt by rash or negligent act) and 338 (causing grievous hurt by rash or negligent act), which, together with fines of varying severity, carry maximum sentences of three months, six months, and six months and two years' rigorous imprisonment respectively. Equivalents under English law are reckless or dangerous driving which is punishable under s 11 of the Road Traffic Act, 1930 ... with two years' imprisonment and fine and causing bodily harm by furious driving which is punishable by s 35 of the Offences Against the Person Act 1861, with two years' imprisonment.

Notwithstanding the opinions of Ratanlal in *Law of Crimes* and the decision of *Cheow Keok* (1940) which was not followed in *Woo Sing* (1954), I am of the opinion that the standard of negligence required for a conviction under s 304A (1) cannot be equated with that required for a conviction for manslaughter and that although the two crimes may and indeed do overlap they are essentially different. The main feature of the offence under s 304A (1) is the causing of death by doing an act which was rash or negligent but which was neither designed nor voluntary. The opinion expressed by the Full Court of Singapore in *Woo Sing* (1954) is, I consider, sound: it is to the effect that the Penal Code is not a codification of English law and it is dangerous, particularly in homicide cases, to try and introduce English case law into the consideration of the Code. English cases stress the grossness of the negligence necessary to constitute manslaughter but I am not prepared to hold that the acts of rashness or negligence which cause death must be of that high degree before an offence under s 304A (1) can be committed.

From the similarity of the words used to describe the degree of rashness and negligence in these sections I am prepared to hold that the degree of rashness or negligence in these sections is the same throughout "for it is a sound rule of construction to give the same meaning to the same words occurring in different parts of an Act"—*Courtauld* v *Legh* (1869) per Cleasby B: The results of the rashness or negligence, however, differs. But I am not prepared to equate the standard of rashness and negligence in these Penal Code sections with that in s 27 or any other sections of the Road Traffic Ordinance 1953 (No 29 of 1953) which has its own provisions regulating the degree of care to be taken in driving motor vehicles and has no direct reference to causing death by rashness or negligence.

In my view and in answer to the Public Prosecutor's certificate the nature and degree of negligence in an act causing death required to support a conviction under s 304A (1) is the same as that in any other act carried out so rashly or negligently as to endanger human life or the safety of others where that act was the immediate cause of death and not the remote cause. It is not possible to assess degrees of negligence and rashness with any precision as we have no precise standard whereby we can measure either negligence or rashness.

Blagden AG J concurred.

Bodley J: It seems to me that s 304A represents the Indian draftsman's attempt to create the statutory offence of manslaughter by negligence: Ratanlal (4th edn); Gours (4th edn, Vol 2).

The section is in the nature of an after-thought and was inserted at a latter period than were its immediate predecessors.

Sections 299 and 300 of the Penal Code create the offence of culpable homicide and enact that the said offence of culpable homicide is murder. This is subject to various exceptions, the effect of any of which would be to reduce the offence to culpable homicide not amounting to murder, or what might accurately be described as voluntary manslaughter. But the common law offence of manslaughter in England takes two forms, voluntary and involuntary, and it is clear that without the insertion of s 304A, the offence of involuntary manslaughter or manslaughter by negligence is entirely lacking.

Process of time revealed that legislation creating the offence was desirable and in my opinion s 304A was the result.

Be it noted that the act has to be one not amounting to culpable homicide which is murder. The section does not say that it must not amount to that form of culpable homicide which does not amount to murder. It would be quite meaningless if it did, as no man commits a rash or negligent act under conditions such as the exceptions envisage. The whole idea of those exceptions is the reducing of a deliberate act causing death which act apart from those exceptions would be murder, to the offence of voluntary manslaughter. No man deliberately commits a rash or negligent act with the intention of harming anyone. So when this section says "not amounting to culpable homicide", it means not amounting to murder and it does not in my opinion mean not amounting to manslaughter.

If this be the correct interpretation of the section then the latter must create the offence of manslaughter by negligence. There is no third standard of culpable homicide. It is true that it is regarded as a less serious offence than that of voluntary manslaughter and that the penalties are correspondingly less severe. This only puts in statutory form what is the invariable practice in England ie the passing of a greatly reduced sentence for manslaughter by negligence than for a manslaughter which is just short of murder.

If manslaughter by negligence is the intended creation of the section, then the test as laid down in *Bateman*'s case (1925) should undoubtedly apply. It was expressly approved by the House of Lords in the case of the *Andrews* (1937) and it is left open to the court to convict of a less serious offence if it is not satisfied that the negligence has been of the *Bateman* standard.

Any less exacting standard would to my mind create a criminal offence out of a tort and would bring within the provisions of s 304A a person who had contributed towards another's death by mere contributory negligence thereby reducing the law to a farcical state.

Mills (1971) has frequently been cited with approval (eg *Kong Siang Ng*, 1966 and cases below). However, although the majority clearly rejected the manslaughter standard, it is not clear what test they preferred. Does Williams CJ approve the civil standard of negligence espoused in *Woo Sing* (1954), or merely its rejection of the manslaughter test?

Anthonysamy v PP (1956) 22 MLJ 247 (HC, KL, Malaya)

The appellant was convicted under s 304(A) of an offence arising out of the manner in which he had driven his lorry. The court adopted the *Woo Sing* (1954) test of negligence. On appeal it was argued that *Cheow Keok* (1940) should be followed.

Buhagiar J: I held the view that the FMS decisions referred to [eg *Cheow Keok*, 1940] were binding on this Court but that in my view the decision in *Woo Sing* ... (1954) was the correct interpretation of s 304(A)....

With regard to the degree of negligence ... I found that ... there was that high degree of negligence to justify a conviction under s 304(A) ... in accordance with ... the FMS decisions....

[His Lordship then explains his reasons for agreeing with *Woo Sing*, 1954:]

In the first place it is, in my opinion fallacious to compare the offence under s 304(A) ... to manslaughter in English law. As Murray-Aynsley CJ ... pointed out in *Woo Sing*'s case (1954), the Penal Code is not a codification of English law....

The word "negligence" must be given the same meaning consistently throughout the Penal Code. Now, on examination of the various sections where this word appears, eg, ss 336, 268, 279, 282 it is apparent that that word cannot have the meaning of "gross negligence" "high degree of negligence" that is necessary in England for a conviction on an indictment for manslaughter. For the purposes of these sections no higher degree of negligence is required than that in civil matters. The gravity of these offences, for which the law provides different degrees of punishment depends on the consequences or possible consequences of the negligent or rash act.

In my opinion the high degree of negligence required in English law for the felony of manslaughter is more akin to the *mens rea* in s 299 of the Penal Code for offences of culpable homicide not amounting to murder, that is "knowledge that he is likely by such act to cause death". In most cases where death has been caused by such a high degree of negligence it will be possible to infer that the offender acted with such knowledge. Thus, if a person drives a motor car at a high speed in a crowded street, it is, I think, possible to infer that he acted with such knowledge and if death results the proper charge would be one of culpable homicide not amounting to murder; and if death does not result or only hurt is caused then the offender could be charged under s 308. Whether such knowledge can be inferred or not is naturally a question which depends on the circumstances of each case; thus, in the case of a cyclist who rides a bicycle in similar circumstances in a crowded street such knowledge would not be inferred and if death results it would be a case of an offence under s 304A.

Support of the view that the negligence necessary for the purposes of s 304A is the same as in civil matters may be found in two sections of the Code which do not seem to have been considered in any reported case where the said section was considered; I refer to ss 32 and 43. Section 32 provides: "In every part of this Code, except where a contrary intention appears from the context, words which refer to acts done extend also to illegal omission"; and s 43 lays down:"the word 'illegal' is applicable to everything which is an offence or which is prohibited by law or which furnishes ground for a civil action ...". In view of these provisions if a doctor causes the death of a person by omitting to do something which the proper skill of his profession required him to do and that omission was such as to furnish ground for a civil action, then the inference is irresistible that there is negligence within the meaning of s 304A.

Appeal dismissed

In *Mah Kah Yew* (1971) the Singapore High Court felt bound as a matter of precedent by *Mills* (1971), as a decision of the Court of Appeal of Sarawak and North Borneo from before Malaysia Day (see ch 1). It considered this result "comforting" on the highly questionable basis (see above, p 485) that *Mills* (1971) adopted the same test as *Woo Sing* (1954). The court also approved the reasons given, obiter, in *Anthonysamy* (1956) in support of the civil standard. However, there are some serious difficulties with the analysis in that case. Buhagiar J argued that gross negligence would generally constitute the necessary *mens rea* for culpable homicide under s 299.3 (see above, p 418) and that the civil standard should therefore be adopted for the lesser offence under s 304(A). There are two problems with this. First, as suggested earlier, negligence, as an objective question, is conceptually different from subjective knowledge under s 299.3 (see above, p 478). There will be cases where, even though the negligence may have been very great, it will not be possible to infer actual knowledge. Consider again the case of *William Tan* (1970, see p 418). At the very least, William Tan seems to have displayed a high degree of negligence but the Singapore Court of Appeal held that he did not have the necessary subjective knowledge for s 299/300 and convicted him of causing death by reckless/dangerous driving under the road traffic legislation; he could also have been convicted of causing death by negligence under s 304(A) (see below, p 496). Second, even if the local courts avoid the manslaughter standard, it does not inexorably follow that the alternative is the civil standard. It is equally possible (and desirable?) to adopt an intermediate standard to demarcate civil and criminal liability more clearly.

Another serious difficulty with the reasoning in *Anthonysamy* (1956) is the rather surprising proposition that ss 32 and 43 of the Penal Code support the civil standard. Sections 32 and 43 are definitional sections. They appear in Chapter 2 of the Penal Code which is headed "General Explanations" and do not in themselves create criminal offences. The sections simply make clear that the word "act" embraces illegal omissions and define the circumstances in which an omission will be regarded as "illegal". The fact that an omission is "illegal" under s 43, in the sense that it could give rise to civil liability, does not in itself establish criminal liability; it is also necessary to establish the other elements of the offence in question. Thus, in the context of s 304(A), once an omission is shown to be illegal, it is necessary to prove that it was the legal cause of death under the restrictive causation rules (see ch 18) and also that the accused was rash or negligent. It does not follow from the wording of ss 32 and 43 that only the civil standard of negligence is appropriate to s 304(A); the sections are equally compatible with either the manslaughter or intermediate standard.

In recent cases the Malaysian courts have moved clearly away from the manslaughter standard. In *Joseph Chin Saiko* (1972) the High Court in Sabah declined to follow the manslaughter standard of *Cheow Keok* (1940) and preferred *Mills* (1971). However, Lee Hun Hoe J encountered understandable difficulty in deciding what the test was; at times he seemed to favour an intermediate standard, based on *Dabholkar* (1948) and *Mills* (1971), and at others to agree with *Woo Sing* (1954).

Adnan b Khamis v PP [1972] 1 MLJ 274 (FC, KL, Malaysia)

The Alor Star High Court ([1971] 2 MLJ 231) felt bound by *Mills* (1971) but did not analyse the standard of negligence. The case was referred to the Full Bench of the Federal Court "in order to resolve the question once and for all".

Ong CJ: In our opinion ... absence of authority, no less than its existence, is as persuasive and significant in showing that over the past 100 years no Indian court has yet declared, in the words of Dr Gour, that s 304A "corresponds exactly" to manslaughter by negligence in English law.

It may be observed that, in *Nidamarti Nagabhushanam* (1872) the court emphasized that "not amounting to culpable homicide" forms part of the definition of the offence created by s 304A. By expressly excluding "culpable homicide" the section must, in our view, logically and necessarily exclude "manslaughter". In any form, "manslaughter" (whether by negligence or otherwise) is "culpable homicide". Where, therefore, the homicide in any case is *not culpable*, it cannot possibly be manslaughter under any circumstances. Hence, with respect to the learned judges who thought otherwise, it cannot possibly be correct to say that what is the essential ingredient in manslaughter by negligence is equally vital to sustain a conviction under s 304A.

A simple illustration will suffice to show why we think the decision in *Cheow Keok* (1940) cannot be supported. Take, for instance, the offence under s 223 committed by a public servant negligently suffering any person in his custody to escape. Where a jailor falls asleep on duty and suffers a prisoner under his charge to pick his pocket and obtain the key to his cell, thereby making good his getaway, his negligence consists merely in falling asleep. How possibly can such passive negligence reach the heights of negligent acts causing loss of life? Should the accused be acquitted of a clear offence under s 223 because the prosecution is required by the *Cheow Keok* decision (1940) to perform an impossible feat? Unless the law is to be stultified, it must be so interpreted that negligence must bear the same meaning throughout the Penal Code.

For the reasons above stated we are unanimously of the opinion that the judgment delivered in *Cheow Keok* (1940) must be regarded as *per incuriam*.

Having overruled *Cheow Keok* (1940), the question remaining to be answered is: How are the courts hereafter to construe "negligence" arising in a wide variety of circumstances and rendered punishable under fourteen different sections of the Penal Code? In other words: what degree of negligence becomes culpable? Unless this is clarified, confusion may be worse confounded.

To serve any practical purpose the answer should be clear and precise. In the first place, mere carelessness or inadvertence, without anything more, is not enough, in our opinion, to establish guilt. An essential ingredient of all offences under the Penal Code is *mens rea*; although, in the context of culpable rashness or negligence, *mens rea* should not be understood as synonymous with "criminal intention" or "wicked mind". Rather, it should be construed as connoting fault or blameworthiness of conduct. In the second place, the fault or blameworthiness must, as in all criminal cases, be proved by the prosecution beyond reasonable doubt–not, as in civil cases, on balance of probabilities. Once these principles have been grasped, we think the test to be applied for determining the guilt or innocence of an accused person charged with rash or negligent conduct is to consider whether or not a reasonable man in the same circumstances would have been aware of the likelihood of damage or injury to others resulting from such conduct and taken adequate and proper precautions to avoid causing such damage or injury. This test is partly objective and partly subjective–objective in the sense that the situation must be one fraught with potential risk of injury to others or whatever consequences contemplated in any particular section of the Penal Code. It is also subjective in that such a situation should have arisen by reason of some fault on the part of the accused: see *Gosney* (1971) *per* Megaw LJ at page 347.

Negligence as an offence, varies in gravity, according to the consequences flowing therefrom. This is reflected in the range of punishment provided for different offences. Accordingly, in the words of Murray-Aynsley CJ we consider that "different degrees of gravity can be treated by a suitable variation in the penalty".

Needless to say, in the case of fatal road accidents, s 304A of the Penal Code seems to have been rendered practically redundant by s 34A of the Road Traffic Ordinance 1958. We can hardly imagine any circumstances in which a charge under s 304A may be resorted to by choice in preference to a charge under s 34A of the Ordinance. Similarly s 279 of the Penal Code must be regarded as obsolescent, if not a dead letter, except for riders of horses.

Reference answered

Although the Malaysian Federal Court has therefore rejected the manslaughter standard, it is still not clear what has been put in its place. *Adnan b Khamis* (1972), followed in *Abdul b Palaga* (1973), only lays down a very general test, couched in terms of the reasonable man. This makes no reference to the standard of negligence required for criminal liability. It is also unclear whether the test differs from *Nidamarti Nagabhushanam* (1872) where the question was whether the *accused himself* would have recognized the risk if he had turned his attention to the consequences of his conduct. The Federal Court suggests that the test of negligence is whether a *reasonable man* would have recognized the risk, but then adds that the accused must be at fault. It is submitted that *Adnan b Khamis* (1972) should be interpreted in the light of *Nidamarti Nagabhushanam* (1872) and, insofar as it may at times suggest a purely objective test, it should be regarded as decided per incuriam. In daily life we blame those who fail to exercise the caution which they are capable of exercising and, in appropriate cases, the law should reflect these commonsense normative judgments by imposing criminal liability (Fletcher, 1978). However, reference simply to an objectively reasonable man can lead to imposing liability on those who, for some reason beyond their control, do not share the hypothetical reasonable man's characteristics–whom we do not blame, and who consequently do not deserve punishment (see above, p 478 and Hart, 1968).

C. Causing death by reckless or dangerous driving

1. Introduction

It will be obvious from the cases discussed above that further difficulties arise because most of the cases under s 304(A) concern vehicular homicide, an area which is also covered by separate road traffic legislation. The Road Traffic Act (Singapore) (Cap 276) (RTA), s 66 and the Road Traffic Ordinance 1958 (Ord 49 of 1958) (Malaysia) (RTO), s 34(A) provide offences of causing death by dangerous or reckless driving. In order to understand and to attempt to rationalize these provisions, the following analysis extends to other road traffic offences involving reckless, dangerous and careless driving. The offences in question are ranked in the following table according to the sentences which may be given.

Offence	*Maximum Sentence (excluding endorsement/disqualification)*
Causing death by reckless or dangerous driving: RTA s 66; : RTO s 34(A)	5 years and fine. 5 years and M$5,000.
Causing death by rash or negligent conduct: Penal Code, s 304(A)	2 years and fine.
Reckless or dangerous driving: RTA s 64	6 months and S$1,000 on first conviction. 12 months and S$2,000 on second/subsequent.
RTO, s 35	1 year and M$2,000 on first conviction. 3 years and M$3,000 on second/subsequent.
Rash or negligent driving or riding: Penal Code, s 279	Singapore: 6 months and S$1,000. Malaysia: 6 months and M$2,000.

Careless driving: RTA, s 65		3 months and S$500 on first conviction. 6 months and S$1,000 on second/subsequent.
	: RTO, s 36	6 months or M$1,000.

The table indicates that causing death by reckless or dangerous driving is the most serious offence, the maximum punishment being more than twice that for s 304(A). Where death is not caused, the maximum punishments under the road traffic legislation are much reduced and there is less disparity with comparable Penal Code provisions (s 279) but the road traffic offences do make express provision for heavier penalties for repeat offenders. In principle, the different penalties should reflect the definition given to the terms used to connote blame, namely, rashness, negligence, recklessness, dangerousness and carelessness. Unfortunately, it is impossible to state with either certainty or clarity the relationship between these degrees of fault. An effort will nevertheless be made.

2. Careless driving

Road Traffic Act (Singapore) s 65; Road Traffic Ordinance (Malaysia) s 36

If a person drives a motor vehicle on a road without due care and attention or without reasonable consideration for other persons using the road, he shall be guilty of an offence....

According to sentence ranking, this is the least blameworthy offence in the preceding table. It should involve more than simply travelling in excess of a speed limit, for which separate provision is made (RTA, s 63; RTO, s 34). According to its ranking, careless driving should also involve conduct which is less blameworthy than negligence under s 304(A). In *Abdul b Palaga* (1973) it was held, following a reference (FC Criminal Appeal No 5 of 1971) to the Federal Court in *Joseph Chin Saiko* (1972), that the evidence necessary to support a conviction for driving without due care and attention would not be sufficient to support a conviction under s 304(A).

It would therefore seem clear that a finding that the accused drove without due care or reasonable attention will not be sufficient to show that he was negligent under s 304(A) or s 279 of the Penal Code. However, since the standard of negligence under the Penal Code, at least in Singapore, is the civil standard (*Woo Sing*, 1954) a fundamental question arises; should criminal liability for careless driving, an offence punishable with imprisonment, arise under the road traffic legislation for conduct which may not be sufficiently blameworthy to give rise to liability in tort?

3. Reckless driving

The difficulties become even greater when any attempt is made to rationalize the remaining mental states of reckless and dangerous driving and rashness and negligence. The statutory provisions are virtually identical in Singapore and Malaysia.

Road Traffic Act (Singapore) s 66:

Any person who causes the death of another by the driving of a motor vehicle on a road recklessly, or at a speed or in a manner which is dangerous to the public, having regard to all the circumstances of the case, including the nature, condition and use of the road, and the amount of traffic which is actually at the time, or which might reasonably be expected to be, on the road, shall be guilty of an offence....

[Section 34A of the Malaysian Road Traffic Ordinance is to the same effect; the only difference, which appears insignificant, is that it refers to the amount of traffic which might be expected to be on the road rather than that which might *reasonably* be expected.]

As we have seen, reckless or dangerous driving is more blameworthy than rashness or negligence according to sentence ranking. However, the cases are obscure on the inter-relationship between the terms. Certainly the courts have generally been unwilling to equate the Penal Code and road traffic legislation terms. In accordance with general principles of statutory interpretation, they have sought to apply different definitions to the different terms. The search for different meanings may be one reason why the local courts have not been attracted by the intermediate standard suggested in *Dabholkar* (1948) where the Privy Council apparently equated negligence under the Penal Code with the degree of fault necessary to constitute dangerous driving (see above, p 480).

Seah Siak How v PP [1965] 1 MLJ 53 (HC, Singapore)

The case concerned s 26(1) of the Singapore Road Traffic Ordinance 1961, now Singapore RTA s 66 and Malaysian RTO s 34(A).

Wee Chong Jin CJ: [I]t is conceded by counsel for the appellant and rightly so I think that ... there was sufficient [evidence] to found a conviction based on negligence and therefore sufficient to found a conviction on a charge under s 304A of the Penal Code.

It was argued however that there was no evidence to support a conviction for driving recklessly and thereby causing death under s 26 of the Road Traffic Ordinance. The argument as I understand it is based on the contention that to bring home a charge of driving recklessly ... there must be shown that the negligence was of such a degree as to amount to the offence of manslaughter in England. "Reckless" according to the Oxford English Dictionary means, in respect of action conduct or things "characterized or distinguished by heedless rashness". That definition in its context has been judicially accepted in a criminal case in England in the case of *Grunwald* (1960) and must in my opinion be the meaning which should be attributed to it under the Road Traffic Ordinance. It follows that to bring home a charge under s 26 in respect of driving recklessly it must be shown that the driving is such as to amount to rash driving and the driver of the vehicle must be heedless of the state of affairs on the road at the time in question....

In my opinion [the] evidence is not sufficient to found a conviction for reckless driving under ... the Ordinance. I would therefore allow the appeal to the extent that the conviction is altered to one under s 304A of the Penal Code.

In defining "recklessness" as "*heedless* rashness", his Lordship was indicating, in line with the structure of the various offences, that recklessness under the road traffic legislation is more blameworthy than rashness; it involves a greater degree of negligence, requiring the additional element of heedlessness. However, it is submitted that this definition of recklessness is of little assistance in explaining the difference between rashness and recklessness. Although the *Oxford English Dictionary* does at one point define "recklessness" as "heedless rashness", in other places it uses reckless as synonymous with heedless and even with the words "careless" and "negligent". It therefore seems that according to ordinary English usage, there is little to differentiate the different terms. This does not prevent the law ascribing a more specific meaning to terms such as "recklessness", but since rashness already requires a subjectively perceived risk, it is hard to see what is added by the word "heedless"; without further explanation, "heedless rashness" appears purely tautologous.

Since recklessness is an English concept and the local road traffic legislation was imported directly from England, it is necessary to consider how far English cases should be followed. The leading English cases now indicate that recklessness connotes not only subjective risk taking but also cases of objective risk taking where the accused has closed his mind to risks which would have been obvious to a reasonable person. This definition, adopted in decisions such as *Lawrence* (1982) and *Caldwell* (1982) is wider than both "*Cunningham* (1957) recklessness" and "*Nidamarti Nagabhushanam* (1872) rashness". No doubt the English cases, as House of Lords decisions, would be considered highly persuasive by local courts. However, their use would lead to a paradoxical situation where the accused might be reckless, thus falling under the road traffic legislation, and liable to up to five years' imprisonment even though he would not satisfy the definition of rashness under the Penal Code with its lower maximum penalty! In the conclusions to this chapter, some tentative suggestions are made as to how the English cases may be distinguished, though serious difficulties still remain.

4. Dangerous driving

Lim Chin Poh v PP [1969] 2 MLJ 159 (HC, Singapore)

This case concerned the interpretation of dangerous driving under s 26(1) of the Singapore Road Traffic Ordinance 1961, now Singapore RTA s 66 and Malaysian RTO s 34A.

Choor Singh J: In my view there are three distinct offences under this section because the use of the word "or" is disjunctive:

(1) causing death by driving a motor vehicle on the road recklessly;
(2) causing death by driving a motor vehicle on the road at a speed which is dangerous to the public, etc, and
(3) causing death by driving a motor vehicle on the road in a manner which is dangerous to the public, etc....

It would appear from the charge that the appellant was charged with elements (2) and (3) abovementioned, the prosecution case being that he was driving at a speed which was dangerous *and* in a manner which was dangerous. Although there is no objection in law to a person being charged under s 26(1) of the Road Traffic Ordinance with driving at a speed and in a manner dangerous to the public, the prosecution must appreciate that by framing a charge in that manner they are taking upon themselves the onus of proving two separate and distinct elements, a speed dangerous to the public and a manner of driving dangerous to the public. In this case the prosecution had to prove both elements of the charge and if they failed to establish either the dangerous speed or the danger to the public, the appellant would be entitled to be acquitted....

Whatever the cause of the accident, there was in my opinion no evidence to support the prosecution's assertion that the appellant drove in a manner dangerous to the public. In my opinion the expression "driving in a manner which is dangerous to the public" indicates some dangerous act or manoeuvre on the part of the driver of a vehicle, eg overtaking a vehicle on the wrong side of it, or overtaking in the face of oncoming traffic, or overtaking when unable to see oncoming traffic, or crossing a junction against traffic light, and so on. There must be some positive act on the part of the driver which is dangerous having regard to all the circumstances.

Counsel for the respondent cited *Evans* (1963) and relied on the following passage from the judgment of the Court of Criminal Appeal...:

> "And it is quite clear from the reported cases that, if a man in fact adopts a manner of driving which the jury think was dangerous to other road users in all the circumstances, then on the issue of guilt it matters not whether he was deliberately reckless, careless, momentarily inattentive or even doing his incompetent best."

Counsel submitted that even if the appellant was merely careless, then, on the authority of the decision in *Evans'* case, the appellant was rightly convicted.

In *Evans'* case (1963), the appellant Evans, a medical practitioner and a very experienced driver with a very long and good record behind him, was driving his Jaguar motor-car along a straight open road. The road was only just over 20 feet wide, so that there clearly would not be room for three vehicles abreast. Ahead of him was a motor-car travelling at about 40 miles an hour. He decided to overtake. In the act of overtaking, he increased his speed to some 60 miles an hour and was driving on his wrong side of the road when he crashed head-on into a motor-car coming from the opposite direction and of whose approach he appeared to have been totally unaware. The driver of the other car was killed. The reason why Dr Evans did not see that approaching vehicle appeared to be that there was a dip in the road ahead of him and at the vital moment when he was deciding to overtake, and commencing to overtake, the approaching vehicle was hidden in this dip, but he knew that the dip was there and he was apparently taking a chance. The question, therefore, in that case, was, viewed objectively, did the course on which and the speed at which Dr Evans drove his car in the particular circumstances prevailing at the time involve danger to another road user? The answer to that question was obviously yes and Dr Evans was therefore rightly convicted and his appeal against his conviction was dismissed by the Court of Criminal Appeal. The passage cited by counsel for the appellant must be understood in the light of the facts of that case. The operative words in that passage are "adopts a manner of driving which the jury think was dangerous" and as stated earlier there must be proved some act or manoeuvre on the part of the accused which could be considered dangerous. Careless driving may well be dangerous though all careless driving are not necessarily dangerous. This court is not going to attempt to lay down what is or is not dangerous driving. The question in these cases always is: "Did the conduct of the accused amount to dangerous driving?" And to answer this question the court must consider whether or not the act or manoeuvre of the accused, viewed objectively, involved danger to other road users in the prevailing circumstances? In the present case, the overtaking of the stationary lorry by the appellant, an experienced bus driver, at 40 mph on an empty road, cannot be said to involve danger to other road users. In my opinion there is no evidence in this case to support a charge of "causing death by driving in a manner which was dangerous to the public". The question is, what offence did the appellant commit? In my opinion, the evidence for the prosecution made out a *prima facie* case of negligent driving and at the close of the prosecution case the learned district judge should have amended the charge [to] one of causing death by a negligent act, an offence punishable under s 304A of the Penal Code and should have called the defence of the appellant on this amended charge.

The appellant's version of the accident was that just as he was about to overtake the stationary lorry, another lorry came from behind him at very great speed sounding its horn furiously in an endeavour to overtake his bus. Consequently he swerved to his nearside to allow this lorry to pass. When this other lorry passed him he swerved back to his offside in order to pass the stationary lorry but failed to clear it. The front nearside of his bus hit the stationary lorry. The learned district judge rejected the appellant's version of the accident because he found that the appellant was not speaking the truth. On the evidence before him he was in my opinion entitled to do so.

Appeal allowed;
Conviction altered to one under s 304(A)

The decision in *Lim Chin Poh* (1969) is interesting for a variety of reasons. The first is that Choor Singh J carefully distinguished passages in the English case of *Evans* (1963) on the grounds that they should be read in the context of the facts of the case. He made it clear that in his view, the offence of careless driving was wider than that of dangerous driving and that there would be cases where the driving was careless but not dangerous. In principle this is correct in terms of the structure of these offences. Furthermore, the decision in *Evans* (1963) was notoriously harsh since "doing one's best" was not enough if one was adjudged to have fallen short of an objective standard of competence. Some English cases even suggested that dangerous driving was an offence of strict liability (*Ball and Loughlin*, 1966) and, although this was not always followed, there was certainly little or no practical distinction between careless and dangerous driving. The willingness to depart from English cases is rare but, at least in this instance, very welcome.

A second important aspect of the decision is that the appellant was convicted under the negligence limb of s 304(A), demonstrating that dangerous driving ranks as more serious than negligence. Although it is extremely difficult to distinguish such degrees of fault in individual cases, this is again in line with the structure of the offences.

D. Conclusions

Despite all attempts at rationalization, fundamental difficulties remain with the current law. One concerns the relationship between the sentences and the degree of fault shown by the accused. The following table ranks the degrees of blameworthiness for vehicular homicide offences (excluding culpable homicide), along with their punishments, if the English House of Lords decision in *Lawrence* (1982) was followed.

(1) *Nidamarti Nagabhushanam* (1872) rashness; maximum two years (Penal Code s 304(A)).
(2) *Lawrence* (1982) recklessness; maximum five years (RTA s 66, RTO s 34(A)).
(3) Dangerous driving; maximum five years (RTA s 66, RTO s 34(A)).
(4) Negligence; maximum two years (Penal Code s 304(A)).
(5) Careless driving, whether death is caused or not; maximum three months (RTA s 65) or six months (RTO s 36).

It is possible that although *Lawrence* (1982) is a House of Lords decision, it would not be followed locally; perhaps the local courts would take their cue from *Lim Chin Poh* (1969) and distinguish English law. This can be done. In England, offences of dangerous driving have now been abolished, though those of careless and reckless driving and of causing death by reckless driving remain. *Lawrence* (1982) could therefore be distinguished as interpreting recklessness in the context of a statute which now contains no reference to dangerous driving. This argument has some attraction since the House of Lords clearly felt that a subjective definition of recklessness would lead to a situation where very high and blameworthy degrees of negligence would not give rise to liability though formerly there might have been liability for dangerous driving (see also Criminal Law Revision Committee, 1980). The recent English cases may therefore be seen as having extended recklessness into some of the area formerly covered by dangerous driving. However, one difficulty with this argument is that the House of Lords has subsequently (*Seymour*, 1983) held that the definition of reckless-ness in *Lawrence* (1982) is applicable throughout the criminal law and is not merely an interpretation of the English Road Traffic Act.

Even if *Lawrence* (1982) was not followed, fundamental problems would remain. So far the cases have been unable to draw a clear dis-tinction between rashness and recklessness. To define "recklessness" as more than rashness–in other words, as requiring something more than the subjective recognition of the risks of the conduct–has not been co-herently attempted and would lead to the boundary between reckless-ness and knowledge becoming even more blurred. Furthermore, although dangerous driving appears less blameworthy than rash driving, it car-ries a heavier maximum penalty.

The previous table explains why prosecutors may still decide, when death is caused, to charge under s 304(A) rather than the road traffic legislation. Since there is no separate offence of causing death by care-less driving, negligence is the easiest of the terms to prove. Contrary to the views of the Federal Court in *Adnan b Khamis* (1972) it seems fair to say that s 304(A) is very far from being "practically redundant" in the case of fatal road accidents. However, the table says nothing about how the degrees of fault are to be distinguished. Although many of the difficulties will not arise in practice if the prosecution charges under the negligence limb of s 304(A), the conceptual difficulties are enormous. The problem is not simply that the terms used to connote blame seem out of line with the sentence ranking; more fundamentally, the degrees of fault are far too closely related for any meaningful distinctions to be drawn between them. One reason the legislature in England abolished dangerous driving was that it had proved impossible in practice to distinguish between careless and dangerous driving. In Singapore and Malaysia, the position is far worse since negligence is interposed somewhere between carelessness and dangerousness, and the term "rash-ness" (unknown in England) is also used.

Many, though not all, of the difficulties have arisen from an English statute being superimposed onto the local criminal law without suffi-cient consideration of how it would relate with existing provisions. The offences of causing death by dangerous or reckless driving were intro-duced in England primarily because juries were unwilling to convict of manslaughter in driving cases. They were, no doubt, influenced by the feeling that "there but for the grace of God go I" and by the fact that "manslaughter" is a serious offence, punishable with life imprisonment, and carries a stigma which "causing death by reckless driving" does not. These difficulties did not exist locally to the same extent because s 304(A) already existed; it is, by definition, not culpable homicide and carries a much lower penalty.

The only way out of the present morass is through legislative re-form. One key policy question is the point at which negligence be-comes a matter for the criminal and not merely the civil law. A second, with which this section concludes, is whether it is useful to perpetuate the distinction between rashness/subjective recklessness and negligence. In *Caldwell* (1982), Lord Diplock compared the case of a person who has foreseen the consequences of his conduct with that of a person who has closed his mind to an obvious risk, and concluded, very controversially: "Neither state of mind seems to me to be less blameworthy than the other." However, his reasoning has attracted little support and enormous criticism. In principle there does seem to be a distinction between the two terms and one we should take into consideration in deciding the appropriate level of criminal liability. As Glanville Williams (1983, p 261) argues:

> [C]an it possibly be said, with justice, that a driver who opens his door being momentarily forgetful of risk is "no less blameworthy" than the driver who realizes the possibility of causing injury to a cyclist whom he sees approaching but flings open his door regardless?

However, Lord Diplock also suggested that even if the distinction existed in theory, it was "fine and impracticable". It is certainly true that in many cases evidence of a high degree of negligence will be sufficient for the court to draw the inference that the accused must have realized the risk he was running. However, this will not always be so. *William Tan* (1970) shows that a high degree of *objective* negligence will not always justify a finding of *subjective* knowledge (see above, p 487); neither will negligence always lead to a finding of rashness/subjective recklessness. In *Lamb* (1967) the accused, in jest, pointed a revolver at his friend. He knew that there were bullets in the gun but thought that since they were not in the chamber opposite the barrel, they would not be fired if he pulled the trigger. Unfortunately the barrel rotated when he pulled the trigger and he shot his friend dead. As Glanville Williams (1983, p 101) points out, he was at most negligent as he did not realize the risks inherent in his conduct. The better view is, therefore, that there is a distinction in blameworthiness between rashness (or "subjective recklessness") and negligence, even though the terms may merge on the facts of some cases. Once recognized, this distinction should also, perhaps, be reflected in different statutory maximum penalties.

Chapter 22

Non-fatal offences against the person

By CMV Clarkson

In this chapter we shall be concerned with those offences where violence or force is directed against other persons, resulting in an injury or threatened injury short of death.

A. Assault

Penal Code, ss 351 and 352

351. Whoever makes any gesture or any preparation, intending or knowing it to be likely that such gesture or preparation will cause any person present to apprehend that he who makes that gesture or preparation is about to use criminal force to that person, is said to commit an assault.

Explanation–Mere words do not amount to an assault. But the words which a person uses may give to his gestures or preparations such a meaning as may make those gestures or preparations amount to an assault.

Illustrations
(a) A shakes his fist at Z, intending or knowing it to be likely that he may thereby cause Z to believe that A is about to strike Z. A has committed an assault.
(b) A begins to unloose the muzzle of a ferocious dog, intending or knowing it to be likely that he may thereby cause Z to believe that he is about to cause the dog to attack Z. A has committed an assault upon Z.
(c) A takes up a stick, saying to Z, "I will give you a beating". Here, though the words used by A could in no case amount to an assault, and though the mere gesture, unaccompanied by any other circumstances might not amount to an assault, the gesture explained by the words may amount to an assault.

352. Whoever assaults or uses criminal force to any person otherwise than on grave and sudden provocation given by that person, shall be punished with imprisonment for a term which may extend to 3 months, or with fine which may extend to $500, or with both.

[FMS Penal Code: Maximum fine is M$1,000.]

No actual force need be used for an assault. We all have a right to be free from *threats* of violence that can cause us apprehension. The object of the offence of assault is to prevent people from trying to frighten others.

499

1.   Actus reus

The *actus reus* of an assault is *making any gesture or any preparation*, for example, shaking a fist or pointing a gun. It must be a physical gesture or preparation.

(a) Significance of words

The explanation to s 351 makes it clear that *mere* words cannot amount to an assault but that words can colour gestures so as to indicate their meaning. For instance, rolling up one's sleeve is prima facie an innocent action but if accompanied by words indicating that this was being done in preparation for punching someone in the face, it would be sufficient gesture or preparation to satisfy s 351 (*Reid* v *Coker*, 1853). On the other hand, pointing a sharp knife at a person could prima facie be indicative of an assault but accompanying words, say, describing the style or design of the knife, would clearly prevent the gesture coming within s 351. In *Tuberville* v *Savage* (1669) the accused placed his hand on the hilt of his sword and told his victim: "If it were not assize-time, I would not take such language from you." This was not an assault because although placing his hand on the hilt of his sword could be a sufficient gesture, the accompanying words indicated that force was *not* going to be used.

There has been much controversy in England as to whether mere words can be sufficient to amount to an assault, the prevailing view being that they *ought* to suffice, as in certain circumstances words can be more menacing and threatening than gestures. Further, if words could not by themselves amount to an assault it would be extremely difficult to prove an assault where the accused uttered menacing verbal threats in the dark or behind the victim's back making gestures that could not be seen. It would mean that if a robber approached one saying: "I have a gun in my pocket. Give me your money or I shall kill you", there is no assault as there is no gesture or preparation. Such controversy need not detain us as s 351 is quite clear that there is no assault in such cases. However s 503 defining criminal intimidation could be used:

> Whoever threatens another with any injury to his person ... with intent to alarm that person ... commits criminal intimidation.

Under this section it is immaterial that the threat is purely verbal.

(b) Causing apprehension

There is one difficult and unresolved problem. Must the victim actually apprehend that physical force is about to be used against him? A literal reading of s 351 would clearly answer this question in the negative. The only *actus reus* requirement is that there be a physical gesture or preparation. If he makes the appropriate gesture or preparation nothing more is required. It is irrelevant whether the victim apprehends immediate physical force. The remainder of the definition in s 351 relates to *mens rea*, ie the accused must *intend* or *know* it is likely that his gestures or preparations *will cause apprehension* of immediate physical force. Accordingly, as long as the accused intends to cause apprehension, it is totally irrelevant whether he succeeds. For example, A sharpens his knife in front of B, saying "I am going to cut your arm." B is deaf and does not apprehend any physical force. According to this view A would nevertheless be liable.

This literal interpretation has not been adopted by the Indian courts and writers. In *Jashanmal Jhamatmal v Brahmanand Sarupanand* (1944) it was stated that the accused "put out his hand towards the woman in a menancing manner *so as to cause her to apprehend* that he was about to use criminal force" and this was therefore an assault. Similarly, in *Ram Singh* (1935) it was held to be an assault when the accused "came sufficiently close to the officers to raise in their minds a reasonable apprehension that actual force was likely to be used". Nelson (1983), drawing on such authorities concludes that "the gist of the offence lies in the effect which the threat creates upon the mind of the victim".

This whole approach is unfortunate in that, yet again, the Penal Code has been ignored with courts and writers simply turning to English law–under which it is well settled that the *actus reus* of an assault is *causing apprehension of immediate physical force*. With respect, the formulation adopted by s 351 is quite different from the English common law making reference to English law inappropriate.

Nevertheless, in terms of policy it must be conceded that there is perhaps a case for continuing to insist on apprehension being caused as this is the sort of readily identifiable harm with which the criminal law is rightly concerned. Under the literal interpretation criminal liability would be imposed upon those who caused no physical harm and no fear or apprehension, but who simply tried to cause such apprehension. It is the law of attempt that should be left to deal with such cases.

(c) Threat of *immediate* force

Threats of future violence are not covered by s 351. The accused must intend or know that his gesture or preparation will cause apprehension that he is *about to use* physical force.

Strictly speaking, following the above literal interpretation, this should be classified as a *mens rea* requirement as it does not matter what the victim apprehends (if anything); if the accused intends or knows that it is likely that his victim will apprehend immediate force, he is liable.

English law has the same requirement that there be a threat of immediate force but has adopted a somewhat flexible attitude in this regard which could well be followed here. For instance, in *Smith* v *Chief Superintendent, Woking Police Station* (1983) a woman was held to be assaulted when she saw the accused looking through her closed bedsitting room window at 11 pm. Although he was outside her room and still had to break the window and climb in before he could actually inflict violence upon her, it was held that the threat of force was sufficiently immediate. Under s 351 he would intend or know that she was likely to apprehend that he was "about to use" criminal force on her.

(d) Conditional threats

A problem arises if the accused makes his threat to inflict force conditional upon the victim doing or refraining from doing something. For instance, the threat could be to hit someone *if they do not keep quiet* or *if they do not hand over their money.*

HS Gour, *The Penal Law of India* (10th edn, 1983) Vol 3, 2990–2991

From the fact that the words, gesture or the preparation are intended or known to be likely to cause another to apprehend that the person uttering the words or making the gesture or the preparation *is about to use criminal force*, it follows that if the words or attitude was to use criminal force not immediately but in a certain contingency dependent upon the volition of the other, there can be no assault, though it is a threat of an assault, which is not by itself an offence. This may be illustrated by an example. A abuses B; the latter warns A that if he persisted in abusing him he should strike him. Here B's attitude may be menacing and he may be prepared and ready to strike A, but his words and gesture do not amount to an assault within the contemplation of this section inasmuch as A has no reason to apprehend that the other is about to use criminal force if he keeps his own mouth shut....

(Gour cites *Birbal Khalifa* (1903) where the accused, objecting to having his thumb print taken by a policeman, produced a *lathi* and said he would break the head of anyone who asked for his thumb print. It was held that because this threat was conditional it did not amount to an assault. Gour then cites *Cama* v *Morgan* (1864) where the defendant threatened to strike the plaintiff if he continued to be impertinent) upon which the court remarked:

... How was the plaintiff to know what a violently incensed man might or might not regard as impertinence?–a look, a gesture, a word, even silence, might be construed as such. The condition of the threat would be held fulfilled and the momentarily suspended violence would become actual criminal force. On these grounds ... we have come to the conclusion ... that the plaintiff ... had reasonable ground to apprehend that the defendant was about to use criminal force to him, and that, therefore, the acts complained of amount in law to an assault.

It is submitted that there is nothing in s 351 to dictate that such an approach should be followed and that local courts would be better advised to follow English law on this point where it is clear that a conditional threat does amount to an assault.

Glanville Williams, *Textbook of Criminal Law* (2nd edn, 1983), 175–176

Then what if one man says to another: "Be quiet or I will blow your brains out", pointing a gun at him a moment afterwards? Is this an assault?

Such a situation is clearly distinguishable from that in *Tuberville* v *Savage* (1669, see above, p 500), for there the words referred to an extraneous condition ("If it were not assize-time") which the victim knew was not fulfilled. There was, therefore, no present threat. But if the words fetter the victim's present freedom, an assault is committed.

In these cases the requirement that the threat should be immediate is qualified: it need only be a threat of force to follow immediately upon disobedience, provided that obedience is required then and there. Were it otherwise, the highwayman who says "Stand and deliver", at the same time pointing a gun, would not be guilty of an assault–a conclusion that is impossible to accept. The victim of the threat realizes that he has to regulate his movements carefully if he is to avoid being shot. Even if he decides to comply with the demand, the fear of being shot, perhaps as a result of misunderstanding by the aggressor, is not absent from his mind. Quite apart from this argument, it is a salutory rule that persons should not be allowed to constrain the conduct of others by threats of immediate physical force, and will be held guilty of assault if they attempt to do so.

2. Mens rea

The *mens rea* of an assault is clearly spelt out by s 351 itself. The accused must either:

(1) *intend* that his victim apprehend immediate physical force; or
(2) *know that it is likely* that his victim will apprehend immediate physical force.

It is thus irrelevant that the accused might be pointing a toy gun at his victim and never intending to harm him at all. As long as he intends (or knows it to be likely) to make his victim apprehensive that he will use the gun, he is liable.

B. Criminal force

Penal Code, ss 350 and 349

350. Whoever intentionally uses force to any person, without that person's consent, in order to cause the committing of any offence, or intending by the use of such force illegally to cause, or knowing it to be likely that by the use of such force he will illegally cause injury, fear or annoyance to the person to whom the force is used, is said to use criminal force to that other.

Illustrations

(a) Z is sitting in a moored boat on a river. A unfastens the moorings, and thus intentionally causes the boat to drift down the stream. Here A intentionally causes motion to Z, and he does this by disposing substances in such a manner that the motion is produced without any other act on any person's part. A has therefore intentionally used force to Z; and if he has done so without Z's consent, in order to cause the committing of any offence, or intending or knowing it to be likely that this use of force will cause injury, fear or annoyance to Z, A has used criminal force to Z.

(b) Z is riding in a chariot. A lashes Z's horses, and thereby causes them to quicken their pace. Here A has caused change of motion to Z by inducing the animals to change their motion. A has therefore used force to Z; and if A has done this without Z's consent, intending or knowing it to be likely that he may thereby injure, frighten or annoy Z, A has committed criminal force to Z.

(c) Z is riding in a carriage. A, intending to rob Z, seizes the horse and stops the carriage. Here A has caused cessation of motion to Z, and he has done this by his own bodily power. A has therefore used force to Z; and as A has acted thus intentionally without Z's consent, in order to cause the commission of an offence, A has used criminal force to Z.

(d) A intentionally pushes against Z in the street. Here A has by his own bodily power moved his own person so as to bring it into contact with Z. He has therefore intentionally used force to Z, and if he has done so without Z's consent, intending or knowing it to be likely that he may thereby injure, frighten or annoy Z, he has used criminal force to Z.

(e) A throws a stone, intending or knowing it to be likely that the stone will be thus brought into contact with Z, or with Z's clothes, or with something carried by Z, or that it will strike water and dash up the water against Z's clothes, or something carried by Z. Here if the throwing of the stone produces the effect of causing any substance to come into contact with Z, or Z's clothes, A has used force to Z; and if he did so without Z's consent, intending thereby to injure, frighten or annoy Z, he has used criminal force to Z.

(f) A intentionally pulls up a woman's veil. Here A intentionally uses force to her; and if he does so without her consent, intending or knowing it to be likely that he may thereby injure, frighten or annoy her, he has used criminal force to her.

(g) Z is bathing. A pours into the bath water which he knows to be boiling. Here A intentionally by his own bodily power causes such motion in the boiling water as brings that water into contact with Z, or with other water so situated that such contact must affect Z's sense of feeling; A has therefore intentionally used force to Z; and if he has done this without Z's consent, intending or knowing it to be likely that he may thereby cause injury, fear or annoyance to Z, A has used criminal force.

(h) A incites a dog to spring upon Z, without Z's consent. Here, if A intends to cause injury, fear or annoyance to Z, he uses criminal force to Z.

(i) A, a schoolmaster, in the reasonable exercise of his discretion as master, flogs Z, one of his scholars. A does not use criminal force to Z because, although A intends to cause fear and annoyance, he does not use force illegally.

349. A person is said to use force to another if he causes motion, change of motion, or cessation of motion to that other, or if he causes to any substance such motion, or change of motion, or cessation of motion as brings that substance into contact with any part of that other's body, or with anything which that other is wearing or carrying, or with anything so situated that such contact affects that other's sense of feeling:

Provided that the person causing the motion, or change of motion, or cessation of motion, causes that motion, change of motion, or cessation of motion in one of the following 3 ways:

(a) by his own bodily power;
(b) by disposing any substance in such a manner that the motion, or change or cessation of motion, takes place without any further act on his part, or on the part of any other person;
(c) by inducing any animal to move, to change its motion, or to cease to move.

Under s 352 the maximum punishment for this offence is the same as for an assault, namely, three months' imprisonment and/or a fine of $500 (Singapore) or M$1,000 (Malaysia).

1. Actus reus

The *actus reus* of criminal force is the use of force to any person without that person's consent:

(a) Force

(i) Elements
The convoluted definition of force in s 349 involves:

(1) either causing motion, change of motion or cessation of motion (this phrase will be hereafter described as "motion, etc");
or causing such motion, etc to any "substance" so as to bring it into contact with the other's body (or anything they are wearing or carrying or that is so situated that such contact affects their sense of feeling);
and
(2) such motion, etc must be caused by one of the three methods specified by the proviso to s 349:

    (a) by his own bodily power (eg Illustration (d)), or
    (b) by disposing substances so as to cause motion, etc without any further act on the part of either party (eg Illustration (a)), or
    (c) by inducing any animal to move, etc (eg Illustration (h)).

Ratanlal and Dhirajlal (1987) assert that this definition is "so wide as to include force of almost every description of which a person is the ultimate object". It clearly is wide as can be seen by the illustrations covering a variety of human activity not immediately associated in the lay mind with "force". In *Jai Ram* (1914) it was held that raising a stick to hit another person was criminal force if it caused the other to flee to save himself or even just to move slightly to avoid being struck. This is causing motion or a change of motion.

Chandrika Sao and Hazari Lal v State of Bihar (1964) 1 SCJ 116 (SC, India)

Singh, a tax inspector, entered a shop to inspect its books. He took up two sets of account books and started examining them. The appellant snatched both books away from him.

Mudholkar J: By snatching away the books which Mr Singh was holding the appellant necessarily caused a jerk to the hand or hands of Mr Singh in which he was holding the books. His act, therefore, may be said to have caused motion to Mr Singh's hand or hands. Further, the natural effect of snatching the books from the hand or hands of Mr Singh would be to affect the sense of feeling of the hand or hands of Mr Singh. We have, therefore, no doubt that the action of the appellant amounts to use of force as contemplated by s 349, Indian Penal Code.

[The learned judge went on to hold that the force had been intentionally caused and caused, at least, annoyance to Mr Singh.]

(ii) Unlawful touching

Despite its apparently all-embracing scope, close analysis of the archaic formulation employed by s 349 reveals a major problem. It appears not to cover cases of unlawful human touching which do not cause motion, etc. (The English crime of battery exists precisely to cover such cases of unlawful touching.) If a man places his hand or other part of his anatomy on a more intimate part of a woman's body, is this a use of criminal force if the woman does not move (ie no motion, etc)? In such a case not only is there no motion, etc but further examining the second portion of the main paragraph of s 349, it is stretching the English language to assert that the accused has brought a "substance" into contact with a part of the woman's body. Can a hand legitimately be described as a "substance"?

This literal interpretation which results in no liability in such cases of unlawful touching must be rejected. There could be little sense in a law that held an accused liable for touching a woman with a feather but not liable for rubbing his hand against her. Even more preposterous would be a law that made him liable if she moved away upon contact but exempted him from liability if the woman, frozen to the spot in terror, failed to move. It is clear that the drafters of the Indian Penal Code intended such unlawful touchings to be covered. Macaulay (1837) thought liability should be imposed for placing an unsolicited arm around a woman. Illustration (d) to s 350, while probably involving some change of motion to the victim is not framed with this as a prerequisite; it simply speaks of A bringing "his own person" into contact with Z. Illustration (f) is even clearer in suggesting that any form of unlawful touching is sufficient. There are no authorities on the point and perhaps this is not surprising. Most persons who are touched in a manner to which they object are going to move in some way–either to escape, to push the toucher away or whatever. Such motion would bring the case within s 349. In cases where the person touched does not move at all, it is going to be difficult for the prosecution to prove beyond reasonable doubt that there was no consent. This proposal would not widen the law unacceptably. The role of s 95 must be recalled. There will be no criminal liability in cases where the force used only amounts to "slight harm".

(iii) Causing hurt

Many of the classic instances of criminal force, for example, pushing someone over or throwing a stone which strikes them, will inevitably, in addition to causing motion, etc, also cause some bodily pain, albeit of a minor nature. It will be seen shortly (p 512) that causing bodily pain is sufficient to satisfy the *actus reus* of the more serious offence of voluntarily causing hurt contrary to s 321 of the Penal Code. This raises an important question. Are these two offences mutually exclusive or is it simply that the prosecutor has a discretion to charge under either, presumably reserving s 321 for cases where a more serious physical harm is caused?

HS Gour, *The Penal Law of India* (10th edn, 1983) Vol 3, 2985

The difference between the two offences is undoubtedly artificial, but if the illustrations appended ... are any indication to the intention of the Legislature, there can be no doubt that the two offences must be held to be mutually exclusive, and therefore, whenever there is a causing of bodily pain it is necessarily a case of hurt and therefore as necessarily (sic) it cannot be a case of criminal force or assault.

There is little merit in this suggestion which even Gour (1983, Vol 3) himself concedes is not accepted by the Indian courts. There might be many cases where a greater physical harm was caused, say, hurt, grievous hurt or even death but the accused might not have had the requisite *mens rea* of such offence. If it is proven that he caused criminal force (the *actus reus*) and had the requisite *mens rea* under s 350, it is difficult to understand the argument that he should be acquitted on the ground that he in fact caused a worse injury than mere force. Thus in *Jai Dayal*

(1876) the accused hit the victim in the course of a quarrel. The victim had an enlarged spleen and consequently died from the blow. The accused had no knowledge of the victim's condition. He could not be convicted of a homicide offence or causing grievous hurt because he lacked the *mens rea* of such offences. He was accordingly convicted of the offence for which he clearly did have *mens rea*, namely, using criminal force contrary to s 350.

(b) "To any person"

The force must be directed "to any person". Thus no offence of criminal force was committed when the lock of a house was broken in the owner's absence (*Bihari Lal*, 1934), nor when the accused removed a ladder thereby detaining the victim on the roof of the house (*Telapolo Sabbad*, 1884).

(c) "Without that person's consent"

There is no offence if the victim consents to the application of force. This consent may be express or implied. In modern conditions where people jostle in queues or run along corridors to get to lectures in time, it is inevitable that force will be applied to those persons pushed or shoved aside. However, this is not criminal force as persons engaged in pursuits wherein they are liable to be pushed (eg catching a bus in a rush hour) are deemed to have consented to the risk of force. It is clear, however, that one is only deemed to have consented to that force which can be reasonably expected in the circumstances. Thus if an accused grabs his victim's arm and roughly pulls him out of the bus queue, there will clearly be no implied consent.

2.   Mens rea

There is a two-fold requirement to be satisfied here:

(a) Intentional use of force

The requisite force (as defined above) must have been intentionally inflicted. Thus it is not enough that the force was accidentally or recklessly inflicted. Indeed, s 350 is not satisfied by proof that the accused knew his actions were likely to cause force. Hence it would not be enough if the accused threw a stone in the general direction of his victim even if he thought it probable that he would hit him. (For discussion of meaning of intention, see ch 3.)

(b) Ulterior purpose

The force must have been intentionally inflicted in order to commit any offence or to cause injury, fear or annoyance.

(i) Committing any offence

If an accused uses force against a woman, say, pushes her over, in order to commit an offence, say, rape, he will have satisfied the *mens rea* requirement of s 350. Of course, this section is only likely to be used in those cases where the ultimate offence has not in fact been committed, or where the accused has not come sufficiently close for there to be attempt liability (see ch 14).

The meaning of "offence" is defined in s 40 of the Penal Code and for purposes of s 350 means an offence punishable under the Penal Code. Accordingly, using force to commit a non-Penal Code offence will not satisfy this requirement.

(ii) Causing injury, fear or annoyance

The force must alternatively have been inflicted with:

(1) the *intention* of thereby illegally causing injury, fear or annoyance; or
(2) knowledge of thereby being likely illegally to cause injury, fear or annoyance.
     ("Illegal" is defined in s 43 and "injury" in s 44 of the Penal Code.)

Gour (1983, Vol 3) asserts that "the section is somewhat inaccurately drawn up and would not bear too close a scrutiny" because all that is required is that the accused have the intention or knowledge of causing the ulterior object, it being irrelevant whether it actually be caused. He asserts that while it is not expressly stated, s 350 must be understood as requiring *the result* of injury, fear or annoyance to be proved. He illustrates this:

> If one intends to push another with an evil mind, but the other takes it in good part, there is no offence whatever the injury, fear or annoyance the act may be calculated to cause in the mind of a bystander (p 2984).

With respect, there is no warrant for such a conclusion. It would be most odd that s 349 should provide such a detailed and complex definition of force if that was only a minor part of the *actus reus*, the essence of the offence being proof of injury, fear or annoyance. Such offences requiring proof of a *mens rea* extending beyond the *actus reus* (known as crimes of "specific intent" by English law) are well known to the common law and are consistent with the general philosophy underlying the Penal Code–one that emphasizes the importance of *mens rea* more than the significance of causing harm. (Again, it should be noted that it is an unlikely scenario where the victim sustains no injury, with its wide definition under s 44, or feels no fear or annoyance and yet satisfies the *actus reus* requirement of not consenting to the force. Normally if motion, etc does not bother us sufficiently to cause injury, fear or annoyance we would be consenting to the force or would probably be deemed to so consent.)

C. Aggravated assault or criminal force

Sections 353–357 of the Penal Code contain offences involving aggravated assaults or use of criminal force, each offence carrying a heavier penalty than simple assault or criminal force.

Section	Offence	Punishment
353	Assault or using criminal force against a public servant in the execution of his duties.	2 years and/or fine.
354	Assault or using criminal force to outrage modesty.	2 years or fine or caning (or any two of these).
[354A]	[Singapore: Aggravated species of s 354 where (1) hurt, etc caused or (2) where offence committed in a lift or against any person under 14 years of age.]	(1) 2–10 years plus caning. (2) 3–10 years plus caning.
355	Assault or using criminal force with intent to dishonour.	2 years and/or fine.
356	Assault or criminal force during theft.	1–7 years and/or caning. [FMS Penal Code: 2 years and/or fine.]
357	Assault or criminal force during wrongful confinement.	1 year or $1,000 fine or both. [FMS Penal Code: Amount of maximum fine is M$2,000.]

[**Note**: Periods such as two to ten years indicate minimum and maximum periods of imprisonment. All other periods, eg two years, indicate a maximum period of imprisonment available for the crime.]

D. Mitigated assault or criminal force

Penal Code, s 358

Whoever assaults or uses criminal force to any person on grave and sudden provocation given by that person, shall be punished with imprisonment for a term which may extend to one month, or with fine which may extend to $200, or with both.

[FMS Penal Code: maximum fine is M$400.]

Explanation–This section is subject to the same explanation as s 352.

Penal Code, s 352

Explanation–Grave and sudden provocation will not mitigate the punishment for an offence under this section, if the provocation is sought or voluntarily provoked by the offender as an excuse for the offence; or

if the provocation is given by anything done in obedience to the law or by a public servant in the lawful exercise of the powers of such public servant; or

if the provocation is given by anything done in the lawful exercise of the right of private defence.

Whether the provocation was grave and sudden enough to mitigate the offence, is a question of fact.

Those who cause harm to others under the influence of grave and sudden provocation are not justified in their actions nor are they to be fully excused. Nevertheless, they are regarded as less blameworthy than their counterparts who cause the same harm but without any excuse. Accordingly, the law regards such persons as *partially excused* and a lesser level of criminal liability with lesser punishment is imposed. (See further ch 4.)

In ch 20 there was a detailed examination of the partial excuse of provocation which had the effect of reducing liability from murder to culpable homicide not amounting to murder. The real significance of the special exception there is that if successfully established the accused escapes the mandatory death penalty. The partial excuse is far less important if facing a charge of assault or criminal force because the judge has a discretion as to sentence and can take provocation into account at the sentencing stage even if all the elements of the partial excuse have not been made out.

The explanation to s 352 adopts the same general principles as Exception 1 to s 300 and local courts will no doubt read in the same reasonable proportion and reasonable man tests. (See ch 20.) There are, however, two important differences in the formulation adopted by the explanation to s 352. First, there is no express reference to the accused's subjective loss of self-control. If read literally this might appear to mean that the offence would be mitigated where there *was* grave and

512 Non-fatal offences against the person

sudden provocation even though the accused actually managed to retain his self-control and was thus not himself provoked. However, it seems highly unlikely that courts would adopt such an interpretation. The better view would be to read in the requirement of loss of self-control into the words "grave and sudden". The second difference between the explanation to s 352 and the exception to s 300 concerns those cases where the assault or criminal force is directed at third parties who did not themselves give the provocation. Exception 1 to s 300 allows the partial defence if the accused causes the death of the provoker or of any other person by mistake or accident. Under the explanation to s 352 it would appear that there can only be mitigation where the accused has assaulted or used criminal force against the person who gave the provocation and not otherwise. The wording does not appear to allow any flexibility in cases involving third parties.

E. Hurt

Penal Code, ss 321, 319 and 323

321. Whoever does any act with the intention of thereby causing hurt to any person, or with the knowledge that he is likely thereby to cause hurt to any person, and does thereby cause hurt to any person, is said "voluntarily to cause hurt".

319. Whoever causes bodily pain, disease or infirmity to any person is said to cause hurt.

323. Whoever, except in the case provided for by section 334 (provocation), voluntarily causes hurt, shall be punished with imprisonment for a term which may extend to one year, or with a fine which may extend to $1,000, or with both.

[FMS Penal Code: Maximum fine is M$2,000.]

The *actus reus* of this offence is causing:

(1) bodily pain or
(2) disease or
(3) infirmity
to any person.

The *mens rea* is:

(1) the intention of causing hurt, or
(2) knowledge that hurt to any person is likely.

These principles are clearly exemplified in the following two Indian cases.

Jashanmal Jhamatmal v Brahmanand Sarupanand AIR (1944) Sind 19 (HC, Sind, India)

The accused, trying to get tenants to leave a building, suddenly confronted a woman in the dark at the bottom of a staircase and uttered a piercing shout, "Haoo" and extended his arm at the woman pointing a pistol at her. The woman collapsed from nervous shock. A doctor found her in a state of hysteria and she was seriously ill from nervous shock for some considerable time afterwards.

O'Sullivan J: There is nothing in ... (s 319) to suggest that the hurt should be caused by direct physical contact between the accused and his victim and we consider it would be unreasonable to interpret the definition in ... (such a) manner.... The matter seems to be placed beyond any doubt by the remarks of the learned Law Commissioners who drafted s 319, to the following effect:

> "... [B]odily hurt may be caused by many acts which are not assaults. A person, for example, who mixes a deleterious poison, and places it on the table of another; a person who conceals a scythe in the grass on which another is in the habit of walking; a person who digs a pit in a public path, intending that another may fall into it, may cause serious hurt...."

The examples ... may, we consider, be extended to cases where serious mental derangement is caused by some voluntary act. It would be ridiculous to say for instance that a person who deliberately set out to cause shock to somebody with a weak heart and succeeded in doing so has not caused hurt; likewise obviously hurt would be likely to be caused to a nervous child, were a person to array himself in a white sheet and suddenly, without warning, spring upon that child on a dark night. Such an act might well cause the victim permanent mental derangement....

[On further inquiry to the District Magistrate it was there] pointed out that:

> "no offence can be held to have been committed, unless it can be proved that the accused did an act with the intention of causing hurt or with the knowledge that he was likely to cause hurt".

Having come to this conclusion he went on to find that:

> "the most that could be said of his action was that he merely wished to frighten the woman or annoy her so that the complainant might be induced to remove from the compound in which he was living"....

The District Magistrate was correct in his assumption that it was necessary to prove that the accused did the act complained of with the intention of causing hurt or with the knowledge that he was likely to cause hurt, but we consider that assuming the prosecution case to be substantially true, more than a mere intention to annoy is to be inferred. Obviously if the facts are well founded, the intention must have been so thoroughly to frighten the woman as to cause her to vacate the premises. If this object was to be served, the scheme of the accused must have been to present himself in the dark before the woman in a sudden and horrifying manner, the inevitable consequence of which would be a sharp shock to the nervous system.... Clearly in order to induce the woman to vacate the premises sufficient reaction upon her nervous system was necessary and the intention must have been to induce in her a sufficient state of fright or hysteria to serve the accused's purpose....

The duration of this state of mental infirmity would be immaterial. Infirmity denotes an unsound or unhealthy state of the body or mind and clearly a state of temporary mental impairment or hysteria or terror would constitute infirmity.... We think therefore if the facts are true, the accused must be deemed to have intended to cause hurt to the woman, and the question whether the hurt was simple or grievous would be dependent on the medical evidence.

Discharge set aside

Manzoor Ahmad v State of Allahabad (1984) 21 ACC 406 (HC, Allahabad, India)

The accused and the 15-year-old victim had an argument. When the boy complained of a headache the accused gave him a glass of milk and added some copper sulphate saying that it was an effective medicine for headaches. Shortly afterwards the boy collapsed; he then vomited and was admitted to hospital for a stomach-wash. The accused was convicted of causing hurt with a poison contrary to s 328 of the Penal Code (see below, p 515) and appealed.

RK Shukla J: But the question remains whether it can be said that the accused knew it to be likely that he will thereby cause hurt to the complainant. Copper Sulphate is a dangerous poison and everybody knows that it is dangerous to life. A person of the age of the appellant must be presume to know that such drug is poisonous.... Under these circumstances, he must be presumed at least to know that it is likely that he will thereby cause hurt to the complainant. The word "hurt" is defined in s 319 IPC as meaning either bodily pain or disease or infirmity to any person. The bodily pain or infirmity may be either permanent or temporary. If a person by the administration of Copper Sulphate is thrown into unconsciousness, vomiting with the possible risk of his life by becoming unconscious for the time being, it is clear that both bodily pain and infirmity are caused. Infirmity has been interpreted ... in *Anis Beg* (1924) as:

> "... inability of an organ to perform its normal function which may either be temporary or permanent...."

I respectfully agree with the above interpretation of infirmity and hold that both bodily pain and infirmity were caused to the complainant by the appellant. It was the grace of God that the condition of the complainant did not deteriorate further and he was saved. In these circumstances, there can be no doubt that the appellant must be deemed to have had knowledge that administering Copper Sulphate was likely to cause hurt to the complainant....

The learned counsel for the appellant relying on the case of *Mrs Veeda Menezes v Yusuf Khan Haji Ibrahim Khan* (1966) urged that it is clear from medical evidence that the condition of the complainant was normal and there was no risk for his life, therefore, this offence will be covered under s 95 IPC. Hence, the appellant has committed no offence. There is no doubt that if the harm is so light that no person of ordinary sense and temper would complain of it, it is excluded by s 95 IPC. The cases of administering poisonous drug like Copper Sulphate to a child of 15 years which caused vomiting green colour, loose motions and made his tongue moisted, will certainly come within the definition of hurt ... [and] it cannot be said that this is such a harm which can be ignored following the above mentioned decision of the Supreme Court. There is no mention of any illustration of poisoning in that case. On the facts and circumstances of this case, I am fully satisfied that this is not such a case which can be ignored under s 95 IPC.

Appeal dismissed

F. Aggravated hurt

Although the injury may be similar the offence and punishment is aggravated in certain specified circumstances where the accused has caused the hurt in a certain manner (eg with a dangerous weapon), or to a particular victim (eg to a public servant in the exercise of his duties), or with a particular specific intent (eg to extort property). The following is a brief outline of these offences.

Section	Offence	Punishment
324	Causing hurt by dangerous weapons or means.	5 years (or fine or caning). [FMS Penal Code: 3 years (or fine or whipping).]
327	Causing hurt to extort property or to constrain to an illegal act.	10 years (and liable to fine or caning).
328	Administering poison with (a) intent to cause hurt, or (b) intent to commit an offence, or (c) knowing hurt is likely.	10 years (and liable to fine).
330	Causing hurt to extort confession or to compel restoration of property.	7 years (and liable to fine).
332	Causing hurt to public servant in discharge of his duty.	5 years (or fine or caning). [FMS Penal Code: 3 years or fine.]

G. Mitigated hurt

Penal Code, s 334

Whoever voluntarily causes hurt on grave and sudden provocation, if he neither intends nor knows himself to be likely to cause hurt to any person other than the person who gave the provocation, shall be punished with imprisonment for a term which may extend to one month, or with fine which may extend to $500, or with both.

[FMS Penal Code: Maximun fine is M$1,000.]

Penal Code, s 335

Explanation–Sections 334 and 335 are subject to the same provisos as exception 1 of s 300.

The test of provocation is thus almost the same as that in Exception 1 to s 300 and is likely to be interpreted in the same manner (eg subjective provocation will be required and a reasonable man test imposed–see above, pp 436–452).

The wording here does, however, differ in one respect from that employed in Exception 1 to s 300. Exception 1 to s 300 allows the provocation defence if the accused causes the death of the provoker or of *any other person by mistake or accident*. Section 334, on the other hand, allows the partial defence provided the accused *neither intended or knew himself to be likely* to cause hurt. Of course, most people who do not intend or know that a result is likely will be held to have acted by mistake or accident and thus generally the result would be the same under either formulation. However, in one situation there could be a material distinction between the two formulations. When a third party is killed Exception 1 requires the accused to act "by mistake or accident". This means (by virtue of ss 79 and 80–see above, pp 186–188; 194–196) that the accused must exercise due care and attention. Thus an accused who is negligent with respect to the death of a third party will be denied the defence of provocation under Exception 1, but if he only causes hurt to the third party he will be allowed the partial defence. This differential approach to innocent third parties does seem reasonable. A stricter test should be required under Exception 1 as there the innocent third party has been *killed* as opposed to merely being *hurt* under s 334.

It is interesting to note that the maximum prison term here is one month's imprisonment. This is the same as that available for assault or criminal force on provocation (s 358). When there is no provocation the greater harm (and *mens rea*) involved in causing hurt is felt to justify a maximum prison term of one year, compared to three months for assault or criminal force. One can only speculate as to why this respective weighting to harm and blameworthiness should have been abandoned in cases of provocation.

Finally, the same observations that were made earlier with respect to s 358 are applicable. Given that the penalty for causing hurt contrary to s 323 is only a maximum penalty (unlike the fixed penalty for murder) and thus any case of provocation could be dealt with more leniently at the sentencing stage, one must question whether s 334 serves any useful purpose at all.

H. Grievous hurt

Penal Code, ss 322, 320 and 325

322. Whoever voluntarily causes hurt, if the hurt which he intends to cause or knows himself to be likely to cause is grievous hurt, and if the hurt which he causes is grievous hurt, is said "voluntarily to cause grievous hurt".

Explanation–A person is not said voluntarily to cause grievous hurt except when he both causes grievous hurt and intends or knows himself to be likely to cause grievous hurt. But he is said voluntarily to cause grievous hurt if, intending or knowing himself to be likely to cause grievous hurt of one kind, he actually causes grievous hurt of another kind.

Illustration

A, intending or knowing himself to be likely permanently to disfigure Z's face, gives Z a blow which does not permanently disfigure Z's face but which causes Z to suffer severe pain for the space of 20 days. A has voluntarily caused grievous hurt.

320. The following kinds of hurt only are designated as "grievous":
(a) emasculation;
(b) permanent privation of the sight of either eye;
(c) permanent privation of the hearing of either ear;
(d) privation of any member or joint;
(e) destruction or permanent impairing of the powers of any member or joint;
(f) permanent disfiguration of the head or face;
(g) fracture or dislocation of a bone;
(h) any hurt which endangers life, or which causes the sufferer to be, during the space of 20 days, in severe bodily pain, or unable to follow his ordinary pursuits.

325. Whoever, except in the case provided for by s 335 (provocation), voluntarily causes grievous hurt, shall be punished with imprisonment for a term which may extend to 7 years, and shall also be liable to fine or to caning.

[FMS Penal Code: Whipping is not an option.]

1. Actus reus

The accused must cause grievous hurt. This involves proof of the following:

(1) that the actions of the accused *caused* the grievous hurt. See ch 18.

(2) that the hurt caused must be *grievous* hurt.

What is meant by "grievous" hurt? Most legal systems choose to mark out those cases where serious injury is caused as opposed to lesser injury. The problem is how this demarcation should be made. English law, for instance, draws a distinction between actual bodily harm and grievous bodily harm but refuses to define these terms leaving it entirely to the jury to determine as a matter of fact the level of injury in any particular case. The Penal Code, on the other hand, enumerates specific harms and designates them "grievous". While this might make for a greater degree of certainty, there is the danger that one's list of grievous hurts might be over-inclusive. Particularly with the advances in medical science since the Penal Code was drafted, the list could include injuries that used to be perceived as very serious, but are now mere temporary injuries easily healed and leaving no trace of the injuries.

Section 320 lists the following kinds of hurt as "grievous":

(a) Emasculation

HS Gour, *The Penal Law of India* (10th edn, 1983) Vol 3 s 2837

Emasculation ... is depriving a man of his virility. It is unsexing the man. Emasculation naturally applies only to man, and the clause was inserted to counteract the practice common in this country for women to squeeze men's testicles on the slightest provocation.... It was suggested that other injuries to the *membera private*, falling short of emasculation, should also be treated as grievous as the act should be repressed by severe penalties, as peculiarly offensive to the feelings of the party injured, and most dangerous–the slightest excess causing the severest suffering. But the Law Commissioners considered the proposed change unnecessary.... Emasculation may be caused in a variety of ways. It may be caused by inflicting such injury to the scrotum of a person as has the effect of rendering him impotent. The impotency caused must be permanent, and not merely temporary and curable....

(b) Permanent privation of sight of either eye

"Privation" means loss or absence. It is thus grievous hurt to cause someone permanently to lose the sight of either eye. This may be achieved by causing blindness (eg by throwing chemicals at a person's eye) or by gouging out the entire eye. Gour (1983) states that "the injury is grievous, both because it deprives a man of an organ of sight, as also because it disfigures him for life".

(c) Permanent privation of hearing of either ear

Causing permanent deafness is similarly classified as a form of grievous hurt.

(d) Privation of any member or joint

Nelson, *The Indian Penal Code* (7th edn, 1983), 1201–1202

The term "member" means nothing more than an organ or a limb, being a part of a man, capable of performing a distinct office. As such, it includes eyes, ears, nose, mouth, hands, feet and, in fact, all distinct parts of the human body designed to perform a distinct office. A "joint" is a place where two or more bones or muscles join. So, there are well known joints in human anatomy at the lower jaw, shoulder, elbow, wrist thumb, hip, knee and great toe.

Causing a person to lose permanently the use of such a limb or joint can be a serious crippling disability, but can, say in the loss of a little finger, have less disabling consequences. Such differences can of course be reflected in the penalty imposed.

(e) Destruction or permanent impairing of powers of any member or joint

Here, any permanent impairment short of privation will suffice. Any injury that diminishes the usefulness of a member or a joint will suffice even if not a major injury in the sense of substantially impairing one's powers.

(f) Permanent disfiguration of head or face

There must be some form of external injury which detracts from the victim's personal appearance. The formulation here is wide. The disfiguration need not be substantial as long as it is permanent. This means that any injury leaving a minor scar would be included.

(g) Fracture or dislocation of bone

The term "fracture" means breaking. With many bones there is little problem in ascertaining whether they are broken. More difficult, however, is the skull bone. How serious must an injury to the skull be for it to be deemed a fracture.

An earlier line of authority had held that for a fracture there should be a break in the bone and that with skull bones it was not sufficient that there was merely a crack but the crack had to extend from the outer surface of the skull to the inner surface. This view was, however, rejected by the Indian Supreme Court in *Naib Singh* (1986) which cited the earlier Supreme Court decision of *Horilal* (1970) with approval:

> It is not necessary that a bone should be cut through and through or that the crack must extend from the outer to the inner surface or that there should be displacement of any fragment of the bone. If there is a break by cutting or splintering of the bone or there is a rupture or fissure of it, it would amount to a fracture within the meaning of cl 7 of s 320. What we have to see is whether the cuts in the bones noticed in the injury report are only superficial or do they effect a break in them.

A "dislocation" in this context means a displacement or putting out of joint of a bone, eg pulling a bone out of its socket.

It is interesting to note that fractured or dislocated bones need cause no lasting injury; indeed, they can often be quickly cured. Such injuries can only be rationalized today as grievous on the ground that they will often be associated with intense pain. (The Indian Penal Code is even wider in that cl 7 extends to a fracture or dislocation of a bone *or tooth*.)

(h) This clause has three subdivisions:

(i) Any hurt which endangers life

Ramla v State of Rajasthan (1963) 1 Cri LJ 387 (HC, Rajasthan, India)

DS Dave J: [A]n injury may be grievous only if it "endangers life". This means that the injury which is actually found should itself be such that it may put the life of the injured in danger. A simple injury cannot be called grievous simply because it happens to be caused on a vital part of the body, unless the nature and dimensions of the injury or its effect are such that in the opinion of the doctor it actually endangers the life of the victim.

Despite the above dictum it is clear that Indian courts have been strongly influenced by the actual organ injured. For instance, injuries to the head and neck virtually raise a persumption of endangering life. In *Vasu Dev* (1982) the court's whole inquiry was to whether the abdomen was a vital part of the human body. Having concluded it was, the court was easily able to hold that the particular injury, "having regard to the delicate nature of the parts which were injured", was one that endangered life.

It should be borne in mind that persons can be convicted of an offence contrary to s 325 even though the victim has in fact died. If the prosecution is unable to prove the requisite *mens rea* under s 300 or 299 it might prefer to proceed under s 325 rather than s 304A because of the relatively light maximum sentence available for the latter. The line, however, between culpable homicide not amounting to murder and grievous hurt is extremely thin. Under s 299 it must be established that there is such bodily injury as is likely to cause death, while s 325 requires that there be such injuries as endanger life. An injury that endangers life is one that raises a definite and identifiable risk of death. Such risk need not, however, be sufficiently great as to amount to a *likelihood* of death.

(ii)   Any hurt which causes the sufferer to be, during space of 20 days, in severe bodily pain

This is one of the most difficult heads of grievous hurt to establish with the onus on the prosecution not only to establish that the victim was in bodily pain for 20 days, but that that pain was "severe". Most injuries capable of causing such prolonged and intense pain would probably qualify more easily under one of the other heads of grievous hurt–perhaps explaining the paucity of cases on this point.

(iii) Any hurt which causes the sufferer to be, during space of 20 days, unable to follow his ordinary pursuits

In *Sahat* v *Hajee Brahim* (1888) it was held that confinement in hospital for treatment raised a presumption that the sufferer was unable to follow his ordinary pursuits for the duration of his confinement. Subsequent Indian cases have, however, emphasized that there is no such presumption. Persons may be easily capable of following their ordinary pursuits but choose to remain in hospital to convalesce fully or because the standard of care and food there may well be higher than at home (*Samaj*, 1969). Such persons are clearly not "unable" to follow their normal pursuits. The onus is on the prosecution to *prove* inability to follow ordinary pursuits; proof of hospitalization for 20 days is not enough (*Sachidanand Pathak*, 1983).

In *Mahinder Singh* (1925) it was held that this head could not be applied if the victim died within the 20-day period. To be unable to follow one's ordinary pursuits for 20 days presupposes that one is alive for such a period!

2. Mens rea

Section 322 makes it clear that the accused must either intend to cause grievous hurt or know himself to be likely to cause grievous hurt. The explanation adds that it is not necessary for the accused to cause the same type of grievous hurt as intended. Thus he would be liable if intending a permanent disfiguration of the head or face he caused a fracture or dislocation of a bone.

I. Aggravated grievous hurt

As was the case with hurt, in certain circumstances when grievous hurt is caused the offence becomes aggravated. The following is a brief outline of these offences:

Section	Offence	Punishment
326	Causing grievous hurt by dangerous weapons or means.	Life imprisonment or 10 years. [FMS Penal Code: 20 years (and liable to fine or caning).]

329	Causing grievous hurt to extort property or to constrain to an illegal act.	Life imprisonment or 10 years. [FMS Penal Code: 20 years (and liable to fine or caning).]
331	Causing grievous hurt to extort confession or to compel restoration of property.	10 years (and liable to fine or caning). [FMS Penal Code: whipping not an option.]
333	Causing grievous hurt to public servant in discharge of his duty.	10 years (and liable to fine or caning). [FMS Penal Code: Whipping not an option.]

J.   Mitigated grievous hurt

Penal Code, s 335

Whoever voluntarily causes grievous hurt on grave and sudden provocation, if he neither intends nor knows himself to be likely to cause grievous hurt to any person other than the person who gave the provocation, shall be punished with imprisonment for a term which may extend to 4 years, or with fine which may extend to $2,000, or with both.

[FMS Penal Code: Maximum fine is M$4,000.]

Explanation–Sections 334 and 335 are subject to the same provisos as Exception 1 of s 300.

This section is phrased in similar manner to s 334 (causing hurt on provocation) and is subject to the same interpretation and comment– see above, pp 515–516. There is, however, one material difference. We saw that the punishment for causing hurt on provocation was the same as for an assault or using criminal force on provocation, suggesting that the focus was not on the degree of harm caused but on the causing of some harm (any harm) while provoked. This thinking has been clearly rejected by s 335. Where the result is *grievous* hurt on provocation, the maximum prison term becomes one that reflects the gravity of the harm, namely, four years.

K.   Non-fatal offences by rash or negligent act

Penal Code, ss 336–338

336.   Whoever does any act so rashly or negligently as to endanger human life or the personal safety of others, shall be punished with imprisonment for a term which may extend to 3 months, or with fine which may extend to $250, or with both.

[FMS Penal Code: Maximum fine is M$500.]

337. Whoever causes hurt to any person by doing any act so rashly or negligently as to endanger human life or the personal safety of others, shall be punished with imprisonment for a term which may extend to 6 months, or with fine which may extend to $500, or with both.

[FMS Penal Code: Maximum fine is M$1,000.]

338. Whoever causes grievous hurt to any person by doing any act so rashly or negligently as to endanger human life or the personal safety of others, shall be punished with imprisonment for a term which may extend to 2 years, or with fine which may extend to $1,000, or with both.

[FMS Penal Code: Maximum fine is M$2,000.]

What is meant by the terms "rashly or negligently"? The meaning of these terms was fully discussed in ch 21 and will not be repeated here on the basis that it has been held that negligence, at any rate, bears the same meaning throughout the Penal Code.

Anthonysamy v PP (1956) 22 MLJ 247 (HC, KL, Malaya)

(The facts are set out above, p 486.)

Buhagiar J: The word "negligence" must be given the same meaning consistently throughout the Penal Code. Now on examination of the various sections where this word appears, eg ss 336, 268, 279, 282 it is apparent that the word cannot have the meaning of "gross negligence".... For the purposes of these sections no higher degree of negligence is required than that in civil matters. The gravity of these offences, for which the law provides different degrees of punishment depends on the consequences or possible consequences of the negligent or rash act.

The concept "rashness" also bears the same meaning throughout the Penal Code in the sense that it requires the accused himself to recognize the risks, ie foresee the possibility of the harmful consequence occurring. (See ch 21 for full discussion.)

However, while there was controversy as to what it was precisely that the accused had to foresee for purposes of s 304A (death or mere injury see p 477), ss 336–338 spell out this requirement clearly. The act must be rash as to human life or the personal safety of others. This means that the accused must himself have recognized that his actions would involve danger to human life or personal safety.

Part VII

Property offences

Chapter 23

Theft

By KL Koh

A. Introduction

Penal Code, ss 378–382

378. Whoever, intending to take dishonestly any movable property out of the possession of any person without that person's consent, moves that property in order to such taking, is said to commit theft.

Explanation 1–A thing so long as it is attached to the earth, not being movable property, is not the subject of theft; but it becomes capable of being the subject of theft as soon as it is severed from the earth.

Explanation 2–A moving, effected by the same act which effects the severance, may be a theft.

Explanation 3–A person is said to cause a thing to move by removing an obstacle which prevented it from moving, or by separating it from any other thing, as well as by actually moving it.

Explanation 4–A person, who by any means causes an animal to move, is said to move that animal, and to move everything which in consequence of the motion so caused is moved by that animal.

Explanation 5–The consent mentioned in the definition may be express or implied, and may be given either by the person in possession, or by any person having for that purpose authority either express or implied.

Illustrations

(a) A cuts down a tree on Z's ground, with the intention of dishonestly taking the tree out of Z's possession without Z's consent. Here, as soon as A has severed the tree, in order to such taking, he has committed theft.

(b) A puts a bait for dogs in his pocket, and thus induces Z's dog to follow it. Here, if A's intention be dishonestly to take the dog out of Z's possession without Z's consent, A has committed theft as soon as Z's dog has begun to follow A.

(c) A meets a bullock carrying a box of treasure. He drives the bullock in a certain direction, in order that he may dishonestly take the treasure. As soon as the bullock begins to move, A has committed theft of the treasure.

(d) A, being Z's servant and entrusted by Z with the care of Z's plate, dishonestly runs away with the plate without Z's consent. A has committed theft.

(e) Z, going on a journey, entrusts his plate to A, the keeper of a warehouse, till Z shall return. A carries the plate to a goldsmith and sells it. Here the plate was not in Z's possession. It could not, therefore, be taken out of Z's possession, and A has not committed theft, though he may have committed criminal breach of trust.

(f) A finds a ring belonging to Z on a table in the house which Z occupies. Here the ring is in Z's possession, and if A dishonestly removes it, A commits theft.

(g) A finds a ring lying on the high road, not in the possession of any person. A by taking it commits no theft, though he may commit criminal misappropriation of property.

(h) A sees a ring belonging to Z lying on a table in Z's house. Not venturing to misappropriate the ring immediately for fear of search and detection, A hides the ring in a place where it is highly improbable that it will ever be found by Z, with the intention of taking the ring from the hiding place and selling it when the loss is forgotten. Here A, at the time of first moving the ring, commits theft.

(i) A delivers his watch to Z, a jeweller, to be regulated. Z carries it to his shop. A, not owing to the jeweller any debt for which the jeweller might lawfully detain the watch as a security, enters the shop openly, takes his watch by force out of Z's hand, and carries it away. Here A, though he may have committed criminal trespass and assault, has not committed theft, inasmuch as what he did was not done dishonestly.

(j) If A owes money to Z for repairing the watch, and if Z retains the watch lawfully as a security for the debt, and A takes the watch out of Z's possession, with the intention of depriving Z of the property as a security for his debt, he commits theft, inasmuch as he takes it dishonestly.

(k) Again, if A having pawned his watch to Z, takes it out of Z's possession without Z's consent, not having paid what he borrowed on the watch, he commits theft, though the watch is his own property, inasmuch as he takes it dishonestly.

(l) A takes an article belonging to Z out of Z's possession, without Z's consent, with the intention of keeping it until he obtains money from Z as a reward for its restoration. Here A takes dishonestly; A has therefore committed theft.

(m) A, being on friendly terms with Z, goes into Z's library in Z's absence and takes away a book, without Z's express consent, for the purpose merely of reading it, and with the intention of returning it. Here, it is probable that A may have conceived that he had Z's implied consent to use Z's book. If this was A's impression, A has not committed theft.

(n) A asks charity from Z's wife. She gives A money, food and clothes, which A knows to belong to Z, her husband. Here, it is probable that A may conceive that Z's wife is authorised to give away alms. If this was A's impression, A has not committed theft.

(o) A is the paramour of Z's wife. She gives A valuable property, which A knows to belong to her husband Z, and to be such property as she has no authority from Z to give. If A takes the property dishonestly, he commits theft.

(p) A in good faith, believing property belonging to Z to be A's own property, takes that property out of B's possession. Here, as A does not take dishonestly, he does not commit theft.

379. Whoever commits theft shall be punished with imprisonment for a term which may extend to 3 years, or with fine, or with both.

379A.–(1) Whoever commits theft of a motor vehicle or any component part of a motor vehicle shall be punished with imprisonment for a term of not less than one year and not more than 7 years and shall also be liable to fine.

(2) A person convicted of an offence under this section shall, unless the court for special reasons thinks fit to order otherwise and without prejudice to the power of the court to order a longer period of disqualification, be disqualified for a period of not less than 3 years from the date of his release from imprisonment from holding or obtaining a driving licence under the Road Traffic Act.

(3) In this section–

"motor vehicle" means a mechanically propelled vehicle intended or adapted for use on roads, and includes a trailer drawn by a motor vehicle;

"component part", in relation to a motor vehicle, includes any tyre, accessory or equipment.

[Sections 379A to 382 deal with the aggravated forms of theft. (See Table below.)]

1. Punishment

In Singapore the punishments for theft and its aggravated forms were increased in 1984 (See Penal Code (Amendment) Act 1984 (Act 23 of 1984). Below is a comparative table of the position in Singapore and Malaysia.

Penal Code of Singapore	*FMS Penal Code*
Section 379 (theft): Imprisonment up to 3 years, or fine or both.	Imprisonment up to 3 years, or fine, or both. For second or subsequent offence,* imprisonment or fine or whipping or any 2 of such punishments.
Section 379A (theft of motor vehicle): Imprisonment for not less than 1 year and not more than 7 years, and fine. Disqualification for not less than 3 years from holding or obtaining driving licence.	No equivalent of s 379A; would be covered by s 379, above.
Section 380 (theft in dwelling house): Imprisonment up to 7 years and fine.	Imprisonment up to 7 years and fine. For a second or subsequent offence,* imprisonment and fine or whipping.
Section 381 (theft by clerk or servant of property in possession	Imprisonment up to 7 years and fine.

of master): Imprisonment up to
7 years or fine.

Section 382 (theft after preparation made for causing death or hurt in order to commit theft): Imprisonment up to 10 years and caning with not less than 3 strokes.	Imprisonment up to 10 years and fine or whipping.*

[**Note: *382A.** Whoever, having been convicted of an offence under ss 379, 380 or 382 subsequently commits an offence under any other of the said three sections, shall be deemed to have committed a second offence under the section under which he has been subsequently convicted.]

2.   Interpretative problems

The offence of theft in s 378 is not drafted too felicitously as the elements of *mens rea* and *actus reus* are not clearly demarcated. As worded, it is open to two interpretations. One interpretation is to regard the *mens rea* as contained in the phrase "... intending to take dishonestly any movable property out of the possession of any person without the person's consent ...", and the *actus reus*, "... moves that property in order to such taking ...".

Another interpretation is to regard the *mens rea* as contained in the element of dishonest intention only, and to regard the other elements, ie (1) taking movable property; (2) out of the possession of another; (3) without the person's consent; and, of course, (4) moving that property in order to take it, to be the *actus reus*. So regarded, the *mens rea* would be the dishonest intention to commit the *actus reus*.

It is proposed to adopt the latter interpretation. However, it may be noted that dishonesty and "consent" are two separate elements and affect both the *mens rea* and *actus reus* in theft (see below, pp 533, 539–541).

"Dishonestly" is defined in s 24 and amplified in s 23:

23.   "Wrongful gain" is gain by unlawful means of property to which the person gaining it is not legally entitled.

"Wrongful loss" is loss by unlawful means of property to which the person losing it is legally entitled.

Explanation–A person is said to gain wrongfully when such person retains wrongfully, as well as when such person acquires wrongfully. A person is said to lose wrongfully when such person is wrongfully kept out of any property, as well as when such person is wrongfully deprived of property.

24. Whoever does anything with the intention of causing wrongful gain to one person, or wrongful loss to another person, is said to do that thing dishonestly.

The definition of "dishonestly" is expressed in artificial terms of causing "wrongful loss" or "wrongful gain" which may not resolve the question of whether or not there is dishonest intention in the case of a bona fide claim of right where there may be no "dishonest intention" even though the person may in fact cause wrongful loss or wrongful gain within the meaning of s 24 (see below, p 532).

B. Dishonesty

Dishonesty requires the intention to cause wrongful gain or wrongful loss. This intention to take dishonestly must exist at the time of moving the property (see s 378, Illustrations (h) and (i)). There is no dishonest intention if a person takes his friend's book, which was carelessly left in a restaurant, intending to return it after he has read it. However, if he subsequently forms the dishonest intention not to return it he may be liable for criminal misappropriation of property under s 403 of the Penal Code (see ch 26). It is not theft as there is no dishonest intention *at the time* of taking. (See *Mehra* 1957.)

The wrongfulness of the taking consists of knowing that the property belongs to another person or, if the property belongs to him (accused), he knows the other person has a right of retention (see Illustrations (f) and (j)). If a person takes lost property there is no dishonest intention in the taking but there may be criminal misappropriation (see Illustration (g) to s 378). (See bona fide claim of right, below, p 534.)

1. Taking another's property as security for debt

There are conflicting decisions on the question whether the taking of property of another as security for a debt constitutes theft under s 379. In some cases courts have held that there is no dishonest intention.

In the Indian case of *Manikant Yadav* (1980), the petitioner removed a bullock from the informant because he (informant) owed him money. The court held the petitioner had no dishonest intention. It stated:

> When a person takes another man's property believing under a mistake of fact and in ignorance of law that he has the right to take it committing an offence and to retain it until compensated, he may not be held guilty of theft in as much as there is no dishonest intention even though he may cause wrongful loss within the meaning of the Penal Code.

Similarly, in *Kadirawail* v *Kader Meedin* (1881), the accused took some
jewellery from the person of the deceased woman who was his debtor.
He made clear to those present there that he intended to retain the jewellery only as security for the debt. It was held that a dishonest intention had not been proved and theft was not committed.

PP v Ramiah (1959) 25 MLJ 204, (HC, KL, Malaya)

(The facts appear in the judgment.)

Thomson CJ: The three accused in this case were prosecuted for house-breaking in order to the committing of the offence of theft in contravention of s 454
of the Penal Code. All three of them were found not guilty and discharged....

[T]he three accused broke into the living room of the complainant and
removed a trunk containing a large quantity of property. Some days later the
trunk with its contents intact was found in the possession of one of them. The
defence of the first accused ... was that the complainant owed him money and
that he removed the property because he thought if he kept it for a few days
the complainant would pay the debt. He had no intention to steal. The defence
of the other two accused was that they thought the property was that of the
first accused and that they had assisted him to remove it.

No complaint has been made regarding the acquittal of the second and third
accused. The prosecution, however, have appealed against the acquittal of the
first accused....

In the Indian case of *Sri Churn Chungo* (1895) the facts were similar to
those of the present case. Petheram CJ, referred to the sections of the Indian
Penal Code corresponding to the sections of our Code which have been quoted
and went on to observe:

> "It is evident that it was the intention of the Legislature that it should be theft under
> the Code to take goods in order to keep the person entitled to the possession of them
> out of the possession of them for a time, although the taker did not intend to himself
> appropriate them, or to entirely deprive the owner of them. This is precisely what a
> creditor does, who by force or otherwise takes the goods of his debtor out of his
> possession against his will in order to put pressure on him to compel him to dis-
> charge his debt; and it must follow that a person who does so is guilty of theft
> within the provisions of the Indian Penal Code."

On this view of the law which I have no hesitation in following the first accused
should clearly have been found guilty of the offence charged against him. The
appeal is accordingly allowed, the order of acquittal and discharge is set aside
and a conviction is substituted for it.

Appeal allowed

There appears to be no distinction on the facts between *Manikant Yadav*
(1980) and *Kadirawail*(1881) on the one hand and *Ramiah* (1959) on
the other. In each of these cases the creditor took the goods of the
debtor as security for a debt.

In *Manikant Yadav* (1980) the court based its decision on the ground that the accused acted under a mistake of fact. It is difficult to see how a mistake of fact can arise. Even if he thought that by taking the goods of his debtor, it might induce him to pay back the loan, there is no mistake of fact if the debtor was not thereby so induced to return the money. The taking of the goods is simply to coerce the debtor into payment and there is no question of mistake of fact about it. It is interesting to note that the court held there was *no dishonest intention even though wrongful loss was caused* within the meaning of s 24 of the Indian Penal Code, if a mistake of fact did occur. As there was no *intention* to cause wrongful gain or wrongful loss, the court thought it immaterial if actual loss or gain was caused.

On policy grounds *Ramiah*'s case can be supported. The law of theft should discourage self-help as it might lead to unnecessary reprisals or violence. The law should therefore take a strict view of a creditor who takes the goods of his debtor as security for his debt–he should be convicted of theft. The creditor should proceed to the civil court to make his claim.

2. Intention to take without consent

The *mens rea* of theft also includes an *intention to take property of another without his consent*. As McElwaine LJ in *Lim Soon Gong* (1939) said: "*Mens rea* is essential to theft and illustration (m) (a) ... show this". Illustrations (l) and (o) also deal with the question of consent and the element of "dishonestly" in theft. (See also, s 378, Explanation 5 and Illustrations (e), (m), (n), and (o).) The provision relating to consent under s 90 of the Penal Code (see ch 6) also applies in this context.

The wording of s 378, as amplified in Illustrations (m), (n) and (o), suggests that the question is whether the accused intended to take property with or without the consent of the person rather than whether or not that person in fact did consent. On this view, which is borne out by the above Illustrations, what is important in determining whether or not there is consent is how the accused "conceives" the situation. If the accused conceived that the person would have consented to the taking because he was on friendly terms with him, there is no theft, even though it turned out that the person would not have consented (see Illustrations (m) and (n)).

So far as the element of consent was concerned, the learned judge in *Packeer Ally* (1916) said that it is a condition which must be in the mind of the accused when he intends dishonestly to remove the property (see below, p 540). (See *Raja Mohamed*, 1963, below, p 541.)

C. Bona fide claim of right

1. Scope

HS Gour, *Penal Law of India* (10th edn 1984) Vol 4, 3283

The right [s 378 Illus (p)] claimed is the right to possession as against the person in whose possession the article is. This right may be claimed on either of three grounds: (i) Because the claimant is owner of the article, and he has not parted with the right of possession involved in ownership in favour of another. (ii) Because he *bona fide* believes himself to be the owner of the article, who has not parted with his possessory rights. (iii) Because another is the owner of the article, or the claimant in good faith believes another to be the owner, and he claims possession on the other's behalf.

Mere assertion of right does not constitute a valid claim of right. Thus, a mere plea by an accused that the property with the theft of which he is accused, is his own property, unsupported by proof of by some circumstances which tend to indicate that there is some truth in the statement is insufficient. The claim must be tried and determined by the Court, and must be proved by evidence to be fair and good, though not necessarily correct.

Mere doubt as to one's right is insufficient; the doubt must be shown to be reasonable, as where the ownership of the property alleged to have been stolen is shown to be the subject of a *bona fide* dispute between the parties. But the Criminal law must not be set in motion to assist a civil action and the mere fact that one who is in possession has no right is no ground for another to claim right to the goods so possessed.

The claim must be one made in good faith, ie, it must be honestly made, and if not so made as where it is a mere pretence, it will be of no avail.

"Good faith" under s 52 of the Indian Penal Code (which is *in pari materia* with its counterpart in Singapore and Malaysia) reads: "Nothing is said to be done or believed in good faith which is done of believed without due care and attention." Gour equates "good faith" with *honesty* (see above).

In England a claim of right is recognized if a person asserts what he believes to be a lawful claim, even though it may be unfounded in law or fact (see *Bernhard*, 1923). The test of honesty under English law could be subjective. It is submitted that the test under s 52 is objective as "due care and attention" is required. Thus it is misleading to equate good faith with honesty.

2. Absence of "claim of right" as an element in mens rea of theft

The *mens rea* of theft is the element of dishonest intention, ie an intention to cause wrongful gain or wrongful loss. If A bona fide believes himself to be the owner of the article, who has not parted with his possessory rights, he does not intend to take dishonestly. In fact, he intends a rightful gain or a rightful loss when he takes under a claim of right. (See ch 26.) Thus the absence of a bona fide claim of right is an element in the *mens rea* of theft. In *Lim Soon Gong* (1939), the respondents were charged with committing theft of sand from the foreshore. One of the issues was whether they had a dishonest intention. The Court of Criminal Appeal of the Straits Settlements said:

> Property may be taken under a *bona fide* though mistaken belief of right or in the *bona fide* though mistaken belief that it belongs to no one or has been abandoned. The circumstances must be such as to show or to raise a presumption that the person intended to do something which he knew or should have known was wrongful. *Mens rea* is essential to theft and illustrations (m) (n) and (p) [s 378] show this.

In the Indian case of *Suvvari Sanyasi Apparao* v *Boddepalli Lakshiminarayana* (1962), the Supreme Court of India said:

> It is settled law that where a bona fide claim of right exists, it can be a good *defence* to a prosecution for theft. An act does not amount to theft unless there be not only no legal right but no appearance or colour of a legal right. In 2 East PCP 659, the law was stated long ago thus (emphasis added):
>
> > "If there be in the prisoner any fair pretence of property or right, or if it be brought into doubt at all, the court will direct an acquittal."

It is misleading for the court to refer to the right as a "defence" in the context of the Indian Penal Code. It is not a true defence insofar as it does not fall within the general exceptions of the Penal Code. Otherwise, the burden is on the accused to prove a bona fide claim of right (see s 107 of the Evidence Act (Singapore) (Cap 97) and s 105 of the Evidence Act 1950 (Rev 1971, Act 56) (Malaysia)). As noted, in the context of theft (see also ch 26), a bona fide claim of right negatives the *mens rea*, even though it may involve a mistake as to the civil law.

Would a mistake as to the civil law relating to sale of goods give rise to a bona fide claim of right?

Lai Chan Ngiang v PP (1930) 1 JLR 30 (Court of a Judge, Johore, unfederated Malay States)

The appellant went to the house of a man who owed him $72 in respect of some "kayus" of cloth. The appellant helped himself to four "kayus", three of which he had sold to the man.

Thorne J: This was apparently a simple process for collecting the value of a part of the debt, and I have no doubt that in doing what he did, the Appellant thought he was justified in taking back from his debtor goods which he had sold, when the debtor failed to pay his debt. That is not the law. I do not forget that one of these bundles of cloth had not been bought of the Appellant but I think it likely that the Appellant made a mistake. The law is that upon a sale on credit, on delivery of the goods sold to the buyer the property in the goods passes to the buyer even though payment of the price be postponed for quite a long period. In taking these bundles of cloth then the Appellant strictly was removing the goods of his debtor. That was an unlawful and improper act. If the Appellant was unable to collect payment he could have had recourse to the Civil Court to enforce payment of the debt. In order to establish a charge under this section it is necessary that the prosecution should prove that the person accused took the goods of another intentionally, dishonestly intending to deprive the owner of his goods.... Here I am satisfied that there was no dishonesty of intent on the part of the Appellant whatever, and the Magistrate was, therefore, wrong in convicting the accused.

Appeal allowed

Thorne J based his decision on the ground that the appellant was not dishonest because he did not intend to deprive the debtor of his goods even though he made a mistake of law. The learned judge pointed out that the appellant thought he was justified in taking back the bundles of cloth when the debtor failed to pay for them. It might well be that the appellant thought he was still the owner of those goods and did not appreciate the fact that on a sale by credit, property in the goods may pass immediately despite the postponement of payment, unless there is an intention to the contrary. Assuming that property had passed, it is a mistake of law, ie civil law if the appellant had thought he was still the owner. This prompted the learned judge to remark that it was "not the law" and that the taking was "an unlawful and improper act". Nevertheless, he held that the appellant had no dishonest intention.

The learned judge did not allude to the question of a bona fide claim of right (see Illustration (p) to s 378). If such a claim of right were to apply, the appellant must exercise good faith. For example, should the appellant have made some enquiry as to whether he could repossess the bundles of cloth that had not been paid for, before taking them? On this question, the Indian case of *Sitabai Purshottam* (1931) should be considered. There the accused (vendor) had sold a barge to the complainant and received part of the purchase price. The accused seized the barge from the complainant when the latter failed to pay the balance of the purchase price. However, before she seized the barge she asked her Pleader to write a letter to the complainant informing him that if he did not pay the balance of the purchase price, the contract would be cancelled. Moreover, as the court observed, the terms of the contract were such that it could be construed that the property in the goods was not to pass until payment of the purchase price. Although the court pointed out that the whole matter should have been litigated in a civil court, nonetheless, it proceeded to consider the position as follows:

> It is quite possible that there may not have been any delivery in law, and it is even more possible that the vendor may have believed that there had been no delivery in law and if the vendor delivered that and that the possession of the barge was still in her in law, then ... she cannot be convicted of theft because she ... has not been shown to have had any dishonest intention in seizing possession of the barge.

It is submitted that, on the facts in *Sitabai Purshottam* (1931), the vendor did act in good faith (s 52) by seeking the advice of the Pleader before she seized the barge. Can *Lai Chan Ngiang* (1930) and *Sitabai Purshottam* (1931) be distinguished? Would the price of the cloth be relevant in determining whether the appellant in *Lai Chan Ngiang* should have first consulted a lawyer before he took the cloth? On the facts, would a bona fide claim of right apply in *Lai Chan Ngiang* (1930)?

D. Actus reus

It may be noted that the subject matter of theft is movable property (see s 22 and Explanation 1 to s 378; *Lim Soon Gong*, 1939; see also ch 26).

The *actus reus* of theft consists of a number of elements set forth below:

1. Taking out of possession: temporary deprivation sufficient

The question that has arisen in a number of cases is whether a *temporary* deprivation of possession of property would suffice to constitute theft.

Ward v PP (1953) 19 MLJ 153 (HC, Johore, Malaya)

Storr J: In this case the two appellants ... were convicted of the theft of certain articles, under s 380 of the Penal Code....

The main point argued in the appeal was that the evidence tended to show that the appellants, although they admitted taking the articles, did not take them with any criminal intention. The idea in their minds at the time of taking the articles was that in due course they would get the consent from the owner and when he required the articles they would return them to him. Although Mr Leonard argued very forcefully that the appellants acted without criminal intention and as the owner would only have been deprived of possession of the articles for a short time there could be no offence, on looking up the authorities I have come to the conclusion that there is very little substance in this argument.... Petheram CJ, in a judgment of the Full Bench in *Sri Churn Chungo* (1895), s 378, after taking into consideration ss 24 and 23, will read as follows:

> "Whoever in order to take with the intention of gaining property by unlawful means moves that property, or whoever in order to take with the intention of retaining by unlawful means property which he does not intend to acquire, moves that property, or whoever moves property in order to take it with the intention of keeping the person entitled to the possession of it out of the possession of it by unlawful means, though he does not intend to deprive him permanently of it, is said to commit theft. When the section is read in this way it is evident that it was the intention of the Legislature that it should be theft under the Code, to take goods in order to keep the person entitled to the possession of them out of the possession of them for a time, although the taker did not intend to himself appropriate them, or to entirely deprive the owner of them."

which, I think, gives a true and fuller definition of the offence defined in s 378. It is therefore quite clear to me that ... the offence of theft under s 380 of the Penal Code had been committed by the appellants.

Appeal dismissed

2.   Property in possession of another

Theft is an offence against possession, not ownership. Thus the person who files a complaint that theft has been committed need not establish that he is the owner of the property. What is relevant is that he must be in possession of it.

The word "possession" is not defined in the Penal Code.

Atchuthen Pillai, *Criminal Law* **(6th edn, 1983) 675**

We [the "Law Commissioners"] believe it to be impossible to mark with precision by any words, the circumstances which constitute possession. It is easy to put cases about which no doubt whatever exists and about which the language of the lawyers and of the multitude be the same. It will hardly be doubted for example, that a gentleman's watch lying on a table in his room, is in his possession, though it is not in his hand; and though he may not know whether it is on his writing table or on his dressing table. As little will it be doubted that a watch which a gentlemen lost a year ago on a journey, and which he never heard of since, is not in his possession. It will not be doubted that when a person gives a dinner, his silver forks while in the hands of his guests are not in his possession; so also when he has deposited them with a pawnbroker as a pledge. But between these extreme cases lie many cases in which it is difficult to pronounce with confidence, either that property is or that it is not in a person's possession.

This term possession plays an important part both in civil and criminal law. It forms the basis of the civil action of trespass and also of the offence of theft. Possession exists in one whenever he has physical control, whether rightful or wrongful over a corporeal thing. It is entirely distinct from property and either may exist without the other; thus when an article is stolen, though the thief has possession, the owner retains the property.

Possession may be *de facto* or *de jure*. The former is mere custody. A servant has only mere custody of the articles which belongs to his master. For example: A, the master of a house gives a dinner party; the plate and other things on the table are in his possession, though from time to time they are in the custody of his guest or servants.

... [P]ossession is a simple question of fact. If I buy a motor car from a person who has the right to sell it, I obtain the right of ownership over it and it is my property. If I let it to another person, or it is stolen, the person to whom it is let or the thief has the possession but I still retain the property.

It is clear that when things are in one's physical possession, one is said to be in possession of that thing. If things are out of one's possession but nevertheless one has control over them, one may still be considered to be in possession of that thing, Section 27 of the Penal Code gives an example of this:

When property is in the possession of a person's wife, clerk or servant, on account of that person, it is in that person's possession within the meaning of this Code.

Explanation–A person employed temporarily or on a particular occasion in the capacity of a clerk or servant is a clerk or servant within the meaning of this section.

Illustrations (j) and (k) demonstrate that a person in lawful custody or control may be said to be in possession.

Possession may be lost or abandoned as when there is no longer control over the thing. For example, A lost his watch when swimming in the sea ten years ago. After such a long period of time he may no longer have the control of the thing. He may even have abandoned the idea of gaining possession of it. (See also Fitzgerald (ed), *Salmond on Jurisprudence* (12th edn, 1985.)

3. No consent to taking

Where a person consents to the taking, the *actus reus* of theft is not committed (see Explanation 5 to s 378).

One interpretation is to consider dishonesty and absence of consent as two distinct and essential consituents of the offence of theft, ie the *actus reus* and the *mens rea*. In the Indian case of *Mehra* (1957) the court said:

Commission of theft, therefore, consists in (1) moving a movable property of a person out of his possession without his consent, (2) the moving being in order to the taking of the property with a dishonest intention. Thus, (1) the absence of the person's consent at the time of moving, and (2) the presence of dishonest intention in so taking at the time, are the essential ingredients of the offence of theft.

The rationale for this approach is that where a person did consent, the fact that the accused thought there was no consent is irrelevant–no theft is committed.

However, this analysis raises the difficult question in cases where there is at least de facto consent as in entrapment cases where, for example, a master suspecting his servant to be dishonest in conspiring with another to remove his property, facilitates the theft by handing to the servant the key to the safe. One approach is to consider whether there is consent of the master to the taking. Another is to consider the intention of the accused to take without consent as the predominant feature rather than the consent of the person from whom the property was taken (see above, p 533).

Packeer Ally v Savarimuttu (1916) 2 CWR 216 (SC, Ceylon)

Ennis J: It appears that the accused approached the storekeeper of an estate and asked him to join with him in taking away rubber from the estate suggesting that they should share the proceeds. The storekeeper reported the matter to the Superintendent. The Superintendent then authorized the storekeeper to let the accused have the rubber, and directed him to cause the accused to be followed to ascertain to whom the rubber was sold. This was done. The only point raised in the appeal is whether in view of the fact of the Superintendent having consented to the removal of the rubber the offence of theft as defined in s 366 has been committed. According to the wording of that section the intention of the accused seems to be the predominent feature rather than the consent of the person from whom the property was taken. The section runs: "Whoever, intending to take dishonestly any movable property out of the possession of any person without that person's consent, moves that property in order to such taking, is said to commit theft." The consent mentioned there seems to have been mentioned as a condition which must be in the mind of the accused when he intends dishonestly to remove the property. The section does not run whoever moves that property without the consent of the person shall commit theft. So far as I understand that section the offence of theft in this case has been committed. There is however an Indian case of the *Troylukho Nath Chowdhry* (1878) where under similar circumstances a doubt was rasied as to whether theft had been committed where consent to remove had been given. The High Court to whom the case was referred held that even if the offence of theft had not been committed the offence of abetment had been, as, under the explanation to the Indian section, equivalent to our s 101, to constitute the offence of abetment it is not necessary that the act abetted should be committed.

The punishment awarded in this case is within the limits of the punishment awardable for the abetment of theft, and whether the offence committed in this case is theft or abetment of theft, no alteration in the punishment is necessary.

In these circumstances I see no reason to interfere with the conviction on technical grounds, and dismiss the appeal.

Appeal dismissed

In *Troylukho Nath Chowdhry* (1878), (mentioned in *Packeer Ally*, 1916) the defendant sought the aid of one Cummins with the intention of committing a theft of the property of Cummins' master. Cummins, with the knowledge and consent of his master, and for the purpose of procuring the defendant's punishment, aided him in carrying out his object. It was held that property removed was taken with the knowledge of the master. Hence, theft was not committed, but the defendant was guilty of abetment of theft.

The law faces difficult questions of public policy in entrapment cases. The law may draw the distinction between the situation where the plan is initiated by the master and one where it originated from the "thief". In the former, if, for example, the master, hands the key to his house over to the servant for the sole purpose that he may entrap the servant and his accomplices the law may regard this approach as an unfair method of entrapment, and may well regard that there is consent by the master to the taking.

Regarding the latter, it may be noted that in *Troylukho* (1878), the plan did not originate from the master. Hence it should be viewed that the master did not consent to the taking of the property. He merely assisted the thief in carrying out the latter's dishonest intention. It is submitted that the defendant should have been convicted of theft, and not abetment of theft.

4. Moving property out of possession

The property must be moved and taken out of possession. Illustrations (a), (b) and (c) to s 378 make it clear that the crux of the offence of theft is the dishonest intention of taking property out of a person's possession upon the moving of the thing (see also, s 378, Explanations 2 to 4 and Illustrations (a), (b) and (c)).

Raja Mohamed v R (1963) 29 MLJ 339 (HC, Singapore)

The appellant removed boxes containing two dozen glasses from the company's ground floor store-room.

Ambrose J: In this case the appellant, who was a chemical mixer employed by the Singapore Glass Manufacturers Co Ltd, was charged with theft of property in the possession of his employer under s 381 of the Penal Code. It was alleged that on the 15th October 1962, at about 7.45 pm at the Company's premises at Henderson Road, Singapore, he committed theft in respect of two dozen drinking glasses valued at $2 in the possession of the Company. He was convicted by the trial Magistrate and sentenced to one day's imprisonment and a fine of $300.

It was submitted on behalf of the appellant that, though the Magistrate found that the two dozen glasses were removed by him from the store on the ground floor of the Company's premises to a box on the first floor, it was not proved that they had been removed out of the possession of the Company. I concede that to constitute theft there must be an intention to take dishonestly any movable property out of the possession of another person without that person's consent. But in my judgment, it is sufficient if the person who has formed such dishonest intention moves that property in order to such taking; and it is not necessary for him to move that property out of the possession of the other person.

Appeal dismissed

Section 378 speaks of moving property "out of the possession" of any person, and to that end moves the property "in order to such taking". The court in *Raja Mohamed* (1963) held that it is sufficient if an accused, who has formed such dishonest intention, moves that property in order to such taking–it is not necessary for him to move that property out of the possession of the other person. For example, A "moves" B's ring into a cupboard near the entrance to the door of B's house, intending to take it away when A goes home. This is theft even though the ring is still in the possession of B. Illustrations (a), (b), (c) and (h) to s 378 bring out clearly that it is the intention of dishonestly taking the thing out of a person's possession without his consent that is the crux of the matter. Once this is satisfied, as soon as the thing is moved, theft is committed. In other words, a moving is complete where the object is moved and the gain or loss contemplated need not be a total acquisition or total deprivation. Thus the accused in *Raja Mohamed* (1963) need not move the glasses out of the premises of the company into his own possession. Indeed, he need not even have moved them to the first floor. It would have been theft even if he had simply lifted up the glasses provided the moving was accompanied by the dishonest intention of taking out of the possession without the consent of the company at the time of the lifting.

Chapter 24

Extortion

By KL Koh

A. Introduction

Penal Code, ss 383–389

    383. Whoever intentionally puts any person in fear of any injury to that person or to any other, and thereby dishonestly induces the person so put in fear to deliver to any person any property or valuable security, or anything signed or sealed which may be converted into a valuable security, commits "extortion".

Illustrations
(a) A threatens to publish a defamatory libel concerning Z, unless Z gives him money. He thus induces Z to give him money. A has committed extortion.
(b) A threatens Z that he will keep Z's child in wrongful confinement, unless Z will sign and deliver to A a promissory note binding Z to pay certain moneys to A. Z signs and delivers the note. A has committed extortion.
(c) A threatens to send men to plough up Z's field, unless Z will sign and deliver to B a bond, binding Z under a penalty to deliver certain produce to B, and thereby induces Z to sign and deliver the bond. A has committed extortion.
(d) A, by putting Z in fear of grievous hurt, dishonestly induces Z to sign or affix his seal to a blank paper and deliver it to A. Z signs and delivers the paper to A. Here, as the paper so signed may be converted into a valuable security, A has committed extortion.

    384. Whoever commits extortion shall be punished with imprisonment for a term of not less than 2 years and not more than 7 years and with caning.

[Sections 385 to 389 deal with aggravated forms of extortion. (See Table below.)]

1. Punishment

In Singapore the punishments for extortion and its aggravated forms were increased in 1984. (See Penal Code (Amendment) Act 1984 (Act 23 of 1984.) Below is a comparative table of the position in Singapore and Malaysia.

Penal Code of Singapore

FMS Penal Code

S 384 (punishment for extortion): Imprisonment for not less than 2 years and not more than 7 years *and* caning.

Imprisonment up to 3 years, or fine, or whipping, or with any 2 of such punishments.

S 385 (putting person in fear of injury in order to commit extortion): Imprisonment for not less than 2 years and not more than 5 years *and* caning.

Imprisonment up to 2 years, or fine, or whipping or with any 2 of such punishments.

S 386 (extortion by putting a person in fear of death or grievous hurt): Imprisonment for *not less* than 2 years and not more than 10 years *and* caning.

Imprisonment up to 10 years and a fine or whipping.

S 387 (putting person in fear of death or of grievous hurt in order to commit extortion): Imprisonment for not less than 2 years and not more than 7 years and with caning.

Imprisonment up to 7 years, and fine or whipping.

S 388 (extortion by threat of accusation of an offence punishable with death, or imprisonment, etc): Imprisonment for up to 10 years and fine or caning: if offence is one punishable under s 377 (unnatural offences), imprisonment for life.

Death or imprisonment up to 20 years. In attempt to induce person to commit such offence– imprisonment up to 10 years and fine or whipping. If offence is punishable under s 377 (unnatural offences), imprisonment up to 20 years.

S 389 (putting person in fear of accusation of offence, in order to commit extortion): Punishable with death or life imprisonment, or imprisonment up to 10 years, and fine or caning; if offence is punishable under s 377, imprisonment for life.

Imprisonment up to 10 years and fine or whipping; if offence is punishable under s 377 (unnatural offences), imprisonment up to 20 years.

B. The law

Extortion is distinguished from theft in two main respects. First, extortion is committed by putting a person in fear of injury thereby dishonestly inducing the person so put in fear to deliver property. In theft, the taking is without consent of the person. Second, the subject matter of extortion is not limited, as in theft, to movable property but extends to immovable property (eg handing over of title deeds) or valuable security.

Under s 383 of the Penal Code, the *mens rea* of extortion consists in *intentionally* committing the *actus reus*, ie putting a person in fear of injury to himself or another; and *dishonestly* inducing that person so put in fear to deliver to any person any property or valuable security.

1. Fear of injury

"Injury" is defined in s 44 of the Penal Code as "any harm whatever illegally caused to any person in body, mind, reputation or property". The word "illegally" is in turn defined in s 43 as "applicable to every thing which is an offence, or which is prohibited by law, or which furnishes ground for a civil action; ...". (See ch 3.)

It is necessary for the prosecution to prove that the victim was put in fear of injury and that the fear must be present in the victim's mind when he made the delivery. The "extortioner" must intend to cause the injury. The element of fear is clearly brought out in s 383 which speaks of putting a person "in fear of any injury to that person or to any other" when delivering the property or valuable security. However, it is not clear whether it is sufficient if the victim is subjectively so put in fear but not a person of ordinary stability. As a matter of policy, since timorous victims are easy preys to extortioners, a subjective view ought to be taken.

The element of fear of injury inducing delivery is not satisfied if the accused were to forcibly take property or valuable security from his victim. In *Jadunandan Singh* (1941), the accused assaulted the victims and forcibly took their thumb impressions on some blank pieces of paper which could be converted into valuable security. He was charged with extortion under s 383 of the Indian Penal Code. Dhavle J acquitted the accused of extortion but convicted him of using criminal force under s 252 of the Indian Penal Code. The learned judge stated:

> It is clear that this definition makes it necessary for the prosecution to prove that the victims ... were put in fear of injury to themselves or to others, and further, were thereby dishonestly induced to deliver papers containing their thumb impressions. The prosecution story in the present case goes no further than that thumb impressions were "forcibly taken" from them. The details of the forcible taking were apparently not put in evidence. The trial Court speaks of the wrists of the victims being caught and of their thumb impressions being then "taken".

Fear of injury may be caused by a person threatening to use his influence of power, whether real or supposed. In *Meer Abbas Ali* v *Omed Ali* (1872), the victim, Omed Ali, gave 2 rupees to Abbas Ali through fear that if he did not give them, he (Omed Ali) would lose his position as *peadah* in the Small Cause Court Judge's establishment. Glover J in holding Abbas Ali guilty of extortion said:

> [T]here is ample evidence to show that Abbas Ali had very great influence in such matter.
>
> We also think it clear ... that any one might reasonably have considered a threat coming from Abbas Ali as a thing not to be trifled with ... there is direct evidence to the fact, that a bad word from Abbas was ordinarily followed by ruin to those against whom he interested himself, and more than one instance is proved of direct and immediate injury resulting from Abbas Ali's influence....
>
> We feel no doubt that Abbas Ali was a man both disliked and feared by the Small Cause Court Judge's establishment and that he made use of his real or supposed influence to induce members of the establishment, to give him money, threatening in case of refusal, the loss of their situations....

(a) Implied threats

Illustrations (a) (b) and (c) to s 383 deal with express threats of injury. However, words uttered may on their face appear to be innocent but if they can be construed by the victim that some injury may be caused unless certain demands are met, such words can constitute an implied threat of injury.

Beh Tuck Seng v R (1947) 13 MLJ 197 (HC, Singapore)

(The facts appear in the judgment.)

Murray-Aynsley CJ: In this case the appellant approached the complainant and said he wanted to collect $10.80 for expenses. He said further "everyone here has joined, what about you?" The complainant, who was a stall-holder, took this as a threat and feared that if he did not pay he would be beaten or his stall upset. He, therefore, paid over a sum of money. There is no suggestion that the appellant had any business to collect any money from the complainant....

All that is necessary under the section [ie 384] is that a person should be intentionally put in fear of any injury and should be thereby dishonestly induced to deliver any property or valuable security.

In this case it is clear that the complainant was put in fear and that he was induced thereby to hand over money.

The whole question therefore turns on whether this was done "intentionally" and "dishonestly".

To anyone with any knowledge of the habits of extortioners the whole transaction has a very familiar sound and it is not surprising that the complainant put upon it the construction that he did. The learned District Judge thought the same about it, and I think one would have to be ingenuous to think otherwise.

Appeal dismissed

In *Beh Tuck Seng* (1947), the court accepted the construction given by the complainant that "everyone here has joined (ie paid $10.80 for expenses) what about you?" meant that if he (the complainant) did not pay he would be beaten or his stall upset. There was no evidence that such incidents had occurred to those who had not "joined". However, Murray-Aynsley CJ took judicial notice of the "habits of extortioners". It can be said that a person of ordinary stability would have construed the words in the same way as the complainant. His Lordship adopted both an objective and subjective viewpoint as he also regarded the complainant's construction of the implied threat as "not surprising".

Lee Choh Pet v PP (No 2) [1972] 1 MLJ 187 (CCA, Singapore)

The deceased's kidnappers–the appellants–commenced negotiations for the payment of $20,000 from the father of the deceased, Ong Yew Kee, for the release of the deceased–the father being unaware that his son had already been killed. The appellants were convicted, *inter alia*, under s 386 of the Penal Code.

Choor Singh J: The evidence on record does not ... support the charge of extortion....

[T]here is not a single word in his [Ong Yew Kee] evidence to the effect that he was at any time put in fear of death or grievous hurt being caused to his son by the kidnappers. The essence of the offence of extortion as defined in s 386 of the Penal Code is the putting of a person in fear of death or of grievous hurt being caused to him or to some other person. To sustain a conviction under this section there must be evidence that the accused person made a threat to the complainant of death or of grievous hurt being caused to him or to any other person. The charge framed by the trial court at the close of the prosecution case states that the appellants together with two other persons in furtherance of the common intention of all of them "committed extortion by putting one Ong Yew Kee in fear of grievous hurt being caused to Ong Beang Leck". The evidence of Ong Yew Kee does not support this charge. According to him all that he was told by the kidnappers on the telephone was that his son would not be released unless ransom money was paid. He does not say that he was put in fear of grievous hurt being caused to his son. The information given by the kidnappers to the father of the deceased that his son would not be released unless ransom money was paid, however alarming it may have been to him, did not constitute an offence under s 386 of the Penal Code. The sum of $20,000 was paid by the father of the deceased to the kidnappers not because he was put in fear of grievous hurt being caused to his son but because he believed that his son would be released upon payment of the said sum. The inducement was the promised release of his son and not fear of the causing of grievous hurt.

Appeals against convictions under ss 364 and 302 dismissed;
Conviction under s 386 quashed

On the face of it, the telephone conversation of the appellants to the deceased's father that his son would not be released unless ransom money was paid did not suggest that the deceased's father was put in fear of death or grievous hurt to his son and it was not given that interpretation by the deceased's father. Be that as it may, the words could constitute an actual threat of injury under s 383, which deals with simple extortion. (See Illustration (b) to s 383, threat of wrongful confinement.)

It is irrelevant that the father did not know that his son was already dead at the time of the telephone conversation. The appellants should have been charged for extortion under s 384 rather than its aggravated form under s 386 of the Penal Code.

Where an actual threat is not expressed it is not always clear whether the interpretation given by the victim represents the injury intended by the accused. The demeanour of the "extortioner" may assist in determining how the victim construes words which on the face of them are innocent but may be a threat of injury.

Tan Cheng Kooi v PP [1972] 2 MLJ 115 (HC, Penang, Malaysia)

The appellants had mooted the idea of forming an illicit partnership for the production of pornographic films. Subsequently, at a meeting in Penang, the complainant decided not to participate. One of the appellants demanded some money.

Chang Min Tat J: Then, according to the complainant, the first accused demanded ... $50. This demand was purportedly for expenses incurred in coming from Kedah. Also, according to the complainant, the first appellant did not appear happy, and he said he would not befriend the complainant anymore. The complainant alleged he then became frightened because he took this to mean a threat.

Complainant had only $30 with him and he said he would go home to fetch the $50 but on his way home, he stopped at the police headquarters where he lodged a report to a Chinese police detective. At the suggestion of the police detective, he returned to the bar. There he told the appellants that he could not get the money, at which in the words of the complainant the appellants were displeased and their *faces became black with anger*. (Emphasis added.) He was frightened. The appellants then produced a booklet for him to sign. Before he could sign it, the four detectives amongst whom were the Chinese detective to whom he had made the report and a Malay detective whom he had met with the Chinese detective, pounced on the appellants and arrested them....

The question, of course, is always whether a specific injury was threatened, in which case one would naturally expect the prosecution to describe the threat that was made or whether a general threat of injury was made without anything specific being mentioned. In the latter case, the prosecution could not conceivably be able to describe the injury threatened. In this connection, regard must, I think, be paid to the predilection of the peoples in the East of never calling a spade a spade. But can the offence of extortion never be committed, if the accused, for instance, asked for a loan in words that never went beyond what would normally be for a loan but in such circumstances as would indicate that the repayment was never within the contemplation of the so-called borrower? To my mind therefore, where an actual threat was expressed, then it should of course be expressed in the charge. Where, however, the threat was implied and it was not possible to infer more than a general threat of injury, then it must be realized that the particulars of a specific threat could not be given and so long as the injury threatened came within the definition of "injury" in s 44 of the Penal Code, then this essential ingredient of the offence of extortion would have been supplied in the charge.

Counsel in this case in answer to a question from me were generous enough to admit that if words innocent on their surface were uttered with overtones or implications of an injury, then there would be the use of a threat of injury.

There is of course at least one judicial decision which supports this view.

It is sufficient for me to say ... that the threat can be an implied one for the offence to be made out....

Appeal allowed

When the complainant in *Tan Cheng Kooi* (1972) returned to the bar and told the appellants that he could not get the money, they were displeased and their "faces became black with anger". The court held that the demeanour of the appellants frightened the complainant. However, it is to be noted that the complainant had gone back to the bar only for the purpose of entrapping the appellants, and he was accompanied by two detectives for this purpose.

It is therefore doubted if a reasonable man would have in fact been "frightened", as the detectives were near at hand ready to act. Even adopting a subjective approach, was the complainant really frightened having regard to the circumstances?

(b) Threats to exercise legal powers

There are two diametrically opposite lines of authorities on the question whether a person who is empowered to exercise certain legal powers pursuant to his office can be held liable for extortion where the fear of injury is caused by his threat to exercise his legal powers if the victim does not pay him a sum of money that he demands.

(i) Not constituting "injury"

Vincent Lee v R (1949) 15 MLJ 296 (HC, Singapore)

(The facts appear in the judgment.)

Murray-Aynsley CJ: In this case the appellant was charged and convicted under s 384 of the Penal Code. It appears that the appellant was what is known as a volunteer special constable and was duly vested with all the powers and privileges of a "Police Officer". It also appears that in spite of this he had never performed any duties as such. It is also alleged that armed with these powers he had to extract money, threatened various persons who were smoking chandu with arrest.

The offence of extortion is defined in s 383 of the Penal Code. It will be seen that an essential part of the offence is putting a person in fear of "injury". In turn "injury" is defined in s 44 of the same code. There "injury" is harm illegally caused. It appears to me to follow from this that the exercise of legal powers however done can never constitute harm.

It is to be regretted that the use of the word "extortion" in this connection, which is very different from the technical use in English law and also from the popular use, has led to confusion. It will be seen that the authorities cited in the commentary both in Gour and Ratanlal are mostly English cases and they are examples of offences very different from that defined in the section. If the appellant is guilty of an offence, it is not that of which he has been convicted.

Appeal allowed

Abu Hassan v PP (1962) 28 MLJ 61 (HC, Penang, Malaya)

The appellant, a customs officer, was convicted of attempted extortion under s 385 of the Penal Code. He had told one Thangavelu that unless he (Thangavelu) paid him $500 he would report him with a view to action being taken against him for attempting to take excess money than permitted to India.

Hepworth J: The first question which had to be decided was whether if the prosecution case was to be believed the offence disclosed was that of attempted extortion. The prosecution conceded that the threat which they alleged had been made by the appellant was a threat to exercise his legal powers. Nonetheless it was submitted that the offence disclosed was extortion, reliance being placed on the observations of Rigby J in *Loh Kwang Seang* (1960). The learned Judge said:

> "If A, knowing that B has committed an offence in respect of which it is A's duty to take action against him, threatens to take such action against him unless B pays him a sum of money, and, in consideration of such money being paid by B, forbears to take such action, then A has committed the offences of both corruption and extortion. The offence is "extortion" because the additional–and I emphasize the word "additional"–element is present of putting B in fear of injury by the threat of bringing a criminal accusation against him. It matters not whether the accusation be true or false: the offence is completed by the act of obtaining the money as a direct consequence of the threat to bring the criminal accusation."

With respect I am unable to agree with the learned Judge. In *Loh*'s case (1960) the learned Judge's attention was not drawn either to the case of *Vincent Lee* (1949) or to s 44 of the Penal Code. An essential part of the offence of extortion is putting a person in fear of "injury". In turn "injury" is defined in s 44 of the same Code. There "injury" is harm illegally caused, and it follows that the exercise of legal powers, however done, can never constitute harm. In my opinion, therefore, the offence disclosed was not that of extortion and if the evidence adduced by the prosecution was to be believed the offence was one under the Prevention of Corruption Ordinance 1950....

Appeal allowed

See also, *Johar* (1965) where Wee Chong Jin CJ accepted the principle laid down in *Vincent Lee* (1949) and *Abu Hassan* (1962) as correct.

The crux of the issue in *Vincent Lee* (1949) and *Abu Hassan* (1962) is whether a person can be said to be put in fear of injury within the meaning of ss 43 and 44 of the Penal Code if he himself has committed an offence which justifies his arrest by a police officer. The threat of arrest by a police officer acting in the course of his duty cannot constitute an injury to the victim in view of the fact that he had brought about it himself. Would it make any difference if the threat of arrest was groundless and was based on improper motive?

It is to be noted that the police officer may be liable under s 213 of the Penal Code (obtaining gratification in consideration of concealing an offence). He could also be liable under s 5 of the Prevention of Corruption Act (Singapore)(Cap 241) (see *Loh Kwang Seang* 1960 below, p 552). (For Malaysia, see Prevention of Corruption Act 1961 (Act 57 of 1961).)

HS Gour, *Penal Law of India* (10th edn, 1984) Vol 4, 3345

Now, since the "injury" here threatened may be of any kind, it follows that the question depends not so much upon the nature of the threat as upon the effect it is intended to and does produce upon the mind of the other. Nor, indeed, is it necessary that the threat should be directed against the victim if, it is intended to influence him. For instance, the son may, for the purpose of extorting money from his father, for an attempt to commit suicide, thereby frightening the father and making him accede to his request. He would then be guilty of extortion as all necessary elements of the offence are present in his case. A corrupt police officer, intending to extort money from a person, took him into custody and threatened to prosecute him for an imaginary offence, intending and knowing that his relations would come forward to ransom him, which was done. Here, the money may be intended to be extorted out of the relation, and yet the injury may not be directed against him. In this respect the English view is coincident, it being held by Lord Russell CJ, the word "menaces" in the English statute includes not merely, threats to person and property, but also involving, no doubt, a threat of injury, but of injury not confined to the person or property of the person threatened. And as was added in the same case, the threats may relate to any threat of a danger by an accusation of misconduct, not amounting to a crime. The threat may, again, be of the exposure of truth; it need not be of a falsehood. For the offence has nothing to do with the truth or falsehood of accusation, but with the intention and its effect upon the mind of the victim. Hence a terror or threat of a criminal charge whether true or false amounts to fear of injury and the act of putting in terror of a criminal charge amounts to an offence of extortion.

So, where the prisoner sent a letter to the prosecutor demanding of him a sum of money, failing which he should summon his daughter in a case as having visited a brothel with an officer, it was contended that the prosecutor had not controverted the fact that the prosecutor's daughter had visited the brothel, but Rolfe B, told the jury that, even if the lady had gone, in fact, to the brothel, it would not make any difference to the charge. The same view was taken in other cases in which the accused had threatened to expose the prosecutor for having been guilty of an infamous crime, unless a certain sum was paid up as hush money, whereupon the Court ruled that the offence had nothing to do with the truth of the accusation.

So the prosecutor while returning home one night met a woman on the way to whom he spoke, whereupon he was accosted by the prisoner who was a policman on duty, who demanded his name threatening to prosecute him for having spoken to a prostitute on the street for which he made himself liable to pay a fine of £1. He, however, proposed to let the matter drop if he was paid 5s. which the prosecutor paid him. He was held to have brought himself within the plain words of the statute. The same view has been taken in this country, it being held that the terror of a criminal charge is a fear of injury within the meaning of this section, and that this offence may be committed whether the charge threatened is true or false.

The above passage from Gour is based mainly on English cases. In the words of Murray-Aynsley CJ in *Vincent Lee* (1949), the authorities cited in the commentary in Gour are "examples of offences very different from that defined in s 384".

(ii) Constituting "injury"

There are three lines of reasoning for the view that a threat to exercise legal powers against a person who has committed an offence, unless a sum of money demanded is paid, constitutes injury.

"Additional element of putting victim in fear of injury"

In *Loh Kwang Seang* (1960), Rigby J said:

> If A, knowing that B has committed an offence in respect of which it is A's duty to take action against him, threatens to take such action against him unless B pays him a sum of money and, in consideration of such money being paid by B, forbears to take such action, then A has committed the offences of both corruption and extortion. The offence is "extortion" because the additional–and I emphasize the word "additional"–element is present of putting B in fear of injury by the threat of bringing a criminal accusation against him. It matters not whether the accusation be true or false: the offence is completed by the act of obtaining the money as a direct consequence of the threat to bring the criminal accusation.

Rigby J stated that the "additional" element present is that of putting the victim in fear of injury by threat of bringing a criminal accusation against him. It is not clear what is meant by the word "additional". There does not appear to be any additional harm done to the victim other than the "harm" brought about by the victim's own unlawful act. It is indeed the duty of the police officer to take action against him (see *Vincent Lee*, 1949, and *Abu Hassan*, 1962, see above, p 550).

Rigby J went on to say that it did not matter whether the accusation was true or false. This statement finds expression in Gour (1984, Vol 4, see above, p 551). It is noted that the authorities relied on by Gour are based on the English law of threatening with "menaces" where the threat may be the exposure of truth and need not be of falsehood. Applying English law, Gour expressed the view that a threat of a criminal charge whether true or false amounts to fear of injury and the act of putting a victim in terror of a criminal charge amounts to an offence of extortion. Gour's view overlooks the technical meaning of "injury" as defined in ss 43 and 44 of the Penal Code.

It is submitted that under s 384 of the Penal Code it makes a difference whether the criminal accusation is based on reasonable grounds or not. If the accusation was false or groundless and was actuated by improper motive, it would constitute an injury within the meaning of s 44 read with s 43 as it might "furnish ground for a civil action" (see s 43), ie malicious prosecution.

It is noted that a distinction should be made between extortion and corruption (see Prevention of Corruption Act (Cap 24) (Singapore) and Prevention of Corruption Act (Malaysia)). Rigby J in *Loh Kwang Seang* (1960) stated:

> A, acting outside the scope of his duty as a Police Officer, represents to B, falsely and inaccurately, that acts done by him constitute a criminal offence, and, under the threat of bringing an original accusation against him in respect

of those acts–and of the consequences that will ensue as a result of that criminal accusation–dishonestly induce B to give him money, then the offence is one of plain extortion and not corruption. It is not corruption for the very good reason that, in making the accusation, A was at no time acting in the course of his duty. It is extortion because, as the very word implies the money was extorted from B as a direct result of the threat of bringing a criminal accusation and of the consequences that would thereafter ensue. In such cases B, as the unwilling victim, is in no sense of the word an accomplice to the offence committed by A and his evidence, if accepted and believed, does not require corroboration.

These examples illustrate the distinction between corruption and extortion. They also serve to show that while the offence of corruption may include the offence of extortion, the latter is by no means a necessary element of the former in that extortion necessarily involves the additional and essential element of dishonestly inducing the victim to part with his money as a direct consequence of being put in fear of injury–whether injury to his person or injury arising from the threat of a criminal accusation. No such element of proof is required to sustain a conviction for corruption.

"Unlawful" demand

Ling Kai Huat v PP [1966] 1 MLJ 123 (HC, Sibu, Malaysia)

The second appellant together with the first appellant, a police constable, extorted money from one TSH by threatening to take action against him for trading without a licence. He was charged, inter alia, with extortion. He was in fact attached to the traffic branch of the police force and had nothing to do with the inspection of trade licences. Further, on the day and time in question he was off duty. The second appellant's main ground of appeal was that the learned magistrate was wrong in convicting him because the threat alleged to have been made by him was a threat to exercise his legal powers.

Lee Hun Hoe J: The definition of "injury" in the Sarawak Penal Code appears to be similar to that of Malaya and Singapore. That is to say "injury" means harm illegally caused. The emphasis is on the word "illegally". It implies an illegal act or omission. The illegality arises not as a result of the exercise of the legal powers but as a result of the unlawful demand. At page 1760 of Gour's (1955–57) the question of demand is discussed:

"Where the making of demand is legal, there is no injury in law, for injury means the causing of harm *illegally*, and no harm, whatever mental suffering it may cause, can be illegal when it is countenanced by law. But while this is conceded, it is said in Madras even in such a case, that, a legal demand may become illegal and extortionate, if it is excessive and out of proportion to the injury sustained. The accused, a village magistrate, had his goat, worth two and half rupees, injured by the complainant, whereupon he demanded a sum of Rs 10 by way of compensation, failing which he threatened to prosecute her. He was convicted of extortion and on the question about the legality of the conviction being referred to the High Court, Best J, said: "Though to threaten to use the process of the law is perfectly lawful, to do so for the purpose of enforcing payment of *more than is due* is illegal, and such a threat made with such an object must be held to be a threat of injury sufficient to constitute the offence of extortion. The fact that the offence with which the complainant was liable to be charged was compoundable can make no difference. The question is, was the complainant induced by such threats to pay the accused more than the latter was entitled to, and the finding is in the affirmative. This is sufficient to justify the conviction.

In the case under appeal there is no question of the demand being justiciable. Second appellant had no such right. The demand was without doubt illegal. Our Penal Code has its origin in the Indian Penal Code. Therefore Indian authority is bound to be persuasive and should be treated with respect. In my view *Loh Kwang Seang*'s case (1960) seems to be more in line with Indian authority.... The definition indicates that the extortioner must first use intimidation to achieve his object and such intimidation must be intentional. The intimidation is the putting of any person in fear of any injury to himself or any other person. The nature of injury is discussed at some length in Gour's *Indian Penal Code*. I refer to a passage at page 1759:

"A corrupt police officer, intending to extort money from a person, took him into custody and threatened to prosecute him for an imaginary offence, intending and knowing that his relations would come forward to ransom him, which was done. Here the money may be intended to be extorted out of the relation, and yet the injury may not be directed against him. In this respect the English view is coincident, it being held by Lord Russell CJ that the word 'menaces' in the English Statute includes not merely threats to any person and property, but also involving, no doubt, a threat to injury, but of injury not confined to the person or property of the person threatened. And as was added in the same case, the threats may relate to any threat of a danger by an accusation of misconduct, not amounting to a crime. The threat may, again, be of the exposure of truth; it need not be of a falsehood. For the offence has nothing to do with the truth or falsehood of the accusation, but with the intention and its effect upon the mind of the victim. Hence a terror or threat of a criminal charge whether true or false amounts to fear of injury and the act of putting a person in terror of a criminal charge amounts to an offence of extortion."

I agree that the exercise of legal powers, if it is lawful, can never constitute harm. It is therefore necessary to ascertain whether the exercise of such powers is lawful or not. To threaten to use the process of the law is lawful. But to do so for the purpose of demanding money or other illegal purpose is unlawful. Consequently using such threat with such an object is unlawful and can amount to a threat of "injury" within the meaning of s 44 of the Penal Code sufficient to constitute extortion. In other words when the exercise of such powers is used as a cover for an illegal purpose then it becomes unlawful and can therefore constitute "injury". For the above reasons I am inclined to support *Loh Kwang Seang*'s case (1960).

In that case at page 273 Rigby J also gave another illustration:

"But if A, acting outside the scope of his duty as a police officer, represents to B, falsely and inaccurately, that acts done by him constitute a criminal offence, and, under the threat of bringing an original accusation against him in respect of those acts–and of the consequences that will ensue as a result of that criminal accusation–dishonestly induce B to give him money, then the offence is one of plain extortion and not corruption for the very good reason that, in making the accusation, A was at no time acting in the course of his duty. It is extortion because, as the very word implies, the money was extorted from B as a direct result of the threat of bringing a criminal accusation and of the consequences that would thereafter ensue. In such cases B, as the unwilling victim, is in no sense of the word an accomplice to the offence committed by A and his evidence, if accepted and believed, does not require corroboration."

The illustration seems to cover the case under appeal. Second appellant went to the 10th and 15th Mile, Oya Road, Sibu, when he was off duty and for his own purpose. If second appellant committed a criminal offence while he was off duty he should not be allowed to claim protection by reason of the fact that he was a police constable. Assuming that as a police constable he could exercise certain legal powers then it follows from what I said previously that once he demanded for money the exercise of such powers became unlawful.

For the reasons given his appeal from conviction is dismissed.

First appellant's appeal dismissed;
Second appellant's appeal against conviction dismissed, sentence reduced

Lee Hun Hoe J states that "[t]o threaten to use the process of the law is lawful. But to do so for the purpose of demanding money or other *illegal* purpose is unlawful" and constitutes injury under s 44 of the Penal Code. Having regard to ss 43 and 44 of the Penal Code, does the learned judge's statement beg the question? Does it confuse the two separate elements of extortion, viz (1) intentionally putting a person in fear of injury and (2) dishonestly inducing the person so put in fear to deliver property, eg money. See *Kang Siew Chong* (1968, below).

Abuse of exercise of legal power

PP v Kang Siew Chong [1968] 2 MLJ 39 (HC, Raub, Malaysia)

The accused, a police constable, was charged with attempted extortion by putting a courting couple, sitting in close proximity, in fear of injury and thereby inducing them to deliver money to him. The man was married and the girl was unmarried. He had threatened to take them to the police station in order to obtain their particulars, unless they gave him M$50.

Raja Azlan Shah J [said obiter]: In my view the learned president had properly directed his mind on the law that the threat to exercise a legal power does not constitute injury within the meaning of section 44 of the Penal Code. But where he had erred was in failing to consider the exercise of the legal power. Under the section it is incumbent to distinguish between the threat to use the process of law and the exercise of that process. The former, for example, as in the present appeal the threat to take the couple to the police station in order to obtain their particulars, does not constitute injury as prescribed in section 44. But if, ... the threat is made with the object of exacting payment of money that is not due, it is an abuse of the exercise of that power and is therefore illegal, and such a threat made with such an object constitutes a threat of injury within the meaning of the section. A close parallel is afforded by the case of *B Appalasami* (1892) which is briefly reported in Ratanlal (1966):

> "Threat to use the process of law for the purpose of enforcing payment of more than is due is illegal and such a threat made with such an object is a threat of injury."

It is equally a threat of injury where money is exacted where none whatever is payable, as where a greater fee is exacted than what is legally due.

The prosecution had, in my view, established *prima facie* case which, if unrebutted, would warrant a conviction.

The defence was a mere denial. The accused said he did not extort or attempt to extort $50 from the couple. He did not threaten them at all. He did not say that he would arrest them if they refused to produce their identity cards. On the facts, a court, acting reasonably, is entitled to conclude that the accused had failed to raise a reasonable doubt as to his guilt....

Appeal allowed

On the facts, the actual decision in *Kang Siew Chong* (1968) may well be correct. However, Raja Azlan Shah J stated, obiter, that if the threat is made with the object of exacting payment of money that is not due, it is *an abuse of the exercise of that power* and is illegal within the meaning of s 44.

This reasoning confuses two distinct limbs in s 383. The first is intentionally putting a person in fear of injury. The second is dishonestly inducing the person so put in fear to deliver property. The two limbs are clearly brought out in Illustrations (a), (b), (c) and (d) of s 383. In each of the illustrations there must first be a threat of injury (s 44) which is illegal within the meaning of s 43, ie it must be an offence, or prohibited by law, or it must furnish ground for a civil action. Illustration (a) gives an example of a threat giving rise to a civil action, ie to publish a defamatory libel against a person. Illustrations (b), (c) and (d)   are examples of threats which constitute offences, eg putting a person in fear of grievous hurt.

The delivering of money or other valuable security must be induced by the threat of injury. With due respect, the learned judge is wrong in saying that a threat is illegal by reason of its being made with the object of exacting the payment of money. It is submitted that a threat by him to take the person to the police station to obtain particulars is not illegal if that person himself has done an act which justified action being taken against him (see above, p 549).

No doubt, the money demanded which is not due would cause wrongful loss to the person delivering it and wrongful gain to, say, the policeman who threatens to bring a person to the police station. While this would have satisfied the element of "dishonesty" in the second limb of s 383, extortion is not committed if the person delivering the money is not put in fear of injury itself within the combined meaning of ss 44 and 43.

The dictum of Raja Azlan Shah J appears to coalesce the two limbs abovementioned.

2. Bona fide claim of right

The *mens rea* consists in *intentionally* putting a person in fear of injury and as a consequence *dishonestly* inducing the person so put in fear to deliver property or valuable security. If a person bona fide thinks he has a right to demand payment there is no dishonest inducement.

R v A'bdul Ka'der Valad Ba'la A'buji (1866) Crown Cases 45 (HC, Bombay)

The accused had purchased from the government the right of carrying any firewood he might find lying on certain parts of the jungle during certain periods of the year. He misconstrued the extent of the right thinking that he had the sole right of removing wood to the exclusion of others. Believing himself to be entitled to all the wood lying in the jungle for a certain period, he demanded payment from the complainants for the wood they had collected. When they declined to pay, he refused to let them go. The complainants claimed that they themselves were entitled to the wood without payment.

Couch CJ: The conviction in this case cannot, we think, be upheld. There was no such fear of injury as is contemplated by s 383 of the Indian Penal Code, in the definition of "extortion", nor was the money given the complainants in consequence of any such fear of injury. If the agreement between the prisoner and the Collector had reserved the rights of the villagers, and the prisoner had a right only to take what remained of the firewood, then the villagers would have a right as against him, and the firewood would be their property. What the prisoner in effect said was: "You shall not have the firewood, unless you pay me for it."... [A]nd the prisoner may have believed in good faith that he had acquired such a right as he put forward. And even though he were wrong in his construction of the agreement, yet, if he supposed that he had the right, he would not have "dishonestly" induced the delivery of property. The right construction of the agreement appears to us to be, that the Government professed by it to give to the prisoner what they had no right to give without interfering with the rights of the villagers.

Conviction and sentence reversed

Chapter 25

Robbery

By KL Koh

A. The law

Penal Code, ss 390–402

390.–(1) In all robbery there is either theft or extortion.

(2) Theft is "robbery" if, in order to commit theft, or in committing the theft, or in carrying away or attempting to carry away property obtained by the theft, the offender, for that end, voluntarily causes or attempts to cause to any person death, or hurt, or wrongful restraint, or fear of instant death, or of instant hurt, or of instant wrongful restraint.

(3) Extortion is "robbery" if the offender, at the time of committing the extortion, is in the presence of the person put in fear, and commits the extortion by putting that person in fear of instant death, of instant hurt, or of instant wrongful restraint to that person or to some other person, and, by so putting in fear, induces the person so put in fear then and there to deliver up the thing extorted.

Explanation–The offender is said to be present if he is sufficiently near to put the other person in fear of instant death, of instant hurt, or of instant wrongful restraint.

Illustrations

(a) A holds Z down, and dishonestly takes Z's money and jewels from Z's clothes, without Z's consent. Here A has committed theft, and, in order to the committing of that theft, has voluntarily caused wrongful restraint to Z. A has therefore committed robbery.

(b) A meets Z on the high road, shows a pistol, and demands Z's purse. Z, in consequence surrenders his purse. Here A has extorted the purse from Z, by putting him in fear of instant hurt, and being at the time of committing the extortion in his presence. A has therefore committed robbery.

(c) A meets Z and Z's child on the high road. A takes the child, and threatens to fling it down a precipice, unless Z delivers his purse. Z, in consequence, delivers his purse. Here A has extorted the purse from Z, by causing Z to be in fear of instant hurt to the child, Z being present. A has therefore committed robbery on Z.

(d) A obtains property from Z by saying, "Your child is in the hands of my gang, and will be put to death unless you send us $1,000." This is extortion, and punishable as such; but it is not robbery, unless Z is put in fear of the instant death of his child.

391. When 5 or more persons conjointly commit or attempt to commit a robbery, or where the whole number of persons conjointly committing or at-

558

tempting to commit a robbery, and of persons present and aiding such commission or attempt, amount to 5 or more, every person so committing, attempting, or aiding, is said to commit "gang-robbery".

392. Whoever commits robbery shall be punished with imprisonment for a term of not less than 2 years and not more than 10 years and shall also be punished with caning with not less than 6 strokes; and if the robbery is committed after 7 pm and before 7 am the offender shall be punished with imprisonment for a term of not less than 3 years and not more than 14 years and shall also be punished with caning with not less than 12 strokes.

393. Whoever attempts to commit robbery shall be punished with imprisonment for a term of not less than 2 years and not more than 7 years and shall also be punished with caning with not less than 6 strokes.

394. If any person, in committing or in attempting to commit robbery, voluntarily causes hurt, such person, and any other person, jointly concerned in committing or attempting to commit such robbery, shall be punished with imprisonment for a term of not less than 5 years and not more than 20 years and shall also be punished with caning with not less than 12 strokes.

395. Whoever commits gang-robbery shall be punished with imprisonment for a term of not less than 5 years and not more than 20 years and shall also be punished with caning with not less than 12 strokes.

396. If any one of 5 of more persons who are conjointly committing gang-robbery, commits murder in so committing gang-robbery, every one of those persons shall be punished with death or imprisonment for life, and if he is not sentenced to death, shall also be punished with caning with not less than 12 strokes.

397. If at the time of committing or attempting to commit robbery, the offender is armed with or uses any deadly weapon, or causes grievous hurt to any person, or attempts to cause death or grievous hurt to any person, such offender shall be punished with caning with not less than 12 strokes, in addition to any other punishment to which he may be liable under any other section of this Code.

399.* Whoever makes any preparation for committing gang-robbery, shall be punished with imprisonment for a term of not less than 3 years and not more than 10 years and shall also be punished with caning with not less than 12 strokes.

400. Whoever shall belong to a gang of persons associated for the purpose of habitually committing gang-robbery, shall be punished with imprisonment for life, or with imprisonment for a term which may extend to 10 years, and shall also be punished with caning with not less than 6 strokes.

401. Whoever shall belong to any wandering or other gang of persons associated for the purpose of habitually committing theft or robbery, and not being gang-robbers, shall be punished with imprisonment for a term which may extend to 7 years, and shall also be punished with caning with not less than 4 strokes.

402. Whoever shall be one of 5 or more persons assembled for the purpose of committing gang-robbery, shall be punished with imprisonment for a term which may extend to 7 years, and shall also be punished with caning with not less than 4 strokes.

1.   Punishment

In Singapore the punishments for robbery and its aggravated forms were increased in 1984 (See Penal Code (Amendment) Act 1984 (Act 23 of 1984). Below is a comparative table of the position in Singapore and Malaysia.

Penal Code of Singapore	*FMS Penal Code*
S 392 (robbery): Imprisonment for not less than 2 years and not more than 10 years and caning with not less than 6 strokes.	Imprisonment up to 10 years and fine.
S 392 (after 7 pm and before 7 am): Imprisonment for not less than 3 years and not more than 14 years and caning with not less than 12 strokes.	(Between sunset and sunrise): Imprisonment up to 14 years and fine or whipping.
S 393 (attempted robbery): Imprisonment for not less than 2 years and not more than 7 years and caning with not less than 6 strokes.	Imprisonment up to 7 years and fine.
S 394 (causing hurt in committing robbery): Imprisonment for not less than 5 years and not more than 20 years and caning with not less than 12 strokes.	Imprisonment up to 20 years and fine or whipping.
S 395 (gang-robbery): Imprisonment for not less than 5 years and not more than 20 years and caning with not less than 12 strokes.	Imprisonment up to 20 years and whipping.
S 396 (gang-robbery with murder): Death or imprisonment for life or up to 10 years and (if no death sentence) caning with not less than 12 strokes.	Death, or imprisonment up to 20 years and whipping.
S 397 (armed robbery): Caning with not less than 12 strokes in addition to any other imprisonment.	Whipping in addition to other punishment under the Code.
S 399 (preparation for committing robbery):	Imprisonment up to 10 years and whipping.

Imprisonment of not less than
3 years and not more than
10 years and caning with not less
than 12 strokes.

S 400 (gang-robbery):   Imprisonment up to 20 years
Imprisonment for life or up to   and whipping.
10 years, and caning with not less
than 6 strokes.

S 401 (wandering gang of   Imprisonment up to 7 years and
thieves): Imprisonment which   fine or whipping.
may extend to 7 years and caning
with not less than 4 strokes.

S 402 (assembling for purpose of   Imprisonment up to 7 years and
committing gang-robbery):   fine or whipping.
Imprisonment which may extend
to 7 years and caning with not less
than 4 strokes.

Robbery is theft or extortion in an aggravated form. Hence, the elements of theft or extortion must be present in addition to the aggravated circumstances set out in robbery.

Section 390 provides for the circumstances when theft constitutes robbery. The words "for that end" in s 390 must relate to the commission of theft. Hence where an assault has no relation to the theft, robbery is not committed. If, for example, the accused first assaulted the complainant and then subsequently formed an intention to take his watch, he cannot be liable for robbery but only for theft.

2. "For that end"

Bishambhar Nath v Emperor AIR (1941) Oudh 476 (HC, Oudh, India)

The applicants tried their luck at a dart shooting stall at a carnival. An altercation ensued with the manager. A scuffle broke out and thereafter the applicants removed a cash box and money from a table.

Ghulam Hasan J: Can it be said in the present case that in order to the committing of the theft of cash or in committing the theft of cash, or in carrying away or attempting to carry away property obtained by the theft, the accused, for that end, voluntarily caused or attempted to cause hurt? The words "for that end" used in s 390, Penal Code, in my opinion, clearly mean that the hurt caused by the offender must be with the express object of facilitating the committing of the theft, or must be caused while the offender is committing the theft or is carrying away or is attempting to carry away the property obtained by the theft. It does not mean that the assault or the hurt must be caused in the same transaction or in the same circumstances. A Bench of the Madras High Court in *Karuppa Gounden* (1917) has held that "the word 'for that end' in s 390, Penal Code, cannot be read as meaning in those circumstances". It was held by the Lahore High Court in *Karmun* (1934) that

> "before a person can be convicted of robbery the prosecution must prove that hurt was caused in order to the committing of the theft or in committing the theft or in carrying away or attempting to carry away the property obtained by the theft. The hurt contemplated must be a conscious and voluntary act on the part of the thief for the purpose of overpowering resistance on the part of the victim, quite separate and distinct from the act of theft itself."

In the present case it cannot be contended with any show of reason that whatever injury was caused it was caused when the assault was made upon the stall manager and his servant with the primary object of enabling the accused to the committing of the theft. I am satisfied, therefore, that the assault or the beating had no relation whatever to the commission of the theft, although there is no doubt that the theft was committed at the same time or immediately afterwards. I am of opinion that the accused are not guilty of an offence under s 394, Penal Code....

Revisions partly allowed

The essence of robbery is that the offender, for the committing of theft or carrying away of or attempting to carry away of property obtained by theft, commits one or the other of the wrongful acts mentioned in s 390. Where a thief after abandoning stolen property uses violence against his pursuers in order to avoid capture, the theft is not converted into robbery. (See *Nga Po Thet*, 1917.)

Where violence is used, for example, firing at a guard while carrying away the booty after the commission of the robbery, it would fall within s 390 and also under the Arms Offences Act (Singapore)(Cap 14) (see below, pp 571–572).

3.   Section 397: armed robbery

In both Singapore and Malaysia, s 397 deals with the situation where the offender is either "armed with" or "uses" a deadly weapon. In India, each of these situations is dealt with separately, the first in the Indian Penal Code s 398 which is punishable with imprisonment of not less than seven years; and, the second, in the Indian Penal Code s 397 which is also punishable with imprisonment of not less than seven years. There is no s 398 under the Singapore and FMS Penal Codes as the two situations are dealt with in s 397.

(a) "Armed with" and "uses"

In the Indian case of *Phool Kumar* (1975, see below, p 563), the two terms "armed with" and "uses" (in ss 398 and 397 of the Indian Penal

Code respectively) were given an identical meaning. Unlike in the Arms Offences Act (Singapore) (see below, p 571) the word "use" is not defined in the Penal Code.

Phool Kumar v Delhi Administration AIR (1975) SC 905 (SC, India)

Untwalia J: "Phool Kumar had a knife in his hand." He was therefore carrying a deadly weapon open to the view of the victims sufficient to frighten or terrorize them. Any other overt act, such as, brandishing of the knife or causing of grievous hurt with it was not necessary to bring the offender within the ambit of s 397 of the Penal Code.

6. Section 398 uses the expression "armed with any deadly weapon" and the minimum punishment provided therein is also 7 years if at the time of attempting to commit robbery the offender is armed with any deadly weapon. This has created an anomaly. It is unreasonable to think that if the offender who merely attempted to commit robbery but did not succeed in committing it attracts the minimum punishment of 7 years under s 398 if he is merely armed with any deadly weapon, while an offender so armed will not incur the liability of the minimum punishment under s 397 if he succeeded in committing the robbery. But then, what was the purport behind the use of the different words by the Legislature in the two sections, viz "uses" in s 397 and "is armed" in s 398. In our judgment the anomaly is resolved if the two terms are given the identical meaning. There seems to be a reasonable explanation for the use of the two different expressions in the sections. When the offence of robbery is committed by an offender being armed with a deadly weapon which was within the vision of the victim so as to be capable of creating a terror in his mind, the offender must be deemed to have used that deadly weapon in the commission of the robbery. On the other hand, if an offender was armed with a deadly weapon at the time of attempting to commit a robbery, then the weapon was not put to any fruitful use because it would have been of use only when the offender succeeded in committing the robbery.

7. If the deadly weapon is actually used by the offender in the commission of the robbery such as in causing grievous hurt, death or the like then it is clearly used. In the cases of *Chandra Nath* (1932); *Nagar Singh* (1933) and *Inder Singh* (1934) some overt act such as brandishing the weapon against another person in order to over-awe him or displaying the deadly weapon to frighten his victim have been held to attract the provisions of s 397 of the Penal Code. JC Shah and Vyas JJ of the Bombay High Court have said in the case of *Govind Dipaji More* (1956) that if the knife "was used for the purpose of producing such an impression upon the mind of a person that he would be compelled to part with his property, that would amount to 'using' the weapon within the meaning of s 397." In that case also the evidence against the appellant was that he carried a knife in his hand when he went to the shop of the victim. In our opinion this is the correct view of the law and the restricted meaning given to the word 'uses' in the case of *Chand Singh* (1970) is not correct....

Phool Kumar (1975) has been followed in two recent Indian decisions: see *Jai Parkash* (1981); and *Jang Singh* (1984).

(b) Creating a substantive offence

This question, whether s 397 of the Singapore and the FMS Penal Codes creates a substantive offence, has been raised in a number of cases in Singapore and Malaysia. One view is that s 397 creates a substantive offence and s 34 (see ch 17) can be invoked. This would mean that other miscreants who were not armed with or did not use deadly weapons could be jointly liable with the offender. Another view is that s 397 merely prescribes an additional punishment for this aggravated form of robbery; there is no scope for the application of s 34.

(i)   Applicability of s 34 to s 397

R v Yeo Kim Watt (1946) 12 MLJ 155 (CCA, Singapore)

The first appellant and the second appellant were jointly charged under ss 392 and 397 of the Code. It was found that the second appellant was armed with a deadly weapon, ie a pistol, but the first appellant was not. The trial judge convicted both the appellants of the offence of robbery under s 392. As the second appellant was armed with the pistol, he was sentenced to an additional punishment under s 397, but not the first appellant.

The trial judge then stated a case for the decision of the Court of Criminal Appeal as to whether he was correct in his view that s 34 of the Code has no application to s 397.

Willan CJ: [T]he question referred to this Court for a decision is as follows:

If one member of a gang is guilty of committing, or attempting to commit, robbery in any one of the aggravating circumstances set out in s 397 of the Penal Code, can the provisions of s 34 of that Code be invoked to support a charge against every member of the gang under the first mentioned section?

As almost all the authorities cited by counsel when arguing the case before us were decisions of Indian Courts, it is necessary in the first place to decide whether the provisions now contained in our Penal Code and in the Indian Penal Code have the same effect....

Until comparatively recent times the various Courts in India were in direct conflict regarding the correct answer to the question which has been referred to this Court, but it now appears to have become settled law in all Indian Courts that the provisions of s 34 of the Indian Penal Code cannot rightly be invoked to render a person convicted under ss 392 and 393 liable to the penalties prescribed by ss 397 or 398. Perusal of the numerous reported cases shows that the decisions are based on two grounds, viz:

(a) "Neither s 397 nor s 398 creates an offence. The effect of these sections is merely to limit the minimum of punishment which may be awarded if certain facts are proved". (Page J in *Ali Mirza*, 1923); and

(b) In both sections it is specifically provided that "the offender" shall be liable to the penalties prescribed by the sections and, being a penal statute, this provision must be construed strictly.

Now it is abundantly clear that the substituted s 397 in our Penal Code does not "merely limit the minimum punishment which may be awarded if certain facts are proved" because no minimum punishment of any kind is in fact prescribed. To this extent therefore the reason advanced by Page J does not apply to our Code. The main ground he set out in support of his decision, however, was that ss 397 and 398 of the Indian Penal Code do not create offences. It is unnecessary to consider whether we are in agreement or not with this decision in so far as the two sections of the Indian Penal Code are concerned, but it is necessary to consider whether s 397 of our Penal Code creates a separate offence or whether it merely prescribes a punishment for an offence already defined in the Code. In other words, is the commission of the offence of robbery in any of the aggravated circumstances set out in that section an offence distinct from robbery which is punishable under s 392 or attempted robbery which is punishable under s 393 of the Penal Code?

Turning to other sections of the Penal Code for guidance, it is clear that committing theft in any of the aggravating circumstances set out in s 382 is an offence entirely different from theft under s 379, and voluntarily causing hurt by the weapons or the means set out in s 324 is not the same offence as is punishable under s 323 for voluntarily causing hurt. There are a number of other instances in the Code where the commission of an offence in specified aggravating circumstances is made an offence quite separate and distinct from the commission of the offence in the absence of such circumstances. Thus comparable provisions in other parts of the Penal Code indicate that in fact a new offence was created when the new s 397 was substituted for the original section, because s 397, when read with s 392 or s 393, creates offences which are aggravated forms of the offences of robbery and of attempted robbery.

Counsel pointed out that since s 397 refers to "the offender ... such offender" whereas s 394 refers to "any person ... such persons", the introduction of the word "offender" in the former section must be assumed to be intentional, and that the object could only have been to limit the application of the section to the robber or robbers who actually committed the aggravated offence. This was one of the grounds on which the decisions of the Indian Courts were based.

As to this, we would first point out that there is no need to have recourse to s 34 when considering s 394 because under that section the guilty act of the robber who causes hurt in committing the robbery is imputed to all the others who are jointly concerned in the commission of the robbery, and it would not avail any one of the others to say that he had nothing to do with the causing of such hurt. We might add that a similar liability attaches itself to each member of the gang under s 396 when one of such members commits murder during the actual gang robbery.

In the second place, if counsel's submission is correct, the anomalous situation arises that whereas, by virtue of the specific provision contained in s 394, if any person in committing or attempting to commit robbery voluntarily causes "hurt", such person "and every other person jointly concerned in committing or attempting to commit such robbery" become liable to an increased penalty, but if in the same circumstances the hurt caused was "grievous hurt" only the actual assailant is liable to be charged, and thus become liable to the increased penalty, under s 397.

An example of such an anomaly would be the case of three persons, each armed with a stick, jointly committing robbery by day and in such robbery causing hurt by blows struck with such sticks. For committing the robbery and causing hurt they would all be liable to imprisonment and a whipping under s 394. If, however, one of the blows had been struck with slightly greater force and grievous hurt caused–say the complainant's little finger had been broken–then, according to the Indian decisions, only the robber who had caused that particular grievous hurt would be liable to the additional punishment of whipping under s 397.

To take the anomalies further. If in a robbery one of the persons is armed with a knife and causes hurt in the commission of such robbery, all the robbers are liable to imprisonment and a whipping under s 394; if the robber with the knife goes further and causes grievous hurt, he only is liable to be whipped under s 397; and lastly, if there are at least five persons committing such robbery and the one armed with the knife causes death in committing what has now become gang-robbery, then all are liable to be punished with death, or imprisonment together with a whipping under s 396.

We cannot think that the legislature intended such anomalies, because in case such as we have instanced it only takes one person armed with a knife or a gun to overawe the inhabitants of the premises to be robbed, whilst the other members of the gang proceed with the actual robbing.

If, without in any way straining the generally accepted rules of interpretation, another construction is possible which would avoid creating these anomalies, that construction should be adopted. In our view this is possible for the following reasons:

(a) Comparison of the language of s 397 with that of s 394 is of no assistance as to whether s 34 applies to s 397 because the provisions of s 394 are sufficient in themselves to deal with all the persons committing robbery with hurt without recourse to s 34.

(b) By s 9 of the Penal Code it is provided that words in the singular include the plural and therefore the word "offender" in s 397 can be interpreted as including more than one person.

(c) Section 397, when read with s 392 or s 393, creates separate and distinct offences from the offences prescribed by the two last mentioned sections to the same extent that the offence of theft in any of the aggravating circumstances set out in s 382 is an offence different from theft under s 379 and just as voluntarily causing hurt by the weapon or the means set out in s 324 is not the same offence as that which is punishable under s 323 for voluntarily causing hurt.

(d) That since s 392 or s 393, read together with s 397, creates separate and distinct offences, there is no reason why s 34 should not apply to those offences to the same extent as it applies to other offences.

With regard to the reference, therefore, this Court decides that the provisions of s 34 of the Penal Code are applicable to s 397 of that Code in respect of the offences defined when that section is used conjointly with s 392 or s 393.

Reference answered accordingly

Willan CJ distinguished the Indian authorities on s 397 on the ground that s 397 does not lay down a minimum punishment. With respect, the type of punishment, ie whether or not there is a minimum punishment is not the crux of the matter in determining whether a substantive offence is created. Section 397 creates an aggravated form of robbery, ie where the offender is armed with a deadly weapon, for which the offence carries a heavier punishment than simple robbery under s 392.

Lee Wai Kam v PP [1976] 2 MLJ 19 (HC, Ipoh, Malaysia)

The appellant and another were charged with armed robbery under ss 392 and 397 of the Penal Code.

Abdoolcader J: [Counsel for the appellant] submits that there was no evidence adduced as to which of the two persons involved in the robbery in question was armed with a knife. Mr Devadas relies on the Indian case of *Labedan Sain* (1931) for the proposition that where two or more persons are involved in a robbery, s 34 of the Penal Code has no application to s 397 of the Code, that it must therefore be affirmatively shown that it was the appellant who was armed with a knife, and that accordingly the charge was bad and the proceedings a nullity.

I pointed out the conflicting decisions on this point in the Indian courts but it is not necessary to go further into this issue as fortunately, or perhaps unfortunately for the appellant, the matter has in fact been conclusively determined by the Court of Criminal Appeal of Singapore in *Yeo Kim Watt* (1946) to the effect that there is no reason why s 34 of the Code should not apply to s 392 or s 393 read together with s 397 of the Code to the same extent as it applies to other offences.

Appeal dismissed

(ii) Non-applicability of s 34 to s 397

Subramaniam v PP [1976] 1 MLJ 76 (HC, KL, Malaysia)

One of the three appellants was armed with a knife which was a deadly weapon within the meaning of s 397 of the Penal Code. The other two were not armed nor did they cause grievous hurt or attempt to cause death or grievous hurt to any person. The appellants were charged under ss 392 and 397 read with s 34 of the Penal Code.

Ajaib Singh J: The appellants were ... charged under ss 392 and 397 read with s 34 of the Penal Code. S 397 provides for the imposition of an additional punishment by way of whipping if at the time of committing or attempting to commit the substantive offence of robbery the offender is armed with or uses a deadly weapon or causes grievous hurt to any person or attempts to cause death or grievous hurt to any person. However, whipping may be ordered by the court only against the particular offender who is thus armed or causes grievous hurt or attempts to cause death or grievous hurt and not against a person who associates with such armed offender in the commission of the offence of robbery but is himself not armed with a deadly weapon and does not himself cause grievous hurt or attempts to cause death or grievous hurt to any person. The joint liability of two or more persons in the doing of a criminal act under s 34 of the Penal Code does not extend to s 397 of the Code. Section 397 provides for the imposition of an additional sentence and its provisions are to be invoked only against an offender who actually acts in contravention of that section and to no other person no matter how much that person may have acted in concert and in furtherance of the common intention to commit robbery.

In the present case only one of the three robbers was armed with a knife which was a deadly weapon within the meaning of s 397 of the Penal Code. The other two were not armed nor did they cause grievous hurt or attempt to cause death or grievous hurt to any person. The additional punishment of whipping under s 397 could therefore be imposed only against the armed offender but unfortunately the facts of the case as recorded by the learned president do not state which one of the offenders was armed with the knife.

Before imposing any whipping under s 397 the learned president ought to have ascertained from the prosecuting officer as to which particular offender was armed. This was not done and in the absence of any evidence that either of the appellants had acted in contravention of s 397 of the Penal Code the learned president had no power to order whipping under that section. It need hardly be stressed how important it is for presiding officers in criminal courts to obtain full and accurate details of a crime of which an accused person pleads guilty for only then can the courts be in a good position to assess the seriousness or otherwise of the case and impose appropriate sentences in accordance with the law.

Convictions and sentences set aside

PP v Pua Kia Sing [1977] 2 MLJ 93 (HC, KL, Malaysia)

Ong Hock Sim FJ: In my view s 397 of the Penal Code does not create any offence and s 34 cannot therefore be invoked for the sole purpose of administering the additional penalty of whipping upon others involved in the offence charged. Section 397 ... does not create an offence but empowers the court to impose a punishment *in addition to* any other sentence provided by law for his offence.

I may add that I am in agreement with *Ajaib Singh J in Subramaniam* (1976) that s 34 cannot be invoked for the purpose of punishing other than the offender armed. I am aware that Abdoolcader J followed *Yeo Kim Watt* (1946) (a Singapore case) in holding in *Lee Wai Kam* (1976) that "there was no reason why s 34 of the Penal Code should not apply to s 392 read together with s 397 of the Penal Code *as it applies to other offences*" (emphasis is mine). With respect those judgments erred in accepting s 397 as creating an offence which, I repeat is not supported by the language of the section. The Penal Code of Singapore had the same ss 397 and 398 as the Indian Penal Code prior to the 1938 amendment. The new s 397 did no more than remove the mandatory minimum imprisonment that was provided under the old ss 397 and 398 but enacted that whipping may be inflicted, as an *additional penalty* to that prescribed for the offence charged in regard to the offender who was armed at the time of the offence. There is no reason to differ from the Indian Courts that s 34 has no application in the construction of s 397.

Order accordingly

Tan Chew Man v PP [1977] 2 MLJ 247 (FC, KL, Malaysia)

Ong Hock Sim FJ: No doubt, Ajaib Singh J [the trial judge] allowed himself to be influenced by *Lee Wai Kam* (1976) where Abdoolcader J held that "there was no reason why s 34 of the Penal Code should not apply to s 392 read together with s 397 of the Penal Code to the same extent as it applies to other offences ... as the matter has been conclusively determined by the Court of Criminal Appeal of Singapore in *Yeo Kim Watt* (1946). That judgment received adverse editorial comment at pp lxxxvii to lxxxix of the same volume (1946). We do not agree with that judgment for the reasons given by the learned editor. In that case and *Lee Wai Kam* (1976), the error was in the view taken that s 397 read with s 392 creates a separate and distinct offence. We would adopt the comments of the learned editor which we now reporduce *seriatim*:

"The point at issue is however whether s 397 constitutes a separate offence in itself. We respectfully submit that it does not and that in fact s 397 only provides for an additional punishment for the person or persons who at the time of committing or attempting to commit robbery are armed with or use deadly weapons or cause grievous hurt or attempts to cause death or grievous hurt" and concluded:

"We feel that the Court of Criminal Appeal should have set a higher value to the present unanimous opinion of the courts in India that s 34 of the Indian Penal Code has no application to s 397 or 398 of that Code."...

(Our s 397 replaced the former sections *in pari materia* which provided for minimum terms to be imposed and prescribed that the punishment for robbery (under s 392) and attempted robbery (under s 393) for an offender armed with a deadly weapon shall be liable to whipping "*in addition to any other punishment* under any other section of the Code").

As Ratanlal (1971) says:

"This section is merely a rider to s 394. It does not create any substantive offence."

We, therefore, allow the appeal of the appellant and set aside his conviction and sentence on the first charge. The co-accused was sentenced concurrently with his sentence on the second charge and no order need be made here in regard to his conviction and sentence on the first charge.

Upon the record we are satisfied that there was ample evidence on the charges against the appellant and his co-accused of offences under ss 4 and 9 respectively of the Firearms (Increased Penalties) Act 1971. They have both pleaded guilty thereto. We therefore dismiss his appeal in respect of the second charge.

The judgment, to the extent as varied, stands.

Order accordingly

KL Koh, "Joint Liability and s 397 of the Penal Code of Malaysia" (1977) 19 Mal LR 383, 385

[T]he aggravating circumstances of robbery under s 397, which carry a heavier punishment, can be regarded as creating an offence separate and distinct from robbery *simpliciter* under s 390. For the ingredients of aggravated robbery under s 397 consist of robbery *plus* the aggravating circumstances set out in the section. The additional ingredients, ie the aggravating circumstances render it different from robbery *simpliciter*. By way of analogy it may be noted that robbery itself is theft or extortion in aggravated circumstances. It has never been suggested that robbery is not separate and distinct from theft or extortion.

(b) *Does the language of s 397 preclude the application of s 34?*
The language of the section must be examined to see if it precludes the application of s 34.

In *Yeo Kim Watt* (1946), which was followed in *Lee Wai Kam* (1976), the question was raised as to whether the word "offender" in s 397 can be interpreted as including more than one person. The Court of Criminal Appeal in Singapore provided a short answer by simply saying that "By s 9 of the Penal Code it is provided that words in the singular include the plural and therefore the word 'offender' in s 397 can be interpreted as including more than one person."

On the other hand, in *Subramaniam* (1976), Ajaib Singh J was of the view that "its provisions [s 397] are to be invoked only against an offender who actually acts in contravention of that section and to no other person no matter how much that person may have acted in concert and in furtherance of the common intention to commit robbery." According to the learned judge, liability under s 397 is confined only to "such offender", ie the person who is armed with or uses any deadly weapon or causes grievous hurt to any person, or attempts to cause death or grievous hurt to any person at the time of committing or attempting to commit robbery. In the instant case, Ong Hock Sim FJ endorsed this view.

With respect, both approaches are incorrect. Whether or not s 34 can be invoked in s 397 does not depend on a substitution of words in the plural for the singular. A substitution would make s 397 read, *inter alia*:

> "If at the time of committing or attempting to commit robbery, the *offenders* are armed with or use any deadly weapon, or cause grievous hurt to any person ... *such offenders* shall be liable to be whipped...".

This will still mean the offenders who are armed or who cause the grievous hurt, etc. But we are concerned with the liability of a person other than "such offender", ie a person who is not armed or who did not himself cause the grievous hurt but who satisfies the conditions set out in s 34.

It is noteworthy that the Code generally employs the singular to describe the person committing an offence. For example, s 302 reads: "Whoever commits murder shall be punished with death." Section 34 has been applied to this section to make others jointly liable. It has never been suggested that the use of the singular in s 302 precludes the application of s 34, nor has it been thought that s 9 is the answer. It is submitted that whether or not the language of s 397 precludes the application of s 34 does not depend on whether the singular or the plural is used. Nor is the application of s 34 precluded by reason that in the later part of s 397, the word "such" is used to qualify the offender. Joint liability in the doing of a criminal act is provided for in s 34 itself. It is s 34 which must be considered in the circumstances of each case to ascertain the liability of any person other than "such offender". Suppose A and B set out to commit robbery. B purchases a knife and hands it over to A. In furtherance of the common intention of both to commit robbery, A stabs the victim and causes grievous hurt. It is submitted that A would be liable as "such offender" under s 397 read with s 392. But B would be liable under s 397 read with s 392 and s 34, even though it was A, the offender, who did the act under s 397.

The confusion has arisen because of the wording of the allied offence in s 394 which reads:

> "If any person, in committing or in attempting to commit robbery, voluntarily causes hurt, such person, and *any other person jointly concerned* in committing or attempting to commit such robbery, shall be punished...." (Italics added.)

The phrase "any other person jointly concerned" in committing or attempting to commit such robbery renders s 34 unnecessary. In fact, s 394 seems wider in scope than s 34. For under s 394 it is not necessary to show that the *criminal act*, ie the causing of hurt, is done by several persons in *furtherance of the common intention* to commit robbery. It is only necessary to prove that the other person is *jointly concerned* in committing or attempting to commit such robbery.

The difference in wording between ss 394 and 397 has led some Indian courts to conclude that the introduction of the word "such offender" in s 397 is intentional, and that the object could only have been to limit the application of the section to the offender who actually commits the aggravated offence.

However, in *Yeo Kim Watt* (1946), Willan CJ rejected the above reasoning and pointed out that if that were correct, the anomalous situations would arise. He said:

> "An example of such an anomaly would be the case of three persons, each armed with a stick, jointly committing robbery by day and in such robbery causing hurt by blows struck with such sticks. For committing the robbery and causing hurt they would all be liable to imprisonment and a whipping under s 394. If, however, one of the blows had been struck with slightly greater force and grievous hurt caused–say the complainant's little finger had been broken–then, according to the Indian decisions, only the robber who had caused that particular grievous hurt would be liable to the additional punishment of whipping under s 397. To take the anomalies further. If in a robbery one of the persons is armed with a knife and causes hurt, in the commission of such robbery, all the robbers are liable to imprisonment and a whipping under s 394; if the robber with the knife goes further and causes grievous hurt, he only is liable to be whipped under s 397."

Willan CJ also pointed out another anomaly under s 396 (which deals with aggravated gang-robbery) where if there are at least five persons committing gang-robbery and the one armed with the knife causes death in committing gang-robbery, then all are liable to be punished, *inter alia*, with death or with imprisonment for life. As in s 394, the above section also renders s 34 unnecessary. Section 396 reads:

> "If any one of five or more persons, who are conjointly committing gang-robbery, commits murder in so committing gang-robbery, every one of those persons shall be punished...".

These anomalies strengthen the view that s 34 is applicable to s 397 in appropriate situations in rendering a person, other than "such offender", liable in the same manner as if the act were done by him alone.

It is unfortunate that the Court in the instant case did not analyse more closely the ambit of s 34 in relation to s 397. It is hoped that the Federal Court of Malaysia will one day resolve the conflicting High Court decisions and choose to follow *Lee Wai Kam* (1976).

(iii) Comparison with Singapore Arms Offences Act

Section 5 of the Arms Offences Act deals with the punishment for accomplices. The section reads:

> Where any arm is used by any person in committing or in attempting to commit any offence, each of his accomplices in respect of the last-mentioned offence present at the scene of the offence who may reasonably be presumed to have known that that person was carrying or had in his possession or under his control such arm, shall, unless he proves that he had taken all reasonable steps to prevent the use of such arms, be guilty of an offence and shall on conviction be punished with death.

"Arm" is defined in s 2:

> "arm" means any firearm, air-gun, air-pistol, automatic gun, automatic pistol and any other kind of gun or pistol from which any shot, bullet or other

missile can be discharged or noxious liquid, flame or fumes can be emitted, and any component part thereof and includes any bomb or grenade and any component part thereof;

The expression "use" is defined in s 2 as follows:

"use", with its grammatical variations, means–

(a) in relation to a firearm, air-gun, air-pistol, automatic gun, automatic pistol and any other kind of gun or pistol from which any shot, bullet or other missile can be discharged or noxious fluid, flame or fumes can be emitted–to cause such shot, bullet or other missile to be discharged or such noxious liquid, flame or fumes to be emitted with intent to cause physical injury to any person; and

(b) in relation to a bomb or grenade–to throw the same, or to cause the same to explode, with intent to cause physical injury to any person or property.

Section 5 of the Arms Offences Act	*Section 397 of the Penal Code*
(1) Committing or attempting to commit *any offence*.	Committing or attempting to commit *robbery*.
(2) *Arm is used.*	Armed with *or* uses any *deadly weapon*.
(3) There must be actual use of arm as defined in s 2, ie an intent to cause physical injury.	Mere possession of a deadly weapon is sufficient, and no actual use is necessary (see above, p 563).
(4) Accomplice liable if present at scene of offence, who may reasonably be presumed to have known that such person was carrying or had in his possession or under his control the arm.	Whether accomplice liable depends on whether s 397 creates a substantive offence–authorities conflicting (see above pp 564–571).
(5) Punishable with death.	Punishable with caning of no less than 12 strokes, in addition to any punishment to which he may be liable under any other section of the Penal Code.

In *Chang Bock Eng* (1979), the two appellants were jointly tried for armed robbery. The charge against the first appellant was for committing an offence punishable under s 4 of the Arms Offences Act 1973 (Act 61 of 1973). The second appellant was charged as an accomplice with an offence punishable under s 5 of the said Act. Choor Singh J, in dismissing the appeal, said:

It is not a requirement of s 5 of the Act that an accomplice in the commission or attempted commission of a criminal offence must be proved to have knowledge at the time he joins the principal that the latter is armed with a firearm. What is required is proof that the accomplice may reasonably be presumed to have knowledge that the person who used the firearm in committing or attempting to commit an offence was either (i) carrying it, or (ii) had it in his possession or (iii) had it under his control during the commission or attempted commission of that offence. The burden then shifts on the accomplice to prove that he had taken all reasonable steps to prevent the use by the principal offender of such firearm in the commission or attempted commission of that offences.

Section 5 of the Arms Offences Act deals with the liability of accomplices to any offence in which an arm is used. Where armed robbery is committed under s 397 and an arm is used, eg firing a gun in the course of gang-robbery, the accomplice should be charged under s 397 and s 5 of the Arms Offences Act. Where there is only possession of a deadly weapon (which would include any "arm" within the meaning of the Arms Offences Act) or where it is not actually used, eg mere brandishing, the accomplice may be charged under s 397 only if it can be read with s 34 of the Penal Code (see above, pp 564–567).

Talib b Haji Hamzah v PP [1976] 2 MLJ 2 (CCA, Singapore)

The appellant was an accomplice in two gang-robberies, an offence under ss 395 and 397 of the Penal Code. In each of these gang-robberies a pistol was used by one of the members of the gang. The appellant was convicted of each of the following charges.

Wee Chong Jin CJ: Counsel for the appellant submits that on the evidence before the trial court relating to both robberies, it was not established beyond a reasonable doubt, that in each case a firearm was used within the meaning of s 2 [Arms Offences Act]. Counsel's contention is that in both cases, a firearm or firearms were discharged indiscriminately in order to intimidate the victims and others who might be inclined to intervene; that because of the definition of "use", a charge under s 5 requires a specific intent on the part of the person who discharged the firearm to be proved, namely the intent to cause physical injury to any person; that there was no evidence of such intent in both cases and that the appellant was therefore not guilty on both charges.

Counsel's second submission is that assuming that a firearm was used within the meaning of s 2 in both robberies, on the evidence tendered, it was unreasonable to presume that the appellant knew in both cases that the robber who so used the firearm in each robbery, was carrying such firearm. Consequently, as the evidence did not support the requisite presumption under s 5, both convictions were wrong in law....

Taking the second submission first, and considering it in relation to the first charge, which arose out of the gang robbery at Nam Yick Jewellers, we find that the trial judges have dealt with this matter in their grounds of decision as follows:

"It was clear to me that five male Malays had committed the offence of armed gang robbery on the premises of Nam Yick Jewellers.... There was also evidence to show that three of the robbers were armed with firearms and that at least one firearm was used during the commission of this robbery. Poon Cheok Ming ... was shot at two or three times and one of the shots had hit him on his left shoulder and injured him.... There was evidence to show that the accused was one of the five male Malays present in the shop at the time of the robbery and had actively participated in the robbery.

The evidence of how this robbery was carried out revealed that it was a carefully planned act executed with great precision and with almost lightning speed. The incident itself took place in broad day light in one of the busy parts of this city.

There was ample circumstances present here from which we considered it reasonable to presume that the accused knew that the person who used this firearm was carrying it."...

In our judgment, to bring home a charge under s 5, the prosecution must prove:

1. that an offence was committed or an attempt to commit an offence was made;
2. that the accused was an accomplice in the said offence or attempted offence;
3. that the accused was present at the scene of the said offence or attempted offence;
4. that an arm was "used", within the meaning of s 2, by a person in the commission or attempted commission of the said offence; and
5. that the accused may reasonably be presumed to have known that the person who "used" the arm was carrying or had in his possession or under his control such arm.

Upon proof of these five elements or ingredients, the burden shifts to the accused to prove "that he had taken all reasonable steps to prevent the use of such arm" and failure on his part to discharge this burden makes him guilty of an offence under s 5 of this Act, which is punishable with death.... [T]he person who used the arm in the "Nam Yick" robbery was carrying such arm.

The robber who was alleged to have used an arm in that robbery, within the meaning of s 2, was the one who shot at, and injured, the proprietor of the shop.... It is clear from his whole conduct that this robber who was the first person to appear at the shop was undoubtedly the ring leader of the gang and after ordering the rest of his gang to enter the shop, he fired several shots into the shop. Now, as soon as this ring leader appeared at the shop and pointed his gun at the watchman, the appellant and the other three robbers became aware, if they were not aware of it earlier, that he was carrying a gun. And the shot which injured the proprietor was fired by this ring leader after the appellant became aware that the ring leader was carrying a gun. It follows therefore that at the time the arm was used within the meaning of s 5 of the Act, the appellant "may reasonably be presumed to have known" that the ring leader was carrying such arm. The appellant did not say what steps, if any, he took to prevent the use of such arm.

Furthermore, the very fact that this was a gang robbery, daringly committed during broad daylight, at a jewelry shop in a busy shopping area, indicates that the five robbers must have discussed and planned this robbery, very thoroughly. They knew there was a guard at this shop and that there may be resistance. It can properly be inferred that they discussed all the relevant matters, such as what arms and how many they should carry, which of them should be armed, which of them would tackle the guard, which of them would collect the jewelry from the show cases, who would give the signal to leave and by what means they will get away from the scene of the robbery. It is therefore extremely improbable that the appellant did not know that the robber who shot at the proprietor was carrying a gun when they were about to rob the jewelry shop....

The next submission is that the robber who fired several shots into this jewelry shop did not intend to cause physical injury to any person; that he fired at random to frighten the persons present in the shop; that the proprietor was injured by a bullet which had ricochetted off the wall or the floor of the shop and that consequently it could not be said that an arm had been used within the meaning of s 2 of the Act....

The real question before the trial judges was the intention with which the gun was fired in the direction of Poon, and on this question there was the evidence of Poon, the evidence of the watchman Jais bin Kasman and the evidence of Poon's son Poon Wai Kong. Furthermore, more than one shot was fired in the direction of Poon. Even when he was running away to escape from the gunman, at least two more shots were fired in his direction. In the light of all this evidence, the trial judges who saw and heard the witnesses came to the conclusion that the gun was fired in the direction of Poon with the intention of causing him physical injury. We cannot see any grounds for disturbing this finding of fact which is supported by evidence which was believed by the trial judges.

Now, turning to the conviction on the second charge, we propose to consider first, whether the trial judges were correct in their finding, that on the evidence tendered by the prosecution the appellant may reasonably be presumed to have known that the person who used the arm in that robbery was carrying such arm. The evidence on this issue in the robbery at Mandarin Jewellers was entirely different from that in the "Nam Yick" robbery. In the gang robbery at Mandarin Jewellers, all the five members of the gang carried firearms. There was therefore no question of how many of them or which of them carried firearms. This means that even the appellant was carrying a firearm. Now, it cannot be that all five were carying firearms by sheer coincidence. It must have been planned that all should go armed with guns. Now, when five persons decide to commit gang robbery, and also decide that all five would carry firearms to commit robbery and all five are in fact seen carrying firearms at the scene during the course of the robbery, in our opinion, it is reasonable to presume in those circumstances that when they arrived at the scene of the robbery, each of them knew that the other four were all carrying firearms. And in those circumstances, if one of the robbers uses his firearm in the commission of the robbery, within the meaning of s 2, then each and every one of the other four may reasonably be presumed to have the requisite knowledge under s 5. In our judgment, on the evidence tendered by the prosecution on the second charge, the trial judges were correct in their finding that "there were circumstances present from which ... it was reasonable to presume that the accused knew that the person who used the firearm was carrying it."

The next submission is based on the definition of "use" in s 2 of the Act. It is submitted that the only person who is alleged to have "used" an arm in the robbery at the Mandarin Jewellers is the person who was sitting next to the driver in the front seat of the gateaway taxi and is alleged to have shot at Idros bin Abu Bakar, the police constable who was standing guard in front of the jewelry shop of Poh Heng Goldsmith Ltd....

There was clear evidence before the trial judges, which if believed, showed that the gun was fired at Idros with intent to cause physical injury to him....

Finally, it is suggested that the gun was fired at Idros after the robbery was over and the robbers were speeding away from the scene of the robbery and that therefore the act of firing at Idros did not fall within s 5 of the Arms Offences Act 1973 because it was not done in the course of robbery.

In our opinion the point taken is without substance in view of the definition of robbery....

As the shot was fired at Idros by one of the robbers while he and his four companions were carrying away the booty, the act of firing was done in the commission of the gang robbery. There is support for this view in *Shyam Behari* (1957).

In our opinion the trial judges were correct in deciding that the case against the appellant on both charges had been proved beyond a reasonable doubt and in convicting him on both charges....

Appeal dismissed

Chapter 26

Criminal misappropriation and breach of trust

By NA Morgan

A. Introduction

1. The basic definitions

The offences of criminal misappropriation (CMA) and criminal breach of trust (CBT) are closely inter-related.

Penal Code, s 403

Whoever dishonestly misappropriates or converts to his own use movable property, shall be punished with imprisonment for a term which may extend to two years, or with fine, or with both.

Illustrations

(a) A takes property belonging to Z out of Z's possession in good faith believing, at the time when he takes it, that the property belongs to himself. A is not guilty of theft; but if A, after discovering his mistake, dishonestly appropriates the property to his own use, he is guilty of an offence under this section.

(b) A, being on friendly terms with Z, goes into Z's house in Z's absence and takes away a book without Z's express consent. Here, if A was under the impression that he had Z's implied consent to take the book for the purpose of reading it, A has not committed theft. But if A afterwards sells the book for his own benefit, he is guilty of an offence under this section.

(c) A and B being joint owners of a horse, A takes the horse out of B's possession, intending to use it. Here, as A has a right to use the horse, he does not dishonestly misappropriate it. But if A sells the horse and appropriates the whole proceeds to his own use, he is guilty of an offence under this section.

Explanation 1–A dishonest misappropriation for a time only is a misappropriation within the meaning of this section.

Illustrations

A finds a Government promissory note belonging to Z, bearing a blank endorsement. A, knowing that the note belongs to Z, pledges it with a banker as a security for a loan, intending at a future time to restore it to Z. A has committed an offence under this section.

Explanation 2–A person who finds property not in the possession of any other person, and takes such property for the purpose of protecting it for, or of

577

restoring it to the owner, does not take or misappropriate it dishonestly, and is not guilty of an offence; but he is guilty of the offence above defined, if he appropriates it to his own use, when he knows or has the means of discovering the owner, or before he has used reasonable means to discover and give notice to the owner, and has kept the property a reasonable time to enable the owner to claim it.

What are reasonable means, or what is a reasonable time in such a case, is a question of fact.

It is not necessary that the finder should know who is the owner of the property, or that any particular person is the owner of it; it is sufficient if, at the time of appropriating it, he does not believe it to be his own property, or in good faith believe that the real owner cannot be found.

Illustrations

(a) A finds a dollar on the high road, not knowing to whom the dollar belongs. A picks up the dollar. Here A has not committed the offence defined in this section.

(b) A finds a letter on the high road, containing a bank note. From the direction and contents of the letter he learns to whom the note belongs. He appropriates the note. He is guilty of an offence under this section.

(c) A finds a cheque payable to bearer. He can form no conjecture as to the person who has lost the cheque. But the name of the person who has drawn the cheque appears. A knows that this person can direct him to the person in whose favour the cheque was drawn. A appropriates the cheque without attempting to discover the owner. He is guilty of an offence under this section.

(d) A sees Z drop his purse with money in it. A picks up the purse with the intention of restoring it to Z, but afterwards appropriates it to his own use. A has committed an offence under this section.

(e) A finds a purse with money, not knowing to whom it belongs; he afterwards discovers that it belongs to Z, and appropriates it to his own use. A is guilty of an offence under this section.

(f) A finds a valuable ring, not knowing to whom it belongs. A sells it immediately without attempting to discover the owner. A is guilty of an offence under this section.

Thus, the *actus reus* of CMA is misappropriation or conversion to one's own use of movable property. The *mens rea* is dishonesty.

Penal Code, ss 405–406

405. Whoever, being in any manner entrusted with property, or with any dominion over property, dishonestly misappropriates or converts to his own use that property, or dishonestly uses or disposes of that property in violation of any direction of law prescribing the mode in which such trust is to be discharged, or of any legal contract, express or implied, which he has made touching the discharge of such trust, or wilfully suffers any other person so to do, commits "criminal breach of trust".

Illustrations

(a) A, being executor to the will of a deceased person, dishonestly disobeys the law which directs him to divide the effects according to the will, and appropriates them to his own use. A has committed criminal breach of trust.

(b) A is a warehouse-keeper. Z, going on a journey, entrusts his furniture to A, under a contract that it shall be returned on payment of a stipulated sum for warehouse room. A dishonestly sells the goods. A has committed breach of trust.

(c) A, residing in Singapore, is agent for Z, residing in Penang. There is an express or implied contract between A and Z that all sums remitted by Z to A shall be vested by A according to Z's direction. Z remits five thousand dollars to A, with directions to A to invest the same in Government securites. A dishonestly disobeys the direction, and employs the money in his own business. A has committed criminal breach of trust.

(d) But if A, in the last illustration, not dishonestly, but in good faith, believing that it will be more for Z's advantage to hold shares in the Oriental Bank, disobeys Z's directions, and buys shares in the Oriental Bank for Z, instead of buying Government securities, here, though Z should suffer loss and should be entitled to bring a civil action against A on account of that loss, yet A, not having acted dishonestly has not committed criminal breach of trust.

(e) A, a collector of Government money, or a clerk in a Government office, is entrusted with public money, and is either directed by law, or bound by a contract, express or implied, with the Government, to pay into a certain treasury all the public money which he holds. A dishonestly appropriates the money. A has committed criminal breach of trust.

(f) A, a carrier, is entrusted by Z with property to be carried by land or by water. A dishonestly misappropriates the property. A has committed criminal breach of trust.

406. Whoever commits criminal breach of trust shall be punished with imprisonment for a term which may extend to three years, or with fine, or with both.

The different maximum sentences for CBT and CMA indicate that CBT is the more serious offence. The essential precondition for CBT of any type is that the accused has been *entrusted* either with property or with dominion over property and it is because of this "breach of trust" that CBT is considered more serious than CMA. Some offences of CBT involving a dishonest misappropriation or conversion of movable property will also involve CMA. However, CBT is not simply an aggravated form of CMA because in certain respects it is wider. CBT covers "property"; this should be given a wide meaning and CBT is not confined to offences involving movable property. The *actus reus* and *mens rea* elements of CBT are also more complex than those for CMA and must be carefully distinguished. There are five alternative *actus reus* terms contained in s 405 which are not limited to misappropriation and conversion:

(1) misappropriation;
(2) conversion;
(3) use or disposal in violation of a direction of law;
(4) use or disposal in violation of a legal contract;
(5) "suffering any other person to do so".

The *mens rea* for the first four of these situations is dishonesty; for the fifth it is wilfully.

2.   Aggravated forms

Penal Code, ss 404, 407–409

404.   Whoever dishonestly misappropriates or converts to his own use property, knowing that such property was in the possession of a deceased person at the time of that person's decease, and has not since been in the possession of any person legally entitled to such possession, shall be punished with imprisonment for a term which may extend to three years, and shall also be liable to fine; and if the offender at the time of such person's decease was employed by him as a clerk or servant, the imprisonment may extend to seven years.

Illustration

Z dies in possession of furniture and money. His servant A, before the money comes into the possession of any person entitled to such possession, dishonestly misappropriates it. A has committed the offence defined in this section.

407.   Whoever, being entrusted with property as a carrier, wharfinger, or warehouse-keeper, commits criminal breach of trust in respect of such property, shall be punished with imprisonment for a term which may extend to seven years, and shall also be liable to fine.

408.   Whoever, being a clerk or servant, or employed as a clerk or servant, and being in any manner entrusted in such capacity with property, or with any dominion over property, commits criminal breach of trust in respect of that property, shall be punished with imprisonment for a term which may extend to seven years, and shall also be liable to fine.

409.   Whoever, being in any manner entrusted with property, or with any dominion over property, in his capacity of a public servant, or in the way of his business as a banker, merchant, factor, broker, attorney or agent, commits criminal breach of trust in respect of that property, shall be punished with imprisonment for life, or with imprisonment for a term which may extend to ten years, and shall also be liable to fine.

[The only difference between the Singapore and Malaysian provisions is that s 409 of the FMS Penal Code was amended in 1976; such offences do not now carry a maximum of life imprisonment but a fixed maximum term of 20 years.]

The aggravated forms of both CMA and CBT carry much longer maximum terms of imprisonment than the simple forms. In practice, many cases of CBT fall under one of these aggravated forms because it is typically a "white collar" crime, generally committed in the course of employment or business (Ricquier and Yeo, 1984, pp 68–69). Although there is generally no easily identifiable single individual victim of such crimes in the same way as for offences against the person and property offences such as housebreaking, robbery and theft, the consequences may be extremely serious for the society at large and for a large number of individuals within the society. In Singapore the life sentence is technically available for aggravated forms of CBT under s 409 but it is inconceivable that it would ever be used; such indeterminate sentences are not thought appropriate in respect of offences against property and are in practice used primarily in cases of culpable homicide not amounting to murder. Consequently, the effective maximum in Singapore is ten years. By contrast, in Malaysia the effective maximum for such offences is 20 years. Without further research, it is not possible to judge whether Malaysian courts steer by the higher maximum and in practice pass heavier sentences than their Singapore counterparts.

Although ss 407–409 make a term of imprisonment mandatory for aggravated CBT cases, it is also noteworthy that there is no mandatory minimum term specified and no provision for corporal punishment. In cases of CBT where large profits may well have been made, it is common for courts to recognize restitution as a strong mitigating factor and, less frequently, they order fines in addition to any prison term, in order to "claw back" some of the profits from the offence (Ricquier and Yeo, 1984, pp 70–72). This is in marked contrast with the approach taken, especially in Singapore, to other property offences such as housebreaking, robbery, extortion, theft and certain offences of vandalism under the Vandalism Act (Singapore)(Cap 341). For these offences, mandatory minimum terms of imprisonment are common and are not infrequently accompanied by mandatory caning. Since the three punishments of imprisonment, fine and caning cannot be inflicted on any person in respect of one offence (Criminal Procedure Code (Singapore)(Cap 68), s 11), there is far less scope for the fine in such cases. The mandatory minimum penalties also leave far less scope for informal mitigating factors. Are such differences justifiable on the basis of retributive or utilitarian reasoning?

B. Criminal misappropriation

1. Movable property

Penal Code, s 22

The words "movable property" are intended to include corporeal property of every description, except land and things attached to the earth, or permanently fastened to anything which is attached to the earth.

Illustration

Writings, relating to real or personal property or rights, are movable property.

Corporeal property is property which has a physical or material being; it is tangible. Land and things permanently attached thereto are corporeal but as they are immovable, they are incapable of being the subject matter of theft or CMA. However, as the Penal Code makes clear, immovable things attached to the earth may be stolen or the object of theft or CMA once they have been severed from the land. In *Lim Soon Gong* (1939), a case of theft, McElwaine CJ held that "land" in s 22 means "an area of the earth's surface and does not mean a sod cut from the earth"; consequently, sand from the foreshore was regarded as movable property. The definitional boundaries of movable property are not entirely clear and there are few local cases in point but by way of illustration, examples may be given of property which is not regarded as movable in other jurisdictions. In *Avtar Singh* (1965), the Indian Supreme Court held that electricity is not movable property. Similarly, movable property presumably does not include obligations and choses ·in action. However, it does include physical manifestations of such obligations such as a cheque (see illustrations to s 403 and *Tuan Puteh* v *Dragon*, 1876).

2. Misappropriation and conversion

Unlike theft, CMA is not an offence against possession. As shown by the Illustrations and Explanation 2 to s 403, and by Illustration (g) to s 378, there can be misappropriation or conversion of property which is found or which comes into a person's possession in what some of the Indian commentaries have termed a "neutral manner".

The generally accepted definition of "conversion to one's own use" is that it means to "appropriate and use another's property without right as if it is one's own" (*Durugappa*, 1956); the accused must not merely retain property to the physical exclusion of the real owner but also divert it to his own use.

As far as misappropriation is concerned, the statute is open to two readings. The first is to read the phrase "to his own use" with misappropriation as well as conversion. Read in this way, the *actus reus* of CMA is either "conversion to one's own use" or "misappropriation to one's own use". This reading seems to receive some support from Illustrations (a) and (c) to s 403 and from Explanation 2 and Illustrations (d) and (e) thereto, all of which refer to A having "appropriated [property] *to his own use*". However, if this interpretation is taken, misappropriation appears to mean much the same as conversion; there will be misappropriation only where the rightful owner has been excluded *and* the property has in some way been "put to use" by the accused. The second interpretation which more clearly distinguishes the terms, is to regard the *actus reus* as either "misappropriation" or "conversion to one's own use". Some of the difficulty in attributing the proper meaning of "misappropriation" arises because of the inherent tautology of the term "dishonest misappropriation". By definition, *mis*appropriation is usually considered to be "*dishonest* appropriation". It is therefore not surprising that in some cases, misappropriation seems to have been read as equivalent simply to "appropriation", with criminal liability hinging on the question of dishonesty. Thus, in *Sohan Lal* (1915), the following definition was suggested:

> The verb "to appropriate" in this connection means setting apart for, or assigning to, a particular person or use; and to "misappropriate", no doubt, means to set apart for or assign to the wrong person or a wrong use, and this act must be done dishonestly.

Although the point was not properly argued, the broader interpretation of misappropriation–perhaps involving nothing more than retention by the wrong person and the exclusion of the rightful owner–was also perhaps favoured in *Tuan Puteh* v *Dragon* (1876). The appellant apparently found a cheque made payable to a Captain Strong; he took it to a bank but it was not cashed as it required Captain Strong's endorsement. It was argued, inter alia, that under the illustrations to s 403, actual conversion was necessary. However, in a very short judgment, the Supreme Court of the Straits Settlements held that "the prisoner had clearly appropriated the cheque, which was wrongful, and a sufficient misappropriation" under s 403.

3. Dishonesty

If "misappropriation" is given a broad interpretation, roughly corresponding to retention to the exclusion of the rightful owner, the factor which will effectively determine criminal liability in many cases will, as recognized in *Sohan Lal* (1915), be the *mens rea*, dishonesty. Dishonesty has been discussed in the context of theft and will also be discussed in the context of CBT (see below, p 592). Although the definition of dishonesty and the basic principles are the same for all the offences, they embrace different fact situations; consequently, some of the factors relevant to an inference of dishonesty are different in each. Three general points must be made here about dishonesty in CMA. First, even if the exclusion of the rightful owner from his property is sufficient to constitute "misappropriation", and is regarded as causing "wrongful loss" to him under the terms of s 23, such conduct will only be criminal if it can be proved that the accused *intended* to cause such wrongful gain or wrongful loss (s 24). The illustrations to s 403, unlike those to theft under s 378, make no direct reference to the bona fide claim of right. However, the most convincing analysis of the legal basis of the bona fide claim is that it is not derived simply from Illustration (p) to s 378 but from the definition of dishonesty; Illustration (p) to s 378 is best regarded simply as an illustration of one situation where the accused is not considered dishonest. Under this analysis, which is also supported by the cases on theft (see p 534), there is no difficulty incorporating the same doctrine into CMA and CBT. The accused is not dishonest if he has a bona fide claim of right over the property in question; even though he may have *caused* "wrongful loss" to the victim or "wrongful gain" for himself, he cannot be held to have *intended* such gain or loss. An analysis of the bona fide claim on the basis of mistake would also allow the doctrine to be used in the context of CMA.

The doctrine of the bona fide claim may be important in the context of CMA because the property will generally have come into the accused's possession in a neutral manner, perhaps by being found. However, a finder's civil law rights are not represented simply by the saying "finders, keepers; losers, weepers" (*Parker*, 1982), and Explanation 2 to s 403 (and Illustrations (a), (b) and (f) thereto) shows that such a belief will not in itself amount to a bona fide claim as far as the criminal law is concerned. Much will depend on the facts of the particular case, but commonsense and the illustrations to s 403 suggest that the key factors in determining liability will generally be the nature and value of the property in question, whether there are any identifying features which indicate the owner, and whether the accused has made sufficient effort to trace the rightful owner or allowed time for the goods to be claimed.

The second point is that it will prove far more difficult to draw an inference of dishonesty where there has been misappropriation in the sense of retention, but there has been no conversion or attempted conversion or use by the accused. In *Menthis* (1960) it was said:

> [T]he nature of the overt act required to constitute conversion depends on the nature of the article converted. If one finds an article which is in common daily use, has no identifying marks, can easily be carried on one's person, and takes it, then, in the absence of other evidence, the mere taking is not sufficient to indicate a conversion because it may be a neutral act consistent with an innocent taking within a view to returning it to the lawful owner.

Although the wording of this passage refers to the question of conversion, the point is more applicable to dishonesty; mere taking may be a neutral act with the intention of returning the goods to the owner; once there has been conversion, dishonesty is more likely to be inferred

The final point about dishonesty in the context of CMA concerns temporary appropriations. Explanation 1 to s 403 expressly provides that a dishonest misappropriation for a time only can amount to CMA. This is in line with the definition of dishonesty, which does not require an intention permanently to deprive, and with the approach in cases of theft (see *Ward*, 1953, above, p 537). An argument based on Explanation 1 was rejected in *Batty* (1899), a case involving a charge of CBT by dishonest misappropriation. The appellant, who had been entrusted with funds in his capacity as Postmaster-General of Penang, appropriated a sum of money to his own use, after he had worked for three months without a salary. Pellereau J ruled that in considering dishonesty, the jury should "take into consideration whether the prisoner had the *intention* of returning the money and the *power and means* of doing so". He said that Explanation 1 to s 403 did not cover this case because in the illustration to that explanation "there never was at any time rightful or legal possession on the part of the finder, and he had made use of the cheque in a manner which put it beyond his control to return it to Z...". The precise grounds of this decision are unclear; it was not argued that the appellant had bona fide claim of right because he had not been paid but the decision seems to suggest that an intention to return the property at a later date negates dishonesty; this is highly debatable. Explanation 1 to s 403 seems to have been distinguished on the basis that its illustration did not cover the case in hand, but illustrations should not be considered conclusive of the scope of a section.

C. Criminal breach of trust

1. Entrustment in any manner of property or dominion over property

(a) Entrustment

In many cases involving CBT, charges of abetment are brought and are treated very seriously. Frequently this will be because although the accused himself was not "entrusted" with the property, he was the "prime mover" in that he abetted the entrusted party to act in breach of the "trust".

The definition of a "trust" in this context has been the subject of considerable debate. At one time the leading Indian cases took the view that it was confined to instances of a trust in the sense that the term is used in equity. The concept of a "trust" defies easy definition. However, as Keeton (1974) puts it:

> A trust ... is the relationship which arises wherever a person called the trustee is compelled in equity to hold property, whether real or personal, and whether by legal or equitable title, for the benefit of some persons (of whom he may be one and who are termed beneficiaries) or for some object permitted by law, in such a way that the real benefit of the property accrues, not to the trustee, but to the beneficiaries or other objects of the trust.

Under a "trust" in this sense, beneficiaries are able to enforce obligations imposed on trustees. In *Ng Chye Giat* (1938) the view was taken that "entrustment" in s 405 means a trust in this sense. In recent years, particularly through the flexible device of the constructive trust, trusts have been implied by the courts in a wide variety of circumstances which were previously not regarded in such a manner (see Hanbury and Maudsley, 1985). Therefore, even if "entrustment" is interpreted in this manner, more situations would now be liable to fall under CBT.

However, resort to equity has been rendered unnecessary by later cases, which have adopted a broad approach to entrustment and have not followed *Ng Chye Giat* (1938).

WJM Ricquier and S Yeo, *Breaches of Trust in Singapore and Malaysia* (1984), 37

The prevailing modern view is that the term [entrustment] also covers those persons whose positions are analogous to that of trustees. These persons become criminally responsible for property belonging to others because of obligations arising out of a relationship similar in confidence and duties as trustees. This view is correct because the phrase "in any manner" appearing in the opening line of s 405 indicates that the legislative draftsmen did not intend any narrow or technical meaning to be attached to the term "entrusted". Furthermore, in none of the illustrations to s 405 was the injured party restricted to a court of equity in enforcing his demands. For example, two of the illustrations deal with ordinary common law bailment and the relationship between bailor and bailee is one of the common law, not equity. Additionally, in ss 407, 408 and 409 of the Penal Code, none of the persons stated therein would ordinarily be described as a trustee in Chancery proceedings.

The local courts have taken a broad view of entrustment in cases of loans:

Gan Beng v PP [1938] FMSLR 318 (Court of a Judge, Perak, FMS)

The appellant borrowed a bicycle; he failed to return it as promised in two hours and the bicycle was only produced much later when the case came up.

Murray-Aynsley J: [In] *Ng Chye Giat* (1938) the learned Judge, relying on a case reported in Gour held that the word "entrusted" is limited to trusts properly so called. The actual words of Gour are "the word entrusted is used in its legal and not in its popular or figurative sense", so far quoting from an Indian case *Ghanasham Das* (1928), the report of which is not available. Gour then adds in his own words "It means that it implies a creation of trust, actual or resultant, as is clear from the illustrations appended to this section".

Examination of the illustrations reveals the fact that not a single one of them is a trust properly so called. By trust I mean that special form of obligation that could only be enforced in Courts of Equity. I think that in none of the illustrations would the injured party have been restricted to a Court of Equity in enforcing his demands. Two of the illustrations are ordinary common law bailments. I think on a proper interpretation of the section any bailment comes within its scope and the relation of bailor and bailee is one of common law, not of equity. The old writers were wont to define bailment as a trust or confidence.... Even Hailsham, Vol 1, p 724, gives a definition which uses the word "trust" but clearly not in its technical sense....

The present case is the same as *Ng Chye Giat*, 1938 except that it concerns the loss of a bicycle.

I have previously said that in my opinion the wording of the section is wide enough to include bailments and I see no reason to exclude that class which Lord Holt following the terminology of Roman Law called *commodatum*. It is true that the bailment is for the benefit of the bailee but the bailor retains many rights, indeed all rights except actual possession during the continuance of the bailment. I do not follow *Ng Chye Giat*, 1938....

Appeal dismissed

In *Chin Wah* (1940) the court followed *Gan Beng* (1938) and held that the "essence of the offence of criminal breach of trust is the dishonest misappropriation or conversion by a person of property entrusted to him. The fact that in this case the entrusting of the property was gratuitous is, in our view, immaterial; the point is, did the accused dishonestly convert to his own use the property of which he was the bailee?" This broad interpretation has not always been followed in India; in *Rajendra Singh* (1960) the appellants went to a goldsmith and represented that their mother wanted a necklace of a particular design in order to copy it. The goldsmith handed over the chain and the appellants promised to return it in the evening. They did not do so and, although they were convicted of criminal misappropriation and cheating, the court held that there had been no entrustment for the purposes of CBT. Although the appellants had been *lent* the necklace, they had not been *entrusted* with it; "...in the case of a trust the article cannot be returned before the object of the trust is carried out whereas in the case of a loan the article can be returned even before the object of the loan is carried out". This technical analysis of a trust seems unduly restrictive; as Ricquier and Yeo (1984) point out, it places excessive weight on the objects of the loan rather than dishonesty, which is regarded as the key factor in *Chin Wah* (1940). In view of more recent decisions (eg *Harihar Prasad*, 1981, below), it is not clear whether the Indian courts would still adopt this approach.

It is clear that where property is received in the course of employment, there is deemed to be "entrustment" for the purposes of CBT, whether the person had any right to receive the property or not (*Bahru Zaman b Ali*, 1949; *Abdul Wahab*, 1939).

Although entrustment is given a broad interpretation, free of the technicalities of whether the obligations are enforceable in equity, the essential factor in determining borderline cases seems to be that the accused must have received the property or dominion thereover in some broadly defined "fiduciary" capacity; or, as Ricquier and Yeo (1984) suggest, he must have been in a position broadly analogous to that of a trustee. The general guidelines were well expressed by the Indian Supreme Court in *Harihar Prased* (1981):

> When s 405 ... speaks of a person being in any manner entrusted with property, it does not contemplate the creation of a trust with all the technicalities of the law of trust. It contemplates the creation of a relationship whereby the owner of property makes it over to another person to be retained by him until a certain contingency arises or to be disposed of by him on the happening of a certain event. The person who transfers possession of the property to the second party still remains the legal owner of the property and the person in whose favour possession is so transferred has only the custody of the property to be kept or disposed by him for the benefit of the other party.

(b) "In any manner"

As Ricquier and Yeo (1984) argue, this phrase supports the view that "entrustment" should be afforded a broad definition under the Penal Code. It also shows that there may be liability for CBT where the entrustment has taken place in the course of an illegal transaction.

R v Tan Ah Seng (1935) 4 MLJ 273 (HC, Singapore)

The respondent had received $40 for the purpose of renting a house to be used by prostitutes, and he misappropriated the money. He was acquitted but the prosecution appealed.

Burton Ag CJ, Terrell J and Williamson J: The justification for this order is no doubt to be found in the case of *Re Yong Ah Kim, complainant v Lee Keng Chiang*, (1905) in which Fisher, J held that a prosecution will not lie for criminal misappropriation of money paid to a person for a criminal purpose.

In that case Yong Ah Kim gave Lee Keng Chiang $4 with which she commissioned him to bribe the Chinese Interpreter of a Police Court, but instead of attempting to bribe the Interpreter he converted the money to his own use.

The reasoning of this decision is based firstly on a proposition of law summed up by Lord Mansfield as "No Court will lend its aid to a man who founds his cause of action upon an immoral or an illegal act" and Fisher J concluded that "the prosecutrix could not have recovered by civil process the money with which she entrusted the prisoner". But the former of these propositions has no application to the criminal law; and the latter is incorrect. It is clear law that the money could have been recovered back by the prosecutrix at any time before the illegal purpose was carried out [*Taylor* v *Bowes*, 1876] and in our case, as in the Penang case *ex hypothesi* the illegal purpose was never carried out....

[Another] ground of the decision is that there was no dishonesty. The learned Judge held that the complainant having no civil remedy, has suffered no wrongful loss....

But we are unable to follow this reasoning. It seems to us perfectly plain that when a person who has received $4 to bribe a detective, puts that $4 into his own pocket, he has wrongfully gained that $4, apart from all question of wrongful loss by the complainant....

Appeal allowed

(c) Dominion

The distinction between entrustment with property and entrustment with dominion over property has been a matter of some disagreement (for a fuller analysis see Canagarayar, 1986, pp 229–231). Particular analytical difficulties arise where A has overall control of the relevant aspect of the operation but B has "day-to-day" control. Opinion is divided amongst commentators on the correct analysis of such cases; some suggest that A is entrusted with "dominion" over the property and that B is entrusted with the property. Others suggest that A is entrusted with the property and B with dominion. Although the two phrases are closely related and are difficult to differentiate conceptually, the inclusion of dominion makes two things clear, whichever analysis is adopted. First, CBT can be committed provided that the accused has a sufficient degree of control over the property even if it is not physically in his possession. Second, there can be CBT even if another person is in "overall control" of the operations in question; or if another person is in charge of the day-to-day running of the operation. The following cases suggest that the factor which effectively determines whether there is entrustment either of property or of dominion is the degree of control exercised by the accused.

Sinnathamby v PP [1948–49] MLJ Supp 75 (HC, Ipoh, Malaya)

The appellant was an employee at a Public Works Department Quarry. He received $10 from a contractor in return for leaving some stone in a place from which it was later removed.

Thomson J: [I]t was argued [inter alia] ... that there was no evidence that the appellant was in effect entrusted with any sort of dominion over the stone....

So far as I have been able to advise myself, no direct authority exists on the point, and I take the view that the section applies not merely in cases where the exercise of possession of dominion over property is one of the legal incidents of the contract of service but in every case where by virtue of the existence of the contract of service the accused person is in fact in a position to exercise dominion as in this cåse. The evidence of the Executive Engineer who was the appellant's official superior was to the fact that while he gave general orders for any one day as to the use of departmental lorries nevertheless circumstances might arise where any other official might amend these orders and give other orders. That being so, the learned District Judge was fully entitled to find in fact that by virtue of his contract of service, the accused was in a position to exercise dominion over the stone from the Public Works Department Quarry, and that in the particular circumstances of the present case he did exercise that dominion prior to committing the breach of trust in respect of the property over which he exercised it.

Appeal dismissed

Chang Lee Swee v PP [1985] 1 MLJ 75 (HC, KL, Malaysia)

The appellant was convicted of criminal breach of trust by an agent under s 409. He was the Executive Director of TDMB and was in charge of that company's financial matters. He transferred $390,000 from TDMB to another company, KJDB. KJDB was a subsidiary of NADEFINCO Holdings. The appellant was a director of KJDB. KJDB had no shares in TDMB and vice versa. However, NADEFINCO Holdings, of which the appellant was a director, held 41% of the shares in TDMB and 46% in KJDB.

It came to be suspected that TDMB funds were being used for other companies, without the knowledge of the Chairman or the Board of Directors. On appeal against conviction, two main arguments were raised. The first concerned the question of entrustment.

Gunn Chit Tuan J: The learned president ... seemed, and this was conceded by the learned deputy, to have made her finding that there was entrustment merely on the evidence of the chairman of TDMB.... who said that once the appellant was appointed as an executive director in charge of finance, he was entrusted with the funds of TDMB. That witness also said that although the appellant was responsible for the financial matters of TDMB, he was not given specific powers by the board to lend money to other companies.... Counsel for the appellant contended that the learned president had abdicated her function in regard to interpretation and construction of legal documents produced in this case and only relied on the oral evidence of witnesses. He pointed out that she had completely ignored and disregarded the directors' resolution appointing one ... "Tan" as the managing director of TDMB....

It was the contention of counsel that the said directors' resolution appointing Tan as managing director considered in the light of the ... articles of association meant that the board of TDMB had delegated all its powers, except the power to borrow and to make calls, to Tan, the managing director.

It was also pointed out by counsel that the learned president, in finding that the ingredient of entrustment has been proved, had not considered the evidence of one of the prosecution witnesses called Chung Shui Tett ... who was a very senior legal practitioner. That prosecution witness told the Court that the said resolution ... of which he was one of the signatories gave the managing director of TDMB extensive powers, with the exception of the powers to borrow and make calls. Under the powers given by that resolution, the managing director did not have to refer any transaction which he has undertaken involving the lending of a large amount of money. Although such transaction was of major importance, it was not imperative that he has to refer the matter to the board. It was up to his discretion and if he considered it impracticable to refer to the board before deciding or taking action in any matter, he need not refer to the board even if it was a matter of major importance. That same witness was also referred to the ... articles of association and agreed that the board of directors could ... entrust all the powers to the managing director except the powers which are exercisable by the directors in a general meeting....

[T]he issue of whether there was entrustment in this case was, in my opinion, not free from difficulties. In my judgment when TDMB was incorporated and the directors appointed to its board in 1965 the board of directors must be considered to have been entrusted with the powers as well as the funds of the company. But the question which the court in this case had to and should have considered was the effect of the directors' resolution appointing Tan the managing director of TDMB.... It was clear from the said resolution that the board of directors had in 1971 given to Tan all the powers and discretions conferred upon the board of directors by the company's articles of association other than the power to borrow and make calls on behalf of it. It would therefore appear from that resolution considered together with the articles of association that the board of TDMB had delegated and entrusted to Tan all its powers except the power to borrow and make calls, but including the power to manage the funds of the company. The court should have also considered the evidence of the other prosecution witness who gave evidence regarding the extensive powers given to Tan. If both the documentary and oral evidence in this case had been carefully considered, the learned president would have come to the conclusion that the appellant, even after he was appointed an executive director in charge of financial affairs five years after Tan, that is in the year 1976, was not in the position to manage the funds of TDMB without the overall control of Tan and was therefore in the circumstances of this case not entrusted with or had complete dominion over its funds. I also agreed with the learned counsel for the appellant that even if there were any doubts on the construction of the directors' resolutions ... such doubts in their construction should have been resolved in favour of the appellant.

Appeal allowed

As Canagarayar (1986, p 231) points out, the decision in *Chang Lee Swee* (1985) seems difficult to reconcile with *Yeoh Teck Chye* (1981, below, p 591). The second accused in that case was the branch manager of a bank. He had apparently approved loans to the third accused in excess of his overdraft facilities. He had no power to authorize such overdrafts without the authorization of the first accused. However, the questions of whether there had been any entrustment to the second accused and, if so, whether it was of "property" or "dominion", were not explored because counsel conceded that "there was entrustment to or dominion over the property of the Bank by accused 2"; in any case, the court felt that "available evidence to that effect is incontrovertible".

2. Actus reus

(a) Misappropriation and conversion

See above, pp 582–583.

(b) Use or disposal in violation of law or contract

A direction of law may be violated where the law gives express directions as to how the accused is to deal with the entrusted property. A good example is Illustration (a) to s 405; the executor of a will may act in breach of his legal obligations. *Mohamed Adil* (1967) may also involve a violation of law though the point was not argued. In cases where there is no direction of law the court may find that there has been a breach of contractual term, express or implied.

PP v Yeoh Teck Chye [1981] 2 MLJ 176 (FC, KL, Malaysia)

The facts of this case were mentioned earlier (see above, p 590). It was conceded that there was entrustment to the bank manager (accused 2); the court then considered whether he had acted in violation of law or contract in authorizing excessive overdrafts.

Wan Suleiman J: Had accused 2 indeed violated any law prescribing the mode in which his trust is to be discharged?

A government functionary holding money on behalf of his principal would for instance have precise directions of law (the Financial General Orders and the Financial Procedure Act) prescribing the manner of disposal of the money. We are however inclined to favour ... [the] view that no law governs or prescribes the manner in which accused 2, a bank manager, may dispose of the bank money entrusted to him as a manager. The prosecution would therefore have to prove that there had been a breach of contract (express or implied) on his part touching the discharge of the money entrusted to him, indeed prosecution would have to adduce *prima facie* evidence that accused 2 did not have authority to grant temporary short term overdrafts....

[After considering the evidence, his Lordship continued:]

In amending the charges against accused 2 before calling upon him to make his defence the learned trial judge had taken the view that his granting of overdrafts in excess of approved overdraft facility, or exceeding the credit balance where no overdraft facility had been approved ... had been done in violation of the direction of law prescribing the mode in which this entrustment may be discharged. We think with respect that for the words "the direction of law prescribing the mode in which such trust was to be discharged" in each instance, there should be substituted the words "of any legal contract made touching the discharge of such trust", for *prima facie* we would say that there is at the very least an impled legal contract governing the manner in which accused 2 was authorized to dispose of the funds of the bank.

Appeal dismissed

Murni b Haji Mohamed Taha v PP [1986] 1 MLJ 260 (HC, Brunei)

The appellant was paymaster of an army camp. He was entrusted with money and was to use cheques issued by the Treasury to pay serving soldiers. Discrepancies were revealed and the appellant was convicted on charges of criminal breach of trust. One question was whether he had used or disposed of the property in violation of law or a contractual term. Certain State Financial Regulations which had been brought into force in 1955 had been revoked by legislation in 1960. However, they had since been followed as a matter of administrative practice.

Roberts CJ: These regulations, therefore, although they do not have the force of law, bind all public servants if adopted administratively, as they have been.
    The defendent ... in common with all public servants was ... obliged to follow these regulations. They are, therefore, part of a contract of service between himself and the Government of the State.

[The learned judge referred to Illustration (e) to s 405.]

I am satisfied, therefore, that although the defendant could not be said to have appropriated the money entrusted to him in violation of any direction of law, he was violating a term of his contract of employment as a public servant which obliged him to follow the State Financial Regulations which had been administratively adopted throughout the service.

Appeal dismissed

(c) Suffering any person to do so

In *Yeoh Teck Chye* (1981) the Federal Court laid down the elements of CBT in the following manner:

> [F]or a person to be guilty of the offence of criminal breach of trust he should be
>
> (i)   entrusted with property;
> (ii) (a) that he should dishonestly misappropriate or convert it to his own use OR
>   (b) dishonestly use or dispose of the property or wilfully suffer any other person so to do in violation of
> (iii) (a) any direction of law prescribing the manner in which such trust is to be discharged OR
>   (b) of any legal contract made touching the discharge of such trust....

This numbering of the elements of the offence is very odd; it suggests that the "wilful suffering" clause applies only to violations of directions of law or contract and not to cases of misappropriation or conversion.

WJM Ricquier and S Yeo, *Breaches of Trust in Singapore and Malaysia* (1984) 47

It is difficult to understand why the words "so to do" should be restricted to clause (b).... Take the case of A, a lawyer, who is entrusted with a client's money. A knows that his clerk, B, is misappropriating the client's money but does nothing to prevent B from doing so. Should not A be guilty of criminal breach of trust in that he wilfully suffered B to misappropriate the client's money? A plain reading of s 405 would find A guilty of this charge. Hence this fifth type of *actus reus* should be that the accused suffers another person either to misappropriate or convert entrusted property, or to use or dispose such property in violation of a law or a legal contract prescribing the mode in which such a trust is to be discharged.

3. Mens rea

(a) Dishonesty

This is the *mens rea* for cases of misappropriation, conversion and use or disposal in violation of law or contract by the entrusted person himself. Generally the comments with regard to CMA are also applicable but the particular factors relevant to the inference of dishonesty may vary. In the context of CBT a series of cases has shown that negligence or a failure to account for entrusted property does not, without more, constitute dishonesty.

Sathiadas v PP [1970] 2 MLJ 241 (HC, KL, Malaysia)

A traffic clerk with Malaysia-Singapore Airways received moneys from consignees of air freight but did not make entries in sales returns or remit the monies to the head office.

Raja Azlan Shah J: Criminal breach of trust is not an offence which counts as one of its factors, the loss that is the consequence of the act, it is the act itself, which in law, amounts to an offence. The offence is complete when there is dishonest misappropriation or conversion to one's own use, or when there is dishonest user in violation of a direction, express or implied, relating to the mode in which the trust is to be discharged.

It may be observed that mere retention of money would not necessarily raise a presumption of dishonest intention but it is a step in that direction. The fact that money entrusted to be used for a particular purpose, was not used for such purpose; that there was retention for a sufficiently long time would, together with other facts and circumstances justify the inference that the appellant had dishonestly misappropriated or converted the money to his own use. There was the intention in the appellant to deprive his employers of their monies, and the appellant misappropriated the monies for a time, intending to make it good eventually when any further retention became impossible.

In the light of the above observations which are in the nature of principles of general application in cases of criminal breach of trust, and after giving careful consideration to the facts and circumstances of the case before this court, I have reached the conclusion that the result of the evidence on record is that what was done or omitted by the appellant was moved by a guilty mind. On two occasions he had received the monies but had failed to carry out the trusts reposed in him. On the third occasion there exists strong circumstantial evidence of guilt.

Appeal dismissed

In most of these cases the accused failed to provide any explanation of his conduct (see also *Md Adil*, 1967). However, there may be other cases involving a bona fide claim or where there is some other explanation which may lead the court to conclude that he was not dishonest. In *Md b Abdul Jabar* (1948) the accused was entrusted with funds as a government servant. He failed to account for certain expenditure and offered no clear explanation of what happened to the money. He was acquitted; the court emphasized that, as a man with little or no accounting experience, he had placed great reliance on his clerk; he was not liable for CBT even though he had been "grossly careless". An extreme example is provided by *Navaretnam* (1973). The officer in charge of a prison was found to have taken money belonging to a prisoner whose belongings had been entrusted to him. He claimed that he intended to use the money to pay a lawyer for the prisoner. Ali FJ concluded:

> The point as it seemed to us is, if there was any truth in the appellant's statement of his intention to pay the lawyer, then his taking of the money did not become dishonest even if he did so without the prisoner's permission.

Since there was nothing in the prosecution's case to dispute the truth of his statement, the appeal was allowed.

(b) Wilfully

This term is not defined in the Penal Code and has not been the subject of careful analysis by the courts.

Yeow Fook Yuen v R [1965] 2 MLJ 80 (HC, Singapore)

YFY was entrusted with money as treasurer of a trade union. He was charged with wilfully suffering JS to dishonestly misappropriate funds. JS faced charges of abetting YFY to commit CBT. On appeal the court rejected the argument that the sums were loans approved by the Union's Executive Council at the time they were taken.

Wee Chong Jin CJ: It seems to me there can be no question but that the first appellant by so permitting the second appellant to take these moneys of the union had intentionally deprived the union of the use of these moneys had thereby intentionally caused wrongful loss to the union and had intentionally caused wrongful gain to the second appellant and the second appellant by so instigating the first appellant to deprive the union of the use of these moneys was guilty of the offence of abetment. There was no evidence on behalf of either appellant that either of them held the *bona fide* belief that the first appellant was acting within the authority of his office as honorary treasurer of the union in making these advances from time to time to the second appellant and indeed the evidence indicated, as the trial judge has found, that both appellants knew it was wrong on the part of the first appellant to allow and for the second appellant to take these advances without the prior approval of the executive council. It was urged before me that so long as both appellants regarded these moneys as advances or loans and *bona fide* believed them to be advances or loans there was no dishonest intention on the part of either of them. This argument is in my view fallacious. The real question to be decided on the issue of dishonest intention is not the question whether either appellant *bona fide* believed these takings to be loans but whether either appellant *bona fide* believed that the first appellant had lawful authority to make these loans to the second appellant. On the facts before the trial judge there was ample evidence to support his finding that both appellants acted "dishonestly" within the meaning of s 24 of the Penal Code.

It was next contended that ... [subsequent ratification of the loans] by the executive council ... afforded a complete defence in law in respect of the present charges. Counsel for the appellants was however unable to draw my attention to any authority in support of his contention and I need only say that in my opinion the trial judge was correct in rejecting this defence contention.

Appeal against conviction dismissed

A number of interesting points emerge from this case. First, the court reduced the sentences but agreed that JS deserved a heavier punishment even though his charges were of abetment. Second, the court's dismissal of the argument that subsequent ratification afforded a defence is perfunctory but supportable on policy grounds. The quality of the accused's conduct should in such cases be judged at the time it occurred and later ratification should, as in *Yeow* (1965), be considered only in mitigation of sentence.

A third point is more problematic. The court did not consider the possible difference between the terms "wilfully" and "dishonestly" but considered both appellants to have been dishonest. Since both terms are used in one section, they should be given different meanings. Ricquier and Yeo (1984, p 51) suggest that wilfulness lies between negligence and dishonesty:

> For a person to have wilfully suffered another person to commit an act, there must be ... evidence showing that he intentionally omitted to comply with the rules or that he deliberately connived at the misappropriation by shutting his eyes to what was going on. Although dishonesty will often be inferred from these circumstances, the prosecution is not required to prove this additional element.

A final question in such cases is whether the third party (here, JS) must have been dishonest; do the words "to do so" refer simply to the *actus reus* requirements or to the *mens rea* too? Since JS was considered dishonest, the issue did not arise. However, there are good reasons for arguing that the third party need not be dishonest.

WJM Ricquier and S Yeo, *Breaches of Trust in Singapore and Malaysia* (1984), 51–52

Firstly, the third party ... is invariably charged with abetment of criminal breach of trust. The concept of abetment does not include the element of dishonesty because there is abetment so long as either instigation, conspiracy or intentional aiding is proven. It is difficult to see why the principal offender should be liable for criminal breach of trust only if the prosecution proves that the third party (ie the abettor) had dishonestly misappropriated the property. Secondly, the principal offender's liability should be based on his "wilfulness" alone. Otherwise, a person who deliberately enables another person to misappropriate property will be acquitted on a mere technicality, namely, the prosecution's failure to prove that the third party had appropriated the property dishonestly.

D. Criminal misappropriation and breach of trust of partnership property

English partnership law applies in Singapore in commercial matters by virtue of the Civil Law Act (Singapore)(Cap 43), s 5(1). In Malaysia, the Partnership Act 1961 (Act 135, Rev 1974) is also based on the English Partnership Act 1890. A difference has emerged between Indian and local courts on the liability of partners for criminal misappropriation and criminal breach of trust.

1. The Indian approach

With one narrow exception, the Indian courts have not been prepared to impose liability for either CMA or CBT on partners. "Breaches of trust" by partners have generally been considered a matter for the civil law. Although local courts have not followed this, the reasons for the approach must be understood.

The Indian approach may appear somewhat strange at first sight; if one partner dishonestly deals with partnership property without the consent of the other partners and for his own personal benefit, why should he not be criminally liable? The major difficulty in imposing liability for either CMA or CBT arises from the nature of a partnership and the way in which partners are considered by Indian decisions to hold the partnership property. In *Velji Raghavji Patel* (1965), the Indian Supreme Court put the point as follows in the context of CMA:

> It is obvious that an owner of property, in whichever way he uses his property and with whatever intention will not be liable for misappropriation and that would be so even if he is not the exclusive owner thereof. As already stated,

a partner has undefined ownership along with the other partners over all the assets of the partnership. If he chooses to use any of them for his own purposes he may thereby be accountable civilly to the other partners. But he does not thereby commit any misappropriation.

The Indian decisions consider the relationship between partners to be analogous to that of joint tenants in the law of real property. Each and every joint tenant is wholly entitled to the whole of the property; each has the full interest and the individual tenants do not hold in distinct shares. They have certain rights against one another but they have the rights of a single owner as against the rest of the world. An illustration of the length to which this principle extends in the law of real property is the "right of survivorship"; when one joint tenant dies, his interest passes to the other joint tenant or tenants irrespective of directions in his will or the intestacy rules. Partners are similarly regarded in the Indian cases; they are considered to be joint owners of the entire partnership property and are not considered to hold individual shares. Under this analysis it is said that a partner cannot be liable for CMA or CBT because he already jointly owns the property in question; he cannot misappropriate his own property.

In the case of criminal breach of trust, a further problem arises. The Indian cases have held that there can generally be no "entrustment" of partnership property to one partner. The difficulty again stems from the manner in which partners are said to hold partnership property. Since each partner is regarded as having a right to the entire property, no single partner can be regarded as "entrusted" either with the property or with dominion over it. The only exception to this which has been recognized in India is where one partner is specifically entrusted with a particular part of the partnership property by special agreement between the partners.

Bhuban Mohan Das v Surendra Mohan Das AIR (1951) Cal 69 (Full Bench, HC, Calcutta, India)

Harries CJ: [23] [T]here is really no patnr's share in the property until an account & it may well be that a patnr who retains an asset, is entitled not only to his share according to the partnership agreement in that asset but on taking an account it may be found that he is entitled to the whole of the asset & considerably more. In such a case how can it be said that he has been guilty of a breach of trust & has acted dishonestly towards his co-patnrs, if an account would show that he was entitled to everything which he had retained?...

[33] Whether or not a patnr can be said to have been entrusted with property must depend upon whether there is any special agreement between the parties. If there is no special agreement he does not receive property in a fiduciary capacity. It might be that if there was a special arrangement between the patnrs, then it could be said that a patnr was entrusted with property or with dominion over it. For example, if by the terms of the partnership agreement one patnr was given the sole right to possession of the partnership assets or to receive moneys on behalf of the partnership then such a patnr might, though it is unnecessary to hold it, be said to have entrusted another patnr with

money if he gave such other patnr money for a specific purpose. It is unnecessary in this case to decide in what circumstances there can be entrustment. But all we need say is that by special agreement between the parties entrustment might be possible, & if entrustment was possible then a breach of conditions or arrangement might render the person accused guilty of fraudulent breach of trust. However I am satisfied that in ordinary cases where a patnr receives moneys or an asset belonging to a partnership, or holds moneys or assets of a partnership, he does not hold that money in a fiduciary capacity. He cannot even be sued for a share in the moneys or assets by his co-patnr.

[34] The only remedy of a co-patnr is an account & until such an account is taken it cannot be said whether the co-patnr has any interest at all in the asset or money.

Bhuban Mohan Das (1951) was followed by the Indian Supreme Court in *Velji Raghavji Patel* (1965).

2. The local approach

The local courts have not followed the Indian decisions and it is now clear that partners may be liable for both CMA and CBT. In *Haji Sahid v Shaik Peroo* (1875) the Straits Settlements Supreme Court rejected the analogy between partners and joint tenants. The appellant was a partner, with two others, in renting betel nut trees. He was given 33 bags of nuts to be taken to S in part payment of a partnership debt. He did not deliver the nuts and faced charges of CMA and CBT in respect of the 33 bags. Ford J placed much emphasis on the fact that such *pro hac vice* partnerships were common place and that honest partners should be protected against the dishonest. The appellant was convicted of CMA but was held not liable for CBT because the court felt bound by Indian decisions which, at the time, restricted liability for CBT to cases of a "trust proper". Once that restriction was removed (see above, p 585), it was only a matter of time before liability was imposed on partners for CBT.

R v Lee Siong Kiat (1935) 4 MLJ 53 (SC, Straits Settlements)

The appellant was a managing partner in a firm which had formed a partnership with seven other firms. The eight firms comprised the Hock Hoe Hup Kee Kongsi which was formed for the purpose of obtaining passenger tickets from another firm called KPM. The appellant was the representative of the Kongsi and the books of the Kongsi were kept by a person under his supervision. KPM issued one free ticket for every 15 tickets paid for; 225 free tickets were issued over time to the appellant. He could not account for all of these. Neither could he account for money which had been paid to him by KPM by way of interest on a sum deposited with KPM jointly by all partners to the Kongsi as security for the payment of the tickets. He was convicted on charges of CBT.

Terrell J: [It was] argued that the conviction could not stand because a partner could never be convicted of criminal breach of trust, as under the English law of partnership, which is law in this Colony, a partner does not stand in a fiduciary relation to his co-partners, that accordingly there is no "trust", and there cannot be a criminal breach of a trust which is not recognized in law. Mr Page further argued that by virtue of Ordinance No 111 (Civil Law) the criminal law of England relating to partners was also introduced into the Colony. Apart from the fact that the English statutes make special provisions for charges of theft and embezzlement being brought against partners in respect of the partnership property, I cannot accept this submission. In criminal matters the law in the Colony is provided by the Penal Code to the exclusion of English Common Law or English Statute Law. Ordinance No 111 (Civil Law) as its name implies is exclusively concerned with civil law, and this is all that need be said.

As to the argument that a partner is not in a fiduciary position to his co-partners, this is no doubt correct in so far as he is not a trustee in the strict sense in which that word would be interpreted in a Court of Chancery. But the word "trust" in the expression "criminal breach of trust" as found in the Penal Code, is used in a far wider and more popular sense. A reference to ss 407, 408 and 409 makes this perfectly clear. In s 407 a person entrusted with property may be a carrier, wharfinger or warehouse keeper; in s 408 a clerk or servant; and in s 409, a public servant, merchant, factor, broker, attorney or agent. Not one of the people in these various categories could ordinarily be described as a trustee in Chancery proceedings. One has to remember what a partnership is. It is an association requiring the utmost good faith between the partners–"in societis contractibus fides exuberet"–each partner owes a duty to his co-partners and each partner is entitled to have confidence in his co-partner and good faith towards him. Again in law every partner is an agent for the partnership and an agent is specifically referred to in s 409.

I have no doubt, therefore, on principle that the relationship between partners is such that one of them may be entrusted with property on behalf of the partnership and may accordingly commit criminal breach of such trust within the meaning of Penal Code.

As regards the authorities, they are rather scanty, probably because the proposition has never been contested. The only local case is *Haji Sahid v Shaik Peroo*, (1875). In that case the magistrate refused to convict under either ss 403 and 405 as the accused was a partner, and on appeal the Supreme Court reversed the findings as regards s 403 only. The Supreme Court did not convict under s 405 as there was an Indian decision–*Re Lall Chand Roy* (1868) to the effect that a partner does not fall within s 405. The Indian decision has however long since been overruled....

The fact is that in partnership cases it is more difficult to prove the offence of criminal breach of trust because *ex hypothesi* the accused has already a partial dominion over the property in question, and it is essential for the prosecution to prove that this limited dominion on behalf of the partnership has been converted into a personal dominion on the accused's behalf. When the person charged with misappropriating property has no right to the property at all, it is easy to infer that any possession is an unlawful possession. In the case of partnerships, however, the position is different. It may be merely a matter of account and that is in fact one of the defences submitted in the present case. That defence cannot however prevail in cases such as the present where the books and conduct of the parties show that the misappropriation has been complete, and that the property has passed from, or never entered into, the possession of the partnership, and has been misapplied by the accused for his own benefit.

Appeal dismissed

WJM Ricquier and S Yeo, *Breaches of Trust in Singapore and Malaysia* (1984) 44–45

Which is the better position: the latest Indian decisions which hold that partners cannot be criminally liable, or the combined effect of *Haji Sahid* (1875) and *Lee Siong Kiat* (1935) which hold that a partner can be guilty of criminal misappropriation as well as criminal breach of trust? It is submitted that the latter position is preferable. To quote Ford J in *Haji Sahid* (1875), "can it be that an act so manifestly deceitful and injurious to his partners is not to be termed dishonest ... upon the sort of paradoxical reasoning that because a partner has a legal property in all the partnership property and a right of possession to it also, a misappropriation is impossible, the property being in fact his own?" Such dishonesty on the part of a partner should give rise to criminal liability.

The courts in *Haji Sahid* (1875) and *Lee Siong Kiat* (1935) also made some interesting remarks regarding English partnership law. In the former case, Ford J highlighted an English statute which makes partners criminally liable. While the learned judge agreed that this statute did not apply to the colony, he was influenced by the fact that the English Parliament regarded as unsound a rule which gives partners immunity from criminal liability. Ford J inferred that, since the colony did not have an equivalent statute, s 405 might be read widely to include partners.

In *Lee Siong Kiat* (1935), counsel for the accused contended that under Ordinance No 111 (Civil Law), the criminal law of England relating to partners was also introduced into the colony. The court dismissed this contention by holding that:

> "In criminal matters the law in the colony is provided by the criminal code to the exclusion of English Common Law or English Statute Law. Ordinance No 111 (Civil Law) as its name implies is exclusively concerned with civil law, and that is all that need be said."

This decision indicates that, in Singapore and Malaysia, the sole determinant of criminal liability among partners is the Penal Code. Hence, all other statutes, particularly civil statutes, are irrelevant. The logical conclusion, then, is that the provisions of the English Partnership Act, adopted in Singapore under the Civil Law Act, do not assist in the interpretation of ss 403 and 405 of the Penal Code. (By the same argument, the Partnership Act 1961 of Malaysia ... does not influence the interpretation of the provisions in the Malaysian Penal Code.)

Chapter 27

Cheating

By NA Morgan

A. Introduction

The approach taken in this chapter is to consider the basic definition of cheating and thereafter the punishments prescribed for the various forms of cheating under the Penal Code.

Penal Code, s 415

Whoever, by deceiving any person, fraudulently or dishonestly induces the person so deceived to deliver any property to any person, or to consent that any person shall retain any property, or intentionally induces the person so deceived to do or omit to do anything which he would not do or omit if he were not so deceived, and which act or omission causes or is likely to cause damage or harm to that person in body, mind, reputation or property, is said to "cheat".

Explanation 1–A dishonest concealment of facts is a deception within the meaning of this section.

Explanation 2–Mere breach of contract is not of itself proof of an original fraudulent intent.

Illustrations

(a) A, by falsely pretending to be in the Government service, intentionally deceives Z, and thus dishonestly induces Z to let him have on credit goods for which he does not mean to pay. A cheats.

(b) A, by putting a counterfeit mark on an article, intentionally deceives Z into a belief that this article was made by a certain celebrated manufacturer, and thus dishonestly induces Z to buy and pay for the article. A cheats.

(c) A, by exhibiting to Z a false sample of an article, intentionally deceives Z into believing that the article corresponds with the sample, and thereby dishonestly induces Z to buy and pay for the article. A cheats.

(d) A, by tendering in payment for an article a bill on a house with which A keeps no money, and by which A expects that the bill will be dishonoured, intentionally deceives Z, and thereby dishonestly induces Z to deliver the article, intending not to pay for it. A cheats.

(e) A, by pledging as diamonds articles which he knows are not diamonds, intentionally deceives Z, and thereby dishonestly induces Z to lend money. A cheats.

(f) A intentionally deceives Z into a belief that A means to repay any money that Z may lend to him, and thereby dishonestly induces Z to lend him money, A not intending to repay it. A cheats.

601

(g) A intentionally deceives Z into a belief that A means to deliver to Z a certain quantity of pepper which he does not intend to deliver, and thereby dishonestly induces Z to advance money upon the faith of such delivery. A cheats; but if A, at the time of obtaining the money, intends to deliver the pepper, and afterwards breaks his contract and does not deliver it, he does not cheat, but is liable only to a civil action for breach of contract.

(h) A intentionally deceives Z into a belief that A has performed A's part of a contract made with Z, which he has not performed, and thereby dishonestly induces Z to pay money. A cheats.

(i) A sells and conveys an estate to B. A, knowing that in consequence of such sale he had no right to the property, sells or mortgages the same to Z without disclosing the fact of the previous sale and conveyance to B, and receives the purchase or mortgage money from Z. A cheats.

(j) A, playing with false dice, or marked cards, wins money from B. A cheats.

The following table shows the different elements of cheating prescribed by s 415.

(1) As a result of deception, the deceived person is induced;

(2) (a) to deliver any property to any person; or — *Mens rea* is either fraudulently (s 25) or dishonestly (s 24).

(b) to consent to any person retaining any property; or

(c) to do or omit to do anything which he would not do or omit if he were not so deceived; and that act or omission causes or is likely to cause damage or harm to that person in body, mind, reputation or property. — *Mens rea* is intentionally.

Deception is therefore common to all forms of cheating and is considered in the next section. Thereafter we shall consider separately the questions of fraudulent and dishonest cheating (2(a) and (b) above) and intentional cheating (2(c) above).

B. Deception

Tan Peng Ann v PP [1949] MLJ Supp 10 (HC, Ipoh, Malaysia)

The appellant had been convicted on two charges which were framed in terms that he had "dishonestly induced" two people to deliver money to him to secure the release of third parties from lawful custody.

Thomson J: It is not ... every form of dishonestly inducing a person to deliver property that amounts to cheating, but only those forms of it in which the dishonesty consists in deceiving of the person concerned....

If the present appellant induced the complainants to pay him money by deceiving them, the deception which he practised upon them must have taken place prior to their handing over the money, for otherwise it could not be said they were thereby induced to part with their money by it, and on the evidence the only such deception that could have been alleged was a representation which the appellant knew to be false that he had a then present intention of using the influence which he clearly possessed on behalf of their friends....

Counsel for the Prosecution [contended] that the accused got money from the complainants by representing that he was able to secure the release of detained persons and that this was false because he had no such powers. At the end of the case, the President arrived at the following result:

> "The basis of cheating is deceiving. The deception in the first charge was that the accused would use his undoubted influence to obtain the release of P.W.1's children. They were not released: from this fact the deduction is that the accused did not use his influence. The detained persons referred to in the second charge were released. The *prima facie* evidence is that it was through no act of the accused."

That is the only passage in which he formulates the question ... and as such it calls for close examination.

In the first place, he rejects the basis on which the case had been opened by Counsel for the Prosecution and finds that it was true that the appellant had some sort of influence with the police. He goes on to find that the appellant represented that he "would" use that influence in the desired direction which I take to mean that he had at the time of making the representation a then present intention of using his influence. His next step should have been to ask himself whether that representation was true or false but if that question was asked I can nowhere find that it was answered.

To say that the appellant did not in fact use his influence, may or may not be justified by the evidence, but it is not an answer to the question whether his representation that he had an intention of using that influence in a particular way was true or false. Nor does it in itself afford any safe ground for saying that the answer to that question is that the representation in question was false. In the absence of anything to the contrary, it may be safe to presume that a man's acts spring from his intentions but it by no means follows as a result either of formal logic or of human experience that his omissions support the inference of any lack of intention.

Appeal allowed

This case shows that deception and dishonesty are distinct requirements; not all dishonesty constitutes deception and the deception must be specified in the charge (see also *Lim Chin Huat*, 1963 and *Khoo Kay Jin*, 1964, below, p 611). However, a "dishonest concealment of facts" may constitute deception (Explanation 1 to s 415) and the judgment in the following case suggests that it is not always easy to distinguish the elements of deception and dishonesty.

Low Cheng Swee v R (1941) 10 MLJ 98 (HC, Singapore)

The appellant insured his car with two companies, AI and CU. A claim was filed in respect of the cost of repair from both companies. The appellant received money from AI and a garage proprietor received money from CU in respect of repairs to the car. The appellant was convicted on a charge of deceiving AI by dishonestly concealing the policy with CU and thereby inducing AI to pay him the money.

McElwaine CJ: Each policy contained a condition to the effect that if at the time of the occurrence of an accident there should be any other insurance existing covering the same loss or damage, the Company should not be liable to pay or contribute more than a rateable proportion of any loss, damage, compensation, costs or expenses.

In connection with the claim against the Commercial Union a claim form was filled in by the appellant. No question was asked on that form as to whether or not there was any other insurance on this car. In the case of the Asia Insurance Co no claim form appears to have been filled in. There is no evidence that in making either claim any express representation was made to either Company that there was no other insurance on this car....

Neither Company asked whether there was another policy, so there was no active misrepresentation on the part of the accused. Each Company just assumed that it was the sole insurer without troubling to make the slightest inquiry of the appellant....

A dishonest concealment of facts is a deception within the meaning of [s 415]....

In making each claim there was a concealment of fact. Was that concealment dishonest?....

Dishonesty ... is ... doing something with the intent of gaining property by unlawful means, and therefore concealment to be an ingredient of cheating must be done with the intent of gaining property by unlawful means. In other words the concealment itself must be unlawful. "Unlawful" is the English form of "illegal", and a thing is illegal if it furnishes ground for a civil action. Non-disclosure of the second policy possibly furnishes the Asia Insurance Co with a cause of action to recover part of the $220 as money paid under a mistake of fact. So whether the appellant has committed a crime by his concealment depends entirely upon whether or not he was aware of the condition in the policy limiting the Asia Insurance Company's liability.

There is no sufficient evidence that he was aware of it. Whether an illiterate Chinese would, in a civil action, be bound by conditions in an English contract which he cannot read and which have not been explained to him and of which he is unaware, does not now arise. But in a criminal case I think that before non-disclosure can be deemed to be dishonest it must be shown that the accused knew that the Company's liability would be lessened by the fact which he failed to disclose, and that the non-disclosure would deceive and lead the Company to act to its detriment. I am not disposed to assume any such knowledge in a criminal case, and such knowledge is not proved....

Appeal allowed

C. Cheating by dishonest or fraudulent inducement

These categories of cheating (2(a) and (b)) refer to the delivery or retention of property. As in the case of criminal breach of trust, there is no reason to limit this to movable property. Dishonesty has already been discussed (see above, p 531). "Fraudulently" is defined in a singularly unhelpful manner.

Penal Code, s 25

A person is said to do a thing fraudulently if he does that thing with intent to defraud but not otherwise.

It is interesting that in the original draft Penal Code prepared by the Indian Law Commissioners (1837), the *mens rea* term "dishonestly" was not used. Instead, "fraudulently" was used and was defined as dishonesty now is under s 24. However, since both terms are used, they must be given different definitions and must mean something different from deception. The following cases suggest, inter alia, that deprivation of property, or the intention to deprive of property, is the basis of dishonesty but is not necessary for fraud. In this sense at least, fraud seems wider than dishonesty. It seems correct to give dishonesty a narrower meaning because of the punishments for cheating; for offences under 2(a) where the *mens rea* is dishonesty, a heavier penalty is attracted under s 420 than for fraudulent cases which are punishable under s 417 (see below, p 615).

Seet Soon Guan v PP (1955) 21 MLJ 223 (HC, KL, Malaya)

Buhagiar J: As a definition ... [s 25] is defective inasmuch as it is content to define one word by another itself requiring definition and the Code does not define "to defraud"....

The correct meaning of the term "fraudulently" is to be sought by consideration of the context in which that term is used in the Code. That term is used either by itself or in juxtaposition with the term "dishonestly" or together with other terms eg s 209: "fraudulently or dishonestly or with intent to injure or annoy"). "Dishonestly" is dealt with in s 24 of the Code; this section in conjunction with s 23, leaves no doubt as to the meaning of "dishonestly". In my opinion there can be no doubt that "fraudulently" used in juxtaposition with "dishonestly" must be something different from, although akin to, "dishonestly". As the Judges in a Calcutta Full Bench Case, *Abbas Ali* (1897) remarked:

> "The word 'fraudulently' is used in ss 471 and 464 together with the word 'dishonestly' and presumably in a sense not covered by the latter word. If, however, it be held that 'fraudulently' implies deprivation, either actual or intended, then, apparently, that word would perform no function which would not have been fully discharged by the word 'dishonestly', and its use would be mere surplussage. So far as such a consideration carries any weight, it obviously inclines in favour of the view that the word 'fraudulently' should not be confined to transactions of which deprivation of property forms a part."

Support for the view that "fraudulently" does not imply deprivation of property is to be found in other sections of the Code. The only instances in which the word "dishonestly" appears by itself and not in juxtaposition to the word "fraudulently" are ss 378 (theft), 383 (extortion), 403 and 404 (misappropriation of property), 405 (criminal breach of trust), 411 and 412 (receiving stolen property), 420 (cheating and dishonestly inducing a delivery of property) and 461 and 462 (dishonestly breaking open any closed receptacle containing or supposed to contain property). In all these sections (with the possible exception of the two last mentioned, where however an offence is committed if there is an intent to commit mischief), deprivation of property is a necessary consequence of the offence.

Although the terms "dishonestly" and "fraudulently" should be distinguished, this is not easy to do. The contrasting approaches of the three judges in the following case provide ample evidence of that difficulty.

King-Emperor v Tha By Aw (1907) 4 BLR 315 (Chief Court, Lower Burma)

Under government regulations people were entitled by law to possess up to three tolas in weight of opium at any one time, obtained from the government or from a licensed vendor. The appellant, whose real name was Tan Sein, did not possess more than three tolas but had obtained more than his proper share by giving a false name and by representing that he was resident in another town.

Irwin Offg CJ: There is no doubt that the Resident Excise Officer at Henzada was deceived by Tan Sein giving a false name and representing himself to be a resident of Henzada town. And ... it is obvious that if Tan Sein had given his true name and address, the Resident Excise Officer would have refused to let him buy any opium. In consequence of the deception he supplied him with opium.

The deception was not dishonest, as it would not cause wrongful loss to anybody, nor would it cause wrongful gain to Tan Sein. He is legally entitled to possess as much opium as he can induce the Resident Excise Officer to permit him to buy, so long as he does not possess more than three tolas at one time.

It remains to be considered whether the deception practised by Tan Sein was fraudulent....

In *Muhammed Saeed Khan* (1898), the learned Judge quoted some observations of Sir James Stephen in his *History of the Criminal Law of England*, viz:

> "Whenever the words 'fraud' or 'intent to defraud' or 'fraudulently' occur in the definition of a crime, two elements at least are essential to the commission of the crime; namely, first, deceit or an intention to deceive, or in some cases mere secrecy; and secondly, either actual injury or possible injury, or an intent to expose some person either to actual injury or to a risk of possible injury by means of that deceit or secrecy. This intent is very seldom the only or the principal intention entertained by the fraudulent person, whose principal object in nearly every case is his own advantage....
>
> A practically conclusive test as to the fraudulent character of a deception for criminal purposes is this–Did the author of the deceit derive any advantage from it which could not have been had if the truth had been known? If so, it is hardly possible that the advantage should not have had an equivalent in loss or risk to some one else, and if so, there was fraud."

If the "practically conclusive test" just described were applied to the present case, without regarding the rest of the passage, Tan Sein's act would at once be pronounced fraudulent, for Tan Sein obtained by deceit a quantity of opium which he would not have obtained without deceit. But if we look for the "actual injury or risk of possible injury" to some other person, or the "equivalent in loss or risk of loss to some one else", what do we find? The object of Government in framing the rules and directions under the Opium Act is to restrict the consumption of opium in order to prevent persons who are deficient in self-control from injuring themselves physically and morally by over-indulgence in the drug. It may be taken that the deception practised by Tan Sein tends in some small degree to defeat that object, but it appears to me that the risk of injury to some persons unknown involved in the success of the deception is too remote and too meagre to be taken as fulfilling the condition suggested by the eminent jurist.

Moreover, causing risk of injury to some persons unknown who have nothing to do with the person deceived does not seem to fulfil the condition laid down in s 25, Penal Code....

I would set aside the conviction and sentence....

Hartnoll J: [His Lordship also approved of the views of Sir James Stephen set out in the judgment of Irwin Offg CJ and continued:]

[F]or the purposes of the present case I am of opinion that it is sufficient to adopt the definition of Sir James Stephen and that it may be taken that, if both the elements mentioned by that learned jurist are present in the case under discussion, there is no doubt that there has been fraudulent conduct within the meaning of s 415 of the Indian Penal Code. It seems to me that in the case alleged against Tha Byaw *alias* Tan Sein both these elements are present. [Government] rules have ... been framed to prevent the consumption of opium generally by the Burmans, as it is considered deleterious to them; and when Government prohibits the consumption of a drug in such a manner, I think that the Courts must consider that its supply to those prohibited from consuming it must cause actual injury to them or at least possible injury or risk of possible injury to them. Where therefore a man by deceit gets possession of more opium than he would otherwise be able to get hold of, there is always the danger–not remote in my opinion, but immediate and present–of his hawking it about to those prohibited from using it....

I consider that the injury, or possible injury, to the Burman nation from the unlawful hawking of opium is far greater and immediate than the possible injury from the harm caused to the public at large by unauthorized persons fabricating certificates so as to enable them to sit at examinations which the recent course of judicial decision in India has held to be fraudulent....

I must therefore hold that on the facts proved against Maung Tha Byaw *alias* Tan Sein his conduct is fraudulent within the meaning of s 415 of the Indian Penal Code.

Ormond J: The accused by means of deceit obtained opium which he would not otherwise have obtained, ie he obtained goods by false pretences. He acted "dishonestly" within the meaning of the Penal Code, ss 24 and 23, because by means of deceit he gained opium which was not his own, and which he would not have gained but for the deceit.

It matters not, I think, that he paid the usual price. If, having given his true name and address, he would have been entitled to this opium at double the price that would have been charged him if he had resided at another place he would clearly be guilty of cheating, if he obtained it at the lower price by a false representation as to his residence; so, too if he obtains it (as in this case) by means of a false representation, when he would not have been able to obtain it at any price without such deceit.

In my opinion the accused is guilty of cheating under s 417 of the Indian Penal Code.

D. Cheating by intentional inducement

Echoing the language used in the Penal Code to define "injury" (s 44), cheating under 2(c) of our earlier categorization requires that the act or omission induced by the accused either caused or was likely to cause harm or damage in body, mind, reputation or property to the deceived person and not to a third party. The definition and limits of such harm or damage were discussed in the following cases.

Baboo Khan v State of Allahabad AIR (1961) All 639 (HC, Allahabad, India)

The accused impersonated an eye surgeon and operated on R, a blind boy. The operation was unsuccessful and the boy's father, Z, did not pay the accused.

[Editor's note; there was no "delivery" by Z, the deceived party, under 2(a) or (b), and the direct harm of the operation had been caused to R.]

Order of court: [I]t is clear that the accused Babu Khan deceived the complainant Zalim by pretending to be Dr Mohan Lal of Aligarh and intentionally induced him to allow an operation to be performed on his son Rajpal, which he would not have allowed to be performed if he had not been so deceived. But before the offence of cheating can be made out it has further to be shown that the act which the person deceived was induced to do by the deception practised on him caused or was likely to cause "damage or harm to that person in body, mind, reputation or property". No harm has been caused to reputation or property in this case.

   Damage or harm in body has been caused to Rajpal who was operated on; but by the definition quoted above it is necessary that the harm should be caused to the person deceived not to any one else, and in this case the person deceived was not Rajpal but Zalim. There remains however to be considered damage or harm in mind; and it seems to me that Zalim himself was harmed in mind by the act which he was induced to do on account of the deception practised by the accused, for his permitting the operation to be performed on his son's eye must inevitably have caused him a good deal of mental anguish.

   "Damage or harm in mind" has not been defined in the Penal Code, but I presume that it covers both injury to the mental faculties and also mental pain (just the same as damage or harm in body would cover wounds or other hurts and also physical pain).

Appeal against conviction dismissed

Johnson v McLarty (1888) 4 Kyshe 430 (SC, Straits Settlements)

S Co wanted to obtain firebars of a particular design. The appellant, an employee, represented to the respondents, P Co, that he wanted the firebars for AH, who often dealt with P Co. When he called to collect the bars, the respondents became suspicious and they refused to deliver the bars.

Wood J: The appellant here intentionally induced the prosecutors [respondents] to believe they were making firebars for Ah Heng and not for another person–but he *never intended to cause damage or loss* to the prosecutors, being ready to pay for the bars when made. It has been urged by the Solicitor-General that the appellant's act might injure the prosecutors in their business, but I consider that, a damage, which, even if shewn to exist, is too remote to be within the meaning of s 415 of the Penal Code.

Appeal allowed

Canagarayar (1987) has argued that *Baboo Khan* (1961) requires only that the accused intended to induce a person to act in a particular manner; by contrast, *McLarty* (1888) requires that he must in addition have intended to cause damage or loss to the deceived person. Given the brevity of both judgments, and of *McLarty* (1888) in particular, this may be reading too much into the decisions. The decisions may be reconciled on the basis that "damage to business" (*McLarty*, 1888) was unproven and/or too remote whereas mental anguish (*Baboo Khan*, 1961) fell within the definition of harm or damage under s 415. However, if the decisions do conflict, the decision in *McLarty* (1888) should be followed as a decision of the Supreme Court of the Straits Settlements. Canagarayar also suggests that *McLarty* (1888) is better on policy grounds and in line with the views of the authors of the Penal Code.

JK Canagarayar, "Dishonoured cheques and the offence of cheating–A Singapore perspective" (1987) 29 Mal LR 41, 47

Macaulay ... indicated in his report:

> "In fact, if all the misrepresentations and exaggeration in which men indulge for the purpose of gaining at the expense of others were made crimes, not a day would pass in which many thousands of buyers and sellers would incur the penalties of the law....
>   Penal laws clearly ought not to be made for the preventing of deception, if deception could be prevented by means of the civil code."

The more restrictive interpretation in *McLarty* (1888) may accomplish some of the objectives that Macaulay had in mind and provide adequate reinforcement to the remedies in civil law in instances where the accused actually intended the harm....

E. Dishonoured cheques

Dishonoured cheques have presented particular difficulties in the context of cheating. The decisions from Singapore and Malaysia demonstrate a lack of clarity and it appears that liability may depend less on the fundamental questions of deception and dishonesty and more on technical questions of whether the sale was on a cash or credit basis or on the date of the cheque.

Yong Yong Peng v R (1947) 13 MLJ 40 (HC, Singapore)

The appellant and another man ran a chop which had a bank account. Most of the money in the account was withdrawn and the premises were vacated. The appellant was convicted on two charges of cheating in respect of dishonoured cheques. On the first occasion the complainant accepted the cheque as he thought it was genuine and previous cheques had been honoured. On the second the cheque was accepted because the appellant said he was unable to obtain cash because the banks were closed.

McElwaine CJ: The appellant was accustomed to dealing with both the persons said to have been cheated and he knew that their terms were cash on delivery....

The giving of a cheque is not necessarily a representation that the drawer is in credit with his bank to the amount of the cheque, but there is an implied representaiton that the cheque is a good, valid and genuine order for payment: *Hazelton* (1874). There was no evidence that the Chop or the appellant had authority to overdraw, and in fact the account never had been overdrawn, so there was nothing to lead the appellant to think that the Bank would honour the cheques.

The appellant and the complainant knew that the transactions were cash transactions, and I think there was an implied representation that the cheques would be met. The appellant kept the books of the Chop and must have known the state of the accounts. The fact that the Chop closed down the very day on which notice of dishonour was given, and that everything of value was removed, is distinct evidence of fraudulent intent, and that evidence is enhanced by the fact that the seals and signboard were left behind–an indication that the Chop was not going to re-open elsewhere.

I think there was false representation as to an existing fact and that the offence charged was committed.

There is no doubt whatever that the appellant represented that he intended to pay for the goods and that he had no such intention. It seems to me that a representation under such circumstances is itself a false representation of an existing fact....

If there was no false pretence as to the cheque still this man had no intention to pay at the time he got the goods. That is indicated by his disappearance with the goods as soon as he received them.

Appeal dismissed

Re DC Henry (1958) 24 MLJ 224 (HC, Penang, Malaysia)

On 10 April 1957 the appellant wanted to purchase goods on credit from a shopkeeper. When the shopkeeper refused, the accused gave him a postdated cheque, dated 15 April. On 13 April he gave another postdated cheque (dated 18 April) in respect of further goods. Both cheques were subsequently dishonoured but the shopkeeper nevertheless continued to supply goods on credit to the appellant.

Rigby J: [T]he learned President found as a fact that the accused deceived the complainant on both these occasions by dishonestly inducing him to deliver to him sundry goods to the value of $50 and $70 on credit on the security of the two post-dated cheques.

"The act of drawing a cheque for payment of goods purchased implies at least three statements as to the state of affairs existing at the time when the cheque is drawn, first, that the drawer has an account with the bank in question; secondly, that he has authority to draw on it for the amount shown on the cheque; and, thirdly, that the cheque, as drawn, is a valid order for the payment of that amount, or that in the ordinary course of events the cheque, on future presentation, will be honoured. It does not, however, imply any representation that the drawer already has money in the bank to the amount shown in the cheque, for he may either have authority to withdraw, or have an honest intention of paying in the necessary money before the cheque can be presented." (*Ratanlal*, 18th edn, p 1058).

Again:

"Where a person orders goods on credit and promises expressly or impliedly to pay for them on a particular date, then if the prosecution proves that at the date of the contract the circumstances of the accused were such that he must have known that it was practically impossible that he would be able to pay for the goods, the offence of cheating is committed." (*Ratanlal*, 18th edn, 1936).

On the facts of this case, having regard to the evidence as to the defendant's Bank account the learned President, in my view, was strictly justified in finding that at the time the accused presented the post-dated cheques maturing and due on the 15th and 18th respectively the financial position of the accused, as a Government servant dependent on his monthly salary, was such that he must have known that he would not have the funds in the Bank to meet the cheques on the dates they were due for presentation. The facts, therefore, within the letter of the law, strictly support the charges of cheating.

Appeal dismissed

Khoo Kay Jin v PP (1964) 30 MLJ 22 (HC, Penang, Malaysia)

(The facts appear in the judgment.)

Hepworth J: The brief facts of the case were that the appellant ordered certain goods from the complainant to a value of approximately $14,000, which goods were delivered by the complainant to the appellant on the 15th August 1962. The complainant in his evidence said that it was a cash transaction. The appellant said in his evidence that it was a credit transaction. Be that as it may counsel for the appellant was prepared to argue the appeal as if the complainant's version that it was a cash transaction was correct. In any event no payment was made on the 15th August 1962, but on the 18th August 1962, the complainant accepted from the appellant 4 post-dated cheques dated the 20th, 22nd, 27th and 31st August 1962, respectively, totalling $14,000 in payment. These 4 cheques were not in fact presented for payment until October 1962, by which time the appellant's account at the Oversea-Chinese Bank had been closed. Evidence was, however, given by a representative of the Bank that had these cheques been presented for payment on the due dates they would not have been honoured....

[His Lordship held that the charge was defective as it did not specify the deception "that rendered this inducement dishonest" and continued:]

It was also submitted on behalf of the appellant that (where goods are delivered at an earlier date and post-dated cheques are accepted in payment at a later date and are subsequently dishonoured, that does not mean that a criminal offence has necessarily been committed.) In the case of *RS Ratra v Ganesh Dass* (1940) it was held that deception is only one element of the offence of cheating and not the only element. There can be no cheating unless by reason of the deception the person deceived is induced to part with any property or to do or to omit to do anything which he would not do or omit to do but for the deception. Therefore the giving of a post-dated cheque in lieu of money due with the knowledge that the drawer had no funds in the Bank does not amount to an offence of cheating in the absence of evidence to show that the person to whom the cheque was issued parted with any property or that he did or omitted to do anything which he would not have done or omitted to do if he had known that the cheque would be dishonoured....

The questions ... which have to be asked and answered are:

(1) What was the complainant induced to do or to omit to do?
(2) What was the deception which constituted the inducement?
(3) Did this induced commission or omission on his part cause or was it likely to cause him some harm or damage in body, mind, reputation or property?

The answer to question (1) according to the charge is that he was induced to allow payment for radios and other goods by post-dated cheques instead of cash. The answer to question (2) does not appear from the charge. Presumably it was making the complainant believe that the cheques would be honoured. Assuming that to be the correct answer to question (2), what is the correct answer to question (3)?

It was argued by the learned Deputy that the complainant had been deceived into accepting these post-dated cheques because he believed they would be honoured, he would not have done that if he had known that the cheques would be dishonoured, and he had therefore suffered damage because he had thereby foregone his right immediately to institute civil proceedings.

The answer to this argument is in my view that the damage spoken of must be the proximate result of the act complained of. If it is a mere possibility and not a necessary consequence of the act an essential element of the offence of cheating is not satisfied....

But in any event there was no evidence that it was ever in the contemplation of the complainant that by accepting the post-dated cheques he was foregoing his right immediately to institute civil proceedings, nor was there any evidence whatever that this caused or was likely to cause him any damage.

On the facts of this case assuming that it was a cash transaction it is quite clear that the liability to pay $14,000 for the goods arose when they were delivered on the 15th August 1962. As from that date the money was due. If he had known on the 18th August 1962, that the cheques would be dishonoured he would not, of course, have accepted them. But by accepting them on the 18th August 1962, he did not put himself in any worse position than he had been from the moment when he had delivered the goods without receiving payment, and the purchase price had then become due, on the 15th August 1962. Accordingly it could not be said that he had suffered any damage as a result of agreeing to accept on the 18th August 1962, the post-dated cheques in payment, whether he had been dishonestly induced to do so or not.

Appeal allowed

PP v Chen Kee Nan [1969] 2 MLJ 239 (HC, Ipoh, Malaysia)

The respondent placed an order with the complainant by telephone for sacks of rice worth $2,055. He promised to pay cash on delivery. On delivery, made by a third party, he offered a postdated cheque for $1,460 as part payment. On receiving the cheque the complainant immediately sought out the respondent who gave another postdated cheque for the balance. The cheques were dishonoured.

Pawan Ahmad J: The learned president in acquitting and discharging the repondent at the close of the prosecution case stated that the prosecution failed to prove dishonest intention on the part of the repondent. In coming to this conclusion the learned president relied largely on the commentary by Gour (1966, Vol IV) which reads as follows:

> "Where, therefore, a person gives a post-dated cheque in payment for goods already received and the cheque is dishonoured, there is only a breach of promise for which the remedy lies in a civil court, but the person cannot be held guilty of cheating. The giving of a cheque in lieu of money due even with the knowledge that the drawer had no funds in the bank does not amount to cheating. If the accused intended to deceive the complainant by falsely inducing him to believe that the cheque would be honoured, there is deception, but deception is only one element of the offence of cheating and not the only element. There can be no cheating unless the person deceived is induced to part with any property or to do or omit to do anything which he would not do or omit to do but for the deception."

In addition, the learned president also relied on the case of *Khoo Kay Jin* (1964).

Now, in Gour (1966, Vol IV) under paragraph "Post-dated cheque", the learned author draws a distinction between a post-dated cheque given to discharge an existing liability and a post-dated cheque issued against delivery of goods. This is what the learned author has to say in the matter:

> "A distinction must be drawn between a case where a post-dated cheque is given to discharge an existing liability and a case where it is issued against delivery of goods, property or cash with an assurance that it will be met on being presented to the bank on the due date and in due course. In the first case the failure to provide the balance is merely a breach of promise, whereas in the latter it may have different consequences. Intention of the drawer at the time the cheque is issued is a material test and if it appears from the circumstances of the drawer that he did not expect that the cheque would be cashed in normal course it would be *prima facie proof* of the intention to cheat."

Apparently, the learned president was not aware of this distinction and therefore he failed to distinguish the case of *Khoo Kay Jin* (1964), from the present case. In the first instance, in *Khoo Kay Jin*'s case, (1964), the post-dated cheque was issued some three days after delivery of the goods and it was therefore issued in order to discharge an existing liability whereas in the present case the first post-dated cheque P2, at any rate, was issued and handed over to PW 3 immediately against delivery of the rice and further when P 4 was issued a little bit later the respondent gave an assurance that both P 2 and P 4 would be met on being presented to the bank on the due dates and in due course....

In order to ascertain the intention of the respondent at the time when he issued the post-dated cheques P 2 and P 4, it will be necessary to examine the surrounding circumstances. First of all when the respondent placed the order for the rice he promised to make the payment in cash but instead issued two post-dated cheques as payment against delivery. The promise to pay in cash was obviously to induce PW 7 to deliver the rice because he must have known if he did not make this promise PW 7 would not have agreed to deliver the rice to him as they were strangers and as they had no dealings with one another previously.

Next, according to the evidence of PW 1, the manager of Bank Bumiputera, Ipoh, the respondent opened an account in the name of Chop Chew Eng Hin (Teck Kee) with the bank on 26th July 1967 with a cash deposit of $500 and on the same day made a withdrawal of $400. Between that date and 16th August 1967 when this account was closed the respondent made two further deposits and two further withdrawals. During this period but after the two said deposits and the two said withdrawals the respondent issued 11 other cheques of various amounts but they were returned with the words "Refer to drawer" stamped on them because there was no money in the respondent's account to meet any of those cheques. Both P 2 and P 4 are included in those 11 post-dated cheques. From these circumstances it is obvious that when the respondent issued P 2 and P 4 he did not expect that they would be cashed in the normal course. In my view this is further strengthened by the evidence of PW 9, the shop assistant employed by Chop Chew Eng Hin (Teck Kee), who said that nearly all the goods in the shop had been removed through the back door a few days before P 2 and P 4 were due to be presented to the bank.

In view of these circumstances, I find that the learned president was wrong in coming to the conclusion that the prosecution had failed to prove a *prima facie* case.

Appeal allowed

The cases on dishonoured cheques do not follow consistent or easily identifiable reasoning and analysis of general principles is hindered by the failure of most cases to consider earlier decisions (see also *Lim Chin Huat*, 1963). However, certain factors are implicitly or explicitly deemed to be relevant, or at least suggested by the judgements. The first is the distinction between cash and credit transactions. *Yong Yong Peng* (1947) and *Khoo Kay Jin* (1964) hint that this is significant but full discussion was avoided in *Khoo Kay Jin* (1964) by the appellant's willingness to proceed on the assumption that it was a cash sale. It is not clear how far the question of a cash or credit sale was deemed relevant in *DC Henry* (1958), or what the precise basis of that decision was. Two fundamental questions should be addressed more clearly if this distinction is to be used. First, when is a transaction made on a cash as opposed to a credit basis? Second, what are the consequences of deciding the first question one way or the other–does liablitiy arise *only* with regard to cash transactions or is it that liability is more likely in such cases?

The other factors on which emphasis is placed in *Khoo Kay Jin* (1964) and *Chen Kee Nan* (1969) are the date of the cheque and the date on which it was accepted by the complainant. In *Khoo Kay Jin* (1964) the complainant accepted postdated cheques some days after the delivery of the goods. Since there had already been delivery, before any deception by the dishonoured cheques, 2(a) was not relevant. It was held that there was no liability under 2(c) because by accepting the cheques at a later date the complainant had suffered no tangible harm or damage. In *Chen Kee Nan* (1969) the court distinguished cases where postdated cheques are given to discharge an existing liability (as in *Khoo Kay Jin*, 1964) and cases where such cheques are given against delivery (as in *Chen Kee Nan*, 1969). Liability may arise in the second case but not in the first. The rationale of these decisions seems to be that in cases of an existing liability the complainant has not been induced to behave in a manner causing, or likely to cause, harm or damage; where the cheques are given against delivery, he has. The distinction is a very fine one. The courts have not tied such arguments clearly with the question whether the sale is cash or credit but it may be that they see postdated cheques as more akin to cash sales (and therefore more likely to give rise to liability) where they are given on delivery. On the facts of the cases and their apparent rationale, it is also difficult to see the relevance of the date on the cheque; the key factor may be not so much the date on the cheque but the date at which the cheque was received. If a cheque is received against delivery then, whatever its date, it is more likely to give rise to liability than where it is given to discharge an existing liability because the complainant may suffer no harm in the second case. The only relevance of the date on the cheque may therefore be that the court might construe a postdated cheque as giving rise to a credit sale; and therefore less likely to give rise to liability even when given against delivery.

There can be no doubt that the courts must develop more coherent and consistent decisions in the area of cheating and dishonoured cheques. The role of the factors identified in the preceding paragraphs must be analysed and articulated in the light of modern needs; at present the reported cases provide little more than vague pointers to factors considered relevant.

F. Punishment and aggravated forms of cheating

1. Simple cheating

Penal Code, s 417

Whoever cheats shall be punished with imprisonment for a term which may extend to one year, or with fine, or with both.

2. Section 420

Penal Code, s 420

Whoever cheats and thereby dishonestly induces the person deceived to deliver any property to any person, or to make, alter or destroy the whole or any part of a valuable security, or anything which is signed or sealed, and which is capable of being converted into a valuable security, shall be punished with imprisonment for a term which may extend to seven years, and shall also be liable to fine.

The usual approach to prescribing punishments in the Penal Code is to provide punishment for the "simple" offence, as defined by one section of the Penal Code, and then to provide separate definitions of the formal aggravating (and less frequently mitigating) factors, and the punishments therefor. However, this approach is not followed in the context of cheating. Certain forms of cheating, as defined by s 415 alone, are punishable with the enhanced penalties prescribed by s 420, not merely under s 417.

Offences falling under s 420 carry a much longer maximum prison term than under s 417 and, on the wording of s 420, a prison term is mandatory. Two main situations are covered by s 420. First are some cases defined in s 415 alone. Canagarayar (1987, p 43) suggests, following some Indian commentators, that s 420 embraces *all* offences of cheating falling under headings 2(a) and 2(b) of our earlier classification, ie all cases of fraudulent or dishonest inducements. With respect, this is wrong. Section 420 provides enhanced punishment for only one specific form of cheating under heading 2(a), namely, *dishonest* inducement of the *delivery* of property; it does not refer either to fraudulent inducements falling under 2(a) or to cases of retention under 2(b). As a penal provision, providing much enhanced punishment, it should be strictly construed. A strict construction also accords with the view espoused in the cases (above) that in the context of cheating, fraud is less blameworthy than dishonesty.

The second situation covered by s 420 is the dishonest (again no reference to fraudulent) inducement of the deceived person to "make, alter or destroy" a valuable security, etc.

Penal Code, s 30

The words "valuable security" denote a document which is or purports to be, a document whereby any legal right is created, extended, transferred, restricted, extinguished, or released, or whereby any person acknowledges that he lies under legal liability, or has not a certain legal right.

Illustration

A writes his name on the back of a bill of exchange. As the effect of this endorsement is to transfer the right to the bill to any person who may become the lawful holder of it, the endorsement is a "valuable security".

KL Koh and Molly Cheang, *The Penal Codes of Singapore and Malaysia*, (1976, Vol II), 445–446

In *Tan Wee Meng* (1955) the question whether a shipping guarantee is a "valuable security" as defined in s 30 was considered. A shipping guarantee is a document issued by a bank which enables a consignee of goods to take delivery of them from the shipping company without the relevant bill of lading, the bank undertaking to indemnify the shipping company against any loss thereby occasioned. This indemnity is known in Singapore as a "shipping guarantee". In determining whether a shipping guarantee is a valuable security, Whyatt CJ examined the first limb of s 30 which reads: "The words 'valuable security' denote a document ... which is or purports to be, a document whereby any legal right is created...". He held that the document itself must create or at least purport to create, a legal right, and consequently if it is necessary to have recourse to matters extraneous to the document in order to create a legal right, the document does not come within the scope of the definition. According to him, a shipping guarantee is at the time of its execution, no more than a written offer by the consignee and the bank to the shipping company. It does not of itself create a legal right in the holder and could be revoked by the offeror prior to its acceptance by the offeree. Hence, a shipping guarantee is not a valuable security. This may well be correct when viewed against the first limb of s 30 only. However, he did not consider the second limb of the section which is wider in scope. It reads: "a document ... whereby any person acknowledges that he lies under legal liability,...". Is a shipping guarantee a document whereby the bank issuing it acknowledges that it lies under legal liability? It is interesting to note that after rejecting the argument that it was a valuable security within the meaning of the first limb of s 30, he further considered whether it was *capable* of being converted into a valuable security for the purpose of s 420. In giving a negative answer he said:

> "But the legal rights and liabilities which thus come into existence at the moment of acceptance flow from the consensus of the parties and not from any newly-acquired vigour in the shipping guarantee. That document remains unchanged and the only new circumstance is the act of the shipping company accepting the offer and creating a binding contract."

Of course, his mind was directed to the first limb of s 30.

The crux of the problem is whether an offer contained in the shipping guarantee to indemnify the shipping company, in the event of the shipping company accepting it, is sufficient to render the shipping guarantee a valuable security under the second limb of s 30. The Indian case of *Kumaran* (1961) affords an analogy. There, a declaration under a proposal for insurance was duly signed by the proposer, stating that in the event of the proposal being accepted by the insurance company and the proposer failing to take up the policy, he (the proposer) would pay to the company the initial expenses incurred by it in connection with the proposal. This was held to be sufficient to make the proposal for insurance a valuable security as defined in s 30 of the Indian Penal Code. The court emphasized that the proposal for insurance was not a mere proposal but contained a stipulation of liability should the proposer fail to take up the policy in the event of its acceptance by the insurance company. In a shipping guarantee there is also an express stipulation that the bank will indemnify the shipping company, should the shipping company act on it. It is submitted that it falls within the scope of the second limb of s 30.

3. Cheating by personation

Penal Code, ss 416 and 419

416. A person is said to "cheat by personation", if he cheats by pretending to be some other person, or by knowingly substituting one person for another, or representing that he or any other person is a person other than he or such other person really is.

Explanation–The offence is committed whether the individual personated is a real or imaginary person.

Ilustrations

(a) A cheats by pretending to be a certain rich banker of the same name. A cheats by personation.
(b) A cheats by pretending to be B, a person who is deceased. A cheats by personation.

419. Whoever cheats by personation shall be punished with imprisonment for a term which may extend to three years, or with fine, or with both.

4. Section 418

Penal Code, s 418

Whoever cheats with the knowledge that he is likely thereby to cause wrongful loss to a person whose interest in the transaction to which the cheating relates, he was bound, either by law or by a legal contract, to protect, shall be punished with imprisonment for a term which may extend to three years, or with fine, or with both.

G. Cheating in the course of an illegal transaction

R v Lim Chong Soo (1946) 12 MLJ 51 (HC, Singapore)

The respondent and others contracted to sell 1,000 forged one dollar notes to the complainant for $388. The complainant received a bundle of blank paper with a couple of genuine notes outside.

McElwaine CJ: There is no doubt that a Civil Court will not enforce a contract to break the law, nor will it help a person who has paid money under such a contract when complete to recover what he has paid....

This is not a proceeding to enforce an illegal contract or to recover money paid for an illegal consideration. It is as the record shows, prosecution on behalf of the King.

Cheating may be a civil wrong, but it is also a crime against the State, and here the Crown seeks to have the accused punished for this crime if they are found to have committed it....

In *Tan Ah Seng* (1935) a Court of three Judges held that a prosecution would lie for criminal misappropriation of money entrusted to the accused for a criminal purpose. I see no reason why a man should escape punishment for a crime because he has conspired with a complainant to commit the same or another crime.

I cannot consider it to be a defence for a pickpocket to prove that the watch which he stole had been stolen by the person from whom he stole it.

Appeal allowed

Chapter 28

Receiving stolen property

By KL Koh

A. Introduction

Penal Code, ss 410–411

410.–(1) Property the possession whereof has been transferred by theft, or by extortion, or by robbery, and property which has been criminally misappropriated, or in respect of which criminal breach of trust or cheating has been committed, is designated as "stolen property", whether the transfer has been made or the misappropriation or breach of trust or cheating has been committed within or without Singapore.* But if such property subsequently comes into the possession of a person legally entitled to the possession thereof, it then ceases to be stolen property.

(2) The expression "stolen property" includes any property into or for which stolen property has been converted or exchanged and anything acquired by such conversion or exchange, whether immediately or otherwise.

[*FMS Penal Code: Substitute "Malaysia" therefor.]

411. Whoever dishonestly receives or retains any stolen property, knowing or having reason to believe the same to be stolen property, shall be punished with imprisonment for a term which may extend to 5 years, or with fine, or with both; and if the stolen property is a motor vehicle or any component part of a motor vehicle as defined in section 379A shall be punished with imprisonment for a term not less than 6 months and not more than 5 years and shall also be liable to fine.

[FMS Penal Code: Imprisonment up to three years, or fine, or both.]

412. Whoever dishonestly receives or retains any stolen property, the possession whereof he knows or has reason to believe to have been transferred by the commission of gang-robbery, or dishonestly receives from a person, whom he knows or has reason to believe to belong or to have belonged to gang-robbers, property which he knows or has reason to believe to have been stolen, shall be punished with imprisonment for life, or with imprisonment for a term which may extend to 10 years, and shall also be liable to fine.

[FMS Penal Code: Imprisonment up to 20 years and fine.]

413. Whoever habitually receives or deals in property which he knows or has reason to believe to be stolen property, shall be punished with imprisonment for life, or with imprisonment for a term which may extend to 10 years, and shall also be liable to fine.

[FMS Penal Code: Imprisonment up to 20 years, and fine.]

414. Whoever voluntarily assists in concealing or disposing of or making away with property which he knows or has reason to believe to be stolen property, shall be punished with imprisonment for a term which may extend to 3 years, or with fine, or with both; and if the stolen property is a motor vehicle or any component part of a motor vehicle as defined in section 379A shall be punished with imprisonment for a term of not less than 6 months and not more than 5 years and shall also be liable to fine.

[FMS Penal Code: Imprisonment up to three years, or fine, or both.]

B.   Definition of "stolen property"

The word "stolen" is a shorthand expression to cover property which, according to s 410, has been stolen, extorted, robbed, or which has been obtained by criminal misappropriation, criminal breach of trust or cheating. Under the Indian Penal Code the definition of "stolen property" excludes property which is the subject of cheating. The transfer of the property in respect of theft, extortion or robbery may take place outside Singapore (or Malaysia under the FMS Penal Code) or the misappropriation or breach of trust may be committed outside Singapore (or Malaysia under the FMS Penal Code). However, the receiving or retention must be within Singapore (or Malaysia under the FMS Penal Code). If the theft is committed in Singapore and the accused is found in possession of stolen property outside Singapore, he cannot be charged under s 411 by a Singapore court as the offence of receiving stolen property is committed beyond the territory of Singapore (for Malaysia, see s 411 of the FMS Penal Code).

1.   "Thief" need not be convicted

It must be proved that the goods had been "stolen", but it is not necessary to prove that a person has been convicted of those offences listed in s 410 before the accused can be convicted of receiving stolen property under ss 411, 412, 413 and 414.

Ajendranath v State of Madhya Pradesh AIR (1964) SC 170 (SC, India)

Some woollen shawls, mufflers and bedsheets despatched by rail were found missing. Soon after, the police found the appellant and a few others. The appellant told the police where the stolen property was and recoveries were made. Six persons were convicted by the magistrate of various offences (conspiracy and theft), and the appellant was convicted of conspiracy and of assisting in concealment of stolen property under s 414 of the Indian Penal Code.

The question arose as to whether the appellant (and others) could be convicted of receiving stolen property if the property was not proved to be stolen property.

Raghubar Dayal J: It is not necessary for a person to be convicted under s 414, IPC that another person must be traced out and convicted of an offence of committing theft. The prosecution has simply to establish that the property recovered is stolen property and that the appellant provided help in its concealment and disposal. The circumstances of the recovery sufficiently make out that the property was deliberately divided into different packets and was separately kept. May be that the property falling to the share of a particular thief was kept separately. It was recovered from several different places in the same house. These places included an iron safe and an underground cellar. The evening before, several persons, including the appellant, were found to be coming out of the back door of the house which had its front door locked. The appellant also knew the whereabouts of the property inside the house of his maternal grandfather. He attempted to sell a few mufflers a day before the recoveries were made. He was seen arriving at the house, during the night, in a car with some persons and then removing property which looked like bales from the car to the house. All these circumstances go to support the finding that he had assisted in the concealment of the stolen property and had thus committed the offence under s 414, IPC.

Appeal dismissed

2. When goods cease to be stolen property

Section 410, which defines "stolen property", provides that "if such property subsequently comes into the possession of a person legally entitled to the possession thereof, it then ceases to be stolen property". Clearly, if the owner of stolen property were to take the goods from the thief and then hand it back to the thief for the purpose of handing it over to the receiver to entrap him, the receiver will not be guilty of receiving stolen property as the property is no longer "stolen".

It would also cover persons who might have to deal with the property legally. The word "legal" is not defined in the Penal Code but the word "illegal" is defined in s 43 as "applicable to everything which is an offence, or which is prohibited by law, or which furnishes ground for a civil action".

Suppose a van was carrying stolen goods from Point X to Point Y to be disposed of by A. On its way, it was stopped by four policemen. In order to trap A the four policemen went into the van and asked the driver to proceed to its rendezvous at Point Y. The policemen disguised themselves as civilians and went into the van. At the rendezvous the van was met by A who began to unload the goods for the purpose of disposing them. When A had unloaded the goods, he was arrested. Are the goods stolen property? (See *Haughton* v *Smith*, 1973.)

When the policemen went into the van they might be considered as having taken lawful "possession" under s 27 of the Penal Code, which includes custody. The police are empowered to deal with stolen property. Indeed, they are legally bound in the discharge of their duty to investigate suspected criminals.

3. Conversion of stolen property

Under s 410(2) "stolen property" includes any property which has been converted or exchanged. Thus if A steals $1,000 from B, buys an air-conditioner with the stolen money and offers the air-conditioner to Z who knowingly receives it, Z is guilty of receiving stolen property; or if A receives money by selling stolen property, the money he receives is stolen property. When stolen goods are exchanged a number of times, for example, if money is exchanged for a watch and the latter is ex changed for a ring, each exchanged article becomes "stolen property". The Indian Penal Code does not have the equivalent of s 410(2).

C. Actus reus

The *actus reus* of s 411 is the receipt or retention of "stolen property". There must be proof that the accused is in possession of the property that is stolen. In *Hong Ah Huat* (1971) Sharma J said:

> The word possession implies a physical capacity to deal with a thing as we like to the exclusion of everyone and a determination to exercise that physical power on one's own behalf. It implies dominion and consciousness in the mind of the person having dominion over the object. Possession must be conscious and intelligent possession and not merely the physical presence of the accused in proximity or even in close proximity to the object.

However, this is the concept of possession under English law; under s 27 of the Penal Code "possession" is wider. It reads:

> When property is in the possession of a person's wife, clerk or servant, on account of that person, it is in that person's possession within the meaning of this Code.
>
> *Explanation*–A person employed temporarily or on a particular occasion in the capacity of a clerk or servant is a clerk or servant within the meaning of this section.

Thus, unlike English law where a distinction is made between possession and custody, under the Penal Code custody would be included within the concept of possession.

For the offence of receiving stolen property under s 411, there must be proof of possession of the stolen property. Whether or not a person is in possession of stolen goods must be inferred from the circumstances of each case. Very often, short of a confession, there is no direct evidence of the physical, constructive, exclusive or joint possession of the stolen property (see *Varia*, 1948).

The mere fact that an accused had knowledge of the place where the stolen property was found is not sufficient to prove that he was in possession of the stolen goods (*Kasmin b Soeb*, 1947).

Where property is found in a house occupied by several persons, none of them can be said to be in possession of the stolen property unless there is some evidence of conscious control.

Goh Peng Meng v PP [1948–49] MLJ Supp 15 (HC, Malacca, Malaya)

The appellant was the second accused who was convicted under s 411 of the FMS Penal Code for retaining (not receiving) stolen property. He was found in a house which was in the joint possession of the first and third accused (first accused was found guilty but there was no evidence against the third accused and he was acquitted).

Callow J: [W]here property is found in a house in the possession of more than one inmate, none of them could be said to be in possession of it unless there is some evidence of conscious control (Gour, 1936). There is no doubt the facts support a charge of assisting in the concealment of stolen property contrary to s 414 of the Penal Code, or of harbouring–this Mr Atkinson conceded, but he submitted there is not sufficient evidence of exclusive control to justify conviction on the charge as it stands....

Was this property in the joint possession of the appellant? There was no evidence of the relationship of the appellant with the 1st accused in the Court below, and the question of whether possession was sufficiently attributed to the appellant is one dependent upon the proved circumstances of the case (Gour, 1936).

Had the appellant as occupier of the house such control over it as to prevent anything coming in, or being taken out without his sanction (Gour, 1936). It would appear from the nature and number of the exhibits that he must have had cognizance of them (*Hari*, 1904, *Budh Lal*, 1907), but even presuming this postulate against the appellant the case must be taken further to sustain the conviction.

I think the fact that the Police had to break in does take it one step further. It meant the appellant was in premises secured from within, and in the room in which he was found was discovered also property recently stolen.

The best proposition of law appropriate to this case which I have at my disposal is contained in *Woodroffe's Evidence* (1931):

> "The finding of stolen property in the house of the accused, provided there were other inmates capable of committing the larceny is of itself insufficient to prove his possession; though if coupled with proof of other suspicious circumstances, it may fully warrant the conviction of the accused."

If the property had simply been discovered in the house occupied by the appellant, with no other circumstances of suspicion it is manifest that no conviction could have ensued. I think, after reference to such authorities as are here available, that there is a clear distinction to be drawn between a person in whose house stolen property is found unaccompanied by any other proved act or conduct of such person, and whose acts and conduct coupled with surrounding circumstances arouse irresistible conclusions of guilt in connection with the receiving or retaining of such property.

Here is a man whose door is barred to the Police, who is found hiding in the roof above property stolen a few days before. Was his conduct and were such circumstances compatible with conscious and voluntary possession?

On the evidence of witnesses seen and heard in the Court below the Magistrate held there was sufficient evidence for the appellant to be called upon for his defence; thereupon the appellant rested his case and the convictions followed.

I agree with the Magistrate....

Appeal dismissed

Albakhar v PP (1960) 26 MLJ 247 (HC, Alor Star, Malaya)

(The facts appear in the judgment.)

Rigby J: The appellant, an 18-year-old student, was convicted of dishonestly retaining stolen property, to wit, 7 plants of orchids which he knew, or had reason to believe, was stolen property, contrary to s 411 of the Penal Code.

For the prosecution to succeed it was necessary to prove:

(1) that the orchids had been stolen; and
(2) that the appellant retained them knowing or having reason to believe that they had been stolen....

It was ... necessary to prove that the stolen orchids, or part of them, were found in the possession of the appellant and that he had retained them knowing, or having reason to believe, that they were stolen property....

[T]he only evidence remaining against the appellant was the fact that 7 pots of orchids subsequently identified as the property stolen a fortnight previously were found in a house which the appellant presumably occupied in common with the other members of his family. There was no evidence whatsoever as to how they got there or when or by whom they were taken. It is relevant to refer to the following passages in Ratanlal's (1953).

> "Where property is found in a house in the possession of more persons than one, mere discovery of any stolen property in that house is not in itself sufficient to prove that the possession was of any of those persons."

and again, at page 1037:

> "Where stolen property is found in a house occupied by several persons, it is not enough to show that the property was found in the house to convict a member of the family who might have had nothing to do with bringing or keeping it there."

There was clearly insufficient evidence to have established a *prima facie* case against the appellant and he should have been discharged at the close of the case for the prosecution....

Appeal allowed

D. Mens rea

The *mens rea* of receiving stolen property under s 411 consists of dishonestly receiving or retaining any property, which is stolen or which the accused knows or has reason to believe to be "stolen". (For the meaning of "dishonestly", see ss 23 and 24 of the Penal Code.)

Knowledge is the highest degree of speculative faculty and consists of the perception of the truth of the affirmative or negative propositions (see ch 3).

Penal Code, s 26 reads:

> A person is said to have "reason to believe" a thing, if he has sufficient cause to believe that thing, but not otherwise.

Belief is weaker than knowledge. Unless the accused confesses, knowledge or reason to believe has to be inferred from the circumstances.

1. Knowledge

There is often no evidence as to who hid the stolen property. Mere knowledge of the whereabouts of the stolen property may not be sufficient to implicate a person when other inferences may be drawn. However, if the accused is the only one who knows where the stolen property is hidden, such exclusive knowledge may point to the fact that he was the one who kept them there and was in control and conscious possession of them.

Moti Lal v State AIR (1959) Patna 54 (HC, Patna, India)

The accused, Moti Lal, was convicted under s 411 of the Indian Penal Code for being found in possession of stolen articles, inter alia, utensils and silver ornaments.

Untwalia J: Now the question arises whether the utensils taken out from the sota by Moti Lal could be held to be in possession of Moti Lal from the simple fact of his going alone to the sota and taking out the utensils from the place of concealment in the sota. In my opinion, it is right to hold that Moti Lal was found in possession of the stolen utensils. The sota was a public place no doubt not in the exclusive possession of Moti Lal. But here we are not concerned with possession of the utensils.

The utensils were kept in a hidden place and, according to the evidence of PW 5 as quoted above by me, other persons who were asked to take out the utensils from the sota failed, it was Moti Lal who went and brought the utensils out. It was, therefore, within his exclusive knowledge as to where the utensils were kept concealed in the sota. From this fact of knowledge, an inference can be drawn under s 114 of the Evidence Act [ie presumption of recent possession; the law being *in pari materia* with the Evidence Act of Singapore and of Malaysia (see below, p 629)], in absence of any other thing on the record to show as to how Moti Lal had knowledge of these things, that he had knowledge because he kept them there and therefore he had control over those articles and had the conscious possession of them. I may quote a sentence from Halsbury's Laws of England, 3rd Edition, Vol 10, at p 811, where while considering the possession of stolen properties it has been said:

> "It is unnecessary to prove a manual possession of the goods by the prisoner; it is sufficient that they were under his conscious control, or that he is in joint possession with the thief."

As soon as it is held that the utensils were in possession of the petitioner, illustration (a) of s 114 of Evidence Act is attracted, and the stolen articles being found in possession of the petitioner soon after the theft, it must be presumed in the circumstances of this case that Moti Lal received the goods knowing them to be stolen because he did not account for his possession. A controversy has arisen in some of the cases and the point was argued by Mr Nageshwar Prasad also before us as to whether mere knowledge of the fact as to where the stolen goods were kept can necessarily lead to the inference that they were in possession of the person having that knowledge.

On this question, in my opinion, every case will depend upon its own facts. There may be cases where a court may not be justified in presuming possession of the person who had mere knowledge of the articles placed but there may be cases where the articles are concealed in a place about where the particular person had the knowledge and it may be assumed in such cases that the articles were in his possession. I may in this connection refer to the case of *Chavadappa Pujari* (1945). In this case a reference is made to an unreported Bench decision of the Bombay High Court in *Rama Balappa* (1948), where it was held that, although the place in which the property was found buried did not belong to the accused, the very fact that he knew that the property was buried there would justify the presumption that he was in possession of it since he would be able to exercise control over it and remove it any time he liked....

The important point is that the circumstances and conduct of the accused point clearly to his knowledge of the exact spot where the ornaments were and, in the absence of any explanation, the reasonable inference is that he put them there himself. I, therefore, hold that Moti Lal, the petitioner, was found in possession of the stolen utensils which he had kept concealed in the sota and, in absence of any explanation of his possession, it must be presumed that the articles having been found, in his possession soon after the theft, were received by him with the knowledge that they were stolen properties. He has therefore, been rightly convicted under s 411, Indian Penal Code, so far as this item of property is concerned....

(23) Now coming to the recovery of the silver ornaments from the well, it will be found that the evidence of the Assistant Sub-Inspector (PW 2) is as follows:

> "Both these accused further pointed out that two chandi Hasulis and one pair of chandi Bajoo were thrown in a well."

No other special part was attributed to Moti Lal, the petitioner. It may be that he had knowledge that the silver ornaments were in the well but the evidence is not very clear as to whether this was within his exclusive knowledge and/or whether the silver ornaments were within his absolute control. Somebody else entered the well the following morning and took them out from the well.

In these circumstances, mere knowledge of the petitioner about the ornaments being in the well will not be sufficient to lead to the inference that he was in possession of those ornaments. There was no evidence as to who had kept the ornaments in the well. The evidence was again in that indefinite form that both the accused pointed out the ornaments in the well. In these circumstances, I do not think it safe to uphold the finding of the lower appellate court that Moti Lal, the petitioner, was in possession of the stolen silver ornaments.

Sentence modified;
Revision dismissed

2. Belief and suspicion

In a number of cases in Malaysia and in India on receiving stolen property, courts have used the test of the reasonable man in determining whether a person has reason to believe that the property is stolen. While it is necessary to show that a person feels convinced in the circumstances that the property is stolen, he need not be absolutely convinced.

Ahmad b Ishak v PP [1974] 2 MLJ 21 (HC, Kuantan, Malaysia)

The accused was convicted under s 414 of voluntarily assisting in disposing a cheque which he knew or had reason to believe to be stolen property.

Arulanandom J: [T]he accused cashed the cheque by purchasing some jewellery and receiving the balance of the amount of the cheque in cash....

Now the counsel for the appellant has also argued at length that the circumstances were such that the accused could not have had reason to believe or the knowledge necessary to warrant a conviction. "Reason to believe" is defined in s 26 of the Penal Code. It says:

"A person is said to have 'reason to believe' a thing, if he has sufficient cause to believe that thing, but not otherwise."

Now, "reason to believe", knowledge, intention, are things in a man's mind and you cannot see it, you cannot hear it. Nobody who receives stolen goods carries a big banner saying that these are stolen goods. Nor does he shout from the roof tops. You must look into the circumstances and consider if the circumstances are such that any reasonable man could see sufficient cause to believe that it was stolen. Firstly, it was a government cheque made out in the name of a person who was not the person handling the cheque. It was made out in the name of Abdul Hamid bin Hussain and it was a crossed cheque. Secondly, the endorsement of the payee on the cheque was not made in the presence of the accused. The learned counsel argued that crossed cheques do change hands very often. As a general statement I agree a businessman who has to deal with transactions involving money may have occasion to handle crossed cheques but not an office boy. In this case it had been passed from an office boy to a Penghulu to the tune of $2,000.90 when the cheque is made out in the name of another person. Thirdly, the cheque was in the hands of the office boy working in a government department who should not normally be in possession of these cheques. The accused knew that the person from whom he got the cheque was a mere office boy and working in a government department. This was a government cheque. Fourthly, the amount of the cheque from the point of view of the office boy was considerable and it is not usual for people to entrust such cheques with office boys for encashment. Fifthly, there was no reason advanced by the office boy as to why the payee himself could not cash it. Sixthly, the office boy did not want to cash it himself. Seventhly, the office boy's reason for not cashing the cheque himself was that he owed the goldsmith money. Firstly, this was not supported by the goldsmith, and secondly, this is again incredible because from the accused's own evidence the office boy was supposed to have owed him $600. Eighthly, the purported explanation of the office boy that he had interest in logging concessions could hardly have been taken seriously. If he had timber concessions or any interest in logging concessions he would not be an office boy and an office boy is not one likely to have interest in logging concessions. So even without invoking the presumption there was sufficient cause for the accused to have reason to believe that the cheque was stolen. Furthermore, the accused's conduct itself when he got the cheque and went to the goldsmith's shop would tend to show that he knew the cheque was stolen. This is what he told the goldsmith. He forgot to bring his identity card and hence did not leave his name and identity card number with the goldsmith. The learned magistrate has made findings of fact that the accused knew or had reason to believe that the cheque he had was stolen. Then after cashing the cheque he kept the jewellery purchased for himself. Whether this was consideration for cashing the cheque or not I am not prepared to say. But his story that he was owed $600 and he received gold to the value of $499 does not ring true. Because if he was owed $600 which again was not supported by any document, he would have retained $100 before giving the remainder of the cash to the office boy. On page 33 of the grounds of judgment the learned magistrate says, referring to the accused:

> "A man of some standing in society, a penghulu, is an acquaintance of an office boy. And this office boy stands above all others in his profession. He indulges in money making industry logging. And this man–the accused–without raising an eyebrow believed him.
>
> To add flavour to the transaction the cheque was handed to him as payment of a six hundred dollar debt. The cheque (P 7) was cashed at a goldsmith by buying certain gold ornament. Accused keeps the gold, the balance in cash was handed back to Adnan. For reasons best known to him (accused) he is satisfied in keeping the gold a hundred dollars less than what was then due.
>
> And before cashing the cheque, accused explained to the goldsmith that he had forgotten to bring his identity card along....
>
> This so called repayment of debt shows that the debt does not exist at all. The cheque was illegally obtained, handed to accused for cashing and in consideration of his part in this illegal transaction he was paid five hundred dollars.
>
> The court accordingly convict the accused and sentence him to twelve months imprisonment."

I can find no reason for my interfering with the learned magistrate's findings of fact....

Appeal dismissed

Courts have drawn a distinction between reason to believe and suspicion. In *Bhaggan* (1935) the High Court of Oudh distinguished the word "believe" in s 411 of the Indian Penal Code and the word "suspect":

> [T]he word "believe" in s 411 IPC, was much stronger than the word "suspect", and involved the necessity of the prosecution showing that the circumstances were such that a reasonable man must have felt convinced in his mind that the property which he was dealing was stolen property, and it was not sufficient in such a case to show that the accused person was careless or that he had reason to suspect that the property was stolen or that he did not make sufficient inquiries to ascertain whether it had been dishonestly acquired.

In *Gulbad Shah* (1888) Rattigan J said:

> A person might be held to have reason to believe property to be stolen within the meaning of s 411.... When the circumstances are such that a reasonable man would be led by a chain of probable reasoning to the conclusion or inference that the property he was asked to deal with was stolen property although the circumstances may fall short of carrying absolute conviction to his mind in the point.

In *Tan Ser Juay* (1972), the appellant was convicted of voluntarily assisting in the disposal of stolen property under s 414. He was asked to arrange the sale of an unusual number of watches without relevant certificates. There was also no receipt from the seller for his purchase. He also seemed to have deliberately shut his eyes to finding out more about the goods by refraining from asking questions. In setting aside the conviction, the High Court in Singapore held that the evidence only raised suspicions and that the appellant did not know or had reason to believe the watches were stolen property.

This case could be compared with the case of *Koh Poh Gek* (1980, Unreported) where the accused was charged with retaining stolen property under s 411 in respect of some transistors.

The accused ran a *karang guni* (rag-and-bone) business, buying and selling "junk" items. He bought the stolen property soon after some thefts. The prosecution case was that since the items were not locally available and in view of the large number sold to the accused, he should have reason to believe that the items he was dealing with were stolen items. The accused in his defence stated that he was at first reluctant to buy the items. However, after the sellers had identified themselves as policemen and had assured him that nothing would happen to him, he bought the items.

The magistrate, in acquitting the accused said:

> He had no knowledge that the items which he said looked like junk to him were stolen items or had reason to believe that they were stolen items because they were sold to him by police officers who had assured him that he could re-sell the items. Furthermore, he was also assured that nothing would happen to him. He had no reason to doubt the words of the police officers.

3. Presumption from recent possession

In most cases of receiving or retaining stolen property there is no direct proof that the accused is receiving stolen property. However, an inference may be drawn from the fact of recent possession, in the absence of reasonable explanation. This presumption of receiving stolen property is contained in s 116 (formerly s 114) of the Evidence Act (Singapore) (Cap 97) which provides:

> The court may presume the existence of any fact which it thinks likely to have happened, regard being had to the common course of natural events, human conduct, and public and private business, in their relation to the facts of the particular case.

> *Illustration*
> (a) The court may presume that a man who is in possession of stolen goods soon after the theft is either the thief or has received the goods knowing them to be stolen, unless he can account for his possession.

(For the equivalent provision in Malaysia, see s 114 of the Evidence Act 1950 (Rev 1971, Act 56).)

What amounts to recent possession will vary according to the nature of the stolen goods and whether they are capable of being passed readily from hand to hand. Under s 116 of the Evidence Act of Singapore possession must be recent before the accused is required to rebut the presumption by explaining how he acquired possession. Mere recent possession is itself insufficient to raise the presumption of receiving stolen property as the proper inference may be that he himself is the thief. If possession is not recent no presumption is raised that the accused knew or had reason to believe the goods to be stolen. Between the two extremes the answer as to what constitutes recent possession may be found, so that an inference of receiving stolen property may be drawn. The accused may adduce evidence to account for his possession.

Mah Kok Cheong v R (1953) 19 MLJ 46 (HC, Penang, Malaya)

Spencer Wilkinson J: Cases of theft or receiving where the *only* evidence against the accused is the possession of property recently stolen. These cases are really in a class by themselves–they may be looked upon not so much as cases where the law has cast a burden of proof upon the accused, but rather as cases where the law has given special significance to a certain class of circumstantial evidence, namely, the possession of stolen goods. The law is that such possession is in itself evidence of the theft or receiving unless explained; and the numerous decisions dealing with the subject, from *Abramovitch* (1949) onwards until the recent decisions of *Garth* (1949), *Aves* (1950) and *Wang Kia Heng* (1951), are all concerned with the degree of explanation which will entitle the accused to an acquittal.

Wang Kia Heng (1951) is a case which turned on s 34(1) of the Minor Offences Ordinance, but the court approved the test laid down by Lord Goddard CJ in the English case of *Aves* (1950) which was a case of receiving. The test in *Aves'* case (1950) was:

> "Where the only evidence is that an accused person is in possession of property recently stolen, a jury may infer guilty knowledge (a) if he offers no explanation to account for his possession, or (b) if the jury are satisfied that the explanation he does offer is untrue. If however, the explanation offered is one which leaves the jury in doubt whether he knew the property was stolen, they should be told that the case has not been proved, and, therefore, the verdict should be not guilty."

In *Soong Chak Sung* (1955) the Federation Court of Appeal held that the principles laid down in *Aves'* case (1950) were "clearly applicable to cases under s 411 of the Penal Code...." See also *Sam Kim Kai* (1960) where Rigby J held that the court below came to the right conclusion that the explanation of the respondent might reasonably be true; it left the court in a genuine doubt as to whether the respondent knew or had reason to believe that the property in his possession was stolen property.

PP v Hong Ah Huat [1971] 1 MLJ 52 (HC, Muar, Malaysia)

(The facts appear in the judgment.)

Sharma J: The accused was charged under s 411 of the Penal Code ... for having dishonestly retained four spray pumps and six tins of paint having reason to believe the same to be stolen. He was also charged in the same court in Arrest Case No 192 of 1969 for having dishonestly retained motor cycle JF 3912 having reason to believe the same to be stolen. The date of the commission of the offence as mentioned in both the charges was 4th May 1969....

PW 3 the investigating officer, went to the house of the accused on the night of 4th May 1969 and it was the accused himself who produced some of the spray pumps from a bush at the back of his house. The accused also led PW 3 to a rubber plantation at Jalan Yong Peng, Labis, and produced motorcycle JF 3912 from among the banana plants. The six tins of paint were also found covered with leaves and it was the accused who led the investigating officer to the place from where they were recovered....

For a charge to succeed under s 411 it must be proved that the accused either dishonestly received the property or having received it honestly retained it dishonestly. So far as the charges in the two cases are concerned, they relate to dishonest retention of stolen property having reason to believe the same to be stolen. The accused had, according to the prosecution evidence, purchased the stolen property (and this does not include the motorcycle) for $228 from PW 4, PW 9 and Hashim bin Chik. PW 4 in his evidence had also stated that he had made arrangements for sale of the stolen goods with the accused and that part of his evidence has remained unchallenged. In every case under s 411 of the Penal Code two facts, namely (i) that a theft was committed and certain articles were stolen and (ii) that the stolen articles were recovered from the possession of the accused have to be established by direct evidence. This the prosecution had proved as far as the charge in case LA 191 of 1969 was concerned. If these two facts are established and the recovery from the possession of the accused is recent, it is open to the court to presume under *Illustration (a)* of s 114 of the Evidence Ordinance that the accused is either the thief or a receiver of stolen goods. This presumption though rebuttable, when explained either by direct evidence or by the character and habits of the possessor or otherwise, is usually regarded by the jury as conclusive. The question as to what amounts to recent possession varies according to whether the stolen article is or is not calculated to pass readily from hand to hand. It depends upon the nature of the article itself. *Wigmore* in his work on Evidence says:

> "On a charge of taking goods, the fact that A was found, subsequently to the taking, in possession of the goods taken is relevant to show that he was the taker. It is true that several other hypotheses are conceivable as explaining the fact of his possession; nevertheless the hypothesis that he was the taker is a sufficiently natural one to allow the fact of his possession to be considered as evidentiary. There has never been any question of this."

Dealing with the matter *Taylor* says:

> "This presumption is in all cases of fact rather than of law. It is occasionally so strong as to render unnecessary any direct proof of what is called the *corpus delicti*. Thus, to borrow an apt illustration from Maule J, if a man were to go into the London Docks quite sober, and shortly afterwards were found very drunk, staggering out of one of the cellars, in which above a million of gallons of wine are stored, this would be reasonable evidence that the man had stolen some of the wine in the cellar, though no proof were given that any particular vat had been broached, and that any wine had actually been missed."...

In these two cases some of the objects were recovered at the back of the house of the accused and the motorcycle a little distance away and it was the accused who led the police to the discovery of these articles. The production of property does not necessary prove possession. In the case of *Chavadappa Pujari* (1945) Divatia J said:

> "*Illustration (a)* to s 114 is not exhaustive but only indicative of the general principle embodied in the section that in making presumptions the court should have regard to the common course of natural events and human conduct in their applica-

tion to the facts of a particular case. The condition precedent for the application of the illustration is that the accused must be in possession of stolen goods. Where they are on the person of the accused, or in the houses or fields exclusively occupied by them, there can be no doubt that they must be deemed to be in their possession. But, in quite a number of cases, stolen property is produced without making any incriminating statement from a place which is not exclusively occupied by the accused or which is of the ownership of another person. In such cases a good deal depends upon whether the production was accompanied by information given by the accused in custody as would be admissible in evidence under s 27. Such information can be relied on by the prosecution as incriminating evidence against the accused along with the producion or discovery of stolen property. But the production of property by itself would not necessarily prove his possession. It would at the most show that he had knowledge where the property was kept or concealed. Thus, where it is proved that the accused made a statement to the effect that 'I have concealed the property at a particular place and I will produce it', and if it is discovered in consequence of that statment, it would be evidence of his possession, even though the stolen articles are kept or concealed in another man's property, because unless he had possession he would not have kept them at that place. Where however the accused, without stating that he had concealed stolen property, merely produces it from a place to which other people could have access, it would not be sufficient to establish his possession even though the property may be concealed, because it is consistent with any other person having done so and the accused might have merely knowledge of it. In the absence of any incriminating statement made by the accused leading to the discovery of the property, its production alone from another man's property would not be sufficient to establish the accused's possession. It may at the most show his knowledge that the property was concealed there. The mere knowledge that stolen property is lying hidden somewhat is not incriminating circumstance for the offence of theft or receiving stolen property, and such knowledge cannot by itself raise a presumption of possession. It is the prosecution that has to establish accused's possession apart from his knowledge, and it is only when his possession is proved that the accused has to account for it in order to escape from the presumption under *Illustration (a)* to s 111.".…

There was sufficient evidence to proceed against the accused under s 414 of the Penal Code. The order of the magistrate in that case is also consequently set aside with the direction that the charge be amended to one under s 414 of the Penal Code and the case sent back for retrial.

Retrial ordered

[See also, *Ahmad bin Ishak*, 1974, and *Moti Lal*, 1959, above, p 625.]

E. Habitual receiving

In *Goh Khiok Phiong* (1954), Smith J said:

It would be necessary to prove at least three prior acts of receiving (that is to say, four acts of receiving in all) before it could fairly be said that the accused was an habitual receiver. It is not necessary that the accused should have been convicted of receiving but it is necessary that the proof of those prior acts should be as convincing as if he had been convicted, for it is those acts which determine the applicability of the offence under s 413 and the enhanced penalty provided therefor–See Gour's *Penal Law of India* (1936).

Index